Critical acclaim for The Battle for Spain

Winner of the 2005 La Vanguardia prize for non-fiction

Reviews of the Spanish edition

'A book which reads extraordinarily well (and this should be no surprise to those who know his very famous *Stalingrad* and *Berlin*), both for new readers as well as for those who already know the immense bibliography on the Civil War. From the very first moment, Beevor recreates the political climate of the period as if it were a present compelling to all. The structure of the book, the rhythm of the action, the insights into the characters, the white terror, the red terror, the revolution and the political infighting, the foreign intervention: all, despite belonging to that "other country", put us right back in the war amid the flames of those years. Yet it is in his account of the military operations that Beevor is at his most brilliant ... This book is destined for the first rank of general histories of the Civil War' Santos Juliá in *El País*

'His narrative capacity, which has fascinated his readers since *Stalingrad*, is confirmed once again in this book, which will contribute, without doubt, to constructing the historical memory of the Civil War which we need: a non-sectarian memory, broad and deep, which covers all sides of the miasma and which explores the reasons which led to that sleep of the reason which was our last civil war ... Beevor strikes again with his golden touch' *ABC*

'All in all, perhaps the best general work on the war to be published in decades' Rafael Núñez Florencio in *El Mundo*

'Beevor has surpassed the challenge he set himself with efficacy, rigour, soundness and clarity. And considering that it is now seventy years since the Civil War, which is still the object of permanent controversy in our country, this book constitutes a work richly deserving of praise' Xavier Casals in *Clio*

'The magnificent book of Antony Beevor on the Civil War, which makes thorough use of the Moscow archives and the recent bibliography of the war, gives a clear explanation of the logic behind the war' *El País*

'He has produced a moving masterpiece' *Times Literary Supplement*

'Most nations are deeply suspicious of foreigners who write books about them. Thus, the most convincing tributes to Antony Beevor's history of the Spanish Civil War come from Madrid's reviewers whose applause kept this book at the top of their bestseller lists for months ... Fascination lies in the human drama, superbly captured by Beevor' *Sunday Times*

'A gripping, revelatory account' *Sunday Telegraph*

'This is an enthralling book. The narrative is masterly, wonderfully clear as a guide through the labyrinth. It is even-tempered and full of good sense ... it is admirable' *Literary Review*

'It is an admirably clear-sighted account. What Beevor does so well is to place the war in the context of Spanish history and world politics ... Beevor's understanding of warfare and tactics is second to none ... This is a great achievement' *Daily Telegraph*

'A very different book, which displays all Beevor's exceptional narrative skills and literary flair. The story he tells is grimly familiar, but he presents it with a freshness, an eye for detail and a degree of detachment that makes this one of the best accounts to date of the Spanish crisis' *Evening Standard*

'Antony Beevor's revised history of the Civil War, which vividly anatomises a state and a society in the process of disintegration, is a tract for our times ... Above all, he has Beevorised the book, given it the richness of detail and the narrative drive that made *Stalingrad* such a success' *Guardian*

'In many ways it's his most impressive book to date because he coolly makes sense of such a complicated story: the narrative sweep is consummate, the seamless use of so many sources masterful, and the eye for detail makes it a superb read' *Mail on Sunday*

'*The Battle for Spain* looks likely to become the standard account of the conflict for at least the next generation' *London Review of Books*

'Every Spaniard now has a brilliantly written, judicious and non-ideological history of the Civil War to contemplate ... that is the scale of Antony Beevor's achievement' *The Tablet*

'For the big picture of the war, all the more powerful for its blending of narrative intensity with emotional restraint, there is no rival to Antony Beevor's masterly *The Battle for Spain*' *Independent*

'Beevor's strength, as established in his earlier works, is his narrative mastery' *Sydney Morning Herald*

'A brilliant account of this dark chapter of Spain's and Europe's history ... With this striking book Antony Beevor strengthens his position as the leading military historian of our time. He tells us in an accessible language about our culture's most heartbreaking conflicts and darkest tragedies' *Svenska Dagbladet*

'Antony Beevor is a contemporary Tolstoy who, with his books on history, is creating a literary masterpiece which will stand the test of time ... [he] proves that history today is one of literature's most vital branches' *Dagens Nyheter*

Antony Beevor is the author of *Crete: The Battle and the Resistance*, which won a Runciman Prize; *Paris After the Liberation, 1944–1949* (written with his wife, Artemis Cooper); *Stalingrad*, which won the Samuel Johnson Prize, the Wolfson Prize for History and the Hawthornden Prize for Literature; *Berlin: The Downfall*, which received the first Longman–*History Today* Trustees' Award; and *The Mystery of Olga Chekhova*. *Stalingrad* and *Berlin* have been translated into twenty-five languages and have sold more than two and a quarter million copies between them. His latest work, *A Writer at War: Vasily Grossman with the Red Army 1941–1945*, is an edition, with his Russian researcher, Dr Luba Vinogradova, of Grossman's wartime notebooks. A fellow of the Royal Society of Literature and Chevalier de l'Ordre des Arts et Lettres in France, Antony Beevor has also been the chairman of the Society of Authors and is a visiting professor at the School of History, Classics and Archaeology at Birkbeck College, University of London.

By Antony Beevor

The Battle for Spain: The Spanish Civil War 1936–1939

A Writer at War: Vasily Grossman with the Red Army 1941–1945
Edited and translated with Luba Vinogradova

The Mystery of Olga Chekhova

Berlin: The Downfall

Stalingrad

Paris After the Liberation (with Artemis Cooper)

Crete: The Battle and the Resistance

Inside the British Army

The Spanish Civil War

THE BATTLE FOR SPAIN

THE SPANISH CIVIL WAR 1936–1939

ANTONY BEEVOR

PHOENIX

A PHOENIX PAPERBACK

First published in Great Britain in 2006
by Weidenfeld & Nicolson
An earlier version of this book was published in 1982
by Orbis Publishing Ltd under the title
The Spanish Civil War
This paperback edition published in 2006
by Phoenix,
an imprint of Orion Books Ltd,
Orion House, 5 Upper St Martin's Lane,
London WC2H 9EA

1 3 5 7 9 10 8 6 4 2

A CIP catalogue record for this book
is available from the British Library.

ISBN 13: 978-0-7538-2165-7
ISBN 10: 0-7538-2165-6

Typeset by Input Data Services Ltd, Frome

Printed and bound by Butler and Tanner Ltd,
Frome and London

www.orionbooks.co.uk

For Gonzalo Pontón with all my gratitude
for all his help

CONTENTS

LIST OF ILLUSTRATIONS

[1] Arxiu Nacional de Catalunya
[2] Agencia EFE
[3] Previous edition of *The Battle for Spain (The Spanish Civil War)*
[4] *La Vanguardia*
[5] Archivo General de la Administración
[6] Getty Images

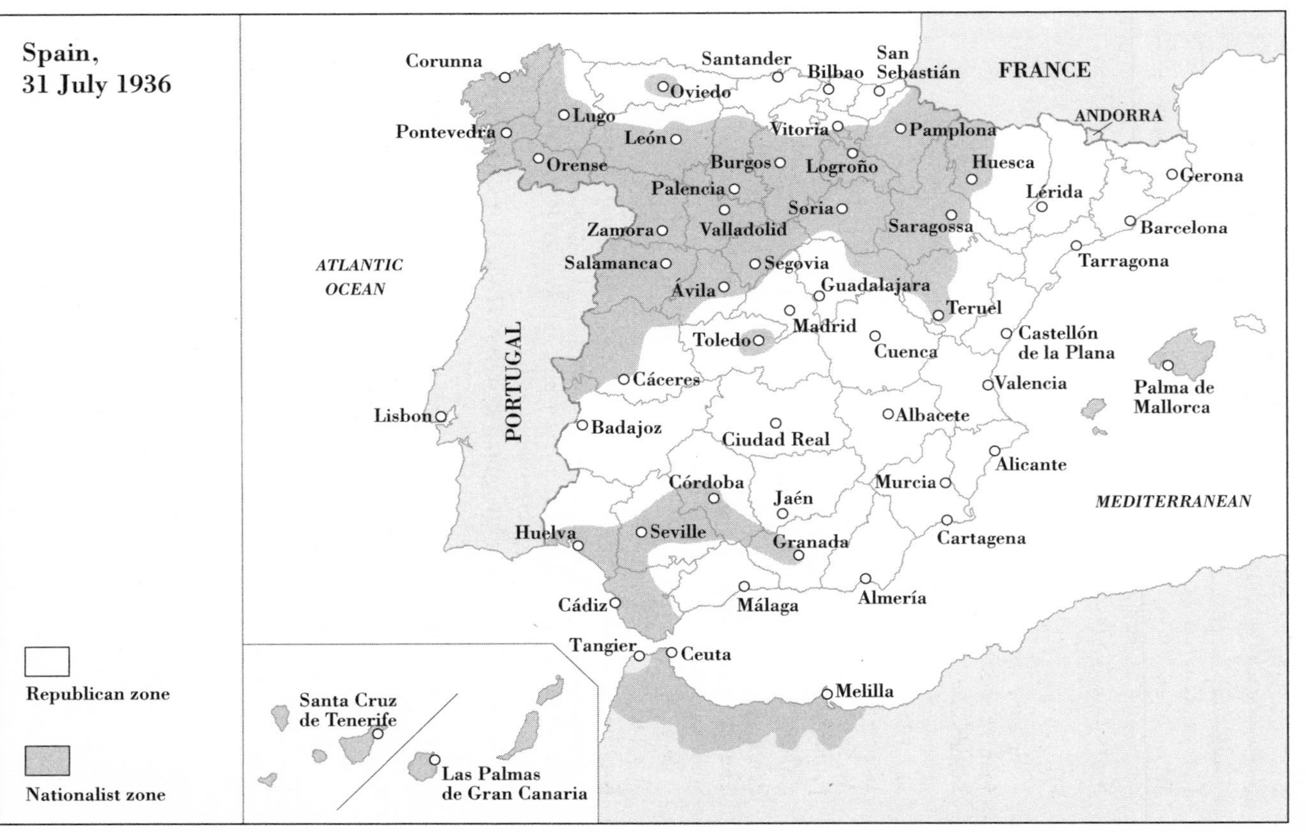
Spain,
31 July 1936
Republican zone
Nationalist zone
FRANCE
ANDORRA
PORTUGAL
ATLANTIC
OCEAN
MEDITERRANEAN
Corunna
Santander
Bilbao
San
Sebastián
Oviedo
Lugo
Pontevedra
León
Vitoria
Pamplona
Orense
Burgos
Logroño
Huesca
Gerona
Palencia
Lérida
Soria
Saragossa
Barcelona
Zamora
Valladolid
Tarragona
Salamanca
Segovia
Ávila
Guadalajara
Teruel
Madrid
Toledo
Cuenca
Castellón
de la Plana
Cáceres
Valencia
Palma de
Mallorca
Lisbon
Badajoz
Albacete
Ciudad Real
Alicante
Córdoba
Murcia
Jaén
Huelva
Seville
Granada
Cartagena
Cádiz
Málaga
Almería
Tangier
Ceuta
Melilla
Santa Cruz
de Tenerife
Las Palmas
de Gran Canaria

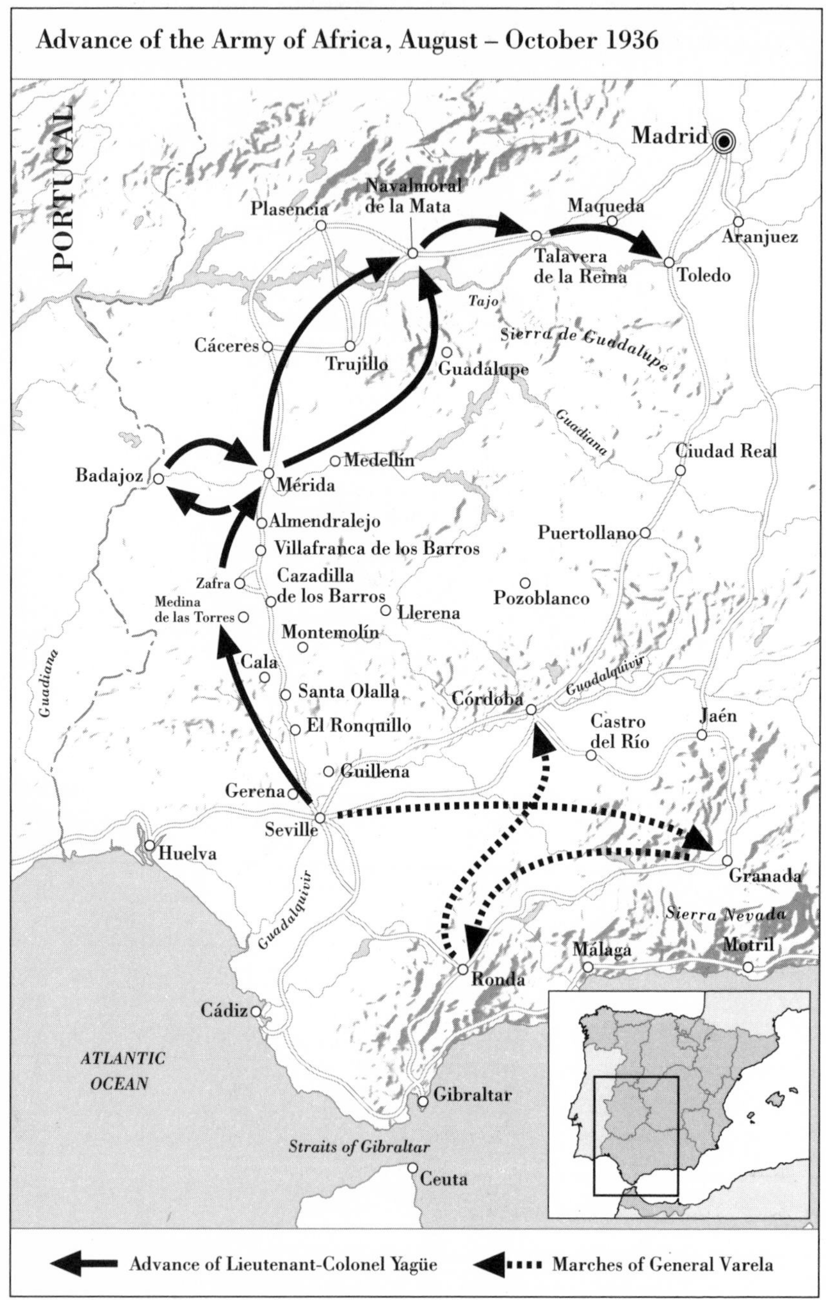
Advance of the Army of Africa, August – October 1936
PORTUGAL
Madrid
Navalmoral de la Mata
Plasencia
Maqueda
Aranjuez
Talavera de la Reina
Toledo
Tajo
Cáceres
Trujillo
Guadalupe
Sierra de Guadalupe
Guadiana
Ciudad Real
Badajoz
Mérida
Medellín
Almendralejo
Villafranca de los Barros
Puertollano
Zafra
Cazadilla de los Barros
Pozoblanco
Medina de las Torres
Llerena
Montemolín
Cala
Guadiana
Santa Olalla
Córdoba
Guadalquivir
El Ronquillo
Castro del Río
Jaén
Guillena
Gerena
Seville
Huelva
Granada
Guadalquivir
Sierra Nevada
Málaga
Motril
Ronda
Cádiz
ATLANTIC OCEAN
Gibraltar
Straits of Gibraltar
Ceuta
Advance of Lieutenant-Colonel Yagüe
Marches of General Varela

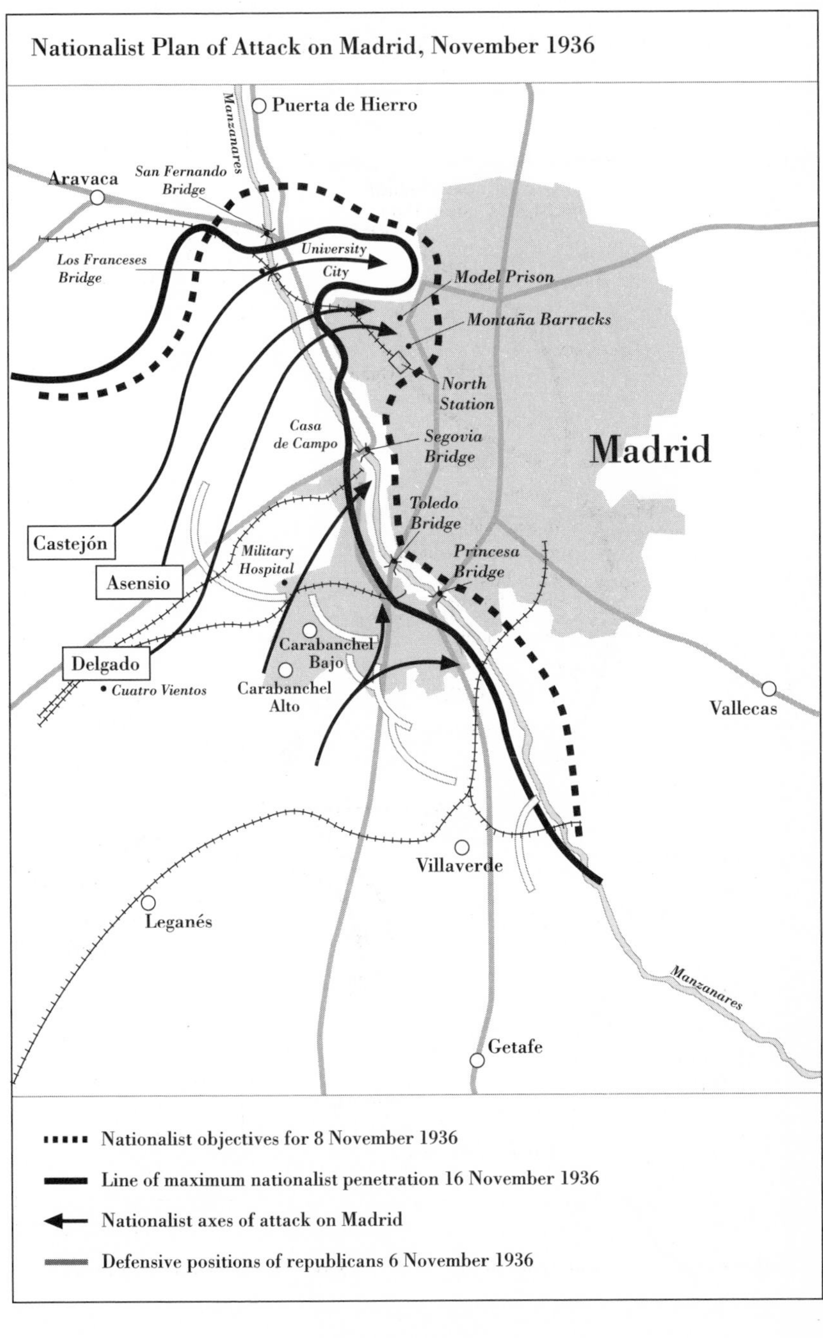
Nationalist Plan of Attack on Madrid, November 1936
Puerta de Hierro
Manzanares
San Fernando Bridge
Aravaca
Los Franceses Bridge
University City
Model Prison
Montaña Barracks
North Station
Casa de Campo
Segovia Bridge
Madrid
Toledo Bridge
Princesa Bridge
Castejón
Military Hospital
Asensio
Carabanchel Bajo
Delgado
Cuatro Vientos
Carabanchel Alto
Vallecas
Villaverde
Leganés
Manzanares
Getafe
Nationalist objectives for 8 November 1936
Line of maximum nationalist penetration 16 November 1936
Nationalist axes of attack on Madrid
Defensive positions of republicans 6 November 1936

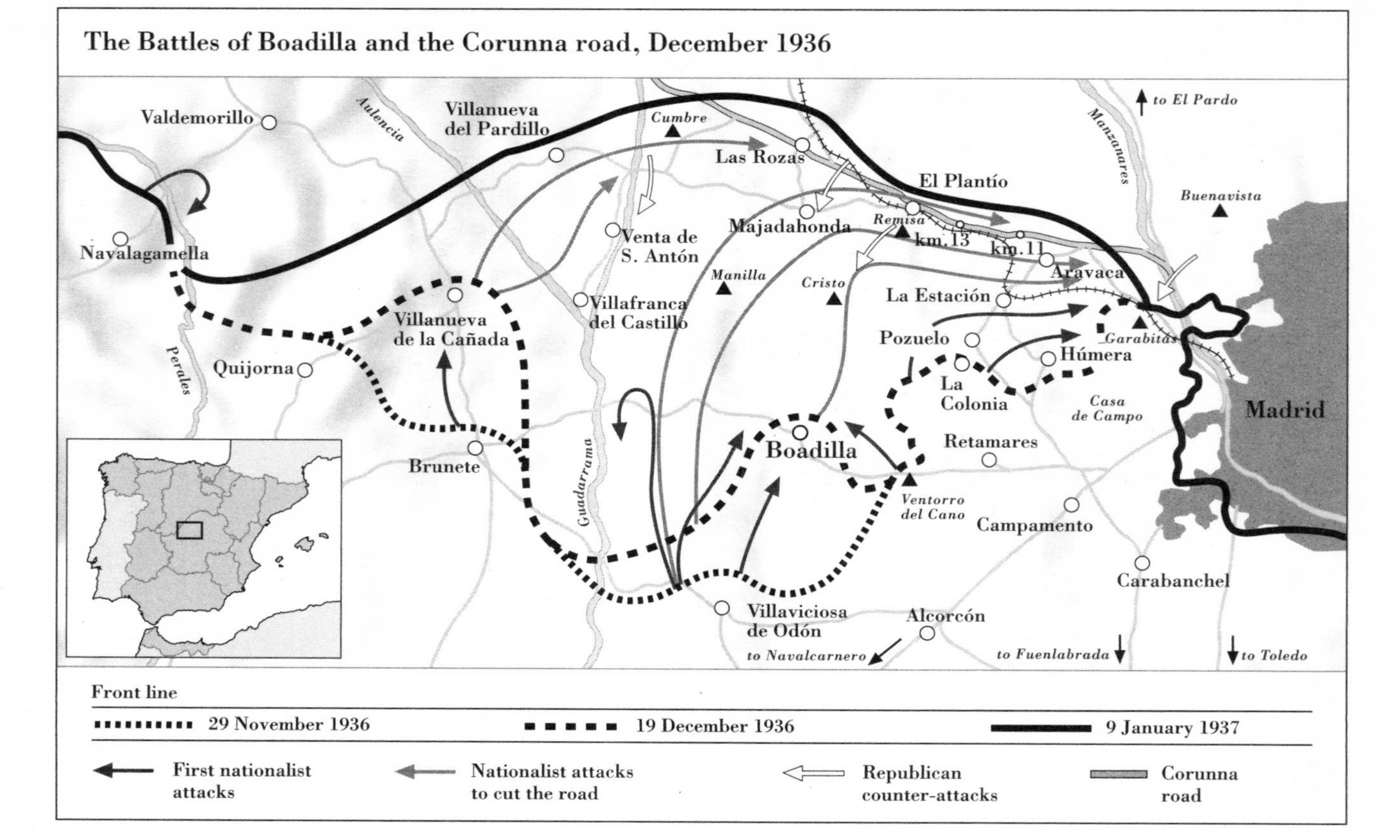

The Battles of Boadilla and the Corunna road, December 1936
to El Pardo
Valdemorillo
Aulencia
Villanueva
del Pardillo
Cumbre
Las Rozas
El Plantío
Manzanares
Buenavista
Navalagamella
Venta de
S. Antón
Majadahonda
Remisa
km.13
km.11
Aravaca
Manilla
Cristo
La Estación
Villafranca
del Castillo
Villanueva
de la Cañada
Perales
Quijorna
Pozuelo
Garabitas
Húmera
La
Colonia
Casa
de Campo
Madrid
Brunete
Guadarrama
Boadilla
Retamares
Ventorro
del Cano
Campamento
Carabanchel
Villaviciosa
de Odón
Alcorcón
to Navalcarnero
to Fuenlabrada
to Toledo
Front line
29 November 1936
19 December 1936
9 January 1937
First nationalist
attacks
Nationalist attacks
to cut the road
Republican
counter-attacks
Corunna
road

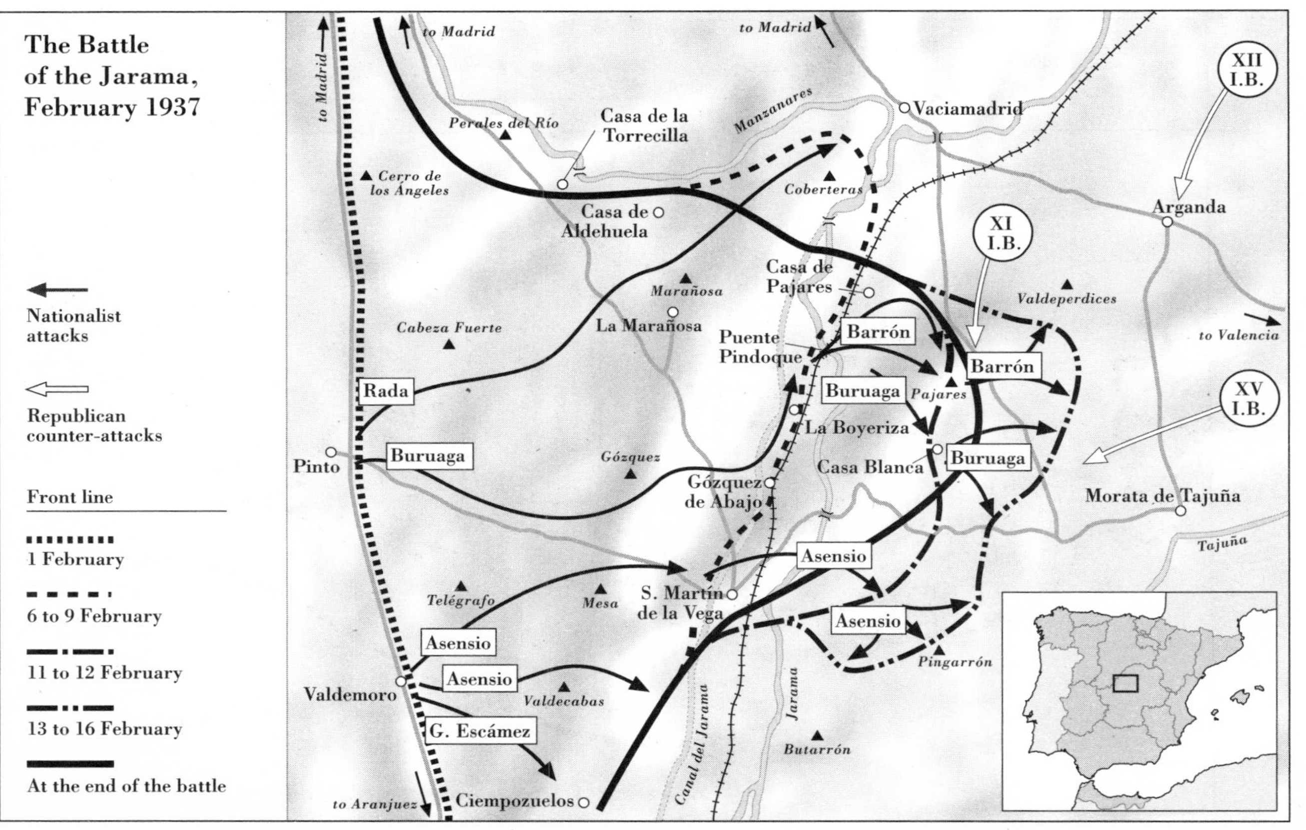
The Battle
of the Jarama,
February 1937
Nationalist attacks
Republican counter-attacks
Front line
1 February
6 to 9 February
11 to 12 February
13 to 16 February
At the end of the battle
to Madrid
to Madrid
to Madrid
Perales del Río
Casa de la Torrecilla
Manzanares
Vaciamadrid
XII I.B.
Cerro de los Ángeles
Coberteras
Arganda
Casa de Aldehuela
XI I.B.
Casa de Pajares
Marañosa
Valdeperdices
La Marañosa
Cabeza Fuerte
Puente Pindoque
Barrón
Barrón
to Valencia
Rada
Buruaga
Pajares
XV I.B.
La Boyeriza
Pinto
Buruaga
Gózquez
Casa Blanca
Buruaga
Gózquez de Abajo
Morata de Tajuña
Tajuña
Asensio
Telégrafo
Mesa
S. Martín de la Vega
Asensio
Asensio
Pingarrón
Asensio
Valdemoro
Valdecabas
Jarama
Canal del Jarama
G. Escámez
Butarrón
to Aranjuez
Ciempozuelos

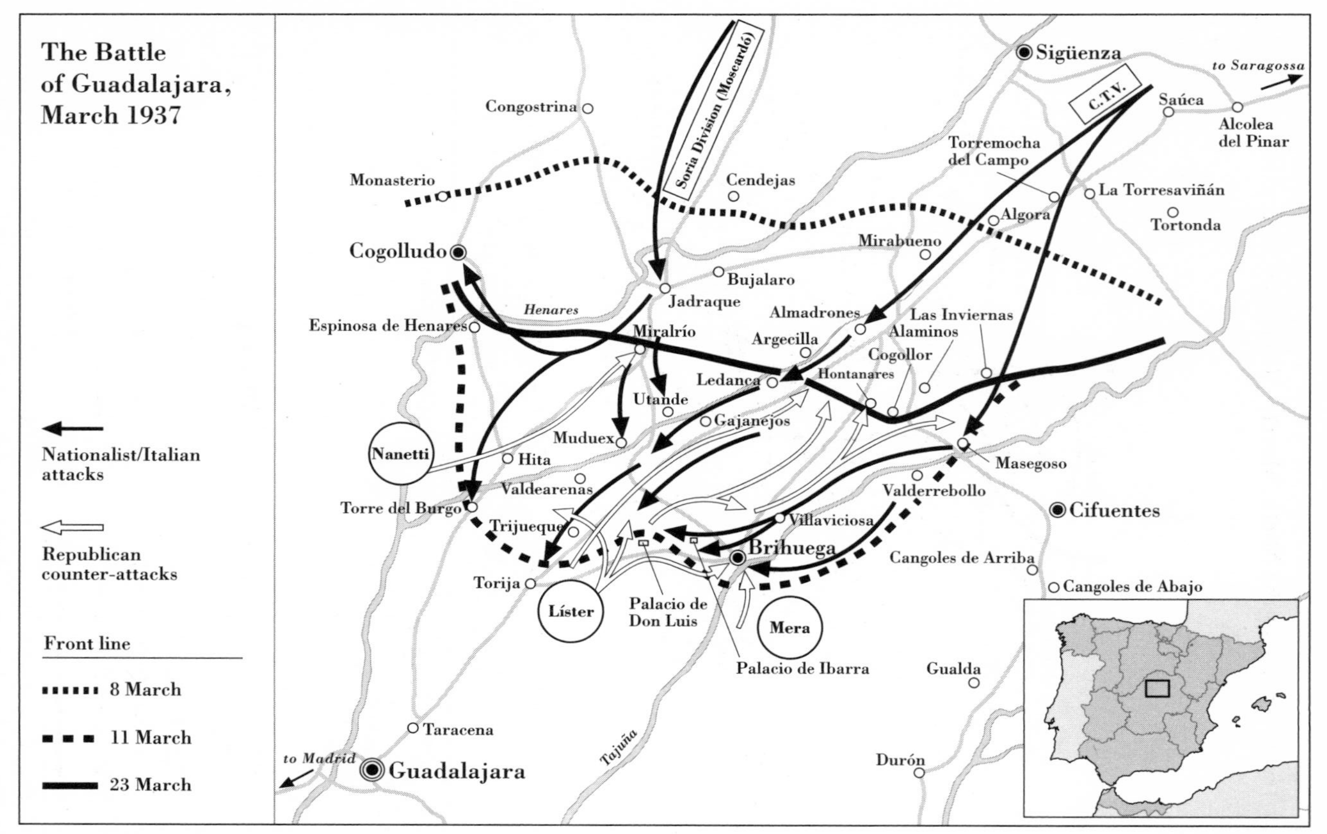

The Battle
of Guadalajara,
March 1937
Nationalist/Italian attacks
Republican counter-attacks
Front line
8 March
11 March
23 March
Sigüenza
to Saragossa
C.T.V.
Saúca
Alcolea del Pinar
Congostrina
Soria Division (Moscardó)
Torremocha del Campo
La Torresaviñán
Tortonda
Monasterio
Cendejas
Algora
Mirabueno
Cogolludo
Bujalaro
Jadraque
Henares
Almadrones
Las Inviernas
Alaminos
Espinosa de Henares
Miralrío
Argecilla
Cogollor
Ledanca
Hontanares
Utande
Gajanejos
Nanetti
Muduex
Hita
Masegoso
Valdearenas
Valderrebollo
Torre del Burgo
Cifuentes
Trijueque
Villaviciosa
Brihuega
Cangoles de Arriba
Torija
Cangoles de Abajo
Líster
Palacio de Don Luis
Mera
Palacio de Ibarra
Gualda
Taracena
Tajuña
to Madrid
Guadalajara
Durón

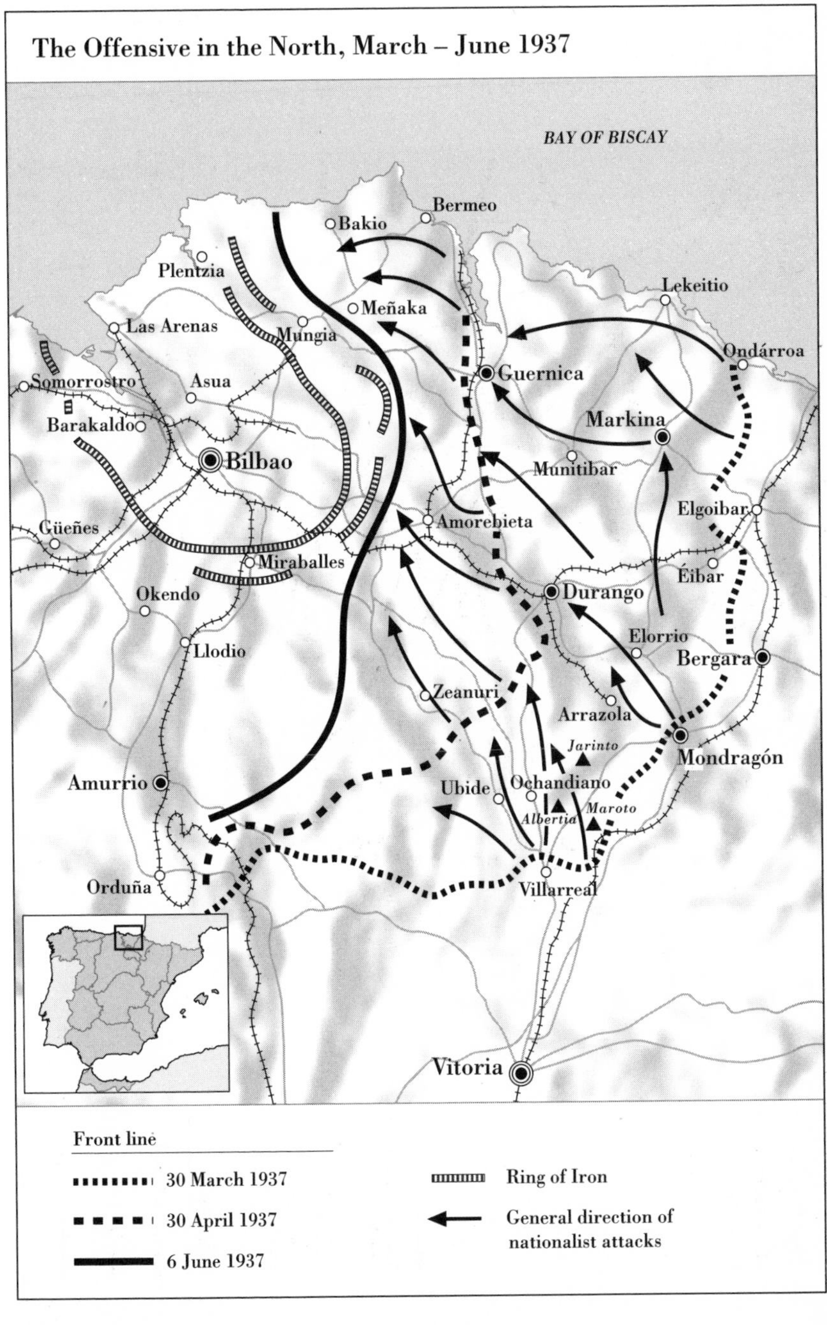
The Offensive in the North, March – June 1937
BAY OF BISCAY
Bermeo
Bakio
Plentzia
Meñaka
Lekeitio
Las Arenas
Mungia
Ondárroa
Somorrostro
Asua
Guernica
Markina
Barakaldo
Bilbao
Munitibar
Elgoibar
Amorebieta
Güeñes
Miraballes
Éibar
Okendo
Durango
Elorrio
Llodio
Bergara
Zeanuri
Arrazola
Jarinto
Mondragón
Amurrio
Ubide
Ochandiano
Albertia
Maroto
Orduña
Villarreal
Vitoria
Front line
30 March 1937
30 April 1937
6 June 1937
Ring of Iron
General direction of nationalist attacks

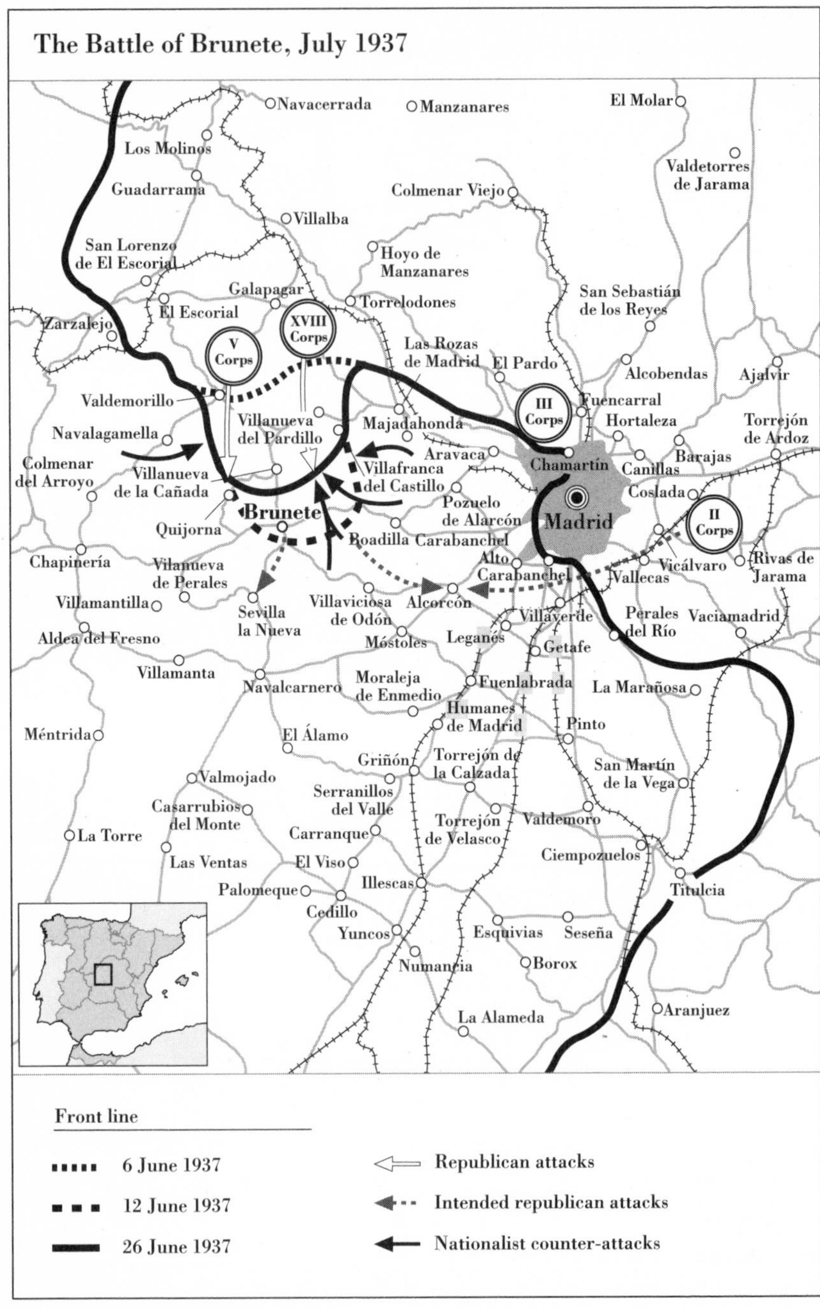
The Battle of Brunete, July 1937
Navacerrada
Manzanares
El Molar
Los Molinos
Valdetorres de Jarama
Guadarrama
Colmenar Viejo
Villalba
San Lorenzo de El Escorial
Hoyo de Manzanares
Galapagar
Torrelodones
San Sebastián de los Reyes
El Escorial
Zarzalejo
XVIII Corps
V Corps
Las Rozas de Madrid
El Pardo
Alcobendas
Ajalvir
Valdemorillo
III Corps
Fuencarral
Villanueva del Pardillo
Majadahonda
Hortaleza
Torrejón de Ardoz
Navalagamella
Aravaca
Chamartín
Canillas
Barajas
Colmenar del Arroyo
Villanueva de la Cañada
Villafranca del Castillo
Coslada
Pozuelo de Alarcón
Madrid
II Corps
Brunete
Quijorna
Boadilla
Carabanchel
Chapinería
Vilanueva de Perales
Alto Carabanchel
Vicálvaro
Rivas de Jarama
Vallecas
Villamantilla
Sevilla la Nueva
Villaviciosa de Odón
Alcorcón
Villaverde
Perales del Río
Vaciamadrid
Aldea del Fresno
Móstoles
Leganés
Getafe
Villamanta
Navalcarnero
Moraleja de Enmedio
Fuenlabrada
La Marañosa
Humanes de Madrid
Méntrida
El Álamo
Pinto
Griñón
Torrejón de la Calzada
San Martín de la Vega
Valmojado
Serranillos del Valle
Casarrubios del Monte
Torrejón de Velasco
Valdemoro
La Torre
Carranque
Ciempozuelos
Las Ventas
El Viso
Illescas
Titulcia
Palomeque
Cedillo
Esquivias
Seseña
Yuncos
Numancia
Borox
La Alameda
Aranjuez
Front line
6 June 1937
12 June 1937
26 June 1937
Republican attacks
Intended republican attacks
Nationalist counter-attacks

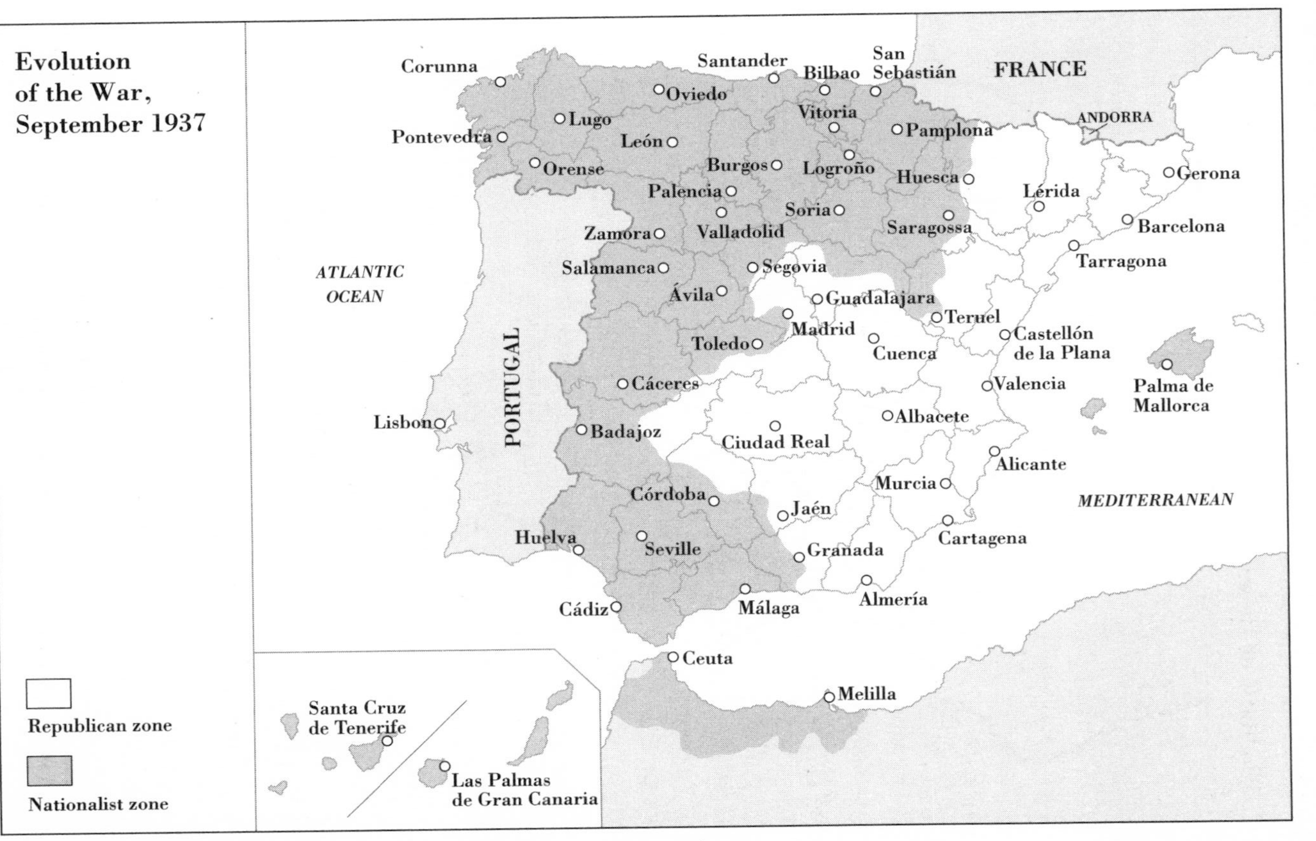
Evolution
of the War,
September 1937
Republican zone
Nationalist zone
Corunna
Santander
Bilbao
San
Sebastián
FRANCE
ANDORRA
Oviedo
Lugo
Vitoria
Pamplona
Pontevedra
León
Orense
Burgos
Logroño
Huesca
Gerona
Palencia
Lérida
Soria
Saragossa
Barcelona
Zamora
Valladolid
Tarragona
Salamanca
Segovia
ATLANTIC
OCEAN
Ávila
Guadalajara
Teruel
Madrid
Castellón
de la Plana
Toledo
Cuenca
PORTUGAL
Palma de
Mallorca
Cáceres
Valencia
Albacete
Lisbon
Badajoz
Ciudad Real
Alicante
Murcia
Córdoba
MEDITERRANEAN
Jaén
Cartagena
Huelva
Seville
Granada
Almería
Cádiz
Málaga
Ceuta
Melilla
Santa Cruz
de Tenerife
Las Palmas
de Gran Canaria

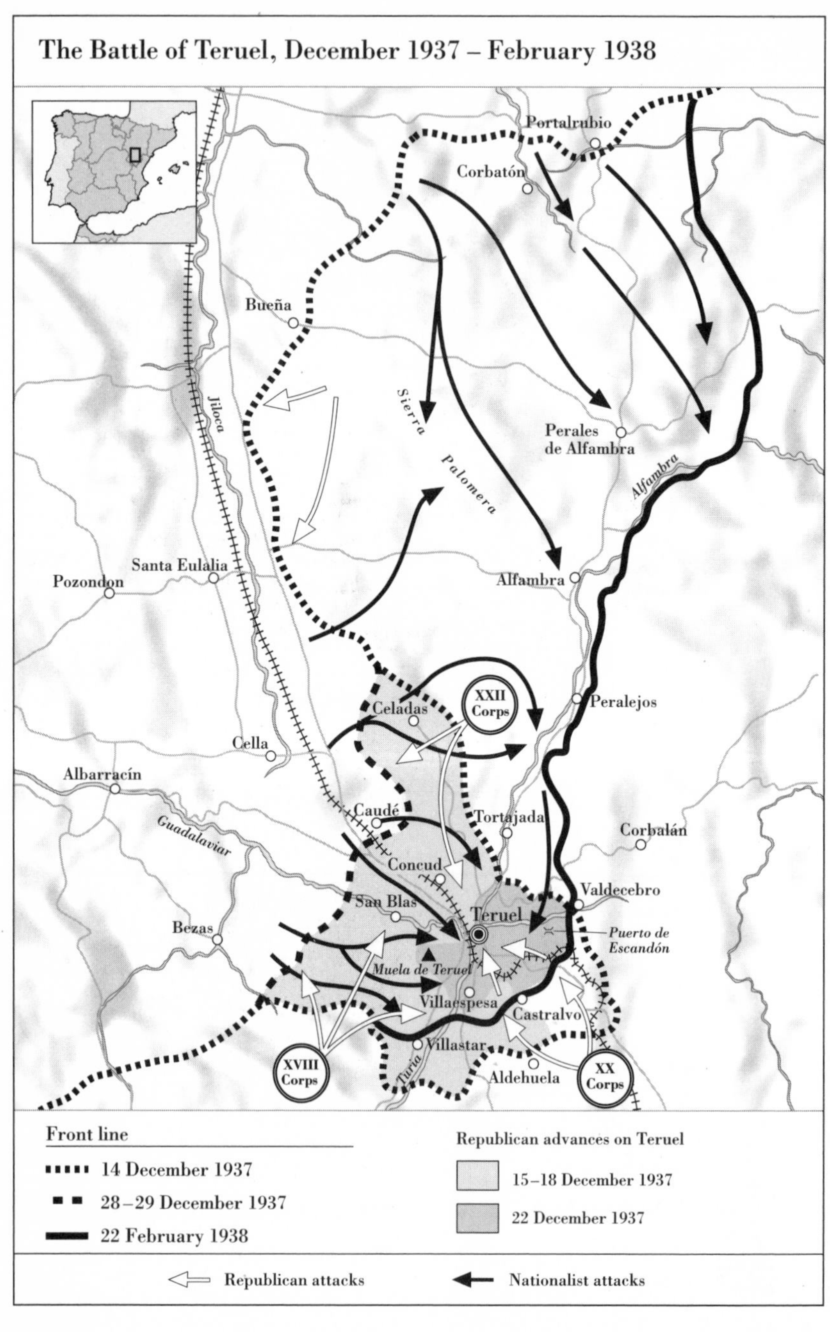
The Battle of Teruel, December 1937 – February 1938
Portalrubio
Corbatón
Bueña
Jiloca
Sierra
Palomera
Perales de Alfambra
Alfambra
Santa Eulalia
Pozondon
Alfambra
XXII Corps
Celadas
Peralejos
Cella
Albarracín
Caudé
Tortajada
Corbalán
Guadalaviar
Concud
Valdecebro
San Blas
Teruel
Puerto de Escandón
Bezas
Muela de Teruel
Villaespesa
Castralvo
Villastar
XVIII Corps
Turia
Aldehuela
XX Corps
Front line
14 December 1937
28–29 December 1937
22 February 1938
Republican advances on Teruel
15–18 December 1937
22 December 1937
Republican attacks
Nationalist attacks

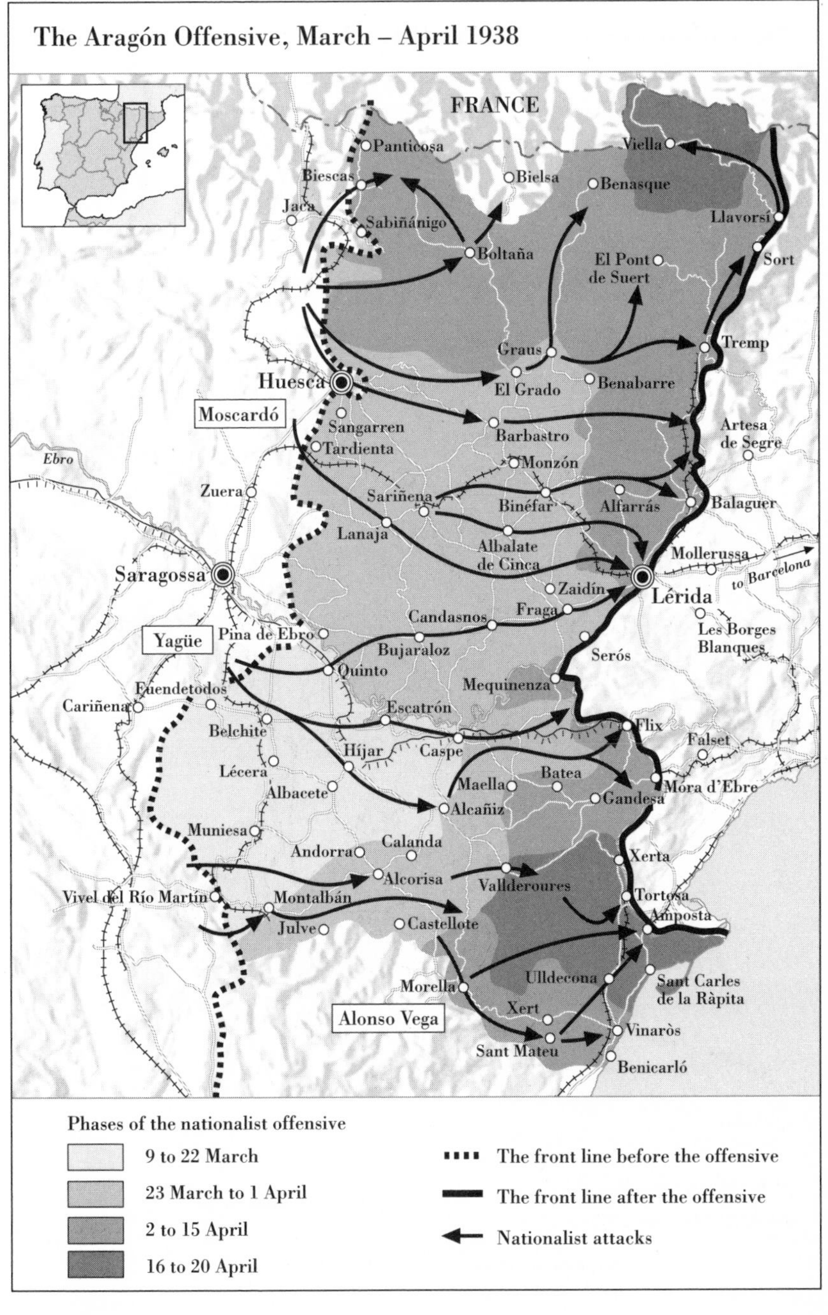

The Aragón Offensive, March – April 1938
FRANCE
Panticosa
Biescas
Bielsa
Benasque
Viella
Jaca
Sabiñánigo
Boltaña
Llavorsí
El Pont de Suert
Sort
Tremp
Graus
El Grado
Benabarre
Huesca
Moscardó
Sangarren
Tardienta
Barbastro
Artesa de Segre
Ebro
Monzón
Zuera
Sariñena
Binéfar
Alfarrás
Balaguer
Lanaja
Albalate de Cinca
Mollerussa
to Barcelona
Saragossa
Zaidín
Lérida
Candasnos
Fraga
Les Borges Blanques
Yagüe
Pina de Ebro
Bujaraloz
Serós
Quinto
Mequinenza
Fuendetodos
Cariñena
Escatrón
Flix
Belchite
Falset
Híjar
Caspe
Lécera
Batea
Maella
Móra d'Ebre
Albacete
Gandesa
Alcañiz
Muniesa
Calanda
Andorra
Xerta
Alcorisa
Valdderoures
Vivel del Río Martín
Montalbán
Tortosa
Amposta
Julve
Castellote
Ulldecona
Sant Carles de la Ràpita
Morella
Xert
Alonso Vega
Vinaròs
Sant Mateu
Benicarló
Phases of the nationalist offensive
9 to 22 March
23 March to 1 April
2 to 15 April
16 to 20 April
The front line before the offensive
The front line after the offensive
Nationalist attacks

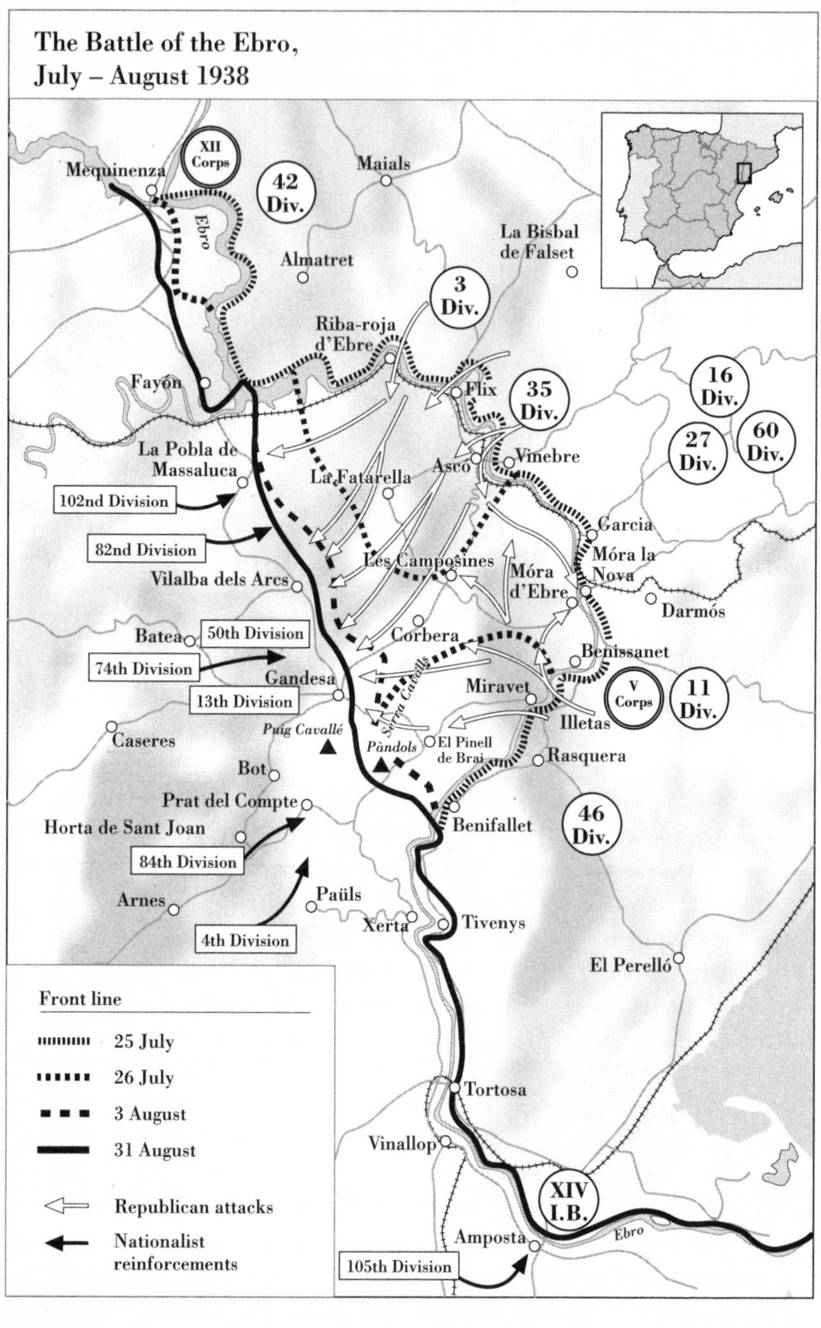

The Battle of the Ebro,
July – August 1938
Mequinenza
XII Corps
42 Div.
Maials
Ebro
Almatret
La Bisbal de Falset
3 Div.
Riba-roja d'Ebre
Fayón
Flix
35 Div.
16 Div.
27 Div.
60 Div.
La Pobla de Massaluca
Ascó
Vinebre
La Fatarella
102nd Division
Garcia
82nd Division
Móra la Nova
Les Camposines
Móra d'Ebre
Vilalba dels Arcs
Darmós
Batea
50th Division
Corbera
74th Division
Benissanet
Gandesa
Serra Cavalls
Miravet
V Corps
11 Div.
13th Division
Illetas
Caseres
Puig Cavallé
Pàndols
El Pinell de Brai
Rasquera
Bot
Prat del Compte
46 Div.
Horta de Sant Joan
Benifallet
84th Division
Arnes
Paüls
Xerta
Tivenys
4th Division
El Perelló
Front line
25 July
26 July
3 August
31 August
Republican attacks
Nationalist reinforcements
Tortosa
Vinallop
XIV I.B.
Amposta
Ebro
105th Division

ACKNOWLEDGEMENTS

This book has had a curious life. I began work on what can now be called the prototype version in 1976, not long after the death of General Franco. It was finally published in 1982 under the title *The Spanish Civil War*, soon after Colonel Tejero held the Cortes hostage at gunpoint in an attempt to overthrow the democracy which had emerged under King Juan Carlos. Then, four years ago, my Spanish publisher, Gonzalo Pontón, persuaded me to rewrite the book completely. The idea was to use all the research carried out so painstakingly by Spanish and other historians over the last quarter of a century, as well as add new material from German archives and especially from Soviet files which had not been accessible.

Gonzalo Pontón, the founder of Crítica, the publishing house which has brought out more books on recent Spanish history than any other, made the project possible by sifting the huge number of books and academic papers on the subject which have appeared in recent years. Quite literally this book, *The Battle for Spain*, would never have been possible without all his help and enthusiasm in completing a project which proved far more extensive than any of us had foreseen when he first raised the idea. It has been an immense pleasure and a privilege to work with him.

For all non-Spanish editions I have included the original, perhaps over-mechanistic, synopsis of the country's history as a very brief reminder for readers. The structure of the book also remains more or less the same as the prototype edition. The real difference lies in the detail and the sources, but interestingly, I find that the huge increase in information available today has tended to swell the number of vital questions rather than reduce them. This, on the other hand, may also be due to the author losing some of the more passionate certainties of youth over the last 24 years.

In any case, this book could never have been completed without a great deal of help from other friends and colleagues. In Russia, I am deeply grateful once again to Professor Anatoly Chernobayev for his advice and above all to my long-standing research assistant, Dr Luba Vinogradova, to whom I owe so much already. As well as the staff of numerous archives, I am particularly indebted to those in the library of 'Memorial' in Moscow. Angelica von Hase once again assisted me greatly in Germany, especially in the Bundesarchiv-Militärarchiv in Freiburg. In Sweden, Björn Andersson and Dr Lars Erickson obtained documents for me from the Swedish Krigsarkivet and Alan Crozier most kindly translated them for me.

In London, I have been extremely lucky to work once again with Ion Trewin, and as always, I am more than happy to have another old friend, Andrew Nurnberg, as my agent. All this turns publishing a book from a fraught and stressful experience into a co-operative and delightful one. And once again, my greatest debt of all is, as always, to my wife, Artemis Cooper, who has had to relive these years.

INTRODUCTION

‘A civil war is not a war but a sickness,’ wrote Antoine de Saint-Exupéry. ‘The enemy is within. One fights almost against oneself.’ Yet Spain’s tragedy in 1936 was even greater. It had become enmeshed in the international civil war, which started in earnest with the bolshevik revolution.

The horrors in Russia had undermined the democratic centre throughout continental Europe. This was because the process of polarization between ‘reds’ and ‘whites’ allowed both political extremes to increase their own power by manipulating fearful, if not apocalyptic, images of their enemies. Their Manichaean propaganda fed off each other. Both Stalin and Goebbels later exploited, with diabolical ingenuity, that potent combination of fear and hatred. The process stripped their ‘traitor’ opponents of their humanity as well as their citizenship. This is why it is wrong to describe the Spanish Civil War as ‘fratricidal’. The divisiveness of the new ideologies could turn brothers into faceless strangers and trade unionists or shop owners into class enemies. Normal human instincts were overridden. In the tense spring of 1936, on his way to Madrid University, Julián Marías, a disciple of the philosopher José Ortega y Gasset, never forgot the hatred in the expression of a tram-driver at a stop as he watched a beautiful and well-dressed young woman step down onto the pavement. ‘We’ve really had it,’ Marías said to himself. ‘When Marx has more effect than hormones, there is nothing to be done.’[1]

The Spanish Civil War has so often been portrayed as a clash between left and right, but this is a misleading simplification. Two other axes of conflict emerged: state centralism against regional independence and authoritarianism against the freedom of the individual. The nationalist forces of the right were much more coherent because, with only minor exceptions, they combined three cohesive extremes. They were right wing, centralist and authoritarian at the same time. The Republic, on the other hand, represented a cauldron of incompatibilities and mutual suspicions, with centralists and authoritarians, especially the communists, opposed by regionalists and libertarians.

Ghosts of those propaganda battles of 70 years ago still haunt us. Yet the Spanish Civil War remains one of the few modern conflicts whose history had been written more effectively by the losers than by the winners. This is not surprising when one remembers the international sense of foreboding after the Republic's defeat in the spring of 1939. Anger then increased after 1945, when the crimes of Nazi Germany came to light and General Franco's obsessive vindictiveness towards the defeated republicans showed no sign of diminishing.

It is difficult for younger generations to imagine what life was really like in that age of totalitarian conflict. Collectivist ideals, whether those of armies, political youth movements or of trade unions, have virtually all disintegrated. The passions and hatreds of such an era are a world away from the safe, civilian environment of health and safety, and citizens' rights in which we live today. That past is indeed 'another country'. Spain itself has changed completely in a matter of decades. Its emergence from the civil war and Francoist era has been one of the most astonishing and impressive transformations in the whole of Europe. This, perhaps, is why it is unwise to try to judge the terrible conflict of 70 years ago with the liberal values and attitudes that we accept today as normal. It is vital to make a leap of the imagination, to try to understand the beliefs and attitudes of the time – whether the nationalistic, Catholic myths and the fear of bolshevism on the right, or the left's conviction that revolution and the coercive redistribution of wealth could produce universal happiness.

Such passionately fought causes have made it far harder to be objective, especially when one looks at the origins of the war. Each side is bound to want to prove that the other started it. Sometimes even neutral factors tend to be neglected, such as the fact that the Republic was attempting to carry out a process of social and political reform in a few years, which had taken anything up to a century elsewhere.

The actual events during the war, however, such as the atrocities committed and the details of the repression that followed, are now beyond serious contention, thanks to the immense and scrupulous work of many Spanish historians in local archives and cemeteries. Most of the military details, including the squabbles between republican commanders, are also clear with the opening of previously secret files in Russia over the last dozen years. We have, too, a much more precise view of Soviet policy in Spain. Yet, inevitably, the interpretation of many facts is still going to be swayed by personal opinion, especially the chicken-and-egg debate of the causal chain that led to the war. Do you begin with the 'suicidal egotism' of the landowners, or with the 'revolutionary gymnastics' and rhetoric which inflamed the fears of bolshevism, pushing the middle class 'into the arms of fascism', as the more moderate socialist leaders warned? A definitive answer is beyond the power of any historian.

Some are strongly tempted to consider that the Spanish Civil War could not have been avoided. This contravenes that informal yet important rule of history that nothing is inevitable, except perhaps in hindsight. On the other hand, it is very hard to imagine how any form of workable compromise could have been achieved after the failed left-wing revolution of October 1934. An increasingly militant left could not forgive the cruelty of the Civil Guard and the colonial troops, while the right became convinced that it had to pre-empt another attempt at violent revolution.

Other even more unanswerable questions remain important, if only because they can provoke us into seeing issues from an unaccustomed perspective. The ideals of liberty and democracy formed the basis of the Republic's cause abroad. Yet the revolutionary reality on the ground, the impotence of the Spanish parliament, the Cortes, and the lack of respect for the rule of law on both sides, must be looked at carefully.

Republican propaganda during the civil war always emphasized that its government was the legally appointed one after the elections of February 1936. This is true, but one also has to pose an important question. If the coalition of the right had won those elections, would the left have accepted the legitimate result? One strongly suspects not. The socialist leader Largo Caballero threatened openly before the elections that if the right won, it would be open civil war.

The nationalists tried from the very beginning to pretend that they had risen in revolt purely to forestall a communist putsch. This was a complete fabrication to provide retrospective justification for their acts. But for the left to claim that the nationalists had launched an unprovoked attack against law-abiding democrats is disingenuous. The left had often shown as little respect for the democratic process and the rule of law as the right. Both sides, of course, justified their actions on the grounds that if they did not act first, their opponents would seize power and crush them. But this only goes to show that nothing destroys the centre ground more rapidly than the politics of fear and the rhetoric of threat.

Some argue that words cannot kill. But this becomes less and less convincing the more one looks at the cycle of mutual suspicion and hatred, all enflamed by irresponsible declamation. In fact, the right-wing leader Calvo Sotelo was assassinated because of his own deliberately provocative speeches in the Cortes. It is also important to consider whether the rhetoric of annihilation tends to become a self-fulfilling prophecy. General Queipo de Llano threatened in one of his notorious broadcasts from Seville that the nationalists would execute ten republicans for every one of their own men killed. This proved in the end to be not that far from the mark.

One must also not forget Largo Caballero's declaration that he wanted a Republic without class warfare, but to achieve that a political class had to disappear. This was an obvious echo of Lenin's openly stated intention to eliminate the bourgeoisie. But would a victory of the left in say 1937 or 1938 have led to a comparable scale of executions and imprisonment as under Franco? It is, of course, impossible to tell, and one cannot judge entirely by the Russian civil war, but it is still a question which must not be brushed aside. The winner in any civil war, as several historians have argued, is bound to kill more because of the cycle of fear and hate.

All these complex and interrelated issues show how it is impossible to separate cause and effect with scientific precision. Truth was indeed the first casualty of the Spanish Civil War. The subject has suffered from more intense debate and more polemics for longer after the event than any other modern conflict, including even the Second World War. The historian, although obviously unable to be completely dispassionate, should try to do little more than understand the feelings of both sides, to probe previous assumptions and to push forward the boundaries of knowledge. As far as is humanly possible, moral judgements should be left to the individual reader.

POLITICAL PARTIES, GROUPINGS AND ORGANIZATIONS

NATIONALISTS

MONARCHIST (ALFONSINE)

Acción Española
Renovación Española

The Alfonsine monarchists supported the descendants of Queen Isabella II, the daughter of Ferdinand VII, as opposed to those of his brother, Don Carlos. Thus the monarchists in the twentieth century were those who backed King Alfonso XIII and then his son, Don Juan, the Count of Barcelona and the father of the present King Juan Carlos. The monarchist faction was strong among conservative army officers and it saw itself as the natural leadership for 'Old Spain'. Popular support was marginal.

CARLIST

Communión Tradicionalista
Requetés (the Carlist militia)
Pelayos (Carlist youth movement)
Margaritas (Carlist women's service)

The Carlists supported the rival Borbón line of Don Carlos, and stood for the idea of a traditionalist ultra-Catholic monarchy as opposed to Alfonsine monarchism, which they felt had been corrupted by nineteenth-century liberalism. The leadership, particularly the Count of Rodezno, tended to be court-orientated, while the base of mainly Navarrese smallholders was populist.

FALANGE

Falange Española de las JONS
Flechas (Falangist youth movement)
Auxilio Social (Falangist women's service)

The Falange was a small fascist-style party founded by José Antonio Primo de Rivera in 1933, which then merged in 1934 with the more proletarian JONS (Juntas de Ofensiva Nacional-

Sindicalista). There was tension between the 'modern reactionaries', who followed José Antonio and who believed in the nationalist ideals of Old Spain above everything else, and the socialist wing, which resented the way its anti-capitalist ideology was overridden by the upper-class *señoritos*. The 'leftist' faction was even more disadvantaged by the vast influx of opportunists in 1936 and 1937. Its influence was crushed when Franco institutionalized the movement, amalgamating it with the Carlists.

Falange Española Tradicionalista y de las JONS (FET)

This amalgam of the nationalist political movements, principally the Falangists and the Carlists, was ordered by Franco in April 1937. He became its chief. The uniform of the movement combined the dark-blue shirt of the Falange and the red beret of the Carlists.

PRE-WAR RIGHT

Confederación Española de Derechas Autónomas (CEDA)

Acción Popular (AP)

Juventudes del Acción Popular (JAP)

Popular Action Youth

Partido Agrario (mainly Castilian landowners)

CEDA, the Spanish Confederation of the Autonomous Right, was a political alliance of right-wing Catholic parties, brought together under Gil Robles. It won the election of 1933, but its failure to win in February 1936 led to its rapid disintegration. JAP, its youth movement, went over to the Falange en masse during the spring of 1936.

Partido Republicano Radical (PRR)

Led by Alejandro Lerroux, a former revolutionary and anti-cleric, who swung to the right, the party was reputed to be the most corrupt of the period. In 1934 its liberal wing broke away under Diego Martínez Barrio to form Unión Republicana.

Derecha Liberal Republicana (DLR)

The Republican Liberal Right party of conservatives, such as Miguel Maura and Niceto Alcalá Zamora, who had turned against the monarchy.

Lliga Catalana (LC)

The Catalan League was the Catalan nationalist party of the *grande bourgeoisie*, and represented the dissatisfaction of Barcelona industrialists with the centralism and taxation of Madrid.

REPUBLICAN

POPULAR FRONT PARTIES AND AFFILIATED ORGANIZATIONS

Unión Republicana (UR)

Martínez Barrio's Republican Union was a centre-right party that broke away from Lerroux's Radicals (who had formed the government of 1934–5 with CEDA participation). It thus represented the right wing of the Popular Front alliance assembled for the February 1936 elections. Its support came from the liberal professions and businessmen.

Izquierda Republicana (IR)

Azaña's Republican Left party came from the fusion in April 1934 of his Republican Action, Casares Quiroga's Galician autonomy party and the radical socialists.

Esquerra Republicana de Catalunya

Lluís Companys's Republican Left Party of Catalonia was the Catalan counterpart to Azaña's Izquierda Republicana.

Partido Socialisto Obrero de España (PSOE)

The Spanish Socialist Workers' Party

Unión General de Trabajadores (UGT). The General Union of Workers was the trade union affiliated to the socialist party.

Juventudes Socialistas (JJSS). The Socialist Youth amalgamated with the Communist Youth in the spring of 1936 to form the United Socialist Youth, but then the whole organization was brought under communist control by its leader, Santiago Carrillo, when the civil war began.

Partido Comunista de España (PCE)

The Spanish Communist Party

Juventudes Socialistas Unificadas (JSU), the United Socialist Youth.

Partido Socialista Unificado de Cataluña (PSUC). The United Socialist Party of Catalonia was an amalgamation of Catalan socialist parties in the spring of 1936, which was completely taken over by the communists.

Partido Obrero de Unificación Marxista (POUM)

The Workers' Party of Marxist Unification was led by Andreu Nin (Trotsky's former secretary from whom he was now disassociated) and Joaquin Maurin. The party was not 'Trotskyist' as the Stalinists claimed, but had more in common with the left opposition in the Soviet Union.

ALLIES OF THE POPULAR FRONT

The Libertarian Movement (anarcho-syndicalist and anarchist)

Confederación Nacional de Trabajo (CNT). The National Confederation of Labour was the anarcho-syndicalist trade union.

Federación Anarquista Ibérica (FAI)

Federación Ibérica de Juventudes Libertarias (FIJL)

Mujeres Libres (the anarcho-feminist organization)

BASQUES

Partido Nacionalista Vasco (PNV)

The Basque Nationalist Party of conservative Christian Democrats.

Acción Nacionalista Vasca (ANV)

Basque Nationalist Action was a much smaller social democrat splinter from the PNV.

Solidaridad de Trabajadores Vascos (STV)

Solidarity of Basque Workers. The Basque nationalist Catholic trade union.

INITIALS

AC	Acción Catalana
AP	Acción Popular
AR	Acción Republicana
CEDA	Confederación Española de Derechas Autónomas
CNT	Confederación Nacional de Trabajo – anarcho-syndicalist trade union
CTV	Corpo Truppe Volontarie – Italian fascist expeditionary corps
DEDIDE	Departamento Especial de Información del Estado
DLR	Derecha Liberal Republicana
FAI	Federación Anarquista Ibérica – anarchist purists
FET	Falange Española Tradicionalista y de las JONS
FRG	Federación Republicana Gallega
GRU	Glavnoye Razvedyvatelnoye Upravleni (Soviet military intelligence)
JAP	Juventudes de Acción Popular – Popular Action Youth
JONS	Juntas de Ofensiva Nacional Sindicalista
NKVD	Narodnyi Kommissariat Vnutrennich Del – People's Commissariat for Internal Affairs (Soviet secret police)
ORGA	Organización Republicana Gallega Autónoma
OVRA	Opera Voluntaria de Repressione Antifascista (Italian fascist secret police)
PCE	Partido Comunista de España – Spanish Communist Party
PNV	Partido Nacionalista Vasco – Basque Nationalist Party
POUM	Partido Obrero de Unificación Marxista – Workers' Party of Marxist Unification
PRR	Partido Republicano Radical
PRRS	Partido Republicano Radical-Socialista
PSOE	Partido Socialista Obrero Español – Socialist Party
PSUC	Partit Socialista Unificat de Catalunya – Catalan Communist Party

RENFE	Red Nacional de Ferrocarriles Españoles (Spanish rail network)
SIEP	Servicio de Información Especial Periférico
SIM	Servicio de Inteligencia Militar (republican counter-intelligence)
SIPM	Servicio de Información y Policía Militar
UGT	Unión General de Trabajadores
UME	Unión Militar Española
UMRA	Unión Militar Republicana Antifascista

PART ONE

Old Spain and the Second Republic

I

Their Most Catholic Majesties

On an unsurfaced road in Andalucia or Estremadura, one of the first automobiles in Spain has broken down. In the photograph a young man grasps the steering wheel. He is not very good-looking, due to a large nose and enormous ears. His brilliantined hair is parted in two and he has a moustache. The driver of the car is King Alfonso XIII.

On either side, men are pushing hard at the mudguards. Their faces are burned a deep brown by the sun and they are poorly dressed, without collars or ties. They are making a big effort. In the background, three or four figures dressed in suits and hats observe the goings-on. A rider, perhaps a local landowner, has reined in his horse. On the right, a landau drawn by two horses, the reins held by a uniformed coachman, waits ready to rescue the monarch if the car's engine fails to restart. The caption announces that the king's greatest wish is to maintain 'direct contact with his people'. Few images better represented the extremes of the social and economic contrasts of Spain in the early part of the twentieth century. But perhaps the most striking aspect of the photograph is the way the peasants and the king must have seemed like foreigners to each other in their own country.

Spain, with its stern tradition of rule from Madrid, was becoming increasingly turbulent at that time, both in the countryside and in the big cities. So not even the tidy-minded could say later that the Spanish Civil War simply began in July 1936 with the rising of the 'nationalist' generals against the republican government. That event signalled the greatest clash in the conflict of forces which had dominated Spanish history. One of those antagonisms was evidently between class interests, but the other two were no less important: authoritarian rule against libertarian instinct and central government against regionalist aspirations.

The genesis of these three strains of conflict lay in the way the

Reconquista of Spain from the Moors had shaped the social structure of the country and formed the attitudes of the Castilian conquerors. The intermittent warring against the Moors, begun by Visigoth warlords in the eighth century, finally ended in 1492 with the triumphal entry into Granada of Isabella of Castile and her husband, Ferdinand of Aragon. For the Spanish traditionalist that event marked both the culmination of a long crusade and the beginning of the country's civilization. This idea permeated the nationalist alliance of 1936, which continually invoked the glory of Ferdinand and Isabella, the Catholic monarchs, and referred to their own struggle as the second *Reconquista*, with liberals, 'reds' and separatists allotted the role of contemporary heathen.

With a feudal army forming the prototype of state power, the monarchy and warrior aristocracy retook possession of the land during the fight against the Moors. In order to continue the *Reconquista*, the aristocracy needed money, not food. The cash crop which could provide it was Merino wool. Common land was seized for sheep grazing, which not only had a catastrophic effect on the peasants' food supply, but also led to soil erosion, ruining what had once been known as the 'granary of the Roman empire'. Few people were needed to tend the sheep and the only alternative to starvation was the army and, later, the empire. In the Middle Ages Spain was estimated to have a population of about fourteen million. At the end of the eighteenth century it was a little over seven million.

Castilian authoritarianism developed from a feudal-military emphasis to one of political control by the Church. During the seven centuries of the *Reconquista*'s uneven course, the Church's role had been mainly that of propagandist for military action, and even of participant. Then, in Isabella's reign the warrior archbishop was superseded by the cardinal statesman. Nevertheless, the connection between Church and army remained close during the rapid growth of Spain's empire when the crucifix was the shadow of the sword over half the world. The army conquered, then the Church integrated the new territories into the Castilian state.

The power which was exerted over the population was an irresistible force, backed by the threat of hell and its earthly foretaste in the form of the Inquisition. A single denouncer, an anonymous whisper from a jealous enemy, was often enough for the Holy Office, and the public confessions extracted before autosda-fé provided a striking foretaste of the totalitarian state. In addition the Church controlled every aspect of education and placed the entire population in a protective custody of the mind by burning books to keep out religious and political heresy. It was also the Church which vaunted Castilian qualities such as endurance of suffering and equanimity in the face of death. It encouraged the idea that it was better to be a starving *caballero* than a fat merchant.

This Spanish Catholic puritanism had been guided by Cardinal Ximénez de Cisneros, the ascetic friar promoted by Isabella to be the most powerful statesman of the age. It was basically an internal reformation. The papacy was being rejected because of its corruption, so Spain had to save Europe from heresy and Catholicism from its own weakness. As a result the clergy practised what it preached, with the exception of forgiveness and brotherly love, and sometimes issued pronouncements on property which were almost as subversive as the original teaching. Nevertheless, the Church provided spiritual justification for the Castilian social structure and was the most authoritarian force in its consolidation.

The third strain of conflict, centralism against regionalism, also developed in the fifteenth and sixteenth centuries. The first major revolt against the united kingdoms had a distinctly regionalist element. The rising of the *comuneros* in 1520 against Isabella's grandson, the Emperor Charles V, was provoked not only by his use of the country as the treasury of his empire and by the arrogance of his Flemish courtiers but also by his disregard for local rights and customs. Much of the country had been assimilated into the Castilian kingdom through royal marriage and the Spanish Habsburgs preferred to let the Church act as the binding force of the realm.

These three determining attributes of the Castilian state, feudal, authoritarian and centralist, were strongly interlinked. This was particularly true when it came to the regional question. Castile had established a central authority in Spain and built the empire, but its administration rigidly refused to acknowledge that feudal economic relationships were growing out of date. The wars in northern Europe, the fight against the French in Italy and the destruction of the Armada meant that the imperial power, developed in less than two generations, had started to decline almost immediately. Castile had the unbending pride of a newly impoverished nobleman, who refuses to notice the cobwebs and decay in his great house and resolutely continues to visualize the grandeur of his youth. This capacity for seeing only what it wanted to see made the Castilian ruling order introverted. It refused to see that the treasures from the Americas in the churches fed nobody and that the vast quantities of precious but useless metal only undermined the country's economic infrastructure.

Catalonia, which was made part of the kingdom of Aragon during the Middle Ages, was very different from the rest of the peninsula. Not surprisingly, friction developed later between Madrid and Barcelona. The Catalans had enjoyed a considerable amount of power in the Mediterranean. Their empire had included the Balearics, Corsica, Sardinia, Sicily and the Duchy of Athens. But as it had been the Castilian Isabella, not Ferdinand of Aragon, who financed Columbus, they did not have direct trading access to the Americas.

In 1640 Catalonia and Portugal rose against Philip IV of Spain and his minister, the Count-Duke of Olivares. Portugal won its independence but Catalonia acknowledged Louis XIII of France as its king, until Barcelona fell to Philip IV in 1652. Then, after the death of the last Spanish Habsburg in 1700, the War of the Spanish Succession started and Catalonia sided with England against Louis XIV's grandson, Philip of Anjou. The Catalans were betrayed by the English in the Treaty of Utrecht, and the Bourbon Philip V abolished Catalonia's rights, after it was reduced in 1714. The castle of Montjuich was built to dominate the city and remind the Catalans that they were ruled from Madrid. With this beginning Philip proceeded to implement the centralist idea of his Sun King grandfather. The unifying force of the Church had waned, so a new centripetal strength was needed if the monarchy was to control non-Castilians. The twentieth-century Basque philosopher Unamuno, who was no separatist, stated that 'the aim was unity and nothing else; unity stifling the slightest individuality and difference ... It is the dogma of the ruler's infallibility.' But ruthlessness did not solve the problem; it only stored up trouble for the future.

The backwardness of Spanish commercial activity during the seventeenth and eighteenth centuries was mainly due to the way that Spanish Catholicism had maintained an anti-capitalist line by clinging to medieval teaching on usury. The code of the *hidalgo* (Spanish nobleman) forced him to despise money in general and the earning of it in particular. The census of 1788 showed that almost 50 per cent of the adult male population was not involved in any form of productive work. The army, the Church and, above all, the vast nobility were a dead weight on the rest of the population. It was perhaps this statistic which provoked the well-known saying that 'one half of Spain eats but does not work, while the other half works but does not eat'.

In reaction against the commercial backwardness and rigidity of the ruling order, Spain was to experience a middle-class revolution in advance of most of Europe. The country enjoyed a brief easing of the chains in the mid eighteenth century, during Charles III's reign, when the influence of the Enlightenment was felt. Reforms severely reduced the Church's influence over the army, while many officers were attracted to Freemasonry. This anti-clerical and, therefore, political movement was inextricably linked with the development of liberalism among Spain's very small professional middle class. Liberalism became a recognizable force early in the nineteenth century as a result of the 'War of Independence' against Napoleon's armies. The faint-hearted Charles IV was overthrown in a popular revolt because of the corruption and scandals of his favourite, Manuel de Godoy, and the arrival of the French army. Napoleon refused to recognize his heir, Ferdinand VII, and much of the Spanish aristocracy sided with the occupying power. Then Murat's executions in Madrid provoked a spontaneous rising by the people on the 'Second of May' 1808, when they ferociously attacked the French emperor's Mameluke cavalry with knives. 'Napoleon's ulcer', as the rising was called, was the first large-scale guerrilla war of modern times and 60,000 Spaniards died in the defence of Saragossa. The bitter resistance came from a popular movement, though some liberal army officers played a major role, especially within the local juntas of defence.

The traditional ruling structure of 'Old Spain' suffered its first formal upset in 1812, when the central junta of defence proclaimed the Constitution of Cádiz, which was based upon middle-class liberal principles. This opportunity of dispensing with the stifling restrictions of monarchy and Church prompted many towns and provinces to declare themselves self-governing cantons within a Spanish federation. These changes did not last. Ferdinand VII was allowed to return on condition that he accepted the constitution, but he later broke his word and invoked the Holy Alliance, under which in 1823 the French King Louis XVIII sent an army, called 'The Hundred Thousand Sons of St Louis', to crush Spanish liberalism. Ferdinand dismantled the liberal army and reintroduced the Inquisition to destroy 'the disastrous mania of thinking'.

Spain in the nineteenth century continued to suffer from the clash between liberalism and traditionalism. After Ferdinand's death in 1833, his heir was the young Queen Isabella II. The liberal army supported her succession (and later provided most of her lovers). But the traditionalist forces grouped themselves around Ferdinand's brother and rival claimant, Don Carlos (and thus became known as Carlists). The main Carlist strength lay among the smallholders of the Pyrenees, especially in Navarre, and his supporters became famous for their religious fanaticism and ferocious rejection of modernity. In the first Carlist War of 1833–40 a British Legion, nearly 10,000 strong and led by regular officers, fought for the liberal side. The civil war of a hundred years later would also attract foreign volunteers, but sympathy for such idealistic ventures changed drastically in British governing circles. Admiration for the Byronic tradition of supporting foreign insurrections disappeared after 1918 with the rise of socialist revolution and recognition of the true horrors of war.

The free-thinking liberalism which permeated the increasingly middle-class Spanish officer corps in the early years of the century declined. Liberals profited from the sale of church lands and developed into a reactionary *grande bourgeoisie*. The governments in Madrid were corrupt and the generals acquired a taste for overthrowing them. This was the age of the *pronunciamiento*, when generals would form up their troops and make long speeches appointing themselves saviour and dictator of the country. Between 1814 and 1874 there were 37 attempted coups, of which twelve were successful.[1] The country lurched along, becoming poorer and poorer, while Queen Isabella exercised her guards officers. She was finally deposed in 1868 after choosing a lover of whom the army did not approve. Two years later Amadeo of Savoy was chosen as her successor, but his earnest goodwill was not enough to win support from a population exasperated with the monarchy. His abdication in February 1873 was followed by a vote in the Cortes establishing a republic.

The First Republic was soon brought down by military intervention. Its federalist programme had included the abolition of military conscription, a very popular measure, but within a few weeks of the first elections sporadic Carlist revolts became a full-scale civil war and the government was forced to break this important promise. The Carlist pretender's most effective troops were the staunchly Catholic Basques, who were primarily motivated by separatist ambitions of throwing off rule from Madrid. Spanish monarchs were only lords of the Basque provinces, which constituted a *señorio* and which had never been subjected to central rule like other parts of the peninsula.

The generals saw the army's main role as enforcing Spanish unity, especially after the loss of the American empire. As Castilian centralists, they were appalled by the prospect of separatist Basque and Catalan nations occupying the Pyrenean frontier. They were also implacably opposed to federalism, so when self-governing cantons were proclaimed in other areas they did not hesitate to crush this movement against government from Madrid as well as the Carlists and Basques. The First Republic lasted only a few months.

The conservative politician Cánovas del Castillo had been planning the re-establishment of the Bourbons since the fall of Isabella. He also wanted to institute stable government while returning the army to barracks. This was achieved when General Martínez Campos proclaimed Alfonso XII king at the end of 1874. Alfonso was Isabella's son (and therefore presumably of good military stock), but he was still only a Sandhurst cadet.

Under Cánovas's constitution, which was to last half a century, Church and landowner were back in strength. They had every intention of keeping it that way and elections were unashamedly manipulated. Peasants and tenants had to vote as their landlord told them or face eviction. Canvassing consisted of the political bosses, the *caciques*, sending out armed gangs known as *El Partido de la Porra* (the Bludgeon Party) and if that did not look like working, then ballot papers were destroyed or substituted. Political and economic corruption spread from Madrid in a way that far exceeded anything known in previous centuries. The courts were rigged right down to the village tribunals, so no poor person ever expected to have his case heard, let alone obtain justice.

Although there may often have been a vicious rivalry between liberals and conservatives in the provinces, there was virtually a gentleman's agreement between their leaders in the capital.

Whenever there was an unpopular measure to carry out, the conservatives retired and the liberals, who had now become almost indistinguishable from their opponents, came in. The two parties resembled those little wooden men who appear alternately to indicate the weather. But any high-minded figure, however aristocratic, who denounced the corruption was regarded as a traitor and shunned. The trinity of army, monarchy and Church, which had originally made the empire, was also to preside over its final collapse. In 1898 the Spanish-American War saw the pathetic rout of the armed forces and the loss of Cuba, the Philippines and Puerto Rico. Most of the soldiers' food and equipment had been sold by their officers.

Even the tawdry end of the *reconquista* vision in Cuba in 1898 did not rouse the rulers of Spain from their myopic complacency. They could not admit that the obsession with empire had ruined the country. To admit that would have been to undermine the institutions of aristocracy, Church and army. This refusal to face reality started to come up against new political forces, which were growing rapidly and which, unlike the liberalism of the early nineteenth century, could not be absorbed into the governing structure. The incompatibility of 'Eternal Spain' with these new political movements developed into the clash which later tore the country apart.

Alfonso XIII, the driver of the broken-down car, became king at the age of sixteen in 1902. Poverty was so great at the beginning of the twentieth century that over half a million Spaniards, out of a population of eighteen and a half million, emigrated to the New World in the first decade of the century alone. Life expectancy was around 35 years, the same as at the time of Ferdinand and Isabella. Illiteracy rates, varying sharply by area, averaged 64 per cent overall. Two thirds of Spain's active population still worked on the land. Yet it was not just a problem of property rights and tensions between landowners and landless peasants. Within the total of five million farmers and peasants, there were huge differences in standards of living and techniques, according to region. In Andalucia, Estremadura and La Mancha, agriculture remained primitive and ineffectively laborious. In many other areas, such as Galicia, León, Old Castile, Catalonia and the north, small proprietors worked their own land with fierce independence while the rich coastal plain of the Levante represented perhaps the best example of intensive culture in Europe.[2]

Industry and mining provided only 18 per cent of the jobs available, little more than domestic and other services.[3] Spain's main exports came from agricultural produce, particularly the fertile coastal region around Valencia, and only a certain amount from mining. But after the collapse of the last vestiges of empire, money was repatriated and along with other investment from Europe, above all from France, a banking boom followed during which some of the major Spanish banks of today were founded.[4] The government subsidized industrial development and, in Catalonia especially, huge fortunes were made.

The country remained neutral in the First World War. Its agricultural exports, raw materials and rising industrial output at such a time created what seemed like an economic miracle, with thousands of new enterprises. The new prosperity led to a significant rise in the birth rate, which would have its effect twenty years later in the mid 1930s. Spain's balance of payments was so favourable that the country's gold reserves increased dramatically.[5] But when the war was over the economic miracle faded away. The governments of the day fell back on protectionism. Expectations had risen, and disappointment and resentment were bound to follow in the unemployment that ensued.

2

Royal Exit

The first attempt to organize some form of trade union in Spain had occurred as early as the 1830s, and there were small non-political associations in existence at the middle of the nineteenth century. Then new political ideas arrived across the Pyrenees and began to take root. The anarchist, or libertarian, form of socialism arrived first and its fundamental disagreement with Marxist socialism was to have great repercussions in Spain. Proudhon had already been translated by Pi y Margall, the president of the First Republic, when Giuseppe Fanelli arrived in Spain in 1868. Fanelli was an admirer of Bakunin, Marx's great opponent in the First International. He came to Madrid without speaking any Spanish and with no money, but the 'Idea', as it became known, found a very enthusiastic audience. Within four years there were nearly 50,000 Bakuninists in Spain, of whom the majority were in Andalucia.

There were several reasons why anarchism in the early days became the largest force within the Spanish working class. Its proposed structure of co-operative communities, associating freely, corresponded to deep-rooted traditions of mutual aid, and the federalist organization appealed to anti-centralist feelings. It also offered a strong moral alternative to a corrupt political system and hypocritical Church. Many observers have pointed to the naive optimism which anarchism inspired among the landless peasants of Andalucia. Much has also been made of the way in which the word was spread by ascetic, almost saint-like characters and how the converts gave up tobacco, alcohol and infidelity (while rejecting official marriage). As a result it was often described as a secular religion. Even so, the intensity of this early anarchism led converts to believe that everybody else must see that freedom and mutual aid were the only foundation of a naturally ordered society. An uprising was all that was needed to open people's eyes, unfetter the vast potential of goodwill and set off what Bakunin called the 'spontaneous creativity of the masses'.

Their frustration at being unable to 'unlock the mechanism of history', as the Russian writer Victor Serge described it, led to individual acts of political violence in the 1890s. The *tigres solitarios*, as their fellow anarchists called them, acted either in the hope of stirring up others to emulate them or in reprisal for the indiscriminate brutality of the Brigada Social, the secret police. The most famous example was the torturing to death in 1892 of several anarchists in the castle of Montjuich in Barcelona. This led to an international outcry and to the assassination of Cánovas del Castillo, the organizer of the restoration. A vicious circle of repression and revenge was to follow.

During the last quarter of the nineteenth century the Marxist wing of socialism, *los autoritarios*, as their opponents called them, developed much less rapidly. In late 1871 Karl Marx's son-in-law Paul Lafargue arrived after the fall of the Paris Commune and within a year the basis of Spanish socialism was laid in Madrid. The Marxists' comparative lack of success was partly due to the emphasis which they placed on the central state. The socialists under Pablo Iglesias, a typesetter who emerged as the leading Spanish Marxist, proceeded cautiously and concentrated on building an organization. Eventually in 1879 they founded the Spanish Socialist Workers' Party (PSOE) and formed their General Union of Labour (UGT) in 1888. Iglesias still insisted that the class struggle should be waged in a moderate and evolutionary manner (the PSOE did not formally repudiate the monarchy until 1914). The socialists accused their anarchist rivals of 'irresponsibility', but they in turn were seen as heavily bureaucratic and received the nickname of 'Spanish Prussians'.

Another reason for the socialists' slow development in a predominantly agricultural society came from Marx's contempt for the peasantry and what he called 'the idiocy of rural life'. He believed that capitalism would be overthrown only by its own creation, the industrial proletariat. However, in Spain, the major part of industry was concentrated in Catalonia, which had become the stronghold of anarchism. As a result the 'Castilian' socialists had to look to Bilbao for support among industrial workers. The central mass of Spain and the northern coast were to be their main spheres of influence, while the anarchist following was greatest down the Mediterranean belt, especially in Catalonia and Andalucia.

From the 1890s until the early 1920s Spain experienced many turbulent years, especially those which coincided with the Russian and German revolutions at the end of the First World War. The main areas of strife were the large landed estates, the *latifundia* of Andalucia and Estremadura, the mining valleys of Asturias and Vizcaya, and industrial Catalonia. In *fin de siècle* Barcelona, nouveaux riches factory owners had indulged in triumphant ostentation, both architecturally and socially.

The cycle of violence between industrial revolt and repression became chaotic at times. The Brigada Social, the secret police, interpreted its role as the guardian of public order in an extraordinary manner, often hiring gangsters to take on the anarchist '*pistoleros*' or strike leaders. The first explosion of urban unrest, the Semana Trágica, or 'Tragic Week', at the end of July 1909, was not, however, caused by industrial dispute in Barcelona. It was a by-product of the colonial war in Morocco. Riffian tribesmen had wiped out a column of soldiers sent to secure mining concessions bought by the Count de Romanones, one of Alfonso XIII's advisers. The government called up the reserves; the poor could not afford to buy themselves out of military service and married workers were the most affected.[1] A strong anti-militarist mood had grown up in the years following the Cuban disaster, and the spontaneous reaction in Barcelona to the Morocco crisis was sudden and overwhelming.

The 'young barbarians' who supported the Radical Party leader Alejandro Lerroux went wild and others followed, with church burning and forms of desecration such as the famous incident of a worker dancing with a disinterred nun. Such symbolic violence was the reaction of a people traumatized by intense superstition. Much of the teaching of the Spanish Catholic Church sounded appropriate to the Dark Ages and this mental repression, together with the political role played by ecclesiastical authorities, made the Church rank with the Civil Guard as the first target of an uprising. Some half a dozen people were killed during this disturbance, but when the army arrived to restore order there was a massacre.

Hundreds were arrested including Francisco Ferrer, the founder of the libertarian Modern School. Although it was evident that Ferrer could have had nothing to do with the rioting, the Catholic hierarchy put heavy pressure on the government to convict their educational opponent. He was sentenced to death on the basis of obviously false testimony and his execution led to a wave of protest in Spain and abroad.

After the Barcelona upheaval of 1909 a majority in the libertarian movement evolved a fresh strategy. This new direction was mainly influenced by the French syndicalist movement, with a union-based policy, the ultimate objective of which was a general strike followed by the reorganization of society based on self-managed industry and agriculture. This led to the setting up of the anarcho-syndicalist National Confederation of Labour (CNT), whose component unions were to be organized by industry, not by craft. The Spanish libertarian movement thus consisted basically of anarchist purists and anarcho-syndicalists.

During the First World War, while industrialists profited enormously, their workers suffered from high inflation – prices doubled between 1913 and 1918 – yet salaries increased by only 25 per cent.[2] Union membership rose dramatically as a result. The UGT increased to 160,000 members, while the anarcho-syndicalist CNT swelled to some 700,000 by the end of 1919. The socialist party itself, the PSOE, soon counted on 42,000 activists. Its leading members included Francisco Largo Caballero, Indalecio Prieto, Fernando de los Ríos and Julián Besteiro, all of whom would be major figures in the years to come. Meanwhile the very moderate Catholic union movement, Confederación Nacional Católica Agraria (CONCA), grew mainly in the agrarian heartlands of Castile and León. Its only hope in industrial centres was in the devout Basque country.[3]

In Spain, the entrenched position of the military establishment proved a major obstacle to gradual reform. The Spanish army was 160,000 strong, commanded by 12,000 officers and 213 generals.[4] This overmanned and incompetent organization was a heavy charge on the state. Its role was never clear. Although basically reactionary, at times it saw itself as an ally of the people against corrupt politicians and a force for national regeneration. Reduced after the loss of empire to an existence of provincial garrisons, its only active area of operations lay in the Spanish protectorate of Morocco, a far smaller area than that accorded to France in 1906 at the Conference of Algeciras. The only economic interest in the territory lay in its phosphate mines, while the local Kabyle population longed to rid themselves of European rule. For Spanish officers keen on promotion, service in Morocco promised real soldiering far from the boredom of barrack life at home. An '*africanista*' mystique developed, making them the elite of the Spanish armed forces and giving them a sense of destiny as well as arrogance.

In 1917 a military and political crisis developed in Spain. Associations known as Juntas de Defensa had grown up in the forces to demand better conditions, but when the government tried to abolish them their leaders published a manifesto attacking the lamentable state of the army. Afraid of a *pronunciamiento*, the conservative administration of Eduardo Dato conceded to some of their demands. But this encouraged in some politicians, above all Francesc Cambó, the leader of the Lliga Catalana, the idea that they could use the opportunity to force through constitutional reforms. They hoped that this would modernize the country and introduce real democracy. Cambó called for an assembly of politicians on 19 July in Barcelona as a step towards a constituent Cortes, a fully representative parliament.

At the same time the socialist PSOE and the UGT, under similar illusions, also imagined that the juntas offered a chance of change. They called a general strike to support their own demands for a constituent Cortes. Dato closed parliament and suspended constitutional guarantees. The strike began on 13 August in Madrid, Barcelona, Bilbao, Saragossa, Oviedo and the mining regions of the Asturias and Andalucia. But the Juntas de Defensa not only refused to join the revolution, their members took part in crushing the strikes, leaving 72 dead, 156 wounded and 2,000 arrested. In Asturias, where the strike lasted a month, General Ricardo Burguete and a young *africanista* major called Francisco Franco were in charge of the repression which included torture. It was a foretaste of a far more serious upheaval in 1934, in which General Franco was to play a leading role. While the socialist leaders were condemned to life imprisonment in Cartagena, nothing happened to Cambó.

Repression alone was no solution to the social problems which increased with the end of the First World War. The population was growing, largely due to a fall in infant mortality, and the cities swelled, with internal migration from the more impoverished areas of the countryside as men and women sought work at a time of rising unemployment. The Church no longer was able to control the population as it had, yet the politicians of the day refused to accept the possibility of change. They did not know, or did not want to consider, how to move 'from an oligarchic liberalism to mass democracy'.[5] Comparatively little had changed in attitude since Ferdinand VII, a century before, had described Spain as a bottle of champagne and himself as the cork to prevent it gushing over.

When the First World War ended and the export boom slackened, the workers became more militant. Also, the news from Russia brought hope to the left. There was talk of Europe blazing with revolution at both ends. The period of 1918–20, with uprisings in Andalucia and strife in Barcelona, was known as the 'three years of bolshevism'. The worst wave of unrest started when the anarcho-syndicalist CNT brought the workers of La Canadiense out on strike.[6] The Catalan employers replied with lockouts and resorted to blackleg labour from depressed areas. In answer to the violence from the unions, especially the CNT, they hired *pistoleros* to shoot down union leaders. To restore order Alfonso XIII appointed General Severiano Martínez Anido as civil governor. His chief of police, General Arleguí, reorganized the police *pistoleros* and 21 union leaders were shot down either at home or in the street in less than 48 hours. The cycle of bitterness was such that it later led to the assassination by anarchists of Eduardo Dato in 1921.[7]

The radicalization of the CNT clashed with the moderate stance of the socialist UGT. The anarcho-syndicalists saw the socialists as reformists, if not traitors to the working class. The Spanish Communist Party was founded in 1921, with both militant socialists and anarchists responding to the call of Andreu Nin and Joaquín Maurín. This third, although still minute, force was to take part in the struggle for leadership of the industrial working class. Meanwhile, in the countryside the day workers in Andalucia continued their own long *jacquerie* of doomed uprisings. The strikes of rural labourers followed each other at a rapid rhythm. The Civil Guard would be called out, and the trouble suppressed by shootings and arrests. The protests spread from Córdoba to Jaén, Seville and Cádiz, with demands for better conditions and the recognition of rural trade unions. But encouraged by news from the other end of Europe, they adopted slogans such as '*¡Vivan los soviets!*', which they daubed on whitewashed walls, confirming landowners in their suspicion that if they weakened, they could face the same terrible fate as Russian landowners.[8] Even the politicians in Madrid recognized that some form of land reform programme needed to be implemented urgently, but few governments remained in place long enough to tackle the problem.[9]

Although the politicians in Madrid managed to maintain a certain status quo for most of the time, in July 1921 a far deeper crisis developed when the Spanish army in Morocco suffered a most ignominious defeat. A division commanded by General Silvestre was ambushed at Annual on 20 July 1921 by Moroccan tribesmen under Abd-el-Krim. For reasons of personal vanity, King Alfonso was said to have wanted an outstanding victory to announce on the feast of St James (the Spanish army's patron saint) and that he had gone behind the minister of war's back to encourage Silvestre in this venture.

The Annual expedition was a classic example of military incompetence: 10,000 soldiers were killed, 4,000 were taken prisoner and Silvestre committed suicide. A week later another major position was lost, another 7,000 soldiers were massacred and all the officers were led away in chains. The reaction throughout Spain was so bitter that the government was forced to set up a commission of inquiry. The king was severely censured in its findings, but shortly before the report was due to be published the new captain-general of Catalonia, Miguel Primo de Rivera, made a *pronunciamiento* on 13 September, appointing himself dictator with Alfonso remaining as head of state. The other generals gave him tacit support to prevent this public condemnation of the army and the king.

General Primo de Rivera immediately declared a state of war throughout the country to halt any unrest or protests in their tracks. Yet he was not a typical dictator of that inter-war period. He was in a way an Andalucian version of those hard-living, hard-riding squires of Regency England. As a young officer he had been sickened by corrupt practices within the army, such as the selling of the soldiers' food and equipment. But he also had that fatal military attitude to politics: all would be well if everyone could be united in a single party, rather like the army itself. He subsequently set up his own organization, the Unión Patriótica, but it never stood a chance of gaining mass support. Primo also had a completely arbitrary approach to justice, trying often to play Solomon with a sense of humour, which fell flat. But there was comparatively little police state brutality under his dictatorship.

Primo's assumption of power was welcomed at first by industrialists and accepted by the liberal middle classes, who felt that nothing could be worse than the recent years of chaos and bloodshed. They hoped that the dictator, even though a member of the aristocracy, might be able to implement agrarian reforms which no landowning government would consider. But although Primo sympathized with the peasants in a patriarchal fashion, any serious attempt to tackle the agrarian problem would have required measures that were too radical for him and unthinkable for those on whom he depended.

He did, however, attempt to end the industrial warfare in Catalonia. Workers' organizations had to be involved, he decided, and the employers controlled. The centralist socialists were the obvious choice for him, and he brought the secretary of the UGT, Francisco Largo Caballero, into his government as a councillor of state, to set up industrial arbitration boards. This idea of working with Primo's administration was firmly opposed by the other main socialist leader, Indalecio Prieto. The anarchists also accused Largo Caballero of shameless opportunism when their organizations and publications were banned.

The Catalan employers, meanwhile, having welcomed Primo's arrival in power, now hated his control over their methods of dealing with union leaders. Primo also took a spiteful pleasure in attacking their nationalism through attempts to suppress Catalan language and culture. Like all patriarchs, he was convinced of his own good intentions. He made grand gestures, took petty measures and was unpredictable. His biggest success, due more to luck than good judgement, was to end the war in Morocco. In April 1925 the great Riffian chief Abd-el-Krim overreached himself by attacking the French zone in a wild fashion. This produced an immediate military alliance between France and Spain. On 8 September French and Spanish troops landed at Alhucemas, trapping Abd-el-Krim's force. The rebellion in Morocco was finally crushed.

In December Primo formed a directorate composed of military officers and civilians. Yet his plans to modernize Spain lacked both judgement and luck. They included overambitious and badly planned engineering projects, such as hydroelectric dams and highways, which resulted in enormous waste.[10] The deficit doubled between 1925 and 1929, and his young finance minister, José Calvo Sotelo, made things far worse by pegging the peseta to the gold standard. Currency speculators made large fortunes at the government's expense and attempts to prop up the value of the currency failed dismally. There was a flight of capital, and by the time the Second Republic was declared in 1931 the peseta had lost nearly 50 per cent of its value.

Under Primo's rule a claustrophobic irritation built up. Bankers and industrialists hated his intervention in matters he did not understand. The middle classes started to react when he interfered with the universities. As a flamboyant product of his profession and background, the well-meaning patriarch had by now become a liability to the monarchy he had stepped in to save. Alfonso XIII began to fear for his throne. Over the previous five years a political opposition to the dictatorship had developed in left-liberal and intellectual circles. The most important became known as the Alianza Republicana and was headed by Manuel Azaña, Alejandro Lerroux, Marcelino Domingo and several others. Its aim was not just to do away with the dictatorship, but also the monarchy. Opposition to the whole idea of collaborating with Primo had also grown within socialist ranks and by 1929 Largo Caballero was forced to realize his mistake in agreeing to work with the regime. When in 1930 the socialists opposed the monarchy and the dictatorship, UGT membership began to rise rapidly. From 211,000 members in 1923 it increased to 277,000 in 1930 and was to reach just over half a million two years later.

Like a stern, insensitive father whose authority is challenged, Primo tried to enforce his will more and more. Hurt and confused at not being appreciated, he appealed to the army to reassure himself of their support. It was not forthcoming, so Primo presented his resignation to the king on 28 January 1930 and went into exile. He died in Paris a few weeks later.

On 30 January Alfonso XIII, who could no longer fall back on the constitution that he himself had openly broken, entrusted the government to another general, Dámaso Berenguer. This outraged General Sanjurjo, then the director of the Civil Guard, who believed himself far better qualified for the post. Alfonso's obstinate recourse to generals and the fact that Berenguer allowed nearly a whole year to pass before summoning the Cortes only exasperated people more as the country was governed by decree and censorship remained in place. Even former monarchist politicians, such as Niceto Alcalá Zamora and Miguel Maura, publicly came out in favour of a republic.

Indalecio Prieto, at first on his own account, then later with the support of the executive committees of the socialist PSOE and UGT union, joined the conspiracy. The republican alliance officially came into being in the Basque coastal resort of San Sebastián on 27 August 1930. Catalan republicans joined the San Sebastián pact, as it became known, on condition that Catalonia received a statute of autonomy. This republican movement strengthened with the support of military officers such as Gonzalo Queipo de Llano, one of General Franco's chief rivals after the military rising of 1936, Ramón Franco, the aviator brother of the nationalist leader, and Ignacio Hidalgo de Cisneros, later the communist commander of the republican air force in the civil war.

In December the UGT called a general strike, which the anarcho-syndicalist CNT did not oppose. Meanwhile Alcalá Zamora became the president of a revolutionary committee, which constituted itself as a government in waiting. University students and workers openly campaigned for the overthrow of the monarchy and a rising, which was planned for 12 December, had to be delayed by three days. Unfortunately, nobody warned Captains Galán and García Hernández of the garrison of Jaca. They rose in revolt at six in the morning, but finding themselves on their own, they had to surrender. Tried for military rebellion, they were executed. This turned them into immediate martyrs of the republican cause. General Emilio Mola, the director-general of security, arrested all the members of the revolutionary committee to be found and the uprising collapsed. But this did little to halt the republican momentum.

In the following month, January 1931, another university strike began, headed by a group known as 'Al servicio de la República'. It included the principal figures of the Spanish intelligentsia: José Ortega y Gasset, Gregorio Marañón, Ramón Pérez de Ayala and their president, the poet Antonio Machado. On 14 February the king, shaken by the agitation, replaced Berenguer with Admiral Juan Bautista Aznar and gave orders that municipal elections should be called for 12 April. This allowed the republicans to turn the vote into a plebiscite on the monarchy itself. On the evening of 12 April the results began to come in. The socialists and liberal republicans had won almost all the provincial capitals of Spain. The excited crowds packing the centre of Madrid instantly acclaimed the shadow government of Alcalá Zamora as the new government, even though these elections had nothing to do with the Cortes.[11]

General Berenguer, who had become minister of war, ordered the army to abide by the will of the people. The Count de Romanones, a member of Admiral Aznar's government, tried in vain to come to an agreement with the republican committee. He then asked the director of the Civil Guard, General Sanjurjo, if he could count on his force. The offended general took his revenge and answered no. The whole of Madrid became 'a fiesta of the people which took on the appearance of a revolution'.[12] That same evening Admiral Aznar presented the king with his government's resignation.

At six in the morning of 14 April 1931 the Republic was proclaimed at Eibar and the news spread almost instantaneously throughout Spain. Romanones had a meeting with the republican leader Alcalá Zamora, who told him that the king and his family should leave Spain that very afternoon. The king, who rejected the idea of another minister, that the army should keep him in power, left Madrid to embark at Cartagena. His departure created no disturbances. 'Well before its collapse,' wrote Miguel Maura, 'the monarchy had evaporated in the consciousness of Spaniards.'[13]

3
The Second Republic

On 14 April 1931 the revolutionary committee headed by Niceto Alcalá Zamora, a Catholic and a landowner from Córdoba, converted itself into the provisional government of the Republic. Alcalá Zamora then became president and head of state.[1]

These leaders of the Republic faced immense problems deeply rooted in Spanish society: agrarian reform, the intransigence of the armed forces, the Catalan and Basque questions, and the issue of relations between the Catholic Church and the state. They also needed to tackle the deficiencies of the educational system in their objective to create a 'Republic of citizens'.

The international situation following the Wall Street crash of 1929 was hardly propitious. The world depression did not affect Spain as severely as some of the more industrially developed countries, yet prices for the country's traditional exports were reduced by nearly half.[2] Protests over the fall in living standards and social unrest awoke fears across much of Europe of more revolutions following the one in Russia. This had contributed to the assumption of dictatorial or authoritarian regimes in a number of countries.[3] In such a climate the fall of the monarchy in Spain and the proclamation of a republic was unwelcome to the international banking community. Morgan's Bank immediately cancelled a loan of 60 million dollars agreed with the previous administration.

The new government also inherited the consequences of the economic mistakes made under Primo de Rivera's dictatorship, the massive debts from public spending projects and the collapse in the value of the peseta. Large amounts of capital had also been transferred abroad in anticipation of increased taxation and a further deterioration of the country's economy.[4] Landowners and industrialists, afraid of the financial effects of the government's likely social programme, immediately cut investment. These fears were influenced by the appointment of one socialist, Indalecio Prieto, as minister of finance, and another, Largo Caballero, as minister of labour.[5]

The government, a coalition from six different parties, proceeded nevertheless to summon the Cortes and draft a constitution for the Second Republic. Throughout April, May and June of 1931 they continued to issue decrees dealing with the question of land reform. These forbade landowners to expel tenants or to hire day labourers from outside their municipality. And they extended employment rights agreed in industry, including the eight-hour day, to agricultural workers. On 21 May the government created the Comisión Técnica Agraria to draft a law, setting up an Institute of Agrarian Reform. It established a programme to resettle between 60,000 and 75,000 families each year, but its budget was only 50 million pesetas, a totally inadequate amount for the task.

The following week the new minister of war, Manuel Azaña, set out to tackle the overmanned military establishment. He offered generals and officers the possibility of passing to the reserve list on full pay. He reduced the sixteen captaincy-generals to eight 'organic divisions', suppressed the rank of lieutenant-general, reduced the length of obligatory military service to one year and ordered the closure of the General Military Academy of Saragossa, which happened to be commanded by General Francisco Franco.[6]

These reforms did not bring about any substantive improvements in the modernization or efficiency of the army. If anything, it provided disgruntled officers with the time and opportunity to plot against the Republic. The government also made the error of keeping General Sanjurjo in the post of commander of the Civil Guard, a corps which had a notorious reputation for its deadly acts of repression.[7] It set up a new paramilitary force, with the unpromising title of Assault Guard. They were known as the *asaltos*, and tended to be deployed in towns and cities while the Civil Guard policed the countryside.

Catalan autonomy was also high on the list of matters to be addressed. It was a question which greatly concerned old-fashioned Castilian centralists, who saw any concessions to the regions as a threat to the unity of Spain. The April elections had proved a victory for the party of the Catalan left, the Esquerra Republicana de Catalunya, an essentially middle-class organization led by Francesc Macià and Lluís Companys. The two of them had proclaimed on

14 April that a Catalan republic would be established within a federal state. This was not exactly what had been negotiated in the pact of San Sebastián, so three days later three ministers left Madrid for Barcelona to discuss with Macià and Companys the best way forward to enable the Cortes to approve a statute of autonomy. On 21 April Macià was named as president of the Generalitat of Catalonia, the name of the medieval Catalan Commonwealth.

The relationship between the new secular Republic and the Catholic Church was unlikely to be simple, with the Concordat of 1851 still in force. No more than fifteen days after the announcement of the Republic, Cardinal Pedro Segura, the primate of Spain, issued a pastoral denouncing the new government's intention to establish freedom of worship and to separate Church and state. The cardinal urged Catholics to vote in future elections against an administration which in his view wanted to destroy religion. The Catholic press followed his lead. The organ of Acción Católica, *El Debate*, dedicated itself to defending the privileges of the Church while the monarchist daily, *ABC*, aligned itself with the most traditionalist positions.

Faced with a revolt by the most important figure in the Spanish Church, republican ministers ordered the expulsion from the country of Cardinal Segura and another cleric, Mateo Múgica, Bishop of Vitoria. In the course of a curious spate of activity Cardinal Segura based himself in the south of France and instructed his priests in Spain to sell Church property without transferring the proceeds into pesetas.[8]

The fanatical mysticism of the Church provoked much of the anti-clericalism in Spain, especially the 'miracles', which in the 1930s often involved a 'red' supposedly committing a sacrilegious act and dropping dead on the spot. The novelist Ramón Sender attributed the left's vandalism against churches, such as the desecration of mummies, to the Church's obsession with the kissing of saints' bones and limbs. Anything, however ridiculous, was believed by the *beatas*, the black-clothed women who obeyed their priests' every word like the devotees of a cult leader. In Spain there were more psychological disorders arising from religious delusions than all other kinds. This atmosphere influenced even unbelievers in a strange way. Workers formed gruesome ideas of torture in convents, and many natural catastrophes were attributed to the Jesuits in the same way as the Church blamed Freemasons, Jews and communists.

On 11 May, two weeks after the publication of Segura's pastoral, serious disturbances were sparked off by an incident outside a monarchist club in Madrid, when a taxi driver was apparently beaten up for shouting '*¡Viva la República!*'. Crowds gathered and the buildings of the monarchist newspaper *ABC* were set on fire. The Carmelite church in the Plaza de España suffered next, followed by more and more churches over the next two days, with the outbreak spreading down the Mediterranean coast and into Andalucia – with arson in Alicante, Málaga, Cádiz and Seville. These disturbances finally obliged a reluctant government to impose martial law. The right, however, would never forget the notorious remark attributed to Azaña that he preferred that all the churches of Spain should burn rather than a single republican should be harmed.

On 3 June the Spanish bishops sent the head of government a collective letter denouncing the separation of Church and state, and protesting against the suppression of obligatory religious instruction in schools.[9] But pressure against the government was also building up from the other side, especially from the libertarian left. On 6 July the anarcho-syndicalist CNT declared a telephone workers' strike throughout Spain. This paralysed lines from Barcelona and Seville, but CNT members also carried out acts of sabotage against the North American-owned Telefónica network, which Primo de Rivera's dictatorship had sold to ITT. The United States ambassador demanded the deployment of security forces and the Madrid government also brought in strike breakers from the UGT.

The CNT declared a national strike and in Seville the funeral of a worker killed by a strike breaker was broken up by the Civil Guard. The ensuing battle produced seven dead, including three civil guards. The Madrid government declared a state of war on 22 July. The army and Civil Guard, the traditional forces of law and order, acted with their customary brutality. They used light artillery as well as the '*ley de fugas*', the excuse of shooting prisoners 'while attempting to escape'. The casualty rate rose by another 30 dead and 200 wounded, as well as hundreds arrested. Spanish workers, who had placed great hopes in the Republic, came to the conclusion that it was as repressive as the monarchy. The CNT declared open war and announced their intention of overthrowing it by social revolution.

*

The Republic, following the elections on 28 June, was just starting its parliamentary business in the Cortes.[10] The first session had taken place under the presidency of the socialist intellectual Julián Besteiro on 14 July. The socialists of the PSOE were for once united, with a rare harmony between Largo Caballero and Indalecio Prieto, the moderate from Bilbao who was a strenuous advocate of a centre-left alliance with liberal republicans. Largo Caballero had agreed to socialist participation in the government because he felt it was in the best interests of the UGT, his overriding concern. Even though his union was growing rapidly, the CNT was outstripping it, since becoming legal again the previous year. (Government figures in 1934 put UGT membership at 1.44 million and CNT membership at 1.58 million.)

At the end of August the first draft of the constitution was debated, including its declaration that 'Spain is a democratic republic of workers of all classes'. The most contentious sections – articles 26 and 27 – provided for the dissolution of religious orders. This precipitated a crisis, which was solved by the persuasive powers of Manuel Azaña. Only the Jesuit order was to be banned and its property nationalized.[11] But article 26 provided for the ending of state subsidies to the Church within two years. The Church faced an acute problem. For the first time it found itself dealing with an administration which rejected the traditional idea that the Church was synonymous with Spain. The fact that religious attendance in Spain was the lowest of any Christian country did not stop Cardinal Segura from declaring that in Spain one was 'either a Catholic, or nothing at all'. Less than 20 per cent of Spain's total population went to mass. In most areas south of the Guadarrama mountains the figure was under 5 per cent. Such statistics did nothing to lessen the Church hierarchy's view, both in Spain and in Rome, that the Republic was determined to persecute it.[12]

The debate over article 44 about the expropriation of land in 'the national interest', demanded by the socialists, produced an even greater crisis and once again (as with article 26) Alcalá Zamora nearly resigned. The policy of agrarian reform needed these powers to work, and even though only uncultivated land would be given to landless labourers, the centre and right were deeply suspicious about where such measures could lead.[13] Finally, on 9 December the Constitution was voted through. Niceto Alcalá Zamora was formally elected president of the Republic and on 15 December Azaña formed a new government.[14]

Manuel Azaña, the most prominent liberal republican, was a strongly anti-clerical intellectual of brilliant wit and lugubrious pessimism. He came to regard himself as the strong man of the Republic, but he lacked consistency and stamina for such a role. His support came mainly from the progressive middle class, such as teachers and doctors, as well as from lower-middle-class artisans and clerks.

The head of the Radical Party, Alejandro Lerroux, who had hoped to lead the government instead of Azaña, found himself vetoed by the socialists. With justification, they considered his party corrupt. From then on Lerroux would look to make his alliances with the right. His support came mainly from conservatives and businessmen who had disliked Alfonso, but had no deep-rooted opposition to the principle of monarchy.

The opponents of republican reform, supporters of the large landowners, the clergy and the army, represented only a small minority of seats within the Cortes, but this did not slow their mobilization to defend traditional Spain.[15] Fascism was a negligible presence at this stage, with a couple of reviews and a handful of right-wing intellectuals gathered round José Antonio Primo de Rivera, the son of the late dictator.[16]

Following the proclamation of the Republic, the anarchists had split between those who followed the syndicalist, or trade union, path, which was the case with '*treintistas*' of Ángel Pestaña and Joan Peiró, and those who belonged to the FAI (Federación Anarquista Ibérica). The FAIistas, including Juan García Oliver and Buenaventura Durruti, believed passionately in the struggle against the state, with strikes and risings, dubbed *la* '*gimnasia revolucionaria*', which was supposed to bring about the social revolution. But it was a small event in the countryside that was to lead to the first major threat to the government.

Castilblanco, a village in the province of Badajoz near the Portuguese border, was on strike during the last days of December 1931. A detachment of the Civil Guard arrived to restore order and one of them opened fire, killing a local man. The reaction of the peasants was ferocious. They lynched four civil guards. The spiral of violence was immediate. In another incident far away in the Rioja, civil guards appear to have avenged their comrades in Castilblanco by killing eleven people and wounding 30 more. Azaña summoned Sanjurjo, upbraided him for the actions of his force and removed him from his post, half-demoting him with the appointment of inspector general of *carabineros*.[17]

General Sanjurjo, who had assisted the arrival of the Republic in April by refusing to support the king, felt badly treated. He began to contact other senior officers with a view to mounting a *coup d'état*. The government was well aware of what was happening and Sanjurjo's coup, when it came in August, was a humiliating failure. It had a momentary success in Seville, but Sanjurjo's inactivity and the CNT's immediate declaration of a general strike finished it off. Sanjurjo tried to flee to Portugal but was arrested at Huelva.[18]

The government in Madrid arrested other conspirators, including José Antonio Primo de Rivera and Ramiro de Maeztu, and deported 140 altogether to Villa Cisneros in the western Sahara. Because a number of aristocrats had been implicated, the government decreed the confiscation of lands belonging to grandees of Spain, a sweeping and illegal measure which naturally hardened their hostility. Sanjurjo was condemned to death, but the sentence was immediately commuted to imprisonment. The general did not have long to wait in jail. As soon as Lerroux came to power he pardoned him. Sanjurjo then went into exile in Lisbon to 'organize a national movement which will save Spain from ruin and dishonour'.

The immediate effect of Sanjurjo's rebellion was to speed up the pace of legislation in the Cortes, of which the next most contentious parts were the statute of autonomy for Catalonia and land reform.[19] The right bitterly opposed Catalan devolution but Azaña, in one of the most brilliant speeches of his career, carried the day. The statute was passed on 9 September, helped by the collapse of the Sanjurjo coup, and on 20 November elections to the Catalan parliament took place, won by Esquerra Republicana de Catalunya led by Lluís Companys.[20]

The year of 1933 began badly for Azaña's government. During the first days of January, as part of the recurring revolts in Andalucia, a wave of violence broke out in the province of Cádiz. A small town, Casas Viejas, with a long anarchist tradition, saw the arrival of 'the day', that is to say the introduction of libertarian communism. On 11 January a group of anarchists besieged the Civil Guard post and firing broke out. More civil guards and assault guards arrived from Cádiz, and they surrounded a house in which an old anarchist known as 'Seisdedos', or 'six fingers', fought them off. The director-general of security ordered an Assault Guard captain, Manuel Rojas, to put an end to the stand-off. Rojas had the house set on fire and two men who escaped from the flames were shot down. Rojas then ordered his men to kill in cold blood twelve of the anarchists who had been arrested previously. Altogether 22 peasants and three members of the security forces died in Casas Viejas.[21]

The right, which had often called for harsh measures to restore order, now attacked Azaña for brutality. He was falsely accused of having given orders to kill the peasants and his reputation suffered. In the Cortes, deputies on the right argued that the events of Casas Viejas proved that the 'rapidity' of social change in the countryside was the problem and attacked the government's socialist measures in the industrial sector. Azaña's government suffered in the April municipal elections and by the autumn it was clear that he and his colleagues were badly weakened. In the circumstances, Alcalá Zamora entrusted a colleague of Lerroux, Diego Martínez Barrio, to form a cabinet which would call fresh elections.

Faced with the possibility of defeating the government, almost all the groups on the right united on 12 October to form a coalition called the Union de Derecha y Agrarios. Alejandro Lerroux's Radical Republican Party presented itself as the moderating force in the centre. The left, on the other hand, was divided when it went into the elections. The socialists were dissatisfied with the reformist caution of their republican colleagues and were pressured by the UGT to denounce what they saw as the reactionary repressiveness of the Azaña government. The anarchists, loyal to their anti-statist ideas and furious at the killings by the Civil Guard, called for abstention.

The elections took place on 19 November 1933. Thanks to the Republic's new constitution, women went to the polls for the first time in Spain, yet many of them voted for the centre-right, which won the most seats.[22] Alcalá Zamora, as president, entrusted the formation of a government to Lerroux. Lerroux's cabinet, composed entirely of Radical Party members, needed the parliamentary support of the CEDA (the Spanish Confederation of the Autonomous Right), which of course extracted its own terms. Its leader, José María Gil Robles, insisted on a range of measures, reversing some of the previous administration's reforms, such as those affecting primary schools, ecclesiastical measures, agrarian reform and labour laws. Lerroux and Gil Robles also agreed an amnesty for all those involved in the coup of General Sanjurjo.

The most dangerous development at this time was the bolshevization of the socialists led by Largo Caballero. On 3 January 1934 *El Socialista* had declared: 'Harmony? No! Class War! Hatred of the Criminal Bourgeoisie to the Death!'[23] Ten days later the socialist executive committee compiled a new programme. Among the points bound to alarm the centre as well as the right were:

Nationalization of the land
Dissolution of all religious orders, with seizure of their property
Dissolution of the army, to be replaced by a democratic militia
Dissolution of the Civil Guard[24]

Following their electoral defeat, the more moderate Indalecio Prieto found himself losing power in the executive committee of the PSOE, which Largo Caballero now controlled. From then on the bulk of the socialists followed a process of radicalization, which led them to focus more outside the Cortes, such as their establishment of an Alianza Obrera – a Workers' Alliance. On 3 February they set up a revolutionary committee ready to create an insurrection against the government, which should take on 'all the characteristics of civil war' and whose 'success would depend on the extent of its reach and the violence which it produces'.[25]

Largo Caballero ignored the warnings of the deposed leader of the UGT, Julián Besteiro, that such a policy constituted 'collective madness' and that an attempt to impose the dictatorship of the proletariat would turn out to be 'a vain, childish illusion'.[26] Manuel Azaña had also warned the socialists that preparing an insurrection would give the army the excuse to re-enter politics and crush the workers.[27] Largo Caballero brushed such cautions aside. The attacks published in his newspaper *Claridad* against Besteiro, Prieto and other moderate socialists 'were even more virulent than those against Gil Robles or the monarchists'.[28] Utterly irresponsible rhetoric and the debasement of political discourse fanned the flames of resentment and created fear. The socialist youth began to arm and train in secret, like the Carlists in the north-east and the minuscule Falange. Ortega y Gasset had warned the previous June of the 'emergence of childishness, and thus violence, in Spanish politics'.[29]

Lerroux's government, as well as bringing land reform to a halt, cancelled in May the confiscation of land belonging to the grandees of Spain and annulled the law which provided agricultural workers with the same protection as industrial employees. Landowners are supposed to have told hungry labourers seeking work to 'eat the Republic'. The agricultural subsidiary of the UGT[30] called for a general strike but it took effect only in the provinces of Cáceres, Badajoz, Ciudad Real and in certain parts of Andalucia. To start a strike in such circumstances, without any parliamentary support, was a serious error for it played into the government's hands.

That summer of 1934 also saw a clash between the Madrid government and the Generalitat of Catalonia, which was involved in its own version of land reform, affecting the tenant farmers of vineyards. On 2 October 1934 the new government of Ricardo Samper, an associate of Lerroux, became a casualty of this imbroglio, under pressure from an intransigent right, and Samper resigned.

President Alcalá Zamora had to manage this crisis in the face of outrage from the left, which claimed that the right was determined to destroy the Republic and that new elections must be held, and the right which wanted to be represented in the government. Gil Robles announced that he would not support a government from the back benches unless it included members of the CEDA.

Largo Caballero himself had acknowledged the previous year that there was no danger of fascism in Spain, yet in the summer of 1934 the rhetoric of the *caballeristas* took the opposite direction, crying fascist wolf – a tactic which risked becoming a self-fulfilling prophecy. Following an outcry over a shipment of arms to socialists in the Asturias, Gil Robles, the leader of the CEDA, announced that they would 'no longer suffer this state of affairs to continue'.[31] Despite being the largest party in the Cortes, the CEDA had received no ministerial posts, and Gil Robles now demanded a share. The UGT, which suspected the CEDA's lack of commitment to the Republic (due primarily to the anti-clerical clauses in its constitution), announced in turn that they 'would not answer for their future action'. Following the fall of the Samper government on 4 October, three members of the CEDA, but not Gil Robles himself, entered the new government of Alejandro Lerroux.

The socialist PSOE, fired up on militant rhetoric and prepared to rise against the government, decided to unleash a revolutionary general strike. Other parties of the left and centre-left, fearing that the Republic was about to be handed over to its enemies, proclaimed that from that moment they were breaking away from legality. The government felt compelled to outlaw the general strike and proclaim a state of war in Spain.

The general strike began on 5 October and took effect throughout most of the country. Largo Caballero and his followers compounded the irresponsibility of their actions. They launched an insurrection without any planning. It was the most obvious way of terrorizing the middle classes and forcing them into the arms of the right, just as Besteiro and others had warned.

When the UGT declared its general strike in Madrid, it asked soldiers and police to join the revolt as if the capital of Spain in 1934 were Petrograd in 1917. Largo Caballero was soon forced to recognize that this did not produce the spontaneous revolution of the masses that he had hoped for. The strikers tried to occupy the ministry of the interior and some military centres, a few of them firing pistols, but they were soon rounded up by the security forces. By 8 October nearly all the members of the revolutionary committee had been arrested.[32]

In Catalonia the general strike took hold, despite the abstention of the CNT, whose leaders wanted nothing to do with a revolution started by socialists and republicans. The Catalan left, on the other hand, exasperated at the Madrid government's treatment of their statute of autonomy, saw in the general strike an opportunity for accelerating their independence. At eight in the evening on 6 October, Companys appeared on the balcony of the Generalitat to proclaim 'a Catalan state within a Spanish federal republic'. He invited 'anti-fascists' from all over Spain to assemble in Barcelona to establish a provisional government. Lerroux ordered the local military commander, General Domingo Batet, to proclaim a state of war and end this sedition. Batet, who was a prudent man, positioned a pair of field guns in the Plaza de Sant Jaume and gave the order to fire blanks. At six in the morning of 7 October, Companys surrendered. He and his followers were arrested and tried. Companys was sentenced to 30 years in prison. Manuel

Azaña, who had been in Barcelona purely by chance, was arrested and confined on a prison ship. The Catalan statute of autonomy was suspended immediately and Manuel Portela Valladares was appointed governor-general of Catalonia.

In the north of the country the revolutionary general strike spread immediately in the mining areas of León, in Santander and in Vizcaya. In Bilbao there were clashes over five or six days with the security forces and in Eibar and Mondragón 40 people were killed. But the arrival of troops and the Spanish air force dropping bombs on the mining areas put an end to the revolt.

In Asturias things were very different. One month before there had been a strike to protest against the CEDA gathering in Covadonga, a sacred spot for the Spanish right for it was regarded as the starting point of the *Reconquista* of Spain from the Moors. Asturias was also the only place in Spain where the CNT had joined the revolutionary coalition, Alianza Obrera, and where the communists had a noticeable following. The revolutionary committee was led by the socialist Ramón González Peña, yet the communists later boasted that they had directed the uprising. This confirmed the worst fears of the centre and right, and later gave Franco an excuse for talking of a 'red conspiracy'.[33]

Estimates of the numbers of armed workers who took part in the uprising range between 15,000 and 30,000. Most of their rifles came from a shipment of arms supplied by Indalecio Prieto, supposedly one of the most moderate members of the parliamentary socialist party. These rifles had been landed by the yacht *Turquesa* at Pravia, north-east of Oviedo.[34] Prieto had promptly fled to France to avoid arrest. Other weapons came from arms factories in the region which were seized. The miners also had their dynamite blasting charges, which were known as '*la artillería de la revolución*'.

On 5 October the first move of the rebels was to attack the Civil Guard posts and public buildings at dawn. They occupied Mieres, Gijón, Avilés and some small towns in the mining region. They also sent columns to seize Trubia, La Felguera and Sama de Langreo. The next day they moved on Oviedo, defended by a garrison 1,000 strong, and took it, fighting street by street and house by house. The revolutionaries set up a commune, replacing money with coupons signed by the committee. They requisitioned trains and transport vehicles, and took over buildings. Some 40 people were murdered, mainly the rich and a number of priests. It was full-scale civil war, although limited to one region.

With the country under martial law the minister of war ordered General Franco to suppress the rebellion. On 7 October General López Ochoa left Lugo with an expeditionary force. The same day the cruiser *Libertad* accompanied by two gunboats reached Gijón, where they fired at the miners on shore. Aircraft also bombed the coalfields and Oviedo. On 8 October Franco sent two *banderas* of the Spanish Foreign Legion and two *tabors* of Moroccan *regulares* under the command of Lieutenant-Colonel Yagüe.[35] López Ochoa took Avilés later that day.

By 11 October the situation of the revolutionaries in Oviedo was desperate. They had run out of ammunition and knew that the rising had failed in the rest of Spain. At dusk on 12 October General López Ochoa's troops were in control of almost the whole town. Six days later the new head of the revolutionary committee, Belarmino Tomás, offered to surrender providing the Moorish troops were kept out of the towns and villages. Yet from 10 October legionnaires and *regulares* had invaded the mining villages and treated them as enemy territory, with looting, rape and the execution of prisoners on the spot. The security forces unleashed a savage repression on the area as a whole. The man most notorious for his cruelty was the Civil Guard commander, Major Lisardo Doval.

The Asturias revolution had lasted no more than two weeks, but it cost around 1,000 lives and created enormous damage. Thousands of workers were sacked for having taken part in the rising and several thousand were imprisoned, of whom many were liberated in January 1935 when the state of war was suspended. Altogether twenty people were condemned to death, but only two sentences were carried out, which was extremely lenient for the age, when one considers how Stalin's or Hitler's regime would have reacted to a revolutionary rising. Responsibility for the appalling brutality of the security forces lay more with their commanders, especially Yagüe and Franco, than with the politicians in Madrid. Azaña had been unfairly blamed for Castilblanco, but this was on a different level. The Asturias rising inevitably demanded stronger measures, which meant even less possibility of control from Madrid over the actions of the army and Civil Guard.

The clearer minds on the left saw that the rising had been a terrible disaster. But for the militants, especially Largo Caballero, it had produced an intoxicating whiff of revolution. For the right, on the other hand, it seemed to show, as Calvo Sotelo argued, that the army – the spine of the state – was the only guarantee against revolutionary change. Yet above all, the rising had been a profound shock to the nation as a whole and a near fatal blow to democracy in Spain. There can be no doubt that such a violent insurrection alarmed the centre as well as the hard right. It certainly appeared to confirm conservatives in their belief that they must do everything possible to prevent another attempt to create the dictatorship of the proletariat, especially when Largo Caballero declared: 'I want a Republic without class war, but for that one class has to disappear.'[36] They did not need to be reminded of the horrors which followed the Russian revolution and Lenin's determination to annihilate the bourgeoisie.

With the defeat of the October revolution the suspension of the Catalan state of autonomy and the dissolution of the left-wing town councils, the Radical-CEDA coalition seemed supreme. The CEDA, however, felt that its presence in the Lerroux government did not do justice to its parliamentary strength. Gil Robles wanted to amend the Constitution to abolish the restrictions on the Church's role in education, but he had little success. Lerroux and his Radicals had at least held on to one principle, and that was their anti-clericalism. Yet the government crisis which ensued had another cause. When President Alcalá Zamora decided to exercise his constitutional prerogative and commute the death sentence passed on González Peña, the CEDA leaders declared their opposition. Lerroux had to form another government and this time include five members of the CEDA. Gil Robles insisted on becoming minister of war. He appointed General Fanjul to be under-secretary and Franco to be the chief of the general staff.[37]

The new government turned back the Republic's clock in certain matters, such as returning property to the Jesuits and indemnifying the grandees for the expropriation of their land. It ignored agrarian reform and public education. Meanwhile, the republican left began to get itself together again. In December 1934 Azaña was cleared of any involvement in the events of October and freed. A few months later he made a pact between the left and the three centrist parties: Izquierda Republiçana, Unión Republicana and the Partido Nacional Republicano. In March 1935 Azaña reappeared in the

Cortes and began a series of mass meetings around the country. In Madrid more than 300,000 people turned up. During this speech he laid out the basis for an electoral alliance of the left which would take them to victory in the elections that took place the following February.

The socialists, on the other hand, remained profoundly divided. Prieto, still in exile in Paris after the October revolution, broke with the followers of Largo Caballero – the *caballeristas* – and once again tried to align himself with Azaña. Largo Caballero himself came out of prison in November, more of a bolshevik than ever, having at last read the works of Lenin in his cell and received visits from Jacques Duclos, the French Comintern representative. The leaders of the uprising received surprisingly lenient treatment.

The alliance between the CEDA and Lerroux's radicals finally collapsed at the end of 1935 as a result of political scandals. In October there was the *estraperlo* gambling scandal, which allowed the president of the Republic to demand the resignation of Lerroux.[38] He entrusted Joaquín Chapaprieta with forming a new government, but the following month another row broke out over corruption, which provided the *coup de grâce* for the Radical Party as a whole.[39]

Gil Robles thought that his time had come to take over the government and he withdrew support from Chapaprieta, but his move proved a mistake. President Alcalá Zamora, who did not like him and wanted to create a large centre party, entrusted the government to a man he trusted, the former governor of Catalonia, Manuel Portela Valladares. Blind to the fact that democracy in Spain had become so fragile, Alcalá Zamora had pushed republican democracy into its endgame. It soon became clear that the clash of attitudes throughout the country was so great that the forces of conflict could not be contained within the Cortes.

4
The Popular Front

When the new head of government, Manuel Portela Valladares, summoned the council of ministers on 1 January 1936 he already had in his hands the decree to dissolve the Cortes. New elections were to be announced for 16 February. They were to be the last free elections held in Spain for 40 years.

The decree was finally published on 7 January and the electoral campaign rapidly became heated. The results of the previous election had underlined the way the law gave such a favourable weighting to political coalitions. This encouragement to both the left and the right to create alliances had the effect of emptying the centre ground.

Any possibility of compromise had been destroyed by the revolutionary uprising of the left and its cruel repression by the army and Civil Guard. The depth of feeling was too strong on either side to allow democracy to work. Both sides used apocalyptic language, funnelling the expectations of their followers towards a violent outcome, not a political one. Largo Caballero declared, 'If the right win the elections, we will have to go straight to open civil war.'[1] Not surprisingly, the right reacted with a similar attitude. In their view a left-wing victory in the polls was bound to lead to violent revolution and the dictatorship of the proletariat which Largo Caballero had promised.

The main group on the right was basically an alliance of the CEDA with monarchists and Carlists of the National Block. José María Gil Robles, the CEDA leader, called it 'the national counter-revolutionary front'.[2] Gil Robles, whose Catholic corporatism had acquired some superficial fascist trappings, allowed himself to be acclaimed by his followers at mass meetings as the leader, with the cry '*¡Jefe, jefe, jefe!*'. (The Spanish for 'chief' was an amateurish imitation of '*Duce!*' or '*Führer!*'.) His advertising for the campaign included a massive poster covering the façade of a building in central Madrid with the slogan: 'Give me an absolute majority and I will give you a great Spain.' Millions of leaflets were distributed saying that a victory for the left would produce 'an arming of the mob, the burning of banks and private houses, the division of property and land, looting and the sharing out of your women'.[3] The finance for such a campaign came from landowners, large companies and the Catholic Church, which hurried to bless the alliance with the idea that a vote for the right was a vote for Christ.

Since the proclamation of the Republic in April 1931, with the subsequent burning of churches and convents and the anti-clerical provisions in the Constitution, the Catholic hierarchy had already demonstrated its hostility. But the rising of October 1934 had pushed it into advocating disobedience to a legally constituted government if it were necessary to protect the interests of the Church. When the Republic suppressed the state subsidy the Church had soon found itself impoverished, and its priests depended even more on contributions from their parishioners.[4]

In 1936 Spain had some 30,000 priests, most of whom were poor and very uneducated, incapable of any other employment. The hierarchy, however, was jealous of its privileges. When Cardinal Vidal y Barraquer, faced with the Church's financial crisis, proposed that the richer dioceses should help the poorer ones, most of the bishops objected furiously.[5]

On 15 January 1936 the parties of the centre-left and left signed a pact to contest the elections as a single group.[6] A Popular Front programme was drafted, concentrating mainly on agrarian reform, the re-establishment of the Catalan statute of autonomy and an amnesty for the prisoners in Spain arrested after the October revolution.[7] Nothing was said about nationalization of banks or division of the land, but the right claimed that there were secret clauses in the pact.[8] This was a natural suspicion in the circumstances. The Popular Front election manifesto was indeed mild, yet the *caballeristas* had already called for the nationalization of the land, the dissolution of the army, Civil Guard and all religious orders with seizure of their property. In May 1935 the manifesto of the Alianza Obrera had called in addition for 'confiscation and nationalization of large industry, finance, transportation and communications'.[9]

The proposal to free all those sentenced for taking part in a violent rebellion against the legally elected government of the day was bound to provoke the right. In fact, the open determination of the left as a whole to release from prison all those sentenced for the uprising of 1934 was hardly an assurance of its respect for the rule of law and constitutional government. The Janus-like nature of the Popular Front alliance was demonstrated one week after the election. On the same day Diego Martínez Barrio said that the Popular Front was a 'conservative enterprise' and *El Socialista* proclaimed: 'We are determined to do in Spain what has been done in Russia. The plan of Spanish socialism and Russian communism is the same.'[10]

The electoral pact, first urged by socialists and left republicans, had been born in the Asturias rising. It coincided with the new policy of the Comintern which called on communists to ally with non-revolutionary left-wing groups to fight the new threat of fascism in Europe. This was a two-stage plan, moderate at first, then revolutionary in the longer term.[11] In June 1936 the Comintern leader Georgi Dimitrov stated that given the present situation in Spain, 'the fundamental and urgent task of the Communist Party in Spain and the Spanish proletariat' was to ensure victory over fascism by completing 'the democratic revolution' and isolating 'the fascists from the mass of peasants and urban petit bourgeoisie'.[12]

The Comintern controllers were hardly interested in preserving the middle class. The Popular Front strategy was simply a means to power. This was confirmed later at the Comintern's meeting on 23 July to discuss the right-wing rising. Dimitrov warned that the Spanish communists should not attempt to establish a dictatorship of the proletariat 'at the present stage'. 'That would be a fatal mistake. Therefore we must say: act under the banner of defending the Republic ... In other words, comrades, we believe that in the present international situation it is advantageous and necessary for us to carry out a policy that would preserve our opportunity to organize, educate, unify the masses and to strengthen our own positions in a number of countries – in Spain, France, Belgium and so forth – where there are governments dependent on the Popular Front and where the Communist Party has extensive opportunities. When our positions have been strengthened, then we can go further.'[13]

Going further also meant that the elimination of political rivals was a high priority right from the start. On 17 July, just as the anarchists were preparing to defeat the generals' rising in Barcelona, the Comintern 'advised' the Spanish communist politburo: 'It is necessary to take preventative measures with the greatest urgency against the putschist attempts of the anarchists, behind which the hand of the fascists is hidden.'[14]

The Spanish Communist Party, as the French Comintern representative André Marty reported later to Moscow, was run almost entirely by Vittorio Codovilla (who had the cover-name 'Medina') and the PSUC in Catalonia by Erno Gerö (alias 'Singer' or 'Pedro'), another Comintern envoy. Marty later dismissed the work of the Spanish Communist Party's politburo as 'terribly primitive'.[15] José Díaz was the only competent member, but he was too ill with liver problems to be effective.

The largest party of the Popular Front was the Partido Socialista Obrero Español (PSOE). Francisco Largo Caballero, now 66 years old, had become its most radical and bolshevized leader. He distrusted the broad alliance with the Left Republicans of Manuel Azaña and allowed himself to be courted by Jacques Duclos, another Comintern representative in Spain, who had identified Largo Caballero as the most suitable leader of the Spanish working class. Not only *Claridad*, the newspaper of the *caballeristas*, but the communist press of Europe began to hail this old trade union leader as the 'Spanish Lenin'. Yet Largo Caballero, carried away by his own rhetoric, began to alarm his new communist friends. His inflammatory and revolutionary speeches at mass meetings around Spain calling for the elimination of the middle class was contrary to Dimitrov's policy. (Some wit at the time coined the slogan 'Vote communist and save Spain from Marxism'.) But whether or not his speeches were the product of revolutionary intoxication or revealed his own intentions at that time, it was hardly surprising that the right, threatened with extinction by the left, should have prepared to strike back.

The influence of the Spanish Communist Party was considerable for an organization which when founded in 1921 had numbered just a few dozen militants. A decade later, at the time of the fall of the monarchy, it mustered a few thousand members. In the elections of November 1933 it received 170,000 votes and its first seat in the Cortes. But in the first half of 1936 it went from 30,000 members to nearly 100,000.[16] The left needed the anarchists to vote if it was to win such a closely fought election. This time the anarchists were prepared to vote, even though it was against their principles. The only hope of getting their comrades out of prison lay with the Popular Front.

On 16 February the voting stations opened in a tense yet calm atmosphere. The two coalitions of both right and left were each convinced that they would win. General Franco's propagandists later tried to claim that there had been serious irregularities and implied that the results were somehow invalid, but this was completely untrue. Even the monarchist newspaper, *ABC*, wrote on 17 February that the poll had taken place 'without strikes, without threats and without any scandals. Everybody voted as they wanted to, in absolute liberty.'

The provincial electoral commissions finally gave their verdict on 20 February: the Popular Front had won by just over 150,000 votes. The electoral law encouraging coalitions, which had favoured the right in 1933, now favoured the left. The Popular Front, despite winning by a margin of less than 2 per cent of the total vote, achieved an absolute majority of seats in the Cortes.[17] Perhaps the most striking figure from the election revealed that the Falangists of José Antonio Primo de Rivera received only 46,000 votes out of nearly ten million throughout Spain: on average less than 1,000 votes per province. That provided a rather more realistic indication of the fascist threat than that proclaimed by Largo Caballero.

The left, ignoring the narrowness of their victory, proceeded to behave as if they had received an overwhelming mandate for revolutionary change. Predictably, the right was horrified to see crowds rush forth to release prisoners themselves, without even waiting for an amnesty. Almost as soon as the results were known, a group of monarchists asked Gil Robles to lead a *coup d'état*, but he would have nothing to do with it personally. Instead he asked Portela Valladares to proclaim a state of war before the revolutionary masses rushed into the streets. Embittered by defeat, Gil Robles also came out with a surprising and hypocritical attack against the rich, the very people who had supported and financed his campaign, accusing them of having demonstrated a 'suicidal egotism' in the way they had reduced wages.

General Franco, the chief of the general staff, sent an emissary to General Pozas, director-general of the Civil Guard, inviting him to take part 'in the decisions which need to be taken in the defence of order and the well-being of Spain'.[18] Franco also tried to convince Portela Valladares that he should not hand over power to the

Popular Front and offered the support of the army. This was evidently the first time that Franco had considered military intervention. He fully realized the importance of the Civil Guard and the Assault Guard.

Franco, not yet convinced that a coup would work, went to see Portela again on 19 February. He said that if he allowed the country to go communist he would bear a heavy responsibility before history. But Portela, although driven to the wall and shattered – he 'gave the impression of a ghost', wrote Manuel Azaña, 'not that of a head of government' – did not cede to Franco's moral blackmail.[19] He resigned that very day. The President of the Republic, Alcalá Zamora, had no alternative but to ask Azaña, whom he disliked, to form a government. Azaña proceeded to assemble a cabinet with members of his own party and that of the Unión Republicana. He did not consider including a single socialist in his government. In any case, Largo Caballero vetoed the participation of the socialist party (PSOE) in the new administration to prevent Prieto forming a social-democratic alliance with the Left Republicans.

Despite the moderate basis of the new cabinet, the right reacted as if the bolsheviks had taken over the government. They were appalled by the rush of people into the streets to celebrate their victory and marching to the prisons to release prisoners. The Church warned that the enemies of Catholicism, 'under the influence and direction of the Judaeo-Masonic world conspiracy, are declaring a war to the finish against us'.[20] The right had decided that to safeguard its idea of Spain, the parliamentary road was no longer an option, if only because their opponents on the left had already demonstrated their own willingness to ignore the rule of law.

On 20 February the first council of ministers of Azaña's government met after he had addressed the nation on the radio. Azaña spoke of justice, liberty and the validity of the constitution. He would undertake, with the approval of the Cortes, 'a great work of national restoration in defence of work and production, encouraging public works, and paying attention to the problems of unemployment and all the other points which had motivated the coalition of the republican and proletarian parties which is now in power'.[21]

Among the many problems which faced his government, perhaps the most urgent was the proclamation of an amnesty, following prison riots in Burgos, Cartagena and Valencia. The government could not wait until the Cortes was assembled. On 23 February it re-established the Generalitat of Catalonia and also the socialist councils suspended throughout Spain after the revolution of October 1934. At the same time Azaña embarked on a reorganization of the army command, appointing generals loyal to the Republic to key posts and sending those suspected of plotting to appointments far from Madrid.

The government then reanimated the work of the Instituto de Reforma Agraria, with the minister of agriculture himself, Mariano Ruiz Funes, overseeing the process in Andalucia and Estremadura. The president of the Generalitat, Lluís Companys, left the prison of Puerto de Santa Maria and was welcomed in Barcelona by an enormous demonstration as he reopened the Catalan parliament. On 16 March Azaña announced that the confiscation of land belonging to aristocrats involved in the Sanjurjo rising would be reactivated. And all those workers who lost their jobs as a result of participating in the October revolution would be reinstated.

The economic situation was not good. Since 1931 private investment had plummeted and in 1936 it dropped to the level of 1913. Not surprisingly, with the new government's programme, capital left the country at an increasing rate. Juan March, the Mallorcan multimillionaire, who had amassed an enormous fortune through tobacco smuggling, fled Spain to avoid prison. Once out of the country, he concentrated on speculating against the peseta on the foreign exchange markets. From his own pocket he provided a tenth of the twenty million pesetas collected by the anti-republican group of whom the Count de los Andes was the president.[22]

Far more serious than March's financial chicanery were the economic consequences of the left's electoral victory. Workers put in huge wage demands, far beyond what the factory or farm could sustain. Strikes multiplied, unemployment rose and the value of the peseta fell sharply on the foreign exchanges. The real problem facing the centre-left government of Azaña was the result of its Faustian pact with the hard left of *caballeristas*, who saw it as the equivalent of the Kerensky regime in Russia, a view shared by the right. This liberal government found that it had no influence on its electoral allies, now set upon a revolutionary course, and could not persuade their followers to obey the law. Luis Araquistáin, the editor of *Claridad* and the voice of the bolshevizing tendency within the socialists and UGT, had argued during the election campaign that Spain, like Russia in 1917, was ready for revolution. He had rejected the earlier warnings of Julián Besteiro, the former leader of the UGT, that revolutionary activities such as factory occupations simply horrified the middle class and destroyed the economy. Each left-wing organization began to form its own militia – the communists' was the most disciplined and effective. And an unprecedented number of people went around armed, ready to defend themselves from the attacks of opponents. The general impression of a breakdown of law and order played straight into the hands of the undemocratic right. The right-wing press blamed the disorders on the left, while the left blamed the right. The right insisted that democracy was not working and that the Cortes had become useless. Women from the middle and upper classes insulted officers in the streets, telling them that they were cowards for not overthrowing the government.

No group on the right did more to cause disorder, and thus to provoke a military coup, than the Falange. It was subsidized from a number of sources – 10,000 pesetas monthly from Renovación Española, money from the Banco de Vizcaya, and later from Juan March, and 50,000 pesetas a month from Mussolini passed through the Italian embassy in Paris.[23] The Nazis, however, had little confidence in them and refused them the million marks of support which they had requested. The Falange needed the money because it was growing at an astonishing rate, largely due to an influx from the youth movement of Acción Popular – some 15,000 of them in the spring of 1936, effectively doubling the size of the Falange to 30,000.[24]

The Falange Española, or Spanish Phalanx, had been born in the Comedy Theatre in Madrid on 29 October 1933. It was founded by José Antonio Primo de Rivera, the elder son of the dictator, a young lawyer of dark good looks and supposedly great charm. He attracted a coterie of fascist intellectuals and appealed to students, especially those from wealthy families, the *señoritos*, as well as many from the lower middle class who felt threatened by social change. The Falange had also been joined by former members of his father's Patriotic Union from a decade before, as well as frustrated monarchists and conservatives appalled by the electoral victory of the left.

Falangism differed from Nazism and fascism in its profoundly conservative nature. Mussolini used Roman symbols and imperial imagery in his speeches merely for their propaganda effect. The Falange, on the other hand, used modern and revolutionary phraseology while remaining fundamentally reactionary. The Church was the essence of *Hispanidad* (Spanishness). The new state would 'draw its inspiration from the spirit of the Catholic religion which is traditional in Spain'. Their symbols were those of Ferdinand and Isabella: the yoke of the authoritarian state and the arrows of annihilation to wipe out heresy. They did not just borrow the symbols, but tried to revive the Castilian mentality. The ideal Falangist was supposed to be 'half-monk, half-soldier'.

Yet the movement suffered from something of a split personality between the nationalist and the socialist elements. José Antonio attacked 'the social bankruptcy of capitalism' and denounced the living conditions of workers and peasants. Yet Marxism he found repugnant as an ideology, because it was not Spanish and because a class struggle weakened the nation. The country had to be united in a system in which the employer could not exploit the employee. At one moment José Antonio was making vain approaches, first to the socialist Prieto, then to the anarcho-syndicalist CNT. The next, he was reminding Franco of Oswald Spengler's remark that in the last resort civilization had always been saved by a platoon of soldiers. But a civilization which has to be saved by soldiers is a conservative's image of a perfect world, rather than that of a revolutionary national socialist.

The Falange constantly sought more firearms for their street fighting and José Antonio put in motion a Bulldog Drummond-style intrigue. Luis Bolín, the London correspondent of the monarchist *ABC*, met a prominent but anonymous Englishman by a secret recognition signal in Claridge's Hotel. They arranged for large quantities of submachine-guns to be packed in champagne cases and shipped from Germany in a private yacht. In fact, they did not arrive in time, but it was not long before Bolín in London began to organize a far more important delivery.

The Falange, however, already had weapons from other sources. On 10 March a Falangist squad led by Alberto Ortega tried to assassinate Professor Luis Jiménez de Asúa, a socialist deputy, but instead killed his police escort. Four days later Falangists made an attempt on Largo Caballero's life. That same day, 14 March, José Antonio met Franco in the house of the general's brother-in-law, Ramón Serrano Súñer, to discuss a joint plan of action. The following day the Falange was outlawed by the government because of the attack on Largo Caballero and José Antonio was arrested for the illegal possession of arms. It is difficult to reconcile José Antonio's famous charm with the brutality of his followers and the outspoken racism of his coterie at their dinner-jacketed gatherings in the Hotel Paris. He cannot, in any case, escape responsibility, because his speeches were a clear incitement, even if violence remained an abstract quantity to the fastidious Andalucian.

The ideal of defending traditional Spain required active preparation, now that the authoritarian right had discarded any further attempt to make use of the parliamentary system. In the Pyrenees the Carlists had started to arm and train their *requeté* militia, famous since the Carlist wars in the nineteenth century for its uniform of a Basque beret in bright red.

The Carlist movement was purely arch-conservative. Its official title was the Traditionalist Communion and it has been described as a form of lay Jesuitry. It believed that a 'judaeo-marxist-masonic' conspiracy was going to turn Spain into a colony of the Soviet Union.[25] Liberalism, in the view of Carlists as well as the Church hierarchy, was the source of all modern evils, and they dreamed of reviving a royal Catholic autocracy in a populist form. The main Carlist strength lay in the Pyrenees, though they did have supporters in a number of other areas, such as Andalucia. The Carlists no longer showed their former sympathy with regionalist aspirations. This had stemmed from their stronghold being in the former kingdom of Navarre and had also been a means of winning Basque and Catalan support for the Carlist wars in the nineteenth century. By 1936 they had come to detest Basque and Catalan nationalism.

A number of Carlist officers were trained in Italy with the help of Mussolini, while their leaders, Fal Conde and the Count of Rodezno, organized the purchase of weapons from Germany. The strength of the *requetés* is hard to calculate exactly, but there were probably more than 8,000 members in Navarre alone early in 1936. A figure of 30,000 for the whole country has been suggested. One of their backers, José Luis Oriol, organized a ship from Belgium which brought 6,000 rifles, 150 heavy machine-guns, 300 light machine-guns, five million rounds of ammunition and 10,000 hand grenades.[26]

In the spring of 1936 the Carlists' Supreme Military Council was set up in Saint Jean de Luz, just over the French frontier, by

Prince Javier de Borbón-Parma and Fal Conde. It was composed of former officers and began to plan a rising in conjunction with the right-wing Unión Militar Española, a secret association of right-wing officers within the army, with Alfonsine monarchists and the Falange. Their contact was Colonel José Varela (later one of Franco's most important field commanders) who had earlier been training the Carlist *requetés* secretly in the Pyrenees mountains. So far only the vaguest rumours of these preparations had reached Azaña's government in Madrid.

5
The Fatal Paradox

Political turmoil in the spring of 1936 created an uncertainty which paralysed industry and finance. Although imports had fallen, Spain's principal exports – oranges, almonds, wine and oil – had fallen much further.[1] The fact that the country's balance of payments depended upon agrarian produce at the very time when agrarian reform represented one of the most bitterly divisive issues, did not of course help. Landowners, faced with worldwide price deflation and four months of almost constant rain in western and southern Spain, were trying to maintain a profit margin just when desperately underprivileged labourers were demanding better living standards. The bill for decades, if not centuries, of social, technological and political immobilism was being presented at the worst possible moment.

The Instituto de Reforma Agraria took up again its task of resettlement as best it could, but this proceeded with great slowness because of the legal actions launched by landlords. This exasperated the peasants, especially since they also had a feeling after the Popular Front's victory in the February elections that they should be able to dictate conditions. In addition they had a longing for revenge after the sackings and wage reductions over the previous two years and the triumphalism of many landowners when the centre-right was in power.

In the first fortnight of March, landless *braceros* began to occupy estates in the provinces of Madrid, Toledo and Salamanca. Then, at dawn on 25 March, 60,000 landless peasants in the province of Badajoz seized land and began to plough it. Over the next few weeks, similar actions were launched in the provinces of Cáceres, Jaén, Seville and Córdoba. The security forces, subdued by the memory of Casas Viejas, acted with indecision, but this did not help. In one of the confrontations with peasants in Yeste, a civil guard was killed. The Civil Guard, known with approval or bitter irony as the Benemérita, replied by killing seventeen day labourers and wounding many others.[2] In any case, during the government of the Popular Front fewer than 200,000 peasants were resettled in the whole of Spain on 756,000 hectares of land, yet it was still more than during all of the previous administrations under the Republic.[3] But none of those who colonized the land had money for seeds or tools. The Banco Nacional Agrario, which had been envisaged in the initial legislation to address the problem, was never set up.[4]

The gradualist lines of social democrats could neither satisfy the inflamed aspirations of the workers, nor reassure landowners that private property would be respected. That spring strikes broke out not in pursuit of a particular demand but to show working-class muscle. There was a fierce satisfaction in the idea that the old saying of the downtrodden might come true: 'when God in heaven wants justice to change/the poor will eat bread and the rich will eat shit'.[5]

Meanwhile in Madrid, on 3 April the Cortes reunited. Indalecio Prieto proposed the impeachment of the president of the Republic. Prieto's accusation was that Alcalá Zamora had dissolved parliament unnecessarily, using a literal and sectarian interpretation of article 81 of the Constitution. His motion was won with 238 votes and only five against. Alcalá Zamora was unseated four days later. Less than a month after that, on 3 May, Manuel Azaña was elected president of the Spanish Republic. Prieto hoped to take over the leadership of the government, but his rival Largo Caballero was determined to prevent it by vetoing any socialist participation in the government. Azaña therefore appointed the Galician politician Santiago Casares Quiroga president of the council of ministers, the equivalent of prime minister.

During the following days a series of assassination attempts convulsed the country. The first victim was a judge, Manuel Pedregal, who had sentenced a Falangist to 30 years in prison for the murder of a vendor of left-wing newspapers. Then a bomb exploded next to the presidential saluting stand at a military parade on 14 April to commemorate the fifth anniversary of the Republic. The escort of assault guards opened fire in error against a junior officer of the Civil Guard. This developed into a running battle between Falangists and members of the Assault Guard and more were killed and wounded. The Falange claimed the deaths of the journalist Luciano Malumbres in Santander, the journalist Manuel Andrés in San Sebastian, and in Madrid the socialist Carlos Faraudo, a captain. On 16 April Falangists opened fire with submachine-guns against workers in the centre of Madrid, killing three and wounding another 40.

The communists had meanwhile set up their own very effective paramilitary arm, the Milicias Antifascistas Obreras y Campesinas (MAOC), and the socialists organized their own column, the 'Motorizada', to take on the fascist squads. Weapons were carried almost as a matter of course, to such a point that members of the Cortes were asked to hand theirs in when they entered the parliament building. In Barcelona, which had been calmer than Madrid, a *pistolero* of the anarchist FAI shot down the two brothers Miquel and Josep Badia, leading members of Estat Català.

Largo Caballero's rhetoric became even wilder. His declaration that 'the revolution we want can be achieved only through violence' was interpreted by the Socialist Youth as Leninist strategy. And on 1 May, when the great May Day parade swarmed through the streets and avenues of central Madrid, conservatives watched in trepidation from their balconies or from behind shutters. They eyed with mounting alarm the red flags and banners and portraits of Lenin, Stalin and Largo Caballero on huge placards, and listened to the chanting of the demonstrators, demanding the formation of a proletarian government and a people's army. But it was not just these obvious political symbols that frightened them. The workers in the street had a new confidence or, in their view, insolence. Beggars had started to ask for alms, not for the love of God, but in the name of revolutionary solidarity. Girls walked freely and started to ridicule convention. On 4 May José Antonio delivered a diatribe from prison against the Popular Front. He claimed that it was directed by Moscow, fomented prostitution and undermined the family. 'Have you not heard the cry of Spanish girls today: "Children, yes! Husbands, no!"?'[6]

Prieto attacked the 'revolutionary infantilism' of the left and warned that excesses in the streets and the burning of churches only pushed the middle classes into supporting a military rebellion. This formed part of his major speech on 1 May at Cuenca.[7] Another socialist leader, Julián Besteiro, professor of logic at the University of Alcalá de Henares, tried to warn his party that Spain in 1936 was not Russia in 1917 and that the Spanish army was not about to mutiny like the Tsarist forces, exhausted by a long and terrible war. He was right, but after the left-wing uprising of October 1934 it was almost certainly too late to expect either side to return to the rules of parliamentary democracy.

During that turbulent spring, the anarcho-syndicalist CNT tried to get work for its unemployed members, competing with the socialist union, the UGT. But anarchist purists of the FAI attacked this as reformist. They were convinced that to have anything to do with capitalist society was to be corrupted. In any case, the threat of a military rising began to unite syndicalists and members of the FAI. On 1 May the CNT held its national congress in Saragossa, 'the second city of anarchism'. The Congress ratified the traditional position of making no pact with any political party, but listened attentively to Largo Caballero's arguments in favour of unity between the UGT and the CNT. Neither he nor the anarchists realized that this also happened to be the communists' secret strategy.

In spite of its restrained militancy, the Spanish Communist Party had a better organization and better discipline than other parties, and a firm will. This was what its recruits so admired as the only way to advance the cause of the working class. The Popular Front alliance was not enough for the communists. They wanted an integration of all working-class parties and unions to help them seize power. Largo Caballero, an unimaginative old trade unionist who was totally out of his depth, had no idea that Álvarez del Vayo, the adviser whom he trusted most and whom he later appointed to be foreign minister, was working closely with the Comintern agent Vittorio Codovilla. They were planning the wholesale defection of the Socialist Youth to the Spanish Communist Party, with promises of power and the argument that only the communists had the professionalism and the international support to defeat fascism.

Ettore Vanni, an important leader of the Italian Communist Party then working in Spain, said that communist discipline was accepted with a fanaticism which at times dehumanized them yet constituted their great strength. The determinist idea of 'scientific socialism' convinced the young militants that nothing could stop the final triumph of Marxism. They believed that absolute control of power was the only way to achieve their ideals. Spanish communists were strongly influenced by their own images of the Russian revolution, which they saw as a mixture of romantic heroism and a ruthless rejection of sentimentality to achieve what they thought would be a better society. They saw themselves as the only ones who could direct the masses correctly. Anyone who wavered or questioned this was a weak petit bourgeois, if not a traitor to the international proletariat. They derided the fears of libertarians on the corruptive influence of power, which they saw as the fussing of dilettantes on the eve of battle with an implacable enemy. Among those who responded to the call of communism was the head of the Socialist Youth, Santiago Carrillo. He had become all-powerful after having merged the socialist and communist youth movements into the Juventud Socialista Unificada. Then, when the civil war broke out Carrillo brought the organization's 200,000 members entirely under communist control in a carefully staged manoeuvre during the chaos of the fighting.

In Catalonia the communists merged with the Unió Socialista, the Catalan arm of the PSOE and the Partit Català Proletari to constitute the PSUC (Partit Socialista Unificat de Catalunya), which soon also came under total communist control. Communists who had followed Trotsky, on the other hand, had grouped themselves in 1935 in the POUM (Partit Obrer d'Unificació Marxista) under the leadership of Joaquín Maurín. In the Basque country the statute of autonomy, was finally approved and in Galicia the statute of autonomy was passed with a massive majority on 28 June.[8]

During that early summer of 1936, the situation in Europe was tense. Hitler was remilitarizing the Rhineland in a flagrant violation of the Treaty of Versailles. He was also putting pressure on the Austrian chancellor, Kurt von Schuschnigg, as part of his strategy to prepare the *Anschluss*. Mussolini invaded Abyssinia and openly considered the possibility of extending his new empire in North Africa. In France the Popular Front won the elections, with Léon Blum leading the new government, but the reaction of the right revealed that France might face political turmoil.

In Spain, the pace of political violence and strikes increased with the onset of summer. On 1 June the UGT and CNT called all building workers, mechanics and lift operators out on strike. During the demonstration of 70,000 workers which followed, the stewards were attacked by armed Falangists, the strikers sacked food shops and the security forces had to be called in. At the beginning of July the UGT accepted arbitration but the CNT fought on. Members of the CNT responded to the Falangist attacks in kind and killed three of José Antonio's bodyguards in a café. The government closed CNT centres in Madrid and arrested the strike leaders, David Antona and Cipriano Mera. Mera later became the most effective anarchist commander in the civil war.

In the middle of June in Málaga, anarchists and socialists became involved in battles condemned by the leaders of both CNT and UGT, while out in the countryside 100,000 CNT labourers declared themselves to be on strike. On 16 June Gil Robles stated in the Cortes that since 16 February 170 churches had been burned, 269 murders had been committed and 1,287 people injured. Altogether 133 general strikes and 216 local strikes had been called. His statistics, it must be pointed out, came from the less than impartial source of *El Debate*, but that did nothing to contradict the general impression that Spain was becoming ungovernable.[9]

Calvo Sotelo backed him up with a list of accusations against the government and warned that patriotic soldiers would save Spain from anarchy. When he personalized his insults, the president of the Cortes forced him to withdraw his words. There can be no doubt that his intention was to increase the sensation of complete disorder. The crescendo of insults and accusations from both sides tended to confirm that parliamentary government had broken down irretrievably.

Black propaganda was being used in a confusing profusion and at times it is hard to know what to believe. For example, the right claimed that the left was spreading rumours that nuns were handing out poisoned sweets to children, while the left claimed that the right itself spread these rumours to provoke anti-clerical outrages. Time and again, the right-wing press compared Azaña to Kerensky and José Antonio reminded the Spanish army of the fate of Tsarist officers.[10]

In 1936 the Spanish army consisted of some 100,000 men. Nearly 40,000 of them were the tough and efficient troops based in Morocco, but the rest in the metropolitan army were of little use. 'In Spain', as one historian pointed out, 'there was not enough ammunition for a single day of warfare, military production was in chaos, and there were hardly any armoured vehicles, anti-tank weapons or anti-aircraft guns.'[11] Several thousand soldiers never received uniforms and many more never received any weapon training. Conscripts were often used as free domestic labour by officers.

The low military efficiency of the army had not stopped *pronunciamientos* in the past and, despite the fighting in Asturias, the officers plotting a rebellion did not appear to have been overly concerned by the opposition that they might face.[12] Azaña's government, while aware of a possible threat, did not deal with it effectively. Immediately after the elections, they took the unfortunate precaution of sending the most suspect generals to appointments far from the capital, such as General Franco to the Canary Islands and General Goded to the Balearics. In an age of aviation it was hardly a true island exile. In addition, Las Palmas was close to Morocco and Mallorca to Barcelona. General Emilio Mola, the main organizer of the conspiracy, who would take the codename the 'Director', was sent as military governor to Pamplona, the fief of the Carlists and their 8,000 *requetés* who were ready to march.[13]

Mola, who had been in Morocco, preparing the garrison there for rebellion, returned to the Peninsula and stopped in Madrid on his way to Pamplona. Between 5 and 12 March he had meetings with other key conspirators: Orgaz, Goded, Ponte, Kindelán, Saliquet, Franco, Varela, Galarza, Fanjul and Rodríguez del Barrio. Mola told Goded that he was drafting 'instructions and directives to set the conspiracy in motion first and then for a possible rising'.[14] The initial plan involving Varela and Orgaz collapsed because José Díaz, the secretary-general of the Spanish Communist Party, read out in open session a confidential document from the plotters and forced the government to take action.

On 25 May Mola, a myopic and meticulous commander who could infuriate colleagues with his caution, sent off his 'Instrucción reservada no. 1'. This indicated that the coup needed to unite the armed forces and non-military groups who supported their cause. They were counting, of course, on the Falangists, the *requetés* and the other right-wing parties. The figurehead of the rising would be General José Sanjurjo, known as 'the lion of the Rif', because he had won fame in the Alhucemas landing of 1925 which led to the defeat of Abd-el-Krim. A large, rather vain man, he was the descendant of Carlist officers who had fought the liberals in the nineteenth century.

Under his command came the man who was undoubtedly the

most competent of the colonial officers known as *africanistas*, Francisco Franco Bahamonde. Franco, the son of a naval paymaster in El Ferrol, had joined the army because of a lack of openings in the navy. He was a hard-working cadet, but not brilliant at the Academy of Infantry – he passed out number 251 out of 312 candidates. In North Africa, however, he received rapid promotion in the Foreign Legion. This corps was modelled on its French equivalent. Unlike his robust soldiers, Franco lacked a military appearance. He was short, had a pot belly and a high-pitched voice, which provoked jokes among his fellow officers. They called him by the diminutives 'comandantín' and 'Franquito'.[15] The young general, although undoubtedly brave, was extremely cautious in his planning. In fact his reticence during the spring of 1936 led many colleagues to think that he might not join the rising because the left hated him so much after repressing the Asturias revolution. He was certainly not an expansive man and rarely gave away his thinking. He was also, at that time, not known for his religious beliefs and in the Legion he stood out for showing little interest in chasing women. He did have one passion, however. He was viscerally anti-communist and devoted himself to reading journals on the subject of the bolshevik threat.[16]

The triumvirate of Sanjurjo, Mola and Franco could hardly have offered greater contrasts. They were then joined most surprisingly by a very eccentric character, General Queipo de Llano. He was assumed to have been a convinced Freemason and republican because he had taken part in a failed plot against the monarchy in 1930.

The left, in the meantime, was seeking allies within the army. They used their own secret society within the armed forces, the Unión Militar Republicana Antifascista (UMRA), but this was concentrated above all in the Assault Guard and the presidential guard.[17] Its members were mostly connected to the socialist PSOE, but the communists, in the form of Vicente Uribe and Enrique Líster, tried to infiltrate it. At the beginning of July 1936 a group of 200 members of UMRA were preparing what they called 'Operation Romerales'. This was a plan to kidnap or assassinate coup leaders in Morocco, but on 8 July the project was discovered and halted immediately by Casares Quiroga. The UMRA leaders met the head of government to warn him of the military plot, which was being prepared for 16 July. They gave him the names of Goded, Mola, Fanjul, Varela, Franco, Aranda, Alonso Vega, Yagüe and García Valiño. Casares Quiroga replied that there was not the slightest danger of a rising.[18]

The political involvement of young military officers on the left would lead to the most important incident before the rising. On 12 July Falangist gunmen murdered Lieutenant José Castillo Sería of the Assault Guard and a known member of the UMRA. He was the second socialist officer to be killed. Several of his comrades, including Captain Fernando Condés of the Civil Guard and the socialist Victoriano Cuenca, decided to take revenge. They first went to the home of Antonio Goicoechea, the head of the monarchist Renovación Española. He was away, so they tried the house of Gil Robles, but he was in Biarritz. Finally they drove in the middle of the night to the apartment of Calvo Sotelo, in the Calle de Velázquez. They ordered him to dress and to accompany them. He was shot dead in their automobile and the body was dumped outside the entrance to the city's eastern cemetery.

The uproar of the right was enormous, even though the government itself had obviously had nothing to do with the murder. Those who were soon to call themselves 'nationalists' always insisted that the assassination of Calvo Sotelo was the final straw. But this is misleading. By the time the event took place in Madrid, civilian conspirators such as Luca de Tena, Juan de la Cierva and Luis Bolín had hired in London, with Juan March's money, a de Havilland Dragon Rapide. This aeroplane was already on its way towards Las Palmas to collect General Franco to take him to Casablanca and then on to Tetuán to join the Army of Africa. In addition, Mola had sent detailed orders with instructions for a rising to take place between 10 and 20 July. For months Falangists had been co-ordinating in secret with rebel officers their involvement as soon as they received the codeword 'Covadonga' – an emotive touch invoking the place where the *Reconquista* of Spain had started against the Moors. And on 29 June José Antonio had smuggled out the order from his prison cell that the Falange Española must join the rising.

On the other hand, nationalists can argue that even though the government bore no personal responsibility for the assassination of the leader of the opposition by uniformed police, this was hardly relevant. They were not rising so much against the elected government as against the total lack of government, which Calvo

Sotelo's murder so starkly demonstrated. And although the mechanics of the rebellion had indeed been set in motion already, the slaying of Calvo Sotelo made many more people support the rising than would otherwise have been the case.

Despite so much evidence of all these preparations, the republican leaders could not bring themselves to believe the terrible truth. Azaña and Casares Quiroga acted a little like Chamberlain faced with Hitler. The president of the Republic seems to have lost all political sense. He suffered moments of depression combined with outbreaks of euphoria. Both Azaña and Casares Quiroga even dismissed warnings from generals loyal to the Republic or from Prieto, or the communist deputy Dolores Ibárruri, always known as 'La Pasionaria', who tried to alert Casares Quiroga to Mola's preparations in Pamplona. But the head of government insisted that 'Mola is loyal to the Republic'. The ultimate paradox of the liberal Republic represented by its government was that it did not dare defend itself from its own army by giving weapons to the workers who had elected it.

Although the atmosphere was still very tense during that third week of July, life still tended to go on out of habit. For the middle classes, it was the time to go on holiday. Very few of them, however, imagined that their lives might well depend on their choice of destination or on a decision to stay at home.

PART TWO

The War of Two Spains

6

The Rising of the Generals

The generals had planned a *coup d'état* with a rising of garrisons in Spanish Morocco and throughout Spain. The success of such an action depended more on the psychological effect of speed and ruthlessness than on numbers. Although the rebel generals did not achieve an outright coup, the Republic failed to crush the rising in the first 48 hours, the most important period of the whole war, when the possession of whole regions was decided.

The hesitancy of the republican government was fatal in a rapidly developing crisis, because the initial uncertainty enforced a defensive mentality. The prime minister did not dare arm the UGT and CNT. He refused to depart from the legal constitution of the state, even though a state attacked by its own 'spinal column' has ceased to exist for all practical purposes. The delay in issuing weapons discouraged pre-emptive or counter-offensive moves against the rebel military. 'The republican authorities were not prepared to give us arms,' recalled a carpenter from Seville, 'because they were more afraid of the working class than they were of the army. We communists did not share the government's confidence that the rising would be suffocated in twenty-four hours.'[1]

Republicans made a virtue of necessity. They encouraged the idea that 'to resist was to win', as a slogan later put it. Even during the rising the communist deputy La Pasionaria had expressed this dangerously appealing idea with '*¡No Pasarán!*' (They shall not pass!), her famous plagiarism of Pétain's phrase at Verdun.

The military plotters seldom had complete surprise on their side, but doubt and confusion were certainly in their favour. If the workers held back on the advice of a civil governor who was afraid of provoking the local garrison into revolt they were lost. They paid for this hesitation with their lives. But if they demonstrated from the beginning that they were prepared to assault the barracks, then most of the paramilitary forces would join them and the garrison surrender.

The final orders, sent out by General Mola in coded telegrams, provided for the Army of Africa to revolt at 5 a.m. on 18 July and the army in mainland Spain to rise 24 hours later. The difference in timing was to allow the Army of Africa to secure Spanish Morocco before being transported to the Andalucian coast by the navy. The rebel generals could count on this force because the rank and file were not conscripts, but regulars or, more accurately, mercenaries, whose reliability had been proved in the crushing of the Asturias rebellion. There were few officers of liberal sympathies, perhaps because colonials always exaggerate what they believe are national virtues. They despised politicians and had a virulent hatred of 'reds', a term including liberals and all those opposed to a right-wing dictatorship. It was an attitude which Mola expressed with all clarity in his instructions for the rising: 'He who is not with us is against us.'

The elite force, and the most introvert, was the Foreign Legion. Composed in large part of fugitives and criminals, its ranks were indoctrinated with a cult of virility and slaughter. They were taught to be useful suicides with their battle cry of '*¡Viva la Muerte!*' (Long live Death!). The Legion was organized in *banderas*, compact battalions with their own light artillery. The Moroccan troops, on the other hand, were divided into *tabores* of some 250 men each. These *regulares* were Riffian tribesmen commanded by Spanish officers. Their ferocious efficiency had been amply proved resisting colonial power during the first quarter of the century. Probably their most important skill was the ability to move across country using the folds in the ground. Such stealth had a decided advantage over the Spanish idea of conspicuous bravery. These Moroccans had been recruited with the offer of higher wages than those which the French colonial authorities paid and also with an engagement bonus of two months' pay. Widespread unemployment in Spanish Morocco prompted thousands to enlist.[2]

The rebels could hardly have failed to take Spanish Morocco. With only a handful of officers loyal to the Republic, the legionnaires obeyed the order to join the rising without question and the *regulares* were told that the Republic wanted to abolish Allah. The Spanish workers, who had virtually no arms and little contact with the indigenous population, found themselves completely isolated.

Towards midday on 17 July the plan for the next morning was discovered in the Moroccan town of Melilla, but General Romerales, a loyal republican described also as 'the fattest of the 400 Spanish generals and one of the easiest to trick',[3] could not make up his mind whether to arrest the officers concerned. Colonel Seguí moved faster and arrested the general, having decided that it would be dangerous to delay, even though the other conspirators would not be ready. The Assault Guard were persuaded to join the rising and key buildings in the town were rapidly seized. The Foreign Legion and *regulares* attacked the *casa del pueblo*, where trade unionists fought to the end. While the remaining pockets were being finished off, Seguí had General Romerales and the mayor arrested.[4] He signalled Colonels Sáenz de Buruaga and Yagüe commanding the garrisons at Tetuán and Ceuta. General Franco in Las Palmas was also informed by telegram about this premature action.

At ten past six the following morning, Franco sent his reply. 'Glory to the heroic Army of Africa. Spain above everything. Accept the enthusiastic greeting of those garrisons which join you and all the other comrades in the Peninsula in these historic moments. Blind faith in victory. Long live Spain with honour!' The same text was sent to all the divisions on the mainland, the headquarters of the Balearic Islands, to the commander of the cavalry division and the naval bases.[5] In Las Palmas, Franco ordered the troops on to the street where, joined by Falangists, they besieged government buildings until they were surrendered. Franco then handed over command of the Canaries to General Orgaz and set off by sea to the aerodrome, which he reached at three in the afternoon of 18 July.[6]

As dusk fell on 17 July in Spanish Morocco, the commanders of the Legion and the *regulares* moved their forces into position in the other garrison towns. The Spanish working-class areas were quickly occupied and prominent unionists shot on sight. The declaration of a general strike was no more than a brave gesture as the Moroccan *regulares* were let loose. In Larache the workers fought desperately with very few weapons through the night, but in Ceuta, Yagüe's legionnaires crushed the resistance in a little over two hours, killing the mayor. All this time the commander-in-chief in Morocco, General Gómez Morato, was gambling. Having carried out Azaña's reshuffle, he was hated by the rebel officers. He knew nothing of the rising until a telephone call for him from Madrid from Casares Quiroga was put through to the casino. He immediately took an aeroplane to Melilla where he was arrested as soon as he landed.

The only remaining centres of resistance at dawn in Morocco on the 18th were the high commissioner's residence and the air force base at Tetuán; both surrendered a few hours later when threatened with artillery. All those who had resisted were executed, including the high commissioner and Major de la Puente Bahamonde, whose fate was approved by his first cousin, General Franco. In a single night the rebels had killed 189 people.[7]

Colonel Beigbeder, who spoke Arabic, approached the Caliph Muley Hassan to secure his support. He warned him that the republican government could declare Morocco independent in order to undermine the rebel cause. And any encouragement of Moroccan nationalism would put him in danger after his collaboration with the colonial power.

In Madrid the republican government had been aware of the rising since the evening of 17 July. The next morning it issued the following communiqué: 'The government states that the movement is confined to certain areas in the Protectorate and that no one, absolutely no one, on the mainland has joined this absurd venture.' At 3 p.m. on 18 July Casares Quiroga firmly rejected offers of aid from the CNT and UGT. He urged everyone to carry on as normal and to 'trust in the military powers of the state'. He claimed that the rising in Seville had been suppressed, still believing that General Queipo de Llano would secure central Andalucia for the Republic. In fact, Queipo de Llano had already done precisely the opposite. 'Thanks to preventative measures taken by the government,' Casares Quiroga proclaimed, 'it may be said that a vast anti-republican movement has been wiped out.' He again refused to arm the workers, saying that 'anybody who hands out weapons without my approval will be shot'.[8]

That night the CNT and UGT declared a general strike over Unión Radio. It was the nearest they could get to ordering mobilization. The news coming in showed the administration's statements to be a mixture of contradictions, lies and complacency. The workers began to dig up weapons hidden since the Asturian events of October 1934 and, although Casares Quiroga's government finally began to understand what it faced, its basic attitude did not change. 'His ministry is a madhouse,' an observer remarked, 'and the maddest inmate is the prime minister. He is neither sleeping nor eating. He shouts and screams as if possessed. He will hear nothing of arming the people and threatens to shoot anybody who does it on his own initiative.'[9]

When the rising was successful in a town, the pattern of events usually started with the seizing of strategic buildings, such as the town hall. If there was no military garrison, the rebel forces would consist of civil guards, Falangists, and right-wing supporters armed with hunting rifles or shotguns. They would proclaim a state of war in official terms, and in several places confused townsfolk thought that they were carrying out the orders of the Madrid government.

The response of the CNT and UGT was to order a general strike and demand weapons from the civil governor. Arms were either refused them or were unobtainable. Barricades were rapidly constructed, but workers who resisted the rebels were massacred, and potential opponents who survived, from the civil governor down to the lowest union official, were executed. On the other hand, if the troops wavered or delayed in coming out of their barracks, and the workers were ready, the outcome was usually very different. An immediate attack, or an encirclement of the barracks, was enough to ensure the rebels' surrender.

A very important factor was the decision of the paramilitary forces, who were much better trained and armed than the conscript infantry. But it was wrong to say that their loyalty or disloyalty to the government was the crucial element. Like the general population, they were often unsure in their own minds, and only the most dedicated would fight when the battle was obviously lost from the beginning. They often hung back to see which way things were going before committing themselves. If the workers' organizations took immediate and firm action, then they usually remained loyal, although the Civil Guard often revealed their true colours later on. Of the two corps, the Assault Guard showed more loyalty to the government than the Civil Guard, but then they tended to be an urban force and the big cities had a better prepared working class.

The city of Seville was of great strategic importance in the plans of the rebels as a base for the advance on Madrid. The intelligent chief of staff there, José Cuesta Monereo, was the true brains behind the coup which enthroned General Queipo de Llano, the commander of the *carabinero* frontier guards, as the 'viceroy' of Andalucia. Queipo was irreverent, cynical, unpredictable and possessed a macabre sense of humour. Early on the morning of 18 July, accompanied by his ADC and three other reliable officers, he marched into the office of the commander of the military region, General José Fernández de Villa-Abrille, who was given no time to recover from the surprise intrusion. When told to decide immediately whether he was with the rising or against it, Villa-Abrille dithered. Queipo arrested him and had a corporal guard the door with orders to shoot anyone who attempted to leave the room.

Queipo next went to the San Hermenegildo infantry barracks where he found the 6th Regiment drawn up on parade, fully armed. He went straight to the colonel to congratulate him on joining the rising. The colonel replied that he was for the government. Queipo suggested that they should discuss the matter in his office. Once inside, he arrested him too. He then tried other officers to see if they would lead the regiment, but Sanjurjo's failure was evidently strong in their thoughts. Eventually a young captain, who was a Falangist, volunteered and all the other officers were locked up.

With the infantry on his side, Queipo managed to persuade the artillery regiment to join him as well. Falangists, who arrived to help, were given weapons from the armouries. Nationalist legend claimed that Queipo seized Seville with only a small force, when in fact he had some 4,000 men.[10] An artillery salvo ensured the surrender of the civil governor and the Assault Guard. Then, despite Queipo's promise to save the lives of those inside if they gave in, they were all shot. Just before the chief of police was due to be executed, he was told that his wife would be given his full salary if he handed over the secret files on the workers' organizations. He explained where they were hidden, but his widow probably received nothing after he was shot.

The Civil Guard joined the rebels as soon as they saw the surrender of the Assault Guard. It was only then that the workers started to react. A general strike was ordered over Radio Seville and peasants were called in from the surrounding countryside to help. Barricades were constructed in desperate haste, but the feud between anarchists and communists undermined the organization of an effective counter-attack. The workers withdrew into their own districts of Triana and La Macarena around the perimeter of the town where they prepared their defence. The rebels captured the radio station, which was used by Queipo to broadcast threats of violence against those who resisted him and, more important, to deny government claims that the revolt had been crushed on the mainland. The rising of 18 July 1936 was the first modern coup in which radio stations, telephone exchanges and aerodromes were of major importance.

On 22 July General Queipo de Llano declared over the radio that he 'was not playing politics' and that what the generals wanted was to 're-establish order subverted by foreign powers, and that the Marxist conglomerate had deformed the character of the Republic'. He added, 'As a Spaniard, I regret the blind obstinacy of those who with weapons in their hands oppose this movement of liberation. This obliges me to be implacable in punishing it.'[11]

In Málaga the workers were strong but they had no weapons. Their leaders maintained contact with the Assault Guard, the only government force they felt they could trust. On the afternoon of 17 July, when the news of the rising in Melilla arrived, a rash young army officer, Captain Agustín Huelin, had led his company out towards the centre of the town. On the way they ran into a strong force of assault guards, who attacked at once. The soldiers came off worse. The senior officer in Málaga, General Paxtot, felt that he had no option but to move immediately. The rest of the garrison was marched out, but their commander changed his mind and marched them back to barracks. The colonel in charge of the Civil Guard was, most unusually for that corps, arrested by his own men when he also declared for the rising. The workers then surrounded the army barracks and set fire to a number of buildings. The garrison surrendered immediately.

In Almería the civil governor refused to arm the workers, using the argument that he did not wish to provoke the military into open revolt. He later claimed that he had no weapons to issue anyway. Only the arrival on 21 July of the destroyer *Lepanto* with a loyal captain secured the port for the Republic. Its guns were trained on the headquarters of the Civil Guard, which surrendered immediately. The threat of shelling proved a strong factor in many towns.

The civil governor in Jaén took a more positive approach. He called in the Civil Guard and persuaded them to lay down their weapons, even though they protested that they were loyal to the Republic. He then gave the weapons to the UGT and CNT for distribution and the town was secured. Obviously many more towns would have been saved if such a course had been followed, but there were few governors prepared to admit the total ineffectiveness of normal channels.

In the naval port of Cádiz, Colonel Varela was freed from prison by the local garrison and took command of the rising there. His troops attacked the *comandancia*, which was defended by the civil governor and members of an improvised workers' militia. The town hall was another centre of resistance, but artillery was brought up. Then at first light on the next day, 19 July, the destroyer *Churruca* arrived with the first reinforcements from the Army in Africa. The insurgents had captured a major naval port on the Andalucian coast.

The rebels were also to secure most of the coast to the Portuguese frontier, including Algeciras, La Línea (where the Carlists shot 200 Freemasons) and Jeréz. The repression was savage. Professor Carlos Castilla del Pino, who was then thirteen years old, described the killings in his birth place of San Roque. 'They took an anarchist couple, whose son was a friend of mine at school, off to a village 25 kilometres away and shot them there. Later, a Falangist who witnessed the execution told me that before being executed, the wife was raped by all the Moroccan soldiers who made up the execution squad ... Five wounded *carabineros* were dragged from their hospital beds. The Moors seized them by their arms and legs and threw them into the back of a lorry ... When they got them out to the highway, there was no way that the wounded could stand up to be shot, so the Moors bayoneted them.'[12]

In Huelva, however, the left retained control for the first few days. The Civil Guard commander in Madrid ordered the local detachment to attack Seville but it joined Queipo's forces immediately on arrival.

In the capital Casares Quiroga resigned as prime minister at four o'clock in the morning of 19 July. The atmosphere in Madrid had been very tense throughout the night. Even the backfiring of a car would lead people to think that the rising had started there too. During the hot night the cafés stayed open and the streets were noisy. Popular frustration and anger at the government was increased by contradictory news items broadcast on the wireless. The UGT and CNT were beginning to suspect treachery.

On receiving Casares Quiroga's resignation, Azaña asked his friend, Diego Martínez Barrio, the president of the Cortes, to form a government. His cabinet was composed of republican parties only and purposely ignored the left-wing elements of the Popular Front alliance, since it was the new prime minister's intention to achieve a reconciliation with the right. This moment of crisis revealed the crucial division between the liberal government of the Popular Front and the left.

Nevertheless, Martínez Barrio's peace overture to General Mola by telephone was firmly rejected. 'It is not possible, Señor Martínez Barrio,' said Mola. 'You have your people and I have mine. If you and I should reach agreement, both of us will have betrayed our ideals and our followers.'[13] It was perhaps ironic that a rebel general should remind the prime minister that he was the representative of those voters to whom he owed his appointment. The workers were furious with what they regarded as an utterly *fainéant*, if not treacherous, government. 'Large demonstrations are formed simultaneously,' an eyewitness wrote. 'They move towards the interior and war ministries like avalanches. The people shout "Traitors! Cowards!"' Militants shouted, 'We've been sold down the river! We'd better start taking them out and shooting them!'[14]

Martínez Barrio's government collapsed instantly. He described the event himself: 'Within a few minutes the political demonstration had brought about the ruin of my government. It was senseless to ask me to combat the military rebellion with mere shadows, stripped of authority and ludicrously retaining the name of ministers.'[15] His ministry had lasted just a few hours.

Azaña asked yet another personal friend to form a government. José Giral, a university professor, was the only liberal politician who realized that the politicians of the Republic could not refuse to face reality any longer. During the morning of 19 July he dissolved the army by decree and ordered that arms should be given to the workers' organizations. Julian Marías, who went to mass with his fiancée Lolita in the Church of the Carboneras near the Puerta del Sol, did not imagine that it would be the last one held there until April 1939. When they emerged on to the street afterwards, it seemed as if the city had changed hands during the church service. Requisitioned motorcars decorated with red or red and black flags careered around with rifles pointing out of the windows. The weapons had been handed out from the Assault Guard barracks in the Calle del Correo nearby.[16]

Even so, there were governors and officials who refused to carry out this instruction. In Madrid the government had to order General Miaja point-blank to comply with the order. More than 60,000 rifles were then delivered in lorries to UGT and CNT headquarters, where the heavy grease was cleaned off with party newspapers. Only 5,000 of them had bolts; the remainder were stored in the Montaña barracks where Colonel Serra, who was one of the conspirators, refused to hand them over.

David Antona described the scene inside CNT headquarters, which the government had closed only a few weeks earlier: 'A narrow dark room. We could hardly move. A jabber of voices, shouts, rifles – many rifles. The telephone never stopped ringing. It was impossible to hear yourself speak. There was only the noise of rifle bolts from comrades who wanted to learn quickly how to handle them.'[17]

The loyalists were lucky that there was also confusion among the conspirators in Madrid. Nobody seemed certain who was to take command, until eventually General Fanjul assumed this ill-fated responsibility. The rebel generals had known how hard it would be to seize Madrid at once. But considering that their strategy was based on a holding action until reinforcements arrived from Pamplona, Saragossa and Barcelona, astonishingly little preparation had been made for a siege.

Late in the afternoon of 19 July Fanjul went to the Montaña barracks, where he addressed the officers and those Falangists who had come to help. But when they attempted to march out, they found that they were hemmed in by crowds of *madrileños* who had been directed there by the UGT and CNT. Fire was exchanged and the troops withdrew into the barracks. The rebels' action had more the air of a ritual than a military operation. Outside, La Pasionaria's speech on the radio calling for resistance was relayed over loudspeakers, then the besiegers settled down to wait for the morning.

While the fighting on the mainland intensified during the afternoon of 18 July, the Dragon Rapide aeroplane, organized by Luis Bolín in London, collected General Franco in civilian clothes. The English pilot was supposed to match half a torn playing card with its counterpart in his passenger's possession. Franco dispensed with such a trivial touch of amateur conspiracy; perhaps he felt it beneath the dignity of a man of destiny. Sanjurjo may have been accepted as the figurehead, but Franco had an unshakeable belief that his own abilities were indispensable to the success of the rebels' great undertaking.

Franco flew to Casablanca, in French Morocco, where Luis Bolín awaited him, but first he needed to be sure that the Army of Africa was in control. He telephoned officers in Larache who advised him not to land in Tangier. At dawn on 19 July he left for Tetuán, changing into uniform in mid flight. Senior rebel officers were waiting for him at the airport. They included Yagüe, Solans, Seguí, Sáenz de Buruaga and Beigbeder.[18] A conference was held around the aircraft. Franco learned that the rising had not been entirely successful. He decided that Bolín should leave at once with an authorization to 'purchase aircraft and supplies for the Spanish non-Marxist army' – a somewhat bland description for the forces of what was later to be called *La Cruzada*.

The second decision which Franco took in Tetuán that day was to order that those loyal to the Republic should be held in a concentration camp near the city and in the castle of El Hecho in Ceuta. After a rapid selection, Falangists came each morning to shoot them in groups.[19]

Reinforcements were needed urgently on the mainland and, since the rising in the fleet had failed, aeroplanes were essential to carry the Army of Africa to Spain. On 22 July the German consul in Tetuán passed on to the Wilhelmstrasse a message from Colonel Beigbeder, a former Spanish military attaché in Berlin: 'General Franco and Lieutenant Colonel Beigbeder send greetings to their friend, the honourable General Kühlental, inform him of the new nationalist Spanish government, and request that he send ten troop-transport planes with maximum seating capacity through private German firms. Transfer by air with German crews to any airfield in Spanish Morocco. The contract will be signed afterwards. Very urgent! On the word of General Franco and Spain.'[20]

On the northern coast of Spain, the port of Santander was secured for the Republic without bloodshed on the morning of 19 July, when the 23rd Infantry Regiment refused to rise. But in Oviedo the left was too confident after the strength it had demonstrated in the Asturian rebellion of 1934. The local military commander, Colonel Aranda, had managed over the previous months to convince the civil governor and most of the workers' leaders that he was loyal to the government. Aranda, insisting that he acted on Madrid's orders, refused to hand over any weapons. The civil governor, reassured by his promises of loyalty, described him to the workers' leaders as a man of honour. Aranda suggested that he hold Oviedo while the miners form a column to go and help in Madrid. But as soon as they had left, he declared for the rising. The trusting governor was among the first to be executed once Aranda's troops and civil guards secured the town. After the workers realized that Aranda had tricked them, they surrounded the town and a long and furious siege began.

In Gijón, the rising failed thanks to the decisive action of dockers who confronted the troops under the command of Colonel Pinilla. They withdrew to the Simancas barracks, where they were besieged for over a month until *dinamiteros* blew up the buildings.

Events were much less dramatic in the Carlist city of Pamplona. On the morning of 19 July General Mola, the 'Director', scrupulously followed his own timetable and declared a state of war in Navarre. There was little resistance in this stronghold of traditionalism, often described as the Spanish Vendée. Those in the *casas del pueblo* who tried to resist perished in a massacre.[21] All that day a continual stream of Carlist farmers arrived in the main square to volunteer. Wearing their large scarlet berets, they shouted the old battle cry, '*¡Viva Cristo Rey!*' A French observer of the scene said that he would not have been surprised to see an auto-da-fé of heretics organized at the same time. A total of 8,000 *requetés* assembled, singing:

> Give me my beret,
> Give me my rifle,
> I'm going to kill more reds
> Than there are flowers in April and May.[22]

Navarre had voted to reject the statute of Basque autonomy offered by the Republic, so the Basques were well aware of the threat posed by the Carlists joining the military rebellion. On 19 July the nationalists also captured the city of Vitoria, heart of the southern

Basque province of Alava, but in Bilbao the civil governor managed to intercept Mola's telephone call to the military commander.[23] A council of defence for the province of Vizcaya was set up, the fortress of Basurto was surrounded and the soldiers were disarmed.

In Basque territory to the east, the initiative came almost entirely from working-class organizations, such as the UGT in Eibar and the CNT in San Sebastián. In San Sebastián events resembled those which had taken place in Oviedo. Colonel Carrasco declared that he was loyal to the government, so a column was sent off to help at Mondragón. When the colonel eventually showed his hand, his men were besieged in the María Cristina Hotel and the Gran Casino Club. San Sebastián, the summer capital and the most fashionable seaside resort in Spain, contained a considerable number of right-wing supporters, but they were unable to withstand the workers' unexpectedly ferocious attack. In their defence of the María Cristina the rebels were alleged to have used live hostages as sandbags in the windows, but this was probably an example of the exaggerated rumours of the time being used as propaganda. The anarchists seized the weapons in the Loyola barracks, since they were not certain that the Basque nationalist party would oppose the rising. This, and their subsequent shooting of some right-wing prisoners, worsened relations with their Basque Catholic allies in the PNV.

In Old Castile, Burgos, the city of soldiers and priests, was 'nationalist to the very stones', as the Countess of Vallellano said later to Doctor Junod of the Red Cross.[24] There was virtually no opposition, but that did nothing to lessen the mass executions once names and addresses had been obtained from police headquarters. Generals Batet and Mena, who stayed loyal to the government, were among the first to be shot. The most prominent right-wing civilians in the conspiracy – Sáinz Rodríguez, Goicoechea, the Count of Vallellano, Vegas Latapié, Yanguas, Zunzunegui and the Marquess of Valdeiglesias – had already gathered at Burgos to welcome General Sanjurjo as the new head of state, but they waited in vain. His aeroplane from Portugal had crashed on take-off and the 'Lion of the Rif' was killed instantly, burned in the wreck along with his dress uniforms and decorations.

In Valladolid, the heart of that austere Castile romanticized by José Antonio, the Assault Guard rebelled against the civil governor, Luis Lavín, and seized Radio Valladolid and the post office. The governor was arrested and the rebel officers he had locked up were freed. Generals Saliquet and Ponte entered the headquarters pistols in hand to take command of the rising. General Nicolás Molero and those loyal to him fought back and in the exchange of fire, three men were killed and five wounded, including Molero himself, who was executed several days later. Saliquet proclaimed a state of war and ordered the troops into the street. The railwaymen of the UGT fought with great bravery, but were soon annihilated. The 478 people who had sought refuge in the *casa del pueblo* were imprisoned.[25]

The failure of the left to secure Saragossa, the capital of Aragón, was a major disaster, especially for the anarchists. The government, suspicious of General Cabanellas's intentions, sent a friend of his, General Nuñez de Prado, to confirm his loyalty to the Republic. Cabanellas declared for the rising and had Nuñez de Prado and his ADC shot. There were about 30,000 CNT members in Saragossa, but their leaders insisted on working through the civil governor, even though he gave them no arms. Troops led by Colonel Monasterio marched into the streets at dawn on 19 July and the virtually defenceless workers suffered a fearful massacre.

Barcelona presented a very different story, even though it had been regarded by the military conspirators as the most certain conquest of all. The nationalists, relying on UME officers who were right-wing and anti-Catalan, had 12,000 troops to bring in from their barracks to dominate the central area. General Goded was to fly in from Majorca, once the island was secured, and take command. The plotters, however, never took into account the determination of the workers' organizations, nor did they foresee that the Assault Guard and, more surprisingly, the Civil Guard, would oppose them.

On the evening of 18 July Companys, the president of the Catalan Generalitat, refused to issue arms to the CNT, even though news of events in Morocco and Seville had reached him and he had been given documentary proof of plans for the rising in Barcelona. Catalan police arrested anarchists carrying arms, but they were released after vigorous protests by the CNT regional committee.

The anarchists, who knew very well what awaited them if the army seized the city, decided not to leave their fate in the hands of politicians. During that night the CNT local defence committees went ahead with full preparations for war. Isolated armouries were seized (a couple with the active assistance of sympathetic NCOs) and weapons were taken from four ships in the harbour. Even the rusting hulk of the prison ship *Uruguay* was stormed, so as to take the warders' weapons. The UGT dockers' union knew of a shipment of dynamite in the port, and once that was seized, home-made grenades were manufactured all through the night. Every gun shop in the city was stripped bare. Cars and lorries were requisitioned and metal workers fixed crude armour plating while sandbags were piled behind truck cabs. Vehicles were given clear identification with large white letters daubed on the roof and sides. The vast majority were the anarchist initials CNT-FAI, but POUM and PSUC were also in evidence. Some bore the letters UHP (United Proletarian Brothers), the joint cry of the workers' alliance in the Asturian revolt.

The atmosphere of that hot night was highly charged. The Popular Olympiad (organized as a boycott of the Olympics in Nazi Germany) was due to open the next morning. The event was forgotten in the threatening crisis, and the foreign athletes waited uneasily in their hotels and dormitories. (Many of them joined the fighting the next day alongside the workers and around 200 later joined militia columns.) Companys, realizing he was superfluous for the moment, went for a walk on the Ramblas, a felt hat pulled down over his eyes to avoid being recognized. The streets were crowded and noisy, with loudspeakers attached to the trees playing music interrupted by announcements. In the favourite anarchist meeting place, the Café La Tranquilidad, CNT members were dashing in and out to hear the latest news and report on the arming of the workers. The members of the regional committee, such as Buenaventura Durruti, Juan García Oliver and Diego Abad de Santillán, maintained a close liaison with the Generalitat despite Companys's decision. In fact a few assault guards ignored the Generalitat's instructions and handed out rifles to the CNT from their own armoury.

Just before dawn on 19 July, the soldiers in the Pedralbes barracks were given rum rations by their officers, then told that orders had been received from Madrid to crush an anarchist rising. Falangists and other supporters wearing odd bits of uniform joined the column as it set off up the Diagonal, one of the major thoroughfares of Barcelona.[26] Almost immediately factory sirens all over the city sounded the alarm. Also at about five in the morning, the Montesa cavalry regiment moved out of its barracks in the Calle Tarragona, the Santiago regiment of dragoons left the Travessera de Gràcia barracks and a battery of the 7th Light Artillery Regiment marched forth from the Sant Andreu barracks, where more than 30,000 rifles were held.

The deployment of troops into the streets was badly co-ordinated. The infantry regiment from the Parque barracks was vigorously attacked and forced to make a fighting retreat back behind its own walls, while the Santiago cavalry regiment was scattered at the Cinc d'Oros. Some units never even broke out into the streets. Those that did manage to march out, advanced to seize strategic buildings near the Plaza de España and the Plaza de Cataluña. They barricaded themselves in the Hotel Colón, the Ritz and the central telephone exchange. Detachments attacked en route made barricades to defend themselves, but these were charged by heavy lorries driven in suicidal assaults. The soldiers were also attacked with home-made bombs lobbed from rooftops and by snipers. Barricades to bar their way to the centre were constructed by almost everyone who could not take part in the fighting. Those made with paving stones could withstand light artillery if properly laid, as the workers knew from the street fighting during the Semana Trágica in 1909.

At about 11 a.m. General Goded arrived from Majorca by seaplane. The island had been easily secured for the rising, although Minorca, with its submarine base at Port Mahon, was won for the left by soldiers and NCOs who resisted their officers. Goded went immediately to the *capitanía* (the captain-general's headquarters), where he arrested the loyal divisional commander, Llano de la Encomienda. It was not long, however, before all the rebel-held buildings in the centre of the city were besieged. The black and red diagonal flag of the CNT-FAI appeared on barricades, lorries and public buildings. Loudspeakers in the streets continued to relay news, instructions and exhortations throughout the long hot Sunday. Churches were set on fire after reports of sniping from church towers (not by priests, as rumour said, but by soldiers who had occupied the belfries of Los Carmelitas and Santa Madrona). Summary executions were carried out, including a dozen priests in the Carmelite convent wrongly accused of firing at people from its windows.

Attacks across open ground surrounding the besieged buildings caused heavy casualties. Then, at about two o'clock, when it was evident that the army would not be able to defeat such determined numbers, Colonel Escobar brought in his civil guards on the side of the workers, with a column of 800 mounting the Vía Layetana to the Commission of Public Order where Companys waited on the balcony. A mounted squadron trotting along the Ramblas gave the clenched fist salute to roars of approval from the crowds. It was the first time that this paramilitary force had been cheered by the workers of Barcelona, though their instinctive suspicion of the Civil Guard did not disappear. With their excellent marksmanship, the civil guards were to prove a great help in the attack on the Hotel Colón and the Ritz, although the anarchists recaptured the telephone building on their own.

The real turning point came in the Avenida Icaria, where barricades were improvised with huge rolls of newsprint to stop cavalry and the 1st Mountain Artillery Regiment on their way to help the besieged rebels in the centre. At one moment during the fighting, a small group of workers and an assault guard rushed across to an insurgent artillery detachment with two 75mm guns. They held their rifles above their heads to show that they were not attacking as they rushed up to the astonished soldiers. Out of breath, they poured forth passionate arguments why the soldiers should not fire on their brothers, telling them that they had been tricked by their officers. The guns were turned round and brought to bear on the rebel forces. From then on more and more soldiers joined the workers and assault guards.

It was a salvo from captured artillery under the command of a docker which brought the surrender of General Goded in the *capitanía*. Many Republicans wanted to shoot this leading conspirator on the spot, but he was saved by a communist, Caridad Mercader, the mother of Trotsky's assassin. Goded was taken to Companys, who persuaded him to broadcast a statement over the radio to save further bloodshed. 'This is General Goded,' he said. 'I make this declaration to the Spanish people, that fate has been against me and I am a prisoner. I am saying this so that all those who are still fighting need feel no further obligation towards me.'[27] His words were of great help to the left-wing forces in other parts of Spain, especially in Madrid where they were broadcast over loudspeakers to the rebels defending the Montaña barracks. But agreeing to make the statement did not save him. A court martial of republican officers in August condemned him to death for rebellion.

By nightfall only the Atarazanas barracks, near the port, and the Sant Andreu barracks still held out. The machine-gun emplacements round the Columbus monument had been silenced in the early evening. The airport at Prat was commanded by a sympathetic officer, Colonel Díaz Sandino, and his planes had attacked the monument, enabling a wave of workers and assault guards to overrun it. In the castle of Montjuich the garrison had shot the rebel officers and then handed over the weapons in the armoury to the CNT.

The next morning the anarchists, insisting that the capture of the Atarazanas barracks was their prerogative, told the paramilitary forces to stay clear. Buenaventura Durruti gave the order for the mass attack: '*¡Adelante hombres de la CNT!*' He led the charge with his companion in arms, Francisco Ascaso, who was killed almost immediately. That final action brought total casualty figures to about 600 killed and 4,000 wounded. As in all the fighting, a desperate, selfless bravery was shown by the attackers. Many of the casualties were unnecessary, especially those suffered in the final assault when the anarchists had artillery and air support available. Nevertheless, the courage of that attack passed into anarchist folklore, obscuring the fact that dash and bravery are dangerous substitutes for military science.

7
The Struggle for Control

The plan for the military rising had given the navy a key role. Their ships were needed to bring the Army of Africa to the mainland. This had been worked out in advance between General Franco and senior naval officers, on fleet exercises near the Canaries. Warships were to make all speed for Spanish Morocco on the outbreak of the rising.

On 18 July General Queipo de Llano demonstrated his confidence in this strategy during the first of his garrulous broadcasts over Radio Sevilla, totally unconcerned that he might be revealing their plans in the process: 'The navy, always faithful to the heartbeat of the nation, has joined us en masse. Thanks to its help, the transport of troops from Morocco to the Peninsula has to be carried out very quickly and soon we will see arriving in Cádiz, Málaga and Algeciras the glorious columns of our Army of Africa, which will advance without rest on Granada, Córdoba, Jaén, Estremadura, Toledo and Madrid.'[1]

Such sweeping assumptions, however, proved premature. The overwhelming majority of officers in the navy certainly supported the rising. In common with the naval officers of most Latin countries, those in Spain were more aristocratic than their counterparts in the army. The Spanish army had acquired liberal pockets, having become a ladder for the social-climbing middle class in the nineteenth century. Spanish naval wardrooms, on the other hand, tended to be strongly monarchist and the average officer's attitude towards the lower deck at that time was scarcely enlightened.

On the morning of 18 July the ministry of marine in Madrid instructed three destroyers to sail for Melilla from Cartagena. They received orders by radio to bombard the insurgent town. The officers on board thus knew that the rising had begun. In two of the destroyers all hands were called on deck, where their captains explained the objectives of the rebellion. But if the officers had been expecting shouts of enthusiasm, they were to be disappointed.

The junior ranks in the navy were far better organized than their counterparts in the army. They had held a secret conference in El Ferrol on 13 July to discuss what they should do if the officers rebelled against the government. In Madrid a telegraphist, Benjamín Balboa, intercepted the message dictated by General Franco in Tenerife. He passed it at once to the ministry of marine and arrested the officer in charge of the radio section, Lieutenant-Commander Castor Ibáñez, who was part of the conspiracy. Balboa, on orders from the ministry, immediately contacted all signals operators with the fleet to warn them of what was going on and asking them 'to watch their officers, a gang of fascists'. As a result of his actions, the majority of ships' crews were informed of events and could not be tricked by false stories. Following this up, Giral, still at this point minister of marine, sent a signal dismissing all officers who refused government orders.

Of the three destroyers off Melilla only the officers on the *Churruca* stayed in command. This was because the radio was out of order. On the *Almirante Valdés* and *Sánchez Barcáiztegui* (the ship on which Azaña had been imprisoned) the crews, forewarned by radio operators, rushed their officers and overpowered them. They then elected a ship's committee, bombarded Melilla and Ceuta, and returned to the loyal naval base of Cartagena. The rebels thus had only one destroyer and one gunboat, the *Dato*, to start ferrying the badly needed reinforcements from the Army of Africa across to Spain.

By the morning of 19 July the government had ordered all available warships to steam to the Straits of Gibraltar to prevent the Army of Africa from crossing. The officers who wished to join the rising could not prevent the news from reaching the lower deck. On the cruiser *Miguel de Cervantes* the officers resisted to the end, but on most ships they surrendered once ratings had seized the ship's armoury. The only seaworthy battleship, the *Jaime I*, was won back by the sailors, as were the cruiser *Libertad* and even the destroyer *Churruca*, after it had landed half a *tabor* of *regulares* at Cádiz. The nationalists later claimed that 'mutinous' sailors had assassinated their officers and accused Giral of being responsible.

After the ministry of marine had sent instructions relieving rebel officers of their command, the following famous exchange of signals occurred: 'Crew of *Jaime I* to ministry of marine. We have had serious resistance from the commanders and officers on board and have subdued them by force ... Urgently request instructions as to bodies.' 'Ministry of marine to crew *Jaime I*. Lower bodies overboard with respectful solemnity. What is your present position?'[2]

The officers of the Royal Navy at Gibraltar were watching events carefully. The very idea of such action by the lower deck sent shudders down their spines. The Invergordon mutiny of 1931, even though it had been little more than a strike, was fresh in their memories, and only seventeen years had passed since the much more serious revolt of the French fleet in the Black Sea.[3] There was no doubt as to where their sympathies lay, and this was to have an appreciable influence in several areas. Voelckers, the German chargé d'affaires in Spain, informed the Wilhelmstrasse in October: 'As for England, we have made the interesting observation that she is supplying the whites with ammunition via Gibraltar and that the British cruiser commander here has recently been supplying us with information on Russian arms deliveries to the red government, which he certainly would not do without instructions.'[4]

With the rising crushed on most ships, many of the rebels were sure that they were doomed, since it seemed the Army of Africa could not cross to the mainland. Mola, convinced that their project had failed, continued only because there was no choice. The German chargé d'affaires reported to the Wilhelmstrasse that the defection of the fleet might frustrate Franco's plans. It could mean the sacrifice of garrisons in the major cities.

This setback did not turn out to be a disaster for the nationalists because they managed to start the first major airlift of troops in history.[5] Although the airlift began almost immediately with a few Spanish air force Breguets, Nieuports and Italian Savoias, it was chiefly effected by Junkers 52s sent by Hitler, who remarked later that Franco should erect a monument to the plane because it was so vital to his victory.[6] But the nationalists also benefited from the fact that the new ships' committees were badly co-ordinated, thus severely reducing the effectiveness of the republican navy. The republican navy was also deterred from attacking ships transporting units of the Army of Africa because they were screened by the German pocket battleships *Deutschland* and *Admiral Scheer*. In this way the rebels managed to bring across the so-called 'convoy of victory' with 2,500 troops and much equipment, including heavy weapons which could not be flown over.

The most furious fighting within the navy did not take place at sea, but in the port of El Ferrol at the north-west tip of Spain. On 19 July the CNT and UGT demanded that the civil governor comply with the order to issue arms, but the head of the naval arsenal refused to hand any over and a state of war was declared by the conspirators. The 29th Marine Infantry and detachments from the 3rd Regiment of Coastal Artillery managed to clear the town for the rebels, but many workers joined with sailors to seize the arsenal.

Loyalist sailors also manned the cruiser *Almirante Cervera*, which was in dry dock, as well as the immobilized battleship *España*. These two ships managed to knock out the destroyer *Velasco*, which had been secured by its officers for the rising, but they could not traverse their heavy guns landwards at the coastal batteries because of installations alongside the dock. The destruction caused by a major naval battle in such a restricted area was enormous. Eventually, on 21 July nationalist officers faked a signal from the ministry of marine ordering the ships to give in and avoid useless bloodshed. The loyalist commander of the *Almirante Cervera*, Captain Sánchez Ferragut, and Rear-Admiral Azarola accordingly offered to surrender on the condition that there were no executions. This was promised, but later ignored.

The military rising elsewhere in Galicia had begun, after a delay, early on 20 July. In Corunna the civil governor, Francisco Pérez Carballo, a personal friend of Casares Quiroga, refused arms to the UGT and CNT. He assured them that the military governor had received a solemn promise from his officers that they would not rebel. But General Pita Romero was then arrested and shot. The divisional commander, General Enrique Salcedo, was shot later, as was Pérez Carballo. The fate of his pregnant wife, Juana Capdevielle, was terrible. She was imprisoned, then miscarried when she heard that her husband had been murdered. She was let out of prison, but in August some Falangists raped and killed her.[7]

Groups of workers with very few weapons held out against the troops and a large detachment of the Falange under Manuel Hedilla. They were finally crushed in a last stand near Sir John Moore's grave, just as reinforcements were arriving in the form of *dinamiteros* and miners from Noya armed with rifles. Finding they were too late and coming up against strong counter-attacks, the relief column fell back into the hills. Some broke up into guerrilla forces, others made their way eastwards towards Bilbao.

In Vigo, which also fell to the nationalists, the soldiers of the Mérida Regiment were given a great deal of alcohol, so the column marched to the centre of the town half-drunk. In the Puerta del Sol the officer in command proclaimed a state of war and, when unarmed civilians shouted protests, gave the order to fire. The soldiers started shooting in every direction.

Early in the morning of 20 July the sparsely armed citizens of Madrid around the Montaña barracks were joined by many others, including women. Two 75mm Schneider guns were towed into place. A retired captain of artillery, Orad de la Torre, sited them in the Calle Bailén some 500 metres from the barracks. Later, a 155mm gun, commanded by Lieutenant Vidal, was brought to within 200 metres of their target.[8]

Thousands of people surrounded the barracks along the Paseo de Rosales and from the North Station. It was a mass which advanced and retreated without order. A lawyer who was with them described the scene: 'Rifle shots were cracking from the direction of the barracks. At the corner of the Plaza de España and the Calle de Ferraz a group of assault guards were loading their rifles in the shelter of a wall. A multitude of people were crouching and lying between the trees and benches of the gardens.' Some loyalist planes arrived from the nearby airfield of Cuatro Vientos where the rising had been suppressed the day before. At first, they dropped leaflets calling on the soldiers to surrender. Later, when they dropped bombs on the barracks the thousands of civilians cheered and jumped for joy, but the machine-guns in the barracks opened up again, killing some of them. The young British poet Jack Lindsay wrote a poem about that day:

> We found an odd gun,
> We brought it up on a truck from a beer-factory.
> We rushed the Montaña barracks
> With some old pistols and our bare hands
> through the swivelling machine-gun fire.
> I was there.
> I saw the officers cowering,
> their faces chalked with fear.[9]

Not surprisingly, emotions were often stronger than common sense. Old revolvers were fired at the thick stone walls by those privileged few who had weapons. The assault on the Montaña barracks was to prove what horrors can result from confusion. Many of the soldiers wanted to surrender and waved white flags from their windows. The crowds ran joyfully forward but the machine-guns commanded by officers opened up again, killing many in the open. This happened several times so the mass of people were utterly enraged by the time the barracks were stormed. This was achieved only because a republican sapper sergeant within managed to throw open the gate before being shot down by an officer. The slaughter which followed was terrible.[10]

In Granada, General Miguel Campins stayed loyal to the Republic and assured the civil governor that his officers could be trusted.[11] But Colonels Muñoz and Leon Maestre set the rising in motion. Campins was arrested on 20 July and shot later on the orders of General Queipo de Llano for having opposed the '*movimiento salvador de España*'. The workers, who had believed that the garrison and the Assault Guard would not revolt, realized too late what was happening that day. The military rebels had seized the centre of the city by nightfall. Their opponents withdrew to the district known as the Albaicín, which they barricaded and defended for three days, but artillery was brought up and scores of families were buried in the rubble of their houses.

Of all the major towns, Valencia experienced the longest delay before the situation was clear because General Martínez Monje, the military commander, refused to declare himself for either side. General Goded's broadcast from Barcelona was a great blow to the conspirators there, who found it very difficult to persuade fellow officers to join. The CNT had already declared a general strike in the Valencian region and joined the executive committee set up by the Popular Front parties in the office of the civil governor. This dignitary had been deposed by the committee because he refused to hand over arms.

The CNT, with its docker membership, was the largest of the worker organizations and insisted on various conditions before co-operating with the Popular Front. One of these was that the paramilitary forces should be divided up among much larger groups of workers in order to ensure their loyalty. This was accepted and the mixed 'intervention groups' occupied the radio station, telephone exchange and other strategic buildings. Even so, when a detachment of the Civil Guard was sent together with some workers to help in another area, they shot their guardians and went off to join the nationalists.

General Martínez Monje continued to insist on his loyalty although he refused to hand over any weapons as ordered by the government. Few were convinced by his protestations, since he was evidently waiting to see how events developed in other towns. The argument over whether to storm the barracks was further confused when a delegation under Martínez Barrio arrived from Madrid. Eventually even those who were afraid of forcing neutrals into the enemy camp agreed that the situation was intolerable. The barracks were finally taken two weeks after the rising had begun. This failure to take Valencia was a grave blow for the plotters, because they could not advance on Madrid from the east.

In Andalucia Queipo de Llano's forces had not managed to secure much more than the centre of Seville and the aerodrome. The private planes housed at the aeroclub were to prove very useful for reconnaissance work and amateur bombing raids. But the vital function of the airstrip was to provide a landing ground for the airlift from Morocco, including the 5th Bandera commanded by Major Castejón. Their arrival on 21 July led to an all-out assault on the working-class district of Triana (where the Emperor Trajan is supposed to have come from). Castejón and his men then attacked the districts of La Macarena, San Julián, San Bernardo and El Pumarejo, which held out until 25 July.

Queipo de Llano's press assistant, Antonio Bahamonde – who later changed sides – described the action against these areas, which were defended by their inhabitants with hardly any weapons, claiming that more than 9,000 had been killed in the repression: 'In the working-class districts, the Foreign Legion and Moroccan *regulares* went up and down the streets of very modest one-storey houses, throwing grenades in the windows, blowing up and killing women and children. The Moors took the opportunity to loot and rape at will. General Queipo de Llano, in his night-time talks at the [Radio Seville] microphone ... urged on his troops to rape women and recounted with crude sarcasm brutal scenes of this sort.'[12]

News of these actions triggered off reprisal killings in the Andalucian countryside, where the peasants had risen against their landlords and the Civil Guard. Then, once Queipo's forces had secured Seville, the rebels started to dominate the countryside around. Some Falangist sons of landowners organized peasant hunts on horseback. This sort of activity was jokingly referred to as the '*reforma agraria*' whereby the landless *bracero* was finally to get a piece of ground for himself.

In many outlying areas of Spain a shocked stillness followed the sudden violence, but there was little pause for breath after control of the major towns had been decided. Columns were rapidly organized to help in other areas, or recapture nearby towns. In Madrid the UGT had organized an effective intelligence system through the railway telephone network to find out where the rising had succeeded and where it had failed. Lorryloads of worker militia rushed out from the capital. Guadalajara was retaken after a bitter struggle, Alcalá de Henares was recaptured from the Civil Guard who had declared for the rising and Cuenca was secured by 200 men led by Cipriano Mera. Other hastily formed militia detachments moved quickly north to block General Mola's troops along the line of the Guadarrama mountains.

A large column of militiamen drove south in a convoy of lorries, taxis and confiscated automobiles across the Castilian plain towards Toledo, where Colonel Moscardó was organizing the nationalists' defence of the military academy in the Alcázar fortress. Only a handful of the cadets assembled, as it was the summer vacation, but a strong force of civil guards had been brought in from the surrounding countryside. A mixed bag of officers and a large number of Falangists brought the total of active defenders to around 1,100. Inside the fortress were also more than 500 women and children and 100 left-wing hostages. Moscardó, who had not been involved in the conspiracy, was acting on his own initiative. He had managed to stall the war ministry's orders to despatch the contents of the Toledo arms factory to Madrid, and his men had withdrawn into their fortress with most of its contents just as the militia column reached the edge of the town. The siege of the

Alcázar had begun. It was to be exceptionally rich in emotive symbolism for the nationalists.

In Barcelona the greatest concern of the anarchists was the fall of Saragossa to the army and the resulting slaughter of their comrades. Flying columns of armed workers assembled in great haste and rushed forth into the Aragón countryside. Villages and small towns which had been secured for the rising by the local Civil Guard detachment and right-wing sympathizers were seized on the way. The militia usually shot all those whom they felt represented a threat before moving on. However, the columns were primarily made up of urban workers. Their fighting effectiveness lay in the streets, not in the countryside where they had no sense of terrain. 'We didn't have maps,' recounted Jordi Arquer, a POUM leader, 'and I am not talking about proper military maps, but a simple Michelin road map.'[13]

During their advance, the anarcho-syndicalist columns, armed with the 30,000 rifles from the Sant Andreu barracks, seized towns and villages which had fallen into rebel hands, and shot suspected supporters of the rising. Of the advancing columns only Durruti's did not fall to the temptation of securing rural areas, which was shown to be a dangerous distraction when the principal town was in enemy hands. The regular commander of the republican forces, Colonel Villalba, even ordered Durruti not to rush on so tempestuously towards Saragossa. A strong detachment of Carlists, sent by General Mola in Pamplona, arrived to reinforce the Saragossa garrison and Durruti's force was unsupported. The militia columns from Barcelona, amounting to about 20,000 men, would have been far more effective if they had been concentrated on fewer objectives. But such a spontaneously mobilized body could not act like troops controlled by a general staff.

The fighting was chaotic. Improvisations on both sides ranged from the inspired to the impractical. Field guns were fixed on to the rear of lorries, forming an early version of self-propelled artillery; armoured cars were built round trucks, sometimes effectively, although often the weight of steel plate was far too heavy for the engine. Every form of grenade, or *petardo*, was tried out (the so-called Molotov cocktail was in fact invented a little later by the Foreign Legion when attacked by Russian tanks outside Madrid that autumn). But with the originality came a contempt for more prosaic military customs, such as digging trenches. To fight from the ground was utterly contrary to the Spanish concept of war. There was a subconscious moral certainty that bravery must lead to victory.

It was not until the early days of August that the respective zones became clear and fronts recognizable. The insurgents had a broad horizontal strip of territory from Galicia and León in the west to Navarre and north Aragón in the east. This surrounded the coastal regions of Asturias, Santander and the Basque country, which had defeated the rising. In the south and west the rebels had seized no more than a small part of Andalucia.[14]

Only at this stage did the realization that Spain faced civil war, rather than a violently contested coup, penetrate people's minds. The republican failure to win outright in the early days, when dash and instinct outweighed weaponry and military science, meant that they were to become involved in a totally different type of fighting, one in which very different qualities were needed to win.

The nationalists' greatest military asset was the 40,000 men of the Army of Africa, with its combat experience.[15] They had also secured 50,000 men from the badly trained and poorly equipped metropolitan army. In addition, seventeen generals and 10,000 officers had joined the rising. They had about two-thirds of Queipo's *carabineros*, 40 per cent of the Assault Guard and 60 per cent of the Civil Guard. In all, this represented about 30,000 men out of the combined strength of the three paramilitary forces. In total they could count on around 130,000 officers and men. The Republic, at the time of Giral's decree dissolving the army, counted on 50,000 soldiers, 22 generals and 7,000 officers, in addition to some 33,000 men from the paramilitary security forces. In theory, this represented a total of 90,000 men.[16]

For a long war it looked as if the Republic had the advantage: the large cities with their industry and manpower, mining areas, most of the navy and merchant marine, two-thirds of the mainland territory, the gold reserves and the citrus fruit export trade from Valencia, which was the country's largest foreign-currency earner. However, the nationalists were more than compensated by help from outside Spain and control of the main agricultural areas. Their primary supply of recruits for some time was to be the Riffian tribes. Hitler and Mussolini were to provide military, naval, air, logistical and technical support, while American and British business interests supplied vital credits and oil.

The nationalists at this point were starting to organize a military state, while in the republican zone revolutionary processes were set on foot. The army's attempt at what they claimed was a pre-emptive counter-revolution had destroyed what little remained of the republican state. Andreu Nin of the POUM described it thus: 'The government does not exist. We collaborate with them, but they can do no more than sanction whatever is done by the masses.' The rising of the right had pushed an unplanned revolution into the eager arms of the left.

8
The Red Terror

The most emotive issue in warfare is that of atrocities. It is nearly always the most visually horrific of them which become fixed in the imagination. Spain witnessed many during its civil war, but it was also one of the very first in which the techniques of mass propaganda played an important role.

The Spanish Civil War was a magnet for foreign correspondents and the enemy atrocities related by press officers provided sensational copy. In the early days little was done, or could be done, by correspondents to check the truth and background of most incidents. Refugees often justified their panic with exaggerated or imagined tales of horror. The gang of Barcelona workers said to be covered in blood from a massacre on 19 July were, in fact, from the abattoirs and had rushed straight out to resist the military rising. Wild estimates of the killing were reported: the nationalists stated at the time that half a million people had been slaughtered in republican territory and claimed the still excessive figure of 55,000 after the war. Perhaps the confusion and speed of events made journalists fall back on clichés, rather than investigate what lay behind the ferocity of the war. Having tended to ignore Spain, Europe did not understand the turbulent cycles of repression and revolt which had now built up to an explosion affecting every corner of the country.

The initial, hasty impressions passed on by journalists with little first-hand evidence seriously affected the Republic's foreign relations when it needed to buy arms in the crucial months of the war. The violent excesses recounted in many papers justified that distaste for the revolution in the republican zone which ran strongly in British conservative and diplomatic circles. The left-wing administration in France under Léon Blum suppressed its own natural sympathies and, alarmed by Hitler's occupation of the Rhineland that spring, felt obliged to follow the British idea of refusing aid to both sides (a policy which was bound to favour the nationalists). Not until the bombing of Guernica in April of 1937 did the battle for world opinion really change in the Republic's favour, but by then the republicans were already losing the war.

The Spanish war saw many terrible acts, but it was those of a religious significance that tended to prevail in people's minds: 'reds' killing priests and disinterring the mummies in convent vaults; it was even said that Dolores Ibárruri, La Pasionaria, had bitten the jugular of a priest; or Carlist *requetés* making a republican lie in the form of a cross before hacking off his limbs to the cry of 'Long live Christ the King!'.

If people in other countries were reminded of the Thirty Years' War, or the religious persecutions of the Dark Ages, and shuddered at this 'new barbarism', it was not surprising. The slaughter did not follow the same pattern on each side. In nationalist territory the relentless purging of 'reds and atheists' was to continue for years, while in republican territory the worst of the violence was mainly a sudden and quickly spent reaction of suppressed fear, exacerbated by desires of revenge for the past.

The attacks on the clergy were bound to cause the greatest stir abroad, where there was little understanding of the Church's powerful political role. The Catholic Church was the bulwark of the country's conservative forces, the foundation of what the right defined as Spanish civilization. Not surprisingly, the outside world had a fixed impression of Spain as a deeply religious country. The jest of the Basque philosopher Unamuno, that in Spain even atheists were Catholic, was taken seriously. Centuries of fanatical superstition enforced by the Inquisition had engraved this image on European minds. Even so, it was surprising how few foreign newspapers made the connection between the religious repression dating back to the Middle Ages and the violent anti-clericalism that developed in the nineteenth century. The rage which led to such excesses in some areas was fired by one great conviction: the promise of heaven for the meek was the age-old trick by the rich and powerful to make the poor accept their lot on earth. For the anarchists, at least, the Church represented nothing less than the psychological operations branch of the state. As such it was a target which ranked in importance with the Civil Guard.

During the war the nationalists claimed that 20,000 priests had been slaughtered; afterwards they said that 7,937 religious persons were killed. This figure was still over a thousand too high. Today, we know that out of a total ecclesiastical community of around 115,000, thirteen bishops, 4,184 priests, 2,365 members of other orders and 283 nuns were killed, the vast majority during the summer of 1936.[1] It was a terrible slaughter, yet liberal Catholics abroad were later to state that the killing of priests was no worse than the right's killing of left-wingers in the name of God. The Spanish Church was furious at this attitude, yet it said nothing when the nationalists shot sixteen of the Basque clergy including the arch-priest of Mondragon. Only the Bishop of Vitoria took a stand and persuaded the Pope to protest to General Franco, who was furious and declared that he would send bishops who supported him to Rome.[2] Some twenty Protestant ministers were also killed by the nationalists, yet protests were useless.[3] The most sensational item of propaganda in the world press involved the raping of nuns, yet the detailed nationalist indictment of republican crimes published in 1946 offers no evidence for any such incident, while hinting at only one.

There were certainly occasions when wanton cruelty was inflicted on priests before they died, particularly in Aragón, Catalonia and Valencia. Some were burned to death in their churches and there are reports of castration and disembowelment, and that some were buried alive after being made to dig their own graves. Many more churches were set alight and vandalized. Copes were used for mock bullfights in the street. A republican who dressed himself in the Archbishop of Toledo's ceremonial garments as a joke was nearly shot by a drunken *miliciano* who mistook him for the primate. Communion wine was drunk out of chalices, stained-glass windows were broken and militiamen shaved in the fonts.[4]

Following the collapse of law and order in the republican zone, the anger of the masses was directed first against the rebel generals and their supporters and then against class enemies: clergy, landowners and their *señorito* sons, factory owners, *cacique* political bosses, members of the learned professions and shopkeepers. This violence of the first days was like a brutal explosion. But the vengeance was not as indiscriminate and blind as has sometimes been claimed.

The killing of the clergy was far from universal and with the exception of the Basque country, where the Church was untouched, there was no marked regional pattern. In depressed rural areas the priests were often as poverty-stricken and ill-educated as their parishioners. Those who had taken as much trouble over burying the poor as the rich were often spared. The same was usually true of the killing of shopkeepers and members of the professional class. A lawyer or shopkeeper who had not taken advantage of the poor or showed arrogance was usually left alone. Factory owners and managers with a reputation for dealing fairly with their workforce were nearly always spared and in many cases kept on in the new co-operative. On the other hand, any 'known exploiter' had little chance of survival if caught in the early days. Obviously there were exceptions to this pattern, but the rumours of people being shot merely for wearing hats and ties were the product of an inevitable middle-class persecution complex.

Left-wing parties and unions requisitioned buildings and set up their own 'commissions of investigation', usually known by the Russian names of *checas*.[5] Supporters of the rising were dragged in front of these revolutionary tribunals when they were not shot out of hand. The names and addresses of those belonging to groups involved in the rising were taken from official departments or the respective party headquarters, if their records had not been destroyed in time. Evidently some victims were denounced by servants, debtors and enemies. With the intense atmosphere of suspicion and the speed of events, many mistakes were undoubtedly made.

This pretence of justice happened mainly in cities and large towns where the socialists and communists were dominant. Fake Falange membership cards, said to belong to the defendant, were often produced so as to ensure that the proceedings were rapid. When declared guilty, prisoners were taken away to be shot. Their bodies were then often left in prominent positions with placards stating that the victims were fascists.[6] Anarchists tended to despise this farce of legality and simply got on with the shooting. Believing in the individual's responsibility for his actions, they rejected any form of corporate 'statism' for officials to hide behind. The other reason for immediate execution was their genuine horror of putting anyone in a prison, the most symbolic of all state institutions.

The establishment of the *checas* was unsurprising, considering the spy mania and the frustration caused by the government's lack of resistance to the military rising. Some of them became gangs ruled by opportunist leaders. One *checa* set up in the palace of Count del Rincón in Madrid was run by García Atadell, a former secretary-general of the Communist Youth, who set off for Argentina with his loot, but was captured by the nationalists en route and later garrotted.

Exploiting the fear and turmoil, a great number of criminals found it easy to act under political flags of convenience. Many of those who took real and imagined fascists for rides (in the movie jargon used at the time) were teenage workers or shop assistants who were not political fanatics, but young men excited by their sudden power. The actress Maria Casares (daughter of the ex-prime minister), who worked at a Madrid hospital with her mother, described what happened when they found blood in their car one morning. Their young driver, Paco, gave 'an imperceptible shrug. Then he said, "We took a guy for a ride at dawn, and I'm sorry I haven't had time to clean up the car." And in the rear-view mirror I saw his indefinable little smile; a smile of bragging and shame at the same time, and also a sort of atrocious innocence. The expression of a child caught red-handed.'[7]

In spite of the wave of political killings in Madrid during the first few weeks, there remained a very large population of nationalists, judging by the numbers to emerge two and a half years later when Franco's troops approached. Those of the upper and middle classes who knew they were in danger usually tried to go into hiding, disguise themselves as workers to flee Madrid, or seek refuge in overcrowded embassies. Foreign legations were estimated to have held a total of 8,500 people at the beginning of February 1937.[8] Some embassies, representing governments sympathetic to the nationalists, acted as espionage centres, using both radio and diplomatic bag to pass information to the other side. One *checa* opened a fake embassy some months later and killed all those who came there for shelter. The indiscriminate killing began to decline only when control was exercised over the criminals released from prison and military action began in the Madrid area.

The worst mass killing in Madrid occurred on the night of 22–23 August, just after an air raid and the arrival of reports of the massacre of 1,200 republicans in the bullring at Badajoz. Enraged militiamen and civilians marched on the Model Prison when rumours spread of a riot and a fire started by Falangist prisoners. Thirty of the 2,000 prisoners, including many prominent right-wingers, several of them former ministers, were dragged out of the prison and shot.[9] A horrified Azaña came very close to resigning as president of the Republic.[10]

In Barcelona the top priorities for revenge (after certain police officials like Miguel Badía) were the industrialists who had employed *pistoleros* against union leaders in the 1920s and, of course, the gunmen themselves. This wave of repression was carried out mainly by 'investigation groups' and 'control patrols' created by the Central Committee of Anti-Fascist Militias, but also by unscrupulous and sometimes psychologically disturbed individuals, taking advantage of the chaos.

There was inevitably a wide-ranging settlement of accounts against blacklegs. One or two killings even went back to old inter-union disputes. Desiderio Trillas, the head of the UGT dockers, was shot down by a group of anarchists because he had prevented CNT members from receiving work. This murder was condemned at once by the CNT-FAI leadership and they promised the immediate execution of any of their members who killed out of personal motives. It was a threat which they carried out. Several prominent anarchists, such as their building union leader, Josep Gardenyes, who had been freed from prison on 19 July, and Manuel Fernández, the head of the catering syndicate, were executed by their own comrades in the FAI for taking vengeance on police spies from the time of Primo's dictatorship.[11]

The army officers who had supported the rising and then been captured soon became victims. A column of militiamen attacked the prison ship *Uruguay* and shot the majority of the rebels held there between 29 and 31 August.[12]

It appears that freed convicts were responsible for a considerable part of the violence and much of the looting. The real anarchists burned banknotes because they symbolized the greed of society, but those they had released from prison did not change their habits with the arrival of the social revolution. The excesses of unreformed criminals caused the CNT-FAI to complain bitterly that the 'underworld is disgracing the revolution', but they were reluctant to admit that they had allowed almost anybody to join their organization. Falangists sought refuge in their ranks, as well as others who had no interest in libertarianism. Many on the left also alleged that civil guards were often the most flagrant killers, as they sought to protect themselves from suspicions of sympathizing with the right.[13]

The worst of the violence occurred in the first few days throughout the republican zone of Spain, though it varied greatly from region to region. On the whole the depressed areas saw more ferocity, especially in New Castile, where over 2,000 people were killed by the left during the course of the war. In Toledo 400 were killed between 20 and 31 July, in Ciudad Real some 600 were killed in August and September. There was great savagery also in parts of Andalucia, such as Ronda where the victims were thrown over the cliffs. (Hemingway used this incident in *For Whom the Bell Tolls*.) But in Ronda, as in many towns and villages, the executions were carried out by groups from other parts. It was a phenomenon which bore a remarkable resemblance to the way in which peasants during the nineteenth century had burned the church of a neighbouring village, but not their own.

There was relatively little violence in Málaga before 27 July, but on that day nationalist aircraft bombed the market, killing women and children. Coming just after Queipo de Llano's boasts over Seville Radio that he knew from spies everything that happened in the town, the air raid had a traumatic effect. Suspects were hauled out of prison and shot against the nearest wall and there was a further round-up in the wealthy areas of the town. Altogether some 1,100 people, including General Paxtot, were killed in Málaga between late July and the end of September. During the same period Valencia and Alicante also experienced terrible violence, which killed 4,715 people throughout the region.

The main characteristics of the situation in the republican zone were the almost total lack of control in the first days of the rising, the intensity and rapidity of the killings, and the attempts by left-wing and republican leaders to stop the violence. There would be one or two renewed outbreaks later in Madrid. At the end of October, 31 prisoners, including Ramiro de Maeztu, the author of *Defensa de la Hispanidad*, and Ramiro Ledesma Ramos, founder of the JONS, were taken out of the Prison de las Ventas and shot. There was an even more infamous event in November, when Franco's forces were at the gates of Madrid and 2,000 prisoners were shot when evacuating them to the rear to prevent them being liberated by the nationalists.

In September Largo Caballero's 'government of unity', made up of socialists, republicans and communists, took firm steps to re-establish law and order. They set up popular tribunals which, although far from perfect, were an improvement, and created municipal councils to replace the patrols whose members were ordered to the front. The cases of looting and murder rapidly diminished.

Even during the worst of the violence, leaders from all organizations and parties did what they could to save people. In Madrid, President Azaña managed to rescue the monks from his old college at the Escorial. Galarza, the minister of the interior, saved Joaquín Ruiz Jiménez. La Pasionaria intervened on behalf of many victims, including nuns. So did Juan Negrín and many others. In Catalonia Companys, Ventura Gassol, Frederic Escofet and other leading members of the Generalitat, the rector of the university Pere Bosch Gimpera, and the anarcho-syndicalist leader Joan Peiró, among others, spoke out strongly against the crimes and helped hundreds of those at risk to escape or to leave the country. And this did not happen only in the big cities. In many towns and villages civil governors, teachers, mayors and others did what they could to protect prisoners from being lynched, even when nationalist forces were close.[14]

In all, the victims of the red terror in the republican zone during the civil war rose to some 38,000 people, of whom almost half were killed in Madrid (8,815) and in Catalonia (8,352) during the summer and autumn of 1936.[15] On the republican side there was a strong mixture of feelings when the worst of the rearguard slaughter was over. The majority of republicans were sickened by what had happened. The anarchist intellectual Federica Montseny referred to 'a lust for blood inconceivable in honest men before'. Although La Pasionaria intervened on several occasions to save people, other communists took a fatalistic attitude to the violence. Stalin's ambassador is said to have commented, with a shrug, that the scum was bound to come to the top at such a time. The dubious rationale that the atrocities had been far worse on the other side was not used until the Republic's propaganda campaign became effective in 1937. And yet the different patterns of violence were probably even more significant than the exact number of victims.

9
The White Terror

The pattern of killing in 'white' Spain was indeed different. The notion of a '*limpieza*', or 'cleansing', had formed an essential part of the rebel strategy and the process began as soon as an area had been secured. General Mola, in his instructions of 30 June for the Moroccan zone, ordered the troops 'to eliminate left-wing elements, communists, anarchists, union members, Freemasons etc.'[1] General Queipo de Llano, who described their movement as 'the purging of the Spanish people', did not specify political movements. He simply defined their enemies as anybody who sympathized 'with advanced social currents or simple movements of democratic and liberal opinion'.[2]

The nationalists in fact felt compelled to carry out a harsh and intense repression, partly to destroy the democratic aspirations encouraged under the Republic and partly because they had to crush a hostile majority in many areas of the country. One of General Franco's press attachés, Captain Gonzalo de Aguilera, even said to the American journalist John Whitaker that they had 'to kill, to kill, and to kill' all reds, 'to exterminate a third of the masculine population and cleanse the country of the proletariat'.[3] Between July 1936 and early 1937 the nationalists allowed 'discretionary' killing under the flag of war, but soon the repression became planned and methodically directed, encouraged by military and civil authorities and blessed by the Catholic Church.

The repression in nationalist Spain began as soon as an area had been conquered. The first to be killed, apart from those captured in the front line who were frequently shot on the spot, were union leaders and representatives of the republican government, above all civil governors and mayors, but also other officials who had remained loyal. From the start, even republicans who were promised their lives in return for surrendering were killed. Officers who had stayed loyal to the government were also shot or imprisoned.

Military custom required that loyalist or neutral regular officers be accorded court martials where possible. On the whole, waverers were imprisoned, while most of those who had continued to serve the government, including seven generals and an admiral, were shot on the grounds of 'rebellion'. This remarkable reversal of definitions had also occurred in the navy, where nationalists described sailors who followed ministry of marine instructions as 'mutinous'.

Once the troops had moved on, a second and more intense wave of slaughter would begin, as the Falange, or in some areas the Carlists, carried out a ruthless purge of the civilian population. Their targets included union leaders, government officials, left-of-centre politicians (40 members of the Popular Front in the Cortes were shot),[4] intellectuals, teachers,[5] doctors, even the typists working for revolutionary committees; in fact, anyone who was even suspected of having voted for the Popular Front was in danger. In Huesca 100 people accused of being Freemasons were shot when the town's lodge did not even have a dozen members.[6]

The nationalist counterpart to the *checas* in republican territory were the local committees, usually consisting of leading right-wingers, such as the major landowner, the local Civil Guard commander, a Falangist and quite often the priest, although some risked their lives trying to prevent massacres. All known or suspected liberals, Masons and leftists were taken before the committee. A few prisoners might try to accuse others in a panic-stricken attempt to save themselves, but otherwise they had either a dazed or a defiant manner. Their wrists were tied behind their backs with cord or wire before they were taken off for execution. In Navarre a priest gave last rites to Basque nationalists en masse in front of an open trench before the volley, but in most places the condemned were taken in batches to the cemetery wall. Those who 'knew how to die well' shouted '*¡Viva la República!*' or '*¡Viva la Libertad!*' in the same way as condemned nationalists called out '*¡Viva España!*'.

The Falange often resorted to using the local prison as a reserve of victims when their squads could not find anyone outside to execute. In Granada alone, some 2,000 people died in this way. Nobody can tell what proportion of the victims were seized at home or at work, then shot at night lined up in front of car headlights. People lying awake in bed would cross themselves instinctively on hearing shots in the distance. The corpses of these 'clients', as they were sometimes called, were left in the open. If they were union members they often had their membership cards pinned to their chest as proof of guilt.

In some areas, as was the case in Seville and Huelva, special lorries were used, known as 'meat wagons', to take the corpses to the cemetery.[7] At times, however, corpses were displayed as a warning, as happened to the body of the mother of the communist leader Saturnino Barnero, which was left for a number of days in the Plaza del Pumarejo in Seville. In Huelva also the body was displayed of a confectioner who had thrown an espadrille at General Sanjurjo after his failed coup in August 1932. The practice of displaying bodies continued for a long time,[8] until the nationalist authorities had to insist on burial for reasons of public health.

It seemed to make little difference to the nationalists whether or not there had been open opposition to their forces. In the military centre of Burgos and the Carlist capital of Pamplona they had not been resisted, yet the purge began immediately. In Burgos, the capital of Castille, groups were taken out each night to be shot by the side of the highway. Ruiz Vilaplana, president of the College of Clerks of the Court, recounted in his memoirs that he witnessed 70 people killed in one batch.[9]

In Pamplona on 15 August, while the procession of the Virgin del Sagrano was taking place, Falangists and *requetés* took 50 or 60 prisoners, including some priests suspected of Basque separatism. Before killing them, the *requetés* wanted to give them the opportunity of confession, but the Falangists refused. In the confusion some prisoners tried to escape but were shot down. 'In order to sort out the situation, priests gave absolution en masse to the remainder. The executions were carried out and the trucks returned to Pamplona in time for the *requetés* to join the procession as it entered the cathedral.'[10] The Association of Families of the Murdered of Navarre have identified 2,789 people executed in the province.[11]

As might be expected, the repression was much more intensive and systematic in places where the UGT and the CNT had many members, especially in areas where the Popular Front had won in the elections of February. In Rioja, for example, over 60 per cent of the victims belonged to Popular Front parties. Over 2,000 people were executed and buried in mass graves outside Logroño.[12] There was practically no village in the Rioja which did not have inhabitants buried in the mass grave of La Barranca.[13] In Teruel the wells of Caudé, 84 metres deep, were used for dumping the corpses of the killed. A peasant living nearby heard and recorded in a notebook 1,005 *coups de grâce*.[14]

In Seville, where Queipo de Llano's bluff had won over the confused soldiers, the initial killing was said to be part of a military operation. But when reinforcements from the Army of Africa arrived under Major Castejón, the mopping-up was nothing more than a fearful massacre, with survivors finished off by knife or bayonet. Immediately afterwards Colonel Díaz Criado was put in charge of public order and almost all the local officials were killed. Because the prison was not large enough, the nationalists used the Jáuregui cinema as a holding centre for more than 2,000 people, also the Variedades music hall, the Falangist headquarters and even two boats anchored near the Torre del Oro. Francisca Díaz, the eighteen-year-old sister of the secretary-general of the Spanish Communist Party was interrogated for a whole night. She saw many of the workers from the olive oil factory roped together. They were going to be taken out to be shot.[15] The nationalist repression in the province of Seville accounted for 8,000 lives during 1936.

Córdoba had been seized on 18 July in a few hours, with little resistance. Queipo de Llano, furious because no reprisal had been carried out, immediately sent Major Bruno Ibáñez of the Civil Guard to the city. He started with 109 people from the lists given him by landowners and clergymen. A few days later they began to shoot the prisoners out on the roads and in the olive groves. 'The basement of Falange headquarters in which people were held was like a balloon which was blown up in the afternoon and was empty the following morning. Each day there were executions in the cemetery and along the roads leading out of the city.'[16] It is calculated that a total of 10,000 were killed in Córdoba during the war, a tenth of the population. 'Don Bruno could have shot the whole city,' a Falangist lawyer recounted. 'They sent him to Córdoba with carte blanche.'[17]

In Huelva, a town which the nationalists did not fully take until the middle of September, more than 2,000 people were killed, including the civil governor, Diego Jiménez Castellano, and the commanders of the Civil Guard and the *carabineros* who had stayed loyal to the Republic. It is calculated that another 2,500 inhabitants disappeared, but many of them may have escaped across the border to Portugal.[18]

When Major Castejón's 'Column of Death' reached Zafra on the road to Badajoz, he ordered the local authorities to provide him with a list of 60 people to be shot. 'Little by little, those on the list were locked up in a room of the town hall. Some inhabitants who came into the mayor's office were shown the growing list. They were allowed to remove three names providing they wrote down three others.' In the end, 48 of the names were substitutes.[19]

One of the great *lieux de mémoire* of the Spanish Civil War was Badajoz itself.[20] The massacre perpetrated there by the troops of Lieutenant-Colonel Yagüe during its capture and the following repression turned into the first propaganda battle of the war. The nationalists exaggerated their losses in the battle and also the numbers of right-wingers killed by the left beforehand. In fact, Yagüe lost no more than 44 killed and 141 wounded. But even after the war, the nationalists could not ascribe more than 243 killings to the left, while estimates on nationalist killings in the province range from over 6,000 to 12,000.[21]

On the road to Madrid the nationalist columns followed the same pattern. They subdued villages along the way, laying waste and daubing on the whitewashed walls graffiti such as 'your women will give birth to fascists'. Meanwhile, General Queipo de Llano menaced republicans who listened to Radio Seville with stories about the sexual powers of the African troops, to whom he promised the women of Madrid as an inducement. War correspondents were held back from Toledo so that they should not witness the events which followed the relief of the Alcázar. There 200 wounded militiamen in hospital were finished off with grenades and bayonets. The conduct of the campaign was compared to the *furia española* of Philip II's infantry in the sixteenth century, which terrorized Protestant Holland in its all-destructive advance.

Near Gibraltar a Falangist reported that the wife of a left-winger was raped by a whole firing squad of Moors before being shot. An American journalist, John Whitaker, was present when two young girls were handed over to Moroccan troops near Navalcarnero by their commanding officer, Major Mohamed Ben Mizzian, who told him calmly that they would not survive more than four hours.[22] The major subsequently reached the rank of lieutenant-general in Franco's army and *regulares* were later made 'honorary Christians' by the nationalists. The horror they inspired in republican territory led to two of them being torn to pieces by a crowd when the truck in which they were being sent back as prisoners stopped to fill up with petrol.

Another of the great places of suffering was Granada, known above all for the murder of the poet Federico García Lorca, the most celebrated victim of the civil war. The fascist and military attitude to intellectuals showed itself to be one of deep distrust at the least, and usually consisted of an inarticulate reaction mixing hate, fear and contempt. This was shown in Granada where five university professors were murdered. García Lorca had returned to his house outside the city in the Huerta de San Vicente just before the rising. (With the start of the summer holidays many on both sides were saved or killed simply by their travel plans.) He was in danger because of his liberal sympathies although he belonged to no party. Even the refuge given him by the Falangist poet Luis Rosales and his family could not save him.

On Sunday, 16 August, a few hours after the murder of his brother-in-law, Manuel Fernández Montesinos, the mayor of Granada, he was seized by a former deputy of the CEDA, Ramón Ruiz Alonso, who later asserted that Lorca 'did more damage with his pen than others with their guns'. He was accompanied by Luis García Alix, secretary of Acción Popular, and the Falangist landowner Juan Luis Trescastro, the perpetrator of the crime, who would say later: 'We killed Federico García Lorca. I gave him two shots in the arse as a homosexual.'[23] H. G. Wells, the president of PEN, demanded details on the fate of Lorca as soon as the news reached the outside world, but the nationalist authorities denied any knowledge of his fate. Lorca's death remained a forbidden subject in Spain until the death of Franco in 1975.

The nationalists justified the brutality of their repression as reprisals for the red terror, but as had been the case in Seville, Córdoba and in Badajoz, and as would be the case in Málaga six months later, the subsequent nationalist killings exceeded those of the left several, if not many, times over. In Málaga the nationalist executions took place after the militia, and undoubtedly almost all those responsible for killing right-wingers, had escaped up the coast. This shows that there was little attempt to identify the guilty. But above all, the contrast in the numbers killed by each side could not be starker.

In August 1944 the British consul in Málaga obtained the nationalists' own figures and forwarded them to the ambassador in Madrid, who passed them on to London. He reported that while 'the "reds" were in control of Málaga from 18 July 1936 until February 7th 1937 ... they executed or murdered 1,005 persons'. But that 'during the first week of Liberation, that is from February 8th to 14th ... 3,500 persons were executed by the Nationalists'. And 'from February 15th 1937 to August 25th 1944, a further 16,952 persons have been "legally" sentenced to death and shot in Málaga'.[24] According to other sources, more than 700 people were shot against the walls of the San Rafael cemetery just between 1 and 23 March 1937,[25] but one local historian put the total figure for Málaga at 7,000 executions,[26] roughly a third of the number given to the British consul. Whatever the exact figure, the nationalist 'reprisals' were clearly not just a question of revenge, they were also motivated by the idea of establishing a reign of terror especially in areas where the right had been numerically weaker.

Even in areas where they were strong, however, the 'killing machine' was also used as a conspicuous message. In Valladolid the Falangist 'dawn patrols' shot 914 people, but the main reservoir of victims was once again the mass of prisoners seized just after the rising. They were locked into tram coaches and most days the Falangists would take out a dozen to execute them in public.[27] 'It wasn't just a crowd of illiterates who came to watch the spectacle,' recounted Jesús Álvarez, a chemist in the town. 'They were people of standing, sons of distinguished families, educated people, people who called themselves religious ... they went so regularly to see the executions that stalls selling coffee and churros were set up so that they could eat and drink while they watched.'[28] On 24 September the office of the civil governor of Valladolid published a statement that it had been noticed recently that although 'military justice' satisfied the need for punishment, large crowds were gathering at the place of execution. The civil governor appealed to pious people that they 'should not come to watch such things, and even less bring their wives and children'.[29]

In the rear areas the Falange had rapidly developed into the nationalists' paramilitary force, assuming the task of 'cleaning up'. The young *señoritos*, often aided by their sisters and girlfriends, organized themselves into mobile squads, using their parents' touring cars. Their leader, José Antonio, had declaimed that 'the

Spanish Falange, aflame with love, secure in its faith, will conquer Spain for Spain to the sound of military music'. The real militants were obsessed with their task of cutting out 'the gangrenous parts of the nation' and destroying the foreign, 'red' contagion. The rest simply seemed to find sanctified gangsterism appealing. The Carlists, on the other hand, were fired by religious fanaticism to avenge the Church by wiping out such modern evils as Freemasonry, atheism and socialism. They also had a far higher proportion of their able-bodied men at the front than the Falange and, despite their violent excesses on many occasions, were reputed to have treated their prisoners of war the most correctly.

Nationalist killings reached their peak in September and continued for a long time after the war was over. Not surprisingly, people wondered if Franco wanted to repeat the deathbed answer of the nineteenth-century General Narváez when asked if he forgave his enemies: 'I have none. I have had them all shot.'

In the course of the last ten years, detailed work has been carried out region by region in Spain to establish the number, the identity and the fate of the victims. Accurate statistics have now been compiled on 25 provinces and provisional figures on another four. For just over half of Spain, this comes to a total of over 80,000 victims of the nationalists.[30] If one takes into account the deaths which were never registered and allows for the provinces not yet studied, we are probably faced with a total figure for killings and executions by the nationalists during the war and afterwards of around 200,000 people. This figure is not so very far from the threat made by General Gonzalo Queipo de Llano to republicans when he promised 'on my word of honour as a gentleman that for every person that you kill, we will kill at least ten'.[31]

10
The Nationalist Zone

A *coup d'état* does not need a positive creed, just an enemy. A civil war, on the other hand, demands a cause, a banner and some form of manifesto. During the preparation for the coup, the military plotters had not concerned themselves greatly over the exact form of government which their *pronunciamiento* would herald. The urgency of the conspiracy did not allow them to waste time discussing hypothetical constitutions. They would discuss the finer points and formulate a detailed justification for their actions after the country was secured. The substance was clear to all: centralized authoritarian rule. The form, however, was not clear, although the possibilities included Falangism, Carlism, a restoration of the Alfonsine monarchy and a republican dictatorship.[1]

Until this problem could be resolved the nominal direction of nationalist Spain was constituted in Burgos on 24 July in the Junta de Defensa Nacional. General Cabanellas, the divisional commander at Saragossa, assumed the presidency supported by nine generals and two colonels. This figurehead establishment was organized by Mola, who commanded the Army of the North. It appears to have been an attempt to reduce the power of Franco, who commanded the most important military formation. Before the rising, General Hidalgo de Cisneros, the loyal commander of the republican air force, had said that 'General Goded was more intelligent. General Mola a better soldier; but Franco was the most ambitious.'[2] (His verdict on Mola was to prove highly inaccurate.)

Mola had talked of a republican dictatorship which would maintain the separation of Church and state. He had even ordered that the monarchist flag be taken down in Pamplona. The Carlists were so horrified by his attitude that in the last few days before the rising there had even been doubts whether they would commit their *requetés*, who were needed to assure the obedience of the regular troops to the nationalist cause. Queipo de Llano's sudden rise to prominence in the rebellion with his seizure of Seville must have worried them almost as much. He not only finished his radio broadcasts with '*¡Viva la República!*' and the liberal anthem, the 'Himno de Riego', but, worst of all, he was a Freemason. The idea of fighting under the republican tricolour was anathema to all traditionalists. Only the military plotters had sworn loyalty to it.

The Carlists' main hope for safeguarding their interests was destroyed on 20 July with General Sanjurjo's death. Major Ansaldo, the monarchist airman, had arrived in Portugal to fly him to Burgos with the announcement that he was now 'at the orders of the head of the Spanish state', which caused very emotional scenes among the general's entourage. Their light aircraft crashed on take-off and Sanjurjo died in the flames. This accident has been attributed either to sabotage by a Franco supporter or to Sanjurjo's vanity in taking so many cases of uniforms. The latter explanation seems the more probable, although Ansaldo claimed it was sabotage.

During this time of uncertainty over the form of the new state, the Catholic Church provided the nationalist alliance with both a common symbol of tradition and a cause to transcend ideological confusion within their ranks. Its authoritarian, centralist nature and its attitude to property were acceptable to all factions, except the left wing of the Falange. Its hierarchy rallied to the cause of the right and prominent Churchmen were seen giving the fascist salute. Cardinal Gomá stated that 'Jews and Masons poisoned the national soul with absurd doctrines'.[3] The most striking piece of ecclesiastical support for the nationalist rising came in the pastoral letter 'The Two Cities' published by the Bishop of Salamanca, Pla y Daniel, on 30 September. It denounced the left-wing attacks on the Catholic Church and praised the nationalist movement as 'the celestial city of the children of God'.[4] Pla y Daniel also demanded the reversal of all anti-clerical restrictions and reforms implemented under the Republic. He was not to be disappointed.

A few brave priests put their lives at risk by criticizing nationalist atrocities, but the majority of the clergy in nationalist areas revelled in their new-found power and the increased size of their congregations. Anyone who did not attend mass faithfully was likely to be suspected of 'red' tendencies. Entrepreneurs made a great deal of money selling religious symbols, which were worn ostentatiously to ward off suspicion rather than evil spirits. It was reminiscent of the way the Inquisition's persecution of Jews and

Moors helped make pork such an important part of the Spanish diet.

The disparate groups that made up the nationalist movement were well aware of the danger in their undertaking, for they controlled less than half of Spanish territory and just under half of the population. It was this uncertainty and the desire for strong leadership which Franco was able to exploit in the following months. He was a great admirer and worthy successor of that most cynical of statesmen, Ferdinand of Aragon, usually cited as the original of Machiavelli's Prince. During August it became almost certain that Franco was to be the nationalists' Caudillo, or leader, but nobody really knew what beliefs were hidden behind his bland, complacent expression, nor to what extent he would be able to reconcile the markedly different opinions about the future form of the nationalist state. The Falange was worried that it would be little more than an auxiliary force under army command. The monarchists wanted Alfonso returned. The Carlists wanted a royal Catholic dictatorship with a populist flavour, although they realized that their pretender to the throne, the eighty-year-old Don Alfonso Carlos, would not be accepted by their allies. (In any case, he died in September without heirs as a result of an automobile accident.)

Franco's constitutional formula for unifying the nationalists was as brilliant in what it included as in what it left unresolved. The basis of his approach was to have a monarchy without a king. Alfonso was not acceptable to the majority of nationalists and he had little popular appeal: yet the arrangement satisfied the traditionalists without provoking the Falange or republicans like Queipo de Llano or Mola. It also avoided the kind of frustration Mussolini felt over King Vittorio Emanuele, which had resulted in serious tensions between royalists and fascists in the Italian armed services.

On 15 August, the Feast of the Assumption, a great ceremony was organized in Seville. The purpose was to pay homage to the old monarchist flag and adopt it as the banner of the 'new *reconquista*'. The ceremony was also a part of Franco's plan to assert his ascendancy over potential rivals for the nationalist leadership. Queipo said that he would not attend, remarking that 'if Franco wants to see me, he knows where I am'.[5] Franco arrived with a large retinue, including General Millán Astray, the founder of the Foreign Legion. He was received by all the local dignitaries, headed by Cardinal Ilundaín, but not Queipo. They proceeded to the town hall on the Plaza de San Fernando. Queipo, who had decided to turn up at the last moment, made a long rambling speech which caused consternation among Franco's entourage. The republican tricolour was lowered, then the monarchist flag of red-gold-red hoisted to the strains of the Royal March. Franco made a much briefer speech, in which he hailed 'our flag, the authentic one, the one to which we have all sworn loyalty, and for which our forefathers died, a hundred times covered with glory'.[6] He then embraced the flag, followed by Cardinal Ilundaín.

Seville had rapidly become the personal fief of Queipo and Franco was galled by his cavalier behaviour. Queipo's portrait was everywhere. His face dominated the town and was reproduced even on vases, ashtrays and mirrors. Households where 'reds' had been killed were the first to be forced to display his photograph in their windows. Against this barrage of publicity Franco's staff desperately sought to obtain exposure for their chief. Eventually they managed to arrange for his photograph to be projected on cinema screens to the tune of the Royal March. The audience gave the fascist salute during the five minutes that this lasted. Later on, public establishments in the nationalist zone were obliged to display his portrait. And whenever the Royal March was played on the radio all those who did not want their loyalty to be suspect rose to their feet and gave the fascist salute.

The publicity of other nationalist groups was just as strident. Posters appeared everywhere. The Carlist message proclaimed, 'If you are a good Spaniard, and you love your country and her glorious traditions, enlist with the *requetés*.' The Falange's slogan was briefer and more threatening: 'The Falange calls you. Now or never.' More than 2,000 new Falange members were said to have enlisted in a 24-hour period in Seville alone. Queipo de Llano was both cynical and accurate when he referred to the blue shirt as a 'life-jacket'. Many a left-winger or neutral who wanted to avoid the *máquina de matar*, the killing machine, rushed to enlist and often tried to prove himself more fascist than the fascists, a counterpart to the phenomenon in republican territory.

José Antonio's pre-war fears were confirmed, when this influx of opportunists swamped the surviving *camisas viejas*, the 'old shirts'. Nearly half of the pre-war veterans had died in the rising. Meanwhile, José Antonio was in Alicante jail guarded by militiamen, Onésimo Redondo had been killed and Ledesma Ramos was also in enemy hands. The Falange was thus in an uncomfortable position. Its membership was greatly swollen just at the time that its leaders were out of action.[7] As a result the Falange operated in an unpredictable fashion. Some militia units went to the front, but the majority stayed in the rear areas to provide an improvised bureaucracy and an amateur political police. The Falangist patrols, supposedly checking suspicious characters, were blue-shirted and flamboyantly conspicuous as they forced passers-by to give the fascist salute and shout '*¡Arriba España!*'. Girl Falangists went into cafés to ask men why they were not in uniform. They then presented them with sets of doll's clothing in a contemptuous manner while a back-up squad of male comrades watched from the door. One German visitor reported to the Wilhelmstrasse: 'One has the impression that the members of the Falangist militia themselves have no real aims and ideas; rather, they seem to be young people for whom mainly it is good sport to play with firearms and to round up communists and socialists.'[8]

José Antonio had been transferred to Alicante jail by the republican authorities early in July, just before the rising. He had been allowed such a lax prison regime that Count de Mayalde managed to pass him two pistols in the meeting room. Dramatic plans to rescue José Antonio never came to fruition, first on the day of the rising and then again the next day. A group of Falangists were discovered by assault guards and three of the rescue team were killed in the shoot-out.[9] Further plans to release him were discussed in October on board the battleship *Deutschland*, but these were opposed both by Admiral Carls, the German squadron commander, and the German foreign ministry. Another failed project involved the German torpedo boat *Iltis*.[10] One more attempt is said to have been thwarted by General Franco, who did not want such a charismatic rival at large.[11]

The proceedings to bring José Antonio and his brother Miguel to trial began on 3 October in front of the Popular Tribunal of Alicante. They were charged with conspiracy against the Republic and military rebellion. When the trial itself started on 16 November, José Antonio was allowed to defend himself, his brother and his sister-in-law, Margarita Larios. His legal training helped him put up an impressive performance. Knowing he was doomed, he did not stoop to ask for clemency. He was, however, successful in having his brother's and sister-in-law's sentences reduced, remarking that 'life is not a firework to be let off at the end of a party'.

José Antonio was executed swiftly by the local authorities on 20 November, in case the cabinet of ministers, which was due to meet that morning, reduced the sentence to life imprisonment. The Falange had a great martyr as a result, but was left without any leader of stature – a situation which could hardly have displeased Franco. He suppressed all news of the execution for two years when the Republic was doomed. Franco, who was far too pragmatic to be jealous of a dead rival, did not mind allowing the cult of José Antonio to develop later.

Behind the military edifice of nationalist Spain, attention had to be given to economic matters. One of the main priorities for the rebel generals was to obtain hard currency from exports to pay for the war. In Andalucia Queipo de Llano proved himself to be a surprisingly competent commercial administrator, albeit one with a pistol in his hand. Smuggling, fraud and the export of capital became capital offences. The foreign exchange earners, such as sherry, olives and citrus fruit, were given the highest priority and he organized trade agreements with the Salazar regime in Lisbon. Exporters had to hand over all their receipts in pounds or dollars to the military authorities within three days.[12] However, the granting of import licences, monopolies and commercial rights led to the corruption and profiteering which was to permeate nationalist Spain. Contributions to the movement were a good investment for those who were quick. At the same time charities mushroomed, occupying the time of clergy, *beatas*, war widows and other civilians with an ambitious eye to the future.

Meanwhile, the loudspeakers in the streets played music such as the violent Legion marching song 'El Novio de la Muerte' (The Fiancé of Death). And at the radio station every evening a bugler stood in front of the microphone to herald the daily bulletin from the Generalissimo's headquarters. It was against this militaristic atmosphere that a remarkable act of moral courage was to take place, an incident highlighted by the emphasis on physical bravery in that war. On 12 October, the anniversary of Columbus's discovery of America, a Festival of the Spanish Race was organized at the University of Salamanca. The audience consisted of prominent supporters of the nationalist movement, including a large detachment of the local Falange. Among the dignitaries on the stage sat Franco's wife, the Bishop of Salamanca who had issued the pastoral letter, General Millán Astray, the founder of the Foreign Legion, and Miguel de Unamuno, the Basque philosopher who was the rector of the university. Unamuno had been exasperated by the Republic, so in the beginning he had supported the nationalist rising. But he could not ignore the slaughter in this city where the infamous Major Doval from the Asturian repression was in charge, nor the murder of his friends Casto Prieto, the mayor of Salamanca, Salvador Vila, the professor of Arabic and Hebrew at the University of Granada, and of García Lorca.

Soon after the ceremony began, Professor Francisco Maldonado launched a violent attack against Catalan and Basque nationalism, which he described as 'the cancer of the nation', which must be cured with the scalpel of fascism. At the back of the hall, somebody yelled the Legion battlecry of '*¡Viva la Muerte!*' (Long live Death!). General Millán Astray, who looked the very spectre of war with only one arm and one eye, stood up to shout the same cry.[13] Falangists chanted their '*¡Vivas!*', arms raised in the fascist salute towards the portrait of General Franco hanging above where his wife sat.

The noise died as Unamuno stood up slowly. His quiet voice was an impressive contrast. 'All of you await my words. You know me and are aware that I am unable to remain silent. At times to be silent is to lie. For silence can be interpreted as acquiescence. I want to comment on the speech, to give it that name, of Professor Maldonado. Let us waive the personal affront implied in the sudden outburst of vituperation against the Basques and Catalans. I was myself, of course, born in Bilbao. The bishop, whether he likes it or not, is a Catalan from Barcelona. Just now I heard a necrophilous and senseless cry: "Long live Death!" And I, who have spent my life shaping paradoxes, must tell you as an expert authority that this outlandish paradox is repellent to me. General Millán Astray is a cripple. Let it be said without any undertone. He is a war invalid. So was Cervantes.[14]

'Unfortunately there are all too many cripples in Spain now. And soon there will be even more of them if God does not come to our aid. It pains me to think that General Millán Astray should dictate the pattern of mass psychology. A cripple who lacks the greatness of Cervantes is wont to seek ominous relief in causing mutilation around him. General Millán Astray would like to create Spain anew, a negative creation in his own image and likeness; for that reason he wishes to see Spain crippled as he unwittingly made clear.'

The general was unable to contain his almost inarticulate fury any longer. He could only scream '*¡Muera la inteligencia! ¡Viva la Muerte!*' (Death to the intelligentsia! Long live Death!). The Falangists took up his cry and army officers took out their pistols. Apparently, the general's bodyguard even levelled his submachine-gun at Unamuno's head, but this did not deter Unamuno from crying defiance.

'This is the temple of the intellect and I am its high priest. It is you who profane its sacred precincts. You will win, because you have more than enough brute force. But you will not convince. For to persuade you would need what you lack: reason and right in your struggle. I consider it futile to exhort you to think of Spain.'

He paused and his arms fell to his sides. He finished in a quiet resigned tone: 'I have done.' It would seem that the presence of Franco's wife saved him from being lynched on the spot, though when her husband was informed of what had happened he apparently wanted Unamuno to be shot. This course was not followed because of the philosopher's international reputation and the reaction caused abroad by Lorca's murder. But Unamuno died some ten weeks later, broken-hearted and cursed as a 'red' and a traitor by those he had thought were his friends.[15]

11

The Republican Zone

From the start, the rising of the generals had fragmented the country into a mass of localized civil wars. But this was not the main reason for the collapse of the republican state. The central government's disastrous response to the crisis was one major factor: perhaps the inescapable paralysis of a centre-left government facing a right-wing revolt on one side and left-wing revolution on the other. Another was the disintegration of the mechanism of state, when so many of its functionaries, from the diplomatic corps to the police, to say nothing of the armed forces, supported the nationalists.

The CNT and the UGT, which had borne the brunt of the fighting, rapidly filled the vacuum, creating revolutionary organizations in republican territory. The only real exception was the Basque country. 'There, the situation is not revolutionary,' it was observed. 'Private property is not questioned.'[1] The membership of the two unions increased enormously, partly out of admiration for what they had done, but mostly for opportunistic reasons as they were now the power in the land. They soon had around two million members each, a striking total when the lost territories are taken into account. The POUM and above all the Communist Party were also to increase rapidly. The communists' vast gains, increasing their strength to 250,000 members in eight months, came from the middle class attracted by the Party's disciplined approach, from the ambitious and from right-wingers afraid of arrest, just as left-wingers joined the Falange to survive in the nationalist zone.[2]

In the early days of the rising Madrid had the air of a revolutionary city. Militiamen of the UGT and CNT could be seen in almost every street checking identities. Their usual dress consisted of dark blue *monos* (which were like boiler suits) and badges or coloured scarves to denote their political affiliation: black and red for the anarcho-syndicalists, red for the socialists and communists.

The lack of opportunity, or the unwillingness, to shave on a regular basis made most of them look especially villainous to foreign observers. None went anywhere without a rifle. 'Idle young men,' wrote Azaña in his diary, 'instead of fighting in the trenches, they show off their martial kit in the streets, rifle slung across the shoulder.'[3]

The government's original refusal to issue arms had left a deep mark. Workers remembered that feeling of impotence when facing the military uprising, and this meant that a vast number of weapons was kept in rear areas during the early months. Also, nationalist ruses like those at Oviedo and San Sebastián meant that there was a reluctance to commit too many men to the front in case there were more unpleasant surprises behind the lines.

The socialist UGT was still the most powerful organization in Madrid, even though the CNT continued to gain rapidly at its expense. Girls wearing the red and blue of the Socialist Youth were everywhere collecting money for left-wing charities, encouraged by their new freedom to talk to whomever they wanted without being thought loose. Schoolchildren dressed as Young Pioneers (an attempt to imitate the Soviet original) might be seen walking along in crocodile chanting slogans in shrill voices like a monotonous multiplication table. Foreign journalists made much of the fact that middle-class jackets and collars and ties were hardly to be seen in the streets any more. However, this probably owed as much to the exceptionally hot weather and the new informality as to the persecution of those in bourgeois clothes.

Once most of the militia left for the various fronts, the revolutionary aspect of Madrid began to wane. There were still beggars on street corners and expensive shops and restaurants soon reopened. The war could almost have been overseas. Only the foreign journalists who crowded the cafés and hotel bars of the Gran Vía seemed to think that the capital was at the centre of events. Meanwhile, the economic situation was deteriorating hopelessly. Because of the shortage of coins and banknotes, the unions began to issue 'coupons', which were then taken over by municipal authorities obliged to find ways to help the civilian population survive when every day became more precarious.

The shock of civil war made Spanish workers both outward-looking in their hope for international support against fascism and inward-looking in the way they trusted only the local community.

Every town and village had its revolutionary committee, which was supposed to represent the political balance in the community. It was responsible for organizing everything the government and local authorities had done before. On the Pyrenean border, anarchist militiamen in their blue *monos* stood alongside smartly uniformed *carabineros*, checking passports. It was the committee of the border town, not an official of the central government, who decided whether a foreigner could enter the country.

The local committees organized all the basic services. They commandeered hotels, private houses and commercial premises for use as hospitals, schools, orphanages, militia billets and party headquarters. In Madrid the Palace Hotel, one of the largest in Europe, was used in the early days as a refuge for orphans and the Ritz as a military hospital. They established their own security forces to stop random and personally motivated killings disguised as anti-fascist operations. Justice became the responsibility of revolutionary tribunals, whose proceedings were an improvement on the sham trials of the early days. The accused were allowed to have legal assistance and to call witnesses, although standards varied widely and in some places justice remained a grotesque piece of play-acting. Once the initial fears of the first weeks had started to abate, the death penalty became much rarer.

In Asturias the CNT established the Gijón War Committee. The CNT's strength came from dockers, seamen and, above all, fishermen, who set up a co-operative covering every aspect of their trade. In Avilés and Gijón the fishermen collectivized their boats, docksides and tinning factory.[4] The UGT was stronger inland, among the miners. Eventually its committee merged with the anarchists, and a socialist became president of the joint council. On the other hand in Santander socialists took over the war committee, prompting anarchists to attack their authoritarian manner.

In the Basque country, things were very different. Juntas of defence were replaced by the autonomous Republic of Euzkadi, which came into existence on 1 October. (The Basque red, green and white flag, the *ikurrina*, had already replaced the republican tricolour.) The formal establishment of the Basque government, with José Antonio Aguirre as president, or *lehendakari*, was confirmed by a meeting of municipal delegates in traditional fashion exactly a week later when oaths were sworn under the sacred oak tree of Guernica. The conservative Basque nationalist party held the most important portfolios, while republicans and socialists were allowed the lesser ones.[5] The anarchists, who were strong in San Sebastián and the fishing communities, neither demanded nor were offered any role in the administration. The Basque nationalists established a very rigid control with their paramilitary militia, the Euzko Godarostea, which excluded left-wingers and non-Basques. However, both the UGT and the CNT later formed their own battalions to fight in the army corps of Euzkadi. The mixed feelings of the Basques, loyal to the Republic which gave them autonomy, yet far closer in social and religious attitudes to the nationalists, was to create a disastrous mistrust within the alliance.[6]

Of all these regional moves to self-government, the most extraordinary and the most important took place in Catalonia. The journalist John Langdon-Davies described the contradictions in Barcelona, calling it 'the strangest city in the world today, the city of anarcho-syndicalism supporting democracy, of anarchists keeping order, and anti-political philosophers wielding power'.[7] On the evening of 20 July Juan García Oliver, Buenaventura Durruti and Diego Abad de Santillán had a meeting with President Companys in the palace of the Generalitat. They still carried the weapons with which they had stormed the Atarazanas barracks that morning. In the afternoon they had attended a hastily called conference of more than 2,000 representatives of local CNT federations. A fundamental disagreement arose between those who wanted to establish a libertarian society immediately and those who believed that it had to wait until after the generals were crushed.

Companys had defended anarchists for nominal fees when a young lawyer. His sympathy for them was unusual among Catalan nationalists, who often referred to them in almost racial terms as 'Murcians', because the major source of anarchist strength had been among non-Catalan immigrant workers. Although some Catalan politicians later denied his words, Companys is said to have greeted the anarchist delegates thus:[8] 'Firstly, I must say that the CNT and the FAI have never been treated as their true importance merited. You have always been harshly persecuted and I, with much regret, was forced by political necessity to oppose you, even though I was once with you. Today you are the masters of the city and of Catalonia because you alone have conquered the fascist military ... and I hope that you will not forget that you did not lack the help of loyal members of my party ... But you have won and all is in your power. If you do not need me as president of Catalonia, tell me now and I will become just another soldier in the fight against fascism. If, on the other hand ... you believe that I, my party, my name, my prestige, can be of use, then you can depend on me and my loyalty as a man who is convinced that a whole past of shame is dead.'

Whether or not these were Companys's exact words, Azaña later described this as a plot to abolish the Spanish state. But the Catalan president was a realist. Official republican forces in Barcelona amounted to about 5,000 men of the paramilitary corps and events elsewhere had shown that it was very dangerous to rely on them entirely. The regular army no longer existed in Barcelona, for most of the rebel officers had been shot and the soldiers had either gone home or joined the worker militias. Meanwhile, with rifles from the Sant Andreu barracks and from elsewhere, the anarchists were estimated to have some 40,000 weapons distributed among their 400,000 members in Barcelona and its suburbs. It would have been folly for Companys to have considered attacking them at their moment of greatest strength and popularity. The anarchists also appeared to be his best allies against the reimposition of Madrid government. Companys expressed the situation drily: 'Betrayed by the normal guardians of law and order, we have turned to the proletariat for protection.'

The Catalan president had presented the anarchists with a fundamental dilemma. García Oliver described the alternatives: 'Libertarian communism, which is tantamount to an anarchist dictatorship, or democracy which signifies collaboration.'[9] Imposing their social and economic self-management on the rest of the population appeared to violate libertarian ideals more than collaborating with political parties. Abad de Santillán said that they did not believe in any form of dictatorship, including their own.[10]

At their Saragossa conference only seven weeks before, the anarchists had affirmed that each political philosophy should be allowed to develop the form of social co-existence which best suited it. This meant working alongside other political bodies with mutual respect for each other's differences. Though genuine, this was a simplistic view, since the very idea of worker control and self-management was anathema both to liberal republicans and the communists. These two groups would in time win, first by forcing the anarchists to renounce many of their principles and then by expelling them from positions of power.[11]

Even if the anarchist leaders sitting in the Catalan president's ornate office, having just been offered the keys of the kingdom, could have foreseen the future, their choice would have been no easier. They had the strength to turn Catalonia and Aragón into an independent non-state almost overnight, but that would have created a major confrontation with the socialists and communists at a critical moment. The Madrid government also controlled the gold reserves, and a boycott by the rest of republican Spain and by foreign companies could have destroyed the Catalonian economy in a very short time. Yet what seems to have influenced their decision the most were the obvious needs of unity to fight the military rising and concern for their comrades in other parts of Spain. The demands of solidarity overrode other considerations. They could not abandon them in a minority which might be crushed by the Marxists.

The libertarian leaders therefore proposed a joint control of Catalonia with other parties. On their recommendation the Central Committee of the Anti-Fascist Militias was set up on 21 July. Although in the majority, they said that they would recognize the right of minorities and take only five of the fifteen posts. Ingenuously, they hoped that they would receive similar treatment in the other areas of republican Spain where they were in a minority.[12]

The Central Committee of Anti-Fascist Militias literally ran everything from security and essential services to welfare; the Generalitat was nothing more than a shadow government, or rather a government-in-waiting, 'a merely formulaic artefact'.[13] Its councillors might make plans and charts, but they had little to do with what was already being put into practice on the ground. The all-important conversion to war industry had been started by Juan García Oliver and Eugenio Vallejo during the initial fighting. The Generalitat did not set up a war industries commission until August and for a long time it had little influence,[14] yet although the Catalan administration had lost the political initiative, it had not entirely lost power. The CNT was incapable of controlling either the economy, which stayed in the hands of the Generalitat, or the banking system, which was now in the hands of the socialist UGT.

The contradictions of political power were to confront the

anarchists in many forms. Their manifesto of 1917, for example, had condemned all festivals, such as bullfights and indecent cabarets which can brutalize the people. But to act as dictatorial censors was an even worse affront to their beliefs. Meanwhile the anarcho-feminist Mujeres Libres, now 30,000 strong,[15] were sticking posters over the walls of the red light district, trying to persuade prostitutes to give up their way of life. They offered and ran training courses for them to acquire skills for productive work, but other anarchists were less patient. According to the sympathetic French observer Kaminski, they shot pimps and drug dealers on the spot.

A notable phenomenon of the war was the spontaneous growth of a women's movement after the 1936 elections. It was born, not of literature or theory from abroad (except perhaps a few translations of Emma Goldman), but of women's instinctive conviction that the overthrow of the class system should mean the end of the patriarchal system as well. The anarchists had always declared the equality of all human beings, but as the Mujeres Libres emphasized, relationships still remained feudal. The most blatant way in which the anarchists had failed to live up to their professed ideals was the different levels of pay for men and women in most CNT enterprises. The Socialist Youth was another major focal point for feminism.

Little headway was made outside the cities, although the greatest demonstration of the new equality was the fact of having militiawomen fighting in the front line. No figures are available, but there were probably not many more than 1,000 women at the front. There were, however, several thousand under arms in the rear areas and a women's battalion took part in the defence of Madrid. (The German ambassador was shocked when, one day, Franco ordered the execution of some captured militiawomen and then calmly continued to eat his lunch.) This move towards equal participation was severely curtailed under the increasingly authoritarian direction of the war effort as the military situation deteriorated. By 1938 women had returned to a strictly auxiliary role.[16]

One observer in Barcelona commented on the attitude towards buildings. He wrote that the people were inclined to destroy symbols, but that they respected in a naive and sometimes exaggerated way everything which seemed useful. Religious buildings, patriotic monuments and the women's prison were demolished or burned down, while hospitals and schools were respected almost with the reverence which the nationalists accorded to churches.

The most important achievement of the republican government of 1931–3 had been in education and reducing illiteracy. The measures limiting Church involvement in education created a great void in the system to begin with, but the school-building and teacher-training programmes were correspondingly ambitious. The Republic claimed to have built 7,000 schools as opposed to only 1,000 during the previous 22 years. An illiteracy rate of nearly 50 per cent in most areas under the monarchy was drastically reduced. Many imaginative projects, such as García Lorca's travelling theatres, were part of an energetic attempt to help the rural mass free itself from the vulnerability of ignorance. All the time, independently of government-sponsored efforts, the *casas del pueblo* of the UGT and the *ateneos libertarios* of the anarchists continued their efforts in this direction.[17] During the war it was above all the earnest study of uneducated militiamen in the trenches which so impressed foreign visitors like Saint-Exupéry.

The outward signs of working-class power were everywhere in Barcelona. Party banners hung from public buildings, especially the black and red diagonal flag of the CNT. The anarchists had installed their headquarters in the former premises of the Employers' Federation, while the communist-controlled PSUC led by Joan Comorera had taken over the Hotel Colón. The POUM had seized the Hotel Falcón, though their main power base was in Lérida. The POUM was growing because it seemed to offer a middle course between the anarchists and the communists. But, as Andreu Nin, their leader, had once been closely associated with Trotsky, the Stalinists hated the POUM even more than the anarchists. They ignored the fact that Trotsky and his Fourth International frequently attacked the POUM.

Barcelona had always been a lively city and the July revolution hardly calmed it. Expropriated cars roared around at high speed, often causing accidents, but such antics were soon stopped when petrol was issued only for essential journeys. Loudspeakers attached to trees on the avenues relayed music and broadcast ludicrously optimistic news bulletins from time to time. These were seized on by groups discussing events such as the attack on Saragossa, whose fall they expected at any moment. It was a world of instant friendship, with the formal expression of address no longer used.

Foreigners were welcomed and the anti-fascist cause was explained repeatedly. Workers possessed a simple faith that if everything was made clear, the democracies could not fail to help them against Franco, Hitler and Mussolini.

All around a heady atmosphere of excitement and optimism prevailed. Gerald Brenan said that visitors to Barcelona in the autumn of 1936 would never forget the moving and uplifting experience. Foreigners who gave a tip had it returned politely with an explanation of why the practice corrupted both the giver and the receiver. Probably the greatest contrast between Madrid and Barcelona was in the use of hotels. In the capital Gaylords was later taken over by the Communist Party as a luxurious billet for its senior functionaries and Russian advisers. In Barcelona the Ritz was used by the CNT and the UGT as Gastronomic Unit Number One – a public canteen for all those in need.

The most outspoken champions of private property were not the liberal republicans, as might have been expected, but the Communist Party and its Catalan subsidiary, the PSUC. Both were following the Comintern line of concealing the revolution. La Pasionaria and other members of their central committee emphatically denied that any form of revolution was happening in Spain, and vigorously defended businessmen and small landowners. This was at a time when rich peasants, *kulaks*, were dying in Gulag camps. The Comintern, without any acknowledgement of such a flagrant contradiction, recorded the communist slogans prescribed for the countryside round Valencia: 'We respect those who want to work their land as a collective, but we also request respect for those who want to cultivate their land individually'; and 'To oppress the interests of petty farmers means oppressing the fathers of our soldiers'.[18]

This anti-revolutionary stance, prescribed by Moscow, brought the middle classes into the communist ranks in great numbers. Even the traditional newspapers of the Catalan business community, *La Vanguardia* and *Noticiero*, praised the Soviet model of discipline. Meanwhile, the anarchist model had already made itself felt throughout the republican zone, but above all down the Mediterranean coastal belt.

This extraordinary mass movement of worker self-management still provokes powerful controversy. The liberal government and the Communist Party regarded it as a major obstacle to their attempts to organize the war effort. They were convinced that central control was vital in a country such as Spain with its strong parochialism and reluctance to react to a threat unless it was close. For example, the anarchists of Catalonia felt that to recapture Saragossa would be tantamount to winning the war. The advance of the Army of Africa in the south-west could almost have been in a foreign country, as far as they were concerned. The exponents of self-management, on the other hand, argued that there would be no motive for fighting if the social revolution were not allowed to continue. Having done the fighting in July when the government refused to arm them, the anarchists bitterly resented the way the government expected them to surrender all their gains. This fundamental clash of attitudes undermined the unity of the Republican alliance. The advocates of a centralized state were to win the struggle in 1937, but the morale of the population was mortally stricken by the Communist Party's bid for power in the process.

The collectives in republican Spain were not like the state collectives of the Soviet Union. They were based on the joint ownership and management of the land or factory. Alongside them were socialized industries, restructured and run by the CNT and UGT as well as private companies under joint worker-owner control. Co-operatives marketing the produce of individual smallholders and artisans also existed, although these were not new. They had a long tradition in many parts of the country, especially in fishing communities. There were estimated to have been around 100,000 people involved in co-operative enterprises in Catalonia alone before the civil war. The CNT was, of course, the prime mover in this development, but UGT members also contributed to it.[19]

The regions most affected were Catalonia and Aragón, where about 70 per cent of the workforce was involved. The total for the whole of republican territory was nearly 800,000 on the land and a little over a million in industry. In Barcelona, worker committees took over all the services, the oil monopoly, the shipping companies, heavy engineering firms such as Vulcano, the Ford motor company, chemical companies, the textile industry and a host of smaller enterprises.

Any assumption by foreign journalists that the phenomenon simply represented a romantic return to the village communes of the Middle Ages was inaccurate. Modernization was no longer feared because the workers controlled its effects. Both on the land and in the factories technical improvements and rationalization could be carried out in ways that would previously have led to bitter strikes. The CNT woodworkers union shut down hundreds of inefficient workshops so as to concentrate production in large plants. The whole industry was reorganized on a vertical basis from felling timber to the finished product. Similar structural changes were carried out in other industries as diverse as leather goods, light engineering, textiles and baking. There were, however, serious problems in obtaining new machinery to convert companies which were irrelevant, like luxury goods, or underused because of raw-material shortages, like the textile industry. They were caused principally by the Madrid government's attempt to reassert its control by refusing foreign exchange to collectivized enterprises.

The social revolution in Catalonian industry was soon threatened in several ways. A sizeable part of the home market had been lost in the rising. The peseta had fallen sharply in value on the outbreak of the war, so imported raw materials cost nearly 50 per cent more in under five months. This was accompanied by an unofficial trade embargo which the pro-nationalist governors of the Bank of Spain had requested among the international business community. Meanwhile, the central government tried to exert control through withholding credits and foreign exchange. Largo Caballero, the arch-rival of the anarchists, was even to offer the government contract for uniforms to foreign companies, rather than give it to CNT textile factories.[20] Recent studies indicate that reductions in industrial output during the course of the war cannot really be attributed to 'revolutionary disorder'.[21]

There were sometimes long discussions and wrangles within the worker committees, but when the issues were clear, little time was wasted. Services such as water, gas and electricity were working under their new management within hours of the storming of the Atarazanas barracks. Using the framework agreed at the Saragossa conference, a conversion of appropriate factories to war production meant that metallurgical concerns had started to produce armoured cars by 22 July. Although not sophisticated, they were not all crudely improvised contraptions. The industrial workers of Catalonia were the most skilled in Spain. The Austrian sociologist Franz Borkenau also pointed out the great difference it made not to have technicians obstructed, as occurred in Soviet Russia.[22]

After defeating the attempted coup in Barcelona and reorganizing production so quickly, the anarchists were angry at the Madrid government's attempt to regain control through the denial of credits. A plan for seizing part of the Spanish gold reserves so as to bypass the central government's denial of foreign exchange was considered, but rejected, by the CNT regional committee. Apart from finance, the other main weakness was the lack of co-ordination between co-operatives within a particular industry. However, government performance on industrial matters was such that it is doubtful whether ministers in Madrid would have done much better.

At the same time as the transformation of industry, there was a mushroom growth of agricultural collectives in the southern part of Republican territory. They were organized by CNT members, either on their own or in conjunction with the UGT. The UGT became involved because it recognized that collectivization was the most practical method of farming the less fertile *latifundia*. It would perhaps also be true to say that in many places the socialists followed this course to avoid being usurped by the anarchists in what they regarded as their fiefs.

In Aragón some collectives were installed forcibly by anarchist militia, especially the Durruti column. Their impatience to get the harvest in to feed the cities, as well as the fervour of their beliefs, sometimes led to violence. Aragonese peasants resented being told what to do by overenthusiastic Catalan industrial workers and many of them had fears of Russian-style collectives. Borkenau showed in an example how much more effective other means could be. The anarchist nucleus achieved a 'considerable improvement for the peasants and yet was wise enough not to try to force the conversion of the reluctant part of the village, but to wait till the example of the others should take effect'.[23] Not surprisingly, a collective begun in that way worked best. Overall, studies of the collectivization conclude that 'the experiment was a success for the poor peasants of Aragón'.[24]

There were some 600 collectives in Aragón but far from all villages were completely collectivized.[25] The individualists, consisting chiefly of smallholders who were afraid of losing what little they had, were allowed to keep as much land as a family could farm without hired labour. In regions where there had always been a tradition of smallholding little tended to change. The desire to work the land collectively was much stronger among the landless peasants, especially in less fertile areas where small plots were hardly viable.[26]

The only alternative systems to the free collectives for supplying the republican zone with food were either state collectives or dividing up the land into smallholdings. The nearest equivalents to state collectives were municipally organized farms. In the province of Jaén, for example, where the CNT was almost non-existent and the UGT weak, the municipality took over the land and organized it. Borkenau recorded that it employed the same *braceros* that the former landowners employed upon the same estates for the same endless working hours for the same starvation wages. 'As nothing had changed in their living conditions so nothing had changed in their attitude. As they are ordered about as before and for the same wages, they start fighting the new administration of the estates as they did the old one.'[27] Borkenau also described how self-managed collectives were much happier when no better off than before. What mattered was that the labourers ran their own collectives – a distinct contrast to the disasters of state collectivization in the Soviet Union, which the peasants had resisted by slaughtering livestock and sabotaging the harvest.

The anarchists attacked the *reparto*, the division of land, because they thought that privately controlled land always creates a bourgeois mentality, 'calculating and egotistical', which they wanted to uproot for ever. But whatever the ideology, the self-managed co-operative was almost certainly the best solution to the food supply problem. The communists attacked the self-managed collectives as inefficient, but in Aragón production increased by a fifth.[28] Not only was non-collectivized production lower, but the individualists were to show the worst possible traits of the introverted and suspicious smallholder. When food was in short supply they hoarded it and created a thriving black market which, apart from disrupting supplies, did much to undermine morale in the republican zone. The communist civil governor of Cuenca admitted later that the smallholders who predominated in his province held on to their grain when the cities were starving.

The other criticism levelled against the collectives was their failure to deliver food to the front line in regular quantities at regular intervals. Obviously there were many cases of inefficiency, but overall the charge was unfair considering that all their vehicles and carts had already been commandeered. Whenever transport did arrive the peasants, not knowing when it would next be available, would pile on every possible foodstuff. The fault lay far more with the militia, who should have organized things the other way round and warned particular collectives of their needs in advance. The army and the International Brigades were also to suffer from bad distribution, often on an even worse scale.

The central government was alarmed by the developments in Aragón, where the anarchist militia columns exercised the only power in the whole of an area predominantly libertarian in sympathy. In late September delegates from the Aragonese collectives attended a conference at Bujaraloz, near where Durruti's column was based. They decided to establish a Defence Council of Aragón and elected as president Joaquín Ascaso, a first cousin of Francisco Ascaso who fell in the Atarazanas assault.

Earlier that summer the government had tried without success to re-establish its control in Valencia by sending a delegation there under Martínez Barrio. It was brushed aside by the Popular Executive Committee, which consisted mainly of UGT and CNT members. Communist pleas for discipline and obedience to government orders went unheeded. Even so, the communists, who opposed free collectives, profited from local conditions in their recruiting drives. The rich Valencian countryside, *la huerta*, was held in smallholdings by extremely conservative peasants, who were joined in their resistance to collectivization by many citrus farmers.

Giral's government in Madrid did not share the anarchists' enthusiasm for self-managed collectives. Nor did it welcome the fragmentation of central power with the establishment of local committees. Its liberal ministers believed in centralized government and a conventional property-owning democracy. They also felt, along with Prieto's wing of the socialist party and the communists, that only discipline and organization could prevail against the enemy. Above all, they were appalled at having no control over the industrial base of Catalonia. But, after Martínez Barrio's failure in Valencia, Giral's administration could do little for the moment except try to keep up appearances. For the future, its continued control of supply and credit held out the prospect that concessions might gradually be wrung from the revolutionary organizations as a first step towards incorporating them into the state.

12

The Army of Africa and the People's Militias

By the beginning of August battle lines had become much clearer. With the two sides developing such markedly different characters in the wake of the rising, it seemed as if two completely separate nations were at war. The rebel generals urgently needed to show rapid gains of territory at the beginning so as to convince a foreign as well as the domestic audience of their success. Having failed to achieve a coup, they required the international recognition, credits and material which a war demanded. General Franco's Army of Africa was to make the most conspicuous contribution to this necessary impression of victory.

Although the forces under General Mola played a less conspicuous role, the 'Director' had rapidly sent three columns from Pamplona mainly made up of Carlist *requetés*. The first left immediately for Madrid, a second force of about 1,400 men moved south to Saragossa to reinforce the nationalist garrison in the third week of July and another, much larger, force was sent north towards the Basque coastline.

The column of 1,000 men under Colonel García Escámez, who had set out for the capital on 19 July, found that Guadalajara had already been captured by armed workers from Madrid. García Escámez then tried another line of advance on the capital, swinging round to the north to cross the Sierra de Guadarrama by the main Burgos road over the Somosierra pass. His force came up against Madrid militias at the summit where, a century and a quarter before, Napoleon's Polish lancers had opened the route to the capital with a suicidal uphill charge against artillery. García Escámez's men captured the pass after several days' fighting, but could do little except consolidate their position since they were virtually out of ammunition.

A nationalist force from Valladolid commanded by Colonel Serrador was joined by some civil guards and part of a signals regiment which had fled from El Pardo.[1] They managed to secure the other pass at the Alto de los Leones to the south-west, but they also suffered from a shortage of ammunition. It was surprising that the chief architect of the conspiracy had not built up reserves in Burgos or Pamplona during the previous months. Mola's difficulties were solved only when Franco sent him large supplies from Germany via Portugal with the assistance of the Salazar regime (the nationalists referred to Lisbon as 'the port of Castile'). Some supplies also arrived on the cargo boat *Montecillo*, when it reached Vigo. But by the time the nationalist columns were resupplied, the militia forces in the mountains had become less haphazard in their organization and had established a front.

Mola's largest force of 3,500 men attacked northwards from Pamplona. The plan was to thrust up the high hills of northern Navarre towards the coast to cut the Basques off from the French frontier, then to capture the summer capital of San Sebastián. On 11 August the column under Major Beorleguí drove a wedge between San Sebastián and the border town of Irún. Six days later the nationalist battleship *España*, the cruiser *Almirante Cervera* and the destroyer *Velasco* arrived to shell the seaside resort. The republican military governor threatened to shoot right-wing hostages if heavy civilian casualties were inflicted. The nationalists called his bluff. Their bombardment was followed by aerial attacks from Junkers 52s on both San Sebastián and Irún.

The defence of Irún demonstrated that untrained workers, providing their defensive position was well sited and prepared, could fight bravely and effectively against head-on attacks backed by modern weaponry. The CNT had been the main contributor to the defeat of the rising in the province of Guipúzcoa, and its members joined with Asturians, Basque nationalists and French communist volunteers organized by André Marty (later the chief organizer of the International Brigades) to make a total force of 3,000 men. Beorleguí's force was numerically weaker, but it had all Mola's artillery, light German tanks and the Junkers 52s in support. In addition, Franco sent a *bandera* of the Foreign Legion 700-strong and a battery of 155mm guns.

There was ferocious hand-to-hand fighting on the Puntza ridge to the south of Irún where positions were captured and retaken several times in the course of a week. The militia fought with remarkable skill and courage. They were aided by French peasants from just across the border signalling the positions of Beorleguí's artillery.[2] The convent of San Marcial was held to the end by a handful of Asturian *dinamiteros* and militiamen. During the final attack, when out of ammunition, they hurled rocks at the Carlists who were storming their position.

In fact, the battle was lost partly because six ammunition trucks failed to reach the defenders after the French border was closed on 8 August. Telesforo Monzón, one of the Basque ministers, had travelled to Barcelona in search of weapons and ammunition. Unfortunately, he did not obtain more than a thousand rifles and six pieces of artillery. A few days later Miguel González Inestal, the head of the CNT fisherman's union, had a meeting with García Oliver, Abad de Santillán and President Companys. They helped him with weapons and a train, which would be sent via France and Hendaye, but it was intercepted by the French authorities.[3]

Irún itself was left a burning ruin when the last of the workers withdrew, some of them having to swim to safety to reach French territory. A parting burst of machine-gun fire hit Major Beorleguí in the calf. The tough old soldier refused treatment and later died of gangrene.

The anarchists in San Sebastián were angry at the lack of support from the Basque nationalists, especially when they heard that the governor was negotiating the surrender of the city with the enemy. They were extremely suspicious after the betrayals which had occurred in the first few weeks of the war, but despite its conservatism the Basque nationalist PNV had not the slightest intention of changing sides. Nevertheless, it was totally opposed to the anarchists' scorched-earth policy, which had led to the burning of Irún during the withdrawal and now meant defending San Sebastián to the last. The PNV prevailed, once their militia shot several anarchists. The nationalists occupied the city on 14 September, which meant that they now surrounded the northern republican zone.[4]

Without any doubt, the most important military development of the summer was the ruthlessly effective campaign of the Army of Africa. Its early arrival on the mainland was mainly due to the help of German and Italian aircraft. Not surprisingly, republican propaganda made much of this foreign intervention at such a vital stage of the war, but the vehement protests tended to obscure two uncomfortable truths. First, republican warships run by sailors' committees seemed to lack the ability or desire for offensive action, especially with the German battleships *Deutschland* and *Admiral Scheer* screening the nationalist convoys across the straits. But they clearly had orders to avoid open conflict and in any case, as the senior Soviet naval adviser later stated, 'The republican ships did not carry out their duty.'[5]

On land, the republican medley of indolent regular officers, urban worker militias and peasants intent on staying close to their *pueblo* proved incapable of launching any effective counter-attack in the vital south-western sector before the colonial troops arrived in strength. The military importance of the airlift by the Savoias and the Junkers 52s must, therefore, not be exaggerated, even though the arrival of 1,500 men between 28 July and 5 August had an enormous influence both on the nationalists' morale and on the international assessment of their chances of victory. Altogether, some 12,000 troops were transported in this way during the first two months of the war, before the nationalists had won absolute control of the straits.

The airlift of legionnaires and Moroccan *regulares* from the Army of Africa was well under way during the first week of August. On 6 August Franco himself crossed to the mainland, leaving General Orgaz in command of the Protectorate. He established his headquarters in Seville, where he decided to split his forces so as to be able to secure Andalucia as well as advance rapidly on the capital.

The main force under Colonel Yagüe was to drive north, parallel to the Portuguese frontier, then swing north-eastwards on Madrid. Yagüe was to prove the most aggressive of all the nationalist field commanders. In many ways these qualities underlined the contrast between the Army of Africa and the apathetic metropolitan army. Colonial officers have always tended to be less fashionable and more professional, but in Spain this difference was even more pronounced than in either the British or French services. Nevertheless Franco, the supposedly archetypal *africanista*, was extremely conventional in contrast to his impetuous subordinate.

A much smaller force of only 400 *regulares* was to secure southern Andalucia under Colonel Varela, a secret instructor of Carlist *requetés* before the rising and the officer released from prison in Cádiz by the insurgents on 19 July. Colonial troops from Seville captured Huelva, before retiring to crush any remaining resistance southwards to Cádiz and Algeciras. Then, in the second week of August, Varela's force moved eastwards to help the beleaguered nationalists in Granada. Once a salient to the city had been established, they prepared to attack Málaga and the coastal strip beyond the mountains. But Córdoba was threatened by a republican force of 3,000 men under General Miaja, so Varela moved rapidly on 20 August to reinforce Colonel Cascajo's small force there. Once the Córdoba front was stabilized in the first week of September (it was hardly to change for the rest of the war), Varela marched southwards and captured Ronda on 18 September.

General José Miaja, the republican commander of the southern front and later of Madrid during the siege, was one of those senior officers who probably stayed loyal from force of circumstance rather than from conviction.[6] His force was composed of loyal regular troops, Madrid militiamen and local volunteers. The ineffectiveness of totally untrained men in conventional manoeuvres was to be expected, but the uselessness and sloth of the regular officers was extraordinary. Franz Borkenau visited the headquarters on 5 September, during heavy fighting which was going badly. 'The staff', he wrote, 'were sitting down to a good lunch, chatting, telling dirty stories, and not caring a bit about their duty, not even trying to establish any contact with the fighting lines for many hours.' Even the wounded were ignored.[7]

Meanwhile, on the northern axis of advance Colonel Yagüe's force was organized in five self-contained columns of some 1,500 men each, with legionnaires and *regulares* mounted in requisitioned lorries and accompanied by 75mm artillery. They were supported by Savoia-Marchetti 81s, piloted by Italians in Legion uniform, and Junkers 52s flown by Luftwaffe personnel. Yagüe struck due north into Estremadura, maintaining a momentum of advance exceeded only by the armoured punches of 1940. His tactics were simple and effective. The lorry-borne force rushed up the main road at full speed until resistance was encountered at a town or village. (No ambushes were made in the open country because the inhabitants wanted to defend their homes and needed the feeling of security which walls gave.) The nationalists would order surrender over loudhailers provided by the Germans. All doors and windows were to be left open and white flags hung on every house.

If there was no reply, or firing, then the troops would dismount and launch a rapid pincer attack.

Concentrations of defenders provided ideal targets for professional troops with artillery backed by bombers. Mobile groups would have inflicted higher casualties and delayed the nationalists' advance more effectively. Once a village was captured, the ensuing massacre was supposed to be a reprisal for 'red' killings, but it was utterly indiscriminate. Queipo de Llano claimed that '80 per cent of Andalucian families are in mourning, and we shall not hesitate to have recourse to sterner measures'.

The nationalist attack demonstrated the psychological vulnerability of the worker militias. In street fighting, caught up in collective bravery, they were courageous to a foolhardy degree. But in the open the shelling and bombing were usually too much for them, since they refused to dig trenches (Irún was an outstanding exception). 'The Spanish are too proud to dig into the ground,' Largo Caballero later declared to the communist functionary Mije.[8] Most of the bombs dropped were, in fact, almost useless, but the enemy aircraft were skilfully handled, causing maximum terror to peasants who had little experience of modern technology. Also, having no idea of how to prepare a defensive position, the militiamen had a desperate fear of finding themselves facing the Moors' knives alone. Outflanking movements which surprised them usually led to a panic-stricken stampede. Chaos was increased when the population of a village clogged the roads with their carts and donkeys as they too fled from the colonial troops. Sometimes they even seized the militias' lorries for themselves. On the other hand, the nationalist tactic of terror provoked heroism as well as flight. Peasants, having seen their families on their way, would take up shotguns or abandoned rifles and return to die in their *pueblo*.

By 10 August Yagüe's force had advanced more than 300 kilometres to Mérida. Just south of the town at the Roman bridge over the River Guadiana, Asensio's forces met fierce opposition. The defence committee of the town was organized by Anita López, who greatly encouraged the ferocious resistance. She was among those killed when Yagüe's troops finally entered the town that night and carried out a fearful massacre.[9] The next day the bulk of the Mérida militia counter-attacked with the aid of a strong detachment of assault guards and civil guards sent from Madrid. Yagüe left part of his force to hold them off while he advanced due west on Badajoz, on the Portuguese border. Franco had insisted on this diversion from the main axis. Apart from not wanting to leave an enemy strongpoint behind his line of advance, he wished to demonstrate that the northern and southern parts of the nationalist zone were now linked.

Badajoz was defended by no more than 2,000 militia, poorly armed, and 500 regulars under the command of Colonel Puigdengolas.[10] They also had to suppress the civil guards, who declared for the rising just before Yagüe's arrival. His troops took up position outside the town walls on 14 August. A pincer attack was then launched at 5.30 in the afternoon, with the Foreign Legion assaulting two of the gates under the cover of artillery fire, while aircraft bombed the town. The colonial troops broke into the town and the slaughter began. Fighting from house to house with grenade and bayonet, the *regulares* made no distinction between combatant or civilian. Militiamen were even shot down on the altar steps of the cathedral. Any survivors were then herded into the bullring. The smell of blood in the heat was sickening.

Meanwhile, the looting of even nationalists' property was explained by one officer as the 'war tax they pay for salvation'. Officers organized the despatch of the *regulares*'s booty back to their families in Morocco because it helped recruiting. The legionnaires did not burden themselves with the often useless impedimenta which the Moors collected. They simply examined the mouths of the dead and smashed out any gold-capped teeth with their rifle butts.

On 2 September Yagüe reached the Tagus valley, where he swung eastwards towards Madrid. He had already ordered Asensio and Castejón's forces to advance on Navalmoral de la Mata via the high hills to the south of the river. They were attacked ineffectively by an international air squadron organized by the French writer André Malraux, and then came up against a militia force of about 8,000 men under General Riquelme. The colonial troops' rapid deployment, however, outflanked the republican forces, making them fall back in disorder. The Moors' tactical movements achieved a surprise, which struck panic into the inexperienced city militiamen. Yet there were independent groups who attacked and harassed the colonial troops in guerrilla fashion.

Yagüe was determined to keep up his momentum. He pushed on to Talavera de la Reina, the last town of any size before Madrid.

The rapidity and success of his advance had seriously demoralized the force of 10,000 militiamen awaiting him there. It seemed as if the Army of Africa was unbeatable. Once again a flanking motion supported by air and artillery bombardment was enough to start a republican retreat. On the evening of 3 September the road to Madrid was littered with abandoned weapons. The capital lay only 100 kilometres away.

Yagüe had advanced nearly 500 kilometres in four weeks. It was a feat which, even allowing for the experience and training of his troops, took all attention away from Mola's Basque operation. The next move of the Army of Africa still provokes discussion. Franco did not force on north-eastwards to Madrid and so maintain the momentum of attack before a proper defence of the capital could be organized. Instead, he switched the axis of advance south-eastwards to Toledo, where nationalists were still defending the Alcázar. Yagüe argued bitterly against this decision, so Franco replaced him with Varela after the capture of Ronda on 18 September.[11]

As many had remarked, Franco was both ambitious and politically clear-sighted. The defence of the Alcázar had become the most potent source of nationalist propaganda. Its resistance was raised to an almost mystical level.[12] Franco was still, at this stage, little more than *primus inter pares*. To be the 'saviour of the Alcázar' would make his leadership of the nationalist movement unchallengeable. It has, of course, been argued that Franco would have achieved the same pre-eminence by capturing Madrid. But that represented a far more difficult undertaking. To outflank and bomb untrained militiamen in the countryside was one thing. Clearing a major city required a totally different operation. Franco was too wily to take an unnecessary risk before his leadership was officially confirmed. Then, too, while foreign backers and financiers might grumble if the war took a long time, only a very serious reverse would induce them to cut their losses. Franco did not believe that the fighting qualities of the Madrid militia, or their weaponry, would improve in the immediate future. He therefore felt that he could afford to wait a couple of weeks for reinforcements to arrive. It was Mola who was to make a fatuous boast about drinking coffee on the Gran Vía in a matter of days, but even Franco never expected Madrid to resist as it did. Another theory is that Franco wanted the advance to be slow so that there was sufficient time to purge the rear areas of potential opponents. The Italian general Mario Roatta recounted much later that Queipo de Llano had told him that military operations were conducted slowly as a sort of 'olive oil press, in order to occupy and pacify, village by village, the whole zone'.[13]

During August the militia troops besieging the Alcázar underestimated both the speed of Yagüe's advance and the resilience of the fortress's defenders. There was a relaxed atmosphere on the barricades surrounding the military academy. Enormous quantities of small-arms ammunition were wasted against its thick walls. It was some time before artillery was brought up and even the 175mm piece which eventually arrived brought down only the superstructure. The Alcázar was like an iceberg. Its strength lay within the submerged rock. There was something Buñuelesque about the scene: militiamen, wearing straw hats against the sun, lay on mattresses behind their barricades and exchanged insults with the Civil Guard defenders. Twice a day there was a tacitly agreed ceasefire as a blind beggar tapped his way along the Calle de Carmen between the firing lines.

The most serious psychological mistake made by the republican besiegers was the attempt to use Colonel Moscardó's son, Luis, as a hostage. On 23 July a local lawyer called Cándido Cabello rang the Alcázar, saying that they would shoot him unless the defenders surrendered. Moscardó refused and, according to the nationalist version, told his son, who was put on the telephone, to die bravely. In fact, Luis was not shot until a month later in reprisal for an air raid.[14] The dramatic appeal of the story also camouflaged the fact that the 100 left-wing hostages, including women and children, whom the defenders had taken into the Alcázar at the beginning of the siege were never heard of again.[15]

None of this stopped the creation of the most emotive symbolism for the nationalist movement. The defenders, believing that Luis had been shot immediately, could not consider surrendering after such a sacrifice. The story was used as a moral lesson for everyone in nationalist territory. In addition, since the old city of Toledo was the centre of Spanish Catholicism and 107 priests were reputed to have been killed there by the left, the incident was projected with all the fervour of the 'anti-atheist crusade'. It was enrobed with mystical implications of Abraham and Isaac, even of God and Christ, by those carried away with the parallel. Dramatic resemblances were also drawn with episodes from Spanish history – Philip II handing over his son to be executed by the Inquisition and Alonzo Guzmán leaving the Moors to crucify his son outside the besieged walls of Tarifa in the thirteenth century. The young cadets of the Alcázar were extolled by the nationalist press and their supporters abroad. In reality, there was only a handful of cadets there, since the rising took place during the Academy's summer holiday. The courageous defence which tied down so many republicans was conducted by members of the less glamorous Civil Guard.

The rapid approach of the Army of Africa during September made the besiegers appreciate the gravity of their situation. Mines were dug into the rock under the fortress and, in a great show witnessed by the world's press, one corner of the Alcázar was blown up. The presence of women and children inside, however, made the propaganda exercise counter-productive, while the rubble left a formidable barrier enabling the defenders to beat off the assault.

Towards the end of September Varela's relief force arrived within striking distance. Some of the militia stayed on and faced the colonial troops with great courage, but the majority fled back towards Aranjuez. Varela ignored Moscardó's promise that militiamen who surrendered would be spared. Blood ran down the steep and narrow streets of the city in reprisal. Many militiamen killed themselves rather than surrender. Pockets of resistance were burned out and in the hospital 200 wounded militiamen left behind in the hospital of San Juan Bautista were killed in their beds with grenades and bayonets.[16] Nationalist troops are also said to have taken twenty pregnant women whom they found in a maternity wing and shot them against the walls of the cemetery.[17]

The gaunt and erect figure of Moscardó waited in his dust-impregnated uniform. He greeted Varela with the words, '*Sin novedad en el Alcázar*' (Nothing to report at the Alcázar). '*Sin novedad*' was also the codeword for the rising which nobody had bothered to ask the passed-over colonel to join. He repeated the same performance for General Franco and the newspapermen the next day, 29 September. Moscardó was compared to the great warrior heroes of medieval Spain.[18]

The nationalists, especially the Army of Africa, had demonstrated their offensive abilities in these first two months of the war, while the republican militias possessed neither the training nor the cohesion to mount effective operations against organized troops. They were also desperately short of arms and ammunition. One of the first Soviet advisers reported back to Moscow that in August and early September 1936 there was only one rifle per three men, and one machine-gun per 150–200 men.[19]

In Oviedo, which had been won for the nationalists by Colonel Aranda's trick, the siege still continued despite ingenious and brave attacks by Asturian *dinamiteros*. Armoured lorries manned by workers with improvised flame-throwers succeeded in making a breach, only to be forced back. Relief for the besieged in the form of a column under Colonel Martín Alonso was on its way from Galicia.

In the south, near Andújar, a detachment of 1,200 civil guards and Falangists was holding out in the mountain monastery of Santa María de la Cabeza under Captain Cortés.[20] Nationalist pilots devised an original method of dropping fragile supplies. They attached them to live turkeys which descended flapping their wings, thus serving as parachutes which could also be eaten by the defenders. The besieged were eventually overcome in April of the next year by a mass assault. It was a defence at least as brave as that of Toledo, but it was given comparatively little recognition by the nationalists, perhaps because it risked stealing glory from Franco.

Although the worker militias represented the only possible response to the generals' rising, since few regular army units remained in formation, the anarchists, the POUM and the left socialists, including Largo Caballero, regarded the militias as a virtue rather than a necessity. There was a powerful belief that morale and motivation must overcome an enemy which depended on the mercenaries of the Army of Africa or brother workers who would desert at the first opportunity. The republican left wing seriously underestimated the Catholic zeal of the conservative smallholders of Galicia, Old Castile and Navarre, who were to become the nationalists' best troops after the colonial professionals.

The Madrid government, the regular officers, centrist politicians and the communists began to advocate a conventional army as the sole means of resisting the nationalists. The communists' attitude derived from the knowledge that a centralized command could be infiltrated and seized. Hence their call for 'Discipline, Hierarchy,

Organization'. Such plans for 'militarization' were greeted with great suspicion by the left socialists, who described them as 'counter-revolutionary' and looked upon them as a tactic in the government's effort to recover control of the workers' movement. The anarchists were even more strongly opposed. For them a regular army represented the worst aspects of the state. They called it 'the organization of collective crime'.

The two unions, the CNT and the UGT, provided the majority of the militia forces, though all the parties had their own. There were units from the republican left, the Catalan Esquerra, the POUM and the communists. A militiaman was paid ten pesetas a day at first by his local organization and later by the government. This was the equivalent of a skilled worker's wage and it became a heavy burden on the ailing economy.[21] Their uniforms consisted of blue overalls and either a beret or, more often, a fore-and-aft cap in party colours. The standard of equipment and weapons varied greatly. Some militiamen were still carrying only shotguns after six months of war. The maintenance of weapons was universally bad. A rifle without rust was almost unknown; hardly any were cleaned and oil was seldom issued. The few machine-guns were old and lacked spare parts. There was also such a wide variety of calibres that as many as sixteen different types of ammunition were needed within some units. Mortars and grenades, when available, were usually more dangerous to the operator than the enemy, so that the home-made variety, dynamite packed into tomato cans, was preferred.

The greatest shortcoming of the militia system remained the lack of self-discipline. At the beginning stories abounded of detachments leaving the front line without warning for weekends in Barcelona or Madrid. Anyone who stayed awake on sentry duty was thought a fool. Ammunition was wasted by firing at planes at impossible distances and positions were lost because nobody wanted to dig trenches. It is interesting that indiscipline was most marked among groups like factory workers, who had previously been subject to external constraints and controls. Those used to leading an independent existence like farmers and artisans had not had their self-discipline undermined. Much has been made of the fact that leaders were elected and political groupings maintained in the militias. But this was not so much a difficulty as a source of strength. It inspired mutual confidence among men suspicious of outsiders. The real problem came in the first few chaotic weeks, when the revolutionary atmosphere made militiamen react immediately against anything that could be remotely construed as authoritarianism. 'Discipline was almost a crime,' admitted Abad de Santillán.[22]

The election of officers and the trial of offenders by rank-and-file courts were regarded by anarchists as fundamental principles. Each section, comprising ten men, elected its own corporal. Each *centuria*, comprising 100 men, elected its own delegate. A militia column varied greatly in its number of *centuria*. Durruti's column had 6,000 men at its peak, while others consisted of only a few hundred. Most columns had a regular officer who acted as 'adviser' to the column leader, but unless he was known as a genuine sympathizer, he was usually distrusted. There were a certain number of very radical officers in the army, such as Colonel Romero Bassart, the colonial officer who resisted the rising at Larache and later became military adviser to the CNT. There was also the unconventional Colonel Mangada, who was treated as a hero in the first days of the war after his column advanced towards Avila and repulsed a column from Salamanca led by Major Doval in a very confused and inconclusive skirmish in which the Falangist leader, Onésimo Redondo, was killed. Generally, however, republican militia suspected the loyalty of army officers, because many had at first declared for the government, only to betray it later. Some genuine supporters of the Republic were probably shot in error and certainly in several cases loyal regular officers were made scapegoats for militia reverses.

In Catalonia, where the militia system was the most entrenched, the air force officer Díaz Sandino became the Catalan councillor of war while the secretary-general, the anarchist Juan García Oliver, took over militia organization. His main work was to arrange training programmes in the rear. Even though about a tenth of the militia force in Aragón were ex-soldiers who had joined the workers, the standard of training in the metropolitan army had been so abysmal that they provided little help.

Militia volunteers were kitted out at the former Pedralbes barracks, now the Miguel Bakunin barracks where García Oliver had based the Popular School of War. The same building was used for foreign anarchists who arrived to fight in the International Column. They came from all over Europe and Latin America. There were many Italians including Camillo Berneri, a philosophy professor who was murdered the following year during the events of May in Barcelona, and Carlo Roselli, who organized the Giustizia e Libertà column of liberals and anarchists, but who was assassinated in France the following June by members of the right-wing Cagoule. A group of Americans formed the Sacco and Vanzetti *centuria* and a detachment of Germans made up the Erich Muhsam *centuria*, named after the anarchist poet murdered two years before by the Gestapo. The POUM also used these barracks for their militia columns, which included foreign volunteers of whom the most famous was George Orwell. The communist PSUC, under Joan Comorera, found itself in a difficult position. Communist policy demanded a regular army, not militias, yet they could not antagonize their allies.

The largest operation in the east at this time was the invasion by Catalonian militia of the Balearic Islands. Ibiza was taken easily and on 16 August 8,000 men invaded Majorca under the command of an air force officer, Alberto Bayo, later to be Fidel Castro's guerrilla trainer. The invaders established a bridgehead unopposed, then paused as if in surprise. For once the militia had artillery, air and even naval support, yet they gave the nationalists time to organize a counter-attack. Modern Italian aircraft arrived and strafed and bombed the invading force virtually unopposed. The withdrawal and re-embarkation, ordered by the new minister of marine, Indalecio Prieto, turned into a rout. The island then became an important naval and air base for the nationalists for the rest of the war.

The Aragón front became a stalemate after the Carlist reinforcements arrived at Saragossa. The only exception was an unsuccessful attack on Huesca organized by Colonel Villalba. The town was defended by 6,000 men against his besieging force of 13,000, but a supply line along the railtrack stayed open, allowing the nationalists to bring up supplies and reinforcements.[23] Militia detachments held each hill in a rough line along the front, while nationalist troops were installed on the far side of the valley. (The day-to-day existence is best described in George Orwell's *Homage to Catalonia*.)

In Madrid the Communist Party already had a military base on which to build. Their Worker and Peasant Anti-Fascist Militia (MAOC) provided the initial cadres for their 5th Regiment. The first communist objective was to make them look and act like disciplined soldiers. Practical military training was secondary to drilling. 'Steel' companies were formed (later to be imitated by other parties) and they paraded ostentatiously through Madrid causing an appreciable effect.[24] Marching in step presented a great contrast to the militias. The mentality of the 5th Regiment was best described by a party official: 'We established special slogans designed to create an iron unity ... "If my comrade advances or retreats without orders I have the right to shoot him."'[25]

The training of the International Brigades was to follow a similar pattern with drill, discipline and political indoctrination taking up most of the precious time before they were sent up to the front. The Party manual said that a soldier would only fight well if carefully instructed on why he was fighting. This ideological drilling was the work of political commissars and the 5th Regiment was responsible for their introduction. Officially they were there to watch over the 'reliability' of the regular commander. In fact, they were agents in the Communist Party's plan to take over the republican army, which would have to be formed if a conventional war was fought. These 'secular chaplains' were later the cause of a great power struggle between the communists and the government.

The first commander of the 5th Regiment was Enrique Castro Delgado, who was assisted by foreign communist advisers. The Party's 'common front' recruiting campaign, led by La Pasionaria, attracted many who admired the 5th Regiment's professional appearance. Some 25 per cent of the new recruits were socialists; about 15 per cent left republicans. Later they discovered that promotion was virtually impossible without Party membership, since the 5th Regiment served chiefly as a training base for future communist officers. The Communist Party claimed that some 60,000 men served in its ranks, but a maximum of 30,000 is probably more accurate.[26] They included Juan Modesto, a former Foreign Legion corporal, and the Moscow-trained Enrique Líster, both of whom were to become important commanders.

Most regular officers preferred to co-operate with the communists because they were horrified by the militia system. On the whole these loyalist officers tended to be the older and more bureaucratic members of the metropolitan army, since the younger, more aggressive elements had sided with the rising. But only colonial soldiers had received any practical experience. The pre-war home army had seldom even carried out manoeuvres.

The republican commanders therefore had little to offer but second-hand theories left over from the First World War. Along with the communists and the government, who wanted all forces controlled through a central structure, they insisted that the militias adapt to an orthodox model. Eventually the militias would have to agree. They could not resist the enemy for long without major changes and their theorists had failed to put forward any alternative strategy. The government and its allies had an additional motive for wanting to create a regular military organization. They believed that the Republic must impress foreign governments as a conventional state possessing a conventional army.

PART THREE

The Civil War Becomes International

13
Arms and the Diplomats

The failure of the military coup by the rebels, matched by the failure of the government and unions to crush it, meant that Spain faced a long and bloody war. The need for weapons in this much longer struggle forced both sides to seek help abroad, the first major step in the internationalization of the Spanish Civil War.

Of the three most important neutral governments, the British played the most crucial role. An isolationist United States was wary of international commitments. The French government of Léon Blum was alarmed by Hitler's rearmament and, despite France's pact with Russia, relied primarily on Great Britain for mutual defence. Yet when Blum received a telegram on 19 July from José Giral's government in Madrid requesting arms, his first reaction was to agree to help. The Republican government wanted twenty Potez bombers, eight Schneider 155mm field guns, Hotchkiss machine-guns, Lebel rifles, grenades and ammunition.[1] He prepared their despatch in secret with Pierre Cot, the minister of aviation.

The reasons for such discretion were that Blum's Popular Front coalition had been in office for only six weeks, and street fighting in France took place between left-wingers and fascist groups, such as the Croix de Feu. The violence, although not comparable to that in Spain during the spring, still made senior army officers restless. Generals Gamelin, Duval and Jouart, as well as the powerful industrialists of the Comité des Forges, warned that the slightest suggestion of involving the country in the Spanish conflict risked provoking a major storm.[2] The Catholic writer François Mauriac warned in the *Figaro*: 'Take care! We will never forgive you for such a crime.'[3]

The despatch of the aircraft may have been organized in secret, but nationalist sympathizers in the Spanish embassy informed the press, and perhaps also Count Welczeck, the German ambassador.

On 23 July he reported to the Wilhelmstrasse, 'I have learned in strict confidence that the French government has declared itself prepared to supply the Spanish government with considerable amounts of war matériel during the next few days. Approximately 30 bombers, several thousand bombs, a considerable number of 75mm guns, etc., are involved ... Franco's situation is likely to deteriorate decisively, especially as the result of the supplying of bombers to the government.'[4] Not only did this pro-nationalist source exaggerate the scale of the intended shipment, in Tetuán, nationalist officers convinced the German consul that they had not been able to delay the rising because 'Soviet ships had arrived in Spanish harbours with arms and ammunition for an uprising planned by the Communists'.[5]

Blum survived the attacks of right-wing newspapers by restricting the agreement to private sales of unarmed military aircraft, but this meant that the Republic was now being treated on a level similar to the insurgents. To make matters worse, the Spanish ambassador in Paris, Juan Cárdenas, joined the nationalists. Giral's government called on Fernando de los Ríos, then on holiday in Geneva, to replace him, but time was lost. De los Ríos could not be recognized by the French government straight away, he lacked accessible funds and he had no idea of weaponry. On the night of 24 July he had a meeting with Blum, Pierre Cot, Édouard Daladier and Yvon Delbos to examine a clause of the 1935 commercial treaty which allowed Spain to purchase arms up to the value of 20 million francs.[6]

The alternative method of helping the Republic was to prevent foreign support reaching Franco. The British Foreign Office feared that the conflict might escalate and warned the French government that helping the Republic would only encourage Hitler and Mussolini to aid the nationalists. Blum and Daladier, his war minister, were aware that French armaments were inferior to those that Franco could obtain from the dictators. Anthony Eden, the British foreign secretary, agreed with the view of Salvador de Madariaga, the former Spanish representative at the League of Nations, that apart from foreign intervention, the two sides were so evenly balanced that neither could win. This sort of reasoning encouraged the French government to believe that it was better for the Republic if no arms were allowed to reach either zone.

The last hopes of the Spanish republican government that it

would not be treated on a par with its enemies disappeared on 25 July. President Albert Lebrun summoned an emergency meeting of the council of ministers to discuss the impact of the right-wing press campaign against aid to the Spanish Republic. Any attempt to sell arms to the Republic was forbidden. The only exception would be the sale of a few unarmed aircraft through private companies or third parties, such as Mexico.[7]

A policy of 'non-intervention' was therefore proposed by Blum's government on 2 August to include the French, British, German and Italian governments, and any others who became involved in the Spanish conflict. There is little doubt that the British government's attitude was crucial. As Eden said, the French government 'acted most loyally by us'.[8] On 3 and 4 August the French foreign ministry sounded out the Germans and Italians on their intentions. They avoided a definite response to gain time while they speeded up their shipments of arms to the nationalists. Meanwhile the British ambassador in Paris put pressure on the French government not to help the Republic.[9] Blum, afraid of alienating the British, suspended further arms sales as well as civilian aircraft on 8 August. The Spanish frontier was closed to all prohibited commerce.

Four days later the French chargé d'affaires in London recommended an international committee of control 'to supervise the agreement and consider further action'. Eden, however, decided to announce that Britain would apply an arms embargo without waiting for other powers to respond. This in effect meant denying arms to the recognized government and often ignoring those going to the rebels, for the British government refused to acknowledge the proof of German and Italian intervention. On the other hand, there were instances of the British being even-handed. For example, it appears from a German foreign ministry report that the British embassy in Portugal put heavy pressure on the Portuguese authorities to prevent the German vessel *Usuramo* from unloading 'a "certain" cargo' (probably ammunition) and the ship had to sail away to unload elsewhere.[10] And later Franco complained to the German ambassador that Britain had put heavy pressure on Portugal not to recognize his regime.[11] Baldwin's government nevertheless told the Labour opposition that any active expression of sympathy with the republican government of Spain would at that time be against the interests of Great Britain and therefore unpatriotic.

The policy of appeasement was not Neville Chamberlain's

invention. Its roots lay in a fear of bolshevism. The general strike of 1926 and the depression made the possibility of revolution a very real concern to conservative politicians. As a result, they had mixed feelings towards the German and Italian regimes which had crushed the communists and the socialists in their own countries. Much of the electorate also held anti-militarist sentiments after the First World War and feelings of guilt about the Allies' humiliation of Germany at the Treaty of Versailles.[12] The British population, moreover, knew little of events abroad. As the British minister in Berlin, Sir Ivone Kirkpatrick, wrote later, the country 'could not be expected to take an enlightened view of the situation when the government had done nothing to inform it'.[13]

When the Spanish Civil War broke out, Eden was to handle the situation virtually on his own. Stanley Baldwin, the prime minister, was ill when the war began and then became preoccupied by the Abdication crisis. 'I hope', he told Eden, 'that you will try not to trouble me too much with foreign affairs just now.' Eden was hardly an impartial observer of the conflict. He is supposed to have told the French foreign minister, Delbos, that England preferred a rebel victory to a republican victory. He professed an admiration for the self-proclaimed fascist Calvo Sotelo, who had been murdered. He abhorred the killings in republican territory, while failing to comment on nationalist atrocities. From his diplomatic staff on the spot he received emotive descriptions of the killings in the capital and Barcelona. The ambassador, Sir Henry Chilton, was a blatant admirer of the nationalists and preferred to stay in Hendaye rather than return to Madrid. The government also listened to Royal Navy officers who supported the rebels. The naval base of Gibraltar had been flooded with pro-nationalist refugees, among whom journalists of the British press searched diligently for 'first-hand' accounts of atrocities. Franco's admission at the end of July that he was prepared to shoot half of Spain was virtually ignored.

Franco's new press officer, Luis Bolín, had, before the rising, organized a discreet but effective anti-republican campaign in London as correspondent of the monarchist newspaper *ABC*. He claimed, with justification, that he had 'developed a not inconsiderable degree of influence in appropriate circles'. His most important ally was the Duke of Alba, who also had the English dukedom of Berwick and was addressed as 'cousin' by Churchill. In these circles Alba, with his affection for English institutions, typified the civilized Spaniard. His quiet conversations in White's club were infinitely more influential on government policy than mass rallies or demonstrations. But then anyone speaking up for the Spanish republican government in such surroundings would have provoked the kind of horrified reaction caricatured in a Bateman cartoon.

Eden did not fully recognize the dangers of Hitler and Mussolini until 1937 and he did not speak out openly against appeasement until early in 1938. During the first part of the civil war he preferred, on balance, a 'fascist' victory to a 'communist' victory. He believed, not unreasonably after the events of the last twenty years, that social upheaval almost certainly led to a communist dictatorship or fascism. But the refusal to sell arms to the Republic in fact strengthened the communists and weakened the forces of the non-communist centre and left. In the summer of 1936 the Spanish Communist Party represented a very small proportion of the republican coalition. Its organization and unscrupulous methods quickly made up for this numerical weakness, but it was mainly the leverage and prestige of Soviet military aid which was to give it a commanding position.

Many Spanish republicans maintained a naive belief that Great Britain would act as the champion of the underdog in its nineteenth-century tradition. Indeed, the belief that the democracies would eventually deliver them from dictatorship persisted until 1946, seven years after the end of the civil war. Certainly, in 1938 there was a conviction in Spain that even British conservatives would be forced to recognize the necessity of 'joining the fight against fascism'. But they underestimated the deep prejudice of certain governing circles.

The only circumstance likely to influence British foreign policy was a direct threat to traditional interests, the most sensitive of which was still the route to India. It was the threat of a permanent Italian occupation of Majorca and Mussolini's immediate breaking of their 'Gentleman's Agreement' which brought Eden to reconsider his position only on 7 January 1937.[14] Meanwhile, the actions of the Royal Navy were astonishing for a non-interventionist power. Not only were communications facilities provided for General Kindelán in Gibraltar to speak directly to Rome, Berlin and Lisbon, but the battleship HMS *Queen Elizabeth* was moved in front of Algeciras bay to prevent republican warships shelling the port.

*

At the same time as the republican government was appealing to France for military aid, the nationalists were turning to their natural allies, Germany and Italy. After delivering Franco to Tetuán on 19 July, Luis Bolín flew to Lisbon. There, just before his fatal crash, Sanjurjo had countersigned the authorization to purchase aircraft and supplies for the 'Spanish non-Marxist army'. Bolín flew on to Rome on 21 July, where he was joined by the Marquis de Viana, the private secretary of ex-King Alfonso. Together they saw Count Galeazzo Ciano, the Italian foreign minister and Mussolini's son-in-law. According to Bolín, 'his reaction was enthusiastic and spontaneous. Without hesitating an instant he promised us the necessary aid. "We must put an end to the communist threat in the Mediterranean," he cried.'[15] But the real decision lay with Mussolini, who was persuaded to help after Italian representatives in Tangier, including the military attaché and the consul general, had a meeting with Franco.[16]

On 30 July, Mussolini sent Franco twelve Savoia-Marchetti 81 bombers bound for Morocco, two transport planes and a ship loaded with fuel and ammunition. Three of the aircraft crashed on the way, one of them coming down in Algeria, providing documentary proof of Italian military aid. The rest were used as aerial cover for the first nationalist convoy across the straits on 5 August.

Mussolini looked forward to the establishment of another fascist state in the Mediterranean, particularly one which would be indebted to him. His great ambition was to rival British naval power and challenge the French in North Africa.[17] A Spanish ally could control the straits by seizing Gibraltar and offered the possibility of bases in the Balearics, yet her fleet was not likely to be a rival. Mussolini's conquest of Abyssinia had greatly increased his delusions of Italian power and Ciano's main task was to obtain recognition of the 'Italian Empire'. The Savoias were soon followed on 7 August by consignments of 27 Fiat fighters, five Fiat-Ansaldo light tanks and twelve field guns, all with ammunition and trained personnel. Six days later three seaplanes were sent and on 19 August another six fighters.[18]

Republican propaganda later tried to prove – with Nazi documents seized from the German consulate in Barcelona – that fascist intervention was pre-arranged and that the generals would not have launched the rebellion without this guarantee. (The nationalists, for their part, pretended to have found papers in Seville which revealed advance planning for a communist *coup d'état*.) In fact, the military plotters had not received any such guarantee. Relations between Italy and Germany had been strained in the early summer of 1936 primarily because of their rivalry over Austria. Nevertheless, their aid to nationalist Spain was to prove the forging of 'the Rome–Berlin axis', a phrase first used by Mussolini on 1 November 1936.

The Nazi government had better information on the situation in Spain, both through unofficial contacts and through their own sources within the German business community. At the beginning of the war their diplomats, led by the foreign minister, Neurath, were opposed to aiding Franco from fear of provoking a British reaction. Hitler despised this traditional branch of the German government and kept his diplomatic staff almost totally uninformed of his actions. He worked instead with German Military Intelligence, headed by Admiral Canaris, who had met Franco in Spain on several occasions and was keen to support his forces in particular.

On 22 July, as already mentioned, Franco told Colonel Beigbeder to ask the German government for transport aircraft. He had visited Berlin in March with General Sanjurjo to obtain German help in establishing a Spanish air force. (Lufthansa had had much to do with the setting up of Iberia in 1927.) Beigbeder made the first approach, using his friendship with General Kühlental. Then Franco's other emissaries, Bernhardt and Langenheim, two Nazi businessmen living in Morocco, arrived in Berlin on 25 July, in a Lufthansa plane which the nationalists had commandeered.[19] They first saw officials from the Wilhelmstrasse, but the German foreign service was extremely nervous about intervening on Franco's side.[20] They tried to prevent the two men from gaining access to senior members of the Nazi Party in Berlin. But one of them, through his contacts, managed to get a message to Rudolf Hess.[21] Hitler saw them in Bayreuth after a performance of *Siegfried* when they handed over a personal letter from Franco. The meeting went on until 1.30 in the morning. Hitler gave orders to Göring and General von Blomberg to expedite the request. Within 24 hours the special staff set up in the air ministry organized the despatch of Junkers 52s (twice the number that Franco had asked for), six Heinkel 51 fighter-bombers, twenty anti-aircraft guns and other equipment.[22] Hitler, having been convinced that Franco was the most competent and ruthless of the Spanish generals, insisted that military aid would be sent only to his troops. Göring, in a typically theatrical touch, gave the plan the codename Operation *Feuerzauber*, or 'Magic Fire', which occurs in the last act of *Siegfried*.

The special staff in the air ministry also selected 'volunteer' pilots. Göring was thrilled at the idea of testing his 'young Luftwaffe in this or that technical respect'. The Germans were far more hard-headed about the whole enterprise than the Italians. They were offering the best machines and experts available and, although Franco was an ideological ally, they wanted payment in copper and iron ore.[23] Dealings between Franco and Nazi Germany were channelled through a company called Hispano-Marroquí de Transportes (HISMA). Its counterpart in Germany was Rohstoffe und Waren Einkaufgesellschaft (ROWAK).

The first delivery of weaponry reached Spain on 1 August and the rhythm was maintained, either directly to Cádiz or via Lisbon. They included Panzer Mark I tanks, as well as 20mm and 88mm anti-aircraft guns. Nevertheless, German intervention became fully established only in November with the creation of the Condor Legion after Franco's failure to seize Madrid.

Hitler's real reasons for helping Franco were strategic. A fascist Spain would present a threat to France's rear as well as to the British route to the Suez Canal. There was even the tempting possibility of U-boat bases on the Atlantic coast. (The Spanish ports of Vigo, El Ferrol, Cádiz and Las Palmas were used on an occasional basis during the Second World War.) The civil war also served to divert attention away from his central European strategy, while offering an opportunity to train men and to test equipment and tactics.

Within a fortnight of the rebellion it had become evident that the nationalists would receive military aid from Germany and Italy, while the democracies refused arms to the Republic. This imbalance was increased by financial support to the nationalists, as vital in a drawn-out war as military aid. In the early days the republican government controlled the country's 635 tons of gold, the equivalent of 715 million dollars, as backing for its peseta, while the nationalists could offer only the probability of victory as collateral for their currency.[24] Nevertheless, Prieto was wrong to claim on 8 August that the gold gave the Spanish government an unlimited resistance, while the financial capacity of the enemy was negligible.

The famous photograph of the young King Alfonso XIII getting to know his people.

The king with General Miguel Primo de Rivera, who seized power with his approval in 1923.

Crowds celebrating in Madrid on 14 April 1931 when Alfonso abdicated and left Spain for ever.

Lerroux, President Alcalá Zamora and Gil Robles in 1934.

Civil guards arrest a socialist in Madrid, October 1934.

Civil guards escort their prisoners after the failed revolution in Asturias of October 1934.

José Antonio Primo de Rivera (seated centre) and fellow Falangists.

April 1936. Shooting breaks out during the funeral of a Civil Guard officer suspected of an attempt to kill President Azaña.

On 18 July 1936, the day after the rising began in Morocco, Franco reaches Ceuta from the Canary Islands to take over command of the Army of Africa.

19 July 1936. Carlist volunteers flock to the main square of Pamplona to become General Mola's main force.

Assault guards and anarcho-syndicalist workers of the CNT with a captured field gun in Barcelona.

POUM militia in the Carlos Marx barracks in Barcelona.

Junkers 52 sent by Hitler with Moroccan regulares during the airlift to Seville, July 1936.

A *bandera* of the Foreign Legion rounds up villagers during Yagüe's advance north, August 1936.

28 September 1936. Colonel Varela's troops advance into Toledo.

Colonel Moscardó, Varela and Franco celebrate the relief of the Alcázar of Toledo.

Franco, as saviour of the Alcázar, became the unchallenged leader of the nationalists. Yagüe (in glasses), Franco (saluting) and Serrano Súñer just behind him.

Luftwaffe pilots with their Heinkel He-45 fighter-bombers.

The nationalists immediately looked to foreign financial institutions for help as well as to Spanish supporters. The principal backing for the conspiracy came originally from the huge resources of the former tobacco smuggler Juan March, who apparently contributed £15 million. In Britain, the devoutly Catholic Marquess of Bute sold the vast freeholds which he owned in the city of Cardiff and denoted the proceeds to the nationalist movement. Much of the capital that had been smuggled out of Spain during the Republic, especially in the first half of the year, was soon transferred back to nationalist territory. The nationalist movement demanded the gold of private citizens, in particular wedding rings, to help pay for the war.

American and British business interests were to make a great contribution to the final nationalist victory, either through active assistance, such as that given by the oil magnate Henry Deterding, or through boycotting the Republic, disrupting its trade with legal action and delaying credits in the banking system.[25]

Oil had now become almost as vital a commodity in war as ammunition. The US Neutrality Act of 1935 did not, however, reflect this change, thus allowing Franco to receive 3,500,000 tons of oil on credit during the course of the war, well over double the total oil imports of the Republic. The president of the Texas Oil Company was an admirer of the fascists, and on receiving news of the rising he diverted five tankers en route for Spain to the nationalist port of Tenerife, which had a large refinery. Since Texaco had been the principal supplier to the government, his decision was a severe blow to the Republic. Standard Oil of New Jersey was another supplier, though on a smaller scale. The Duchess of Atholl, one of the few British conservatives to support the Republic from the beginning, claimed that the Rio Tinto Zinc company helped finance Franco by supplying foreign exchange at over double the official rate. Later on Ford, Studebaker and General Motors supplied 12,000 trucks to the nationalists, nearly three times as many as the Axis powers, and the chemical giant Dupont of Nemours provided 40,000 bombs, sending them via Germany so as to circumvent the Neutrality Act.[26] In 1945 the under-secretary at the Spanish foreign ministry, José María Doussinague, admitted that 'without American petroleum and American trucks and American credit, we could never have won the civil war'.[27]

Shunned by the democratic powers and the international business community, the Republic could count only on the support of Mexico and the USSR. As a result, the nationalists' warnings of an 'international communist conspiracy' carried some conviction, even though Soviet policy was hardly consistent. After Lenin's death Trotsky's policy of worldwide revolution had been based on the premise that Russian communism could not prosper so long as it was surrounded by a hostile capitalist world. The opposing Stalinist policy of 'socialism in one country', which triumphed in 1927, implied an abstention from involvement in revolutions abroad. The Chinese communists, for example, were sacrificed to Chiang Kai-shek's Kuomintang to further Russian interests, and Stalin gained recognition from the United States government in 1933 by promising not to indulge in subversive activities there.

On 25 July Giral sent a message to Stalin's government via the Soviet ambassador in Paris requesting modern armaments and ammunition 'of all types and in large quantities'. But the Soviet Union was fearful of the international situation and the possible consequences. This did not, however, stop the Kremlin from authorizing less controversial help, with the instruction: 'To order NKVT [People's Commissariat on Foreign Trade of the USSR] to sell fuel oil immediately to the Spaniards, at reduced prices, on most favourable conditions, any amount that they need.'[28]

Giral's request for arms received no reply. For the first two weeks of the Spanish Civil War the lack of comment on events from Moscow raised alarm in foreign communist circles. Stalin was about to purge the Red Army, Trotsky's creation, and he was deeply concerned at the prospect of a foreign adventure which might provoke Hitler at such a time of Soviet weakness. But the exiled Trotsky made use of this silence to accuse Stalin of betraying the Spanish revolution and aiding the fascists. Whether or not it was Trotsky who goaded him into action, Stalin must have realized that Soviet communism would lose all credibility, and probably the loyalty of European parties, if nothing was done to help the Republic. Stalin therefore decided to send aid to the Spanish government, but little more than the necessary minimum. In this way he would neither frighten the British government, which he needed as a potential ally, nor provoke the Germans.

On 3 August 'popular demonstrations' and 'spontaneous indignation meetings' took place all over Russia. Factory workers made 'voluntary contributions' to help the Republic and the government sent its first non-military supplies. Comintern officials, using false names, were also sent to Spain to make sure that the young Spanish Communist Party should not step out of line. Only at the end of September did Stalin decide to provide military help.[29] The first shipment left the Crimea on 26 September and did not reach Cartagena until 4 October.

Mexico, the other country to support the Republic, refused to join the non-intervention agreement. President Lázaro Cárdenas, despite his country's limited resources, provided the republicans with 20,000 Mauser rifles, 20 million rounds and food. These rifles from Mexico were used to arm the militias facing the Army of Africa as it advanced on Madrid.[30]

The Spanish war was no longer simply an internal struggle. Spain's strategic importance, and the coincidence of the civil war with the Axis powers' preparations to test their secretly developed weaponry in Europe, ensured that the war lost its amateur character. The nationalists were inundated with foreign advisers, observers, technical experts and combat personnel. Within a month of the rising Franco had received 48 Italian and 41 German aircraft. The Republic, on the other hand, received no more than thirteen Dewoitine fighters and six Potez 54 bombers. These aircraft lacked weapons and even their basic mountings. The French government could not provide pilots, so the Republic had to resort to very expensive volunteers.

Malraux, the author of *La Condition Humaine* and supposedly a communist sympathizer, set up the air squadron España crewed by mercenaries and paid for by the republican government. This provoked the suspicion and contempt of the Comintern representative André Marty, who regarded Malraux with a good deal of justification as an 'adventurer'. When Soviet advisers arrived, they criticized him for ignoring republican commanders, making 'absurd proposals' and for knowing 'little about aerial tactics'. They also berated his group for 'a complete lack of discipline and lack of participation in battle'. To be fair, their obsolete aircraft stood little chance against Heinkel or Fiat fighters, but this did not stop Malraux from extracting exorbitant rates of pay for very little action, as the Soviet officers reported to Moscow. 'He had recruited the pilots and technicians himself in France. Most of them have come here in order to make good money. Due to his insistence, the Spanish government was paying 50,000 francs a month to pilots,

30,000 francs to observers, and 15,000 to mechanics. This was during the period when the government had no air force at all and it was easy for Malraux to persuade them to pay whatever he wanted.'[31]

The Republic, ignorant of the murky world of mercenaries and the armament industry, suffered from numerous confidence tricksters. Malraux stands out, not just because he was a mythomaniac in his claims of martial heroism – both in Spain and later in the French Resistance – but because he cynically exploited the opportunity for intellectual heroism in the legend of the Spanish Republic.

Relations between foreigners and Spanish were seldom smooth on either side. Franco and his officers hated being indebted to their allies, while their often arrogant German advisers might perhaps have agreed with the Duke of Wellington's comment on the Spanish officers attached to his staff that 'the national weakness was boasting of Spain's greatness'. The Republic, however, was to suffer far more from its only powerful ally, the Soviet Union.

14
Sovereign States

The nationalists also needed a formalized state structure to impress foreign governments, but there was no pretence of democracy. The authoritarian values of all its component groups – army, Falange, Carlists and monarchists – demanded a single leader. Franco, who had established his headquarters at Cáceres on 26 August, refrained from any overt manoeuvring until the relief of the Alcázar became certain in late September. As with his military strategy, he did not make any political move until everything possible was in his favour.

His command of the most professional force, the Army of Africa, had made him a contender for the leadership from the start. Then the German proviso of giving military aid only to his forces greatly strengthened his claim. But Franco knew that if his long-term ambitions were to be satisfied, he needed to gain a complete moral, as well as military, ascendancy over his rivals. That he achieved with the relief of Toledo. To challenge the 'Saviour of the Alcázar' for the leadership of the nationalist movement would have required rash courage.

The first major step to resolve the leadership issue came when Franco requested a meeting of the Junta de Defensa Nacional at the military aerodrome outside Salamanca on 21 September. General Kindelán, the air force commander, had prepared the ground, assisted in the background by the rest of Franco's *camarilla*, including his brother Nicolás Franco, Orgaz, Millán Astray, Luis Bolín and the diplomat José Antonio Sangróniz. They had worked painstakingly to place their chief in the most advantageous position. Colonel Walter Warlimont, Hitler's envoy, had also applied discreet pressure on the question of military assistance.

All the possible candidates for the leadership were present at Salamanca airfield that day: Franco, Mola, Queipo de Llano and Cabanellas, the nominal president of the junta, who chaired the meeting.[1] The military were to take a decision on behalf of right-wing Spain. With the CEDA leader, Gil Robles, in self-imposed exile in Portugal (many nationalists blamed the civil war on his lack of nerve), José Antonio in Alicante prison, where he was to be executed, and Calvo Sotelo dead since just before the rising, only the wishes of the monarchists and the Carlists had to be considered. Mola, Queipo and Cabanellas were all tainted with republicanism or Freemasonry in varying degrees, so Franco benefited greatly from a lack of obvious defects and his political inscrutability.

In a charade which was accepted with varying degrees of enthusiasm, the monarchist General Kindelán proposed at the end of the meeting that Franco should be appointed supreme commander of all land, sea and air forces, with the title of Generalissimo. Mola, conscious that his reputation had suffered because his plan for the rising had not succeeded, gave in almost sycophantically. 'He is younger than me,' he acknowledged, 'and of higher professional standing. He is extremely popular and is well-known abroad.'[2] Queipo, with his habitual lack of tact, ran through the possibilities later. 'So who were we going to nominate? Cabanellas could not take it on. He was a convinced republican and everyone knew that he was a Freemason. We couldn't possibly nominate Mola either, because we would lose the war ... And my reputation was badly damaged.'[3] Only Cabanellas dissented. He demanded a military directory and it cost him dear. Six days later Toledo fell. Kindelán, believing that Franco would restore Alfonso to his throne, helped with the preparations for 28 September, when the 'Saviour of the Alcázar' was to return to Salamanca to be accepted as supreme commander by the other generals.

The most active supporter of Franco behind the scenes was his brother Nicolás. He arranged for a mixed guard of Falangists and Carlists to hail his brother as chief when all the generals came together in Salamanca. Then, by omitting or changing key words in the text of the decree, he made Franco 'Head of the Spanish State', as opposed to 'head of the government of the Spanish State', for 'the duration of the war'.[4] This trick did not endear Franco to his colleagues, who found themselves presented with a fait accompli, one might almost say a *coup d'état* within the coup. Even Mola was deeply irritated that Franco had taken over supreme political power as well as military. It is said that Queipo called Franco a 'son of a whore', or according to other sources a 'swine'. But Kindelán and Dávila somehow persuaded the other generals that Franco had simply been proclaimed head of government for the duration, as the original decree had stated. But there was in any case little that either Mola or Queipo could do once the event had been reported in the newspapers. To protest now could be represented as disloyalty to the nationalist cause.

On 1 October 1936 Franco was invested with his powers in the throne room of the captain-generalcy in Burgos, in front of the diplomatic representatives of Portugal, Germany and Italy. General Cabanellas had been forced to accept total defeat. 'Señor Chief of the Spanish State,' he proclaimed. 'In the name of the Council of National Defence, I hand over to you the absolute powers of the state.' Franco went out on to the balcony to receive the cheers of the crowds. In his speech to them he promised 'no home without a hearth, nor a Spaniard without bread'. The anniversary of this day was to be celebrated for almost 40 years as 'The Day of the Caudillo'.[5] The military junta, which had been led by Cabanellas, was immediately replaced by a 'Junta Técnica del Estado' with General Dávila at its head.[6]

Once Franco became the Caudillo, he never allowed opposition to develop. His speeches skilfully selected compatible aspects of the rival nationalist ideologies. He affected an intensity of religious feeling to woo the Carlists and the Church. The Falangist slogan '*Una Patria, Un Estado, Un Caudillo*' was converted to '*Una Patria: España. Un Caudillo: Franco*'. But it was not long before the chant of 'Franco! Franco! Franco!' was heard.

Historical parallels were drawn by nationalist writers with the first *Reconquista*. This safely inspired the appropriate image in the appropriate mind. For the Falangists, it was the birth of the nation; for Carlist and Alphonsine monarchists it represented the establishment of a royal Catholic dictatorship; for the Church the age of ecclesiastical supremacy; and for landowners the foundation of their wealth and power. Franco was very different from Mussolini and Hitler. He was a cunning opportunist who, despite his rhetoric, did not suffer from overly dangerous visions of destiny.

Franco's new position was reinforced with good news. The recently completed nationalist cruiser *Canarias* had sailed round the Portuguese coast from El Ferrol, the Caudillo's birthplace, to attack republican warships off Gibraltar. She managed to sink the destroyer *Almirante Fernández* and force the others to seek shelter in Cartagena harbour. The blockade of the straits was now finished and Moroccan reinforcements could be brought across without diverting aircraft from bombing raids.

In the republican zone, Giral's government had resigned on 4 September. It had never been able to reflect the reality of the situation, let alone win enough support to influence it. All the political parties recognized that there was only one man able to gain the trust of the revolutionary committees. Largo Caballero was enjoying a great wave of popularity after his visits to the militia positions in the Guadarrama mountains. 'Largo Caballero', wrote his fellow socialist Zugazagoitia, 'retained in the eyes of the masses his mythical qualities and his pathos had started to work the miracle of a difficult rebirth of collective enthusiasm.'[7]

Even Prieto, the middle-class social democrat, recognized that his great rival, the obstinate, often blinkered proletarian, was the only suitable successor to Giral.[8] Both Prieto and the communists tried to maintain the liberal façade as far as possible, but Largo Caballero wanted a coalition which was preponderantly socialist. He felt strongly that he had been exploited by the liberals in the first republican government, undermining his work as minister of labour.

The new government was presented as symbolizing unity against the common enemy since it brought together the liberal centre and the revolutionary left into one administration. This administration called itself 'the government of Victory' and was the first in Western Europe to contain communists. It marked also an important move towards the progressive recuperation of power from local committees. Faced with the nationalist successes (Talavera and Irún were about to fall), even the anarchists found it difficult to challenge its development. Nevertheless, the Republic was still far from that middle-class state which communist propaganda attempted to portray to the world outside. La Pasionaria and Jesús Hernández insisted that Spain was experiencing a 'bourgeois democratic revolution' and that they were 'motivated exclusively by the desire to defend the democratic Republic established on 14 April 1931'.

In fact, the Spanish communists were far from happy that Largo Caballero, the man they had so recently lauded as 'the Spanish Lenin', was now leading the government. They reported to Moscow on 8 September that 'despite our efforts, we were not able to avoid a Caballero government'. They had also tried, following Comintern orders, to evade being included themselves, but 'everyone emphatically insisted on the participation of communists in the new government, and it was impossible to avoid this without creating a very dangerous situation. We are taking the necessary measures to organize the work of our ministers.'[9]

Marty, meanwhile, knew that communist power did not have to reside within the council of ministers. It lay in infiltrating the army and the police, as well as in its propaganda methods. 'The political influence of the Communist Party has exceeded all expectations ... Only our party knows what must be done. The slogans of the party are quickly taken up and reprinted by all the newspapers ... Our party supplies cadres for the police ... The main strength of the army has been directed towards the creation of what has become the pride of the People's Army – the 5th Regiment of the militia. The 5th Regiment, enjoying well-deserved military glory, numbers 20,000 warriors. All the commanders of the regiment are communists.' The aptly named Comrade Checa, the party official responsible for the army and the police, gave 'directives for conducting the interrogation of those under serious arrest'.[10]

President Azaña, who remained as a figurehead of liberal parliamentarianism, objected to the inclusion of communists in the government, but Azaña was increasingly isolated and Caballero's will prevailed. The two communist ministers accepted their posts only after instructions to do so from Moscow. Jesús Hernández became minister of education and Vicente Uribe was given the agriculture portfolio; Alvarez del Vayo, whom Largo Caballero did not yet know to be a communist supporter, became foreign minister.

Caballero's government also included three of his left socialist supporters and Prieto with two of his social-democrat followers, one of whom, the future prime minister Juan Negrín, became minister of finance. Largo Caballero kept the ministry of war for himself and gave Prieto the air force and the navy. There were also two republican left ministers (one of whom was José Giral), one Catalan Esquerra, one Basque nationalist and two representatives of the centrist Republicans.[11]

Caballero had invited his old rivals, the anarchists, to join the governing coalition to broaden the representation of the anti-nationalist groups. The anarchists made the counter-proposal (which was not accepted) of a National Defence Council with Largo Caballero as president, five CNT members, five from the UGT, four liberal republicans and no communists. Such a structure was no more than a euphemism for government and thus a sop to their conscience. They had tacitly admitted the necessity of central co-ordination and collaboration in conventional war. No anarchists, however, joined the government.

The committees started to be given new names and, although most of the original delegates stayed on, they gradually submitted to control from above. A new form of political parity also crept into the municipal councils which replaced the local committees. This distorted their reflection of local political strengths, especially in Catalonia, and assisted the communists, who gained more representation than the actual size of their following justified.

In Valencia the Popular Executive Committee, which had so contemptuously waved aside Martínez Barrio's delegation from the previous Madrid government, acknowledged the new one on 8 September. But the Comintern envoys were furious when a 'very popular anarchist from Valencia' declared at a mass meeting in Madrid on 25 September, 'There is one party that wants to monopolize the revolution. If that party continues its policy, we have decided to crush it. There is a foreign ambassador in Madrid [the Soviet envoy, Marcel Rosenberg] who is interfering in Spanish affairs. We warn him that Spanish affairs concern only the Spanish.'[12]

The effective administration in Catalonia, the Central Committee of the Anti-Fascist Militias, merged with the Generalitat in a new government on 26 September. It was led by Josep Tarradellas and all the workers' organizations and all the parties of the Popular Front were represented. This brought together the anarchist CNT, the communist PSUC and the anti-Stalinist POUM. It marked the first outright acceptance of government by the anarchists. They compromised their principles because they knew that the Madrid government would otherwise continue to starve their self-managed collectives of credits and currency for raw materials.

The POUM had been the most outspoken critic of the CNT leadership's refusal of power in Catalonia; this was partly because it advocated an authoritarian route to the new society, but mainly because it was more aware of the Stalinist threat than the Catalonian anarchists, who could not imagine themselves being challenged in

Barcelona. Andreu Nin, the POUM leader and now councillor of justice, had lived long enough in Russia to appreciate how the infiltration of key posts made the size of the Communist Party's following almost irrelevant. From the Catalan nationalists' point of view, Companys's moderate policy was starting to prove its effectiveness. The anarchists might call the Catalan government, which they had joined, the Regional Defence Committee, but what mattered was that three of them were now members of it. This marked the first major step in the loss of anarchist power in Catalonia.[13]

By the end of September the Defence Council of Aragón was the only major non-governmental organization in the southern part of republican territory which retained control over its own area. This anarchist creation, controlled by the FAI and headed by Joaquín Ascaso, was under heavy pressure from the communist campaign for centralized control. By October its committee acknowledged that it would have to make concessions in order to survive. Popular Front parties were brought into the council and Joaquín Ascaso made a successful diplomatic visit to Madrid. Mutual recognition was agreed upon without compromises that appeared to be too damaging, but it later became clear that the central government and the communists had no intention of allowing the Aragonese council to remain in existence any longer than necessary.[14]

Largo Caballero did not realize at this stage that he was being used to re-establish central state power by the liberals, social democrats and communists. Not until November did he start to understand that he had reloaded what Lenin called 'the pistol of the state' and that others were waiting to take it from him.

Although Caballero's appointment had been greeted with joy by many, the Comintern was the least impressed. Marty described him in a report to Moscow on 17 October as 'a bad union bureaucrat', and recorded that he and Prieto spent most of the time attacking each other in their respective newspapers, *Claridad* and *El Socialista*.[15]

One of the arguments for central control was that evidence of a stable, authoritative government in Madrid might persuade the British and French governments to change their policy on arms sales. This hope was dashed when the reality of non-intervention became clear. The first interventionist states, Germany and Italy, had initially given the non-intervention plan a very cool reception.

But then they realized the potential advantage. Ciano soon agreed to the policy in general, but insisted that it should cover every facet, even 'propaganda aid'. Italy and Germany would then be able to accuse Russia of violating the agreement and so justify their interventionist activities. The Germans agreed to the pact in principle, but argued that it would require a blockade to be enforced. The Soviet government, eager not to be outmanoeuvred, followed similar tactics by insisting that Portugal must be disciplined. Portugal was to become Stalin's whipping boy on the Non-Intervention Committee, since attacking the dictators was too risky for his tastes.

There seems to be little doubt that the French government had been sincere in its original intentions. The same cannot be said of Eden. His later realization that the ambitions of the Axis were only encouraged by appeasement tends to obscure his conduct in 1936. It was hypocritical to duck responsibility by saying that 'the Spaniards would not feel any gratitude to those who had intervened', when the British government failed to act impartially while maintaining its pretensions to being the 'international policeman'. Moreover, Eden's argument that supplying the Republic with arms would make Hitler aid Franco was already shown to be fallacious. Even the nationalist recruitment of Riffian mercenaries, a blatant contravention of the Treaty of Fes in 1912 which established the Spanish protectorate, was ignored. And the republican government was so concerned not to upset the French and British empires that it neither granted Morocco its independence nor made serious attempts to stir up anti-colonial feelings there.

Meetings of the Non-Intervention Committee began in London on 8 September, after numerous delays. These were caused mainly by Germany's refusal to participate until a crash-landed Junkers 52 was returned by the Republic. The committee was organized by the British Foreign Office in London. Lord Plymouth was chairman and the rest of the committee consisted of the ambassadors of the signatory nations, which included every European country except Switzerland. The ambassador of the Republic in London, Pablo de Azcárate, referred to 'confused discussions, embroiled and sterile at which denunciations and counter-denunciations took place'.[16] Eden himself had to admit that 'the lengthy meetings continued ... accusations were met with flat denials and the results of both were sterile'.

The British foreign secretary tried to claim that in October 'the Russians were openly sending supplies to Spain and the evidence we had at this time was more specific against them than against the dictators in Rome and Berlin'.[17] Yet in Geneva at the end of September he had recorded that Álvarez del Vayo, the Republic's foreign minister, 'left with me documents and photographs to prove the extent to which Hitler and Mussolini were violating the agreement'. Even the German chargé d'affaires was concerned at the way Wehrmacht uniforms were being cheered openly on the streets of Seville. And considering the sympathies of the Royal Navy in Gibraltar, it was perhaps not surprising that a blind eye had been turned on the streams of Junkers and Savoias over Gibraltar, which had ferried the Army of Africa between Tetuán and Seville. The American ambassador to Spain, Claude Bowers, later condemned the whole procedure: 'Each movement of the Non-Intervention Committee has been made to serve the cause of the rebellion ... This Committee was the most cynical and lamentably dishonest group that history has known.'[18]

15
The Soviet Union and the Spanish Republic

During October 1936 the nationalists concentrated their best forces on the renewed attack towards the capital from the south-west. Their relentless advance made it look as if the Spanish Republic was mortally stricken, but the defence of Madrid soon became a rallying call throughout Europe to all those who feared and hated the triumphant forces of 'international fascism'. The communist slogan that 'Madrid will be the grave of fascism' was powerfully emotive and the battle for the capital was to help the party to power. From 38,000 members in the spring of 1936, the Communist Party was to increase to 200,000 by the end of the year and 300,000 by March 1937.[1]

The Spanish Communist Party was ordered by the Comintern leaders, Dmitri Manuilski and Georgi Dimitrov, to collaborate in the defeat of the rebellion and the defence of a democratic and independent Spanish Republic. This strategy, decided at the time that the Soviet Union was joining the Non-Intervention Committee, conformed to various political objectives: first, to combat the impression that Spain was undergoing a revolution to install a communist regime; second, to counter the claim of their enemy, relying on outside help, that theirs was a national movement; third, to try to reconcile Leninism with the traditional idea of Spanish liberalism.[2]

Nevertheless, the situation was hardly encouraging. The military position became worse day by day. Madrid appeared doomed after the defeat at Talavera while Bilbao was threatened after the loss of Irún and San Sebastián. The republicans had still not managed to take Oviedo, they had failed at Toledo and the anarchists' offensive against Saragossa had come to a halt. They managed to hold on north of Madrid in the Sierra de Guadarrama, but that, like all republican successes, was purely a defensive action.

These setbacks and the strong German and Italian support

for the nationalists made Dimitrov, the secretary-general of the Comintern, consider intervention by the Soviet Union. On 28 August he wrote in his diary: 'The question of aiding the Spanish (possible organization of an international corps).' On 3 September he wrote: 'The situation in Spain is critical.' And on 14 September he noted: 'Organize help for the Spanish (in a covert form).'[3]

For some years, the question of Soviet intervention in the Spanish Civil War has been polarized between two schematic versions: it was either a Comintern strategy to establish a Soviet regime serving the orders of Moscow, or on the other hand a heroic USSR, motherland of the proletariat, disinterestedly helping the legally constituted Republic. Neither of these two conflicting interpretations is correct, but the latter is definitely further from the rather complicated truth.[4]

Since the 1920s the Soviet presence in Spain had increased, mainly in the form of cultural propaganda. The Comintern had done no more than it had in other Western countries: infiltrate and wait. On receiving news of the *coup d'état* of 18 July 1936, the Comintern had gathered as much information as possible from its principal agents, especially the Argentinian Vittorio Codovilla, who had been the Spanish Communist Party's controller since 1932, while the Soviet authorities considered their position. Stalin, as we have seen, did not come to a decision to intervene until September, two months after the rising. Only then did the Soviet regime consider the possibilities of exploiting the conflict and gaining domestic and international support. The Politburo in Moscow ordered huge demonstrations to be organized while the Comintern initiated an international campaign. Soviet citizens contributed 274 million roubles (approximately £11,416,000) for humanitarian purposes in republican Spain.[5]

The Soviet government sent Mikhail Koltsov, the most famous *Pravda* correspondent, to Spain, followed by two film-makers, Roman Karmen and Boris Makadeev. Three weeks after their arrival newsreels from the Spanish front were being screened in Moscow cinemas and articles were published almost on a daily basis in the Soviet press. On 21 August the Soviet government appointed Marcel Rosenberg ambassador in Madrid, and a month later the old bolshevik who led the assault on the Winter Palace, Vladimir Antonov-Ovseyenko, as consul-general in Barcelona. In the meantime Ilya Ehrenburg, the correspondent of *Izvestia*, kept

Rosenberg informed on the conflict of Catalan politics and Companys's complaints against the central government. The Politburo also appointed Jacob Gaikis to the embassy secretariat and Artur Stashevsky as commercial attaché.

Among the military advisers were General Jan Berzin ('Grishin'), Vladimir E. Gorev ('Sancho') as military attaché, Nikolai Kuznetsov ('Kolya') as naval attaché and Yakov Smushkevich ('Duglas') as air force adviser. The majority of the senior military men in Spain were from Soviet military intelligence, the GRU. The Soviet embassy was set up in the Hotel Palace until eight weeks later when it followed the government to Valencia. The Comintern sent its own team, with Palmiro Togliatti ('Ercole' or 'Alfredo'), the leader of the Italian Communist Party in exile and one of the chief influences on Comintern decision making. He later became the main adviser to the Spanish Communist Party. The Hungarian Erno Gerö ('Pedro') performed a similar role with the PSUC in Barcelona. The most terrifying adviser to come to Spain was Aleksandr Orlov, the representative of the People's Commissariat for Internal Affairs, the NKVD, who was to take charge of the secret police.[6]

At first, the French Communist Party and its leaders provided the main source of communication for the Comintern's directives. Soon, communications on arms shipments, reports from GRU officers and Soviet military advisers were radioed either in the morning or in the evening direct to a transmitter in the Sparrow Hills next to what is now Moscow University.[7]

The government of Largo Caballero approved on 16 September the establishment of an embassy in Moscow. Five days later the socialist doctor Marcelino Pascua, who spoke Russian and had visited the Soviet Union to study public health, was named ambassador. Dr Pascua was received in Moscow with great ceremony and deference, and allowed access to Stalin. On the other hand the republican government did nothing to make Pascua's task easy.[8]

The Soviet authorities knew from their intelligence service, the NKVD, and from Comintern representatives of the critical situation in which the Republic found itself towards the end of August. The secretary-general of the French Communist Party, Maurice Thorez, presented a report on 16 September to the Comintern outlining the Republic's lack of a regular army and chain of command. On 22 September Codovilla called for 'arms above everything else'. As a result, Soviet military intelligence prepared a contingency plan for military assistance and the organization of a GRU group to carry it out. It was completed on 24 September and bore the codename Operation X. Kliment Voroshilov, the minister of defence and an old crony of Stalin's from the Russian civil war, informed the Kremlin ten days later that the sale had been prepared for 80 to 100 T-26 tanks, based on a Vickers model, and 50 to 60 fighters. Stalin gave his approval.[9]

More important than the quantity of armaments sent was their quality. This varied enormously. Rifles and field guns were often in a bad state and obsolete. One batch of guns of Tsarist vintage was known as 'the battery of Catherine the Great'. The ten different sorts of rifles came from eight countries and required rounds of six different calibres. Many of them had been captured during the First World War and some of them were 50 years old.[10] The T-26 and later BT-5 tanks, on the other hand, were entirely modern and better than the opposing German models. The aircraft, although modern by Soviet standards, were soon out-fought and out-flown by the new German aircraft which came into service the following year.

The main barrier to achieving the best use of all this matériel came from the sectarianism of the communists, who jealously kept it for the use of their own forces. Regimental commanders were sometimes forced to become members of the Communist Party to ensure that their men received ammunition and medical care. The advisers, especially the tank commander General Pavlov ('Pablito') and the air force adviser Smushkevich, took all the decisions, often without consulting their Spanish colleagues. Prieto, the minister for air, found that the Soviet advisers and the senior Spanish air force officer, Colonel Hidalgo de Cisneros y López de Montenegro, an aristocrat with strong communist leanings, would not even tell him which airfields were being used, or how many aircraft were serviceable. Prieto's fellow socialist, Luis Araquistáin, said that the real minister of air was the Russian general.

This was no exaggeration. One report back to Moscow clearly demonstrates that Smushkevich, or 'Duglas' as he was known, controlled the republican air force completely. 'The Department is headed by Colonel Cisneros. [He is] a very honest and strong-willed officer who enjoys a great authority both in aviation and in governmental circles, and is a friend of the Soviet Union. There is no doubt that at this moment he lacks both theoretical knowledge and tactical experience to lead the air force on his own. He realizes this and accepts our help with honesty and gratitude. S[mushkevich] as the Chief Adviser has established the best possible relations with him ... It can be said quite clearly that while remaining officially in the position of an adviser, Smushkevich is in fact the commander of all of the air force.'[11]

One of the most important issues of the Spanish Civil War is the payment of Soviet aid with the gold reserves of Banco de España.[12] Spain at the time had the fourth largest gold reserves in the world, due mainly to the commercial boom during the First World War. It would appear that Artur Stashevsky, the Russian economist, was the one who suggested to the minister of finance, Dr Juan Negrín, the idea of keeping 'a current account in gold' in Moscow. Madrid was threatened by the advance of the Army of Africa and this arrangement could be used to buy arms and raw materials.[13] The gold would be converted into foreign exchange through the Banque Commerciale pour l'Europe du Nord, or Eurobank in Paris (both part of the Kremlin's financial organization in France).

On 24 July Giral had authorized the first despatch of gold, in this case to Paris, to pay for armament purchases in France. When the Non-Intervention Committee began its work, gold was still sent until March 1937 in order to buy arms from other sources. Altogether 174 tons of gold (27.4 per cent of the total Spanish reserves) went to France.[14]

On 13 September 1936 the council of ministers authorized Negrín to transfer the remaining gold and silver from the Banco de España to Moscow. Two days later 10,000 crates full of precious metal left the Atocha station and reached the magazines of La Algameca in the port of Cartagena on 17 September. Another 2,200 cases were sent to Marseilles and the rest, 7,800 cases, was shipped to Moscow via Odessa. This consignment was accompanied by NKVD personnel and guarded by a detachment of *carabineros*. On reaching Odessa the 173rd NKVD Rifle Regiment took over guard duties.[15] These 510 tons of precious metals were worth at least $518 million at 1936 values.[16] One of the first bills the Republic had to pay with the gold amounted to $51,160,168. It was for the 'fraternal military support' already provided.[17]

It is very hard to judge the Soviet method of accounting when they calculated what the Republic owed for arms and other expenses, such as shipping and the training of republican troops and specialists. Nothing was free and many charges appear to have been exaggerated to say the least. The Soviet Union claimed that with the credits it provided in 1938 (after the current account in gold had been exhausted, according to their calculations), the Republic had received $661 million worth of goods and services, yet only $518 million in gold had been sent to Moscow. But the Soviet figure does not reveal the creative accounting which took place when changing gold into roubles, and roubles into dollars, and dollars into pesetas. At a time when the rouble–dollar exchange rate was fixed at 5.3:1, the Soviet Union was using the figure of 2.5:1, a difference which netted it a very considerable profit.

When news leaked out of the transfer of the gold reserves to Paris and Moscow, the value of the republican peseta collapsed on the foreign exchanges, falling by half between November and December. The cost of imports became a terrible burden for an already battered economy and the cost of living shot up.[18]

Negrín's role at this time was important for future developments. While organizing the despatch of the gold to Moscow, he became extremely close to Stashevsky, a Pole sent by Moscow as the Soviet economic attaché. Stashevsky immediately recognized that Negrín was more than just somebody the Soviet Union could trust. Negrín believed fervently in the centralization of political power and that also meant economic power. 'Our opinion', Stashevsky reported to Moscow, 'is that everything possible has to be done to support the concentration of all the exports and imports – i.e. all foreign currency operations – in the same hands.'[19]

Both Negrín and Stashevsky were furious with the Generalitat and the anarchists in Catalonia for taking financial affairs into their own hands. 'Catalonians are seizing without any control hundreds of millions of pesetas from the branch of the Banco de España,' Stashevsky reported to Moscow.[20] In their view the fact that the central government had done nothing to help Catalan industry was irrelevant. They also hated the Soviet consul-general in Barcelona, Antonov-Ovseyenko, who clearly sympathized with Companys and got on well with the anarchist leader García Oliver. 'García Oliver does not object to the unified leadership or to discipline in battle,' Antonov-Ovseyenko recorded, 'but he is against the restoration of the permanent status of officers, this foundation of militarism. It is with obvious pleasure that he listens to me when I express agreement with his military plan.'[21]

Antonov-Ovseyenko also noted the comments of the Esquerra minister, Jaume Miravitlles: 'Anarcho-syndicalists are becoming more and more cautious in their management of industry. They have given up their idea of introducing egalitarianism in large enterprises.' Antonov-Ovseyenko, the old bolshevik leader, had become an associate of Trotsky and a member of the left opposition, but his abject statement that August, confessing his faults and condemning his former comrades, did not save him from Stalinist suspicion.[22] He may well have been one of those functionaries sent to Spain as a way of preparing their downfall later. The old bolshevik completely failed to see the danger he was in. He asked Soviet advisers and the central government to support an offensive in Catalonia. On 6 October 1936 the consul-general sent a detailed report to Rosenberg, the Soviet ambassador in Spain: 'Our view of anarchism in Catalonia is an erroneous one ... The government is really willing to organize defence and it is doing a lot in that direction, for example they are setting up a general staff headed by a clever specialist instead of the former committee of anti-fascist militias.' His words were ignored. Comintern propaganda regarded Catalonia and Aragón as 'the kingdom of the Spanish Makhnovist faction'. And since it had been the Red Army which had destroyed the Makhnovist anarchists in the Ukraine, Antonov-Ovseyenko should have seen the warning signs.[23]

He then moved into the realm of international relations, supporting the Generalitat's contacts with Moroccans, and promising them independence for the colony in the hope of creating an uprising in Franco's recruiting ground. 'Two weeks ago', he reported to Moscow, 'a delegation of the national committee of Morocco, which can be trusted because it has a lot of influence among the tribes of Spanish Morocco, started negotiations with the Committee of the Anti-Fascist Militias. The Moroccans would immediately start an uprising if the republican government guaranteed that Morocco would become an independent state if it succeeded and also on the condition that Moroccans would immediately receive financial support. The Catalan committee is inclined to sign such an agreement and sent a special delegation to Madrid ten days ago. Caballero didn't express an opinion and suggested that the Moroccan delegation negotiates directly with [the central government].'[24] Although such a move was considered by the central government and the Spanish Communist Party, this démarche was angrily rejected by Moscow. The last thing Stalin wanted was to provoke France, whose own colony in Morocco might be encouraged to revolt, and to give the British the impression that communists were stirring up worldwide revolution.

Antonov-Ovseyenko appears to have been doomed by the criticisms of Stashevsky and Negrín. This came to a head the following February when Antonov-Ovseyenko 'showed himself to be a very ardent defender of Catalonia'. Negrín remarked that he was 'more Catalonian than the Catalans themselves'. Antonov-Ovseyenko retorted that he was 'a revolutionary, not a bureaucrat'. Negrín declared in reply that he was going to resign because he regarded the statement by the consul as political mistrust and while he was ready 'to fight the Basques and Catalans, he did not want to fight the USSR'. Stashevsky reported all this to Moscow (one even wonders whether he and Negrín provoked Antonov-Ovseyenko on purpose) and the consul-general's days were numbered.[25]

As a result of the reports from Spain expressing total frustration with Largo Caballero's determination to thwart communist power in the army, the Kremlin was looking for 'a strong and loyal' politician who would be able to control events internally, impress the bourgeois democracies, especially Britain and France, and put an end to the 'outrages committed by some of the provinces'. Stashevsky had already seen Negrín as the ideal candidate. In late 1936 he reported to Moscow: 'The finance minister has a great deal of common sense and is quite close to us.'[26] But although Stashevsky's advice was followed, he was to suffer the same fate as Antonov-Ovseyenko. In June 1937 he, Berzin and Antonov-Ovseyenko were all recalled to Moscow where they were executed. Stashevsky's great mistake was to have complained in April 1937 about the vicious activities of the NKVD in Spain, a curious blunder from one so politically aware.

16

The International Brigades and the Soviet Advisers

During the Spanish Civil War the Comintern was best known for having created the International Brigades. Although the exact origin of the idea remains uncertain, it came with the first calls for international support for the Spanish Republic – a form of solidarity, it was felt, which should have a military dimension.[1] On 3 August the Comintern approved a first resolution in general terms, no doubt waiting for a clear signal from the conspicuously silent Kremlin. Only on 18 September, after Stalin had made up his mind, did the secretariat dictate a resolution on 'the campaign of support in the struggle of the Spanish people', of which point No. 7 read: 'proceed to the recruitment of volunteers with military experience from the workers of all countries, with the purpose of sending them to Spain'.[2]

A meeting was then held in Paris when Eugen Fried ('Clément') presented the instructions which he had brought from Moscow. Maurice Thorez and the other leaders of the French Communist Party were to organize the recruitment and training of volunteers destined to fight fascism in Spain. Communist Parties and organizations, such as Red Help International, Friends of the Soviet Union, Rot Front, la Confédération Générale du Travail, the Paix et Liberté movement and the various local committees to aid the Spanish Republic organized by the Soviet intelligence officer Walter Krivitsky, from The Hague, were all to play their part.[3]

In Spain there were already several hundred foreign volunteers. Most had just arrived in Barcelona for the People's Olympiad when the rising took place. A number of them volunteered to form the first nucleus of the International Brigades, the *centuria* Thaelmann, then attached to the PSUC in Catalonia. This unit was led by Hans Beimler, a member of the central committee of the German Communist Party and a deputy in the Reichstag. After Hitler's seizure of power, Beimler had been locked up in Dachau, from where he had managed to escape, reaching Barcelona on 5 August 1936. During the course of the whole civil war between 32,000 and 35,000 men from 53 different countries served in the ranks of the International Brigades.[4] Another 5,000 foreigners served outside, mostly attached to the CNT or the POUM.

The main recruitment centre chosen for the International Brigades was Paris, where volunteers were organized by leaders of the French and Italian Communist Parties. André Marty, a leader of the PCF and a member of the executive committee of the Comintern, had Luigi Longo ('Gallo'), who had been in Spain during the rising, as his second in command. Giuseppe di Vittorio ('Nicoletti') became head of the commissars. Another key figure was Josip Broz ('Tito'), who was also in Paris. The Comintern claimed publicly that the International Brigades consisted of a wide group of spontaneous volunteers, democrats and anti-fascists. It denied that young communists had been ordered to Paris as part of an organized recruitment. Towards the end of the 1960s Moscow admitted that in September 1936 the Comintern had decided to infiltrate 'volunteers with military experience to send them to fight in Spain'.[5] Esmond Romilly, the young nephew of Winston Churchill who enlisted in the International Brigades, wrote that French communists reprimanded those who shouted '*Vive les Soviets!*'.[6]

With right-wing dictatorships forming a belt from Hamburg to Taranto, it required careful organization to bring the East Europeans to Spain. Poles in exile from their country's military regime started to arrive in Paris, together with Hungarians fleeing from Admiral Horthy's dictatorship and Romanians escaping from the Iron Guard. Yugoslavs avoiding the royalist police came along Tito's 'secret railway'. Even White Russians, hoping that service with the Brigades would allow them to return home, joined the mass of East European exiles. Most of them had a hard and painful journey before reaching their destination. 'Often on foot, across fields and mountains, sleeping in the open, hidden in coal tenders or in the bilges of a ship, they managed to get through police control points and frontiers to reach France.'[7] Volunteers from North America did not arrive until much later. The first detachment from the United States left New York on Christmas Day and the Lincoln Battalion saw action in the battle of the Jarama in February 1937.

The story of the International Brigades later became distorted in many ways, not simply from the propaganda motive of exaggerating their role out of all proportion to that of Spanish formations. An impression arose, especially in Great Britain and America, that they consisted of middle-class intellectuals and ideological Beau Gestes such as Ralph Fox, John Cornford, Julian Bell and Christopher Caudwell, who were all killed in action. This came about partly because the intellectual minority was newsworthy and partly because they were articulate and had ready access to publishers afterwards.

In fact, almost 80 per cent of the volunteers from Great Britain were manual workers who either left their jobs or had been unemployed. Photographs of them show scrubbed faces with self-conscious expressions, short hair, cloth caps clutched in hand and Sunday suits with boots. Some of them were glad to escape the apathy of unemployment, others had already been fighting Mosley's fascists in street battles, as their French equivalents had fought Action Française and the Croix de Feu. But most had little notion of what warfare really meant. Slightly over half of them were Communist Party members. Jason Gurney of the British battalion described the drawing power of the Party in the 1930s: 'Its real genius was to provide a world where lost and lonely people could feel important.' Interminable, deeply serious meetings at branch level gave members a feeling of being involved in 'the march of History'.[8] Yet all the time they were made eager to have the responsibility and effort of original thought taken from them. Slogans in 'pidgin agit-prop', as Victor Serge termed it, became an inwardly soothing mantra despite the outward protest.

George Orwell later attacked the left's intellectual dishonesty in the apparently effortless switch from pacifism to 'romantic warmongering': 'Here were the very people who for twenty years had hooted and jeered at the "glory" of war, atrocity stories, at patriotism, even at physical courage, coming out with stuff that with the alteration of a few names would have fitted into the *Daily Mail* of 1918. The same people who in 1933 sniggered pityingly if you said that in certain circumstances you would fight for your country, in 1937 were denouncing you as a Trotskyist-Fascist if you suggested that the stories in *New Masses* about freshly wounded men clamouring to get back into the fighting might be exaggerated.'[9]

In their own countries some young middle-class idealists were ill at ease with workers and perhaps wary of the way their earnest social potholing could risk derision. Like Marx before them, they had often despaired of England's 'bourgeois' proletariat. The Spanish proletariat, on the other hand, had never respected or aped their social superiors. Even in the eighteenth century foreign travellers were amazed at the cavalier way Spanish servants and labourers treated their aristocracy. Also, the fact that the Andalucian peasant had never been crushed by the seizure of the common land or contained by religion meant that the Spanish working class could be romanticized in a way which their own working class seemed to thwart. Consequently, the Spanish conflict offered Anglo-Saxon intellectuals a breath of pure and uncloseted emotion in comparison to the suffocating complacency at home. Middle-class guilt feelings and an urge to sublimate a privileged identity in the mass struggle made many of these intellectuals ideal recruits for communist authority.

There were, perhaps, many volunteers who went to Spain partly in search of excitement, but the selflessness of the International Brigaders' motives cannot be doubted. They saw fascism as an international threat, and the Brigades appeared to offer the best way of fighting it. Spain was seen as the battleground which would decide the future. This belief was maintained long afterwards, so that even to this day there are those who argue that a republican victory would have prevented the Second World War.

Paris was the marshalling yard for volunteers of all nationalities. The secret networks directed them there from eastern, central and south-eastern Europe. From the north, British workers without passports crossed the channel on excursion tickets. On arrival at the Gare du Nord, left-wing taxi drivers drove them to the reception centres in the 9th Arrondissement. Almost every day, young men, brown paper parcels under their arms, could be seen waiting for the Perpignan train at the Gare d'Austerlitz, conspicuously trying to look inconspicuous.

Once safely on the train, they would fraternize with those whose glances they had just been avoiding so studiously. Wine was passed round, food shared and the 'Internationale' sung endlessly. The two principal routes were either to Marseilles, where they were smuggled on to ships for Barcelona or Valencia, or else to Perpignan and then over the Pyrenees at night. Some anarchists, who still controlled the Pyrenean frontier, wanted to turn them back. Their argument was that weapons were needed, not men, but their main fear was that a communist-controlled 'Foreign Legion' was being built up to crush them later.[10] In the fields peasants straightened up to watch the young foreigners pass, singing, in their trains or lorries. The reaction to them was warmest in the towns, where most of the population, especially the children, cheered them and gave the clenched-fist salute. In Barcelona the welcome was unstinted despite the misgivings of the libertarian movement.

On 12 October the steamer *Ciudad de Barcelona* reached Alicante with the first 500 volunteers who had embarked two days earlier in Marseilles. They then boarded a train which took them to Albacete, the base chosen for the International Brigades. Their barracks in the Calle de la Libertad had been seized from the Civil Guard after the rising.

The barracks where many of the nationalist defenders had been killed was used as the induction centre. It was in a disgusting state until a party of German communists cleaned it out thoroughly. Hygiene was a problem, especially for those who were weakened by the malnutrition of unemployment. Certainly the rations of beans in oil contributed to the dysentery suffered by the British working-class volunteers who, like the Canadians and Americans, were unused to foreign food. As soon as they arrived, the German communists put up a large slogan in their quarters proclaiming 'We Exalt Discipline', while the French posted precautions against venereal disease. (With the lack of antibiotics, the latter was to take almost as heavy a toll as in the militias.)

In Albacete, the Brigaders were given their initial indoctrination and issued with 'uniforms' – often either woolly Alpine hats or khaki berets, ski jerkins, breeches, long thick socks and ill-fitting boots. Some found themselves in army surplus uniforms from the First World War, and the Americans later turned up almost entirely kitted out as 'doughboys'. It was rare to find anything that fitted satisfactorily. Senior Party cadres and commissars were conspicuously different. They favoured black leather jackets, dark-blue berets, and a Sam Browne belt with a heavy 9mm automatic pistol. This last item was the great status symbol of the Party functionary.

The recruits were lined up on the parade ground for an address by André Marty, the Brigades' controller who had earlier brought the French volunteers over the border during the fighting at Irún. Marty, a squat man with white moustache, drooping jowl and outsize beret, had made his name in the 1919 mutiny of the French

Black Sea fleet. The heroic legend woven around him in Party mythology made him one of the most powerful figures in the Comintern. Almost nobody dared challenge his authority. At that time he was starting to develop a conspiracy complex that rivalled Stalin's. Influenced by the show trials in Moscow, he became convinced that 'Fascist-Trotskyist' spies were everywhere, and that it was his duty to exterminate them. Although Marty did not order the executions of as many as 500 Brigadiers, as he was alleged to have claimed, he certainly helped to create an atmosphere in which summary execution by commanders played a terrifying part.[11]

The organizational committee of the International Brigades transformed itself on 26 October into a military council, which included Vital Gayman ('Vidal') and Carlos Contreras as well as General Walter. Constancia de la Mora, the niece of the conservative prime minister Antonio Maura and the wife of the communist commander of the republican air force, Hidalgo de Cisneros, acted as interpreter. The military council installed itself in a villa on the outskirts of the town and André Marty requisitioned other buildings in Albacete. The Brigades' military commander was General 'Kléber' (alias Lazar Stern), a tall, grey-haired Hungarian Jew and veteran of the Red Army, who was later to be shot on Stalin's orders. He had travelled under the name of 'Manfred Stern' on a Canadian passport faked by the NKVD.[12]

The parade ground at Albacete was used for drill, after which battalion commissars gave the volunteers long lectures on 'why we are fighting'. These talks were followed by group discussions, used by the commissars to introduce 'ideas' which were then 'discussed and voted upon democratically'. The International Brigades followed the 5th Regiment in introducing the saluting of officers. 'A salute is a sign that a comrade who has been an egocentric individualist in private life has adjusted to the collective way of getting things done. A salute is proof that our Brigade is on its way from being a collection of well-meaning amateurs to a precision implement for eliminating fascists.'[13]

Such meetings and 'democratic procedures' provided tempting targets for the iconoclasts to mock, but these light-hearted jokers were marked down by the commissars. They were likely to be the first suspected of 'Trotskyist-Fascist leanings'. Other sceptics, especially the old sweats from the Great War, were bitterly critical of the 'training'. Most of the volunteers were very unfit, as well as ignorant of the most elementary military skills. As one of the veterans remarked, they were not preparing to go over the top with *Das Kapital* in their hands.

Marty told the volunteers that 'when the first International Brigade goes into action, they will be properly trained men with good rifles, a well-equipped corps'. This was all part of the Party's myth of the professional, when in fact sheer courage, bolstered by the belief that the world depended on them, had to make up for appalling deficiencies in the Brigaders' basic training. Men who were to be sent against the Army of Africa had to project the aura of experts to impress the militias, but they could do little except form ranks, march and turn. Many of them had never even handled a rifle until they were on the way to the front, and the few Great War veterans had to show them how to load their obsolete weapons of varied calibres. From a box of assorted ammunition, inexperienced soldiers had to find the right bullets to fit their rifles. The number of jammed weapons through wedged and separated casings was predictably high.

The militias had suffered from similar disadvantages, but they had no pretensions to being an elite force arriving in the nick of time to save the situation. Nevertheless, the foreign innocents, who felt a 'moment of awe' on being handed a rifle, had several advantages over the Spanish militiamen on first going into battle. They had a slightly greater knowledge and understanding of modern military technology, they understood the value of trenches and, most important of all, they had men in their ranks who 'had been through it before'. Spain's neutrality in the Great War made the first shock of battle much more traumatic to the militia.

The Soviet authorities did everything they could to camouflage the number of Red Army personnel in Spain, even making some of them enlist as volunteers in the International Brigades. The most obvious examples were the commanders, Kléber, Gal, Čopić and Walter, while in the Polish Dombrowski Battalion there was a significant nucleus of Red Army officers. Altogether 30 Soviet officers were sent to Spain as commanders in the International Brigades.[14] The Palafox Battalion appears to have had an even larger Soviet contingent than most. It was commanded by a Major Tkachev ('Palafox'), most of the four companies were commanded by Red Army lieutenants and many of the men, it would appear, were Soviet citizens. 'There was all sorts of nationalities in it,' wrote one member in the official account, 'such as Jews, Poles, Ukrainians, Belorussians, Lithuanians, etc.'[15] In addition, a training centre for International Brigade officers was set up in Tiflis with a capacity for 60 infantry officers and 200 pilots.[16] The Soviet military advisers were ordered to keep out of range of artillery fire (*podalshe ot artillereiskogo ognia*), so that captured officers could not be paraded in front of the Non-Intervention Committee.

Although it is hard to establish exactly the number of Soviet personnel who served in the Spanish Civil War, it is clear from documents that there were never more than 800 present at any one time. The total appears to have been a maximum of 2,150, of whom 600 were non-combatant, including interpreters. There were, in addition, between 20 and 40 members of the NKVD and between 20 and 25 diplomats. Altogether, 189 were reported killed or missing: 129 officers, 43 NCOs and 17 soldiers.[17]

On 16 October, in a coded telegram, Voroshilov, the People's Commissar for Defence, ordered Gorev to 'send advisers to work in divisions and brigades'.[18] The vain Voroshilov, who adopted the codename of 'The Master' for Operation X, was eager to impress Stalin. He hoped, while sitting in his office in Moscow with a map of Spain, to control events on the ground thousands of kilometres away.[19] Advisers, exasperated by his interference, started to refer to him ironically as 'the great strategist'. Voroshilov started sending messages to Madrid telling the chief military adviser to 'use his brains and display some will-power, so that the situation would start looking different'.[20] He also threatened the most senior advisers that 'if the aforementioned instruction is not implemented [on the concentration of forces to attack on the Madrid front], strict disciplinary measures will be taken against all of you'.[21]

The trouble was that many of the advisers were so junior that they had as little experience of command as the Spanish officers they were supposed to advise. Colonel (later Marshal) R. Malinovsky ('Malino') wrote that advisers to some divisional commanders were 'very good lieutenants, wonderful commanders of companies or squadrons, but, of course, were not ready to command a division – and how could one offer advice on something that one has no idea about?'[22] Some advisers were extremely undiplomatic in the way they worked with republican officers and 'rudely interfered in the operational orders given by the commanders'.[23]

Soviet advisers, however, were soon complaining bitterly in their reports back to Moscow about the incompetence and inertia with which they had to deal. 'Sometimes my hands itch to take some of these bastards out of their offices and stand them up against a wall,' wrote General Berzin to Voroshilov. 'Such unpunished, unbridled sabotage of necessary measures, such sloppiness and irresponsibility as reign here in the general staff and in the bureaucracy of the administration at the front, I could never have imagined before. People simply do not carry out the orders of the war ministry, or they do the opposite and calmly continue to stay where they are.'[24]

One of the main problems in the relationship between Soviet personnel and their Spanish allies stemmed from a clash of very different cultures, political as well as social. Soviet soldiers had never had the opportunity to mix with foreigners, especially with ones who disagreed with Stalinist policy, and this was clearly a shock. A commissar with a Soviet tank battalion reported that the first 'specific feature of the local situation which we had failed to take into account' was the fact that 'people around us belong to different political parties'. Another problem was the 'practice of a completely open consumption of alcohol (wine is served with meals)'. Perhaps predictably, a number of Soviet advisers tended to over-exploit the opportunity. An aviation commissar reported that alcohol 'was also a great threat' for the Soviet pilots. 'A local tradition is to drink wine with meals. There is always a lot of wine in our canteens. At first, our men got carried away.'

The tank battalion commissar was also shocked by the existence of legalized brothels in republican Spain. 'I have to mention that it took a while for a number of our comrades to understand how disgraceful it is to visit brothels. About twenty men have visited prostitutes without permission before 3 December. After the party collective stopped these visits to brothels, discipline has changed dramatically for the better.' Clearly few precautions were taken, since 22 men were infected with venereal diseases. He also reported on a 'carefree and offensive attitude towards women: Morkevich, a Komsomol member and commander of a tank, offered 200 pesetas to one woman, who refused and reported this to the Antifascist Women's Committee'.[25]

The small detachment of Soviet naval advisers, led by Kuznetsov, had one overriding priority. It was to organize the safe arrival of ships bringing armaments and ammunition from the Soviet Union. Each vessel was identified by a cypher, consisting of Y followed by a number, and given a different route. Those leaving the Crimea would pass through the Dardanelles, then find an island in the Aegean to carry out a superficial refit to change identity, including the name of the ship and flag of convenience. A fake funnel or superstructure would be added to camouflage the ship's profile. Some pretended to carry tourists, with members of the crew strolling around in hats and pretending to take photographs. The captain was instructed to avoid crossing dangerous stretches in daylight.

Once into the central Mediterranean, the Y ships would keep close to the coast of Africa. They turned north towards Cartagena only when level with Algeria. The most dangerous part of the journey came towards the end, with Italian submarines as well as aircraft patrolling the blockade area. When 48 hours from their destination, Kuznetsov's staff, who had been tracking the progress of each ship, arranged for Spanish republican warships to escort them in.[26]

One young Soviet sailor was clearly fired up with his mission, to judge by the poem he wrote:

> I am a brave sailor from the Red Navy
> I am exactly twenty years old.
> I am sailing out into the vast expanse of the sea
> To bring the Great October to the whole of the world.
>
> Oh, our noise and uproar,
> Resound against the bourgeois shores,
> Our Soviet fleet is the stronghold.
> All the working people, forward![27]

The first ship with Soviet military supplies to reach Spain was the *Campeche*, which berthed in Cartagena on 4 October 1936. The second ship, the Soviet vessel *Komsomol*, reached Cartagena eight days later with the first shipment of T-26 tanks. These two shiploads arrived just in time to play a major part in the imminent battle for Madrid.

17
The Battle for Madrid

The success of the Army of Africa in putting to flight the militias had greatly raised the optimism of the nationalists and the expectations of their allies. Reports were sent to Germany that Madrid had no food reserves, no anti-aircraft defences and no fortifications. The militia were badly armed with old rifles of varying calibres and they had few machine-guns that worked. The republican fighters and bombers, consisting mainly of French Dewoitines and Potez, were no match for the Heinkel and Fiat fighters. It was the combination of artillery fire and air attacks which had completely demoralized the militia columns. Even many regular officers began to shake uncontrollably when they heard aero engines.

It is often forgotten that the Spanish metropolitan army had no battle experience and the majority of its officers had not handled troops even on manoeuvres. This lack of training, as much as the instinctive dislike which most officers felt for the militia system, contributed to the chaotic retreat of the republican forces from Estremadura. As headquarters' staff frequently retreated without attempting to warn their forward units, it was not surprising that militia groups, feeling abandoned, should make a run for it before they were cut off. In fact, with communications virtually non-existent, a formalized command structure could not have co-ordinated the different sectors, even if it had been run efficiently. General Carlos Masquelet attempted to establish defences close to Madrid, with four concentric defence lines, roughly ten kilometres apart. They were not continuous, but concentrated on the most important road junctions.[1]

The nationalist advance on the capital started at the end of the first week of October. The Army of Africa began a three-pronged attack: northwards from Toledo, north-eastwards along the Navalcarnero road and eastwards from San Martín de Valdeiglesias.

Mola was given official command of the Madrid operation, which appears to have been a calculated ploy by Franco, in case anything went wrong,[2] while Colonel Varela was in command of the colonial troops. Yagüe was back with the Army of Africa, but in a subordinate position. The columns, composed of around 10,000 men each, were commanded by Lieutenant-Colonels Carlos Asensio, Fernando Barrón, Heli Rolando de Tella, Delgado Serrano, and Major Castejón while Colonel Monasterio commanded the cavalry. The left flank of the attack was strengthened by 10,000 men from Mola's army, made up of Carlist *requetés*, Falangist militia and regular soldiers. The plan was for the nationalist forces to enter the capital on 12 October, the day of the Feast of the Spanish Race. Mola claimed that he would drink a cup of coffee that day on the Gran Vía and, although the attack on Madrid was delayed, even Franco's staff began to prepare for a triumphal entry. The seemingly inevitable capture of Madrid would not only mean a crushing psychological blow to the republicans. It should guarantee belligerent rights, if not de facto recognition, from foreign powers.

After Navalcarnero on the north-east axis had fallen, Illescas on the Toledo road was occupied on 19 October. Torrejón, also on the Toledo road and some 30 kilometres from the capital, was taken several days later. The nationalists were not alone in believing that Madrid would fall to them rapidly. Foreign journalists and diplomats were sure that the advance of the Army of Africa, backed by squadrons of the Luftwaffe and Italian air force, could not be stopped. The Republic's administration seemed paralysed by a strange mixture of frantic activity and inertia. Many blamed 'sabotage by reactionary civil servants', but however true, such charges did little more than divert attention from the government's own chaos.

In the second half of October Largo Caballero began to issue decrees extending mobilization in an effort to improve Madrid's defences; yet for much of the capital's population the war still seemed remote. Militiamen, criticized for being on 'excessive guard duty' in the capital rather than at the front, tended to ignore official communiqués. Nor could the prime minister himself forget old rivalries. He refused to assign UGT construction workers to the digging of trenches in case they defected to the CNT. And yet the speed of the nationalist advance was such that on 18 October, when Caballero had tried to telephone the republican commander in Illescas, he had found himself talking to the nationalist commander who had just occupied the town.

Of the government decrees issued at this time, the one on 18 October was to have the most far-reaching effect. This announced the establishment of 'mixed brigades' of 4,000 men each. Although not implemented immediately, it marked the first major step away from militia columns towards a formalized army. The brigades were to consist of four battalions, with supporting artillery.[3] A few days later, XI and XII International Brigades were formed at Albacete under the command of Kléber and Lukács. The Republic soon had 80,000 men under arms, most of whom were to bear the brunt of defending Madrid.

Aleksandr Rodimtsev, one of the key commanders at Stalingrad six years later, described his arrival at the Madrid front at this inauspicious moment. He had come from Albacete by truck. Each time they had stopped on the way, village boys had admired their uniforms and stroked their pistol holsters. There had been an air attack on the convoy, and everyone had jumped out cursing in different languages. In Madrid he had reported to the war ministry, accompanied by an interpreter. He was taken to meet General Pozas, commander of the Army of the Centre, who was about to become a member of the Communist Party. Pozas warned him that discipline was weak in the militias. Soldiers went home from the front on their own accord.

Rodimtsev visited the front and encountered a young woman machine-gunner and anarchist *dinamiteros* festooned with grenades. One of them fired a pistol in the air, demanding to see his documents. Rodimtsev was attached to Líster's brigade and he found its headquarters in an abandoned village. Some of the staff were having a siesta. Others were out in a meadow singing a melancholy song. Their commander came over. 'Líster was stocky and swarthy,' wrote Rodimtsev. 'He had a high protruding forehead, black hair which was long and its ends bleached by the sun. When he smiled, dimples appeared in his cheeks, which made his face look kindly and almost childlike. He said in Russian with a slight accent, "Hello, Pablito. I've been expecting you. I had a telephone call in the morning to say that you had left." He introduced me to his commissar and officers. They clapped me on the shoulder, and shook my hand vigorously. All had a few words of Russian: "Come here. Have a coffee. Have a cigarette."' Líster warned him in a whisper that he must be careful. There were 'people around from the "fifth column"'.[4] The 'fifth column' was a phrase attributed to General Mola, who apparently claimed to a journalist that he had four columns attacking the capital and a 'fifth column' of sympathizers within the city ready to revolt.

The rhythm of the nationalist advance was so fast that on 21 October, three days after reaching Illescas, the column of Heli de Tella, supported by Monasterio's cavalry, occupied Navalcarnero, 30 kilometres from Madrid. The militiamen, faced with Ansaldo light tanks, had fled from their triple line of trenches on the western side of the town.

In his final orders for the attack on Madrid, Franco emphasized the need to concentrate forces to provoke the fall of the city. On 23 October Junkers 52s bombed Getafe and Madrid itself for the first time. 'Everyone who can flee the city is fleeing,' wrote Koltsov in his diary the next day. 'By means fair or foul, all the rich people, all top officials escape. Only four or five correspondents have stayed. The streets are completely dark in the evenings. Everywhere patrols are checking people's passes, and it's become dangerous to drive around unarmed. Aragon arrived suddenly from Paris. He came accompanied by Elsa Triolet.'[5]

Four days later the nationalists took Torrejón de Velasco, Seseña, Torrejón de la Calzada and Griñón. The next day, 28 October, Largo Caballero, in an astonishing radio broadcast designed to boost morale, revealed the republican plans: 'Listen to me, comrades! Tomorrow, 29 October, at dawn, our artillery and our tanks will open fire on the enemy. Then our air force will appear, dropping bombs on them and machine-gunning them. At the moment of the air attack, our tanks will attack the enemy's most vulnerable flank sowing panic in their ranks ... Now we have tanks and aircraft! Forward comrades of the front, heroic sons of the working people! Victory is ours!'[6]

Next morning, as he had said, fifteen T-26 tanks commanded by Captain Pavel Arman of the Red Army attacked Seseña. They were the spearpoint of the first mixed brigade commanded by Líster. Pavel Arman was an adventurous character who, despite his heroism in Spain, later fell foul of the Stalinist authorities and died fighting on the Eastern Front. The crews were mainly made up of Russian instructors, with their Spanish trainees acting as gunners.[7]

Taken by surprise, the nationalist infantry retreated and

Monasterio's cavalry suffered a number of casualties. But a detachment of *regulares*, having made a batch of petrol bombs, managed to knock out three tanks, a fifth of Arman's force. The skirmish was claimed as a victory and Arman was made a Hero of the Soviet Union, but the attack had failed completely because Líster's men could not, or would not, keep up with the tanks. Koltsov, who was present, wanted to find out what had gone wrong. 'Líster was standing by the door of the little house in Valdemoro waiting for the group to return. He explained, a grimace upon his face, that his units had been moving well at first, but after 1,500 metres, they had felt tired and sat down. They began to "get stuck" in little groups among the hills. Once they lost sight of the tanks, the infantry on the main axis stopped, then they moved forward again, reached Seseña and after encountering a rather weak fire there, turned back ... While the tankists were being congratulated, bandaged and fed, they kept asking quietly why the infantry had never caught up with them.'[8]

At the beginning of November Largo Caballero again asked the anarchists to join the government, since they constituted the largest group involved in the fight against the nationalists. The other Popular Front parties supported this attempt to end the anti-state within the state. The only prominent dissenter was President Azaña, whose intense dislike of the anarchists appears to have dated from the Casas Viejas incident, the event which had led to the fall of his first government.

Once again CNT-FAI leaders were faced with a fundamental dilemma. They believed the state could not change its nature, whatever the politics of its leaders; yet they were extremely worried by growing communist strength. Federica Montseny, an FAI intellectual, later explained to the American historian Burnett Bolloten: 'At that time we only saw the reality of the situation created for us: the communists in the government and ourselves outside, the manifold possibilities and all our achievements endangered.'[9]

The CNT-FAI asked for five ministries including those of finance and war so as to protect themselves in the two areas where they felt most vulnerable. They settled, however, for four minor posts: health, which had previously only been a directorate-general, justice, industry and commerce. The 'purists' were persuaded to accept this compromise by the 'reformist' syndicalists, such as

Horacio Prieto, the secretary of the CNT National Committee, Joan Peiró, the new ministry of industry, and Juan López, who took the ministry of commerce. Federica Montseny cast aside misgivings and the warnings of her father to become Spain's first woman minister. García Oliver proved an unconventional minister of justice. Legal fees were abolished and criminal dossiers destroyed.

The CNT-FAI leaders had only just taken up their posts when, on the morning of 6 November, Largo Caballero called a cabinet meeting and stated that the government must move to Valencia. Azaña had already abandoned the capital for Barcelona without warning and most ministers, especially Largo Caballero and Prieto, were convinced that Madrid would fall immediately. It was argued in cabinet that if they were captured, the Republic would have no legal leadership and the rebels would instantly achieve international recognition. (In fact, the fall of the capital alone would have had much the same result and Barajas aerodrome to the east was not threatened if they had wanted to escape at the last moment.) The new CNT-FAI ministers opposed this plan strenuously, saying that the government should not abandon the defenders. But the anarchists were alone in their objections and it was decided that the capital would be ruled by a junta in the absence of the administration.

While the government was preparing to quit the city, the streets were filled with peasants and their livestock. 'Many refugees are moving through Madrid,' noted Koltsov that day. 'They are mostly from villages close to the capital. A big flock of sheep was driven past the "Palace" [Hotel], the parliament buildings and the Castellana. Sheep in the streets and plazas of Madrid surprise no one now.'[10]

General Pozas, the former commander of the Civil Guard and soon a Communist Party member, was given command of the Army of the Centre, while General Miaja was to lead the junta in charge of the capital. The orders to these two generals were put in the wrong envelopes, but luckily they opened them immediately instead of waiting as ordered. Pozas alleged that Miaja nearly wept with rage at what he saw as an attempt to sacrifice him in Madrid.

Meanwhile, on that night of 6 November the government loaded its files on to an enormous convoy of lorries which set off for Valencia. Fears that the Valencia road might be cut at any moment by a nationalist thrust were misplaced; instead the convoy was stopped by CNT militia at Tarancón. For desertion in the face of the enemy, the anarchists arrested Álvarez del Vayo, the foreign minister, General Pozas, Juan López, their own CNT minister, and General Asensio, the under-secretary of war, who was reputed to have discriminated against anarcho-syndicalist militias. They also stopped the Soviet ambassador to tell him what they thought of communism. Eventually Horacio Prieto of the CNT National Committee persuaded the militia to let the convoy pass.

The effect of the government's flight from Madrid was remarkable. The anarchist attitude immediately changed to 'Long live Madrid without government!' and the cry was echoed by others as a new feeling came over the capital. The sense of urgency which had marked the early days of the rising returned. The communists called for the formation of local committees, the very bodies which they had resolutely opposed before. The establishment of the Madrid junta was, in itself, a step back towards the fragmentation of power that had occurred in July. Slogans, which would have been taboo only a few days before, were now on the lips of every communist cadre. The gut instinct of defending the city against 'the fascists and their Moors' stirred the population. The parallel with the defence of Petrograd against the whites in the Russian civil war was repeatedly drawn and cinemas showed films like *Sailors of Kronstadt* and *Battleship Potemkin*. The communist deputy La Pasionaria was tireless in her exhortations to resistance, both on the radio and at mass rallies.

As in Barcelona in July, the decision to defend Madrid inspired mass bravery. The terror and loathing which the colonial troops aroused in the *madrileños* helped turn panic into a spirit of fierce resistance. In the Plaza de Atocha a large placard warned: 'In Badajoz the fascists shot 2,000. If Madrid falls they will shoot half the city.' Chains of women and children passed rocks and stones for the construction of barricades. Trenches were dug on the threatened western flank of the city. Houses in the south-west suburb of Carabanchel were prepared for a street-by-street defence.

At this moment of crisis, when the fighting reached the southern suburbs, there was a mass mobilization. Metal workers created the slogan 'Every union syndicate a militia, every union member a militiaman'. The UGT and CNT syndicates formed themselves into battalions of railwaymen, barbers and tailors. There was a battalion of schoolmasters and a graphic arts battalion. Transport and buildings were requisitioned and, as in Barcelona, the Ritz Hotel was turned into a canteen for the homeless and refugees. The junta itself took over the palace of Juan March, where typists worked in the ballroom under huge chandeliers, which jangled ominously once the air raids and shelling started.

Miaja's junta was a strange mixture. Nearly all the members were young and energetic, several being still in their twenties; as a result they were known as 'Miaja's infant guard'. On the other hand the old general, myopic, loquacious and incapable of staying with a subject, was no revolutionary. In fact, he had been a member of the Unión Militar Española, which played an important part in the early planning for the rising. However, he craved popularity and was easily flattered. The communists promoted him as the hero of Madrid, giving him an idealized treatment in their press throughout the world. Miaja was thrilled and even became a Party member to repay the compliment, though joining as many political organizations as possible seemed to be his major indulgence. Azaña laughed at Miaja's 'communism', remembering that the general had told him only four years previously that socialists should be shot.[11]

A chill warning of future developments came with Rosenberg's veto of any POUM representation on the junta. This overtly ignored the principle of political parity, which had so benefited the communists up to then. Rosenberg made it clear that there would be no Soviet weapons if the 'Trotskyists' were included. (Andreu Nin had, in fact, broken with Trotsky, who was critical of the POUM, but Nin remained an anti-Stalinist.) 'Public order' in Madrid was to take on a frightening aspect; NKVD officers remained in the capital after all the other non-military Russian personnel had left. The situation was worsened by Mola's use of the phrase 'fifth column'. Not surprisingly this ill-judged remark greatly increased the fear of treachery from within and unleashed another round of repression.

The Civil Guard, now the Republican Guard, was ruthlessly purged. This drastic act was encouraged by memories of their revolt at Badajoz on Yagüe's approach. The Assault Guard were treated in a similar manner and sent down to Valencia. The communist 5th Regiment took control of the vast majority of security operations, and the security delegate, Santiago Carrillo, presided over a spate of arrests and summary executions which may have exceeded those of July and August. There is no doubt that there were many nationalist supporters in Madrid, but the overwhelming majority of attacks attributed to the fifth column came from a frightened population mistaking the direction of machine-gun fire or confusing artillery shells with 'grenades dropped from windows'.

It is difficult to know whether the junta authorities acted out of genuine fear of a 'stab in the back', or whether they purposely exaggerated incidents in order to justify the security forces' ruthless methods. Spy mania was at its height, and the telephones were cut off to prevent nationalist sympathizers from telephoning intelligence to the Army of Africa in the suburbs. The activities, real and imagined, of the fifth column could not, however, justify the decision to evacuate inmates of the Model Prison to Paracuellos del Jarama and then shoot them. Many were leading nationalist supporters.[12]

It is not known for sure whether this order was given by Carrillo's assistant, José Cazorla, or by Koltsov, the *Pravda* correspondent and special envoy, who declared that 'such important elements must not fall into fascist hands'. Immediate and outspoken condemnation of the killings came from Melchor Rodríguez, the anarchist director of prisons newly appointed by Juan García Oliver, but few others dared to criticize the communists at such a critical moment.

The decision to deal with the prisoners was taken on 8 November at 10.30 during a meeting between representatives of the United Socialist Youth and the local federation of the CNT. The prisoners were classified according to three groups:

> First group: Fascists and dangerous elements. Immediate execution, concealing [our] responsibility.
>
> Second group: Non-dangerous prisoners. Immediate evacuation to the prison of Chinchilla, with full security.
>
> Third group: Prisoners not responsible [for any crimes]. To be set at liberty immediately to demonstrate to foreign embassies our humanitarianism.[13]

There is no evidence to suggest that either Miaja's Junta of Defence or the government in Valencia were informed of this decision taken by Santiago Carrillo and Amor Nuño, both just twenty years old, which cost at least 2,000 lives. (Santiago Carrillo was later the leader of the Spanish Communist Party and the great proponent of Euro-Communism in the latter part of the Cold War, an attempt to distance Western communist parties from the rusty iron hand of the Soviet Union.) It has been claimed that their ruthless policy prevented a revolt by the 'fifth column', but although there is no doubt that there were many nationalist supporters still hidden in the city, they had neither the arms nor the organization to undertake such an action.

Meanwhile, militia units were falling back into the capital, exhausted and demoralized. Some had fled openly, even seizing ambulances to get away from the Moors, but others were fighting back with a dogged courage which slowed the nationalist advance. In fact, it would appear that the militia collapse was exaggerated by newsmen who saw only those who were fleeing. On 4 November Getafe and its aerodrome were captured, prompting Varela to tell journalists that they could 'announce to the world that Madrid will be captured this week'. To the west Brunete had been taken two days before. The newspaper *ABC* in Seville declared: 'We are only a 4.60 peseta taxi ride from the city.'

The nationalists were already organizing food convoys so as to be able to feed the population once they entered the city. Even the cautious Franco felt the outcome was virtually certain, so certain, indeed, that he decided to allow republican troops a line of escape so that they were not forced to fight by being cornered. As a result, no push was made towards Vallecas to cut the Valencia road. It was a decision the nationalists greatly regretted later.

In spite of the republicans' retreat, there had been a major development to improve the morale of the militias. Russian aid purchased with the gold reserves was starting to arrive. Maisky, the Russian ambassador in London, and thus representative on the Non-Intervention Committee, had declared on 28 October that his country felt itself no more bound by the agreement than Germany, Italy or Portugal. This was the day before the T-26 tanks attacked Seseña.

The first batch of Russian aid, which arrived in October, included 42 Ilyushin 15 (Chato) biplane fighters, and 31 Ilyushin 16 (Mosca) monoplane fighters. On 29 October a squadron of Katiuska fast bombers, which had just arrived, raided Seville, and on 3 November Chato fighters were seen over Madrid. A day later they dispersed a formation of Fiat fighters and held their own against the Heinkel 51s. The streets of Madrid were thronged with crowds staring up into the skies and cheering whenever an aircraft was hit; it was always assumed to be an enemy. They did not know, however, that Soviet 'fighters over the Madrid sector were ordered to conduct air battles over their own territory, and to enter enemy territory only so far that they would be able, should the engine stop, to glide back to our own lines'.[14] The arrival of this modern Soviet weaponry, especially the tanks and the stubby I-16 Mosca monoplane, made the Nazis decide to increase their aid. With Franco's agreement it was to be organized within an independent German command and named the Condor Legion.

Having advanced the last few kilometres to the south-western outskirts of the city, Varela began to make probing attacks on 5 November as he tried to decide the best approach. The western side of Madrid had no suburb buffer because the old royal hunting ground of the Casa de Campo stretched down to the River Manzanares. Madrid's centre and key buildings all lay within a kilometre of this exposed triangle, bound by the Corunna road running north-west, and the Estremadura road stretching to the south-west. On the north of the wedge lay the new university city with its widely spaced modern blocks. Varela, who had some 15,000 men altogether, wanted to make a left-flanking attack round the northern tip of the Casa de Campo, in the area of the San Fernando bridge, but Franco insisted on attacking straight on. He wanted to reduce street fighting, especially in working-class districts, to a minimum. Nationalist troops were clearly superior in open country while the majority of their casualties, especially among the *regulares*, had been sustained in house clearing.

The next day Varela issued his orders for the attack scheduled for 7 November. There would be feint attacks against the Segovia and Princesa bridges to distract the defenders, while the main thrust would take place towards the sector which ran from the University City to the Plaza de España. Castejón's column would protect the left flank and occupy Garabitas hill and part of the Casa de Campo. Asensio, with his column, was to advance from the centre of the wedge towards the sector of Rosales and Princesa. Delgado Serrano was ordered to head for the Plaza de España. He would be supported by the Italian Ansaldos and the Panzer Mark Is of Colonel von Thoma.

*

Miaja had established his military headquarters in the finance ministry on 6 November, the day the government left for Valencia. His chief of staff was Colonel Vicente Rojo, described by his opponents as 'one of the most competent members of the Spanish army'.[15] But not all agreed. General Alonso Baquer wrote later that Rojo was a 'mixture of Russian populism and French scholasticism', which meant in the latter case that, as a graduate of the Ecole Supérieure de Guerre, he was anchored in the French doctrines of the First World War. Curiously, the republican army's slavish respect for French military doctrine later convinced Franco and his Axis allies that officers from the French army were secretly directing operations.[16]

Neither Miaja nor Rojo, however, knew what forces they had under their command, nor who was on their staff. Many officers had taken advantage of the confusion to flee the city and some of them, including the former chief of operations, had joined the nationalists. Even Miaja's orders from the central government were contradictory, for he was told to hold Madrid at any cost yet also given detailed instructions for retreat towards Cuenca.

General Gorev, the man said by many to be the real commander in Madrid, was established in the ministry as well. One of his officers, Colonel Nikolai Voronov, controlled the artillery, although few batteries had any shells because of incompetence at the ministry of war. (Six years later Voronov commanded the artillery at Stalingrad and took Paulus's surrender.) He and his Spanish counterpart established their observation post at the top of the Telefónica, a building which later attracted more nationalist artillery fire than any other. Ironically, this skyscraper belonging to the American corporation International Telephone and Telegraph, ITT, became the symbol of left-wing resistance during the course of the battle. Downstairs its chairman, Sosthenes Behn, entertained journalists with brandy while awaiting the arrival of General Franco. According to Hitler's interpreter, Paul Schmidt, he had prepared a banquet to greet the conquerors.[17]

The international press was already describing 'the last hours of Madrid'. Several French journalists even sent details of the capital's capture so as to beat their rivals to the story. The correspondent of *L'Illustration* declared, 'Decisive victory is imminent', and Léon Bailby wrote, 'Nothing can be done to prevent the evident truth.

Madrid will be taken rapidly, and that will be the final victory for the nationalists.'[18] Portuguese radio gave vivid details of General Franco's triumphal entry, mounted on a white charger. It also claimed that José Antonio Primo de Rivera had escaped and was advancing on Madrid at the head of a column of civilians.[19] Telegrams from the Austrian and Guatemalan governments congratulating Franco on his victory were delivered to General Miaja instead. The nationalists and their allies simply did not consider that their success was in doubt. According to the *Daily Telegraph* correspondent, Carlist *requetés* were hurried forward so that Spanish Catholic troops were present at the entry. Reprisal tribunals and Civil Guard detachments allocated to each district waited behind the front line. Even the usually cautious General Franco had declared that he would attend mass in Madrid on 7 November and ordered his staff to make travel arrangements for Church leaders.

The world awaited the outcome of 'a decisive battle' between progress and reaction, or between civilization and red barbarism, depending on one's point of view. Liberals and the left everywhere believed that international fascism had to be defeated at Madrid before Europe fell beneath a totalitarian ice age, while conservatives felt it to be the chance to halt the tide of communism. At this crucial moment the defenders were greatly aided by a fortunate discovery, following Varela's decision to delay his attack by a day. On 7 November, the day before the postponed attack, a militia detachment searched the body of Captain Vidal-Quadras, a nationalist officer in an Italian tank which had been knocked out. In his jacket they found the operational orders.

The plan was to 'occupy the zone between, and including, the University City and the Plaza de España, which will constitute the base of departure for further advances into the interior of Madrid'.[20] Now knowing that the assault on Carabanchel was only a feint, the republican general staff switched the bulk of its forces to the Casa de Campo sector and prepared defensive positions for the next morning. Non-militia members of the UGT organized themselves at their *casas del pueblo* and CNT members at their *ateneos libertarios* before going to the front as reserves. They and everyone else, including the refugees from the south-west, were to wait in batches immediately behind the front line, ready to dash forward and take over the weapon of anyone killed. The reassuring presence of such a mass of comrades may have been like an injection of courage, but that night inexperienced sentries on their own took fright at shadows and opened fire. This inevitably led to fusillades into the dark across the whole sector, resulting in a wastage of ammunition. Any indiscriminate firing was serious as there were apparently fewer than ten rounds per rifle; the departing officials of the war ministry had not left word of where the ammunition reserves were kept.

On the morning of 8 November Varela's three main assault forces under Yagüe attacked out of the cover provided by the low trees on the Casa de Campo. Castejón's column came under heavy fire and he was severely wounded. At the same time Barrón's and Tella's smaller columns moved on Carabanchel in their diversionary attack. Being forewarned, Miaja had maintained only about 12,000 of his 40,000-strong force in Carabanchel; the rest were positioned opposite the Casa de Campo. This heterogeneous mass of militia, including a women's battalion at the Puente de Segovia, mixed with *carabineros* and regular soldiers, and backed by totally untrained volunteers, was twice the size of their opponents. But that does not belittle their achievement that day, considering the difference in armament and experience. Probably less than half of the republicans had been involved in earlier fighting and had only learned how to operate the bolt and aim a rifle the evening before. Many still had no idea of how to clear a stoppage, an operation difficult enough for steady fingers. Nevertheless, the nationalist assault columns were held at the western edge of the city that day, a victory of great psychological importance. The Army of Africa no longer appeared invincible. Republican spirits were further raised by the deployment that evening in the Casa de Campo sector of the first of the International Brigades.

The arrival of XI International Brigade, commanded by General Kléber, had a powerful effect on the population of Madrid. It was generally regarded as the best of the Brigades. Its steadiness, ammunition discipline and trench digging was to have a good influence on the militias. As the 1,900 foreigners marched up the Gran Vía in well-drilled step, the *madrileños* cheered them with cries of '*¡Vivan los rusos!*', on the mistaken assumption that they were the infantry counterpart of the fighter aircraft. 'There were many old women among the locals who welcomed us,' wrote a Serbian serving under the *nom de guerre* of Karl Anger. 'They were wiping tears from their eyes with one hand, while the other hand was raised, with the fist clenched, in a Rot Front greeting ... These clenched fists of old Spanish women made us more courageous and determined.'[21]

The almost suicidal bravery of XI International Brigade, especially the Germans, cannot be doubted, but the exploitation of their devotion was particularly unpleasant. General Kléber (alias Manfred Stern) was turned into a hero, but this was dangerous for him later when he was accused by fellow Soviet officers of 'Kleberism', which meant claiming all the glory for yourself at the expense of the Spanish.[22] Madrid was to be the Communist Party's victory alone. Communist troops under the Italian commissar, Luigi Longo, had tried to stop Major Palacios with two battalions of volunteers and a battery of Vickers 105mm field guns from reaching the capital the day before XI International Brigade arrived. They forced their way through, nevertheless, and were welcomed by General Miaja and Colonel Rojo just before the Brigaders turned up. Soon after dawn on the next morning, these two battalions counter-attacked over the San Fernando bridge on the nationalist left flank in the Casa de Campo, losing nearly half their men and retaking the north-eastern part lost on the previous day. But nothing was heard of this in the outside world, nor were other militia actions reported. It was forgotten that the Brigaders had not appeared in time to affect the fighting on 8 November and that they represented only 5 per cent of the republican forces. So successful was Comintern propaganda that Sir Henry Chilton, the British ambassador, was convinced that only foreigners defended Madrid. Meanwhile, the nationalists also exaggerated the Brigaders' importance, so as to justify their own failure and emphasize the 'threat of international communism'.

Líster's brigade was transferred to the University district by the bridge across the Manzanares. Rodimtsev in the command post saw Moroccan *regulares* advancing, shouting wildly as they moved in towards the bridge, one group at a time running forward while the others covered them. Miguel, one of Líster's machine-gunners, was firing at them in short bursts, but then the gun ceased firing. Rodimtsev, a machine-gun instructor, ran over. 'The belt was jammed. I hit the handle hard with my palm and it fell into place. I started firing at the Moroccans running towards me. The Maxim was working really well. There was a bottleneck on the bridge.

The Moroccans at the front turned back and collided with those coming up behind.' Another machine-gunner, Gómez, later told him that the Soviet Union had sent them bad machine-guns. They could not kill Moroccans. 'We fire at them but nothing happens. Then the enemy shell us with mortars.' Rodimtsev told him to camouflage the machine-guns. The Moroccans were using dummies to attract their fire. Then the nationalists shelled the republican machine-gunners when they revealed their positions.[23]

Having been severely checked on the west flank, Varela switched his attack on 9 November towards Carabanchel. Fierce house-to-house fighting ensued in this working-class suburb, where the militias, on familiar ground, not only held back the *regulares*, but inflicted heavy casualties. That evening, two kilometres to the north, XI International Brigade suffered severe losses when forcing the nationalists to retreat a few hundred metres in the central part of the Casa de Campo. The fierce fighting continued in Carabanchel over the next few days, then on 12 November General Miaja (or more probably General Gorev), concerned that the nationalists might thrust through to cut off the Valencia road, sent XII International Brigade and four Spanish brigades to attack the important hill, Cerro de los Angeles, as a diversion. This second International Brigade had received even less training than the first and, despite the Great War veterans in their ranks, the attack collapsed in chaos. Much of this was due to language and communication problems, but the fact remains that the Brigaders were hardly more skilful at mounting attacks than the militias.

At this stage the anarchist leader, Buenaventura Durruti, arrived with more than 3,000 men from the Aragón front. He had been persuaded to go to Madrid by Federica Montseny, who was representing the government in Valencia. At a meeting with García Oliver at Madrid CNT headquarters, Cipriano Mera, the delegate-general of their militia battalions, warned Durruti against attempting a frontal attack on the Casa de Campo, even though the anarchists had become alarmed at the influence the communists were achieving through the International Brigades. Durruti insisted that he had no option but to attack from the University City in the direction of the Casa de Velázquez. The assault took place on the morning of 17 November, but the covering artillery and air support he had been promised failed to materialize. (Whether that was through oversight or intention, anarchist suspicions of communist tactics were greatly increased.) Durruti's men, who had shown such reckless bravery in the Barcelona fighting, broke back to their start line when they met a concentrated artillery barrage and heavy machine-gun fire, neither of which they had experienced before.

'Endless air battles have been going on all day,' wrote Koltsov that evening. 'At 16.00 a republican fighter aircraft lost its group and attacked a Junkers bravely on its own. Several Heinkel aircraft chased and damaged it. The pilot bailed out with a parachute and landed safely right on a sidewalk on the Paseo de Castellana. The admiring crowd carried the brave man to a car. Five minutes later he was brought to the war ministry. Members of the junta applauded him and hugged the pilot, Pablo Palancar.'[24]

On 19 November the nationalists attacked with the support of heavy artillery and Asensio's column found a gap in the republican line. As a result the nationalists were able to cross the Manzanares and establish a bridgehead deep in the University City in the Faculty of Architecture. The legionnaires and *regulares* held on despite furious counter-attacks from XI International Brigade and other units in that sector, which was to become the most bitterly contested stretch of territory in the whole front. In a foretaste of Stalingrad, the legionnaires of the 4th Bandera and the Edgar André Battalion of XI International Brigade fought a savage battle in the buildings there. 'Once at the University Campus,' wrote Karl Anger, 'we started a ruthless fight for every path, every house, every floor, and every threshold. Here, the front line sometimes goes through the most valuable laboratories and libraries. Sometimes breastworks are constructed from huge volumes of the *Encyclopaedia Britannica*. Here the fascists have come the closest to Madrid: it is only between three and five hundred metres from the Casa Velázquez to the nearest café in town.'[25]

Durruti was mortally wounded during the fighting that day. He died the next morning in the improvised hospital set up in the Ritz, at the same time as José Antonio Primo de Rivera was executed in Alicante.[26] A rumour soon started that Durruti had been shot by one of his own men who objected to his severe discipline. The anarchists, for reasons of morale and propaganda, claimed that he had been killed by a sniper's bullet when in fact his death had really been an accident. The cocking handle of a companion's '*naranjero*' machine pistol caught on a car door, firing a bullet into his chest. Durruti was without doubt the most popular anarchist leader. He had been an unrelenting rebel throughout his life and had earned the reputation of a revolutionary Robin Hood. His funeral in Barcelona was the greatest scene of mass mourning that Spain had witnessed, with half a million people in the procession alone. His reputation was so great, not just among anarchists, that attempts were made after his death to claim his allegiance. The Falange said that, like his two brothers, he was a Falangist sympathizer at heart, while the communists felt certain that he was on the way to joining them.

The nationalists' failure to break through on 19 November made Franco change his strategy. He could not risk any more of his best troops in fruitless assaults now that a quick victory looked much more difficult. So, for the first time in history, a capital city came under intense air as well as artillery bombardment. All residential areas except the fashionable Salamanca district were bombed in an attempt to break the morale of the civilian population. The Italian Aviazione Legionaria and the Luftwaffe conducted a methodical experiment in psychological warfare with their Savoia 81s and Junkers 52s. The bombing did not, however, break morale as intended; on the contrary, it increased the defiance of the population. In London, Prince Otto von Bismarck, the German chargé d'affaires, derided British fear of air attacks 'since you see what little harm they have done in Madrid'.

After the statement that the Salamanca district would be spared, the whole area was packed to overflowing and the streets became virtually impassable. Meanwhile, in a remarkably effective operation, the UGT reorganized the transfer of Madrid's most essential industries to unused Metro tunnels. The artist Josep Renau, the director-general of the Bellas Artes, organized the evacuation of paintings from the Museo del Prado to Valencia. The air raids destroyed hundreds of buildings in Madrid, from slum dwellings to the Palacio de Liria belonging to the Duke of Alba. Alba, in his bitter charges accusing the Republic of responsibility for the damage, did not seem to find it incongruous that the nationalist crusade was destroying its own capital with foreign bombers, but then Franco had already declared to the correspondent of *The Times*: 'I will destroy Madrid rather than leave it to the Marxists.'

That week saw the air war escalate. On 13 November the largest dogfight so far took place, with fourteen Fiats and thirteen Chatos locked in combat over the Paseo de Rosales.[27] The next day Miaja issued an order against shooting at pilots baling out. On 16 November nationalist allies bombed the Prado, the Museo Antropológico, the Academia de Bellas Artes de San Fernando, the Biblioteca Nacional, the Museo de Arte Moderno, the Museo Arqueológico and the Archivo Histórico Nacional, as well as various hospitals: the Clinic of San Carlos, the Hospital Provincial and the Hospital de la Cruz Roja. These attacks were described by Malraux in his novel *L'Espoir*.[28] One bomb hit a school and photographs of the rows of dead children strengthened the determination of *madrileños* to prevent a nationalist victory.

Estimates of the bombs dropped on Madrid vary a great deal, but we know from Colonel Wolfram von Richthofen's personal war diary that on 4 December alone, his Junkers 52s dropped 36 tons on the city.[29] In comparison to Second World War bomb loads, when a single British Lancaster could drop ten tons, this was not intensive, but as the first concerted bombing campaign against a capital city, the psychological effect was considerable. The Chilean poet Pablo Neruda, who lost his house, 'the one of the flowers', experienced a sense of outrage which had nothing to do with his own material loss:

> Come and see the blood in the streets
> Come and see
> The blood in the streets
> Come and see the blood
> In the streets.[30]

The fierce fighting on the western edge of Madrid continued. 'The morning had been hard,' wrote a French volunteer called André Cayatte. 'The battalion was relieved for a few hours' rest. To the west, the noise of shelling rolled on. In all the European languages, people talked and sang with so much friendship that one worked out what one could not understand.' They went back into action at Palacete de la Moncloa on 20 November. 'Major Rivière, a smile on his lips, died with elegance, as he had lived. Rivière, with 115 volunteers, was defending a weekend house surrounded by enemy tanks. Three times the survivors attempted a sortie. Finally, the Moors set the house on fire. Rivière lit a last cigarette from the flames. "Nobody will ever know", he said, "everything that we have done." A moment later he was dead.'[31]

*

The reversion to local committees was proving of great value. Despite an evacuation programme, refugees still crammed the city (its million inhabitants had been increased by half); only such a system could have helped both them and those made homeless by the bombing. The committees supervised the construction of shelters, commandeered empty apartments and organized essential supplies and canteens. In contrast to these efforts a black market boomed and inevitably damaged morale.

The Soviet advisers, commissars, senior officers and important Party cadres had their luxurious and well-stocked base in Gaylords Hotel. The large number of visitors, fact-finding missions and committed supporters from abroad were also well looked after. Foreign journalists ('conspicuous as actresses' in Auden's phrase) suffered little. But for the majority of the population the daily allowance was meagre. A horse or mule killed by the bombing or shellfire would be stripped to its skeleton by housewives, while starving dogs hovered around. One International Brigader recorded that a militiaman, having shot a stray which was lapping at the brains of a dead man, shrugged apologetically and explained that dogs were acquiring a taste for human flesh. Cats and rats were also used as food, if only to improve the thin lentil soup. The killing of one bird in the Madrid zoo was not provoked by hunger, however, but by the way the wretched creature learned to imitate the whistle of incoming shells.

Life in Madrid was full of contradictions. Near the Puerta del Sol two foreign journalists, Sefton Delmer and Virginia Cowles, passed an old woman on the pavement selling black and red anarchist scarves to enter a tailor's shop which made cavalry and opera capes. Delmer and Cowles were fascinated by the continued existence of such an establishment in the middle of revolutionary Madrid. The proprietor, who clearly lacked customers, welcomed his visitors with enthusiasm. Delmer asked him how business was going. 'It is very difficult, señor,' he replied sadly. 'There are so few gentlemen left in Madrid.'[32] They left for lunch on the Gran Vía, 'having to take shelter along the way from the daily pre-prandial artillery salvoes'. Cowles was most impressed at the way the streets filled again after the last round had landed, shopkeepers emerged to take down shutters and people strolled along pavements again.

An English International Brigader told her later that what had struck him the most on reaching the country was to see a Spaniard, standing in the road during a bombardment, nonchalantly picking his teeth with a match. Foreigners were intrigued by the Spanish cult of conspicuous fearlessness. A Serbian International Brigader noted: 'Spaniards are very brave in the fighting. But this courage, too, is of a knightly, poetical sort. It is hard for them to adapt to the volatile, pedantic and prosaic demands of modern war.'[33]

Even with the intense air attacks of 19–23 November life was almost normal. People went to work each day and the trams still ran, even though their tracks had to be repaired continually. The underground was, of course, safer, though people joked that at least the tram had to stop before the front line, whereas on the metro you might come up behind it on the far side. These communication systems meant that reinforcements and supplies could be moved rapidly over the relatively short distances involved. Hot food for the front-line troops was far easier to provide than in normal defensive positions and the troops themselves could be relieved frequently, or even visited at the front.

The troops, and particularly the International Brigades, received visits in their trenches from the large numbers of foreigners brought to Madrid by the siege. These groups included journalists and a few war tourists, as well as politically committed supporters of the Republic. Some of the visitors were there for 'pseudo-military excitement' as one International Brigader described it. On visits to the front line they would often borrow a rifle or even a machine-gun to fire off a few rounds at the nationalist lines. Ernest Hemingway was a good example of the genre and, much as the men may have liked seeing new faces, especially famous ones, they became less enthusiastic when the thrill seekers provoked enemy bombardments.

By the end of November the struggle for Madrid had settled into a cold, hungry siege, punctuated by bombardment, air raids and the occasional flare-up. In Carabanchel, where the front line cut through the middle of streets, a strange deadly struggle continued, with sniping, flame-thrower attacks and tunnelling under houses to lay dynamite. The Carlists lost most of a company in one explosion. Nevertheless, the enthusiastic commitment of Madrid's population diminished as the immediate danger receded. This was accompanied by the gradual replacement of the committees by centralized control. The activities of the communist secret police continued even after the danger was past, which also damaged morale. Anarchist militiamen clashed violently with communist authorities and attempts were made to censor the anarchist press. It was the beginning of a process which led to a major explosion in May of the next year, the start of a virtual civil war within the civil war.

At this time the communists made their first open move against the POUM, as mutual accusations between the Marxist rivals increased. The POUM had outraged the communists on 15 November, when its newspaper, *La Batalla*, analysed Russian policy too accurately. 'Stalin's concern', the article said, 'is not really the fate of the Spanish and international proletariat, but the protection of the Soviet government in accordance with the policy of pacts made by certain others.' Soviet advisers immediately accused *La Batalla* of having 'sold out to international fascism'. With the great increase in direct Soviet control, the Party line in Spain began to reflect the witch-hunt for Trotskyists in the USSR. Having kept them off the Madrid junta, the communists now stopped pay and supplies to the small POUM force on the Madrid front. The POUM militia in the region thus had no option but to disband and its members joined either UGT or CNT units.

The capital was saved and political passions aroused through much of the world, but it had certainly not proved 'the grave of fascism' as the communist slogan had hoped. The battle of Madrid marked only a change in the war. Checking the nationalists there turned a *coup d'état* into a full-scale civil war with international ramifications, almost a world war by proxy. This meant that even more help was needed from abroad. On 2 December 1936, Colonel von Richthofen recorded in his diary: 'Salamanca wants German ground troops – at least two divisions.'[34] (In fact, one German and one Italian.) But a cautious Hitler decided to restrict his aid to Franco to the Condor Legion.

PART FOUR

World War by Proxy

18

The Metamorphosis of the War

History seldom proceeds in straight lines. In December 1936 a series of battles, more in the style of the First World War, began around Madrid, yet the last of the militia defeats, in the pattern of the previous summer, did not take place until February 1937, in the brief Málaga campaign.

Generalissimo Franco became trapped in an unimaginative strategy. The enormous expectations aroused in October for what German diplomats cynically called 'the bullfight',[1] and the failure to take Madrid in November, created an obsessive determination. He insisted to Faupel, the new German chargé d'affaires, 'I will take Madrid; then all of Spain, including Catalonia, will fall into my hands more or less without a fight.' Faupel described the statement as 'an estimate of the situation that I cannot describe as anything but frivolous'.[2]

After Varela's attacks had been checked and the bombing had failed to break the morale of the city, there were basically three options left. One was to try to encircle Madrid from the north-west, and at least cut off water supplies and electricity from the Sierra de Guadarrama. This was to be the first target for the nationalists. The other was to strike eastwards across the River Jarama from their large salient south of the capital. Republican territory around Madrid was like a peninsula, vulnerable at its base formed by the corridor of land along the Valencia road. This would be the second offensive. And with the central front curling back round the Sierra de Guadarrama and across the province of Guadalajara, there was the possibility of striking down at the Valencia road from the north-east. This would be the sector for the third nationalist offensive in March 1937.

On 29 November 1936 Varela launched the first of a series of attacks on the Corunna road to the north-west of Madrid. The intention was to achieve a breakthrough towards the sierra, before swinging right to the north of the capital. This first attack, mounted with some 3,000 Legion and Moroccan troops, supported by tanks, artillery and Junkers 52 bombers, was directed against the Pozuelo sector. The republican brigade retreated in disorder, but the line was re-established by a counter-attack backed by T-26s. Both sides then redeployed so as to reinforce their fronts to the west of Madrid.

The German tanks, however, do not appear to have been used very effectively by their Spanish nationalist crews. 'Inexplicable tank operations,' wrote Richthofen scathingly in his war diary on 2 December. 'German panzer personnel drive the tanks up to the combat zone, then Spaniards take over. They take the tanks for a ride and fiddle around.' He also observed the republican air force. 'Red pilots avoid coming in range of our flak,' he noted four days later.[3] Richthofen, a cousin of the famous Red Baron air ace, was a hard, arrogant man, disliked by German and Spanish officers alike. He was to become infamous as the destroyer of many towns and cities: Durango and Guernica in Spain, then Rotterdam, Belgrade, Canea and Heraklion in Crete, followed by many cities in the Soviet Union, most notably of all, Stalingrad, where 40,000 civilians were killed.

On the nationalist side General Orgaz was put in charge of the central front, where a renewed offensive began on 16 December, after a 48-hour delay due to weather conditions. Varela retained the field command with 17,000 men divided into four columns. The first objective, after a heavy bombardment with 155mm artillery, was the village of Boadilla del Monte, some twenty kilometres west of Madrid. It was captured that night and the general staff in Madrid, realizing that they faced a major offensive rather than a diversion, sent XI and XII International Brigades, backed by the bulk of Pavlov's T-26 tanks. XI Brigade counter-attacked at Boadilla, only to find themselves virtually cut off in the village. The nationalists withdrew to take advantage of such a clearly defined artillery target and attacked again with their infantry. The International Brigades established defensive positions within the thick walls of country houses belonging to rich *madrileños*. They resisted desperately and on 19 December the slaughter was enormous on both sides. The next day Orgaz halted the offensive, having gained only a few kilometres. He lacked reserves and the republicans enjoyed numerical superiority.

Karl Anger, one of the Serbs in XI International Brigade, described their arrival in the village of Majadahonda just south of the Corunna highway at the start of the fighting. 'It was still an untouched little place, far from beautiful, a little dirty because of poverty, but warm, quiet and sweet, like a lamb. We filled it with our troops, services, guns, trucks, armoured vehicles, and all things that an army drags behind it during a campaign. Quiet Majadahonda became crowded, noisy and dirty, as if on a market day. On the first morning after our departure enemy aircraft started dropping bombs on the village. The inhabitants scattered, abandoning all their property. Livestock, pigs, unmade beds and unattended houses. On the first evening and first morning there still was life at Majadahonda. One could see mysterious silhouettes of young Spanish girls behind the poorly lit windows of houses. The next day the windows were already black, gaping – frightening holes in the shells of the houses. Only stray dogs, supply people and stragglers were left in the village, and also a woman who had gone mad. She screamed terribly on a moonlit night in an empty house, and the screams echoed frighteningly in the dead moonlit streets.'[4]

It is also important to understand the chaos which resulted in the driving sleet and the winter darkness. The International Brigades lacked intelligence on the enemy. They had no maps or compasses, and blundered around just managing to avoid attacking each other. A battalion would start digging its trenches, only to find later that they were completely out of line with the neighbouring units. Language problems within the International Brigades did not help. Anger, a Serbian within a German battalion, also indicates in his account the extraordinary mixture of nationalities and of motives within the International Brigades. 'In Majadahonda we were joined by a young Chinese volunteer, the first Chinese to join us. On the next day, when we had just started thinking how to incorporate him better into our Serbian team, he was brought back with both his legs smashed to bits. We hadn't even had time to learn his name.' He went on to add that 'in all the International Brigades, including the first [i.e. XI International] brigade, there was a number of former Russian White Guardists or sons of White Guardists'. These were the desperately homesick Russian émigrés hoping to earn a safe passage back to the Soviet Union.

When nationalist reinforcements arrived towards the end of

December, Orgaz prepared to relaunch his unimaginative offensive along the same axis. During the breathing space the republican general staff had redeployed their units in the Pozuelo-Brunete sector in a very uncoordinated manner and without attending to the supply of ammunition. When the nationalist offensive was relaunched on 3 January 1937 the republican right flank fell back in disorder. At first the republican troops on the left managed to hold Pozuelo, in a battle 'which was the most complete chaos'. Koltsov said that 'despite all their heroism, our units suffered from the confusion, stupidity, and perhaps treason in headquarters'.[5]

Varela then concentrated most of his eight batteries of 105mm and 155mm artillery, together with his tanks and available air power, on the *pueblo*. The republican defence collapsed and the retreat of Modesto's formation, based on the former 5th Regiment, became virtually a rout as men lost all sense of direction in the fog. General Miaja gave the 10th Brigade the task of disarming all those who fled. The only mitigating factor was the destruction of two companies of German light tanks with the 37mm guns of Russian armoured cars. The superiority of Soviet armoured vehicles in Spain later influenced the Wehrmacht's development of heavier tanks.

The ammunition supply was appalling. On average only a handful of rounds per man remained, while some battalions had run out altogether. The fault lay partly with Miaja and his staff for reacting so slowly to the problem, but mainly with Largo Caballero and officers in the ministry of war in Valencia. Largo Caballero replied to Miaja's request for more ammunition with the accusation that he was simply trying to cover up his responsibility for the defeat.

While the whole republican sector looked as if it were about to collapse, Miaja placed machine-guns at crossroads on the way to Madrid to stop desertion. He ordered in XII International and Líster's Brigade. In addition XIV International Brigade was brought all the way round from the Córdoba front. On 7 January Kléber ordered the Thaelmann Battalion to hold the enemy near Las Rozas, telling them 'not to retreat a single centimetre under any circumstances'. In a stand of sacrificial bravery they followed his order to the letter. Only 35 men survived.

Once reinforcements arrived, the front line eventually stabilized. Both sides were exhausted and by mid-January the battle was over, the opposing armies having established themselves in defensive positions. The nationalists had overrun the Corunna road from the edge of Madrid to almost a third of the way to San Lorenzo del Escorial, but the Republic had prevented any encirclement of Madrid from the west flank. Each had suffered around 15,000 casualties in the process.

The two battles for the Corunna road, as they were sometimes called, proved a hard testing ground for French and other volunteers with the tank brigade. The French arrived with what Soviet advisers regarded as an insouciant manner. 'From the very first days', the report back to Moscow stated, 'the French disliked the discipline here. They said, "What kind of life is this, one isn't allowed to drink wine, or go to the brothel, and one has to get up early." They particularly disliked getting up at reveille and going on 25-kilometre marches. But when we explained to them, they understood and proved themselves to be heroes on the field of battle. And when they came back from the battle, they declared, "We don't regard ourselves as Frenchmen, we are internationalists and anti-fascists."' The report admitted that fighting conditions were terrible for the tank crews. 'Men get very tired. After a day's work, men leave the tanks as if drunk, most of them suffer from a shortage of oxygen in their tanks. In some cases they vomit, in some cases they are in a very nervous state.'[6]

The Soviet woman commissar of the tank brigade's medical unit described the far superior medical facilities provided for Soviet advisers in comparison to the terrible conditions in the makeshift hospital in El Escorial for Spanish soldiers. The tank brigade commander, presumably Pavlov, showed an unusual commitment to the care of his men – especially rare in the Red Army. It went beyond just getting trained tankists, who were badly needed, back into their tanks. The commissar's work and observations also provide some of the very few Soviet accounts of battle shock cases.

'Medical vehicles of International Brigades are rushing along the highway. Some of them are painted in a mosaic-like pattern of green–yellow–black–grey, they blend in with the general surroundings. Medical transport is a weak spot here. There are few ambulances and most of them are modified little trucks or assembled from odd bits and pieces. Most of them have enough space for only four stretchers. Two tanks are crawling up from a turn of the road. In the second one is the body of mechanic-driver Ulyanov, who was killed on the spot by a direct hit on his tank. Malyshev and Starkov were wounded.

'The field hospital [for tankists and the International Brigades] is stationed in a big room in one of the houses in a forest nature reserve. Double mattresses with clean linen and blankets have been put on the floor. There is a stove, they feed firewood into it, keeping up the temperature which is important for those who had come back from the front. During the whole operation near Las Rozas there had been a severe fog, penetrating one's entire system ... Besides water and soap, the hospital has petrol and alcohol – to wash the tankists' faces and hands ... The doctor and I go to the main hospital, to look for our wounded men. The hospital in Escorial is overflowing with wounded ... I take note of the types of wounds while passing through the wards and the hall where the wounded men are received. Most of the wounded men are infantry, wounded by artillery shells. Wounds from bullets – in the back and sides.

'During the night of 14 January I found the corpse of a Frenchman in the room next to Starkov. He had been brought back from the battle unconscious, with a heavy wound. The nurse told me that he had shouted in French, "Comrades, look out! Shells are coming from the left." He then started to sing the "Internationale" and died. He had no documents on him. The nurse and I did not have a camera to take a photo of this dead unknown comrade. Upstairs, in an empty ward, lies a dying Italian, wounded in the neck. In the ward next to him there's a wounded Moroccan, with a heavy wound in his leg. He does not talk and rejects food ... It is unbelievably cold in the hospital. We cover Starkov [whose leg had been amputated] with several blankets, dress him in warm underwear which we've brought from brigade headquarters. The brigade commander asked if he could get anything for Starkov. I asked Starkov and then informed the brigade commander that he would like to have a watch. The brigade commander ordered us to take Starkov his own watch ... All the wounded tankists who are now in hospitals in Madrid are sent food on a daily basis from brigade headquarters: canned milk, cocoa, oranges, apples, chocolates, sausage, cookies ... In Madrid we have found the full collections of works by Gorky and Chekhov. The wounded men are supplied with newspapers and magazines, commissars keep visiting them.

'Types of wounds varied from day to day at the front field hospitals and also at hospitals in Madrid. In the wards and operation theatres, which I visited directly after the battles, I happened to see some Spanish infantrymen who were wounded in the back, rear, backs of their legs, and shoulders. At first aid stations at the front we sometimes came across cases of "self-inflicted wounds" among Spanish infantrymen, who, while seized with animal fear, had shot through their own arms and legs, in order to be taken to hospital.'

The woman commissar also recounted the case of a tank crewman called Soloviev, with a broken right arm, who 'developed abnormal psychic reactions', clearly a euphemism for battle shock or what we know today as post-traumatic stress disorder. Soloviev was evacuated on 15 January to the Palace Hotel in Madrid, the Soviet fortress base. His ravings were perhaps an interesting product of propaganda. 'Soloviev would become extremely agitated, he would talk and talk of his recollections. He spoke incessantly about his training and his time in the Red Army, mentioned the names of commanders, sites of their camps, location of units, then turned to the Spanish Civil War, matériel and people dispatched on ships, and about anarchists and Trotskyists. On the order of the brigade commander, Soloviev was moved into a separate room ... On 20 January he showed symptoms of sharp delirium: "Anarchists came here during the night, and they took me upstairs!" "Anarchists will slaughter us all, they came for me, they told me about it last night!" The brigade commander ordered us to evacuate Soloviev from Madrid. Although his fits of delirium have become more frequent, we evacuate Soloviev in one of the brigade's ambulances. We take him to a hospital in Archena. In this hospital, he can be isolated from the outside world and will get the necessary treatment. While he was at "Palas Hotel" [sic], no strangers were allowed into his ward. Political workers from the brigade kept visiting Soloviev and controlling his state.'[7]

It is important at this point to understand what fighting in the field was like for the militiamen who had now become part of the People's Army. The majority were industrial workers who had little experience of the country. Even those who had done military service knew few of the old campaigner's tricks for making life more bearable in general and more durable in battle. Their columns and new 'mixed brigades' were marched or driven out of Madrid in commandeered trucks. Maps were so scarce that they were seldom available at company level and few could read them properly when they were issued. Once at the position which they had been ordered to defend, the soldiers, equipped with little more than a rifle, ammunition pouches and a blanket, started to dig trenches with bayonets and bare hands. They did not bother with latrines, since that would only have meant more digging in the stony Spanish earth and visiting them involved a dangerous journey. In most cases they simply used their trenches, a practice which horrified International Brigaders, accustomed to the First World War idea of digging everything into the ground.

The Castilian winter is renowned for the cold winds coming down off the sierras, and the militias froze in their trenches, often having little more to wear than their boiler suits and rope-soled canvas *alpargatas*, which rotted quickly. With mud everywhere it was impossible to keep clean, owing to the lack of water tankers to bring up fresh water and the general scarcity of soap.

In theory each battalion had a machine-gun company in addition to its three rifle companies, but only the International Brigades or picked communist formations had anything approaching the full establishment. Automatic weapons were the key to repulsing frontal attacks and the lack of them, and of experienced operators, put the People's Army at a grave disadvantage. The Moroccan *regulares* became well known as the most effective machine-gunners in the war in addition to their other remarkable ability to use dead ground. The barren terrain in which they had fought the Spanish so successfully in the colonial wars had taught them to take maximum advantage of the slightest fold in the ground. Not only did this reduce their casualties enormously, but together with their reputation for knife work, it inspired a tremendous fear in republican troops. Their skill often enabled them to creep in between carelessly sited positions and take the defenders by surprise.

Nationalist generals, most of whom proved as rigidly conventional as their republican counterparts, did not make full use of the *regulares*. The majority of the fighting was limited to set-piece offensives, which were often assaults across an open no-man's land, with attack followed by counter-attack. The only discernible difference from First World War tactics was the growing co-ordination between infantry and armour, together with the integration of artillery and air bombardment. This development, however, was almost entirely restricted to the nationalist side and their Condor Legion advisers.

The new breed of republican commander emerging at this time was young, aggressive, ruthless and personally brave, but as utterly conventional and unimaginative as the old officers of the metropolitan army. The outstanding examples of this type, such as Modesto and Líster, were communists from the 5th Regiment. Some, like Manuel Tagüeña, became communists in the early months of the war, having started in Socialist Youth battalions which had affiliated to the 5th Regiment during the fighting in the sierra the previous summer. Their rigidly traditional approach to tactics and their military formality were strongly influenced by Stalinist orthodoxy. The purging of Marshal Tukhachevsky and his supporters who advocated the new approach to armoured warfare returned communist military theory to the political safety of obsolete tactics. In Russia saluting had been reintroduced and the 5th Regiment followed suit. The officers of XI International Brigade had even carried swords when marching up the Gran Vía on 8 November. The exhortation of the new republican brigades may have been revolutionary in language, but the manoeuvring was Tsarist.

After the battle of the Corunna road Kléber left for Moscow in the company of André Marty, having been relieved of his command. It has been said that jealous Spanish communists made him the scapegoat for the Pozuelo collapse, while others, such as Borkenau, believed that Miaja resented Kléber rivalling him as the hero of Madrid. Whatever the explanation, Kléber had become much less flamboyant when he returned to Spain in June to command a division. Despite the idealized portraits of many foreign journalists, who 'played him up sensationally' as one of them admitted, Kléber never really exceeded the level of a tough First World War commander who was unsparing with the lives of his men.

In between the two parts of the Corunna road offensive, the republicans had fought an unsuccessful action in the south when Queipo de Llano's forces advanced to capture the rich olive-growing area of Andújar. It was a singularly inauspicious start for the new XIV International Brigade under General 'Walter', a Polish communist, who later commanded the Second Polish Army in the Red Army's Berlin operation. This brigade included the French

Marseillaise Battalion, which had a British company. The main action, around a village called Lopera just after Christmas, became famous for the death of the two English communist poets John Cornford and Ralph Fox, and for a frightening foretaste of International Brigade justice.

The battle began on the morning of 28 December and finished 36 hours later. Walter had been ordered to retake Lopera, but he had no telephone communications with his units and no air or artillery support. The nationalists decimated their ranks with machine-gun fire, mortars and artillery. XIV International Brigade was virtually untrained. Like the militia in similar circumstances, many of its men turned and ran on being surprised by machine-gun fire. Some 800 corpses were left under the olive trees and 500 men deserted the front line.[8] The commanding officer of the Marseillaise Battalion, Major Gaston Delasalle, was arrested and accused, not only of incompetence and cowardice, but also of being a 'fascist spy'. He was found guilty by a court martial hastily gathered by André Marty. Ilya Ehrenburg later described Marty as speaking, and occasionally acting, 'like a mentally sick man', and Gustav Regler remarked that Marty preferred to shoot anyone on suspicion, rather than waste time with what he called 'petit bourgeois indecision'.[9] Some Brigaders, however, admired him greatly. 'A true revolutionary,' Sommerfield called him, 'compounded of patience, granite firmness and absolute unswerving determination.' Tom Wintringham, who later commanded the British battalion, described the proceedings as 'a thoroughly fair court martial'. But Nick Gillain, serving in XIV International Brigade, wrote later, 'The guards dragged the condemned man out of the court room, while he continued to protest his innocence. There was the sound of two or three shots. Then, a man came back into the room and placed on the table a watch and some money ... Revolutionary justice had been carried out.'[10]

The nationalists and their Axis backers began to adjust themselves to a protracted war. Hitler was not surprised by the turn of events, informed as he was by accurate assessments from Voelckers, the German chargé d'affaires. He was also unperturbed by the long pessimistic reports from his ambassador to Franco, Faupel, and the Condor Legion commander, General Sperrle, because an extended war suited his purposes better. It would distract attention from his expansionist plans in central Europe. Mussolini, on the other hand, was eager to win military glory in Europe, but his mood fluctuated wildly according to the performance of his troops.

The most urgent task facing Franco's staff was to create a trained army of sufficient size. German assistance in this task was almost as important as their combat contribution. The Falangist militia trained by Condor Legion officers at Cáceres in Estremadura bore little resemblance to the gangs of *señoritos* involved in the summer fighting. The Carlist *requetés*, the nationalists' most effective troops after the Army of Africa, now numbered about 60,000. At least half of them came from Navarre, which led to the Carlist claim that 'Navarre had saved Spain'. This arrogance, combined with open contempt for the Castilian Church, which they thought corrupt and pharisaical, did not make them popular with their allies. The famed discipline of the *requetés* derived, not from strong respect for hierarchy, but from the self-discipline of the hill farmer. (Their leader, Fal Conde, exaggerated when he described Carlism as a movement guided from below, but it was a uniquely populist form of royalism.) Their medieval crusading faith made them fearless. Colonel Rada described his *requetés* as men 'with faith in victory, with faith in God; one hand holding a grenade, the other a rosary'.

In early December 1936 the Carlist war council decided to establish a 'Royal Military Academy' to ensure a supply of trained Carlist officers. Franco, jealous of their strength, declared that such an unauthorized move would be considered an act against the nationalist movement. The war council backed down and Fal Conde went into exile in Portugal. The Caudillo followed up this victory with a decree which subordinated all political militias to the code of military justice and the army chain of command.

By the end of 1936 the nationalist army's strength approached 200,000 men, with over half this figure made up by the Carlist and Falangist forces. The Army of Africa was increased to over 60,000 men by early 1937, chiefly as a result of intense recruiting in the Rif. Foreign volunteers also joined the Legion. The largest group was Portuguese and consisted of about 12,000 men known as the *Viriatos*. There was also a detachment of right-wing French volunteers and 600 Irish blueshirts under General Eoin O'Duffy, but their contribution was small. They were withdrawn after only one action in which they found themselves attacked by their own side.[11]

In January Franco set up a joint German-Italian general staff in the hope of deflecting criticism from his allies over the way the war was being conducted. He simply intended it as a sop so as to be able to request more military aid, and implicate his advisers in the responsibility of any reverse. The nationalists' most valuable assistance undoubtedly came from the increased German contribution. The Nazi government had reacted quickly in early November to the appearance of Russian weaponry. Hitler evidently did not realize that Stalin was afraid of provoking him and that he was unwilling to let Spanish affairs embarrass Soviet foreign policy. The first contingents of the Condor Legion arrived in Spain in mid November. General Sperrle was the overall commander and Colonel von Richthofen the commander of Luftwaffe operations. German air power in Spain grew to four fighter squadrons of Heinkel 51 biplanes (to be replaced gradually with Messerschmitt 109s in the early summer of 1937) and four squadrons of Junkers 52 bombers. Other aircraft were sent out later; in fact, all the important machines used by the Luftwaffe at the beginning of the Second World War were tested in Spain.

The Wehrmacht reinforcements came under Colonel von Thoma's command and included anti-tank and heavy machine-gun detachments, artillery and the equivalent of two Panzer battalions. This tank force of 106 Mark I Panzers assembled at Cubas north of Toledo. Their large black berets bore a badge based on the skull motif of the Death's-Head Hussars of the old Prussian army. In support there were 20mm flak batteries and 88mm anti-aircraft guns. The signals corps, too, helped with equipment and training. There was a large contingent of engineers and civilian instructors, who later included Gestapo 'advisers', as well as a naval advisory staff, based on the pocket battleships *Deutschland* and *Admiral Scheer*, both of which stayed in western Mediterranean waters. On 16 November, 5,000 German servicemen disembarked in Cádiz and another 7,000 arrived ten days later.[12]

The great increase in Italian aid followed the secret pact signed by Franco on 28 November at Salamanca. The Caudillo agreed to Mussolini's policy of Italian primacy in the Mediterranean in return for military aid 'to restore political and social order in the country'. During the first months of the war the Italian pilots flying the Savoia 81s and Fiat fighters had in theory been attached to the Spanish Foreign Legion, whose uniform they wore. But in his desire for glory Mussolini now wanted an independent command and recognizable Italian formations in the land battles. As a result the CTV (Corps of Volunteer Troops) was organized. Its commander, General Mario Roatta, formerly of Italian military intelligence, had been Admiral Canaris's counterpart. Roatta had already been to Spain at the beginning of the war with the German liaison officer, Colonel Warlimont.

The Italian infantry sent to Spain consisted mainly of fascist militia, many of whom had been drafted or press-ganged. Having been told that they were going to Abyssinia, they arrived in Spain in midwinter wearing tropical uniforms. The CTV's strength later reached a total of about 50,000 men, but many Spaniards were transferred to their formations and fought under Italian officers. The number of Fiat Ansaldo miniature tanks was greatly increased, but these were little better than closed-in Bren gun carriers. Italian field guns were of good quality, though old, but then artillery has always been the strongest section of Italian military industry. The 'Legionary Air Force', so called to summon up images of imperial Rome, was increased to some 5,000 men. Many more Fiat fighters and Savoia bombers were also sent. Their principal base was Majorca, from where they could attack shipping and, in Ciano's words, 'terrorize Valencia and Barcelona'.[13] This reorganization left Franco's air force commander, General Kindelán, in a similar position to his republican counterpart, Hidalgo de Cisneros, who, even after he became a communist, was lucky if the Russian General 'Duglas' told him what was happening.

The Málaga campaign, the Italian CTV's first action in Spain, took place while the opposing armies in the Madrid region were preparing for the next round. The southern extremity of the republican zone was no more than a long strip between sea and mountain, stretching from Motril to Estepona within 50 kilometres of Gibraltar. Only the overriding priority given to the assault on Madrid had delayed the nationalists from attacking it earlier. Queipo de Llano had grown particularly impatient at what he regarded as a continuing insult to his control of Andalucia. The nationalist field command was given to a Borbón prince, Colonel the Duke of Seville. Franco asked Roatta to join this offensive with his 10,000 fascist militiamen and the Legionary Air Force in close support. It was a clever move, since victory was certain, and Mussolini would therefore be encouraged to continue his aid at a time when he had suddenly become worried about international opinion.

If any campaign was fated to be lost by the Republic it was this one. The terrain and the elongated sector meant that the nationalists could cut it almost wherever and whenever they wanted. The state of the defence was pitiful, for Málaga had led a revolutionary existence cut off from the reality of the war. Within the town there was strong antagonism between the communists and the CNT, while in the countryside the predominantly anarchist peasants were immersed in their collectives. The mountain range provided a most dangerous sense of security.

The republican forces consisted of no more than 12,000 militiamen, a third of whom had no rifles. There was little ammunition even for those who were armed. This state of affairs was largely the result of the deliberate neglect of the government, which disliked the continuing independence of the province. Largo Caballero is reputed to have said 'not a round more for Málaga'. The performance of Colonel Villalba, the commander, moreover, was more than just unimpressive. There are strong grounds for believing that he sabotaged the defence deliberately, since he was treated so well by the nationalists after the defeat of the Republic.[14]

The Duke of Seville's offensive began slowly in mid January with the capture of small pieces of territory. The first major section to be seized was the extreme south-west, including Marbella. Then a small force from Granada occupied a chunk of territory to the north-east of Málaga, endangering its communication with Motril, which lay at the exit of the bottleneck. Yet the attack on Málaga itself in the first week of February still came as a surprise. The Duke of Seville's force advanced up the coast, rolling back the militia detachments with ease; the blackshirt militia under Roatta cut down to the sea; and the Granada force pushed further towards the coast road, although they left this escape route open so as not to provoke resistance. Within three days the nationalist and Italian forces had entered the outskirts of Málaga, after a naval bombardment by units of the nationalist fleet, backed by the *Admiral Scheer*. The republican warships at Cartagena never even left port.

The weather hampered operations and the Condor Legion could do little to help until almost the end. 'At last the fighter squadrons can get off the ground,' wrote Richthofen on 6 February. 'Italians advancing with difficulty. One He 51 shot down. Italians are standing still four kilometres short of Málaga. Spaniards want fighters here there and everywhere. And today again in Saragossa because a red [aircraft] was there. That's not how it should be. Today the Legion Condor had its fourteenth casualty.' But just two days later, on 8 February, he was able to write: 'Málaga taken! Great victory fiesta in white Spain.'[15]

Descriptions of the fleeing civilians and exhausted militiamen along the coast are harrowing.[16] Crazed mothers nursed dead babies and the old and weak died by the roadside. It seemed to the writer Arthur Koestler and his host Sir Peter Chalmers-Mitchell, who had a house in Málaga, as if only a few solitary figures were left in the abandoned landscape of the city. Smoke drifted upwards from houses ruined in the shelling. In the shock of defeat odd militiamen waited apathetically to be put up against a wall. The nationalist revenge in Málaga was perhaps the most horrific of the war, judging by the British consul's report of 20,000 executions between 1937 and 1944. The nationalist prosecutor in Málaga, Carlos Arias Navarro, eventually became the last prime minister under Franco and the man inherited by King Juan Carlos in 1975.

The Málaga disaster brought tensions to a head between the communists and Largo Caballero, whom the Comintern and Soviet advisers referred to in their reports to Moscow as 'the Old Man'. They were furious at Caballero's attempts to restrict communist power within the army, partly because he could not forgive their successful infiltration of the Socialist Youth and the consequent loss of the whole organization to the PCE. André Marty even suggested later that Caballero and Prieto were in the pocket of the British who were urging them to resist the communists.[17]

'He [Caballero] fears the exceptional influence that the Party has in a significant part of the army and strives to limit this,' Berzin reported to Moscow on 12 January 1937. He went on to claim that General Asensio, the assistant minister for war, and General Cabrera, the chief of staff, 'despite repeated exposures of their sabotage in the carrying out of useful measures for fortified fronts, up to now enjoy great trust from the premier and war minister, left socialist Largo Caballero. Some of them have not been exposed, but are undoubtedly agents of Franco ... The fall of Málaga in particular was, for the most part, caused by treason.' He levelled similar accusations against the anarchists and the 'counter-revolutionary Trotskyists' of the POUM, a leitmotif in almost every report back to Moscow. 'It goes without saying that it is impossible to win the war against the rebels if these scum within the republican camp are not liquidated.'[18] Colonel Krivoshein, in a report forwarded to Stalin by Voroshilov, concluded that 'the Communist Party ought to come to power even by force, if necessary'.[19]

The communists were also outraged by the 'impudently slanderous position' taken by Prieto, the minister for the navy, 'at the last council of ministers (where he in essence repeated almost word for word the attacks of the Trotskyist *La Batalla* against the Soviet Union)'.[20]

The transformation of the militia columns into a formalized army started in earnest in December 1936. At the beginning of 1937 republican forces totalled about 320,000 men, although only about half this number were at the various fronts at any one time. These forces were split among the central and southern zone with about 130,000, the three northern zones (Euzkadi, Santander and the Asturias) with over 100,000 and Aragón with about 30,000. The remaining 80,000 or so in rearguard areas included the Assault Guard, the National Republican Guard, formed from loyal civil guards, the *carabinero* frontier police and the MVR, the Militias of Rearguard Vigilance, which were a government incorporation of irregular forces. The *carabineros* came under Negrín, the minister of finance, who built them up as a personal force to about 40,000 strong. The main reason for lack of precision in army figures is inaccurate reporting, both of ration returns (minor and major frauds were carried out by staff and quartermasters) and of unit strengths (commanding officers sometimes adjusted the figures for personal and political reasons).

These greatly increased figures were achieved mainly by increasing the call-up of the classes of 1933, 1934 and 1935. It is impossible to gauge what proportion of the intake was prompted by idealism, circumstances, or even hunger, for the rations were considerably better than those which the civilian population enjoyed. An English International Brigader in hospital later observed that the local people were so desperate that they would eat what they had left on their plates, even if it had been chewed. Meanwhile, with a mixture of encouragement, manipulation and blackmail, the militias were forced into the command structure already prepared on paper. Columns were turned into battalions and brigades during the winter of 1936. In the spring of 1937 divisions and even army corps started to be formed.

The other development which went ahead rapidly was the practice of attaching commissars to every brigade and battalion headquarters. The commissars' official role was to watch over regular commanders and look after the welfare of the troops. However, Álvarez del Vayo, the foreign minister and secret communist supporter, persuaded Largo Caballero to make him commissar-general and with his assistance the communists managed to take control of this powerful branch. By the spring, 125 out of 168 battalion commissars were from the Party itself (PCE and PSUC) or from the Joint Socialist Youth.

The Generalitat in Catalonia followed the policy of the central government, but at the same time it tried to establish the eastern forces as an independent Catalan army. This was an ambitious policy, intensely disliked by the central government. The communists refrained from criticizing the Generalitat, since their policy was to aid Companys, the Catalan president, to assert state power at the expense of the anarchists. Once that was close to being achieved, they would use their Catalan PSUC to help bring the Generalitat under central government control. On 6 December, the *Diari Oficial de la Generalitat* published the decree creating the Exèrcit Nacional de Catalunya, an army composed of three divisions instead of mixed brigades. But in February 1937, when the Generalitat called up the classes of 1934 and 1935, it also had to place its army under the control of the central general staff.[21]

In Euzkadi, meanwhile, Aguirre's Basque government organized its own independent army, the Euzko Gudarostea, with 25,000 men, nominally forming part of the Army of the North. War industries were militarized and work started on constructing the 'iron ring' of Bilbao, a defence line to defend their capital.[22]

The only offensive in the north was General Llano de la Encomienda's push southwards in the mountains towards Villarreal in early December. The Basques and their ill-assorted allies had virtually no air support and only a few field guns hauled by oxen. But morale was high. Pierre Bocheau, a French communist volunteer with the Larrañaga Battalion, recorded his impressions. His unit, an international detachment, was named after Jesús Larrañaga, the Basque communist deputy and chief commissar of the army.

'Friday, a grey, rainy morning, we have assembled in the courtyard of the barracks and we are filling our ammunition pouches, checking our machine-guns, revolvers and rifles. Suddenly one of us, almost a boy, starts singing a song ... We cross Bilbao. At the railway station are the sisters, fiancées and mothers of our Spanish comrades. Some of them are crying. And we Italians, French and Bulgarians from the international detachment are thinking about our mothers, fiancées and sisters who are not here. Spanish women surround me. They offer me bread and oranges. They say with much tenderness in their voices: "Muchacho! Your family is not here to kiss you goodbye."

'In the train, one of my comrades – Piero, I think – spoke of death with much indifference. "To die is nothing. The main thing is to win." ... We begin to sing the "Carmagnole". Then, we sang in Spanish "The Young Guards". It seemed to me for a minute that we are immortal. That not one of us is going to die, even if a bullet strikes the head or the heart.

'Elorrio. The train stops. Night. We call to each other while lining up in companies. It's pouring with rain. Our battalion of workers and peasants is marching forward between the black, silent fences of the village.

'Tuesday. "Comrades! Get up!" It is two in the morning and the night is dark. The company is ready to fight in two minutes. In fact, all we had to do was to put on our boots. Dudul said suddenly, "And actually when you are going into battle, your heart really does beat fast."

'Bullets are hitting the branches of the trees. Bullets are flying past our ears. Bullets hit the ground round our feet. A whisper is heard. "Comrades, we're going to advance now." Then, a loud cry: '*Adelante!*' We move forward, knee deep in mud. We move forward through a curtain of bullets. My body is shaking and I am not a coward. It is flapping around like a pennant in the wind. I have to take my own body by the shoulders and push it forward ...

'It is so heavy to carry a wounded man. The wounded men seem so heavy when you have been on your feet from dawn till dusk. At times, we stumbled into shell holes, tripped and dropped the man we were carrying. Every moan broke our hearts. I collapsed when we reached the wood where the French battalion was fighting. That's all I remember.'[23]

The conduct of the war on the Aragón front, particularly the lack of action, soon became a major cause of tension between the anarchists and the communists. It is true that once the possibility of recapturing the key towns of Saragossa, Teruel and Huesca had diminished, lethargy seemed to descend on the Catalonian militias. Nevertheless, the communist charges (such as the football matches with the enemy, which Hemingway accepted as gospel) were often inaccurate and misleading. The communists made sure that none of the new equipment went to the Aragón front, certainly no aircraft or tanks, which were reserved for their own troops and were, therefore, concentrated around Madrid. Some of the best Catalonian troops were helping on the Madrid front, and many of those left behind were armed only with shotguns. Under such conditions it was unrealistic to expect conventional offensives to be mounted, particularly since XIII International Brigade failed in seven attacks on Teruel.

Even so, anarchist inactivity in a region which they had promised to turn into 'the Spanish Ukraine' was remarkable. Nothing was done by the CNT-FAI leadership to organize guerrilla groups and prosecute a Makhnovista-style campaign, which would have avoided the military conventions which they detested. It is surprising that a man such as García Oliver, who was energetic and imaginative, did not realize that extending enemy forces over wide areas through a vigorous guerrilla campaign would be far less costly in human lives than the slaughter into which they were being inexorably drawn. The nationalists did not have the troops to fight both an anti-guerrilla campaign in their rear areas and a conventional war at the front. There were, it is true, many guerrilla groups behind nationalist lines. But, as will be seen later, a considerable proportion of them were simply refugees from the nationalist execution squads trying to survive. Nevertheless, there was active resistance in Galicia, León, Estremadura and Andalucia, where an irregular brigade under the Granadine cabinetmaker Maroto operated.

The GRU and especially the NKVD carried out 'active work' in Spain. This meant that apart from purely intelligence missions, they conducted sabotage work in the rear areas of the nationalists. 'Orlov', the NKVD chief in Spain, was in overall charge, but Kh.

U. Mamsourov, under the name of Colonel Xanthé, worked in Spain from August 1936 to October 1937 guiding all partisan activities there. He set up *aktivki*, small sabotage groups who crossed the lines for a mission. Mamsourov, who was made a Hero of the Soviet Union, later claimed when a colonel-general that he was the person on whom Hemingway based his hero, Robert Jordan, in *For Whom the Bell Tolls*.[24] Mamsourov was replaced by Naum Eitingon, still one of the great heroes of Soviet foreign intelligence who had been an expert in 'wet operations': it was he who organized the assassination of Trotsky. In his letter to Largo Caballero in December 1936 Stalin also advocated the formation of detachments behind enemy lines. Later on, Orlov claimed to have trained 1,600 guerrillas in his schools and put 14,000 'regulars' in the field, but the latter figure is probably a gross exaggeration.

The conversion of militia forces into the People's Army was known as 'militarization' and it was not a smooth process. Those anarchists, poumistas and left socialists, who defended the militia system on the basis of principle, obstinately refused to see that it could not answer the needs of the situation. They also drew false parallels with the French and Russian revolutions.[25] A 'military machine' can be defeated only by a better machine or by the sabotage tactics of irregular warfare. The militia fell between the two roles. Their improvisation had been a revolutionary necessity, not a military virtue, and as a force to resist a relatively sophisticated enemy they were utterly obsolete.

The theory used to justify the militia system depended almost entirely on morale, which is only one part in the military mix, and the most vulnerable of all. There were too many anarchists who allowed morale to serve as a substitute for practicality, who did not replace the discipline they rejected with self-discipline and who sometimes let their beliefs degenerate into an ideological justification of inefficiency. But there were others, like Cipriano Mera, who realized that they were now committed to a course of action, which they had to pursue even if it conflicted with their ideals. More and more anarchists came to accept this during the autumn and winter of 1936. They were alarmed by the increase in communist power, but they knew that the war against the nationalists was a war of survival.

There were two main stumbling blocks in the process of militarization. One was the principle of 'unified command', which worried the anarchists and the POUM because they feared the communists, even though they came to recognize its necessity in conventional war. The other was the imposition of traditional military discipline. The POUM wanted soldiers' councils like those formed in the Russian revolution, an idea which horrified the communists, while the anarchists were split among themselves. Mera emphasized on several occasions that the instinct of self-preservation had proved itself too strong to be controlled solely by individual will-power in the unnatural atmosphere of the 'noise of artillery, the rattle of machine-guns, and the whistle of bombs'.[26]

The anarchists' beliefs usually made them extremely reluctant to accept any form of command position, which of course made them vulnerable. (This was not new; in 1917 Trotsky became head of the Petrograd Soviet when Voline refused the post on the grounds of anarchist principle.) The conflicts between the anarchists and the military hierarchy were solved by a series of compromises. Saluting, the formal term of address and officers from outside were rejected by the anarchists, and delegates they had already elected were confirmed with the equivalent rank. (As only regular officers could become colonels, militia column commanders remained majors.) The problem over pay differentials was usually solved by officers contributing everything they earned above a militiaman's wage to the CNT war fund.

It was not only the militias who were forced to alter their attitudes in the winter of 1936. In less than six months an attempted *coup d'état* had turned first into a full-scale civil war and then into a world war by proxy. On 31 December 1936 nationalist artillery opposite Madrid rang in the new year by firing twelve shells into the centre of Madrid on the stroke of midnight. Ten of them hit the Telefónica. The Caudillo was said to have been angered by this unprofessional levity. Nevertheless, even such a career-minded general as Franco could not have liked the words of Captain von Goss of the Condor Legion: 'No longer in the spring of 1937 could one talk merely of the *Spanish* war. It had become a real war.'[27]

19

The Battles of the Jarama and Guadalajara

After the bloody shock of the Corunna road had ended in a stalemate, Franco began to prepare a new operation against Madrid. He refused to abandon the idea of taking the capital before spring, but although his strategy of a pincer attack to the east of Madrid was sound, he did not follow it through.

During the second half of January 1937, the front ran southwards from Madrid along the line of the road to Aranjuez. The new offensive was planned in the centre of this sector, thrusting north-eastwards across the River Jarama to cut the Valencia road. This was to be accompanied by an attack of the Italian Corpo di Truppé Volontarie under Roatta, which would strike down towards Guadalajara from the northern part of the nationalist zone. The pincers were planned to join round Alcalá de Henares, thus cutting off Madrid completely. But these two assaults did not coincide because the bad weather in January had delayed the redeployment of Italian troops after the Málaga campaign. There was little chance that they could be in position by the first week of February, yet Franco decided to launch the Jarama offensive without waiting for his Italian allies. The weather was indeed a problem. 'Raining, raining, raining,' wrote Richthofen in his diary at the end of January. 'Airfields are completely sodden. Ice and mist!'[1]

Franco was slow in appreciating how the war had changed in the last few months and that his best troops could not put the republican forces to flight as they had done in the previous autumn. It was no longer a war of rapid manoeuvre, but of head-on slogging, and as a result the advantage of his troops' fieldcraft and tactical skill was greatly reduced. Even the increase in air and artillery support was not enough to ensure victory, especially since the Soviet fighters made the Heinkel 51 obsolete. Delivery of the new Messerschmitt 109 to the Condor Legion was accelerated, but the first models did not arrive until March. In any case, the republican forces were already better prepared to survive air or artillery bombardment.

Although General Mola had supreme command, General Orgaz was in charge of the front. Once again Varela was the field commander. He had five brigades of six battalions each, with a further eleven battalions in reserve, totalling some 25,000 men. They were backed by two German heavy machine-gun battalions, von Thoma's tanks, six batteries of 155mm artillery, and the 88mm guns of the Condor Legion, which were to be battle tested for the first time. Colonel García Escámez commanded the brigade on the right flank by Ciempozuelos near Aranjuez. Colonel Rada was on the left or northern flank, which was bounded by the River Manzanares as it flows eastwards to join the Jarama. In the centre were the brigades of Asensio, Barrón and Sáenz de Buruaga with an axis of advance towards Arganda. The majority of the troops were Moroccan *regulares* and legionnaires. Rada also had a Carlist regiment and Barrón ten squadrons of cavalry.

The republican general staff, too, were planning an offensive in this sector, but jealousies between General Miaja in Madrid and General Pozas commanding the Army of the Centre had held it up. Even so, the Republic mustered some 50 battalions in the area, making the opposing infantry forces roughly level.

When the rain finally eased on 5 February, Mola gave the order for the attack to begin the next morning. On the left Rada's force assaulted La Marañosa, a hill almost 700 metres high, which was defended ferociously by two republican battalions. Five kilometres to the south, Sáenz de Buruaga's brigade took the hamlet of Gózquez de Abajo, only one kilometre short of the River Jarama. Asensio's brigade thrust eastwards from Valdemoro and overran San Martín de la Vega, while García Escámez's force captured Ciempozuelos after heavy fighting in which the defending 18th Brigade lost 1,300 men. By the morning of 8 February the nationalists controlled most of the west bank of the Jarama. On the following day Rada's men occupied the high ground in the loop formed by the confluence of the Manzanares and the Jarama opposite Vaciamadrid. Varela's strategy was correct in allocating the Rada and García Escámez brigades to secure his flanks, but the remaining three columns in the centre proved too small a force to ensure a breakthrough.

The republicans had no idea where the next attack was going to take place, so they decided to reinforce the Madrid road and right bank of the Manzanares. The nationalist offensive was held up for the next two days because heavy rain had made the Jarama unfordable. On 11 February at first light, Moroccan troops from Barrón's brigade, using their large triangular knives, killed the French sentries of the André Marty Battalion (XIV International Brigade) who were guarding the Pindoque railway bridge between Vaciamadrid and San Martín de la Vega.[2] The bridge had been prepared for demolition and the charges were detonated just after its capture, but the metal construction, which was similar to a Bailey bridge, went up in the air a few feet and came down to rest again.

Barrón's brigade, followed by Sáenz de Buruaga's troops, crossed rapidly, but they were then held up for some time by heavy fire from the Garibaldi Battalion from XII International Brigade on higher ground. Later in the day 25 T-26s counter-attacked twice, but each time they were driven back by the nationalist 155mm batteries on La Marañosa. Downstream, Asensio's *regulares* captured the bridge at San Martín de la Vega in a similar attack at dawn the next morning, despite Varela's order to wait until the other bridgehead was established. His brigade then swung south-east towards the high ground at Pingarrón, which like other key features in the area had not been prepared for defence.

General Pozas, the republican commander of the Army of the Centre, had immediately hurried to Arganda to organize a counter-attack. Matters were not helped by his squabble with Miaja, whose chief of staff, Colonel Casado, described their differences as 'fundamentally childish'. Miaja refused to send the five brigades he had available to join the battle unless he was given command of the front. He had his way, but by then the nationalists were across the river in strength, despite air attacks against the two crossing points, during which the Chatos faced heavy fire from Condor Legion 88mm guns and lost one aircraft.

During the night of 11 February the newly formed XV International Brigade arrived under the command of General 'Gal' (Janos Galicz). His chief of staff was Major George Nathan, widely regarded as one of the most competent officers in the International Brigades. The British battalion was on the left, under the command of Tom Wintringham, the Franco-Belgian '6th of February' Battalion in the centre and the 'Dimitrov' on the right. The brigade advanced through the sodden olive groves under heavy enemy fire, which allowed them no respite.[3] Gal's orders were to attack the troops of Sáenz de Buruaga on the San Martín–Morata road. The American battalion was being hurried through induction at Albacete to be ready to reinforce them.

The next day Asensio's troops captured the commanding feature of Pingarrón, while to the north XI International Brigade and the 17th Brigade just held on at Pajares. The British battalion bore the brunt of the attack on the south of the road. They lost over half their men in capturing, then defending, 'Suicide Hill' with their Maxim machine-guns until they ran out of ammunition.[4] The French '6th of February' Battalion on their right was forced back. The British received no warning of what had happened and their machine-gun company was captured by a group of *regulares* from their exposed side. They claim to have been surprised when a group of nationalist troops came up singing the 'Internationale'.[5] 'Suicide Hill' could be held no longer and the whole brigade had to fall back. But a breakthrough in the centre had been prevented, because the nationalists believed republican forces to be much stronger. They also failed to discover the weakness on XV International Brigade's southern flank.

The British battalion had lost 225 men out of 600. Wintringham himself fell badly wounded and the communist novelist Christopher Caudwell was among those killed. Meanwhile, on its right flank, the brigade's Dimitrov Battalion of Balkan exiles and the re-formed Thaelmann Battalion of XI International held off an equally severe attack. Very heavy casualties were inflicted on the *regulares* until the old Colt machine-guns jammed.

In the rolling hills and olive groves to the east of the Jarama between Pajares and Pingarrón, attack followed attack throughout 13 February, as Varela became desperate to achieve his breakthrough. Eventually the Edgar André Battalion of XI International Brigade was forced back as a result of fire from a Condor Legion machine-gun battalion and 155mm bombardment from La Marañosa. The shellfire also destroyed brigade headquarters and cut all field telephone lines to the rear. Barrón's column took advantage of this gap at Pajares and his attack turned the right flank of XV International Brigade. Since the other nationalist formations had already been fought to a standstill, Barrón's troops pushed on alone towards Arganda on the Valencia road.

The front was on the point of disintegrating that night as XI International Brigade and its flanking formations fell back trying to re-establish a line. Varela was worried by the fact that Barrón's brigade was exposed, so he ordered him to halt until the other columns could protect his flanks. It was to be the furthest point of their advance, for the next day 50 of Pavlov's T-26s counter-attacked in what could best be described as a confused charge of mechanized heavy cavalry. Although not a success in itself, this attack gave the republicans enough time to bring forward reserve units to consolidate the centre of the sector.

Richthofen jotted down what he heard from nationalist officers. 'Red opponents before Madrid – tough fighting. French, Belgian and English prisoners are taken. All shot except for the English. Tanks well concealed in the olive groves. Many dead are lying around. The Moors did their work with hand grenades.'[6] Why British prisoners were spared is not clear. Perhaps Franco, on German advice, had judged it safer not to outrage the organizers of the Non-Intervention Committee.

Mola was by now extremely concerned at the way the offensive had halted. He, too, was obsessed with the idea of Madrid and he had persuaded Franco to let him commit the last six battalions in reserve, but these units could not even replace the losses the columns had suffered. Both sides had fought to a temporary standstill. Front-line troops had sustained fearful casualties in charges of hopeless bravery. Both sides were also weakened by hunger because the intensity of the fighting had often prevented the arrival of rations. The republican general staff had reacted so slowly to the crisis that fresh units were not in position to take advantage of the nationalists' exhaustion by counter-attacking. The only reinforcement available at this point was XIV International Brigade, which consolidated the centre of the sector between Arganda and Morata.

On 15 February Franco ordered Orgaz to continue the advance, despite nationalist losses. It was an obstinate and unjustifiable decision, since the Italian forces were still regrouping for transfer to the Guadalajara front. Any further push should at least have been co-ordinated with their offensive. The nationalists lost more of their best troops for an insignificant gain in ground.

On the same day, on the other side of the lines, Miaja's control over the Jarama front came officially into effect. With Colonel Rojo he reorganized the republican formations into four divisions.

On 17 February the republican forces went on to the offensive. Líster's 11th Division moved on Pingarrón in a frontal attack which brought appalling casualties; the 70th Brigade, attached from Mera's 14th Division, lost 1,100 men, over half its strength. On the same day Modesto's division crossed the Manzanares from the north to attack La Marañosa, which was defended by Rada's Carlists. A communist battalion called the 'Grey Wolves of La Pasionaria' was shot to pieces in a doomed attack over a long stretch of open ground. Peter Kemp, an English volunteer serving as a Carlist subaltern, records how his aim was not helped by their chaplain screaming in his ear to shoot more of the atheist rabble.[7]

The only effective part of the republican counter-attack forced Barrón's brigade back to the Chinchón–Madrid road. The Soviet tank brigade played a key role with its T-26s emerging from their camouflaged positions under the olive trees. Moscow was informed how a junior officer named Bilibin managed to evacuate a damaged tank under heavy machine-gun and shellfire. And on 19 February 'Junior officer Novikov's tank received three direct hits. His loader was killed and his mechanic-driver was mortally wounded. Novikov himself was heavily wounded but for more than 24 hours he would not let the enemy approach his burning tank. He was later rescued by his comrades.' This tale of survival in a burning tank for a day and a night strains one's credulity, but Soviet battlefield reports of often genuine heroism had to be as preposterously exaggerated as the Stalinist claims of labour achievements.[8]

Krasilnikov, a tank commander and Communist Party member, also revealed the insane influence of a Stakhanovite mentality on military affairs. 'During the battles near Jarama, battalion commander Comrade Glaziev considered that the best crews were those that fired off the most shells. Yet they were firing these shells while three kilometres away from the enemy.'[9]

Little then happened for the next ten days, until General Gal threw his newly formed division into an impossible attack on Pingarrón. His orders stated that it 'must be taken at any cost', and he persisted with the attack even though the air and tank support, which had been promised, never arrived. Those behind with binoculars could see bodies strewn around, and watched the wounded struggling to crawl back, away from the killing zone. Once again both Brigaders and Spanish troops were paying for the deficiencies of their commanders and staff.

On the morning of 21 February the Scandinavian company in the Thaelmann Battalion took the opportunity of a lull to deepen their trenches and cut more branches for camouflage. It had finally stopped raining. Conny Andersson, a Swedish survivor of the battle, described the scene: 'The morning sun caressed our earthen-grey faces and slowly dried the damp blankets.' Some men crept back to fetch coffee from a huge green container which had been brought up to just behind the front line. Dates and biscuits were handed out. 'We dozed a little in the sunshine, talking about nothing, rolled up the blankets as they dried, cleaned our rifles and prepared ammunition. A German poncing around with a helmet to tease the snipers was despatched to eternity with a professional crack. Some medical orderlies silently carried him down the road and extended the communal grave.' The second company of the battalion was reinforced that day by some Austrians, 'all of whom were bold and hearty and kitted out in short sheepskins. They aroused considerable attention wherever they went – at least the sheepskins did.' Those who saw them coveted them, thinking of the cold hours of sentry duty in the early hours of the morning.[10]

The tight political control of ambitious commissars made propaganda motives interfere with military sense. There were a few extremely competent officers, like the French Colonel Putz, or the English Major Nathan (who was not promoted because he refused to become a Party member), but most senior officers bluffed their way through, relying on rigid discipline. Often their decisions resulted in massive casualties for little purpose. Their bravely dramatic orders like 'stand and die' or 'not a centimetre's retreat', when ammunition was exhausted, sounded well in the propaganda accounts, but it was not the staff who suffered from them.

One of the most tragic episodes involved the men of the Lincoln Battalion, who had arrived in the middle of February fresh in their 'doughboy' uniforms. They were put under the command of an English charlatan who pretended to have been an officer in the 11th Hussars. He ordered them into attack after attack, losing 120 men out of 500. The Americans mutinied, nearly lynched the Walter Mitty character who had been imposed on them and refused to go back into the line until they could elect their own commander. Soon after these last attacks at the end of February the front stabilized, because both sides were now completely exhausted. The Valencia road had not been cut and the nationalists had suffered heavy losses among their best troops. (It would seem that casualties were roughly equal on both sides, although estimates varied from 6,000 up to 20,000.)

The battle of the Jarama saw a closer co-ordination between ground and air forces on the nationalist side, but not on the republican, as a commissar with the Soviet squadrons reported back to Moscow: 'The air force keeps working all day under a great strain, giving its greatest effort to the fighting. It defeats the enemy in the air [an over-optimistic claim] and on the ground, tank units break the front line. All that the infantry needs to do is to secure the results of the air and armoured operations. But the weak rifle units fail to do this. Our men, when they learn about this, feel that their work is being wasted. For example, the fighter pilots said after the air battles over the Jarama: "We don't mind making another five or six sorties a day, if only the infantry would advance and secure the results of our work." After our fighters had had a successful day of fighting over the Jarama sector, the pilots asked what the rifle units had achieved, and when they found out that the infantry had even retreated a little, this caused a lot of unhappiness. Pilot Sokolov became very nervous, he even wept.'[11]

The nationalists had used the Condor Legion Junkers 52 to counter the T-26 attack on the Pindoque bridge and Modesto's advance on La Marañosa. The republican air force had managed to maintain an effective umbrella for most of the early days of the battle, but after 13 February their supremacy was challenged by the Fiat CR 32s of the nationalists, which engaged the Chatos in a large-scale dogfight over Arganda. Five days later the 'Blue Patrol' Fiat group, led by the nationalist ace Morato, was transferred to the front. Together with Fiats of the Legionary Air Force they inflicted heavy losses on a republican group comprising a Chato squadron with a flight of American volunteers, a Russian Chato squadron and a Russian Mosca squadron. It would appear that the Soviet pilots were ordered to act with great caution as a result of these disastrous engagements, in which three Chatos were shot down while the nationalists lost only one Fiat.[12]

After digging in, this second stalemate became a monotonous existence in the damp olive groves. It was a life of rain-filled trenches, congealed stew, occasional deaths from odd bursts of firing and useless attempts to get rid of lice in the seams of clothes. The commissars tried to keep up morale with organized political 'discussions' and by distributing pamphlets or Party newspapers. The lack of fighting also brought to the International Brigades at the front such diversely famous visitors as Stephen Spender, Henri Cartier-Bresson, the scientist Professor J. B. S. Haldane and Errol Flynn.

The events of recent months, especially the fall of Málaga, provoked dissension within the government over the handling of the war. The communists led a determined attack on General Asensio Torrado, the under-secretary of war, whose conduct Largo Caballero had successfully defended against criticism the previous October. (Earlier the communists had tried to flatter Asensio Torrado as the 'hero of the democratic republic', but he rejected their advances and took measures against them, such as insisting on an inquiry into irregularities in their 5th Regiment's accounts and trying to stop their infiltration of the Assault Guard.) As they could not accuse him of incompetence after the qualified success at the Jarama, they attacked him for not having sent enough ammunition to prevent the fall of Málaga.

Álvarez del Vayo openly supported the communist ministers, thus finally ending his friendship with the prime minister. The anarchist ministers did nothing to help the general because they felt he had consistently discriminated against their troops. The republicans and right socialists also disliked him, mainly because of Largo's obsessive reaction to any criticism of his chosen subordinate. The general was finally removed on 21 February. His place was filled by Carlos de Baráibar, a close colleague of Largo Caballero. The communists were disappointed not to have one of their own men appointed.

André Marty, in a long report to Moscow, gave his explanation for Caballero's dogged resistance to the communists. 'Caballero does not want defeat, but he is afraid of victory. He is afraid of victory, for victory is not possible without the active participation of the communists. Victory means an even greater strengthening of the position of the Communist Party. A final military victory over the enemy means for Caballero and the whole world the political hegemony of the Communist Party in Spain. This is a natural and indisputable thing ... a republican Spain, raised from the ruins of fascism and led by communists, a free Spain of a new republican type, organized with the help of competent people, will be a great economic and military power, carrying out a policy of solidarity and close connections with the Soviet Union.'[13] Although this blatant declaration of communist ambitions in republican Spain did not coincide with Stalin's plans, the Comintern does not appear to have discouraged the idea in any way.

The political infighting over Asensio Torrado at Valencia came immediately after the power struggle between Miaja and Pozas. Having increased his responsibilities to include both the Jarama and Guadalajara fronts, Miaja was to have overall command during the largest battles of the first year of the civil war, including the only well-known republican victory, Guadalajara.

Franco's decision to continue with the second half of the pincer operation was as unjustifiable as launching the Jarama offensive on its own.[14] Varela's troops were supposed to recommence their advance towards Alcalá de Henares, but the nationalist forces on the Jarama front were incapable of recreating any momentum.[15] It may be that Franco continued with the operation in response to the misplaced optimism of the Italians after the Málaga walkover. The advance was to be almost entirely an Italian affair.

General Roatta now had some 35,000 men in General Coppi's *Llamas Negras* Division, General Nuvolini's *Flechas Negras*, General Rossi's *Dio lo vuole* Division and General Bergonzoli's *Littorio* Division. The last had regular officers and conscripts; the other formations contained fascist militia. This force of motorized infantry was supported by four companies of Fiat Ansaldo miniature tanks, 1,500 lorries, 160 field guns and four squadrons of Fiat CR 32 fighters, which poor visibility and water-logged airfields were to render virtually non-operational. Mussolini's appetite for military victory pushed on the officers commanding these 'involuntary volunteers' whom he had now managed to have concentrated in an independent command.

The republican general staff appears to have been aware of the growing threat to the Guadalajara sector on the Madrid–Saragossa road, but only one company of T-26 tanks was sent to reinforce the thinly spread and inexperienced 12th Division under Colonel Lacalle.

On 8 March, at first light, Coppi's motorized 'Black Flames' Division, led by armoured cars and Fiat Ansaldos, smashed straight through the republican lines in the *Schwerpunkt* manner. On their right the 2nd Brigade of the Soria Division commanded by the recently promoted Alcázar defender General Moscardó also broke the republican front, but they were on foot and soon fell behind. During that day fog and sleet reduced visibility to 100 metres in places. Bad weather continued on 9 March and the Italians allowed their attack to slow down while they widened the breach in the republican front. That night they stopped to rest because their men were cold and tired (many of their militia were still in tropical uniforms). This break in the momentum of the attack was incompatible with blitzkrieg tactics and was all the more serious since there was no co-ordinated attack on the Jarama front. Roatta sent urgent requests to Franco, but nothing was done.[16] English and French strategists (with the notable exceptions of Liddell Hart and Charles de Gaulle) were to point to the Guadalajara offensive as proof that an armoured thrust was a worthless strategy. The Germans, on the other hand, knew that it had not been followed properly and that the Italian forces were ill trained for such a manoeuvre in the first place.

Miaja and Rojo, reacting more rapidly to the threat than they had at the Jarama, rushed in reinforcements and reorganized the command structure. Colonel Jurado was ordered to form IV Corps based on Guadalajara. Under his command he had Líster's division astride the main Madrid–Saragossa road at Torija, Mera's 14th Division on the right, opposite Brihuega, and Lacalle's 12th Division on the left. Colonel Lacalle was furious not to be offered the overall command, but few people were impressed by this professional officer. The Soviet adviser, Rodimtsev, who visited the front just before the offensive began, was horrified by what he saw. After three days of battle, Lacalle claimed he was ill and the Italian communist Nino Nanetti was given his command. There was a large degree of foreign communist control at headquarters and Jurado's staff was closely supervised by Soviet advisers, including Meretskov, Malinovsky, Rodimtsev and Voronov.

Rodimtsev, who was to be made a Hero of the Soviet Union for his bravery in the forthcoming battle, and later became world famous as the commander of the 13th Guards Rifle Division at Stalingrad, was attached to the 2nd Brigade commanded by Major González Pando. La Pasionaria had just visited Líster's 11th Division. Dressed in male uniform and a fore-and-aft cap, she had been in the trenches talking to the soldiers, including two young women machine-gunners who, in Rodimtsev's view, looked no more than sixteen or seventeen years old.[17]

On 10 March, the Black Flames and Black Arrows reached Brihuega almost unopposed and occupied the old walled town. In the afternoon the Italian Garibaldi Battalion of XII International Brigade was moved up the road from Torija, and one of their patrols came across an advance group of their fellow countrymen fighting for the nationalists. The fascist patrol spoke to them, and went back to report that they had made contact with elements of the *Littorio* Division which was advancing astride the main road. Soon afterwards a fascist column led by Fiat Ansaldos came up the road from Brihuega assuming the way to Torija was open. An Italian civil war then began, later concentrating around a nearby country house called the Ibarra Palace. Making use of the propaganda opportunity, Italian communists led by Nenni and Nanetti used loudspeakers to urge the fascist militia to join their brother workers. Republican aircraft also dropped leaflets promising safe conduct and 50 pesetas to those who deserted, and 100 pesetas for those who crossed over with their weapons.[18]

The next day the Black Arrows pushed Líster's troops back down the main road, but the advance was halted by the Thaelmann Battalion with the help of tank support just short of Torija. On 12 March the republican forces counter-attacked. They were greatly aided by having a concrete runway at Albacete, where General 'Duglas' directed operations. Nearly 100 Chato and Mosca fighters, as well as two squadrons of Katiuska bombers, harried the Italians while they were pushed back in the centre by counter-attacks supported by Pavlov's T-26 tanks and some of the faster BT-5s. The Legionary Air Force Fiats could not get off the ground to support them because of water-logged runways, and the Italian forces withdrew down the Saragossa road and back into Brihuega. General Roatta then proceeded to change the positions of his motorized divisions, a complicated manoeuvre which resulted in many vehicles becoming stuck in the heavy mud, where they were easy targets for the fighters.

Líster's 11th Division began to advance at dawn up the 'French highway', with its 2nd Brigade in the lead. It was cold, with snow and mud, which made movement off the road impossible. This produced traffic jams and chaos. Rodimtsev witnessed a furious argument over who had priority between a battery commander and a supply officer. 'Artillery is everything,' shouted the battery commander. 'It determines the success of a battle and an operation.'

'So perhaps you'll start firing at the enemy with Italian spaghetti?' retorted the supply officer. 'Who's going to bring you ammunition if we don't?' The artillery officer, still furious, told his men to push the supply wagons off the road, whereupon the supply officer drew his pistol.[19]

XI International Brigade and El Campesino's brigade retook Trijueque and advanced up the Brihuega road, dispersing the Italians they found. The inhabitants of Trijueque had been traumatized by the shelling and the air attacks. Fathers were pulling beams and rubble out of the way to find survivors. Among those killed was an eighteen-year-old heroine called Antonia Portero who, according to one Soviet account, had been leading a company. She was one of the first to enter Trijueque, but she was killed by an Italian bombing raid and buried in the ruins of a house.[20] Karl Anger, who witnessed the scenes, also saw the arrival of Mikhail Koltsov, the leading Soviet journalist and plenipotentiary: 'A car arrives. Koltsov climbs out of it and greets us silently, like in a house where someone has just died.'[21]

But Koltsov's morale soon rose when he saw evidence of the Italians' rapid retreat. 'The highway is jammed with Fiat tractors, which they used to transport guns, as well as huge Lancia trucks and cars. The road is littered with rucksacks, weapons and cartridges. There is lots of stuff inside the trucks . . . An excited young fellow is persuading the passing troops to take half a dozen hand grenades and as much sponge cake as they can. The soldiers fill their bags with grenades and cake without stopping their march.'[22]

The next day, 13 March, the republican IV Corps started to prepare for a major counter-offensive, while the Republic's own representatives protested to the League of Nations and the Non-Intervention Committee with documentary proof from prisoners of the presence of Italian formations.[23] The republican plan was straightforward. Líster's division and all available tanks were to be concentrated on the Saragossa road, while Mera's 14th Division was to cross the River Tajuña from the south-east bank and assault Brihuega. Franco's chief of operations, Colonel Barroso, had warned the Italians that republican forces might attack their flank in this way, but he was ignored.

Soon after midday Pavlov's T-26s charged up the Saragossa

road, with infantry clinging to the outsides and firing away from the rattling tanks. The Italians, who had been preparing to advance again, had no defensive positions and were caught in the open. The tanks even managed to ambush a convoy of Italian trucks. The Spanish infantry leaped off the tanks, which then proceeded to ram the lorries and crush some under their tracks. One group of tanks found a camp concealed in a ravine and began shooting it up. But the republican soldiers were tired after the long approach march the night before and heavy going in the mud. And as they neared Trijueque, they were repulsed by machine-gun fire. They also found themselves counter-attacked by Italians with flame-throwers attached to their Fiat-Ansaldo miniature tanks. An Italian infantry battalion then appeared out of an olive grove. Major Pando and Rodimtsev organized an all-round defence at the base of a small hill. Their machine-gun company, commanded by a woman, Captain Encarnación Fernández Luna, managed to hold off the battalion until Líster organized a counter-attack with tanks and reinforcements. Rodimtsev and Pando ran over to the machine-gunners to hug their commander in gratitude, only to find her calmly combing her hair while looking into a fragment of broken mirror.[24]

Meanwhile, Mera's preparations for his part of the counter-offensive were not without problems. He had placed a battalion of *carabineros* by the river to guard a small bridge prepared for demolition by his *dinamiteros*, in case the enemy made a further attempt to advance, but the *carabinero* commanding officer blew it up despite his orders.[25]

A serious setback was avoided only because Mera was helped by local CNT members acting as spies and scouts who were able to advise him of the best places to throw a pontoon bridge across the swollen river. At dawn on the morning of 18 March his division crossed the pontoon bridge and occupied the heights above Brihuega. Heavy sleet shielded them from the enemy's view, but it also caused the general offensive to be delayed. Mera had no alternative but to keep the division lying in the wet with instructions not to fire, hoping that the Italians would not discover them.

The weather did not start to clear until after midday; only then did the Chato and Katiuska squadrons become operational. Jurado gave the order for a general attack. Líster's division advanced up the main road, supported again by T-26 tanks, and this force crashed into Bergonzoli's *Littorio* Division, made up of regular troops. XI International Brigade also went on to the offensive. Karl Anger wrote excitedly of 'the tap-dance of machine-guns'.[26]

On the republicans' right flank, Mera's division had almost managed to surround Brihuega when the enemy became seized by panic and fled. The CTV was saved from an even greater disaster by the fall of darkness, the more orderly retreat of the *Littorio* division and the number of Italian trucks available for their escape. Even so, their offensive had cost the Italians 5,000 casualties and the loss of a considerable quantity of weapons and vehicles. Captured Italian documents stated that many of their supposedly wounded soldiers were found to have nothing wrong with them under their bandages.

For the republicans, the end of the battle brought a moment of respite. Food was brought up on mules and wine was issued. Some of the men cooked paella in their trenches. Commissars issued three cigarettes to each man and trucks brought up new *alpargatas* to replace those shoes which had rotted in the mud and snow.[27] Italian morale, on the other hand, was devastated and Mussolini was furious. Since Moscardó's troops had suffered very few casualties, Franco's officers refused to see the engagement as a nationalist defeat. They were scathing about their allies' performance and composed a song to the tune of '*Faccetta nera*' which went: 'Guadalajara is not Abyssinia; here the reds are chucking bombs which explode.' It ended: 'The retreat was a dreadful thing; one Italian even arrived in Badajoz.'

As the only publicized republican victory of the war, the battle became a propaganda trophy. The communists claimed that the town of Brihuega was captured by El Campesino's brigade and even added several anecdotal touches. In fact, El Campesino arrived alone at dusk on a motorcycle and was fired at by outlying pickets from the 14th Division. He raced back to report that the town was still in enemy hands. Considering that Líster's division was supposed to be advancing up the Saragossa road, El Campesino had no official reason for being anywhere near Brihuega. The communist version of events was dropped in later years after he was disgraced during his Soviet exile and sent to a labour camp.

In that dangerous year of 1937, Soviet officers were to disappear into camps much sooner than El Campesino. Stalinist spy mania was reaching a peak. Suspicions in Spain and suspicions back in the Soviet Union fed upon each other. Regimental Commissar A.

Agaltsov reported to Moscow in 1937 that the 'fascist intervention in Spain and Trotskyist–Bukharin gangs that are operating in our country are links of the same chain'.[28] And some of the Soviet military advisers who returned from special missions in Spain accelerated the 'mincing machine' of the purges. G. Kulik, the commander of III Rifle Corps, wrote on 29 April 1937 to Voroshilov: 'One cannot help asking oneself, how could this happen that the enemies of the people, traitors to my motherland, for whose interests I have fought at the front in Spain, could have managed to receive leading positions? ... As a bolshevik, I don't want the blood of our people to be shed unnecessarily because of the career makers, hidden traitors and mediocre leaders of troops, whom I have seen in the Spanish army. I consider it necessary that a careful review is conducted of all our commanders, in the first place, high-ranking ones, both in the army and in headquarters.'[29] Stalin's purge of the Red Army was under way.

The failure of the Guadalajara offensive was excellent for morale, but it was not the turning point which the Republic and its supporters abroad tried to portray. Herbert Matthews of the *New York Times* even wrote that 'Guadalajara is for fascism what Bailén was for Napoleon'.[30] From a political point of view, however, some argued that 'Guadalajara aroused the enthusiasm of all anti-fascists ... and represented a hard blow for the prestige of fascism and Mussolini'.[31] Yet, paradoxically, Mussolini's desire for vengeance to wipe out the humiliation only tied him closer to Franco's cause.[32] As the Wilhelmstrasse put it, 'The defeat was of no great military importance, to be sure, but on the other hand it had unfavourable psychological and political reactions which needed to be stamped out by a military victory.'[33] Mussolini replaced Roatta with General Ettore Bastico and devoted even more money and armaments to the war at a terrible cost for Italy.

The only certain consequence for the nationalists was that Franco had to abandon his obsession with entering Madrid quickly and to adopt a longer-term strategy. After the casualties suffered at the Jarama, German advisers were able to argue more strongly for a programme of reducing vulnerable republican territories first. For a number of reasons the most attractive target was undoubtedly the northern republican zone along the Bay of Biscay.

20

The War in the North

The isolated northern zone along the Cantabrian coast was the logical military target for the nationalists after four unsuccessful attempts to cut short the war by capturing Madrid. The German advisers put strong pressure on Franco to change his strategy. A longer war would deflect attention from Hitler's plans in Central Europe, but they were also interested in obtaining the steel and coal of the region for their accelerating armaments programme. In any case, Franco had finally realized that he could not muster sufficient troops to mount a decisive offensive around the capital where the Republic had the advantage of interior lines as well as numbers. The only way to improve the ratio of forces was to crush a weaker sector first in order to release troops for the tougher objectives in the centre. As both the Aragón and Andalucian fronts could be reinforced by the republicans fairly rapidly, the beleaguered northern zone was the obvious choice.

The northern zone had been left untouched by the centralization carried out by Largo Caballero's government. The councils of Asturias and Santander still reflected the union-based organization which followed the rising, while the Basques regarded themselves as autonomous allies of the Republic. Although Basque volunteer units had fought at Oviedo, and Asturian and Santanderino militia helped in Vizcaya, the northern regions were not united, except in their objection to a centralized republican command. The Basques, in particular, rejected the idea that the 'Army of Euzkadi' should simply be part of the Army of the North, commanded ultimately from Valencia. Largo Caballero then agreed to this without telling General Llano de la Encomienda, the army commander.

On 1 October 1936 the statute of Basque autonomy had come before the Cortes sitting in Valencia. It took effect four days later. On 7 October the municipal councillors of the region met in the Casa de Juntas in Guernica, 'the sacred city of the Basques', in accordance with their ancient customs. The purpose of this meeting was to elect a president or *lehendakari*. The proceedings had been kept secret in case of air attack, and this small country town to the east of Bilbao was unmolested as José Antonio Aguirre, the 32-year-old leader of the Basque Nationalist Party, swore his oath in the Basque language under the oak tree of Guernica.

Afterwards he named his government, which included four members of the Basque Nationalist Party, three socialists, two republicans, a communist and a member of the social-democratic Basque Action. The Basque Nationalist Party, or PNV, whose motto was 'God and our old law', controlled the ministries of defence, finance, justice and the interior.[1] The programme of the PNV made superficial concessions to the left, with its social-Christian doctrine, yet also insisted on the defence of religious freedom, the maintenance of public order and upheld the Basque people's sense of national identity.[2] During its nine months of existence, the Basque government created the administrative structure of an independent state, with its own currency, its own flag – the red, green and white *ikurriña* – and judicial system.

Telesforo Monzón, the minister of the interior, was a young aristocrat who some 40 years later became the leader of Herri Batasuna, the political front of the ETA guerrilla organization. His first move was to disband the Civil Guard and the Assault Guard. Then he started to recruit his new police force among Basque-speaking supporters. They were heavily armed, selected for their height and dressed in shiny leather uniforms. This elite corps, the Ertzaña, under the sole control of the PNV, was hardly reassuring to some of their left-wing allies, particularly the anarcho-syndicalist CNT.

Friction, however, came less from political than military differences. The CNT had shown in its furious assaults on the rebel-held buildings in San Sebastián during the rising, in its burning of Irún when it was almost surrounded by the nationalists and later in its intention to lay waste to San Sebastián before Mola's troops occupied it, that it wished to fight a war to the finish. The CNT stated openly its preference for dying in the ruins rather than submitting to Franquist rule. The Basques, in line with the character of a mountain people, were content simply to defend themselves when directly attacked. They even had their symbolic Maloto tree on the border marking the point beyond which their forces should never advance. The Basque nationalists made it clear from the beginning of the civil war that, apart from their anti-fascist feelings, they were on the side of the Republic because it promised them autonomy. They proudly proclaimed their Catholic faith and attacked the anti-clericalism in other parts of republican territory. Nevertheless, their resistance to the military rising was supported by the great majority of their priests in spite of the unqualified backing of the Vatican and the Spanish Church for General Franco.

The Basque nationalists also pretended that there were no class divisions in Euzkadi. This had been partly true of agriculture, where feudalism had been weak, but the seafaring side of Basque life, dominated by local shipping magnates, with international empires, was scarcely classless. And in the nineteenth century industrialization attracted cheap labour from Castile, Galicia and Asturias. It was from this non-Basque workforce that the memberships of the socialist UGT, the CNT and the Communist Party were largely recruited. Indigenous workers were represented by the STV, Solidarity of Basque Workers.

The left believed fervently that the nationalists must be defeated. The Basque nationalists, on the other hand, seemed to know in their hearts that the republicans would be defeated. It may be that they learned the idea of being good losers from the English. At any rate, they treated their prisoners extremely well, sending many to France for release in the hope that this might induce the enemy to be a good winner. The nationalists made no reciprocal gestures to this attempt at 'humanizing the war', as Manuel de Irujo, the Basque minister in the central government, called it. They merely stepped up their campaign of hate, using such self-contradictory phrases as 'soviet-separatists' to describe the Basques.

To have the Catholic Basques as enemies was an embarrassment to the nationalist crusade and Franco was later to attack 'these Christian democrats, less Christian than democrat, who, infected by a destructive liberalism, did not manage to understand this sublime page of religious persecution in Spain which, with its thousands of martyrs, is the most glorious the Church has suffered'. The Archbishop of Burgos called Basque priests 'the dross of the Spanish clergy, in the pay of the reds'. The professor of moral theology at Salamanca, having described 'the armed rising against the Popular Front' as 'the most holy war in history', said 'all who positively oppose the national government in present circumstances, trying to weaken its strength or diminish its power or obstruct its role, should be considered as traitors to the fatherland, infidels to religion and criminals to humanity'.

Cardinal Archbishop Gomá also accused the Basque clergy of taking part in the fighting. Even though most modern military chaplains carry sidearms to protect the wounded, it would appear that only a few, if any, Basque priests were given a pistol, and there is no evidence that they used them. The primate also chose to overlook the fanatical Carlist chaplains on his own side. Many of these *requeté* almoners, purple tassels hanging from their large red berets, were in the tradition of the ferocious nineteenth-century Carlist priest Santa Cruz, who used to absolve his prisoners en masse before shooting them. It was the Navarrese Carlists who were chosen as the main instrument to reduce their Basque neighbours in the spring of 1937.

There had been two major areas of action on the northern front during the winter. The fierce siege of Oviedo continued and a Basque offensive was mounted against Villarreal on 30 November 1936, when General Llano de la Encomienda secretly assembled nineteen infantry battalions, six batteries of artillery and some armoured vehicles. A breakthrough to capture Vitoria might have been achieved if they had not been spotted by a nationalist reconnaissance aircraft from Burgos. The nationalist counter-attack prevented the capture of Villarreal, but the Basques were left in control of the three mountains, Maroto, Albertia and Jarinto, whose peaks they proceeded to fortify. Establishing uncamouflaged defensive positions on peaks was to be one of their most serious mistakes. The Basques did not appreciate the ground-attack capabilities of fighters or the effects of bombing.

By the spring of 1937 the Basque nationalists and their left-wing allies had raised some 46 battalions, of which about half were Basque militia, the Euzko-Gudaroztea. The rest were UGT, CNT, communist or republican units. (Many Basques were shocked by the idea of women fighting in some of the left-wing ranks.) These formations were reinforced by ten battalions from Asturias and Santander who did not get on well with the local population. The general staff under Llano de la Encomienda consisted of professional officers, none of whom seem to have been either energetic or efficient. The greatest liability, however, was the shortage of weapons.

At the beginning of the war Telesforo Monzón's trip to Barcelona had produced only limited supplies. Other means had to be used. The gold reserves in the Bank of Spain were seized. Weapons were purchased abroad, or even stolen, and smuggled back by fishing vessels through the nationalist blockade or brought in aboard English ships. In the late autumn, even though the republican battleship *Jaime I* had left the area, some larger ships still managed to get through. One of these was the Russian *A. Andreev*, which brought the Basques two squadrons of Chatos, 30 tanks (T-26 and Renaults) and fourteen Russian armoured cars with 37mm cannon, 40 mortars, 300 machine-guns and 15,000 rifles.[3] Food was also a major worry, with seldom more than two weeks' supply. The monotonous and sparse diet of chickpeas from Mexico was all that separated the Basques from starvation. There were few cats left alive in the Basque country and ingenious methods of catching seagulls were tried.

The nationalist naval force off the Cantabrian coast consisted of the battleship *España*, the cruiser *Almirante Cervera* and the destroyer *Velasco*. The Basques had only an ancient destroyer and two scarcely serviceable submarines. They therefore improvised by mounting 101mm guns from the battleship *Jaime I* on four deep-sea fishing vessels.

The problem for the republican forces, wrote a Soviet adviser, was the naval leadership, especially Captain Enrique Navarro. 'According to the local people and sailors, Navarro was not paying serious attention to the operations of the flotilla. He has avoided visiting the ships, as he is afraid of the sailors. He wears civilian clothes while in town and at his headquarters on the shore. During our first meeting, Navarro complained about the lack of discipline among the sailors, about the threats from committees of ships, and said that a plot existed to attempt to assassinate him ... There was not a single socialist, to say nothing of communists, among the personnel of the headquarters.' Warships of the flotilla were staying passively in Bilbao, following, apparently, a silent agreement between officers at the headquarters and on the ships. Repairs lasted for indefinite periods of time under different pretexts. The republican flotilla was given the scornful nickname of the 'Non-Interference Committee'.[4]

On 5 March the nationalist cruiser *Canarias* was spotted off the mouth of the River Nervión with a small vessel, the *Yorkbrook*, which she had captured. Basque 105mm and 155mm shore batteries opened fire immediately to drive her off; they knew that armed trawlers, escorting a boat from Bayonne, were due. When they appeared out of the mist, the *Canarias* left her prize to engage them. One of the trawlers, the *Bizkaya*, nipped round the *Canarias* and made off with her prize, while the other two replied to her 8-inch guns with their much smaller armament. One of them, the *Guipuzkoa*, caught fire and had to make for the shelter of the shore batteries, but the crew of the other one, the *Nabarra*, continued the attack and fought on into the night until all ammunition was used and the trawler sunk.[5] This incident, reminiscent of Tennyson's 'The Revenge', was commemorated in an epic poem by Cecil Day Lewis.

In mid March the nationalist commanding general, Emilio Mola, issued his preliminary orders for the campaign. His chief of staff, Colonel Vigón, was the most capable planner in the nationalist army and about the only senior Spanish staff officer to be respected by his German colleagues, who described him as 'one of the most outstanding phenomena in the new Spanish nationalist army'.[6] However, even Vigón could do little to overcome Mola's excessive caution. Richthofen claimed that 'the leadership is practically in the hands of the Condor Legion'.[7]

The nationalist force was based on the Navarre Division of four Carlist brigades. In addition, there was the Black Arrows Division, with 8,000 Spanish infantry commanded by Italian officers and supported by Fiat Ansaldos. In this mountainous region, however, the Condor Legion was to prove the nationalists' biggest advantage. The thin coastal strip allowed the defenders little warning of raids, while the terrain greatly restricted their choice of airfields from which defending fighters could be scrambled. The Basques had only a minute fighter force, so the Condor Legion was able to risk using obsolete Heinkel 51s as ground-attack aircraft while waiting for more of the new Messerschmitts to arrive.

The Condor Legion fighter wing was concentrated at Vitoria, the bomber squadrons at Burgos, because the airfield at Vitoria was too narrow. General Sperrle stayed with Franco's GHQ at Salamanca, leaving Colonel Wolfram von Richthofen as the operational commander of the strike forces. On the northern front these consisted of three squadrons of Junkers 52 bombers, an 'experimental squadron' of Heinkel 111 medium bombers, three squadrons of Heinkel 51 fighters and half a squadron of Messerschmitt 109s, although they were suffering from engine problems.[8] The Italian Legionary Air Force also flew missions in support of troop attacks, with Savoia Marchetti 81s and 79s as well as their Fiat CR 32 fighters.

After issuing his ultimatum that 'if submission is not immediate I will raze Vizcaya to the ground', Mola ordered an advance from the south-east. The offensive opened on 31 March with an assault on the three mountains – Albertia, Maroto and Jarinto – which had been taken by the Basques in the Villarreal offensive the previous year. The nationalists showed on this first day that they meant to make use of their crushing superiority in the air. The towns of Elorrio and Durango, behind the front line, were bombed in relays by the heavy Junkers 52s and Italian S-81s from Soria.

Durango, a town of 10,000 inhabitants, had no air defences nor any form of military presence. A church was bombed during the celebration of mass, killing fourteen nuns, the officiating priest and most of the congregation. Heinkel 51 fighters then strafed fleeing civilians. Altogether, some 250 non-combatants died in the attack. The objective of the raid appears to have been to block the roads through the town with rubble, though that does not explain the activities of the fighters.[9] General Queipo de Llano stated on Seville radio that 'our planes bombed military objectives in Durango, and later communists and socialists locked up the priests and nuns, shooting without pity and burning the churches'. On 2 April, the nationalists claimed on Radio Valladolid that 'in Durango only military objectives were attacked. It has been confirmed, on the other hand, that it was the reds who destroyed the church. The church of Santa María was set on fire while it was full of church-goers.'[10]

The main objectives that day included the three mountains and bombing raids were combined with an artillery barrage just before the Navarrese troops of Alonso Vega went into the attack. Condor Legion bombers went in at 8 a.m.: '60 tons of bombs dropped within two minutes,' Richthofen recorded. Richthofen, in his command post, had 'a very good view'. The Navarrese troops, in order to be recognized clearly by the German aircraft, 'have white tunics on their back. The national flag is carried ahead.'[11] The

Basque militiamen, known as *gudaris*, hardly knew what had hit them before they were overrun by red-bereted Carlists screaming their war cry of '*¡Viva Cristo Rey!*'. Reserves could not be brought up because of air strikes on all communications leading to the front. The artillery barrage had also cut field telephone wires from the forward positions.

The Basque counter-attack on Mount Gorbea was successful and they were to hold it for another eight weeks, thus securing their extreme right flank. But two other mountains were lost the next day, while the air attacks on and around the town of Ochandiano smashed a hole in the front. The *gudaris* were demoralized by this overwhelming air power. They could fight back against the fierceness of a Carlist infantry attack, but they lacked both anti-aircraft guns and fighter cover. Twenty battalions lacked proper automatic weapons and some units' machine-gun companies had only a handful of machine pistols. On 4 April Richthofen noted: 'The fighters are strafing the reds up and down the mountain. 200 dead 400 taken prisoner.' The Basque forces were pushed back, but they dug in and fought on. 'We are always surprised by the toughness of the red infantry. The reds are bleeding heavily.'[12]

Later that day, to Richthofen's exasperation, Mola gave orders for a pause in the offensive. 'War here is a tedious business,' Richthofen wrote on 5 April. 'First Spaniards are brought to an operation. Then operational orders have to be worked through. Then reconnaissance, then visiting headquarters. Look at the operational orders and suggest changes, perhaps with the threat "without us". Checking if orders have gone out and were followed.' The next morning his bombers attacked as agreed, 'but the infantry does not intervene, then asks for more support'. Mola ordered another attack for the next day. 'We are dropping bombs for no reason at all,' wrote Richthofen. 'Protest telegram to Franco.'[13]

On 6 April the nationalists announced a blockade of republican ports on the Cantabrian coast. The same day the nationalist cruiser *Almirante Cervera*, with the moral support of the pocket battleship *Admiral Scheer* in the background, stopped a British merchantman. However, HMS *Blanche* and HMS *Brazen* of the British destroyer flotilla assigned to the Bay of Biscay raced up and the cargo ship was allowed into Bilbao.

Baldwin's government was alarmed that Anglo-Basque trade might force Great Britain to take sides in Spain. It did not wish to recognize either the nationalists or the republicans as belligerents, because that meant allowing them to stop and search British ships en route to Spanish ports. Nevertheless, in the light of subsequent events it is difficult to credit the cabinet or its advisers with impartiality. Admiral Lord Chatfield, the First Sea Lord, was an admirer of General Franco and his officers in the Bay of Biscay had an undoubted sympathy for their nationalist counterparts. Sir Henry Chilton, the ambassador at Hendaye, who still had the ear of the Foreign Office though he was not on the scene, acted as a mouthpiece for the nationalists. Chatfield and Chilton informed the British government that the blockade of Bilbao was effective because the nationalists had mined the mouth of the River Nervión and would shell British ships if they did not stop. Although no unit of the Royal Navy had been near the area in question for months, the Basques' assurances that all mines had been cleared were ignored. The Royal Navy flotilla was ordered by London to instruct all British vessels in the Biscay area en route to Bilbao to wait in the French port of Saint Jean de Luz until further notice. As if to mitigate any damage to British prestige caused by this implicit support of the nationalists, the battle-cruiser HMS *Hood* was ordered to Basque waters from Gibraltar.

The Royal Navy's view of the blockade's effectiveness led to furious scenes in the House of Commons. There were only four nationalist ships watching 200 miles of coast and the Basque shore batteries controlled an area beyond the three-mile limit. The government was taken aback at the onslaught it received but Sir Samuel Hoare, the First Lord of the Admiralty, would not admit the truth about the mines in the Nervión, for his source of information was the nationalist navy.

On 20 April the *Seven Seas Spray*, a small British merchantman which had decided to ignore all Royal Navy instructions and warnings, arrived off Bilbao from Saint Jean de Luz. There were neither nationalist warships nor mines; only an ecstatic welcome from the population of Bilbao awaited them. The British government and the Admiralty were totally discredited. Other vessels waiting near the French Basque coast immediately set out for Spain. One of them was stopped ten miles from Bilbao by the cruiser *Almirante Cervera*. The merchantman radioed for help and this time the Royal Navy, in the form of HMS *Hood*, had to take a firm line with the nationalists. In the Basques' view it was poetic justice that the battleship *España* struck a nationalist mine off Santander nine days later and sank.

The Basques could not now be starved into surrender, but the fighting which had begun again on 20 April was going badly for them. The combination of nationalist air power, the fighting qualities of the Carlist troops and republican units pulling out of line without warning brought the front close to collapse. Yet Richthofen's frustrations did not decrease. On 20 April he was furious with the Italian air force. 'There you are. They dropped their bombs on our own troops. A day full of mishaps. Führer's birthday. Sander [Sperrle] has been promoted to lieutenant-general.'[14] Whatever the imperfections on the nationalist side, chaos among the republican forces was increased by the slowness and incompetence of the general staff. Its chief, Colonel Montaud, was notorious for his defeatism and the regular officers were widely criticized for 'their civil service mentality'.[15] The situation was so bad that Aguirre tried to intervene. Luckily for the Basques, Mola's cautious advance failed to take full advantage of the republican disarray.

On 23 April Richthofen noted: 'Weather very good. 4th Brigade has, despite orders, deployed two battalions not twelve. They are to be relieved. Infantry is not moving forwards. What can one do? Condor Legion pulls out at 1800 hours. One cannot lead infantry which is not willing to attack weakly held positions.' The next day he complained again, exasperated that the Italians had bombed the wrong town. 'These are burdens for the leadership which one cannot imagine ... Should we destroy Bilbao after all?'[16] The Italians had been concerned that an attack on the Catholic Basques in the north would provoke the Pope and were reluctant to bomb the main Basque city. One can only speculate, but perhaps Richthofen's frustrations played a part in the most notorious of all the Condor Legion's operations.

During 25 April many of the demoralized troops from Marquina fell back on Guernica, which lay some ten kilometres behind the lines. On the following day, Monday 26 April, at 4.30 in the afternoon, the main church bell in Guernica rang to warn of air attack. It was market day and, although some farmers had been turned back at the edge of the town, many had still come in with their cattle and sheep. The refugees from the advancing enemy, together with the town's population, went down into the cellars which had been designated as '*refugios*'. A single Heinkel 111 bomber of the Condor Legion's 'experimental squadron' arrived over the town, dropped its load on the centre and disappeared.[17]

Most people came out of their shelters, many going to help the injured. Fifteen minutes later the full squadron flew over, dropping various sizes of bombs. People who rushed back into the shelters were choked by smoke and dust. They became alarmed as it was evident that the cellars were not strong enough to withstand the heavier bombs. A stampede into the fields around the town began, then the Heinkel 51 fighter squadrons swept over, strafing and grenading men, women and children, as well as nuns from the hospital and even the livestock. The major part of the attack had not even started.

At 5.15 the heavy sound of aero engines was heard. The soldiers immediately identified them as 'trams', the nickname for the ponderous Junkers 52. Three squadrons from Burgos carpet-bombed the town systematically in twenty-minute relays for two and a half hours. (Carpet bombing had just been invented by the Condor Legion when attacking the republican positions around Oviedo.) Their loads were made up of small and medium bombs, as well as 250kg bombs, anti-personnel twenty-pounders and incendiaries. The incendiaries were sprinkled down from the Junkers in two-pound aluminium tubes like metallic confetti. Eye-witnesses described the resulting scenes in terms of hell and the apocalypse. Whole families were buried in the ruins of their houses or crushed in the *refugios*; cattle and sheep, blazing with white phosphorus, ran crazily between the burning buildings until they died. Blackened humans staggered blindly through the flames, smoke and dust, while others scrabbled in the rubble, hoping to dig out friends and relatives. According to the Basque government, approximately a third of the town's population were casualties – 1,654 killed and 889 wounded – although more recent research indicates that no more than between 200 and 300 died.[18] Those hurrying towards the town from Bilbao had their original disbelief at the news changed by the orange-red sky in the distance. The parliament buildings and the oak tree were found to be untouched because they had been just outside the flight path which the pilots had followed so rigidly. The rest of Guernica was a burned skeleton.

On the following day, 27 April, news of the destruction of Guernica appeared in the British press. The next morning *The*

Times and the *New York Times* published the article of George Steer which was to have a tremendous effect internationally.[19] Aguirre denounced the event in the following words: 'German aviators, in the service of the Spanish rebels, have bombed Guernica, burning the historic city venerated by all Basques.'[20]

As with the account of Durango, the nationalists set out to reverse the story. Using the precedent of Irún, they said that the town had been destroyed by its defenders as they withdrew; Queipo de Llano specified Asturian *dinamiteros*.[21] Franco's GHQ issued a statement on 29 April: 'We wish to tell the world, loudly and clearly, a little about the burning of Guernica. Guernica was destroyed by fire and gasoline. The red hordes in the criminal service of Aguirre burned it to ruins. The fire took place yesterday and Aguirre, since he is a common criminal, has uttered the infamous lie of attributing this atrocity to our noble and heroic air force.'[22]

The Spanish Church backed this story completely, and its professor of theology in Rome went so far as to declare that there was not a single German in Spain and that Franco needed only Spanish soldiers, who were second to none in the world. It was a version that even Franco's most fervent supporters abroad had difficulty in sustaining. General Roatta himself informed Count Ciano on 8 May that General Sperrle had told him that the Condor Legion had bombed Guernica with incendiaries.[23] An American journalist, escorted by a Falangist, met a staff officer from the Army of the North a few months later in August. Her Falangist escort, who totally believed the story put out by Salamanca, told the staff officer that 'reds' in Guernica had tried to tell them that the town had been bombed from the air, not burned. 'But of course it was bombed,' the staff officer replied. 'We bombed it and bombed it and bombed it, and *bueno*, why not?'[24]

Condor Legion veterans were later to claim that their squadrons were really trying to bomb the Renteria bridge just outside Guernica, but that strong winds blew their loads on to the town. The bridge was never hit, there was virtually no wind, the Junkers were flying abreast and not in line, and anti-personnel bombs, incendiaries and machine-guns are not effective against stone bridges. According to Richthofen's personal diary, the attack had been planned jointly with the nationalists. Mola's chief of staff, Colonel Vigón, agreed to the target the day before the raid and again a few hours before it. No nationalist officer mentioned the importance of Guernica in Basque life and history, but even if they had, the plan would not have been changed.

Richthofen's war diary entry for 26 April, although terse, could hardly be clearer and completely contradicts the nationalist version of events. 'K/88 [the Condor Legion bomber force] was targeted at Guernica, in order to halt and disrupt the Red withdrawal, which has to pass through here.' The following day, he simply wrote: 'Guernica burning'. And on 28 April, he wrote: 'Guernica must be totally destroyed.'[25] The Condor Legion's *Gefechtsbericht* (combat report) for the day does not appear to have survived for some reason. One intention of the raid may have been to block the roads, as he wrote, but everything else points to a major experiment in the effects of aerial terrorism.[26]

As the retreat continued in this sector there were several brave and effective rearguard actions. At Guernica the communist Rosa Luxembourg Battalion under Major Cristóbal held back the nationalists for a time, despite the extraordinary incompetence of their formation commander, Colonel Yartz, who appears to have been incapable of reading a map. Then, on 1 May, as the withdrawal steadied, the 8th UGT Battalion laid a highly successful trap at Bermeo, on the coast, putting 4,000 men of the Black Arrows and their Fiat Ansaldos to flight.

For the Army of Euzkadi, however, it was now necessary to start retreating to the 'Iron Ring' round Bilbao. This defence works, with a perimeter of some 80 kilometres, had been started the previous winter. With 15,000 men working on it, as well as civilian contracting companies who installed concrete strong points, it was wrongly compared to the Maginot Line. It had no depth – in many places nothing more than a single line of trenches – and it was incomplete. There was no attempt at concealment and the officer in charge, Major Goicoechea, had gone over to the nationalists with its detailed plans. President Azaña had no illusions about the defensive capability of these positions. 'What the people have called the "ring of Bilbao" . . . is nothing more than a fantasy. Furthermore, I fear that the city of Bilbao will not be defended when the enemy are at its gates.'[27] His scepticism was echoed by Colonel von Richthofen, who commented on 29 April, 'Photographs show that for the moment large parts of these positions have not been fortified.' Two days later he departed on holiday, having just heard of the Condor Legion's most serious loss of the whole war. Republican fighters had intercepted a Junkers 52 carrying seven of his fighter pilots, all of whom were killed when it was shot down.[28]

The Italians were increasing the size of their forces in the north and the nationalists' four Navarrese brigades were each brought up almost to divisional strength. The republicans, meanwhile, raised more *gudari*, UGT, CNT and communist battalions, and brought in Asturian and Santanderino reinforcements. The Valencia government tried to help by sending aircraft via France, but the Non-Intervention Committee frustrated it on two occasions. That the non-intervention policy was effective only on the French frontier increased republican bitterness greatly. It was thought too dangerous to fly the aircraft straight to Bilbao and risk arriving with little fuel and no protection against nationalist fighters. There were now only six Chatos left in the Basque country and, although their pilots had managed to shoot down the first two Dornier 17s to arrive in Spain, morale seemed to sink after their ace, Felipe del Río, was killed.

Relations between the Basques and the Valencia government became strained by misunderstandings. The republican government in Valencia suspected Aguirre and his ministers of trying to arrange a separate peace, while they became convinced that help was denied them on purpose. The Republic knew that the conquest of the north would not only give the nationalists vital industries, but also release large numbers of enemy troops for deployment in the centre. They therefore planned to launch two attacks in May, the Huesca offensive and an attack in the Sierra de Guadarrama towards Segovia. Neither of these attempts, however, forced the nationalists to divert troops from the northern front.

On 22 May the 4th Navarre Brigade reached the eastern side of the Iron Ring. The nationalists' progress was slower as the Basques and their allies were now fighting more effectively and seemed less affected by air attack. They were beginning to fire back, a tactic which, even if not successful, kept the Fiat and the Heinkel fighters at more of a distance. (Almost a third of the Fiats destroyed in action during the war were brought down as a result of small-arms fire.)

Some of the incompetent senior officers had also been replaced. But Aguirre's attempts to animate the army staff during the campaign had done little to improve the situation. His interference stopped when Llano de la Encomienda was replaced by General Gámir Ulíbarri, a Basque regular officer sent from Valencia. Some new brigade and divisional commanders were also appointed, such as the remarkable mechanic Belderrain, who had organized the effective defence of the Inchortas, Cristóbal, the communist smuggler, and the French Colonel Putz from the International Brigades. On the other hand the Russian General Gorev stayed on despite his unimpressive performance.

A change in the nationalist command was at the same time made necessary by the death of General Mola, in an air crash, on 3 June. His death could be described as a setback for the Basques, because his caution, which so exasperated the Germans, had saved them at critical moments. On the nationalist side there were many who suspected that the Caudillo or his supporters were somehow involved, but the suspicion was almost certainly groundless. Franco's other great rival, Sanjurjo, had died in similar circumstances, but air crashes were frequent and accounted for nearly as many lost machines as enemy action.

Mola's place was filled by General Dávila, who was also methodical, but far more stable than his predecessor. Dávila rearranged his forces, ordering the assault on the Iron Ring to begin on 12 June. Major Goicoechea's plans, confirmed by air reconnaissance, pinpointed the weakest spot in the defence line. A bombardment with 150 artillery pieces and air attacks was swiftly followed by the advance of troops commanded by Colonels García Valiño, Juan Bautista Sánchez and Bertomeu.[29] With no depth to the defences, the whole sector crumbled. Nevertheless, it was certainly not a rout. Many units held their ground and slowed the advance.

The Basque nationalist leaders had meanwhile been in contact with the Italian government and the Vatican to try to prevent the nationalists from destroying Bilbao, as Mola had threatened.[30] On 6 May, Pius XI had asked Cardinal Gomá to act as mediator. He saw Mola and obtained a promise that if Bilbao surrendered there would be no bloody reprisals. Cardinal Pacelli, the secretary of state, sent a telegram on 12 May to Aguirre proposing a separate peace for the Basque country, but the telegram was sent to the Valencia government by mistake. This caused great suspicions. Then a more collaborationist wing of the Basque Nationalist Party attempted to negotiate with the Italians through their consul in San Sebastián.

In Bilbao the Basque government decided to evacuate the city on 16 June after agonized discussions. The Basque nationalist leaders also decided to blow up bridges, but not the steelworks and war industries. Their republican allies in Valencia were horrified when they heard of this later. The coast road to the west was soon packed with refugees and, although only a small part consisted of Santanderino units heading for home, the whole mass was strafed by Heinkel fighter squadrons. A junta of defence under Leizaola, the minister of justice, stayed in the city, while the government withdrew towards Santander. Other senior Basque officials and officers fled on ships leaving the harbour.

The republican forces were assigned new positions along the line of the River Nervión, which curves around Bilbao to the east. With the imminent arrival of the nationalist forces the right-wing fifth columnists in Arenas, on the east of the river's mouth, started shooting into the streets in their excitement. The anarchist Malatesta Battalion, positioned on the other side of the river, stormed across and dealt with them rapidly. Their final action before withdrawing was to set fire to the church. The commander knew that its priest was a nationalist sympathizer; he was his brother.

The city was under continual artillery bombardment. Eventually the republican forces had to withdraw because they were threatened on their southern flank, where troops under the Italian commissar, Nino Nanetti, had withdrawn without blowing the bridge behind them. The fifth columnists in the city had another shock when they gathered in the main square with monarchist flags to greet the Carlist troops. A Basque tank suddenly appeared round the corner, fired at some nationalist flags hanging from balconies and disappeared. At five in the afternoon the 5th Navarrese Brigade under Colonel Juan Bautista Sánchez entered Bilbao. The cheers for the nationalists when they arrived sounded hollow in the half-empty city.[31]

The nationalist casualties for the campaign were high – about 30,000 – but the proportion of fatalities was low. The Basques and their allies suffered only slightly more in total, but their death rate was nearly a third, mainly due to air attacks. The Basque army had operated in a markedly different way from the republican army in the centre. There was far less waste of men's lives through futile counter-attacks over open ground.

The nationalist conquerors held summary court martials in the newly occupied territory, and thousands, including many priests, were sentenced to prison. There were, however, fewer executions than usual, because of the strength of feeling that Guernica had provoked abroad. Nothing, however, stopped the conquerors' resolution to crush every aspect of Basque nationalism. The Basque flag, the *ikurriña*, was outlawed and use of the Basque language suppressed. Threatening notices were displayed: 'If you are Spanish, speak Spanish.' Regionalist feelings in any form were portrayed as the cancer of the Spanish body politic.

The units which retreated along the coast to Santander were demoralized. They knew that it was only a matter of time before Santander and the Asturias fell as well. They were at least given a chance to reorganize, when the nationalist advance was delayed by the major republican offensive at Brunete in the Madrid sector on 6 July. Once this had been repulsed, General Dávila redeployed his troops. They included six Carlist brigades under General Solchaga, the Italian force now commanded by General Bastico, which comprised Bergonzoli's *Littorio* Division, the 'March 23rd' Division, the Black Flames and the mixed Black Arrows. The air support consisted of more than 200 planes, split between the Condor Legion, the Legionary Air Force and the nationalist squadrons, which were being given the Heinkel 51s as Messerschmitts arrived in greater numbers.

General Gámir Ulíbarri's force of some 80,000 men had not only less infantry than the nationalists, but also only 40 operational fighters and bombers, many of which were obsolete. On the opening day of the offensive, 14 August, Solchaga's Carlist brigades attacked from the east and smashed through the 54th Division. The Italians were held up by fierce resistance in the Cantabrian mountains to the south-west, but with overwhelming artillery and air support they captured the Escudo pass two days later. The three republican divisions sent to hold the breach were not quick enough and the breakthrough was complete.

Many of the republican formations then carried out a fighting retreat into the mountains of Asturias. The remainder were bottled up in the area of Santander and the small port of Santoña. In Santander the desperation was so great that many men sought oblivion in drink. Officers organized parties of soldiers to go round destroying the wine stocks. The general staff arranged to escape in ships, but the small boats were swamped by panic-stricken men and many capsized. The 122nd and 136th Battalions tried to organize a defence, but apathy seemed to take over once the last chance of escape had gone. They waited for the nationalists and their firing squads. Since many nationalist supporters had been killed in the previous year, mainly on the orders of the socialist Neila, little mercy was expected.

In Santoña, the Basques arranged surrender terms for their *gudaris* with the Italian commander of the Black Arrows, Colonel Farina. These had already been discussed in Rome between Count Ciano and Basque PNV representatives, who felt that the Valencia government had let them down badly. It was agreed that there would be no reprisals and that no Basque soldier would be forced to fight on the nationalist side. Spanish officers announced immediately that this agreement was invalid and Basque soldiers were taken off British ships in the port at gunpoint. Summary trials followed and a large proportion of the officers and many soldiers were executed. It was this dishonouring of the articles of surrender which the Basque ETA guerrillas advanced in later years as a reason why the Republic of Euzkadi was still at war with the Franquist state.[32]

Mussolini and Count Ciano were overjoyed at this 'great victory'. Ciano wanted 'flags and guns captured from the Basques. I envy the French their Invalides and the Germans their Military Museums. A flag taken from the enemy is worth more than any picture.'[33] They felt that their decision to keep Italian troops in Spain after the débâcle of Brihuega had been vindicated. Their jubilation was premature, however, for approximately half of the republican forces had pulled back into the Asturian mountains, where there was to be a much tougher campaign lasting until the end of October, followed by a further five months of ferocious guerrilla warfare. Franco was not able to bring down the Army of the North as quickly as he had hoped.

The relative speed of the nationalists' victory in the Basque campaign was due to the Condor Legion's contribution. The Nazi government did not delay in taking payment. German engineers moved into the factories and steel mills which the Basque nationalists had refused to destroy and most of the industrial production went to Germany to pay the Luftwaffe's expenses for destroying the region. Franco, on the other hand, had to wait longer for his benefits, although he knew that the reduction of the north would eventually give him infantry parity in the centre and south. Combined with his increasing superiority in air and artillery support, it would ensure ultimate victory, unless a European conflict broke out first. The war was now little more than straight pounding and he could pound the hardest, for this campaign had shown that his allies possessed far better means of delivering high explosive than his enemies' allies.

21

The Propaganda War and the Intellectuals

'History to the defeated', wrote W.H. Auden in his poem 'Spain 1937', 'may say Alas but cannot help or pardon.' The Spanish Civil War is one of the comparatively few cases when the most widely accepted version of events has been written more persuasively by the losers of the conflict than by the winners. This development was of course decisively influenced by the subsequent defeat of the nationalists' Axis allies. At the time, however, the Republic may have won many battles for international public opinion, but the nationalists won the key engagement by concentrating on a select and powerful audience in Britain and the United States. They played on the fear of communism in an appeal to conservative and religious feelings, and their audience's suspicions about the Republic were confirmed by Soviet military aid.

The nationalists argued that they represented the cause of Christianity, order and Western civilization against 'Asiatic Communism'. To bolster this version of events, they alleged, on the basis of forged documents,[1] that the communists had planned a revolution with 150,000 shock troops and 100,000 reserves in 1936, a coup which the nationalist rising had pre-empted. They declared that the election results of February 1936 were invalid, even though CEDA and monarchist leaders had accepted the results at the time. They concentrated on presenting life in the republican zone as a perpetual massacre of priests, nuns and innocents, accompanied by a frenzied destruction of churches and works of art. And to justify their failure to take Madrid, they claimed that half a million foreign communists were fighting in Spain.[2]

The republican government's oversimplified case was that it had been elected legally in February 1936 and was then attacked by reactionary generals aided by the Axis dictatorships. Thus the Republic represented the cause of democracy, freedom and enlightenment against fascism. The Republic's foreign propaganda emphasized that their government was the only legal and democratic one in Spain. This was of course true, when compared with the illegality and authoritarianism of their opponents, but liberal and left-of-centre politicians had hardly respected their own constitution at times. The rising of October 1934, in which Prieto and Largo Caballero had participated, greatly undermined their case against the rebels.

The passionate supporters of the Republic refused to acknowledge that the left's threat to extinguish the bourgeoisie and the pre-revolutionary situation which was developing in the spring of 1936 was bound to react to defend itself. The unspeakable horrors of the Russian civil war and the Soviet system of oppression that emerged – the dictatorship of the proletariat, which Largo Caballero had demanded – was a lesson unlikely to be forgotten. And once the war had started, the Republic's democratic credentials began to look increasingly tattered when the Cortes was reduced to a symbolic body with no control over the government. Then, from the middle of 1937, the administration of Juan Negrín developed marked authoritarian tendencies. Criticism of the prime minister and the Communist Party virtually became an act of treason.

Both sides had a very selective and manipulative view of history. In later years supporters of the Republic held that the Spanish conflict represented the start of the Second World War. The Franquists, on the other hand, said it was simply the prelude to a third world war between Western civilization and communism, and that any Nazi or fascist aid they received was incidental.

The Republic's need to convince the outside world of the justice of its cause was greatly increased by the effects of British foreign policy. In addition, the already strained political atmosphere of the 1930s and the internationalized aspect of the civil war made foreign opinion seem of paramount importance to the outcome. The Spanish workers and peasants believed, with innocent earnestness, that if the situation were explained abroad, Western governments must come to their aid against the Axis dictatorships. Foreign visitors were asked how it was possible that in a democracy like America, where the majority of the population supported the Republic (over 70 per cent according to opinion polls), the government refused it arms for self-defence. Republican leaders were much more aware of the reasons for the actions of Western governments, but even they were wrong in believing that the British and French governments would eventually be forced to accept that their interests lay in a strong anti-Axis policy before it was too late.

Under such circumstances it was inevitable that journalists and famous writers should be courted by the Republic. There was a great deal of ground to be made up after the first reports of the 'red massacres', and the tide started to turn in the Republic's favour only in November 1936 with the bombing of working-class areas and the San Carlos hospital during the battle for Madrid. Five months later the destruction of Guernica gave the Republic its greatest victory in the propaganda war, particularly since the Basques were conservative and Catholics. The non-interventionist policy of Western governments, however, remained unaffected.

In July 1936 the Catholic press abroad sprang to the support of the nationalist rising and castigated the anti-clericalism of the Republic, the desecration of churches and the killing of priests. The most sensational accusation was the raping of nuns, a similar fabrication dating back to the Middle Ages, when it was used to justify the slaughter of Jews. Two unsubstantiated incidents became the basis for a general campaign of astonishing virulence. The nationalists were on firmer ground when they condemned the murder of priests and they were supported by the Pope, who declared the priests to be martyrs.[3]

On 1 July 1937 Cardinal Gomá issued an open letter to 'the Bishops of the whole World' calling for Church support of the nationalist cause, a letter in which he stated, somewhat defensively, that the war was 'not a crusade, but a political and social war with repercussions of a religious nature'.[4] Only Cardinal Vidal y Barraquer and Bishop Mateo Múgica failed to sign it. This was in contrast to the statement of the Archbishop of Valencia a month earlier that 'the war has been called by the Sacred Heart of Jesus and this Adorable Heart has given power to the arms of Franco's soldiers'. In addition, the Bishop of Segovia had said that the war was 'a hundred times more important and holy than the *Reconquista*' and the Bishop of Pamplona called it the 'loftiest crusade that the centuries have ever seen ... a crusade in which divine intervention on our side is evident'. Leaflets with photomontages of Christ flanked by Generals Mola and Franco were issued to nationalist troops.

The political role of the Church was ignored when the religious victims were made into martyrs, although some Catholic writers abroad made the connection. One was François Mauriac, who turned against the right-wing cause after a nationalist officer told him, 'Medicine is in short supply and costly. Do you honestly think that we'd waste it for no purpose? ... We have got to kill them in the end, so there is no point in curing them.'[5] 'For millions of Spaniards,' Mauriac wrote to Ramon Serrano Súñer (Franco's brother-in-law and main political adviser), 'Christianity and fascism have become intermingled, and they cannot hate one without hating the other.' Mauriac defended his fellow Catholic writer Jacques Maritain when the pro-Nazi Serrano Súñer derided him as 'a converted Jew'. The publication in 1938 of Georges Bernanos's book *Les Grandes Cimetières sous la Lune*, which described the nationalist terror on Majorca, greatly strengthened the liberal Catholic reaction against the Church's official support for Franco.

In the United States, the Catholic lobby was very powerful. Luis Bolín recounted that a young Irishwoman, Aileen O'Brien, 'spoke on the telephone to every Catholic bishop in the United States and begged them to request their parish priests to ask all members of their congregations to telegraph in protest to President Roosevelt'.[6] As a result of her efforts, Bolín claimed, more than a million telegrams were received at the White House and a shipment of munitions for the Republic was stopped. The power of the pro-nationalist lobby was best demonstrated in May 1938. A group led by the ambassador to Great Britain, Joseph Kennedy, managed to frighten Congressmen who depended on the Catholic vote into opposing the repeal of the arms embargo. They did so even though no more than 20 per cent of the country and 40 per cent of Catholics supported the nationalists.

Nevertheless, in 1937 the nationalists sensed that they had started to lose the battle for international public opinion. Several factors operated against them. First, there was a fundamental difference of attitude between the opposing military commands in their dealings with the press. The nationalists often regarded journalists as potential spies and allowed them little freedom of movement, especially when they might witness a mopping-up episode. As a result their correspondents could not compete in the 'din of battle' personal accounts so beloved by the profession. Also, not all the nationalist press officers were as articulate and urbane as Luis Bolín. One of his successors was Gonzalo de Aguilera, Count de Alba y Yeltes, a landowner from Salamanca, who drove around nationalist Spain in a yellow Mercedes with two repeating rifles in the back. He proudly announced to an English visitor that 'on the day the civil war broke out, he lined up the labourers on his estate, selected six of them and shot them in front of the others – "*pour encourager les autres*, you understand".'[7]

Foreign journalists allowed to enter nationalist Spain soon discovered to their amazement that a hysterical relationship with the truth existed there. Anyone who doubted an invention of nationalist propaganda, however preposterous, was suspected of being a secret 'red'. The American journalist Virginia Cowles, who had just been in republican Spain, discovered in Salamanca that people were eager to ask how things were in Madrid, but refused to believe anything which did not accord with their own grotesque imaginings. The degree of political self-hypnosis she encountered was so strong that 'it was almost a mental disease'. When she told her questioners that bodies were not piled in the gutters and left to rot, as they had been told, and that militiamen had not been feeding right-wing prisoners to the animals in the zoo, they instantly assumed that she must be a 'red' herself. Pablo Merry del Val, the chief of Franco's press service, admiring the gold bracelet that she was wearing, said with a smile, 'I don't imagine that you took that to Madrid with you.' Cowles replied that in fact she had bought it there. Merry del Val was 'deeply affronted' and never spoke to her again.[8]

A modern public relations officer would blanch at some of the extraordinary speeches of General Millán Astray, the founder of the Foreign Legion, who had been so mutilated in the colonial wars. 'The gallant Moors,' he once proclaimed, 'although they wrecked my body only yesterday, today deserve the gratitude of my soul, for they are fighting for Spain against the Spaniards ... I mean the bad Spaniards ... because they are giving their lives in defence of Spain's sacred religion, as is proved by their attending field mass, escorting the Caudillo, and pinning holy medallions and sacred hearts to their burnooses.'[9] Franco, of course, avoided such indelicate contradictions when he spoke of 'the Crusade'.

One technical factor undoubtedly told against the nationalist version of events for much of the war. The overseas cable heads were in republican territory, so that journalists in that zone usually had their copy printed first. Accounts from nationalist Spain were, therefore, often out of date. Nevertheless, the nationalists had won the first round for several reasons. There were very few journalists representing foreign newspapers on its territory during the first days of rearguard slaughter, while Barcelona and Madrid had attracted vast numbers, so that the initial killings on republican territory were reported the most rapidly. The other key point for the early reports was Gibraltar, where many upper-class refugees were arriving, especially from Málaga.

On 21 August 1936 the *New York Herald Tribune* reporter Robert Neville wrote, 'In Gibraltar I found to my surprise that most of the newspapermen had been sending only "horror" stories. They do not seem to be awake to the terrible international implications in this situation.' Sensational accounts sold newspapers, but the initial 'white terror' just to the north in Andalucia was reported only by one or two correspondents, one of them Bertrand de Jouvenal of *Paris Soir*. This can be explained in part by the fact that most journalists were incapable of understanding the peasants who had fled from the Army of Africa, whereas middle- and upper-class Spaniards were more likely to speak a foreign language. However, journalistic or editorial bias could work both ways.

The battle lines of the war in Spain were rapidly taken up in France, Great Britain and the United States. A foretaste of the propaganda struggle came in Great Britain just before the rising, when reports appeared claiming that Calvo Sotelo's eyes had been dug out with daggers, a story to which even Spanish right-wing papers had not given credence. The Republic was supported by the *News Chronicle* and the *Manchester Guardian*. The *Times* and *Telegraph* remained more or less neutral, while the rest supported the nationalists. Immediate sympathizers with the rising were the *Observer*, whose editor, Garvin, was an admirer of Mussolini, and the Northcliffe press, which had backed Mosley's British Union of Fascists. Its *Daily Mail* correspondent, Harold Cardozo, was accordingly accredited to the nationalist forces.

The practice of a newspaper sending a reporter to the side it supported became customary. In fact, Kim Philby, already a secret communist, developed a conservative image as *The Times* correspondent with the nationalists. An exception in the early days was another secret communist agent, the writer Arthur Koestler. Although representing the left-wing *News Chronicle*, he started with the nationalists in Seville, but had to escape when seen by a

German journalist called Strindberg, who knew he was a communist. Luis Bolín, the nationalist press officer, was too late to arrest him as a spy. Koestler returned to republican territory, but Bolín caught up with him at the fall of Málaga, and only pressure from the British and American press saved him from execution.[10]

In the majority of cases the correspondent reflected, or adapted himself to, the political stance of his paper. As a result, Richard Ford's comment of 1846 was equally true 90 years later: 'The public at home are much pleased by the perusal of "authentic" accounts from Spain itself which tally with their own preconceived ideas of the land.' At the beginning of the war correspondents were rushed to Spain, regardless of whether they spoke the language or understood the country's politics. But then even a respected expert like Professor Allison-Peers was unable to differentiate the parties of the left accurately and attributed the peasant troubles in Andalucia to agitators who were profiting from improved communications. The ideas that Latin people had 'violence in the blood' and that military dictatorships were natural to them were reflected in the shorthand of headlines. As always, the pressure of space and journalistic simplification to make accounts easy to digest were bound to distort the issues.

Newspapermen were as much affected by the emotions of the time as anybody else. Many became resolute, and often uncritical, champions of the Republic after experiencing the siege of Madrid. Their commitment affected their coverage of later issues, such as the Communist Party's manoeuvring for control. The ideals of the anti-fascist cause anaesthetized many of them to aspects of the war that proved uncomfortable. It was a difficult atmosphere in which to retain objectivity. In the United States, the Republic was supported by Herbert Matthews and Lawrence Fernsworth of the *New York Times*, and by Jay Allen and John Whitaker of the *Chicago Tribune*.

There were also various types of censorship and pressure, which affected the accounts printed at home. These ranged from propaganda-orientated briefings from government press officers and republican censorship through to the political or commercial prejudices of the editor. At the end of the war Herbert Matthews of the *New York Times* was told by his editor not to 'send in any sentimental stuff about the refugee camps'. In 1937 Dawson, the editor of *The Times*, blocked some of Steer's accounts from the

Basque country because he did not want to upset the Germans. On 3 May, a week after Steer's report on Guernica, he wrote that he had 'done the impossible night after night to keep the paper from hurting their susceptibilities'.[11] The most famous dispute was the one between Louis Delaprée and his editor on the right-wing *Paris Soir*. Shortly before his death (he was flying back to France when his plane was shot down), Delaprée complained that his reports were suppressed. He finished his last despatch by observing bitterly that 'the massacre of a hundred Spanish children is less interesting than a sigh from Mrs Simpson'.

Republican propaganda was often little different from its nationalist counterpart.[12] Both sides seized upon isolated incidents to make general points. The republicans spread horror stories of Moorish *regulares* chopping off the hands of children who clenched their fists, in case they were making the left-wing salute. They also recounted secular miracles, like the nationalist bombs which did not go off because they contained messages of solidarity from foreign workers instead of explosive. There were undoubtedly cases of sabotage by munitions workers, but the exaggeration of republican propaganda developed such addiction to misplaced hope that it became a major liability. Colonel Casado argued with justification that it was a major contribution to the republican defeat. Once the government had excited wild optimism over an offensive, it became virtually impossible to admit failure and this led to the loss of vast quantities of men and matériel in the defence of useless gains.

The major problem of the republican government was the need to provide two incompatible versions of events simultaneously. The account for external consumption was designed to convince the French, British and United States governments that the Republic was a liberal property-owning democracy, while domestic communiqués tried to persuade the workers that they were still defending a social revolution. Censorship came under Álvarez del Vayo's control. The aide responsible for English-speaking journalists stated that he 'was instructed not to send out one word about this revolution in the economic system of loyalist Spain, nor are any correspondents in Valencia permitted to write freely of the revolution that has taken place'.[13]

The Spanish Civil War engaged the commitment of artists and intellectuals on an unprecedented scale, the overwhelming majority of them on the side of the Republic. The conflict had the fascination of an epic drama involving the basic forces of humanity. Yet they did not just adopt the role of passionate observers. The slaughter of the First World War had undermined the moral basis of art's detachment from politics and made 'art for art's sake' seem a privileged impertinence. Socialist realism took this to its logical extreme by subordinating all forms of expression to the cause of the proletariat. The support given by intellectuals to the republican cause was usually moral rather than practical, although a few writers, including André Malraux, George Orwell and John Cornford, fought, and others like Hemingway, John Dos Passos, the Chilean poet Pablo Neruda, W. H. Auden, Stephen Spender, Cecil Day Lewis, Herbert Read, Georges Bernanos, Antoine de Saint-Exupéry, Louis Aragon and Paul Eluard spent varying amounts of time in Spain. Malraux's novel *L'Espoir* was regarded by many as the great novel of the Spanish Republic's resistance, but it would not be long before this great political opportunist became a ferocious anti-communist.

No organization could match the intellectual mobilization for which the Communist Party aimed. In the 1930s the Communist Party succeeded in attracting to its cause many writers, particularly poets, who included Miguel Hernández and Rafael Alberti, Stephen Spender, Cecil Day Lewis, Hugh MacDiarmid and Pablo Neruda. The most famous writer to support the Republic, and lend his weight to the campaign which the communists organized so effectively, was Ernest Hemingway. Nevertheless, the two sides to his character are of great interest when seen against the conflict of political forces within republican Spain. Hemingway was an individualist who believed in discipline for everybody else. He supported communist broadsides against the anarchists, but backed their methods only because he thought them necessary to win the war. 'I like the communists when they're soldiers,' he remarked to a friend in 1938. 'When they're priests, I hate them.' The communists did not realize, when they accorded him such special attention, that his deep and genuine hatred of fascism did not mean that he admired them out of any political conviction. Even so, the brutal way in which Hemingway informed Dos Passos of the communists' secret execution of José Robles (Dos Passos's great friend) ended their association. Hemingway found fault with Dos Passos for supporting the anarchists and for not being 'regular enough in his attitude towards the commissars'.[14]

It is difficult to ascertain how much Hemingway was influenced by the privileged information he received from senior party cadres and Soviet advisers. Being taken seriously by experts distorted his vision. It made him prepared to sign moral blank cheques on behalf of the Republic: hence his absurd statements that 'Brihuega will take its place in military history with the other decisive battles of the world', and that the Republic was 'licking the rebels', as if the fight were almost between Yankees and Southern slave owners. The American civil war haunts his major work, *For Whom the Bell Tolls*. This novel, written just after the Republic's defeat, reveals both a lingering admiration for communist professionals and yet also the author's own selfish libertarianism. Its hero, Robert Jordan, one of Hemingway's self-images, asks, 'Was there ever a people whose leaders were as truly their enemies as this one?'

A number of other writers were to have their idealism undermined far more by the events they witnessed. Simone Weil, who supported the anarchists, was distressed by killings in eastern Spain. She was particularly affected when a fifteen-year-old Falangist prisoner from Pina was captured on the Aragón front and shot after Durruti spent an hour with the boy trying to persuade him to change his politics and giving him until the next day to decide. Stephen Spender, who wrote *Poems from Spain*, was shaken by the executions in the International Brigades and left the Communist Party soon afterwards. Auden, who had written an enthusiastic description of the social revolution at the end of 1936, returned from Spain, after hoping to serve with an ambulance unit, saying little and evidently disillusioned. He nevertheless wrote his long poem 'Spain 1937', with its famous line – 'But today the struggle' – in less than a month and donated the proceeds to Medical Aid for Spain. Yet Orwell's subsequent criticism of the work helped turn him against his own creation.

Not all writers were pro-republican. The nationalists had the support of Charles Maurras, Paul Claudel, Robert Brasillach, Henri Massis and Drieu La Rochelle, as well as the South African Roy Campbell, who wrote a 5,000-verse epic poem, violently racist, which was entitled *Flowering Rifle*. Evelyn Waugh, having said that he would support Franco if he were a Spaniard, then emphasized, 'I am not a Fascist, nor shall I become one unless it were the only alternative to Marxism. It is mischievous to suggest that such a choice is imminent.' Ezra Pound replied that 'Spain is an emotional luxury to a gang of sap-headed dilettantes' and Hilaire Belloc, a supporter of the nationalists, had already described the struggle as 'a trial of strength between Jewish Communism and our traditional Christian civilization'. Yet the majority of those questioned for Nancy Cunard's 'Writers Take Sides' declared their opposition to Franco in varying forms. Samuel Beckett replied, '¡UPTHEREPUBLIC!' In the United States, William Faulkner and John Steinbeck simply declared their hatred for fascism, while others qualified their position by supporting a particular faction on the republican side. Aldous Huxley specified his opposition to communism and sympathy for anarchism (which led Nancy Cunard, a fellow traveller, to mark him down as a neutral).[15] Other supporters of the CNT-FAI included John Dos Passos, B. Traven and Herbert Read.

While the Republic won the propaganda battle, greatly helped by Comintern efforts, the communists were winning the conflict on the left. The bolshevik coup in Russia had given them the unique position of 'controlling the only beacon of revolutionary hope' in the world. Bertrand Russell remarked that any resistance or objection 'was condemned as treachery to the cause of the proletariat. Anarchist and syndicalist criticisms were forgotten or ignored, and by exalting State Socialism, it became possible to retain the faith that one great country had realized the aspirations of the pioneers.'[16] The triangular nature of the civil war in Spain could, in fact, be said to echo the Kronstadt rising against the bolshevik dictatorship in 1921. Three years later, when Emma Goldman condemned the communist regime vehemently at a dinner of 250 left-wing intellectuals, held to welcome her to London, Bertrand Russell was the only person to support her. The rest sat in shocked and embarrassed silence. Yet even Russell wrote soon afterwards that he was 'not prepared to advocate any alternative government in Russia'.

The split between Spanish intellectuals was more complex. Many had gone into exile, appalled both by the nationalist right and the revolutionary left. On the whole, the best known and the majority of those who had stayed in Spain supported the Republic.[17] Literary output during the war was very uneven, with some strong poems and mostly disappointing novels.[18] The republicans devoted great efforts to popular culture through organizations such as the theatre section of the Alianza de Intelectuales Antifascistas and the company

'New Scene', which had writers of the calibre of Rafael Alberti, José Bergamín and Ramón J. Sender preparing material for it.[19] There were also the Militias' Cultural Service, the 'Front Loud-Speaker', and the 'Guerrillas del Teatro'. Every sort of medium was used – books, pamphlets, press, radio, cinema and theatre.

Behind the lines, political organizations and unions produced a wide range of newspapers. At the front, almost every army corps, division, brigade and sometimes even battalions produced their own publication.[20] But perhaps one of the most innovatory methods of propaganda was the use of posters, urging loyalty and confidence in victory as well as warning against spies and venereal disease. They were known as 'soldiers of paper and ink'.[21] Poster art, especially the Soviet example, had had a great influence in artistic circles even before the civil war. The Republic made use of the best poster designers in Spain, while the nationalists had comparatively few of any merit.[22]

Both sides made all possible use of radio stations for information, recruiting and propaganda.[23] The republicans, however, deployed the cinema with great effect. Right from the start of the war, cinemas screened a series of Soviet films. *Chapaev*, the heavily romanticized story of a red partisan hero of the Russian civil war, was shown the most. He urged the peasants to defend the revolution and died heroically at the end. In Spain, however, they often left out the last reel to bolster their audiences with the impression that Chapaev had survived.

The other film which caught the imagination of the Spanish communists was *The Sailors of Kronstadt*, by Yefim Dzigan, which depicted the transformation of a group of anarchist sailors from the naval base of Kronstadt into a disciplined unit of the Red Army. Needless to say, anarchists who knew the truth about the bolshevik crushing of the Kronstadt uprising were less enthusiastic about the film. *The Battleship Potemkin* by Sergei Eisenstein was also screened many times, as well as a number of other Soviet films. Documentaries made in Spain during the war were also shown. The Soviet film-makers Roman Karmen and Boris Makadeev made *Madrid se defiende* (*Madrid Defends Herself*), *Madrid en llamas* (*Madrid in Flames*) and the full-length *Ispaniia*.

The republican government subsidized newsreels and propaganda films, such as *España Leal en Armas* (*Loyalist Spain under Arms*), on which Luis Buñuel worked, and later when the Republic's own film studios were set up, they made *Madrid*, directed by Manuel Villegas López; *Viva la República*; *Los Trece Puntos de la Victoria* (*The Thirteen Points of Victory*); and, most famous of all, André Malraux's and Max Aub's *L'Espoir*, which did not appear until after the war was over. Even the Generalitat set up its own organization, Laya Films, which produced weekly newsreels, *España al día*, and nearly 30 documentaries.[24]

In the spring of 1937, when the republicans were at last starting to win the propaganda war, the International Exhibition of Arts took place in Paris. The Republic's pavilion became famous with the display of Picasso's *Guernica*, but also the work of many other great artists, including Joan Miró, Alexander Calder, Luis Lacasa, Josep Lluís Sert, Horacio Ferrer and Antoni Bonet. The nationalist government put on its own exhibition, but it had to be under the Vatican flag. Its main work was an altarpiece painted by José María Sert, *Intercesión de Santa Teresa por la guerra española*.[25]

The other great event was the International Writers' Congress for the Defence of Culture, which had sessions in Valencia and Madrid, and finished in Paris. This was entirely a communist front organization, with writers from Spain, the Soviet Union, France, Britain, the United States and South America, as well as exiles from the Axis countries.[26] But the communist attempt to create a cultural as well as political hegemony on the left was not helped by events in Moscow.

Less than a month after the start of the Spanish Civil War the first of the great show trials started. Anyone who criticized them was accused of being a crypto-fascist. Victor Serge, speaking against them in Paris, was heckled by a communist worker: 'Traitor! Fascist! Nothing you can do will stop the Soviet Union from remaining the fatherland of the oppressed!'[27] Apart from rare exceptions, like the poet André Breton, socialists dared not speak out because 'the interests of the Popular Front demanded the humouring of the communists'. André Gide prepared a statement on the Soviet dictatorship, but when Ilya Ehrenburg heard of it he organized communist militiamen on the Madrid front to send telegrams begging him not to publish a 'mortal blow' against them. Gide was appalled: 'What a flood of abuse I'm going to face! And there will be militiamen in Spain who believe that I am actually a traitor!' In Spain the POUM's *La Batalla* published critical accounts of the trials, thus greatly increasing the enmity the communists felt for their Marxist rivals. Even CNT leaders tried to prevent their press from attacking Stalin's liquidations at a time when Soviet arms were so desperately needed. The blind, short-term reaction of Western governments and their weakness in the face of Hitler and Mussolini gave the Comintern an apparent monopoly of resistance to fascism.

All this time, the Republic suffered from its dependence on Soviet supplies, which confirmed the fears and prejudices of the minority to whom nationalist propaganda was addressed. In December 1938 Churchill finally came round to the view that 'the British Empire would run far less risk from the victory of the Spanish government than from that of General Franco'. And he said of Neville Chamberlain that 'nothing has strengthened the Prime Minister's hold upon well-to-do society more remarkably than the belief that he is friendly to General Franco and the nationalist cause in Spain'.[28] This section of the population cannot have made up much more than 20 per cent of the total, yet it would appear that it had far more influence over British, and therefore Western, policy towards Spain than the large majority who supported the Republic. On this basis the communists' role on behalf of the Republic probably helped the nationalists become the effective winners of the propaganda war. Appeasement and the Western boycott of the Republic had greatly strengthened the power of the Comintern, which was able to present itself as the only effective force to combat fascism.

Another important lesson from the time was that mass self-deception is simply a sedative prescribed by leaders who cannot face reality themselves. And as the Spanish Civil War proved, the first casualty of war is not truth, but its source: the conscience and integrity of the individual.

PART FIVE

Internal Tensions

14 October 1936. Dolores Ibárruri, 'La Pasionaria', who coined the slogan '*¡No pasarán!*', making a speech.

The captain of a Soviet ship (left) is welcomed by Companys (centre) and Antonov-Ovseenko (right).

Mikhail Koltsov (right) and the Soviet documentary film-maker Roman Karmen (left) in the trenches before Madrid.

The fighting in the Casa de Campo, November 1936.

Refugees sheltering in the Madrid metro during an air raid.

International Brigade troops march through Madrid.

Propaganda photo of a Soviet pilot with his 'Chato'.

Women in Málaga terrified by a nationalist air raid.

The war in the north. Carlist *requetés* being blessed before going into battle.

Colonel Wolfram von Richthofen (centre right looking at camera) with nationalist and Condor Legion officers.

El Campesino making a speech.

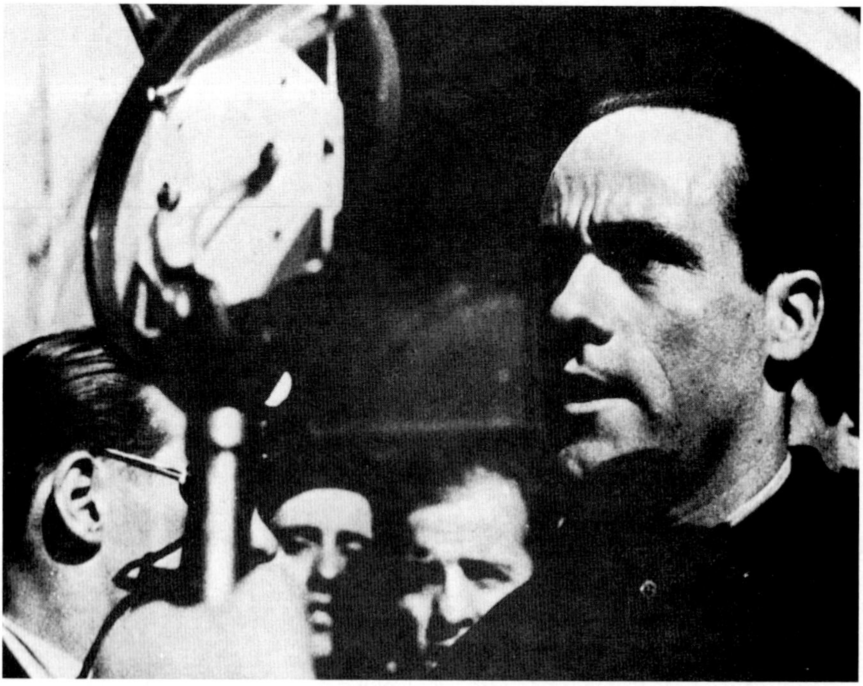

Juan García Oliver broadcasts an appeal for calm during the May events in Catalonia.

6 May 1937. Assault guards brought in to restore order marching through Barcelona.

General Pozas and communist officers take over the Catalan council of defence, May 1937.

The Battle of Brunete, July 1937. Juan Modesto, the communist commander of V Corps.

Republican wounded at Brunete with T-26 tanks in the background.

22

The Struggle for Power

The failure of four attempts on Madrid in five months did not only strain Franco's relations with his German and Italian allies. It also provoked rumblings of discontent within the nationalist coalition. The Carlists had not forgotten Franco's strong reaction to their attempt to maintain the independence of their *requeté* formations. Meanwhile, Falangist 'old shirts' shared their dead leader's fears that the army would annex them, even though they had grown from 30,000 to several hundred thousand members in a year.

Franco kept himself well informed of developments within these two parties. He was not unduly worried, because the nationalist alliance required a single commander and he had no effective rival, either within the army or outside. The main Carlist leader, Fal Conde, was exiled in Portugal and the Count of Rodezno, who remained, was far more amenable. The continued suppression of any announcement of the execution of José Antonio Primo de Rivera at Alicante encouraged wishful rumours among the Falange that he was still alive. This prevented the appointment of a permanent replacement. The German ambassador, Faupel, repeated in a report to the Wilhelmstrasse the astute remark of an Italian attaché: 'Franco is a leader without a party, the Falange a party without a leader.'[1]

In addition, the Falange was still weakened by the potential split which came from the inherent contradiction in José Antonio's philosophy: socialist aspirations had been swamped by reactionary nationalism. José Antonio could be quoted by the proletarian 'old shirts', led by the provincial chief, Manuel Hedilla, to show that the 'socialist' aspect of their movement was fundamental. At the same time the reactionary wing, which was growing more powerful than the 'old shirts', could point to other statements to show that recreating 'traditional Spain' was uppermost in the mind of José Antonio.

It was the latter group, the modern reactionaries, who contacted the Carlists during the winter of 1936–7 for secret talks about an alliance, while the proletarian elements, led by Hedilla, opposed such a move. Sancho Dávila, a cousin of José Antonio, had been in touch with Fal Conde since before the rising and proposed a union of the two parties. Franco heard privately of these discussions, which took place in Lisbon on 16 February, and although they came to nothing, he saw that trouble was more likely to come from Falangist ranks than from the Carlists, who were disciplined fighters uninterested in political intrigue.

Hedilla had been the Falangist chief in Santander and he was lucky to have been in Corunna when the rising began in the north, for his home town was held for the Republic. In Corunna he played an important role, both in bringing the well-armed Falange to help the rebels secure the town and in conducting the subsequent repression, which was among the worst in Spain. Yet this former mechanic soon became the most outspoken critic of indiscriminate nationalist killing on the grounds that it alienated the proletariat from their cause. On Christmas Eve 1936 he told the Falange not to persecute the poor simply for having voted for the left 'out of hunger or despair. We all know that in many towns there were – and are – right-wingers who are worse than the reds.'

Such statements made Hedilla and the left-wing Falangists highly suspect in the eyes of the Spanish right. Many senior army officers – only Yagüe was a committed left Falangist – saw them as little better than 'reds'. A count in Salamanca even declared indignantly to Virginia Cowles that 'half the fascists were nothing but reds', and that in the north 'many of them were giving the Popular Front salute and talking about their brothers in Barcelona'.[2] On the other hand, the *señorito* wing of the Falange, which was strongest in Andalucia, was viewed much more favourably by other nationalists. This faction attracted many from the professional middle class.

During the winter of 1936, the German ambassador had started to cultivate the admiration which the 'old shirts' held for the Nazis. It seems that Faupel was trying to curry favour at home, not acting on orders. He encouraged Hedilla to resist the middle-class takeover of the Falange and advised Franco that the nationalists could win the war only if they introduced social reform. Nevertheless, he wrote to the Wilhelmstrasse that if a clash occurred between Franco and the Falange 'we are in agreement with the Italians that despite our sympathy for the Falange and its healthy tendencies, we must support Franco at all costs'. Franco tolerated his allies' interference in military affairs because he had no choice, but he would not brook their involvement in the political future of Spain. He demanded von Faupel's replacement, even though he had not been involved in any attempt to change the nationalist leadership.

On the night of 16 April 1937, Hedilla's followers attempted to seize the Falange headquarters in Salamanca in a move to oust the rightists led by Sancho Dávila. A gun battle broke out around the Plaza Mayor during which two Falangists were killed. The Civil Guard had to be sent in to restore order and arrests were made. Hedilla was fortunate to have stayed clear of the disturbance. On 18 April he arranged a meeting of the Falange council at which he was elected leader. He thought his triumph was complete when he went round to the bishop's palace, where Franco resided, to announce his election and state that he was at his orders. Franco congratulated him, but the wily Caudillo, who had allowed the Falange's internal strife to continue without interference, made his well-prepared move the next evening.[3]

The Falange, the Carlists, the Alfonsine monarchist Renovacíon Española and the remnants of other right-wing groups, like the CEDA's Popular Action, were amalgamated by decree into one party under his direct orders.[4] The party was to be called the Falange Española Tradicionalista y de las JONS (Traditionalist Spanish Falange and the National Syndicalist Offensive Juntas). As the choice of name indicated, the Carlists came off worst in this forced union, with a programme based on 26 out of José Antonio's 27 points.[5] But, as Franco had calculated, the Carlists were more obedient and less politically minded. The new uniform consisted of the Falangist blue shirt and the Carlist red beret. The fascist salute was officially adopted and the movement's slogan was to be '*Por el Imperio hacia Dios*' (For the Empire towards God). The Caudillo was proclaimed chief of the new party and his brother-in-law, Ramón Serrano Súñer, was appointed executive head. (This produced a new Spanish word, *cuñadismo*, meaning 'brother-in-lawism', as a variant on nepotism.) Serrano Súñer, an intelligent and ambitious lawyer who had been a friend of José Antonio, had become a vice-president of the CEDA, then moved towards the Falange in the spring of 1936. He was captured in Madrid after the rising and held in the Model Prison, where he witnessed the killings in revenge for the news of Badajoz. This experience and the death of his two brothers made him one of the most intransigent advocates of the *limpieza* after he escaped from hospital (in circumstances which have never been satisfactorily explained) and reached nationalist territory in February 1937.[6]

The suddenness of Franco's coup increased its effect. By the time the announcement had been fully appreciated, anyone who wanted to object only exposed himself to the charge of treachery towards the nationalist movement. Hedilla, somewhat unimaginatively, believed that he could maintain a position of power as the head of the Falange and guarantee its independence. He refused to join the council of the new party and tried to mobilize his supporters. He was arrested on 25 April, and condemned to death a month later for 'a manifest act of indiscipline and subversion against the single command of nationalist Spain'.[7] On Serrano Súñer's advice, however, the sentence was commuted to life imprisonment. In fact, he served only four years, but it was enough to remove him from any position of influence during a critical period. The new puppet council appointed by Franco was no longer challenged, after the rest of the Falange was rapidly brought into line by dismissals and about 80 prison sentences.

As commander of the most important formation in the nationalist army, the Army of Africa, Franco had started his climb to leadership from an advanced position. He had no effective rival and the very nature of the nationalist movement begged a single, disciplined command. As a result he had achieved supreme power in two well-timed stages: September 1936 and April 1937. With the first he became de jure leader; with the second, suppressing all potential opposition, de facto dictator. Now he was in position to tackle a long war and to construct his idea of what Spain should be.

A power struggle had also begun in republican territory during the winter of 1936 and the spring of 1937, although the winners, the communists, were never to achieve the same degree of power as Franco. They started from a very restricted base and their policies to centralize power were resisted by one of the major components of the republican alliance, the anarchists. At the same time the Valencia government was exasperated at its lack of control over independent regions, especially Catalonia and Aragón.

In December 1936 the central committee of the Comintern had

met on several occasions to analyse the course of events in Spain and the position of the Spanish Communist Party. On 21 December Stalin sent a letter, counter-signed by Molotov and Voroshilov, to Largo Caballero. Stalin first of all underlined the fact that the republican government had asked for Soviet advisers to help them, and that the officers sent to Spain had been told 'that they should always remember that, in spite of the great solidarity which now exists between the Spanish people and the peoples of the USSR, a Soviet specialist, being a foreigner in Spain, can be really useful only if he stays strictly within the limits of an adviser and adviser only'.[8]

He then went on to emphasize the Comintern line that Soviet aid to republican Spain was to safeguard democracy and insisted that the government followed the Popular Front strategy, which helped landowning peasants and attracted the middle classes. In fact, Stalin was interested in avoiding any embarrassments to his foreign policy, which on one hand wanted to evade provoking Nazi Germany, and on the other to seek a rapprochement with Britain and France. A parliamentary republic should be maintained 'to prevent the enemies of Spain seeing her as "a communist republic"'.

Comintern agents were meanwhile instructed to construct a disciplined army, with a single command, to develop the war industries and achieve united action among all political groups. Codovilla was to convince Largo Caballero to bring forward this programme, a difficult task considering how bad relations were after the communists had taken over the Socialist Youth. The fall of Málaga and the arrival in Spain of the Bulgarian Comintern agent Stoyán Minéevich ('Stepánov') were to put an end to such optimism. On 17 March Stepánov informed Moscow that the person ultimately responsible for the fall of Málaga was Largo Caballero because of his connivance with traitors on the general staff. The Comintern convinced Stalin that it was essential to remove Largo Caballero from the ministry of war and told the Spanish Communist Party to do everything necessary to ensure that '"Spaak" [Largo Caballero] remained only as head of the government'.[9]

The communist tactic was to block ministers from exercising control over the People's Army. This they regarded as essential both in the interests of winning the war and in order to increase their own power. But the anarchists from the beginning had warned clearly that any attempt to impose non-anarchist officers on their troops would be met by force. Faced with such resistance, the communists solicited the support of regular officers. They approached the most ambitious, presenting themselves as the true believers in iron discipline and good organization. Experts in the manipulation of bureaucracy, they infiltrated their own members into key positions. They managed to place Lieutenant-Colonel Antonio Cordón as head of the technical secretariat of the ministry of war, where he controlled pay, promotion, discipline, supplies and personnel. They also removed Lieutenant-Colonel Segismundo Casado from the post of chief of operations on the general staff because he had denounced their machinations and they replaced him with a member of their own party. A report to Moscow in March 1937 reveals that 27 out of the 38 key commands of the Central Front were held by communists and three more by sympathizers.[10] Another report claimed later that 'the Party therefore now has hegemony in the army, and this hegemony is developing and becoming firmly established more and more each day both in the front and in rear units'.[11]

The communists set out to remove General Asensio Torrado, whom they called the 'general of defeats', accusing him of incompetence and treason. The most prominent attack came from the Soviet ambassador, Marcel Rosenberg. Since January 1937, Rosenberg had been behaving like 'a Russian viceroy in Spain', continually harassing Largo Caballero, telling him what to do and what not to do. On one occasion the old trade unionist had thrown him out of his office. The irony of the affair was that on 21 February, while the communists were still calling for Asensio Torrado to be shot, Rosenberg was recalled to Moscow, where he was executed soon afterwards in the purges. Although Rosenberg's successor, Gaikis, played a less dominant role, he continued to urge the fusion of the socialist and communist parties, a step to which Largo Caballero was now completely opposed. Strong-arm tactics became less necessary at such a high level, because the Party controlled most of the bureaucracy.

The Soviet military advisers nevertheless continued to exert pressure by saying to any Spanish officer who objected to their plans that they ought to ask their government whether Soviet assistance was still required. Such activity took place despite the statement in Stalin's letter that Soviet personnel had been 'categorically ordered [to] keep strictly to the functions of an adviser, and an adviser alone'. After the socialist newspaper *Adelante* published on 30 April 1937 an article 'which contained provocative attacks addressed at the USSR and its leaders', Voroshilov, in a coded telegram, gave orders to the chief adviser, General Stern. 'Visit Caballero personally and declare, in response to his request for us to send our pilots, etc., to Spain, that considering this disloyal attitude, we not only cannot send them any more of our men, but we will also have to withdraw the men who are in Spain now, unless they disavow this provocative article in *Adelante* and punish the ones who are guilty for its publication, and unless they apologize to us.'[12]

Largo Caballero's position was also being eroded from within. He could no longer ignore the fact that his close friend, Álvarez del Vayo, the foreign minister, was an active Party supporter. The communist Enrique Castro described their attitude to the foreign minister when he said in a paraphrase of Lenin that 'he is a fool, but more or less useful'. Largo Caballero tried to limit Álvarez del Vayo's control over the appointment of commissars to the army. On 17 April he published a decree placing the corps of commissars directly under his orders.[13] The communist press exploded in outrage. 'Who can feel hostile to this corps of heroes?' it demanded. 'Who can show themselves to be incompatible with those forging the People's Army? Only the declared enemies of the people.'[14] Once hailed as 'the Spanish Lenin', Largo was now a 'declared enemy of the people'. La Pasionaria gave a remarkable example of what Orwell later called double-speak. According to her, restricting the commissars would 'mean leaving our soldiers at the mercy of officers, who could at a moment disfigure the character of our army by returning to the old days of barrack discipline'. Yet the communists were the chief advocates of drill, saluting and privileges for officers.

Caballero's attempts to prevent communist recruiting drives within the armed services also came to nothing. A Soviet officer reported back to Moscow: 'As Largo Caballero has banned party work in units, we have taught our friends to carry out their party work under the guise of amateur creative activities. For example, we organized a celebration dinner on the eve of the [1 May] holiday to which representatives of the anti-fascist committee were invited, as well as those from the Party committee, the editorial office of

Mundo Obrero, and the best commanders of other units of "friends" (Líster and others).'[15]

The communists also set up a police school in Madrid, where students who refused Party membership were failed. The secret police was taken over by NKVD agents in the late autumn of 1936 and it soon became the communists' most feared weapon. Even Wenceslao Carrillo, the director-general of security, found himself powerless against them. Many of the Spaniards who were recruited for this work could hardly be described as 'anti-fascist', but they were given Party cards nevertheless. When the first Soviet ambassador, Rosenberg, made his comment about scum always coming to the top in revolutions, he failed to add that much of it was creamed off into the secret police afterwards. Meanwhile, the campaign to win over the paramilitary forces like the Assault Guard was helped by Margarita Nelken, a socialist member of the Cortes and another secret communist. This was the manoeuvre to which General Asensio Torrado had objected, earning the Party's bitter enmity.

On frequent occasions the communists in the police, stirred up by the paranoia of their NKVD controllers, arrested and interrogated members of other parties. Soon after the battle of Brihuega, Antonio Verardini, the chief of staff of Mera's 14th Division, went to Madrid on a 24-hour leave. There he was arrested on the orders of José Cazorla, the communist councillor of public order, and accused of espionage and treason. As soon as Mera found out he left for the capital with Sanz, the commander of the 70th Brigade, and a lorryload of heavily armed soldiers. On his arrival he told General Miaja that if Verardini was not freed by the communists his men would free him by force. Miaja obtained his release immediately. Mera was to return to Madrid on a similar mission when the communist persecution of the POUM reached its height. On the second occasion he had heard that Mika Etchebehere, the woman militia commander, had been arrested for 'disaffection to the Republic'. It was only by seeing the director-general of security that he obtained her release and had her brought to his headquarters so that she could not be snatched again.

During that spring of 1937 the communist police and the anarchist militia confronted each other in Madrid in an increasingly bitter struggle. The CNT exploded the greatest scandal by publishing the accusations of Melchor Rodríguez, the delegate in charge of prisons, who had put an end to the evacuation and killing of nationalist prisoners the previous November. Melchor Rodríguez revealed that José Cazorla, the communist in charge of public order, had organized secret prisons holding socialists, anarchists and republicans, many of whom had been freed by popular tribunals, to torture and execute them as spies or traitors. Largo Caballero used this on 22 April to dissolve the Junta de Defensa controlled by the communists and re-establish the authority of the Valencia government over Madrid. Nevertheless, there was little he could do to rein in the actions of the NKVD, known in the Soviet Union as 'the unsheathed sword of the revolution'.

The prime minister realized, however, that he could not reveal the dangerous growth of communist power without confirming the suspicions of the British government. At the same time he could count on fewer and fewer allies in his own cabinet. The moderate socialists, such as Prieto and Negrín, were considering the amalgamation of the Socialist Party with the Spanish Communist Party and agreed with the communist arguments that the fragmentation of power must be ended in order to win the war.[16]

The liberal republicans of Martínez Barrio's Unión Republicana and Manuel Azaña's Izquierda Republicana followed a similar path to the moderate socialists in their opposition to Basque and Catalan separatism, and the revolutionary collectives of the anarchists. Lacking the support of liberals and social-democrats, Largo Caballero could only count on the four ministers of the CNT-FAI as allies against the communists and their plan to take over control of the army. Yet the anarchist movement itself was starting to suffer from a split between its reformist leadership collaborating with the government and its militants in Barcelona and in the militia columns.

One radical group, 'The Friends of Durruti', was led by a former Catholic and separatist, Jaime Balius. Since March, the Friends of Durruti in its pamphlets and publications had been denouncing the 'Stalinist counter-revolution' and the 'collaborationism' of the CNT leadership. They claimed to be the guardians of the spirit of 19 July, and demanded a government made up uniquely of the UGT and the CNT. But the basic problem was a deep frustration among the libertarian movement that it was losing all its influence and power. There was a deep regret that they had failed to seize the opportunity the previous July to establish libertarian communism in Catalonia.

The change of atmosphere in Barcelona was remarked upon by observers who returned after a year's absence. The camaraderie and the optimism were gone. Nightclubs and expensive restaurants supplied by the black market had reopened, while the bread queues started at four in the morning. The anarchists blamed the food crisis on Joan Comorera, the communist PSUC leader who was the Generalitat councillor in charge. Comorera had disbanded the food committees, which the CNT set up in July 1936, and ended bread rationing. The food distribution committees had certainly had their deficiencies, but these were overshadowed by the hoarding and profiteering which followed their abolition. The communists, meanwhile, blamed the anarchist agricultural collectives.[17] Angry scenes outside shops were frequent. The Assault Guard often rode their horses into the bread queues or dispersed the women with blows from rifle butts.

There had been many more serious developments to make the anarchists and the POUM feel threatened in Catalonia. In the winter the PSUC had set out to exclude the POUM from the Catalan government. The anarchists, who until then had regarded the communist-POUM battle simply as a Marxist rivalry, began to realize that its outcome would affect them too. The Generalitat, now feeling that it had sufficient power to face down the anarchists, issued a decree on 4 March, dissolving the control patrols and the security council dominated by the FAI. At the same time it amalgamated the Assault Guard and the Republican National Guard into a single force under the command of the councillor for internal security, Artemi Aiguader. The decree also demanded the surrender of weapons.

The communist PSUC stepped up the pressure over the following month. It issued a 'victory plan', which demanded the complete integration of Catalan forces in the People's Army, the call-up of all classes between 1932 and 1936, the nationalization of war industries, the militarization of all transport and the government control of all weapons.[18] The anarchists, although torn in two directions, felt that they had given up enough to their colleagues in the government. 'We have made too many concessions and have reached the moment of turning off the tap,' declared their newspaper, *Solidaridad Obrera*.[19]

Andreu Nin, the leader of the POUM, was exultant that the CNT had reached the end of its tether. He wanted the anarchists to join the POUM in an attack 'on the counter-revolution'.[20] The battle lines of the so-called 'events of May' were being drawn. The POUM could not be defined as 'Trotskyist', as Stalinist propaganda continually proclaimed, and certainly not as 'Trotskyist-Fascist', which was the usual Comintern epithet – a death sentence in Soviet terms. But Stalinists refused to acknowledge that Trotsky's Fourth International had condemned the POUM for having joined the Popular Front in the elections, with Trotsky himself repudiating his former colleague in furious articles.[21]

For Nin, everything that was not revolutionary was reactionary, which was why he despised republican institutions and called on the CNT to install a workers' democracy. The POUM in its revolutionary fanaticism had even convinced itself that the government of the Popular Front was secretly hatching a plot with the nationalists, a curious mirror image of Stalinist suspicions. It was, however, on more rational ground in its belief that the communists were preparing a purge similar to those taking place in the Soviet Union.[22]

23

The Civil War within the Civil War

In Barcelona towards the end of April a series of developments and incidents increased an already tense situation. On 16 April Companys reshuffled his government, giving the post of minister of justice to Joan Comorera, the leader of the communist PSUC. This caused deep unease, especially among the POUM, whom he had threatened with liquidation. On 24 April an unsuccessful assassination attempt was made against the Generalitat's commissioner for public order, Eusebi Rodríguez Salas, another leading member of the PSUC.

The next day, 25 April, *carabineros* sent by Juan Negrín took control of the Pyrenean frontier posts, which up until then had been in the hands of CNT militia. They clashed with anarchists in Bellver de Cerdanya and killed several, including Antonio Martín, president of the revolutionary committee of Puigcerdà.[1] In Madrid, José Cazorla, infuriated by Melchor Rodríguez's denunciation of his secret prisons, closed down the CNT newspaper *Solidaridad Obrera*. Also on that day, in Barcelona, the communist and UGT leader, Roldán Cortada, was killed in Molins de Rei, probably by an anarchist, but there have long been other theories.[2] The PSUC organized a public funeral, which was to be used as a mass demonstration against the CNT. Meanwhile, Rodríguez Salas unleashed an aggressive sweep through the anarchist bastion of Hospitalet de Llobregat to search for the killers of Cortada.

The fear of open conflict on the streets of Barcelona prompted the Generalitat, with the agreement of the UGT and the CNT, to cancel all May Day parades. On 2 May *Solidaridad Obrera* asked workers not to allow themselves to be disarmed under any circumstances: 'The storm clouds are hanging, more and more threateningly, over Barcelona.'[3]

The very next day the Generalitat, deciding to take back all the power lost since 19 July 1936, seized control of the Telefónica in the Plaza de Cataluña. Although this telephone exchange was directed by a mixed committee of CNT and UGT, together with a delegate from the Catalan government, the anarchists had considered it their own since capturing it the previous July. It allowed them to listen in on any conversations made to and from Barcelona, including those of Companys and Azaña.

At three in the afternoon, the communist commissioner for public order, Rodríguez Salas, arrived at the Telefónica with three trucks full of assault guards. (It is assumed, but not certain, that he was acting on the orders of the councillor for internal security, Artemi Aiguader.) They surprised the sentries and disarmed them, but were then halted by a burst of machine-gun fire from the floor above. The anarchists fired shots out of the windows as an alarm call and within a matter of minutes news of the event had spread to all the working-class quarters of the city.

Dionisio Eroles, director of the control patrols, went to the Telefónica and tried to persuade the assault guards to lift their siege of the building, but without success. During the next few hours, people began to tear up paving stones and cobbles to make barricades in Las Ramblas, the Paralelo, the old city, the Vía Layetana and also in the outlying *barrios* of Sants and Sant Andreu. Shops closed and trams ceased to circulate. On one side were arrayed government forces, the communist PSUC and the Unified Socialist Youth, as well as some people from Estat Català; on the other were the CNT and the FAI, the Libertarian Youth, the Friends of Durruti, the POUM and its youth affiliate, the Juventudes Comunistas Ibéricas.

The leaders of the CNT went to the palace of the Generalitat to meet Companys and the chief councillor, Josep Tarradellas. They demanded the immediate resignation of Aiguader and Rodríguez Salas to calm things down, but after a marathon session, which lasted until the early hours of the morning, the negotiations reached a dead end. In the meantime the regional committee of the CNT had declared a general strike for the next day.

The network of barricades which were erected on Tuesday, 4 April, reminded many of the Semana Trágica in 1909 and almost everyone of 19 July 1936. Groups of workers shared out arms on the barricades while others prepared buildings for defence. A German agent of the Comintern in Barcelona reported a week later to Moscow, 'No vehicle which did not belong to the CNT was allowed to pass and more than 200 police and assault guards were disarmed.'[4] Ambulances with large red crosses evacuated the first of the wounded and, because of the random firing, the CNT brought out some of the home-made armoured vehicles from the previous summer. There was fighting on the Paralelo, on the Paseo de Colón, in the Plaza de Palau, in the railway stations and around the building of the Generalitat. The paramilitary police fired from the Colón and Victoria Hotels. Government forces and the PSUC occupied only a few areas in the centre, while the anarcho-syndicalists and their allies controlled the greater part of the city as well as the heavy guns in the fortress of Montjuich.

Whenever the assault guards attempted to seize a building, they were met by a hail of bullets. Firing echoed in the streets from rooftops and balconies, fortified by sandbags. 'From time to time,' Orwell recounted, 'the bursts of rifle-fire and machine-guns were mixed with the explosion of grenades. And at longer intervals, we heard tremendous explosions which, at the time, nobody could explain. They sounded like bombs, but that was impossible because there were no aircraft to be seen. Later they told me – and perhaps it is true – that agents provocateurs had set off large amounts of explosive to increase the noise and sense of panic.'[5]

In the middle of the afternoon, Juan García Oliver and Mariano Vázquez, the national secretary of the CNT, reached Barcelona with two leaders of the UGT. They had been sent by the government in Valencia to try to find a way out of the very dangerous situation which put the Republic in an extremely embarrassing position, especially vis-à-vis the European press. A meeting was held with the Generalitat, which continued to oppose the forced resignations of Aiguader and Rodríguez Salas. Companys told them that taking into account the turn of events, he saw no other option but to request the Valencia government to take matters in hand, even if this meant the end of the Generalitat's Council of Defence.

The anarchist leaders made an appeal over the radio for a ceasefire while Abad de Santillán talked to the control patrols.[6] The council of ministers met that same evening in Valencia. They decided to appoint Colonel Escobar as government delegate in Catalonia, but he was unable to take up the position due to a serious injury. The communist General Pozas was given command of all the forces on the Aragón front.

While anarchist leaders were trying to calm the situation, *La*

Batalla, the POUM's newspaper, argued that the best method of defence was attack and called for the immediate establishment of committees for the defence of the revolution. On Wednesday, 5 May, the anarchist leaders had another meeting with Companys and agreed a compromise solution of a new Catalan government which excluded Aiguader. But the tension in the streets did not lessen. That day, at 1 p.m., the secretary-general of the UGT in Catalonia, Antonio Sesé, was shot in his car on the way to the Generalitat to take up his new appointment as councillor of defence. Later, the corpses of the Italian anarchists Camillo Berneri, who had been professor of philosophy at Florence University, and Franco Barbieri were discovered, as well as that of Francisco Ferrer, nephew of the pedagogue executed at Montjuich after the Semana Trágica, and Domingo Ascaso, brother of the anarchist hero who had been killed the year before in the assault on the Atarazanas barracks.[7]

The middle classes in Barcelona, exasperated by the disturbance and shooting in the streets, wanted governmental authority to be re-established. The central government asked Federica Montseny to go to Barcelona to make an appeal over the radio to beg her fellow anarchists to lay down their arms. She had no success and was forced to accept that order could be reimposed only by force. 'They were the most terrible and bitter days of my life,' she was to say many years later.[8]

Largo Caballero found himself in a difficult position. He needed the CNT, yet events in Barcelona were giving ammunition to the communists. He felt there was no alternative but to agree to the transfer of Assault Guard reinforcements from the Jarama front. In addition Prieto despatched two destroyers packed with paramilitary forces from Valencia. Meanwhile, in other parts of Catalonia and Aragón the communists had taken advantage of events to broaden their offensive by seizing the telephone buildings in Tarragona, Tolosa and several smaller towns. All these attempts were resisted and developed into street fighting, causing the Assault Guard column, which was heading for Barcelona from the Jarama, to stop in Tarragona and crush resistance there.

The same day a group of over 1,500 men from the Red and Black column, the 127th Brigade of the 28th Division and the Lenin Division of the POUM, left the front for Barcelona, but were halted at Binéfar by republican aircraft. They were finally persuaded to return to the front, but only after venting their fury on Barbastro and other Aragonese villages.[9]

Hidalgo de Cisneros flew to the airfield of Reus with two squadrons of fighters and two of bombers 'to undertake operations against the region in the event that the insurgents won'.[10] The reinforcements which had meanwhile arrived in Barcelona on board the destroyers *Lepanto* and *Sánchez Barcáiztegui* increased the government's forces towards the level of the rebel troops the previous July, but they had even less hope of taking the city. The anarchists had an overwhelming numerical superiority, holding almost 90 per cent of Barcelona and its suburbs, as well as the heavy guns of Montjuich. These overwhelming advantages were not used because the CNT-FAI knew that further fighting would lead to a full civil war within the civil war, in which they would be cast as traitors, even if the nationalists were unable to take advantage of the situation.

During the day the famous pamphlet of the Friends of Durruti was distributed on the barricades and published the next morning in *La Batalla*. It had been drafted with the POUM on the evening of 4 May and was addressed to the workers, demanding 'A revolutionary Junta – execution of those responsible – the disarming of the paramilitary police – the socialization of the economy – the dissolution of the political parties which had attacked the working class', and declared, 'We do not give up the streets! – The revolution before everything! – Long live the social revolution! – Down with the counter-revolution!' That afternoon, the CNT and the FAI disowned the pamphlet.

At dawn on Thursday, 6 May, the CNT-FAI leadership proposed a pact with the government. They offered to take down the barricades and order a return to work on condition that the assault guards were withdrawn and did not carry out reprisals. The Generalitat replied positively at five the next morning. *Solidaridad Obrera* made a general appeal: 'Comrades of the government forces, back to your barracks! Comrades of the CNT, back to your unions! Comrades of the UGT and the PSUC, also to your centres! Let there be peace.' But the communist publication *El Noticiero Universal*, referring to the leaflet of the Friends of Durruti, attacked 'the criminal Trotskyism' which had encouraged the anti-fascists of Catalonia to fight among themselves. Other communist publications also raised the temperature with similar attacks.

On Friday, 7 May 150 trucks, bringing 5,000 assault guards and *carabineros*, reached Barcelona. The regional committee of the CNT appealed over the radio for everyone to assist in the re-establishment of law and order. There were the odd shots, but the barricades began to be taken down. But the PSUC and the Assault Guard did not give up their positions and carried out violent reprisals against libertarians.

The libertarians had not won even a pyrrhic victory. Companys had repudiated Rodríguez Salas's attempted seizure of the telephone building and removed Aiguader from the government, but in fact both the libertarian movement and Companys suffered a defeat, while the communists had also gained the lever they wanted to force Largo Caballero from power.

The moral outrage of the communist press knew no bounds when expressing the Party line of Trotskyist treason. This was also reflected in the reports to the Comintern in Moscow, which claimed that the disturbances had been planned well in advance. One Comintern representative claimed that the events in Barcelona were simply a 'putsch', and added that there were 'very interesting documents proving the connection of the Spanish Trotskyists with Franco ... The preparations for the putsch began even two months ago. This is also proved.'[11]

'We have succeeded in revealing close connections', wrote another, 'between Gestapo agents, agents of OVRA, Franco's agents living in Freiburg, Trotskyists and Catalonian fascists. It is known that they have systematically transported weapons and machine-guns over the frontier of Catalonia and that Spanish fascists have sent valuable objects from Catalonia abroad as a payment for these weapons ... The fact that the rebellion in Catalonia was quickly suppressed is regarded by fascist organs as a great failure.'[12] Another report stated, 'There isn't the slightest doubt that people from the POUM are working for Franco and Italian and German fascists.'[13]

At times, the Stalinist delusion appears to have developed into wishful fantasy. 'Some most repulsive looting has started in a number of places,' another report said. 'Gangs of Trotskyist-bandits took all the scarce supplies that the civilian population had, and all their more or less valuable belongings. Those Spanish people who had weapons in their hands replied to this immediately. The Trotskyist traitors were literally wiped out within a few hours.'[14]

Orlov's NKVD officers were sent to Barcelona to investigate and report back. They soon concocted an even more grandiose conspiracy theory of the sort which was already becoming the norm under the Stalinist terror, known in the Soviet Union as the *yezhovschina*, after the head of the NKVD. 'While investigating the rebellion in Catalonia, organs of state security discovered a large organization committing espionage. In this organization Trotskyists were working in close co-operation with the fascist organization "Falange Española". The network had its branches in army headquarters, at the war ministry, the National Republican Guard, etc. Using secret radio stations, this organization was passing to the enemy the information on the planned operations of the republican army, on the movements of troops, on the location of batteries, and directed air attacks using light signals. A plan was found on one of the members of this organization, with marked targets that fascists planned to bomb, and the following message was written in invisible ink on the reverse side of the map: "To the Generalissimo. We are able at the present time to inform you on all that we know about the situation and movements of red troops. The latest information broadcast by our radio station shows a great improvement in our information service."'[15]

As many disillusioned communists later acknowledged, the greater the lie, the greater the effect, because only a committed anti-communist could disbelieve it. The Spanish Republic was infected by the grotesque Stalinist paranoia of the NKVD, yet some Russian historians have recently argued that events in Spain also served to accelerate the 'mincing machine' of the Great Terror back in the Soviet Union. In any case, faced with the barrage of communist lies, any question of republican unity was now dead, whatever the gains in central government control and the restoration of military discipline.

Franco was, of course, delighted with the turn of events in Barcelona, even though the nationalists had not profited from it in military terms. He claimed in an empty boast to Faupel that 'the street fighting had been started by his agents', and Nicolás Franco also told the German ambassador that 'they had in all some thirteen agents in Barcelona'.[16]

The virtual collapse of CNT and POUM influence allowed the judicial system in Catalonia to be reorganized. Joan Comorera, the communist councillor of justice, introduced Special Popular

Tribunals, which were more like military tribunals. The following month, under the authority of the central government, a Special Tribunal for Espionage and High Treason was set up. Of the many thousands accused of taking part in the 'events of May' and arrested, 94 per cent were freed by the ordinary popular tribunals, but only 57 per cent by Comorera's variety.[17] At the same time, there were many political prisoners locked up with the common prisoners. Others were detained by the communist-run counter-intelligence service, the DEDIDE, which became the Servicio de Investigación Militar. They were held in a number of secret prisons, including the Palacio de las Misiones, Preventorio C (the 'Seminario'), Preventorio G (convent of the Damas Juanas), as well as the state prison on the Calle Déu i Mata. There were also labour camps holding 20,000 prisoners.[18]

While the communists blamed the disturbances on 'Trotskyist-Fascist' provocations, the CNT and the POUM accused the PSUC of having planned the attack on the Telefónica to provoke a revolt and crush their opponents. The timing was perfect for the communists, by then desperate to get rid of Caballero and longing to crush anarchist power in Catalonia, which they estimated was weakening rapidly. But this is far from certain. If this had been the case, the communists would have mustered a far greater force in Barcelona well in advance and, according to Companys, armed police in the city on 3 May numbered no more than 2,000.

In any case it was a defeat for the CNT and the POUM. Their newspapers now faced a strict censorship. The POUM in particular was unable to reply to the barrage of invective, however ludicrous. They were accused even of planning the assassination of Prieto and the communist General Walter, 'one of the most popular commanders in the Spanish army'. The very brazenness of the lies had an initial effect of disorientating people. They were tempted to believe what they heard on the grounds that nobody would dare to invent such allegations. Jesús Hernández, the communist minister who turned against the Party after the war, said with some exaggeration, 'If we were to decide to show that Largo Caballero, or Prieto, or Azaña, or Durruti were responsible for our defeats, half a million men, tens of newspapers, millions of demonstrators, and hundreds of orators would establish as gospel the evil doing of these citizens with such conviction and persistence that in a fortnight all Spain would agree with us.' However, several of the

Spanish communist leaders were uneasy at the brash tactics insisted upon by their Soviet and Comintern advisers. La Pasionaria realized that such methods were 'premature' in Spain, where the communists did not have a total control of the media.

On 9 May, just after the ceasefire in Barcelona, José Díaz of the Party's central committee advanced their strategy of deposing Largo Caballero and dealing ruthlessly with the POUM. 'The fifth column has been unmasked,' he declaimed, 'we need to destroy it ... Some call themselves Trotskyists, which is the name used by many disguised fascists who use revolutionary language in order to sow confusion. I therefore ask: If everyone knows this, if the government knows it, then why does it not treat them like fascists and exterminate them pitilessly? It was Trotsky himself who directed the gang of criminals that derailed trains in the Soviet Union, carried out acts of sabotage in the large factories, and did everything possible to discover military secrets with the object of handing them over to Hitler and the Japanese imperialists. And, in view of the fact that all this was revealed during the trial ...' With these words the communists revealed their plans for a spectacular arraignment of the POUM. A renewed attack on the POUM by Trotsky's Fourth International was, of course, ignored by the Stalinists who were determined that their label should stick.[19]

At a cabinet meeting on 15 May (two days before measures introduced by Largo Caballero against communist infiltration of the commissar department became effective) the communist minister, Uribe, demanded on Moscow's orders that the POUM be suppressed and its leaders arrested. Largo Caballero refused, saying that he would not outlaw a working-class party against whom nothing had been proved. The anarchist ministers backed him and proceeded to charge the communists with provoking the events in Barcelona. Uribe and Hernández walked out, followed by the right socialists Prieto and Negrín, the Basque nationalist Irujo, Álvarez del Vayo and Giral.[20] Largo Caballero was left with the four anarchist ministers and two of his old socialist colleagues.

Azaña had been warned by Giral eight days earlier that the social-democrats and liberals would back the communists at the next cabinet meeting. They took this decision partly because they identified with the communist policy of increased central government power and partly because they felt that any other course would put the Republic's arms supply at risk. Prieto insisted that as the coalition was broken, Largo Caballero must consult the president, but Azaña wished to avoid any complications. He told Largo to carry on so that continuity of planning might be maintained on the Estremadura offensive, which was due to be launched later in the month. The anarchist press joined their leaders in supporting Largo Caballero and his 'firm and just attitude which we all praise'. But without Soviet approval of the government there would be no arms. Largo Caballero had not appreciated his growing isolation. He knew about Álvarez del Vayo; he may well have suspected Negrín; but, although he had quarrelled frequently with Prieto, he never expected him to come out on the communists' side.

When, on 14 May, Azaña asked Largo Caballero to continue as prime minister, the old unionist knew that he would not be able to form another administration with the existing distribution of ministries. He therefore returned to the idea of a basically syndicalist government. This was similar to the National Defence Council, which the anarchists had proposed the previous September, with Largo Caballero at its head and the bulk of the ministries split between the UGT and the CNT. He had resurrected the idea in February, when he first became alarmed at the growth of communist influence, but Azaña had angrily rejected the proposal. Soviet control of their arms supply made the proposal totally impracticable. Largo Caballero was therefore allowed to continue only if he gave up the war ministry, as Stalin wanted. This he refused to do, believing that his presence there was the last barrier to a communist coup.

On 17 May Largo Caballero resigned, the final point in a long governmental crisis. Some historians argue that the origins of the ministerial crisis of May 1937 went back to the rising of October 1934 and that Caballero was not destroyed by the communists, but by the split with the moderate wing of the socialist party.[21]

The communists had approached Negrín at the end of the previous year and obtained his agreement to be the next prime minister.[22] General Krivitsky, the NKVD defector, claimed that this had first been prepared the previous autumn by Stashevsky. The other important communist renegade, Hernández, asserts that the decision was taken at a Politburo meeting early in March when foreign communists including Marty, Togliatti, Gerö and Codovilla outnumbered Spanish Communist Party members. Prieto and the liberal republicans agreed with their choice, and Azaña asked Juan Negrín to form an administration on 17 May.

Negrín kept the ministry of finance as well as his new position of president of the council of ministers. Prieto was minister of defence, Julián Zugazagoitia minister of the interior, Giral foreign minister and Irujo, the Basque conservative, minister of justice. To hide communist influence according to Stalin's instructions, the Party received just two minor portfolios: Jesús Hernández as minister of education and health, and Vicente Uribe as minister of agriculture.[23]

The governing system of the Republic became what Negrín and the communists later described as a 'controlled democracy'. This basically meant government from above in which the leaders of the main parties negotiated the distribution of ministries. Normal political life and argument was made difficult under war conditions, and contact between leaders and party members was severely restricted. Azaña complained at the lack of parliamentary debate and its result: 'The newspapers seem to be written by the same person, and they don't print anything more than diatribes against "international fascism" and assurances of victory.'[24] The infrequent proceedings of the Cortes were no more than the trappings of democracy. Only the surviving members from the Popular Front parties remained to take part in its cosmetic role.

Negrín tends to be portrayed either as a puppet of Moscow or else as a man who, recognizing necessity, tried to ride the communist tiger for the benefit of the Spanish Republic. Both interpretations are misleading. Juan Negrín López was born in 1892 into a rich upper-middle-class family in the Canary Islands. In his youth he showed sympathy for the autonomist movement in the Canary Islands and agreed with the PSOE's federalist programme. He was, above all, convinced of his own abilities and there are signs that he felt unsatisfied with the seemingly effortless success of his medical career which, after studies in Germany, led to his becoming professor of physiology at Madrid University at the age of 29. He soon became more actively involved in politics and his talents were undoubtedly greater than those of the professionals. Like many men who are conscious of their ability, he showed himself to be a firm believer in hierarchy, an authoritarian with few scruples who knew what was best for others. Not surprisingly he soon acquired a strong taste for power, once it was offered to him. In his case it appeared to run parallel to gross tastes for food and sex rather than act as a substitute.

Negrín's credentials and his 'iron hand' were applauded by official circles in London and Washington. Yet this government, which was welcomed by Churchill for its 'law-and-order stance', was to leave the NKVD-controlled secret police unhindered in its persecution of persons who opposed the Moscow line and to sacrifice the POUM to Stalin in order to maintain arms supplies in his determination to win the war.

On its first day, Negrín's government agreed to the closing of the POUM's *La Batalla* newspaper. Soviet and Comintern advisers were under great pressure to achieve results quickly. Lieutenant-Colonel Antonio Ortega, the new communist director-general of security, took his orders from Orlov, not Zugazagoitia, the minister of the interior. On 16 June, when the POUM was declared illegal, the communists turned its headquarters in Barcelona into a prison for 'Trotskyists'. The commander of the 29th Division, Colonel Rovira, was summoned to army headquarters and arrested. POUM leaders who could be located, including Andreu Nin, were also arrested. The wives of those who could not be found were taken in their place. These actions were given a veneer of legality by the retroactive decree a week later which created the Tribunals of Espionage and High Treason.

The POUM leaders were handed over to NKVD operatives and taken to a secret prison in Madrid, a church in the Calle Atocha. Nin was separated from his comrades and driven to Alcalá de Henares, where he was interrogated from 18 to 21 June. Despite the tortures he was subjected to by Orlov and his men, Nin refused to confess to the falsified accusations of passing artillery targets to the enemy. He was then moved to a summer house outside the city which belonged to Constancia de la Mora, the wife of Hidalgo de Cisneros, and tortured to death. A grotesque example of Stalinist play-acting then took place. A group of German volunteers from the International Brigades in uniforms without insignia, pretending to be members of the Gestapo, charged into the house to make it look as if they had come to Nin's rescue. 'Evidence' of their presence was then planted, including German documents, Falangist badges and nationalist banknotes. Nin, after being killed by Orlov's men, was buried in the vicinity. When graffiti appeared on walls demanding 'Where is Nin?' communists would scribble underneath 'In Salamanca or in Berlin'. The official Party line, published in *Mundo Obrero*, claimed that Nin had been liberated by Falangists and was in Burgos.[25]

Despite the protests in republican Spain and the petitions from abroad, Negrín, who cannot have believed such a version of events, did nothing when the communists claimed that they were ignorant of Nin's fate. This shameful behaviour opened up a deep split in the new government. When Negrín repeated the communist version to Azaña the president did not believe a word. 'Isn't it too novelettish?' he asked.[26]

With the passage of time since the Moscow show trials and the mood in Spain in 1937, it is very hard to understand how anybody could have believed the accusations of fascism thrown at the POUM, nor why the government did nothing to stop the Stalinists' dirty war against Nin and his followers, who were tortured and 'disappeared'. The 'disciplined machine' had taken over, but it now lacked the energy of popular support. For many, there seemed to be few ideals left to defend. The anarchist theorist Abad de Santillán remarked, 'Whether Negrín won with his communist cohorts, or Franco won with his Italians and Germans, the results would be the same for us.'[27]

24
The Battle of Brunete

Early in 1937 Nikonov, the deputy chief of Red Army intelligence in Spain, had written enthusiastically to Voroshilov, 'The war in Spain has revealed a number of extremely important aspects in the use of modern military equipment and has brought some valuable experience for studying operational, tactical and technical problems.'[1] But both Soviet advisers and communist commanders had learned very little, as the Republic's first major offensive of the war would demonstrate. The 'active war policy' of set-piece attacks adopted for propaganda reasons by the Comintern would rapidly destroy the Republic's ability to resist.

During April 1937, when nationalist troops were advancing on the northern coast towards Bilbao, Largo Caballero's general staff had begun to prepare an ambitious offensive in Estremadura, with 23 brigades and Pavlov's tanks.[2] The plan had been drawn up by General Asensio Torrado before he was removed. The idea was a major attack in the south-west to split nationalist territory in two and to finish with the cycle of battles around Madrid, which always ended in a useless bloodbath. Another reason for choosing Estremadura and not New Castile was that the nationalist troops in the area were inexperienced, badly armed and spread out. For Franco, it would have been much more difficult to bring in reinforcements by rail when republican guerrillas operated behind his lines. On the other hand it would have been extremely hard for the republicans to have deployed their troops and tanks in secret so far from Madrid; it would have left the capital vulnerable; and resupplying an army in Estremadura would have been very difficult.

The Soviet advisers and communist leaders opposed the plan mainly for political reasons. They had invested a huge international propaganda effort in the defence of Madrid, to say nothing of sacrificing many of their best troops in four battles. They were, in fact, as obsessed with the capital as Franco had been over the previous six months. They therefore had informed Largo Caballero that neither their tanks nor their aircraft would support the Estremadura offensive and that General Miaja would not transfer any men from the capital for the operation. Instead, they wanted an offensive to the west of Madrid, attacking very close to where the battle of the Corunna road had been fought.

The dispute over the Estremadura offensive produced the first reaction of regular officers against communist control of the republican army. A number of them, who had at first welcomed communist ideas on discipline, now began to suspect the communists might be more interested in increasing their power than in winning the war. They were alarmed that military affairs could be manipulated for purely propagandistic reasons, and they were horrified by the Party's infiltration of the command structure and its vitriolic campaigns against any officer who resisted.

The fall of Largo Caballero in May, and the appointment of Negrín as head of government, intensified the situation. Prieto, as minister of defence in charge of all three services, was prepared to collaborate closely with the communists and follow their advice on military operations. Yet he was to become one of their fiercest opponents later.

The situation in the north was critical, with the nationalists threatening Bilbao. Republican leaders decided on two operations, one in May and one in June, to take nationalist pressure off the Basques. The first, which was launched on 30 May, took place in the Sierra de Guadarrama. It consisted of an attack on La Granja de San Ildefonso 'to seize Segovia by surprise in an energetic attack', according to Prieto's instructions. This offensive was later used by Hemingway as the background for his novel *For Whom the Bell Tolls*. Bertolt Brecht also set his only poem about the Spanish Civil War there.

My brother was a pilot,
He received a card one day,
He packed his belongings in a box
And southward took his way.

My brother is a conqueror,
Our people are short of space,
And to gain more territory is
An ancient dream of the race.

The space that my brother conquered
Lies in the Guadarrama massif,
Its length is six feet, two inches,
Its depth four feet and a half.[3]

Taking part in the republican operation were the 34th Division under the command of José María Galán, the 35th Division under General Walter and Durán's 69th Division, supported by artillery and Pavlov's tank brigade. All these forces were under the command of Colonel Domingo Moriones, the head of I Corps.

At dawn on 30 May the attack began after a heavy bombardment of nationalist positions around the Cabeza Grande, Matabueyes and La Cruz de la Gallega. The infantry of the 69th Division launched its assault lacking air cover. The republican air force did not arrive until eleven in the morning, and then bombed republican positions.[4] Nevertheless, the 69th Division managed to occupy Cruz de la Gallega and continued its advance towards Cabeza Grande, from where it would be able to deploy direct fire on the Segovia road. Walter ordered XIV International Brigade to launch a frontal attack, which left the pinewood hillside scattered with corpses. Walter's cynicism was revealed in a report back to Moscow in which he wrote, 'the XIV, which heroically, but passively, allowed itself to be slaughtered over the course of five days'.[5]

On 1 June Varela's forces, with one division from Avila and the reinforcements which Barrón had brought from the Madrid front, counter-attacked with strong support from bombers and fighters. They forced the republicans back from Cabeza Grande and threatened the whole advance on La Granja. The next day Walter was relieved from operational command of the offensive and on 6 June Colonel Moriones ordered his troops to withdraw to their start lines. According to Moriones, the attack cost 3,000 men, of whom 1,000 were from XIV International Brigade. And as for the original purpose of the operation, the nationalist assault on Bilbao was delayed by no more than two weeks at the most.

The operation failed partly because the nationalists appeared to have got wind of what was being prepared, but mainly because the republican command had greatly underestimated the speed of the nationalists' reactions and the effectiveness of their air power. The nationalist Fiat fighter force, led by García Morato, even managed to machine-gun Moriones's headquarters.[6] The Soviet pilots of the republican aircraft, on the other hand, demonstrated a distinct lack of aggressive action. Colonel Moriones in his report wrote, 'Our own aircraft carried out bombing attacks from a great height and carelessly ... our fighters kept at a respectable distance and rarely came down to machine-gun the enemy ... enemy aircraft were highly active and extraordinarily effective.'[7]

This action in the Guadarrama produced the first example of unrest in the ranks of the International Brigades as a result of being sacrificed for little benefit. And the brutality of their commanders when some of their men broke in the face of strafing by nationalist fighters was extreme. Captain Duchesne, who commanded the punishment company of XIV International Brigade, 'designated five men at random and shot them, one after another, in the back of the head with his pistol in Soviet style'.[8] When the 69th Division retreated from Cabeza Grande, an infuriated Walter (before he was relieved) had ordered 'the machine-gunning of those who pull back, executions on the spot, and the beating of stragglers'.[9]

The second tactical operation to take pressure off the northern front was an attack on Huesca with the newly constituted Army of the East commanded by General Pozas. General Lukács was ordered up from Madrid with XII International Brigade, which included the Garibaldi Battalion, as well as four other brigades from the Central Front. He was put in charge of the operation, but found that many of the soldiers were badly armed, and that they would have little artillery or armoured support.

Lukács launched the offensive against Huesca on 12 June. The infantry had to attack across a kilometre of open ground. The nationalists, who were well dug in, forced them back with machine-gun fire and artillery. To compound the disaster, the vehicle in which General Lukács and his aides were travelling was hit by a shell. Lukács and his driver were killed, and Gustav Regler, the commissar of XII International Brigade, was badly wounded.[10]

At dawn on 16 June the republican troops launched a new attack against the villages of Alerre and Chimillas, but the intensity of enemy fire forced them back. On 19 June, after another two days of desultory firing, the offensive was cancelled. The Navarrese brigades had just entered Bilbao. Walter reported that XII International Brigade's performance 'was nothing like what it had been during earlier battles.'[11]

The Huesca offensive, recounted by Gustav Regler in his book *The Great Crusade*, contributed to a defeatist mood in republican ranks. It had taken place soon after the events of May in a sector where there were many anarchist formations and the POUM's 29th Division, which included the British *centuria* led by George Kopp, who had just been arrested and accused of espionage. Newspapers from Valencia and Barcelona were intercepted so that the troops should not hear of the denunciations of members of the POUM as traitors.[12]

Total losses for the Huesca offensive rose to nearly three times those of the Segovia offensive. The losses among anarchist and POUM members were very heavy. (Orwell himself received a bullet through the throat, a wound which took him out of the war.) As it had been a communist-led operation and the nationalists appeared to have been forewarned, this only increased their suspicions and their bitterness.

The major operation, however, which the republican government planned to replace the Estremadura offensive, was to take place against Brunete, a village some 25 kilometres to the west of Madrid. The idea was to penetrate the weakly held nationalist lines and cut off the salient, which extended to the edge of the capital. The Communist Party had been carefully preparing the Brunete offensive to demonstrate its power and military effectiveness.

All five International Brigades and the communists' best-known formations were given key roles, and every important officer had a Soviet adviser at his elbow. Miaja was overall commander. Under him were Modesto's V Corps on the right with Líster's 11th Division, El Campesino's 46th Division, and Walter's 35th Division; Jurado's XVIII Corps on the left with 10th, 15th and 34th Divisions. (Jurado, the only non-communist senior commander, became ill and was replaced by Colonel Casado during the battle.) There was also a forward reserve of Kléber's 45th Division and Durán's 69th Division. In support of this force of 70,000 men, Miaja could count on 132 tanks, 43 other armoured vehicles, 217 field guns, 50 bombers and 90 fighters, although only 50 turned out to be serviceable.[13] It was by far the largest concentration of strength yet seen in the war. To the south of Madrid, II Corps commanded by Colonel Romero was to attack towards Alcorcón to meet up with XVIII Corps. And II Corps was to make a diversionary attack in the area of Cuesta de la Reina. 'If we cannot succeed with such forces,' wrote Azaña with his usual lucid pessimism, 'we will not be able to manage it anywhere.'[14]

The great operation, however, concealed crucial weaknesses. The People's Army supply services were not used to coping with such large numbers and the Segovia offensive had shown up the bad communications between commanders as well as their lack of initiative. This last defect, which was to prove so serious in the Brunete offensive, is usually attributed to a fear of making independent decisions among Party members. Such caution may seem surprising in aggressive 30-year-olds like Modesto and Líster. Yet among this new breed of formation commander only Modesto and El Campesino had seen service in Morocco as NCOs, while Líster had received some training in Moscow. Their first experience of military command had come during the sierra engagements of the previous summer. They had often shown themselves daring and resourceful at battalion level, but now they commanded formations with anything up to 30 battalions and had to cope with unfamiliar staff procedures. Azaña disliked the fact that these 'crude guerrillas', 'improvised people, without knowledge', pushed aside regular officers. Despite all their efforts, they could 'not make up for their lack of competence'.[15] But if the new leaders of the People's Army were intimidated by their responsibilities or conscious of their limitations, they certainly did not allow it to show. As with the International Brigades at the Jarama, ignorance was hidden behind a bluff confidence sustained by a ferocious discipline.

The offensive started in the early hours of 6 July, when the 34th Division from XVIII Corps attacked Villanueva de la Cañada. The nationalist resistance was unexpectedly fierce, and when the troops seemed reluctant to keep going into the assault, Miaja gave orders to 'take Cañada at all costs and if the infantry will not go forward place a battery of guns behind our own troops to make them'. Though outnumbered by nine to one, the defenders held off the republicans for a whole day.

Líster's 11th Division swung past this action and attacked Brunete, defended by a very small nationalist force and a handful of medical orderlies.[16] He took the village on the morning of 7 July, but then failed to advance towards Sevilla la Nueva and Navalcarnero. He was concerned that El Campesino's 46th Division had failed to crush the Falangist battalion defending Quijorna to his right rear. (A similar hold-up due to a brave defence occurred on XVIII Corp's left flank at Villanueva del Pardillo.) Instead of advancing while the way ahead lay open, Líster and his Russian adviser, Rodimtsev, ordered their troops to dig in just south of Brunete, where they waited for El Campesino's troops to finish off the Falangists in Quijorna. That took three days, partly because they had not surrounded it properly. This gave Varela time to send a Moroccan *tabor* of *regulares* to reinforce the Falangists.[17]

In the meantime two republican reconnaissance soldiers captured by the nationalists admitted that Navalcarnero was indeed the objective.[18] The town had no defences and no garrison, save a handful of civil guards and supply detachments. Líster's delay saved the nationalists. Within 24 hours of the offensive starting, Varela could count on Barrón's 13th Division, and the next day Sáenz de Buruaga's 150th Division arrived from the north in several hundred trucks, acquired on credit from the United States.[19]

He ordered the 150th Division to attack between Brunete and Quijorna. This threat was met by Walter's 35th Division, which filled the gap between Líster and El Campesino.

On the left flank 15th Division, supported by artillery and aircraft, attacked towards Villanueva de la Cañada and managed to take the village at ten o'clock that night, after heavy fighting against the nationalist division defending that sector. At the end of that first day the nationalist front had been forced back only in the centre, where part of Líster's 11th Division advanced to within two kilometres of Sevilla la Nueva. Nationalist resistance around Quijorna and Villafranca del Castillo, held by no more than a *centuria* of Falangists from Salamanca,[20] had been fierce. The republican advance could only be sustained if the enemy line was broken and the two attacking corps could join up. The republicans had a numerical advantage at this stage in men, artillery and aircraft. But Líster still did not dare advance further with both his flanks exposed.

While Líster waited, General Gal's 15th Division advanced strongly on Boadilla del Monte. But on their line of advance his men came across a small hill, which they called 'Mosquito hill' because of the whistling bullets. It was to form as terrible a memory as 'Suicide Hill' at the Jarama. The troops of Asensio were waiting for them, supported by two Navarrese brigades, as well as the Galician 108th Division, which had just arrived. A desperate battle ensued, which cost many casualties on both sides. Oliver Law, the black commander of the Americans' Washington Battalion, was killed that night and buried there. Meanwhile, republican troops had finally occupied Quijorna, which by then was little more than a pile of smoking ruins.

Although at the start of the battle the republican air force enjoyed air superiority, with up to 30 fighters in each sortie, the nationalists dominated the skies from 11 July.[21] Their aircraft, first the Junkers 52s, Fiats and Heinkel 51s piloted by Spanish airmen, then the Condor Legion, hammered the eight republican divisions concentrated on less than 200 square kilometres of the bare Castilian plain. The first target of the nationalist planes were the T-26 tanks, which presented easy prey in the open. Within two days, once the nationalists had established their maximum rhythm of sorties, the republicans were left with only 38 armoured vehicles. Day and night, Junkers 52s and Heinkel 111s bombed the republican lines at will. From 12 July the Condor Legion deployed its Messerschmitt 109s, flown by pilots such as Adolf Galland, later one of the great Second World War aces. The Chatos and Moscas could not match them above 14,000 feet. On that day 'more than 200 aircraft could be seen in the air at the same time'.[22]

On 10 July XII International Brigade finally took Villanueva del Pardillo, which had been bravely defended by a battalion of the San Quentin infantry regiment. Meanwhile the nationalists counter-attacked to the south-east between Quijorna and Brunete with 10th and 150th Divisions. They had come up against General Walter's 35th Division, which had been pushed forward to seal the gap between the troops of El Campesino and Líster. During this fighting 3,000 republican soldiers were killed and the International Brigades were totally exhausted.[23] On 16 July a bomb splinter hit George Nathan, the commander of the British battalion, in the shoulder and he died a few hours later. His devastated comrades buried him on the banks of the Guadarrama.

Republican troops were also desperately short of ammunition and without water in the July heat. Miaja's staff had woefully underestimated the resupply needs for such a battle. The lessons of the La Granja offensive had not been learned. The Castilian landscape, bleached a pale brown by the sun, became a furnace, especially for the tank troops. The inside of each vehicle was like an oven. The infantry also suffered from the lack of vegetation for camouflage and the difficulty of digging trenches in the baked earth. Corpses, swollen and black from the sun, lay in all directions and the stretcher-bearers suffered heavy casualties trying to remove the wounded.

During that week, little ground was lost or gained in a terrible stalemate. But then on 18 July, the anniversary of the rising, the nationalist infantry, supported by 60 batteries of artillery and aircraft, attacked on all sectors. Richthofen, who had hurried back from his leave to take command of the Condor Legion squadrons, recorded, '18 July. Attack on the red infantry who are much better than expected. Air attacks very good despite strongest red flak as never experienced before. 4 Brigade gets ahead well. Heavy losses on both sides. 4 Brigade has lost eighteen officers by lunchtime and about 400 men. Art[illery] shot badly. Three waved bombing attack went off well, but it did not help. Right wing did not engage at all as art[illery] still not in position. *Manaña!*'[24]

'19 July,' he wrote the next day, 'Red flyers drop heavy bombs even on their own red infantry! Their command post also got its share. The reds have attacked 4 Brigade heavily but they are beaten back. Red attacks to the south at Brunete. Right wing cannot move forward. Our flyers are deployed against the red positions around Brunete.

'20 July. We fly and attack red airfields to keep the opponents down. Richthofen and Sander [Sperrle] with Franco for a big conference with his generals, army commander, and aviation General Kindelán. Clean up here and then quickly back to the north. Franco hopes that the heavy losses are demoralizing the reds. Franco demands that Richthofen concentrates on heavy artillery.' What emerged clearly once again was that the German and nationalist pilots were far better trained and more resourceful than their opponents. Even the Heinkel 51, which was inferior to the Soviet aircraft, was inflicting greater losses. Nationalist aircraft attacked the International Brigades near the River Guadarrama. That day Julian Bell, the nephew of Virginia Woolf, died, having arrived in Spain only a month before.

The Condor Legion's bombers and fighters had little trouble finding targets on the exposed plain. While the Heinkel 111s flew sorties against artillery batteries, headquarters and forming-up areas, the Heinkel 51s strafed, bombed and shot up republican tanks. In addition each fighter carried a load of six ten-kilo fragmentation bombs. Flying wing-tip to wing-tip, they released their loads simultaneously. Trenches, unless dug in a zigzag pattern, provided little protection. One German squadron leader boasted that in a 200-metre stretch of trench, 120 bodies had been found after one of their attacks.[25]

From 23 July nationalist troops, supported by concentrated artillery fire, tanks and aircraft, went over to the offensive. The next day they reached the edge of Brunete. 'Because of bombing attacks,' wrote Richthofen, 'the terrain is full of smoke and visibility is bad. As the mist clears, there is a red counter-attack. Red flyers in the air very strong. Heavy infantry losses on our side. Today for the first time all aircrew are deployed. As the red infantry is thrown back by this deployment of air power, seven new battalions arrive to support them.'[26]

The 'red infantry' thrown back was presumably Líster's division which, despite its reputation for iron discipline, collapsed on 24 July, as the chief Soviet adviser reported back to Moscow later: 'Líster's division lost its head and fled. We managed with great difficulty to bring it back under control and prevent soldiers fleeing from their units. The toughest repressive measures had to be applied. About 400 of those fleeing were shot on 24 July.'[27] 'There was a general panic and flight,' Walter reported to Moscow. 'The International Brigades, except for XI and units of XV, which held their positions, were not much slower in their inexplicable but hasty movement backwards.'[28]

'All the red attacks have been rebuffed,' Richthofen noted exultantly next day. 'Countless red casualties, which are already decomposing in the heat. Everywhere shot-up red tanks. A great sight! Our Heinkel 51s and Spanish fighters attack north of Brunete.' Two days later he claimed the victory as one for the Condor Legion and the nationalist air force: 'The situation here has been saved by the aircrews. The ground forces are not up to it.'[29]

The general staff and the communists proclaimed that the Brunete offensive was a masterpiece of planning. General Rojo even suggested that it had 'a beautiful technical rigorousness, almost perfect'.[30] This was optimistic to say the least. Brunete was intended to be an encirclement operation, taking the enemy by surprise, in many ways a foretaste of the Second World War. The theory of 'deep penetration', using tank units as armoured fists, had already been developed by the finest minds in the Red Army. The tactic had been used in Arman's attack at Seseña the previous autumn. But there was no question of using such a technique at Brunete in July 1937. Marshal Tukhachevsky, its greatest proponent, had been tortured into confessing to treason and espionage for the Germans. A month before the battle of Brunete he had been tried and executed along with seven colleagues. They were shot in sequence just after they left the courtroom. No Soviet adviser, therefore, dared follow his tactical theories.

The divisions were spread out and so were the tanks. And instead of leaving strong points to be dealt with by a second line, the breakthrough force was allowed to halt. Most astonishing of all was that the attack from the north was supposed to be met by another attack coming from the southern suburbs of Madrid towards Alcorcón to complete the encirclement. This never got off the ground, so the plan was rendered virtually useless from the start. Not only did the planners grossly underestimate the enemy's ability to react quickly, they also failed to foresee that as soon as the nationalists achieved air superiority their already overstretched supply system would collapse.

As well as the basic problems of staff failures and republican inferiority in the air, communications between headquarters were disastrously bad. Field telephone lines were continually cut by shelling and runners could not be expected to get through when there was no cover. But these natural hazards of warfare without radios were compounded by the lack of initiative shown by republican commanders. Nationalist field commanders, on the other hand, reacted instinctively and rapidly to the situation as it developed and did not wait for orders from above. Nor did they blindly follow instructions that were out of date when circumstances on the ground had changed dramatically.

Matters were not helped on the republican side by the failure of the staff to provide maps. The International Brigades found that they had to draw them for themselves.[31] The problems of command and control were also made far worse by the way commanders under pressure would claim to have reached a particular point when they were nowhere near it. (This emerged as a common failing in the Red Army later during the Second World War.) Some republican commanders, out of vanity, lied to their superiors deliberately. For example, El Campesino shamelessly exaggerated nationalist casualties in Quijorna, when it finally fell, to justify his initial lack of success. Líster, in his report, quadrupled the number of enemy defending Brunete and even claimed at one point that his troops had reached Navalcarnero, when in fact they were twelve kilometres short of it. When Mera's 14th Division moved towards Brunete to replace the 11th Division, Líster claimed not to know that the village had been retaken by the enemy. Miaja's chief of staff, Colonel Matallana, thought that Líster's men were still occupying some small hills beyond it.

Prieto, who was at Miaja's headquarters when Mera complained that his orders did not correspond to the reality on the ground, became even more furious at the commander-in-chief's protests that he had been misled. General Walter, in his usual scathing terms, reported that the reason why the 11th Division's commanders 'were so touchingly ill informed about the dispositions of their own battalions' was because Líster had far too many officers on his staff.[32] Yet Modesto, the commander of V Corps, may have been trying to save the reputation of the most famous communist formation from responsibility for the loss of Brunete. After the battle, Líster was ordered to 'withdraw his division for retraining and reinforcements', which was perhaps necessary after the 400 executions. Rodimtsev, his military adviser, was summoned to a suburb of Madrid to see 'Comrade Malino[vsky] who wanted to know how things were'.[33]

Nevertheless, the major factor in the disaster, as in the Segovia offensive, lay in the air superiority of the nationalists. Prieto rightly stated that the Achilles heel of the People's Army consisted of 'the commanders and the air force'.[34] The whole of the Republic's Brunete offensive managed to achieve an advance of only 50 square kilometres at the cost of 25,000 casualties, the loss of 80 per cent of its armoured force and a third of the fighter aircraft assigned to the front.[35] The loss of equipment was particularly serious at a time when the blockade of republican ports was becoming much more effective. The nationalists suffered 17,000 casualties, but a much lower proportion were killed, and their losses in equipment and aircraft were far lighter.

The first great offensive of the Republic, which had taken little pressure off the northern zone, perhaps a respite of five weeks, signified a major setback. The blow to morale, with the loss of many of their best troops, was exacerbated by the knowledge that the nationalists were soon to achieve parity in ground forces.

Franco declared that the battle was over on 25 July, the day of Santiago, the patron saint of the Spanish army, and claimed that Saint James had given them victory. If at that moment he was tempted to exploit republican weakness around Madrid and attack again towards the capital, General Vigón took on the task of persuading him that it was essential to liquidate the northern zone first.[36]

Flying in the face of reality, the communists declared to the world at large that Brunete had been a victory. In XV International Brigade, commissars told their men that it 'had totally vindicated the active war policy of the Negrín government following the laissez-faire attitude of Largo Caballero'. The premature and wildly exaggerated claims about the operation's success in the first two days had forced Miaja and his staff to persist at horrendous cost rather than admit failure. The communists defended the operational plan furiously, but such a concentration of slow-moving forces on a restricted front enabled the nationalists to profit from the vastly superior ground-attack potential of their combined air forces. With both Avila and Talavera airfields less than 30 minutes' flying time from Brunete, they were able to establish a bombing shuttle and fighter sortie rhythm, which the advocates of the offensive must have seriously underestimated.

The communists' obsession with propaganda, often at the expense of their men's lives, contributed to the growing unrest within the International Brigades. The minor mutinies which broke out among the Americans, the British and the Poles of XIII International Brigade were described in reports back to Moscow as 'unpleasant events'. Members of the Lincoln Battalion were forced back to duty at pistol point, while the British, who were down to 80 men, accused Gal of incompetence and only returned to the front when Walter Tapsell, their commander, was threatened with execution. The Poles, who had been at the front for several months without respite, decided to return to Madrid. The brigade commander, Vincenzo Bianco ('Krieger'), attempted to crush the revolt by hitting the men and shooting one of them in the head. The International Brigade cavalry detachment, which had done nothing during the battle, was brought in to restore order and prevent anyone leaving the front. Meanwhile, Modesto had resorted to deploying machine-guns behind the line with orders to open fire on anyone who retreated on whatever pretext. The troops were angry about the enormous losses, above all because they suspected that most of them had served no purpose in a senseless butchery.[37]

Soviet reports emphasize the appalling state in which the International Brigades found themselves after Brunete. They had suffered 4,300 casualties out of a strength of 13,353, and nearly 5,000 men were in hospital.[38] International volunteers now formed around only 10 per cent of the strength of the XI Brigade. The rest were Spaniards who naturally resented being commanded by foreign officers who could not speak their language. XIV and XV Brigades were both reduced from four to less than two battalions. Gómez, the head of the International Brigade camp at Albacete, reported to the Red Army's intelligence directorate in Moscow that the performance of the brigades at Brunete had been affected by 'the systematic work of the fifth column'.[39]

The degree of paranoia at this time of Trotskyist witch-hunting is almost incredible. Every blunder, of which there were many, was attributed to deliberate sabotage. General Walter was so convinced that the brigades had been infiltrated that, like Modesto, he set up machine-guns behind the lines to prevent battalions from surrendering to the enemy. 'On the first night of the operation', he reported to Moscow, 'it was necessary to disarm and arrest the entire company of one of the brigade's battalions. Eighteen men from it, led by a lieutenant and three non-commissioned officers, were shot by sentence of an army tribunal for organizing the company's defection to the enemy. The divisional commissar and brigade commander (anarchists) were shot by Líster on the second night of the operation for refusal to obey a military order and for persuading the command staff to surrender. Moreover, during the course of 22 days, while the brigade was in the front line, up to twenty enemy agents were exposed and removed from the division. A good half of these were officers. The surrender of Brunete and the flight of many brigades were to a significant extent the result of panic sown by the "fifth column" that the fascists had spread around our forces.'[40]

Morale in all cases was extremely bad, as General Kléber reported back to Moscow: 'I have begun to worry a great deal about the state of the International Brigades. There is a lot going on there: the attitude of Spaniards towards them and of their attitude towards Spaniards; the questions about morale; the chauvinism of certain nationalities (especially, the French, Poles and Italians); the desire for repatriation; the presence of enemies in the ranks of the International Brigades. It is crucial that a big man be despatched quickly from the big house especially for the purpose of providing some leadership in this matter.'[41]

A further report added that 'the International Brigades are considered to be a foreign body, a band of intruders ... by the vast majority of political leaders, soldiers, civil servants and political parties in republican Spain'. Meanwhile, the foreign volunteers felt 'that they have been treated like a foreign legion ready to be sacrificed', because they were always selected for the most dangerous attacks, and saw it as 'a concerted effort to annihilate and sacrifice the international contingents'. Some International Brigades had been at the front 'for 150 consecutive days'. In XIII International Brigade, Captain Roehr 'committed suicide in battle because he could no longer accept the responsibility of demanding renewed effort from his exhausted men, and at the same time felt he did not have the right to demand rest for his men from his superiors'.[42]

Another report to Voroshilov, passed on to Stalin, noted 'a pessimistic mood and the lack of confidence in victory (the latter has especially strengthened since the operation at Brunete)'. Many Brigaders felt cheated. They had volunteered for six months and were not being allowed home.[43] Most striking of all was the fact that the International Brigades had established their own 'concentration camp', called Camp Lukács. No less than 4,000 men were sent to this camp in the course of three months from 1 August.[44]

25
The Beleaguered Republic

Although the 'active war-policy' of Negrín's government had not started auspiciously, the new prime minister hoped that his cabinet's moderate and disciplined image would succeed in persuading Western governments to change their policy towards Spain. He managed to impress Eden and Churchill, but the former had scarcely six months left before his resignation in protest at Chamberlain's policy, while the latter remained 'in the wilderness' until after the end of the war.

The British government had continued to keep France in the non-interventionist camp by working on its fear of isolation in the face of Hitler. The Non-Intervention Committee, with eight countries participating, had approved on 8 March a new control plan to observe Spanish land and sea frontiers, and control the flow of arms and volunteers. Naval patrols were to watch the Spanish shores, with the Germans and Italians taking responsibility for the Mediterranean coastline.[1]

The diplomatic charade of non-intervention received a severe shock on 23 March 1937, when Count Grandi, the Italian ambassador, openly admitted to the Non-Intervention Committee that there were Italian forces in Spain and asserted that none of them would be withdrawn until the war was won.[2] Even so German and Italian intervention continued to be 'unrecognized'. The only practical step taken had been a measure on foreign enlistments, which meant that each of the signatories passed laws preventing private citizens from volunteering. This, of course, would stop those trying to join the International Brigades, while the Axis powers' contribution of military units was ignored. In addition, the only effective control on importing war material proved to be the Pyrenean frontier, so again only the Republic suffered. Yet even this did not satisfy the nationalists. In Salamanca, Virginia Cowles encountered a great sense of bitterness against the British government, based on the firm belief that non-intervention was 'a communist plot to weaken Franco by excluding foreign aid'.[3]

The isolationism of the United States helped the nationalists, who were aided by many influential sympathizers in Washington. Roosevelt's government had tacitly upheld the non-intervention policy from the beginning. Then, in January 1937, when aircraft were to be shipped to Spain by the Vimalert company of New Jersey, Congress introduced legislation to prevent it. The vote in both houses was overwhelmingly in favour of the ban, but a technical error in the Senate gave the Vimalert company time to load the aircraft and aero engines on the *Mar Cantábrico* in New York harbour. The ship sailed on 6 January, just over 24 hours before the resolution became law. This Spanish merchantman took on more matériel in Mexico and then, disguised as British, made for Basque waters. The deception was no use, for the nationalist cruiser *Canarias* put to sea from El Ferrol on 4 March to await it. The *Mar Cantábrico* was captured on 8 March and all the Spanish seamen were executed. It is still not known who warned the nationalists of its route, but the German embassy in Washington DC had passed a considerable quantity of intelligence on the subject back to Berlin.[4]

On 20 April the scheme to patrol ports and frontiers came into effect. Naval patrols furnished by Great Britain, France, Germany and Italy watched the coasts. The uselessness of the scheme was shown by the fact that not a single breach of the agreement was reported by the time it collapsed in the autumn. The incidents with the greatest potential danger in this period occurred on 24 and 29 May, when the port of Palma de Mallorca was attacked by Russian-piloted bombers from Valencia. On 24 May there were near misses on two Italian warships, the *Quarto* and the *Mirabello*, the German destroyer *Albatross* and the British destroyer HMS *Hardy*.

On 29 May republican aircraft in another raid dropped a bomb which hit the Italian battleship *Barletta*, killing six members of the crew. The same day two direct hits were made on the German battleship *Deutschland*, killing twenty sailors and wounding 73. Hitler, on hearing the news, worked himself up into a fit of terrifying proportions. Neurath only just managed to persuade the Führer not to declare war on the Republic. Hitler instead ordered units of the German navy, including the *Admiral Scheer*, to bombard the undefended town of Almeria in reprisal. The local authorities there estimated that more than 200 shells were fired at the town, killing twenty people, wounding 50 and destroying 40 buildings.

Prieto wanted the republican air force to attack all German warships in reply, which would have constituted a declaration of war. The communists were greatly alarmed and radioed Moscow for instructions. Stalin, not unexpectedly, was entirely opposed to Prieto's suggestion, since provocation of Hitler alarmed him more than anything else. It was later rumoured that orders had been given to liquidate Prieto if he persisted. In the council of ministers, Giral and Hernández formally opposed the plan. Negrín and Azaña decided to send protest notes to the secretary-general of the League of Nations and to the French and British foreign ministries. But both the Foreign Office and the Quai d'Orsay felt that the Germans had been justified in their response. Álvarez del Vayo then demanded an extraordinary meeting of the League of Nations, but with no success.[5]

On 30 May Germany and Italy withdrew from the Non-Intervention Committee. Neville Chamberlain, who had become prime minister on 17 May, tried to calm Hitler with 'definite and considered' attempts to persuade Germany to return to the committee. The Germans, realizing that they could take further advantage of the situation, claimed on 15 June that an unidentified submarine had fired torpedoes at their cruiser *Leipzig* off Oran, and they demanded sanctions against the Republic. They used this incident as their justification for withdrawing from the naval patrol. The Republic denied any part in the event.

The German and Italian policy on Spain was even more closely co-ordinated than that of England and France. Having recognized the Burgos regime the previous November, they recommended that belligerent rights should be granted to both sides so that non-intervention controls should no longer be needed. The British were opposed to the granting of belligerent rights, which would mean interference with British shipping. The French government (now led by Camille Chautemps, but still containing Blum and Delbos) knew that nationalist naval power, with covert help from Italian submarines, could blockade the Republic into surrender. Negrín visited Paris and received a sympathetic hearing. The French promised that they would not concede belligerent rights to the nationalists. But the British government suggested a compromise formula, which involved granting belligerent rights only when foreign troops had been withdrawn. This was then amended to 'substantial reductions', which led to haggling over figures and percentages.

At the end of July the Italians began a random campaign of maritime attacks from Majorca, with 'Legionary' submarines and bombers. In August alone they sank 200,000 tons of shipping bound for republican Spain, including eight British and eighteen other neutral merchantmen. On 23 August Ciano made notes of a visit from the British chargé d'affaires in Rome: 'Ingram made a friendly démarche about the torpedo attacks in the Mediterranean. I replied quite brazenly. He went away almost satisfied.'[6] On 31 July the Italian submarine *Iride* fired torpedoes at the British destroyer HMS *Havock* north of Alicante. On 3 September Ciano wrote, 'Full orchestra – France, Russia, Britain. The theme – piracy in the Mediterranean. Guilty – the fascists. The Duce is very calm. He looks in the direction of London and he doesn't believe that the English want a collision with us.'[7] It was not surprising that Mussolini made such an assumption. Lord Perth, the British ambassador, was later described (perhaps optimistically) by Ciano as 'a genuine convert', a man who had 'come to understand and even to love fascism'. In any case Chamberlain, ignoring Eden's advice, wrote to Mussolini directly in the friendliest terms, thinking he could woo him away from Hitler. Meanwhile, he had instructed Perth to start working towards a treaty of friendship with Mussolini. He was also to use as a personal envoy his sister-in-law, Lady Chamberlain, who proudly wore fascist badges and insignia.

There were the beginnings of a small group in the Conservative Party and its supporters who were sensitive to the dangers of Chamberlain's policy. Harold Nicolson, who was one of them, agreed with Duff Cooper that 'the second German war began in July 1936, when the Germans started with their intervention in Spain'. He went on to say that 'the propertied classes in this country with their insane pro-Franco business have placed us in a very dangerous position'.[8] The only area where the Conservative government was prepared to display a semblance of firmness was in the Mediterranean, the sea lane to the Empire. Its main concern was that Axis bases should not exist on Spanish territory once the civil war was over.

On 22 June Eden argued in the wake of the *Leipzig* incident that 'submarines of the patrol powers in Spanish waters (including the western Mediterranean) should not proceed submerged, and that the Spanish parties should be informed that they must follow this procedure'.[9] The patrol powers would then be justified in attacking any submarines under the surface. This proposal was blocked by the Italians with German support as 'pointless'. Their 'Legionary' submarines would have been the most at risk. The French, no doubt using Eden's proposal, called a conference at Nyon on the shore of Lake Geneva to discuss the situation in the Mediterranean, but Italy and Germany refused to attend. The Nazi government claimed that the *Leipzig* incident had still not been resolved, and the Italians protested at the Soviet Union's direct accusation of continued submarine attacks. The British and French governments 'regretted this decision', adding that they would keep the Axis powers informed of what happened.

Neurath warned Ciano that British naval intelligence had intercepted signals traffic between Italian submarines. Knowing there was little to fear, Ciano replied that they would be more careful in future. The Nyon conference decided with remarkable speed that any submerged submarines located near a torpedoing incident would be attacked by the naval forces of the signatories.[10] Nothing, however, was said of air or surface attacks. That had to be added later at the League of Nations in Geneva. The British then proceeded to make such large provisos in an attempt to persuade the Italians to join the agreement that the whole exercise was rendered virtually worthless. Mussolini boasted to Hitler that he would carry on with his 'torpedoing operations'.

On 16 September Negrín took part in the League of Nations debate over events in the Mediterranean. He demanded an end to the farce, but his words had no effect. He continued to argue that maintaining the fiction of non-intervention was tantamount to assisting the war and demanded that the aggression of Germany and Italy be officially recognized. Only the Mexican and Soviet governments supported him.

At the League of Nations that autumn, Eden tried to justify the non-intervention policy by claiming, untruthfully, that it had reduced the inflow of foreign forces. The British government also tried to prevent the Spanish Republic from publishing details of Italian intervention. Eden admitted that 'it would be idle to deny that there have been wide breaches of the agreement', but he went on to recommend the maintenance of the non-intervention agreement because 'a leaky dam may yet serve its purpose'.[11] For the nationalists it proved no barrier at all. Eventually, the League decided that if it 'cannot be made to work in the near future, the members of the League will consider ending the policy of non-intervention'. The Spanish republican representative asked for a more precise definition of 'the near future'. The French foreign minister, Delbos, hoped it meant not more than ten days and the British representative replied 'probably an earlier date than the Spanish delegate thinks'. The near future had still not arrived eighteen months later when the Spanish Republic ceased to exist.

British Conservative politicians may have started to see the republican government in a more positive light, but they had no idea of the power struggle going on behind the scenes in Valencia. Senior communists and Soviet advisers were in a state of anger and alarm as they found former political allies turning against them.

On 30 July Dimitrov passed to Voroshilov a report from a senior Soviet official in Valencia about the state of relations within the Negrín government. This document reveals the determination of the communists to seize total power in Spain. 'The honeymoon is over ... The government family is far from what might characterize it: friendship, love and peace ... It is true that with this government our party has more opportunities for work, for exerting pressure on government policy, than it had with the preceding government. But we are still far from the desirable minimum.' Again a bitter attack was launched against Prieto for having freed Rovira, the POUM commander, from prison. Prieto even ordered that the POUM's 29th Division be rearmed, but the communists had already managed through their members in the army to disband it entirely.

Prieto, the report continued, 'is afraid that the Popular Army, headed by commanders who come from among the people [i.e. loyal communists], hardened in battle, represents a huge revolutionary force and, as a result of this, will play a decisive role in determining the economic and social life, the political system of a future Spain'. Prieto therefore was trying to prevent political activity, 'especially communist activity, and in this the professional military, including Rojo, supports him. He at least wants the command staff not to consist of active revolutionaries. This policy of Prieto is fundamentally linked to his overall political conception, which does not allow the development of the Spanish revolution to step beyond the limits of a classical bourgeois-democratic republic ... I must add that Prieto's conception about the army is completely supported by Martínez Barrio and the Republicans ... The Republicans are beginning more and more to change their relationship with the Communist Party. Not long ago they regarded the Communist Party with great respect. In June this began to change.' This was presumably influenced by the disappearance of Andreu Nin.

The report then described Zugazagoitia, the socialist minister of the interior, as 'a disguised Trotskyist': 'It was he who sabotaged the pursuit of the POUMists. What is more: he himself organized and supported a number of campaigns of a blackmailing nature, provocations whose goal is to turn the Trotskyist spy affair against the party. He forbade and prevented the publication of materials exposing the connection between Nin and the POUMists and Franco's general staff. It was he who removed Ortega, the communist, from his post as the director-general of public security.' The attacks continued against other ministers. Irujo, the Basque minister of justice, 'acts like a real fascist ... Together with Zugazagoitia, Irujo does everything possible and impossible to save the Trotskyists and to sabotage trials against them. And he will do everything possible to acquit them.'

The report also accused Giral, the minister of foreign affairs, of infiltrating Trotskyists into his ministry. Negrín was the only one to support the Communist Party, but he was not strong enough. 'Our party insisted on the following three points: to carry out a purge of the military apparatus and to help promote to the top ranks the commanders who come from among the people, and to put a stop to the anti-communist campaign; to carry out tirelessly a purge of Trotskyist elements in the rear; once and for all to stop indulging the press, groups and individuals who are carrying out a slanderous campaign against the USSR. If he will not do this, then the Party is strong enough, understands well enough the responsibility that it bears, and will find the necessary means and measures to protect the interests of the people.' The survey of the political situation concluded with the statement: 'The popular revolution cannot end successfully if the Communist Party does not take power into its own hands.'[12]

26

The War in Aragón

After the failure of the Brunete offensive in July, the republican general staff finally admitted that nothing could be achieved by major operations in the central region. But even though another attack on such a massive scale could not be considered after their losses in matériel, a further effort to help Santander and Asturias was demanded. If the republican forces in the north could hold out until the winter snows blocked the passes of the Cordillera Cantábrica, Franco would not be able to bring down his Navarrese, Galician and Italian troops (which would bring him numerical parity) or the major part of his air power before the late spring of 1938.

The Aragón front was chosen for the next republican attack. The reasons for deciding on the east rather than the south-west were primarily political. The communists and their senior supporters in the army could not select Estremadura, because it would be a virtual admission that the Brunete strategy had been wrong and Largo Caballero's project right. The major reason, however, for switching the emphasis of the war to the east was the intention of Negrín's government and the communists to establish complete control over Catalonia and Aragón.

In the wake of the May events in Barcelona, the central government had taken over responsibility for public order in Catalonia, dissolved the Generalitat's Council of Defence, which had been run by the anarchists since its inception, and appointed General Pozas to command the newly designated Army of the East. This represented the first stage in ending the Generalitat's independence and anarchist power in Catalonia. The next stage in reasserting central government control was to be the crushing of the Council of Aragón by bringing in communist troops and placing the three anarchist divisions under overall communist command. The composition of republican forces in the east was changed radically in the summer of 1937. Before Brunete the only communist formation in the region had been the PSUC's 27th (Carlos Marx) Division, but during the last days of July and the first part of August all the elite communist formations were transferred from the central front, including Kléber's 45th Division and Modesto's V Corps (with Líster's 11th Division, Walter's 35th Division and El Campesino's 46th Division). For the first time the anarchists were threatened in their 'Spanish Ukraine'.

At the end of July, after the battle of Brunete, the communists launched a propaganda offensive against the Council of Aragón's president, Joaquín Ascaso, who was a controversial and flamboyant figure. The communists accused him of acting like a Mafia chieftain. His libertarian supporters, on the other hand, defended him vigorously when he was accused of smuggling jewellery out of the country. Ferocious attacks were made on the system of self-managed agricultural collectives in the main Party newspapers *Mundo Obrero* and *Frente Rojo*, because it ran counter to the 'controlled democracy' which Negrín and the communists advocated.

At the end of July the *carabineros*, which Negrín had built up when finance minister, were used to harass the collectives by confiscating their produce. Then, on 11 August, the central government dissolved the Council of Aragón by decree while its members were gathering in the last of the harvest. The anarchist 25th, 26th and 28th Divisions were kept occupied at the front and cut off from news of what was happening, so that Líster's 11th Division, backed by the 27th and 30th Divisions, could be sent against the anarchist and joint CNT-UGT collectives. These 'manoeuvres', as they were officially described, involved mass arrests and the forcible disbandment of the Council of Aragón along with all its component organizations. CNT offices were seized and destroyed, and the collectives' machinery, transport, tools and seed grain were given to the small proprietors whom the communists had encouraged to resist the co-operatives.[1]

The anarchist members of the Council were the first to be arrested and they were fortunate not to have been shot out of hand. Around 100 of them were put in the prison of Caspe, and were still there when the nationalists occupied the town in March 1938.[2] The communists counted on arranging a show trial for Ascaso, but he had to be released on 18 September when they could produce no evidence. (La Pasionaria tried to revive the accusations in 1968, saying that Ascaso had fled to South America where he was living in luxury on his booty. He was, in fact, still working as a servant in a hotel in Venezuela.)

The justification for this operation (whose 'very harsh measures' shocked even some Party members) was that since all the collectives had been established by force, Líster was merely liberating the peasants. There had undoubtedly been pressure, and no doubt force was used on some occasions in the fervour after the rising. But the very fact that every village was a mixture of collectivists and individualists shows that peasants had not been forced into communal farming at the point of a gun.[3] It is estimated that there were up to 200,000 people belonging to the collectives and 150,000 individualists.[4] Perhaps the most eloquent testimony against the communists is the number of collectives that managed to re-establish themselves after Líster's forces had left. Meanwhile, the degree to which food production was disrupted and permanently damaged became a matter for bitter debate. José Silva, the head of the Institute of Agrarian Reform, later embarrassed his communist colleagues considerably when he admitted that the operation had been 'a very grave mistake, which produced a tremendous disorganization in the countryside'.[5]

The exact part in these events played by the non-communist members of Negrín's government, especially Prieto, is the subject of dispute. Negrín himself backed the communist action without reservation, while the liberals and the other right socialists continued to support measures which destroyed 'cantonalism' and increased centralized power. Prieto, the minister of defence, and Zugazagoitia, the minister of the interior, certainly gave instructions for the dismantling of the Council of Aragón and were prepared to use force if necessary. But Prieto denied Líster's claim that he was given carte blanche to destroy the collectives as well.[6] In any case the libertarian revolt, which the authorities had feared, did not take place.

The events in Aragón also caused the rift between the CNT leadership and its mass membership to widen. The weakness of the CNT leaders in their refusal to condemn Líster's action outright provoked much frustration and anger. The only attempt to restrain the communist action came from Mariano Vázquez, the CNT secretary-general, who asked Prieto to transfer Mera's division to Aragón immediately. But he was satisfied by the minister of defence's reply that he had already reprimanded Líster. (Vázquez, a 'reformist' syndicalist and the chief advocate within the CNT of complete obedience to government orders, was a great admirer of Negrín, who is said to have despised him.) The CNT leaders claimed that they had prevented death sentences from being carried out by the special communist military tribunals, but the prospect of three anarchist divisions turning their guns against Líster's troops probably carried greater weight. In any case the whole episode represented a considerable increase in communist power and a corresponding blow to anarchist confidence.

While these events took place, Rojo had been preparing a new operation to be undertaken by the Army of the East. The objective was to distract the nationalists from their final offensive in the north by attacking Saragossa. The recapture of this regional capital offered more than just symbolic significance. It was also the communications centre of the whole Aragón front. The first year of the war in this part of Spain had emphasized that the possession of a key town was of far greater importance than the control of wide areas of open countryside. The nationalists had only the 51st, 52nd and 105th Divisions spread across 300 kilometres of front, with the majority of their troops concentrated in towns.

General Pozas and his chief of staff, Antonio Cordón, set up their headquarters at Bujaraloz. Their plan was to break through at seven different points on the central 100-kilometre stretch between Zuera and Belchite. The object of splitting their attacking forces was to divide any nationalist counter-attack and to offer fewer targets for bombing and strafing shuttles than at Brunete. On the north flank the 27th Division would attack Zuera, before swinging left on Saragossa itself. In the right centre Kléber's 45th Division was to attack south-eastwards from the Sierra de Alcubierre towards Saragossa. Meanwhile, the 26th Division and part of the 43rd Division would attack from Pina, cross the Ebro and cut the highway from Quinto to Saragossa.

The main weight of the offensive, with Modesto's V Corps including Líster's 11th Division and Walter's 35th Division, was concentrated up the south side of the Ebro valley. Líster's 11th Division would thrust along the southern bank towards Saragossa, spearheaded by nearly all the T-26 and BT-5 tanks allocated to the offensive.[7] The BT-5s had been grouped in the International Tank Regiment commanded by Colonel Kondratiev. All the drivers were members of the Red Army.[8] The majority of the 113 republican aircraft on the front were also reserved for the Ebro valley attack. They greatly outnumbered the nationalists' obsolete Heinkel 46 light bombers and Heinkel 51 fighters.[9]

The republicans enjoyed an overwhelming local superiority, both on the ground and in the air. Modesto was certain that the operation was bound to be successful. The general staff orders emphasized that the opposing troops were of low quality, that the nationalists had few reserves in Saragossa and that an uprising would take place in the city to help them.[10] Modesto seemed to be more interested that Líster's division, supported by the tanks, would have the glory of being the first formation to enter the city than in considering contingency plans in case the operation did not turn out to be the walkover he expected. It had been only six weeks since Brunete and Modesto appears to have forgotten what happened there, unless he believed the propaganda that had turned defeat into a victory.

The offensive in Aragón began on 24 August, the day the nationalists were on the point of entering Santander on the north coast, so the main point of the attack was lost. To maintain the advantage of surprise, there was no artillery bombardment nor attacks by the republican air force.[11] In the north, the 27th Division occupied Zuera towards midday. Kléber launched his 45th Division into the attack and reached Villamajor de Gállego, some six kilometres from Saragossa, and halted there because he lacked intelligence on enemy defences. The troops of the 25th Division took Codó after overcoming the fierce resistance of Carlists from the *tercio* of Nuestra Señora de Montserrat, which blocked the road from Belchite to Medina. Meanwhile, Líster with his 11th Division advanced on Fuentes de Ebro but failed to capture it. They took time trying to smash one defensive position after another. An attached cavalry brigade was shattered in the process and lost all its fighting capacity. The most disastrous part of this action affected the International Tank Regiment, which the infantry failed to support when it broke through. Almost all the BT-5s were destroyed. A furious Modesto blamed Líster for the disaster and from then on the mutual hatred of the two great communist leaders became a major problem. This too was blamed on 'the interference of fascist elements who roused mutual hostility between the two and thus weakened the strength of V Corps'.[12] A more rational report to Moscow, however, put the blame on 'the open sabotage of Líster, who did not want to be subordinate to Modesto'.[13]

Quinto was attacked by the 25th Division, which managed to take it on 26 August, despite the nationalist troops' courageous defence of the chapel of Bonastre. With the 11th Division locked in a stalemate in Fuentes de Ebro, the 35th Division had to be sent to its aid. Republican commanders were obsessed once again with crushing every defensive position, when they should have forged ahead towards the main objective and left them to second-line troops. At this point Modesto proposed changing the original plan of taking Saragossa into one of capturing Belchite, which was defended by only a few hundred men. These nationalist defenders had good machine-gun positions, some of them made in ferro-concrete and others in specially prepared houses, as well as the seminary and church of San Agustín.

The attack on Belchite began at ten in the morning on 1 September. It was supported by artillery and aircraft flown by the first Spanish pilots to graduate from training schools in the Soviet Union. Much of the town was reduced to rubble. Then the tanks advanced, a very unwise manoeuvre, since they were extremely vulnerable in streets partially blocked by collapsed buildings. The next day resistance was crushed in the seminary and the fighting revolved around the church of San Agustín. The Calle Mayor became the main line of fire while the nationalists defended their positions in the Calle Goya and the town hall from behind sand-bagged emplacements. The desperate fighting continued until 6 September when the whole of Belchite was a smoking ruin of death, smashed masonry, dust and corpses, both human and animal. The 'nauseating stench' drifted out over the countryside around.[14]

The whole operation had lasted thirteen days, during which the republican troops lacked water in stifling heat amid the over-whelming smell of rotting bodies so powerful that those who had gas masks wore them in spite of the temperature.[15] The delays caused by the nationalists' fierce defence of Quinto and Codó had given them time to bring up Barrón's 13th Division and Sáenz de Buruaga's 150th Division. This was a repeat of the republicans' mistakes at Brunete. They wasted totally unnecessary numbers of men and time reducing resistance points that should have been contained and bypassed. The small nationalist garrisons never posed a serious threat to Modesto's rearguard if he had continued the advance. In the end this huge effort by the republicans, who enjoyed overwhelming superiority, succeeded only in advancing ten kilometres and taking a handful of villages and small towns. It was a total failure in its main objectives of taking Saragossa and diverting the nationalists from their campaign in the north.

Once again the Republic suffered a considerable loss of badly needed armament, especially the tanks. And once more Stalinist paranoia blamed the failure on a 'Trotskyist' fifth column. General Walter considered the situation worse than at Brunete. 'The 35th Division's medical unit', he reported, 'registered several instances of wounded internationalists who were in Spanish hospitals for treatment dying because of maliciously negligent or completely unnecessary surgical operations and diagnoses and methods of treating the sick that were patently the work of wreckers.' In addition, 'a large-scale Trotskyist spy and terrorist organization' was suspected in XIV International Brigade. They were supposedly planning to murder Hans Sanje, its commander, and Walter himself. Walter called the NKVD in Barcelona to come to investigate, but 'Brigade Commander Sanje took it upon himself to carry out the investigation. He went to work so ardently and clumsily that the arrested man, a French lieutenant, quickly died during interrogation, taking with him the secret of the organization.'[16]

General Pozas held Walter responsible for the failure of the operation, by concentrating on secondary objectives and not the main one. Prieto was furious at the handling of the battle and his bitter criticism aroused the Party's anger against him. Along with a growing number of senior officers, he had begun to recognize that communist direction of the war effort was destroying the Popular Army with prestige operations which it could not afford and triumphalist propaganda that was counter-productive. The Catalonia press claimed on 4 September, while the fighting still raged in Belchite, that 'an intelligent and relevant act of the government has given for the first time mobility to all battle fronts. The Spanish people are starting to sense the longed-for and welcome consequences of an efficient policy of national unity facing the fascist invasion.'[17]

The Aragón offensive had certainly come too late to help the defence of Santander. Nor did it delay the start of the third and final stage of the war in the north. Well aware of the importance of reducing the remaining Asturian territory before winter set in, General Dávila redeployed his forces rapidly to continue the advance westwards from Santander.

27

The Destruction of the Northern Front and of Republican Idealism

On 29 August, while the battle of Belchite was reaching its height, the Provincial Council of Asturias assumed all military and civil powers. It proclaimed itself to be the Sovereign Council of the Asturias, under the presidency of Belarmino Tomás. Its first act was to replace General Gámir Ulíbarri with Colonel Adolfo Prada, who took command of the remnants of the Army of the North, now less than 40,000 men strong.

Prada's chief of staff was Major Francisco Ciutat and its main formation was XIV Corps, commanded by Francisco Galán. The republican air force in the north was down to two flights of Moscas and less than a squadron of Chatos.[1] Republican territory was now reduced to some 90 kilometres deep between Gijón and La Robla, and 120 kilometres along the coast, with the Oviedo salient sticking into the western flank.

Dávila's attack on this last piece of republican resistance in the north came from the east and south-east aimed at Gijón. His force was at least twice the size of the republicans' and included Solchaga's four Carlist brigades, three Galician divisions under Aranda and the Italian CTV. They were supported by 250 aircraft, including the Condor Legion.

Nevertheless, the advance, which began on 1 September, averaged less than a kilometre a day, even with the nationalists' crushing air superiority. The Picos de Europa and the Cordillera Cantábrica gave the republican defenders excellent terrain to hold back the enemy and they did so with remarkable bravery. It has been said that they fought so desperately only because the nationalist blockade gave them no hope of escape, but this can never have been more than one factor. When most of the senior officers managed to escape in small boats, the rank and file fought even more fiercely.

Solchaga's Carlists did not reach Llanes until 5 September. These Navarrese brigades then launched themselves against the El Mazuco pass, which they seized and lost and then recaptured, then lost again. The defence of the pass, led by a CNT worker from La Felguera, continued for 33 days. The Carlists finally took it at bayonet point, suffering many losses. Meanwhile, the Condor Legion relentlessly bombed and strafed the republican rear,[2] finding it too difficult to hit their mountain positions with conventional bombs. The German squadrons experimented with a prototype of napalm, consisting of cans of petrol attached to incendiary bombs.

On 18 September Solchaga's Carlists opened the bloodiest part of the whole campaign. After fierce fighting, the 1st Navarre Brigade managed to enter Ribadesella; on 1 October the 5th Navarre Brigade occupied Covadonga; and ten days later they cleared the west bank of the upper Sella. On 14 October Arriondas fell. In the meantime Colonel Muñoz Grandes managed to break through Tama, one of the best fortified positions of the Asturian miners, and advance to Campo de Caso, thus sealing the encirclement. The Condor Legion completed the work, machine-gunning the republicans falling back on Gijón. On 20 October Solchaga's forces joined up with those of Aranda.[3]

The republican government in Valencia instructed Colonel Prada to begin a general evacuation, but Franco's fleet, waiting for the collapse, asked the Condor Legion to bomb the republican destroyer *Císcar*, sent to take off as many people as possible. The *Císcar* sank and foreign ships were intercepted by the nationalist warships. Many senior officials and officers managed to escape on gunboats and other small vessels to France. Yet the bulk of the republican troops continued fighting ferociously until the afternoon of 21 October, when the 4th Navarre Brigade entered Gijón. Part of the republican troops slipped away into the mountains where they joined up with remnants of units which had escaped from Santander. Guerrilla warfare continued in the Cordillera for another six months, tying down considerable bodies of nationalist troops.

Once the nationalists had taken Gijón, the process of 'cleaning up the reds' began in earnest throughout the region. The bullring in Gijón filled with prisoners, as did the Luarca theatre and other buildings in the city. The execution squads worked without rest.[4] The northern front had ceased to exist. For Prieto, the basic cause of the defeat lay in the lack of a unified command.[5] The minister of defence promoted Rojo to general and offered his resignation to Negrín who refused to accept it.

*

The real effects of the conquest of the north were not to become apparent until the new year, when the nationalists started to deploy the Carlist formations, the Italian corps and Aranda's Galician troops in the southern zone. Nationalist warships in the Bay of Biscay were transferred to the Mediterranean, increasing its control of the coastline there. A new naval and air command under Admiral Francisco Moreno was set up in Palma de Mallorca.[6] But for Franco, one of the most important gains lay in the coal and other mines, much of whose produce would go to paying his debt to Nazi Germany.

The considerable growth in nationalist manpower at this time was assisted by drafting more than 100,000 prisoners from the northern campaign into their infantry units as well as labour battalions. This manner of increasing their forces was not always successful, because a large proportion deserted as soon as they reached the front line. There were at least two cases of rebellion caused by left-wingers in their ranks. At Saragossa anarchists drafted into the Foreign Legion started a revolt and attempted to release their comrades from prison. And 200 sailors in El Ferrol, chiefly on the *España*, had been discovered preparing a mutiny during the previous winter. In both cases all those involved were executed.

Meanwhile in republican Spain the autumn of 1937 witnessed the continued decline of anarchist power, the isolation of the Catalan nationalists, discord in socialist ranks and the development of the secret police. Negrín's government presided over these developments and as a result of communist power the repression of dissenters was far greater than it had been during Primo de Rivera's dictatorship. The prime minister's pretended ignorance of secret police activities was unconvincing while, as Hugh Thomas has pointed out, his attempt to restrict political activity through censorship, banning and arrests was parallel to Franco's establishment of a state machine where ideological divergence was also contained.[7] Nevertheless, most of the Republic's supporters abroad who had defended the left-wing cause on the grounds of liberty and democracy made no protest at these developments.

The need to collaborate with the Soviet Union, together with the seriousness of the military situation, was later used by Negrín's supporters to justify the actions of his administration. But it was

Negrín who had persuaded Largo Caballero to send the gold reserves to Moscow, so he bore a major responsibility for the Republic's subservience to Stalin in the first place. Yet during his administration the flow of Soviet military aid decreased dramatically. This was partly the result of the nationalists' naval blockade, but it was also a consequence of Stalin's increasing desire to extricate himself from Spain when he realized that the British and French governments were not going to challenge the Axis. And now the Soviet Union was helping China against Japanese aggression. Paradoxically, Stalin's unease was probably increased by Negrín's obvious hope that the Republic would be saved by a European war.

President Azaña had encouraged the prime minister's firm rule in the early days of his administration, but his attitude was to change when he came to understand Negrín's character better. Both men disliked Companys and Azaña supported Negrín's plans to bring Catalonia under central government control. The president still resented Companys's initial success in increasing the Generalitat's independence during the turmoil of the rising. The reduction of Catalonia's identity was both symbolized and effected by moving the Republic's government from Valencia to Barcelona, and Negrín took every opportunity to emphasize the Generalitat's reduced status.[8] 'Negrín avoided almost any direct contact with Companys,' wrote the communist Antonio Cordón, then undersecretary for the army. 'I don't remember any event or ceremony in which they took part together.'[9]

Largo Caballero realized after his fall from power that the Socialist Party and the UGT were in an even worse state than he imagined. He still had his loyal supporters, especially the inner circle of Luis Araquistáin, Carlos de Baráibar and Wenceslao Carrillo (the father of Santiago Carrillo). But many right socialists, a powerful faction within the UGT, and the majority of the Joint Socialist Youth were collaborating closely with the communists.[10] Some groups responded to their call for unification. A joint newspaper, *Verdad* (meaning 'truth' and intended as a Spanish *Pravda*), had been founded in Valencia. It was the first to praise the socialists in Jaén, who had established their own party of socialist-communist unification called the PSU (United Socialist Party).

The PSOE newspaper, *El Socialista*, and even Largo Caballero's *Claridad*, had already been taken over by the pro-communist wing of the party. But the most disturbing event for Largo Caballero came at the end of September, when his supporters were disqualified from voting at the national plenum of the UGT. Nevertheless, many pro-communist socialists, including even Negrín, still held back from the fateful step of outright union with the PCE. Largo Caballero's speech on 17 October (the first he had been allowed to make since May) explained the fall of his government and gave strong warnings of the dangers the party faced. Largo Caballero did not, however, recover any power, for he was kept off the executive committee, and his supporters on it remained in a minority. At the end of October he moved to Barcelona where, in a form of internal exile, he busied himself in minor affairs.[11]

Probably the most ominous of all the developments in republican territory at this time was the rationalization of the security services, on 9 August 1937, into the SIM, Servicio de Investigación Militar.[12] Prieto had been the architect of this restructuring to increase central control. He believed that the fragmented growth of counter-espionage organizations was uncontrolled and inefficient. One intelligence chief complained that 'everyone in our rearguard carried on counter-espionage'. Independent services with their own networks of agents were run by the army, the Directorate-General of Security, the *carabineros*, the foreign ministry, the Generalitat and the Basque government in exile (now based in Barcelona). Even the International Brigades had their own NKVD-run branch of heretic hunters based at Albacete. Its chief, 'Moreno', was a Yugoslav from the Soviet Union who was shot on his return.[13]

The new department was out of its creator's control as soon as it was constituted in August, since the communists had started to infiltrate and control the police and security services in the autumn of 1936. The first directors, the socialists Ángel Díaz Baza and Prudencio Sayagüés, were not up to the work, while others such as Gustavo Durán, whom Prieto named chief of the SIM for the Army of the Centre, had to be removed because he recruited only communists. The next director was Colonel Manuel Uribarri, who reported solely to Soviet agents and managed to flee to France with a booty of 100,000 francs.[14] Only the following year was communist control reduced. The organization did indeed manage to destroy a number of nationalist networks – 'Concepción', 'Círculo Azul', 'Capitán Mora', 'Cruces de fuego' and others – but there can be no doubt that during its first eight months of existence the SIM, later described as 'the Russian syphilis' by the German writer Gustav Regler, was a sinister tool in the hands of Orlov and his NKVD men.

SIM officers included both unquestioningly loyal Party members and the ambitious. Its unchallenged power attracted opportunists of every sort to its ranks. The core of executive officers then created a network of agents through bribery and blackmail. They even managed to plant their organization in resolutely anti-communist formations as a result of their control of transfer and promotion. For example, a nineteen-year-old rifleman in the 119th Brigade was suborned and then promoted overnight to become the SIM chief of the whole formation with a greater power of life and death than its commander.[15]

Because of the destruction of records, it is difficult to know the total number of agents employed by the SIM. There were said to have been 6,000 in Madrid alone and its official payroll was 22 million pesetas. Its six military and five civilian sections, including the 'Z Brigade', covered every facet of life and its agents were present in every district and command.[16] The most feared section was the Special Brigade, which was responsible for interrogation. When its infamous reputation became known abroad, it simply changed its name. The government insisted that it had been disbanded, but in fact there was an increase in the number of its victims who 'crossed over to the enemy' (the euphemism for death under torture or secret execution). It worked with a network of 'invisible' agents both at the front and in the rear.[17]

In the central region the SIM made use of mainly secret prisons which had belonged to the DEDIDE. The first was the religious college of San Lorenzo, which held 200 suspects. The second was Work Camp No. 1 in Cuenca. Those who had the misfortune to be held there are united in their evidence: maltreatment, the use of cold and hunger to extract confessions, punishment cells called 'the icebox' and the 'fridge', in which prisoners were left naked with water up to their knees, or they were sprayed with freezing water during winter months.[18]

In Barcelona the SIM had two main prisons, one in the Calle Zaragoza, the second in the Seminario Conciliar, although it also used other locations, such as the Portal de l'Ángel, which held 300 people in the summer of 1937, the so-called 'Nestlé dairy', the Hotel Colón, one in the Calle Vallmajor and others. Interrogators worked ruthlessly to extract confessions which matched their conspiracy theories. In September 1937 the security organs in Barcelona reported that they had exposed 'an espionage organization even larger than the one in Madrid. This organization, too, was set up by Catalonian Trotskyists. Its identifying sign was the letter TS and each one of its agents had a personal identification number. Documents that were found in the mattress of one of its members show that this gang had committed a number of sabotage acts and that it was preparing assassination attempts against some top leaders of the People's Front and the Republican Army.' It then went on to give a list of the republican leaders targeted for assassination, perhaps in the hope of encouraging non-communist ministers to support them.[19]

Under NKVD direction, the SIM performed inhuman atrocities. The nationalists exploited and exaggerated this, creating a black legend. Yet although all documents were destroyed, there can be no doubt from oral testimony, and from the continual denunciations of Manuel de Irujo and Pere Bosch Gimpera, that the Soviets were applying their 'scientific' methods of interrogation. The SIM's interrogation methods had evolved beyond beatings with rubber piping, hot and cold water treatment and mock executions which had been carried out in the early days. Cell floors were specially constructed with the sharp corners of bricks pointing upwards so that the naked prisoners were in constant pain. Strange metallic sounds, colours, lights and sloping floors were used as disorientation and sensory-deprivation techniques. If these failed, or if the interrogators were in a hurry, there was always the 'electric chair' and the 'noise box' but they risked sending prisoners mad too quickly.

There are no reliable estimates of the total number of SIM prisoners, nor of the proportions, though it seems fairly certain that there were more republicans than nationalists. It was alleged that any critics of Soviet military incompetence, such as foreign volunteer pilots, were as likely to find themselves accused of treason as a person who opposed the communists on ideological grounds. The minister of justice, Manuel de Irujo, resigned later in protest, although he remained in government as a minister without portfolio. Many other leading republicans were appalled by such judicial practices and above all by the SIM. Negrín simply dismissed critical accounts of SIM activity as enemy propaganda. Only in 1949 did he admit that he had been wrong to the American journalist Henry Buckley.[20]

The communists had been remarkably successful in creating a large degree of control over the government, the bureaucracy and the machinery of public order, while retaining a token presence of only two minor ministries in the cabinet – a requirement of Soviet foreign policy. They had made themselves indispensable to the centrist politicians who had wanted to restore state power and who were now too involved in the process to protest. Nevertheless, a reaction against communist power was starting to develop, especially within the army.

In the autumn of 1937 communist propaganda was making great claims about the progress of the People's Army. It is true that there had been improvements at unit level. But few commanders or staff officers had displayed competence or tactical sense, and the supply organization was still corrupt and inefficient. Above all, damage to morale had been increased by events behind the lines. Communist preferment and proselytizing at the front had reached such levels that former communist supporters among the regular officers were horrified. Prieto was shaken when he heard that non-communist wounded were often refused medical aid. Battalion commanders who rejected invitations to join the Party found weapon replacements, rations or even their men's pay cut off. Those who succumbed were given priority over non-communists. They were promoted and their reputations were boosted in despatches and press accounts.

Co-operation was withheld from even the most senior non-communist officers. Colonel Casado, when in command of the Army of Andalucia, was not allowed to know the location of airfields or the availability of aircraft on his front. Commissars given recruitment targets to fulfil by the Party hierarchy went to any lengths to achieve them. Prieto later stated that socialists in communist units who refused to join the Party were frequently shot on false charges such as cowardice or desertion. After the battle of Brunete, 250 men from El Campesino's division sought protection in the ranks of Mera's 14th Division because of the treatment they had suffered for not becoming communists. Mera refused to return them when El Campesino arrived in a fury at his headquarters. General Miaja, though officially a communist, backed him against a Party member.

Perhaps the most dramatic deterioration in morale after mid 1937 occurred in the ranks of the International Brigades, who in October had lost 2,000 men through a typhus epidemic.[21] There had always been non-communists in their ranks who refused to swallow the Party line, but now even committed communists were questioning their position. At the beginning of 1937 the Irish had nearly mutinied after the Lopera débâcle, when they were prevented at the last moment from forming their own company. The American mutiny at the Jarama in the early spring had been successful, though that was seen as an aberration which had been put right. Some Italians from the Garibaldi Battalion deserted to join the liberal and anarchist Giustizia e Libertà column. During the Segovia offensive XIV International Brigade had refused to continue useless frontal attacks on La Granja and foreigners in a penal battalion mutinied when ordered to shoot deserters.

The anger at futile slaughter was accompanied by a growing unease at the existence of 're-education' camps, run by Soviet officers and guarded by Spanish communists armed with the latest automatic rifles. At these camps labour was organized on a Stakhanovite basis, with food distribution linked to achieving or exceeding work norms. The prisoners were mostly those who wanted to return home for various reasons and had been refused. (It was not known until later that several Brigaders in this category were locked up in mental hospitals, a typically Soviet measure.) One of the most sordid camps was at Júcar, some 40 kilometres from Albacete, where disillusioned British, American and Scandinavian volunteers were held. Some British members were saved from execution by the intervention of the Foreign Office, but those from other nationalities were locked up in the prisons of Albacete, Murcia, Valencia and Barcelona.[22]

The persistent trouble in the International Brigades also stemmed from the fact that volunteers, to whom no length of service had ever been mentioned, assumed that they were free to leave after a certain time. Their passports had been taken away on enlistment and many of them were sent to Moscow by diplomatic bag for use by NKVD agents abroad. Brigade leaders who became so alarmed by the stories of unrest filtering home imposed increasingly stringent measures of discipline. Letters were censored and anyone who criticized the competence of the Party leadership faced prison camps, or even firing squads. Leave was often cancelled and some volunteers who, without authorization, took a few of the days owing to them were shot for desertion when they returned to their unit. The feeling of being trapped by an organization with which they had lost sympathy made a few volunteers even cross the lines to the nationalists. Others tried such unoriginal devices as putting a bullet through their own foot when cleaning a rifle.

Comintern organizers were becoming disturbed, for accounts of conditions had started to stem the flow of volunteers from abroad. Fresh volunteers were shocked by the cynicism of the veterans, who laughed at the idealism of newcomers while remembering their own with bitterness. Some of the new arrivals at Albacete were literally shanghaied. Foreign specialists, or mechanics who had agreed to come for a specific purpose only, found themselves pressganged and threatened with the penalty for desertion if they refused.[23] Even sailors on shore leave from foreign merchantmen in republican ports were seized as 'deserters' from the brigades and sent to Albacete under guard. On 23 September 1937, Prieto issued a decree incorporating the International Brigades into the Spanish Foreign Legion, which brought them under the Spanish Code of Military Justice. He also established a regulation that International Brigade officers in any one unit should not exceed Spanish officers by more than 50 per cent.[24]

The greatest jolt to the attitudes of those in the International Brigades was the persecution of the POUM. Communist ranting against the POUM continued unabated. 'We have in our country', declared one Party orator late in 1937, 'a long chain of very recent facts that prove that Trotskyists have long been engaged in these grotesque criminal activities and as the difficulties increase and decisive battles approach, they start, more and more openly, to popularize the enemy's slogans, to sow the seeds of defeatism, mistrust and split among the masses, and engage more actively than ever in espionage, provocation, sabotage and crime.'[25]

The Party's version of events was so obviously dishonest that only those terrified of the truth could believe it. The majority, however, realizing that they had been duped, resented the insult to their intelligence. They had to hold their tongues while in Spain so as to avoid the attentions of the SIM. Then, when they did reach home they usually remained silent, rather than undermine the republican cause as a whole. Those who spoke out, like Orwell, found the doors of left-wing publishers closed to them.

Uncritical supporters of the Republic were forced to justify the Moscow line. Nevertheless, the attempt to export the show-trial mentality to Spain ignored the fact that, however authoritarian Negrín's government might be, it was not totalitarian. As a result, the sealed maze of distorting mirrors that had replaced reality in the Soviet Union was not duplicated in Spain.

PART SIX

The Route to Disaster

28

The Battle of Teruel and Franco's 'Victorious Sword'

Towards the end of 1937 the nationalists' increase in military superiority became apparent. The occupation of the northern zone had indeed proved to be the essential intermediate step if they were to be assured of victory. For the first time in the war they equalled the republicans in manpower under arms (between 650,000 and 700,000 on each side) and the scales were to continue moving further in their favour. The conquest of the Cantabrian coast had not only released troops for redeployment in the centre; it had also yielded vital industrial prizes to the nationalists. The most important were the arms factories in the Basque country, the heavy industry of Bilbao, and the coal and iron ore of the northern regions (though much of the latter was taken in payment by Germany).

The nationalist army was reorganized, with five army corps garrisoning the fronts, and the five most powerful, including all their elite formations, organized into an offensive Army of Manoeuvre.[1] Although faced with this formidable war machine, the republican general staff and the Soviet advisers refused to admit that their ponderously conventional offensives were gradually destroying the People's Army and the Republic's ability to resist. They would not see that the only hope lay in continuing regular defence combined with unconventional guerrilla attacks in the enemy rear and rapid raids at as many points as possible on weakly held parts of the front. At the very least this would have severely hindered the nationalists' ability to concentrate their new Army of Manoeuvre in a major offensive.

Most important of all, it would not have presented large formations of republican troops to the nationalists' superior artillery and air power. A blend of conventional and unconventional warfare would have been the most efficient, and least costly, method of maintaining republican resistance until the European war broke out. Nevertheless, the pattern of set-piece offensives continued until the Republic's military strength was finally exhausted on the Ebro in the autumn of 1938. Propaganda considerations still determined these prestige operations and the principle of the 'unified command' was vigorously maintained by the communists, the government and regular officers, even though it had hardly demonstrated effective leadership.

The inflexibility of republican strategy became even more serious at the end of 1937, when nationalist air support was increased. Spanish pilots took over the older German aircraft, especially the Junkers 52s, the Italian S-79s and S-81s, and four nationalist fighter squadrons were now equipped with Fiats.[2] The Italian Legionary Air Force had nine Fiat squadrons and three bomber squadrons on the Spanish mainland, apart from those based on Majorca. Soviet intelligence was certain that Mussolini's son, Bruno, who arrived in Spain in October, commanded one of the S-79 bomber squadrons supporting the CTV on the Aragón front.[3] The Condor Legion replaced the Junkers 52 with the Heinkel 111 entirely. In addition, it had a reconnaissance squadron of Dornier 17s, two squadrons of Messerschmitt 109s and two with the old Heinkel 51. All told, the nationalists and their allies deployed nearly 400 aircraft.[4]

The republican air force was inferior in numbers and in quality after its losses in the north and at Brunete. It was reduced to a few squadrons of Chatos and Moscas, and two squadrons of bombers.[5] The nationalists' main fighter, the Fiat, had shown itself to be rugged and highly manoeuvrable, while the Messerschmitt was unbeatable if handled properly. Finally, republican pilots, especially Soviet ones, did not seem prepared to take the same risks in aerial combat as the nationalists. Whole Mosca squadrons sometimes fled from the determined attack of a few Fiats.

The Soviets, who had been withdrawing pilots for service in the Chinese–Japanese conflict, were handing over more and more machines to Spanish pilots who arrived back from training in Russia. Two of the Mosca squadrons were now entirely Spanish, while the four Chato squadrons had Spanish pilots. These biplanes were being manufactured at Sabadell-Reus, near Barcelona, but the replacement of Moscas was limited by the increasingly effective blockade in the Mediterranean. (The nationalists' cruiser *Baleares* had sunk a whole convoy from Russia on 7 September.) The republicans did, however, receive a consignment of 31 Katiuska bombers, bringing their bomber force up to four squadrons of Natashas and four of Katiuskas.

The Republic's only aerial success had come during an intense series of strikes each side made against its opponent's airfields. On 15 October during a further unsuccessful attack on Saragossa, republican fighters and bombers attacked the nationalist airfield near Saragossa, wiping out almost all the aircraft at dispersal. As a defensive measure against counter-strikes the republican air force made great use of dummy aircraft and switched their machines from one airfield to another.

Having crushed the northern zone, Franco felt justified at mounting another offensive on Madrid at the end of 1937. His new strength more than compensated for the Republic's advantage of having interior lines in this region. The nationalist Army of Manoeuvre was deployed behind the Aragón front for an assault south-westwards down the Saragossa–Madrid road, which the Italians had used as their centre line on Guadalajara in March. Varela's Army Corps of Castile was on the left, the Italian CTV in the centre, the Army Corps of Morocco on the right, the Condor Legion and the Legionary Air Force in support, and the two Army Corps of Galicia and Navarre in reserve. But the nationalist alliance was undergoing a crisis, as Richthofen observed on 3 December, because of 'incredible tensions between Spaniards and Italians'.[6]

The threatened sector of the Guadalajara front was held by the Republic's IV Corps, now commanded by Cipriano Mera. As had happened before the battle of Brihuega, Mera was helped by fellow anarchists who crossed the lines into enemy territory gathering intelligence. This time the information was far more valuable. Nationalist sources later said that Mera himself had crossed, disguised as a shepherd, and had read the operational plans in their headquarters. In fact, as Mera himself recounts, the spying mission was suggested and carried out by a young anarchist called Dolda who did not go near their headquarters. Reports from CNT members in nationalist Aragón, whom he visited secretly, warned of major troop concentrations from Saragossa to Calatayud. Dolda's return via Medinaceli confirmed his hunch that the nationalists were preparing for the biggest offensive yet and that it was to be directed at the Guadalajara sector. Dolda returned back through the lines by 30 November. He briefed Mera, who in turn informed Miaja.

Rojo then shelved his plans for an Estremadura offensive towards the Portuguese frontier to split the nationalist zone in two. Instead, an attack to disrupt the nationalist Guadalajara operation was examined. The town of Teruel was chosen for a pre-emptive strike because it formed the corner where the Aragón front turned back north-westwards to run through the province of Guadalajara. One of the great dangers of this project was the proximity of Franco's Army of Manoeuvre, which could be redeployed quite rapidly. Rojo, however, described the operation as an 'offensive-defensive' battle, aiming for a 'limited destruction of the adversary' and to obtain a 'definite advantage for further exploitation'.[7]

Rojo gave orders to transfer the Republic's strike force to the Teruel front: XVIII Corps commanded by Enrique Fernández Heredia, Leopoldo Menéndez's XX Corps and the XXII Corps under the command of Juan Ibarrola. In addition, XIII Corps and XIX Corps were brought in. Colonel Juan Hernández Saravia, the commander of the Army of Levante, was to direct the operation. In all, Rojo deployed 40,000 men.[8] The tank force, in the inefficient Soviet manner, was split up among the attacking divisions and not concentrated.

To begin with, Rojo felt that he could not count on the International Brigades because of the state they were in. Walter, who visited the British and Canadian battalions of XV International Brigade, found it 'difficult to convey in words the state of the weapons and how dirty [they were], especially the rifles'. Walter was also disturbed by 'petty squabbling and strong antagonism in the international units' and by anti-semitism in the French detachments. He was unhappy, too, about the continuing arrogance towards Spaniards – which also came under the heading of 'Kléberism'. 'For more than a year,' he wrote of the Germans in XI International Brigade, 'German chauvinism has been persistently implanted and cultivated, and all of this time an openly racist nationality policy has been carried out.' In too many cases the Spanish troops fighting in the International Brigades had not received proper medical attention and the internationalists did not share with them the rations and cigarettes which they received from home.[9]

The nationalist forces defending the Teruel salient consisted of the 52nd Division which, even when supplemented with volunteers from the city, amounted to less than 10,000 men. Colonel Domingo Rey d'Harcourt, the commander, had established a line of trenches and strong points, supported by others situated on hills, such as La Muela, which dominated Teruel. General Rojo's plan of attack was to encircle the town with the 11th and 25th Divisions attacking from the north-east towards the villages of Caudé and Concud, while the 34th and 64th Division from XVIII Corps would attack from the south-east towards the Pico del Zorro and La Muela de Teruel. Two more divisions, the 40th and 68th from XX Corps, would advance on Escandón and El Vértice Castellar. If the manoeuvre went according to plan, Teruel would be cut off from nationalist territory. In the next stage, units from XVIII and XXII Corps would establish a line of defence to repel the inevitable nationalist counter-attacks, while XX Corps, supported by tanks, would fight into the city.[10]

The provincial capital of Teruel, a gloomy town in bleak terrain, was famous for its cold in winter, but in mid December of 1937 the conditions were almost Siberian. Snow was falling at dawn on 15 December when the 11th Division, in which the communist poet Miguel Hernández was serving, broke through the weak nationalist lines. By 10 a.m. they had taken Concud. The republican forces achieved complete surprise, partly as a result of the weather and partly by forgoing a preliminary bombardment.

Many of the attacks, however, were often wasted. On 17 December the 3rd Tank Company of Captain Gubanov started an assault five times, but the infantry failed to support it. The international tank regiment consisted mainly of Soviet volunteers who were fighting at the most dangerous sectors of the front.[11] Captain Tsaplin was particularly heroic. His tank was hit, with one of his tracks damaged only 50 metres from the enemy trenches. He stayed in his tank for eight hours, 'resisting the ferocious attacks of the enemy. When he ran out of ammunition, he disabled the tank, climbed out and escaped.'[12]

XVIII Corps, having cut through the weak opposition and bypassed the town, captured the Muela de Teruel at midday on 18 December. Two days later its troops joined up at San Blas with XXII Corps and began to prepare the defensive line north-west of the city. On 19 December the 40th Division, which had experienced heavy fighting in Escandón, reached the outskirts of Teruel. Prieto and Rojo arrived that day to visit the front, accompanied by a large retinue of foreign journalists including Hemingway, Matthews and Robert Capa, waiting for the moment when they could announce to the world that the People's Army had captured a provincial capital.[13]

The nationalist high command was taken aback on hearing of the offensive. 'Alarming news,' wrote Richthofen in his war diary. 'The reds have breached the front near Teruel.'[14] Franco was the most disturbed. He was torn between continuing with his plan to attack

Madrid, as he was counselled by his German and Italian advisers, or react to the red cape brandished in his face by the republicans. To the intense frustration of his advisers, Franco could not allow the republicans to enjoy their minor triumph. 'The Generalissimo', reported the Condor Legion to Berlin, 'decided from the start, for reasons of prestige of a special political nature, and at the cost of the already prepared attack via Guadalajara towards Madrid, to re-establish the front around Teruel along the line as it was on 15 December.'[15] Franco's first instinct was to send in the Condor Legion immediately, but Richthofen was cautious. 'Weather situation is quite serious,' he noted.[16]

To seal the breach, Franco sent Aranda to Teruel with three divisions and ordered Dávila to move the 81st Division from the upper Tagus. On 20 December he issued a directive putting together an army for the relief of the city. It would be commanded by Dávila and include the Army Corps of Galicia, which would operate north of the River Tuna, and the Corps of Castile, reinforced with two Navarrese divisions, which would deploy to the south. These forces would be supported by all the artillery and air units available, especially the Italian artillery and the Condor Legion. But for almost a whole week aircraft were grounded by bad visibility and unusually harsh frosts, affecting engines, wings and runways. Only the Condor Legion's anti-aircraft batteries could be sent into action against the breakthrough.

On 21 December fierce street fighting began in Teruel itself. The republican 68th Division with T-26 tanks seized the suburb round the bullring. Slightly blurred photos of republican tanks in Teruel were published around the world. The nationalist garrison under Rey d'Harcourt pulled back towards the centre of the city and prepared to defend the buildings around the Plaza de San Juan and its church. These included the Comandancia Militar, the Civil Governor's office, the Banco de España, the Hospital de la Asunción and many other public buildings. Colonel Barba commanded the defence of the Seminary, the Convent of Santa Clara and the churches of Santiago and Santa Teresa. The republican infantry advanced into the city behind a curtain of machine-gun fire. 'You could make out the *dinamiteros* running up the first streets,' wrote Herbert Matthews of the *New York Times*, 'and the flashes of their explosive charges exploding inside houses. A great moment had arrived: one of those dramatic moments in history and journalism.'[17] But such excited optimism was badly misplaced. The winter fighting in Teruel rapidly turned into the most horrific of all the battles of the civil war.

The republicans had to advance up frozen streets, dodging from one pile of rubble to another under nationalist fire. House after house had to be cleared, using grenades and small arms. Holes were blasted in floors during the fighting, and in side walls as soldiers made their way from house to house, avoiding the killing zone of the street outside. Civilians cowering in cellars were in just as much danger of being killed or maimed by grenades, or buried in masonry from the explosive charges. 'We suddenly saw', recorded one republican soldier, 'someone holding a baby out of a window, shouting at us not to fire because there were civilians in the house.'[18]

The republicans, following Prieto's personal instructions to protect the civilian population, were evacuating women and children back to the cellars of the houses near the Plaza del Torico. But many of the women, despite the risk of being shot, looted what they could. In the temperatures, which dropped to around minus 15 centigrade, there was little water available in the city, with pipes frozen solid. Furniture was smashed to provide fuel to melt snow, as well as create a little warmth. Fighting continued during the night, with soldiers on either side bayoneting each other in the intimate anonymity of close-quarter combat. Conditions in Stalingrad, five years later, would not be much worse.

From 22 December the republican artillery was firing at point-blank range into the public buildings held by nationalist defenders. Miners, directed by Belarmino Tomás, were trying to lay charges under those occupied by Rey d'Harcourt and Barba. When the civil governor's offices were taken 'some of the defenders slipped into the adjoining building, the Hotel de Aragón, where they carried on this cruel struggle. In the civil governor's building some prisoners were taken and many corpses brought out. The majority were children who had died of hunger.'[19] The war photographer Robert Capa described the scene: 'More than fifty people, women and children, most of them blinded by the light, showed their cadaverous faces stained with blood and dirt. They had spent fifteen days below ground, living in continual terror, living off the scraps of food left by the soldiers and a few sardines. Very few had the strength to get up; they had to be helped away. It is impossible to describe such a painful scene.'[20]

Teruel was still not completely occupied by the republicans, but the government proclaimed victory. On Christmas Eve promotions and awards were made: Hernández Saravia was made a general and Rojo was decorated. The communists claimed the victory for themselves. Even Prieto suffered an attack of optimism and joked that he was now minister of defence and attack.[21] Professor Haldane, a great supporter of the Republic, had invited the famous singer Paul Robeson to Teruel, and for most of a night he sang spirituals to the British battalion.[22]

The terrible weather conditions prevented the nationalists from launching their counter-attack until 29 December. This opened with the greatest artillery bombardment yet seen in the war. That day the visibility had improved, the blizzards had died down and the nationalist squadrons were able to operate at full strength, dropping 100 tons of bombs on the republican positions. The republican Moscas were not even able to approach the bombers because of the strong escort of Fiat fighters. The combination of aerial and ground bombardment lasted two hours.[23] As soon as the firing ceased, ten nationalist divisions attacked south-eastwards but the republican line held. The Condor Legion acknowledged that the effect was 'not great'. The Galicia Corps gained only 300 to 400 metres of ground, while the Corps of Castile 'remained on their start line'.[24]

The weather improved next day and the nationalist artillery thundered again. The Condor Legion's Heinkel 51s attacked the 'trench systems and reserve positions', while the highly accurate 88mm guns of its flak batteries focused on key points. 'As we had already tried out in the Asturias,' the Condor Legion staff reported to Berlin, 'the enemy was rendered incapable of fighting when shot up in their trenches by a combination of strafing and flak.'[25]

During 31 December 1937, fresh blizzards reduced visibility to just a few metres. That night the temperature dropped to below minus 20 centigrade. Despite the weather, the Condor Legion managed to get both bombers and Heinkel 51s off the ground, even though it meant carefully chipping the ice off the wings. Tanks and vehicles were frozen to a standstill. And soldiers who resorted to alcohol to warm up died of cold if they fell asleep. Casualties from frostbite rose dramatically.

On this last day of 1937 the two Navarrese divisions commanded by García Valiño and Muñoz Grandes retook the Muela de Teruel. General Rojo informed Prieto of the development by teleprinter and he replied in an ill humour.[26] But worse was still to come. That night,

Major Andrés Nieto, commander of the 40th Division who had been appointed military commandant of the city, inexplicably ordered his troops to abandon Teruel. The besieged nationalists do not appear to have realized what had happened. 'For several hours', observed Zugazagoitia, 'Teruel belonged to nobody.'[27] General Walter was scathing. He called it 'a difficult, panic-stricken day when the republican forces fled from the front and cleared out of Teruel itself. [This] was to a significant degree the result of a panic organized by fascist agents among our units.'[28]

On 1 January 1938, General Rojo ordered Modesto to bring up V Corps to halt the nationalists' advance on the city. Hellish blizzards filled the trenches with snow and made movement almost impossible. Troops in the open stood out as dark silhouettes and became easy targets. Conditions were so bad that the Condor Legion could not take off. The Germans were highly critical of the Italian artillery, which fired from maps and did not observe the fall of shells 'which at no point during the attack' found their targets.[29]

Republican troops reoccupied most of the city and the fighting began again. Just over a week before, on 23 December, Franco had sent a message to Colonel Rey d'Harcourt to stimulate his resistance with the promise of immediate reinforcement. 'Have confidence in Spain, as Spain has confidence in you.'[30] But Teruel was not the Alcázar de Toledo and the republican forces were not the militias of 1936. On 7 January, after 24 days of fighting, Rey d'Harcourt surrendered. The nationalists blamed the loss of Teruel on 'the weakness and incompetence of the sector commander who agreed with the reds to surrender his post of duty'.[31] The republican authorities evacuated the wounded, some 1,500 people, and took most of the civilian population in trucks to Escandón in terrible weather conditions.

Ten days after the surrender of Teruel the nationalists launched a counter-attack from the north towards the Alto de Celadas and El Muletón, which dominated the valley of the River Alfambra. The onslaught with aircraft and artillery was immense. Over a hundred aircraft fought in the skies over the Alfambra valley. Walter brought up the International Brigades in the 35th Division to halt Aranda's Galician Corps. XI International Brigade fought well and deserved 'the highest praise', Walter reported.[32]

Two days later, on 19 January, the 5th Navarrese Division attacked El Muletón defended by XV International Brigade.

Republican casualties were very heavy, but they re-formed their line. The order was given to counter-attack, but commanders expected far too much of their troops. They were almost out of ammunition due to the difficulties of resupply, they had received very little food and had to eat snow as there was no drinking water, nor wood for fuel to melt it. Only in Teruel itself could wood be found, stripped from houses. On that same day soldiers of the 84th Mixed Brigade, part of the 40th Division, refused to return to the front. Altogether, 46 of them were executed without trial the following dawn.[33]

On 5 February, 'in perfect weather conditions' for flying,[34] the nationalists launched their major attack towards the Alfambra. General Juan Vigón directed this operation with three corps, those of Galicia, Morocco and Navarre, together with the Italian CTV and Monasterio's cavalry division. Some 100,000 men and nearly 500 guns were concentrated in the Sierra de Palomera along a front of 30 kilometres.

Peter Kemp, the English volunteer now serving in the Foreign Legion, gives a vivid description of the beginning of this offensive. It was a bright, freezing dawn in the Sierra de Palomera as divisions of red-bereted Carlists and green-coated Legionnaires waited for the bombers to soften up the enemy. Only the sound of the pack-mules' accoutrements broke the silence. Then, waiting on the ridge, the nationalist troops heard the heavy drone of the Italian bombers coming from their rear. To their sudden horror, they realized that the Savoia-Marchettis had mistaken them for the enemy. Two waves in succession bombed the rocky mountainside, despite the recognition strips and arrows laid out behind. The nationalists' casualties, however, were much lighter than might have been expected. The operation was hardly delayed.

The attack was accompanied by Monasterio's 1st Cavalry Division, which made the one great mounted charge of the war in the valley below them. The republican troops manning this part of the front had never seen action before and they were broken immediately by the onslaught. The nationalist formations then swung south, forcing the main republican force to withdraw rapidly. The republicans suffered nearly 20,000 casualties and lost a huge quantity of arms and equipment. On 19 February the nationalists cut the Teruel–Valencia road, leaving El Campesino's 46th Division surrounded in Teruel. At dawn on 22 February the last republicans slipped out of the city, trying to break through the nationalist lines. Three days later

Modesto managed to form a defence line along the right bank of the Alfambra, but this was not the end of the battle. Further operations continued for another four weeks, grinding down the republican forces and pushing them back.

The battle of Teruel, with its cold and street fighting, was one of the most terrible in a terrible war. The nationalists suffered around 40,000 casualties, a quarter of which were from frostbite. The republican losses had been even more appalling, around 60,000 men altogether.[35] In the air battles, the nationalists destroyed far more republican planes than they lost themselves, twelve on 7 February alone,[36] but the greatest danger for all pilots was the weather, which accounted for more crashes than enemy action.

The republican infantry suffered its worst casualties after Teruel itself had been taken. This underlined the tragedy and futility of the whole operation. The Republic had set out to seize a city of no strategic value, which it could never have hoped to hold, all at a catastrophic cost in lives and equipment. Once again, the obstinacy of republican leaders, trapped by premature claims of victory for propaganda purposes, sacrificed a large part of their best troops for no purpose. The pathetic state of the survivors, and their demoralization and exhaustion, was to lead straight to another greater disaster in a matter of weeks.

Republican commanders argued furiously among themselves over who was to blame. The report of the political department of the People's Army listed numerous causes: the strength of the enemy air force, its combined effect with artillery, the reduced republican strength, their inferiority in weapons, the decline in morale and so on.[37] Nothing was said about the ineptitude of the plan or the incompetence of commanders.

The Communist Party tried to put the major part of the responsibility on Prieto or Rojo. Comintern advisers even blamed Prieto for 'distancing himself from the communists'.[38] With his usual sinister insinuation, Stepánov reported to Moscow that the failure at Teruel was due, among other things, to the 'erroneous or treasonous conduct of the general staff, Rojo in particular'.[39]

During the early spring of 1938, the Republic had only two consolations. One was the opening of the French frontier on 17 March to allow through military equipment. The other came from an unexpected source: the republican fleet, which throughout the war had done little to challenge the nationalist and Italian blockade, mainly because of the inertia and inefficiency of its ships' crews. Meanwhile, the nationalist fleet had grown with the help of Mussolini, who sent two submarines. These were renamed the *Mola* and the *Sanjurjo*, hardly reassuring choices for traditionally superstitious submariners. In addition, seven Italian 'Legionary' submarines continued to operate throughout the Mediterranean, ready to hoist the royal Spanish flag if forced to the surface. Mussolini also gave Franco four destroyers and, later in 1938, an old cruiser, the *Taranto*.

The end of the war in the north meant that the nationalist Mediterranean fleet was reinforced by units from the Cantabrian coast, including the cruiser *Almirante Cervera* and two seaplane squadrons of Heinkel 60s. One of these went to Palma de Mallorca, where Admiral Francisco de Moreno had set up his joint-staff headquarters with the Italian navy and air force. Palma was used as the principal Italian bomber base for attacks on shipping and republican coastal cities, chiefly Barcelona and Valencia. The Italians dominated the partnership and the island was almost entirely under their occupation. It had been their private fief ever since the early days of the war, when a Bluebeard-like Italian fascist calling himself the Conte Rossi terrorized the island.[40]

It was against this formidable control of the western Mediterranean that the republican navy took everyone by surprise in March. How large a part luck played in their success is difficult to estimate. A flotilla of torpedo boats, backed by two cruisers, the *Libertad* and the *Méndez Núñez*, and nine destroyers left Cartagena on 5 March to strike at the nationalist fleet in Palma de Mallorca. Meanwhile, a nationalist squadron escorting a convoy from Palma was heading in their direction. It comprised three cruisers, the *Baleares*, *Canarias* and *Almirante Cervera*, three destroyers and two minelayers. The two forces made contact just before 1 a.m. on 6 March. Three of the republican destroyers sighted the *Baleares*, the flagship, and fired salvoes of torpedoes. The nationalist cruiser sank rapidly; Admiral Vierna was among the 726 men lost. Although this was the largest battle at sea, it did not have important results because the nationalists soon refitted the old cruiser *República* and renamed her the *Navarra*. Their navy was much more cautious as a result of this action, but its control of the coast was not affected. And only a few days later Heinkel bombing raids on Cartagena crippled the Republic's only capital ship, the *Jaime I*.

*

News of the loss of the *Baleares* reached the nationalist Army of Manoeuvre just as it was about to launch the most devastating offensive yet seen in the war. It is not certain whether Franco decided after Teruel to give up short cuts to victory once again, and continue with the strategy of dismantling key regions, or whether he was persuaded to take advantage of the weakness of the People's Army before it could recover from the effects of the winter battle. The opportunity of dealing the enemy's most experienced formations a further severe blow, while at the same time separating Catalonia, the main source of republican manpower and industry, from the rest of the zone, was obviously attractive. This could then be followed by the reduction of Catalonia and the severing of the Republic from France. Without Catalan industry and supplies from abroad, the central region would fall in a short space of time. It was a less spectacular strategy than a breakthrough to Madrid, but it was more certain of success.

The nationalists began this campaign with a major advantage. They had redeployed their formations far more rapidly than the republican general staff thought possible. Although warned of the threat by spies, the republican commanders somehow convinced themselves that the Guadalajara front was still the nationalists' target. They assumed, also, that the enemy's troops must be as exhausted after Teruel as their own. Within two weeks of the recapture of Teruel, General Dávila's chief of staff, General Vigón, had finalized his plans. The Army of Manoeuvre positioned itself behind the start line, which consisted of the southern half of the central Aragón sector. Starting on the left flank, which was marked by the south bank of the Ebro, there were Yagüe's Moroccan Corps, the 5th Navarrese Division and the 1st Cavalry Division, the Italian CTV and Aranda's Galician Corps. Three other corps were deployed, those of Castile, Aragón and Navarre. Altogether, Dávila had 27 divisions, comprising 150,000 men, backed by nearly 700 guns and some 600 aircraft.

On 9 March the nationalist campaign opened with a massive ground and air bombardment. By the time the nationalist infantry reached the republican trenches, their occupants were hardly in a state to hold a rifle. The superiority of nationalist artillery, to say nothing of the Condor Legion, the Aviazione Legionaria and the Brigada Aerea Hispana, left the republicans at a total disadvantage. This campaign saw the Junkers 87, the Stuka dive-bomber, in action for the first time. Luftwaffe officers in Spain claimed that it could drop its load within five metres of a target.

Those republican defenders who endured such bombardments then had to face von Thoma's tanks, which were used with great effectiveness: 'the real blitzkrieg'.[41] Nationalist infantry casualties were the lowest of any major offensive during the war. In fact, after many of the bombardments the Foreign Legion had little to do except bayonet the shocked survivors in their trenches. General Walter once again blamed the disaster on 'the immense and intensive activity and work of defeatist elements and agents of the fifth column within republican units ... Those were the days when the most stinking, fetid, treacherous activity by all the bastards of all shades and colours flourished the most.'[42] Another report to Moscow, however, admitted that 'we thought [that the nationalist attack] was only a feint and stubbornly continued to expect a general battle at Guadalajara'.[43] This, needless to say, was a rather more accurate appreciation of the situation.

On the first day of the offensive Yagüe's Moroccan Corps, supported by tanks, smashed through the 44th Division and advanced 36 kilometres along the south side of the Ebro. Belchite, still in ruins, fell to the Carlist *requetés* of the second wave on the next day, 10 March. Yagüe, meanwhile, maintained the momentum of his attack. Any defensive line which the republicans patched together crumbled almost as soon as it was formed. The same day the Condor Legion sent all its Heinkel 111s, Dornier 17s and Heinkel 51s to attack republican airfields. They apparently inflicted with 'astonishing effect severe damage to the enemy air force on the ground'. The next day the 5th Division's rapid advance from Belchite was assisted with German tanks from the Gruppe Droehne and Condor Legion 88mm guns.[44] Without worrying about threats to his flanks, Yagüe pushed forward to Caspe.

After Teruel the republican forces were exhausted and badly equipped (many of them had still not received proper ammunition resupply), while the fresh troops in the front line were inexperienced conscripts. The retreat was more a rout than a withdrawal. 'A large part of the army, which survived the fascist offensive,' wrote Stepánov, 'the overwhelming majority of whom were officers and commanders, were confounded and seized by panic, lost their heads and fled to the rear.'[45]

One or two brave stands were made, but demoralization quickly set in, as the republicans saw that they were incapable of resisting the nationalist onslaught either on the ground or from the air. The situation was made worse by the increase of anti-communist feeling after Teruel. Almost any story of communist perfidy was believed. Non-communist units thought that their ammunition supplies were being cut off deliberately. These suspicions stemmed from isolated incidents. During the battle of Teruel, for example, part of the 25th Division was refused replacement weapons and ammunition when one of their senior officers refused to join the Communist Party. There were also bitter arguments among field commanders and staff, particularly the communist officers, many of which dated from Teruel. Líster had refused to obey Rojo; El Campesino claimed that Modesto had deliberately left his division to be cut off during the withdrawal;[46] and Modesto and Líster still hated each other, as they had done ever since the loss of the BT-5 tanks at Fuentes de Ebro.

During the chaos which ensued from the Aragón débâcle, the mutual recriminations involved both Marty and Líster, who each tried to justify his behaviour by accusing the other of treason and carrying out arbitrary executions. Leaders of the Spanish Communist Party demanded that several International Brigade commanders, including Walter and Čopić, should be dismissed for their failures.

In the first ten days of the Aragón offensive the nationalists took the centre-right of the front to depths varying from 50 to 100 kilometres. On 22 March they began their assault on the sector from the Ebro up to Huesca. Moscardó's Corps and Solchaga's Carlist divisions pushed down south-eastwards, while Yagüe crossed the Ebro to take the retreating republicans in their rear left flank. With the whole of central Aragón now captured the advance to the sea was launched at the end of March.

On 14 March advance units of the Italian CTV entered Alcañiz, which eleven days before had been smashed by fourteen Savoia-Marchettis dropping 10,000 kilos of bombs, killing 200 people. The nationalist *Heraldo de Aragón* announced that the town had been 'set on fire by the reds before fleeing'. The Aviazione Legionaria now had its own Guernica.[47] The nationalists halted briefly on 22 March to regroup. Its next action was to be to the north of the Ebro towards Lérida. Moscardó's Aragón Corps and Solchaga's Navarrese divisions continued to push to the south-east and took Barbastro and Monzón, while Yagüe, having crossed the Ebro near Quinto on 23 March, chased the republicans withdrawing on his left flank. The same day the nationalist command ordered the bombing of Lérida to prepare for their attack.

For the republicans it was a retreat which slowed only when the enemy paused to rest. The withdrawal of a flank formation set off a panic; in the confusion nobody seemed to warn his neighbouring unit. Rations and ammunition seldom got through. And all the time the enemy fighters harried the retreating troops like hounds. Circuses of fighters dived in turn to drop grenades and strafe the republicans. The old fear of being cut off, which had broken the militias in the early days of the war, now affected the People's Army. The senior communist officer, Manuel Tagüeña, reported that by 1 April the 35th and 45th International Divisions near Mora del Ebro had 'completely lost all capacity to fight'.[48]

On 3 April the former POUM stronghold of Lérida fell to Yagüe's troops, but the Italians were held for a time by Líster's 11th Division at Tortosa, which had been reduced to rubble by bombing. The Aragón and Navarre Corps seized the reservoirs of Tremp and Camarasa with the hydroelectric plants which provided power to industry in Barcelona. Balaguer fell on 6 April after a terrible bombardment by 100 aircraft. Berti, with the CTV, and Monasterio's cavalry entered Gandesa, where they were welcomed by the Duchesses of Montpensier and Montealegre and the Countesses of Bailén and Gamazo, waiting to pay homage to the victorious troops.

Meanwhile Aranda's Galician Corps, together with the 4th Navarrese Division, fought on towards the coast just below the Ebro's mouth. On 15 April they took the seaside town of Vinaroz, thus establishing a corridor which separated Catalonia from the rest of republican Spain. On that day, which was Good Friday, the Carlist *requetés* waded into the sea as if it were the River Jordan. All the nationalist press competed in describing how General Alonso Vega dipped his fingers in the water and crossed himself. The nationalists believed that the end of their Crusade was near, because 'the victorious sword of Franco had cut in two the Spain occupied by the reds'.[49]

29

Hopes of Peace Destroyed

During that spring of 1938, while the nationalist Army of Manoeuvre was overrunning Aragón, the Republic faced a growing economic crisis and low morale in the rear areas. There was distrust between political groups, fear of the SIM secret police and resentment against the authoritarian nature of Negrín's government, acute food shortages, profiteering and defeatism. At the same time the population of Barcelona – now the capital of the Republic – suffered from the heaviest bombing raids of the war.

The republican zone lived in a spiral of hyperinflation. The cost of living had tripled in less than two years of war.[1] The greatest burden on the economy at the beginning of the war had been the militia wage bill. The rate of pay, however, was not raised from the original ten pesetas a day, despite the high level of inflation, so that by the winter of 1936 arms purchases from abroad had become by far the greatest expenditure. Spain had no arms industry, apart from small factories in the Basque country and Asturias. It was therefore unrealistic to expect metallurgical industries in Catalonia to be able to convert themselves for war production when the expertise was lacking. In fact, it was remarkable what their factories managed to improvise during the first six months of the war, when the central government, determined to take control from the CNT collectives and the Generalitat, refused to provide foreign exchange for the purchase of machinery from abroad.

All the arms which the Republic needed had to be purchased abroad, with payment in advance in gold or hard currency. From the moment it was known that the Republic's gold reserves had been transferred to France and the Soviet Union, a form of gold fever started in Europe among governments, and above all arms dealers, who saw the chance of huge profits at little risk.

Right from the start of the conflict the republican authorities, ignorant of the arms trade, had created a seller's market in Europe and North America by their obvious desperation. On 8 August 1936 Álvaro de Albornoz, the republican ambassador in Paris, signed a contract with the Société Éuropéenne d'Études et d'Entreprises, giving it exclusive rights 'for the purchase in France and other countries of all products', committing the Republic to pay a commission of 7.5 per cent for its services. Yet this company was largely owned by merchant banks (such as Worms et Cie and the Ottoman Bank), newspapers (*Le Temps* and *Le Matin*) and major industrialists such as Schneider-Creusot, all of whom supported General Franco.

Republican purchasers found themselves facing a barrier of blackmail, when government ministers and senior officials demanded huge bribes, ranging from $25,000 to $275,000, for their signature on export licences and other documents. Sometimes they took the money and then blocked the shipment later.[2] Because of the non-intervention policy, the Republic was entirely vulnerable to such tricks. And often when the weapons – paid for in advance – finally arrived, the crates contained inferior or even unserviceable weaponry. The necessity of obtaining arms wherever they were available meant equipping the People's Army with a wide variety of calibres involving many different types of ammunition. A very large proportion, perhaps even half, of the weapons purchased never arrived, either because of fraud, or the blockade, with torpedoings at sea and the bombing of ports.

Spanish governments had purchased weapons from Germany since well before the arrival of the Nazis in power. The colonial army in Morocco had demanded mustard gas to use against the Riffian tribes, who later became their most effective auxiliaries. Yet during the civil war the Republic purchased arms from Nazi Germany, General Franco's most important ally. Recent research[3] has now shown that what had long been suspected is true: Colonel-General Hermann Göring, Minister President of Prussia and commander-in-chief of the Luftwaffe, was selling weapons to the Republic while his own men were fighting for Franco.

On 1 October 1936 the Welsh cargo ship *Bramhill* reached Alicante, having come from Hamburg with a consignment of 19,000 rifles, 101 machine-guns and more than 28 million cartridges, all ordered by the CNT in Barcelona for its militia columns. The presence of the *Bramhill* in Alicante was observed by officers on HMS *Woolwich*. Her captain immediately informed the Foreign

Office, which investigated the matter. The German government made excuses, saying that Hamburg was a free port, yet it was clear that this cargo had arrived with official blessing. The Foreign Office left the matter there. In fact, the architect of this secret sale of arms to the Republic was Hermann Göring. He used as intermediaries the well-known arms trafficker Josef Veltjens, who had already sold arms to General Mola before the rising, but above all Prodromos Bodosakis-Athanasiades, a piratical Greek on close terms with the country's dictator, Metaxas. Bodosakis-Athanasiades was the chief shareholder and chief executive of Poudreries et Cartoucheries Helléniques SA, whose main associate and backer was Rheinmetall-Borsig which, in turn, was controlled by Göring personally.

Bodosakis passed the demands for weapons which he received to Rheinmetall-Borsig and the Metaxas government provided end-user certificates stating that the equipment was destined for the Greek army. When the shipment reached Greece, Bodosakis transferred it to another vessel supposedly sailing to Mexico, but in fact to Spain. As Bodosakis was dealing with the nationalists as well as the Republic, he had to split shipments between vessels, with the best and latest weapons destined for the nationalists and the oldest and least serviceable for the republicans.

In 1937 and 1938, when the sale of German weapons to the Republic was reaching its peak, Bodosakis's company was ordering shipments from Rheinmetall-Borsig worth anything up to 40 million Reichsmarks (£3.2 million at the time). These consignments were almost all for the Republic and one can be fairly sure that Bodosakis was charging five or six times what he had paid Göring. It is more than likely that he then had to pay a significant share of his immense profits to Göring personally, rather than to Rheinmetall-Borsig, and this was on top of payments to the Metaxas regime and other officials.[4]

There was even a Soviet angle to this very free market trade between Nazi Germany and republican Spain. In November 1937 Bodosakis travelled to Barcelona in a Soviet aircraft, accompanied by George Rosenberg, son of the purged Soviet ambassador. Rosenberg, who was a shipping agent and wheeler-dealer, and Bodosakis came to sign a contract with the Republic for £2.1 million to supply ammunition. On this occasion, as on all others, they insisted on full payment in hard currency in advance. The supply of German weaponry to the Republic continued until the very end of the war, as the international commission for the repatriation of foreign volunteers established in January 1939.[5]

The nationalists, exasperated by this extraordinary racket, protested on many occasions to the German authorities.[6] They identified eighteen vessels with such shipments to republican ports between 3 January 1937 and 11 May 1938, but received little explanation. As far as Hermann Göring was concerned, republican hard currency was as good as nationalist.[7] The decoration of Karinhall, his country house of magnificent vulgarity north of Berlin, was no doubt subsidized by his enormous profits from the Spanish Civil War.

The Republic could not go on paying for their weapons in gold and hard currency.[8] By early 1938 the current accounts in gold in Paris and Moscow were running low.[9] In April Negrín started to sell in the United States the silver of the Banco de España. This was bitterly contested by the Burgos government, which had engaged as its lawyer John Foster Dulles (later the US Secretary of State under Eisenhower), but their attempt failed. On 29 April Francisco Méndez Aspe, the minister of finance, signed the decree of authorization.[10] That summer the government introduced regulations to requisition jewels and precious metals, and confiscate property of 'declared enemies of the Republic' for resale. All these sales of silver, jewels and other property raised $31 million, yet the Republic was spending $27 million a month, *excluding* the costs of Soviet arms shipments.[11]

The only hope lay in approaching the Soviet Union again. In March, the Republic had been granted a credit of $70 million, negotiated by Pascua, the ambassador in Moscow, the previous autumn at 3 per cent interest, with half repaid in gold. This had forced a second despatch of gold to the Soviet Union. Now another credit was requested, this time for $85 million, mostly for purchasing Soviet arms. The Republic had to wait a long time for a reply and by then it would be too late.[12]

Many requests for military assistance from the republican government were simply ignored by Stalin. When the situation became especially hard in the spring of 1938, appeals to the Soviet Union were ignored. 'I passed Negrín's request for help to the respective institution (the Politburo),' wrote Litvinov on 29 April to Marchenko, the Soviet chargé d'affaires in Spain, 'but no decision has been made so far.'[13] Finally, Litvinov wrote on 7 August to Marchenko in Barcelona, 'So far no decisions have been adopted on the requests from Ispanpra [Spanish government]. I think that the reason for this delay is that the answer is going to be negative.'[14] Some arms shipments continued, but Stalin had lost interest in Spain because of the situation in Europe and in the Far East. It was quite clear that the republican government was going to lose and he had other priorities.

As well as the huge cost of importing arms, the Republic had to buy oil, supplies of all sorts, and now food after the loss of Aragón's agricultural regions. Chickpeas and lentils bought from Mexico became the staple of the republican zone's diet. Food shortages were serious everywhere, but Barcelona had to cope with refugees from Aragón, in addition to those who had come earlier in the war from Andalucia, Estremadura and Castile, now a million in total.[15] The scenes of peasants from the Aragónese collectives, herding in livestock and bringing their few belongings on carts as they fled from the nationalists, were even more pathetic than those in Madrid during the autumn of 1936. Food queues were worse than ever and women were killed and maimed during the bombing raids because they would not give up their places. The daily ration of 150 grammes of rice, beans or, more usually, lentils (known as Dr Negrín's little pills) could not prevent the effects of vitamin and protein deficiency among those unable to afford black market prices. Children, especially the increasing number of war orphans (the Quakers reported that there were 25,000 in Barcelona alone), suffered from rickets. In 1938 the death rate for children and the old doubled.[16]

The local population responded to the crisis with its customary ingenuity. Balconies in Barcelona were used for keeping chickens or breeding rabbits and the city woke at dawn to the crowing of the cocks. Pots too were used for growing vegetables, as well as many plots of ground all over the city. Pigeons had disappeared from the streets into casseroles, so had cats, which were served up as 'rabbit'. Orange peel was sliced and cooked as ersatz fries, lettuce leaves were dried to make tobacco, but this was only tinkering at the edges.[17] Mothers used to get up before dawn and walk up to twenty kilometres out to farms in the surrounding countryside in the hope of bartering something for food.

Politicians and senior officials, however, did not seem to be losing much weight; a banquet organized in Negrín's honour in Barcelona led to angry demonstrations of protest. On the whole the troops were much better fed than the civilian population, but they were very conscious of the way their families were suffering. Inevitably they became bitter at the scandals involving theft by the staff and supply services of petrol, rations and equipment for resale on the black market.

Barcelona, already suffering such hardship, was also subjected to continual bombing raids by the Italian air force. The city had already been bombarded in February 1937 by the Italian fleet, then from March of that year the Italian bomber squadrons based on Majorca harried the city. The worst raids were on 29 May and 1 October. But in 1938 the attacks became more concentrated. In January they bombed the harbour areas and surrounding neighbourhoods, terrorizing the civilian population. Ciano was thrilled by the account of the destruction, which he found 'so realistically horrifying'.[18]

These raids prompted a retaliation by the republican air force on nationalist cities, causing several dozen deaths.[19] A diplomatic attempt was made to have such actions suspended on both sides. The republicans ceased their raids when Eden promised to help. It was later revealed, however, that the British had made no attempt to do anything. Mussolini halted the bombing in February, out of pique with the nationalists for not allotting the CTV a sufficiently glorious role at Teruel. But during the advance to the sea he decided, without warning Franco, to relaunch the raids on a far more intensive scale.[20] Ciano noted, 'Mussolini believes that these air raids are an admirable way of weakening the morale of the reds.'[21]

On the night of 16 March the Savoia-Marchetti squadrons from Majorca started an around-the-clock bombing relay to Barcelona. There were no anti-aircraft guns and republican fighters were not scrambled from airfields in the region until the afternoon of 17 March. The casualties were about 1,000 dead and 2,000 wounded.[22] One bomb appears to have struck an explosives truck in the Gran Vía, causing a huge explosion. This gave rise to false rumours that the Italians were experimenting with giant bombs. Mussolini was greatly encouraged by the international reaction. '[He] was pleased by the fact', noted Ciano, 'that the Italians have managed to provoke horror by their aggression instead of complacency with their mandolins. This will send up our stock in Germany, where they love total and ruthless war.'[23]

War weariness had set in on the republican side, exacerbated by cynicism at the behaviour of their leaders. More people came to persuade themselves that it was time to reach some sort of compromise with the nationalists, either directly or through international mediation. Already in October 1936, Azaña had entrusted Bosch Gimpera to make peace overtures via London, but this had been stopped by the ambassador there, Azcárate. The suggestion finally reached the Foreign Office via the French government. In May 1937 Azaña tried again when Julián Besteiro went to London as the representative of the Republic for the coronation of King George VI.

Few soldiers thought of the end of the war except in the despair and panic of retreat, because the Republic's propaganda diet fed their hunger to believe in ultimate victory. Middle-class liberals and social-democrats, on the other hand, were more aware of the implications of an extended war. Some like Martínez Barrio convinced themselves that they would suffer far more than the workers from Franco's victory.

By 1938 demoralization was particularly strong among Catalan nationalists, whose support for the Republic in 1936 had been more solid than that of the Basques. The unity of the Catalan left, Esquerra, had been severely stretched in 1937 and once the central government moved to Barcelona, Companys was ignored. The majority of the Esquerra had gravitated towards the communist insistence on discipline and respect for private property, but they had felt betrayed when Negrín's government rapidly dismantled the Generalitat's independence in the wake of the May events. They were also angry at the failure of their old trading partners, France and especially Great Britain, to help them. They became defeatist and swelled the silent Catalan centre, which had disliked both the nationalists and the revolutionary left. Most of them now longed for the end of the war, persuading themselves that the initial harshness of Franco's regime would not affect them for long.

The main antagonisms, however, broke out within the government, first between Prieto and the communists. His last venture with them in the re-establishment of state power had been Líster's destruction of the collectives in Aragón; but from then on the tempo of minor and major quarrels built up rapidly. There was a dispute over whether a Messerschmitt 109 captured intact should be handed to the French or to the Soviet Union. But the greatest struggle was over the Communist Party's infiltration of army commands.

Prieto attempted to limit communist power in the army by first tightening up on the commissar network. He forbade proselytizing to hamper the communists and he replaced the philo-communist Álvarez del Vayo with one of his own colleagues, Crescenciano Bilbao. He also sacked many communist officers, including Antonio Cordón from the post of chief of staff of the Army of the East. He even ordered Francisco Anton, the young commissar-general of the Army of the Centre who was thought to be La Pasionaria's lover, to transfer to a front-line position. Many of his instructions, including this one, were ignored because all communists were told by the Party that only its instructions should be obeyed. Prieto was also hated by the communists for revealing that the Party made money for itself out of the Republic's merchant navy, which had been reorganized through British holding companies so as to beat the blockade.

Prieto attacked the communists' control of his own SIM when he realized what a terrifying machine it had become, but he was too late. His measures against individuals within this state-spawned state enraged the communists and the Russian NKVD 'advisers', without lessening the secret executions and torture. The rare occasions on which the SIM was effectively challenged occurred at the front, when SIM agents seeking out dissidents were sometimes killed by 'stray bullets'.

Prieto combined this frenzy of moral courage and political decisiveness with a terrible pessimism, at times worse than that of Azaña and much less discreet. The minister of defence did not restrain himself from assuring the French ambassador, Labonne, that the war was as good as lost. His tendency to say in public exactly what he thought became a grave problem for Negrín. This was the beginning of the end of their friendship.

Prieto had hoped that the seizure of Teruel would provide a position of strength from which to start negotiations with Franco, but like Negrín a few months later, and Colonel Casado at the very end of the war, he totally underestimated Franco's obsessive desire to crush his enemies utterly and impose his vision of Spain on the whole country. The collapse of the offensive and its disastrous sequel in Aragón left him utterly demoralized.

The communist press began to attack his policy of depoliticizing the army. In February, his cabinet colleague Jesús Hernández wrote an article in *Frente Rojo* denouncing him as a defeatist.[24] As the communist attacks, including those of La Pasionaria, increased, Prieto told Negrín that he could not work with Hernández. Negrín raised the matter at the council of ministers, supporting Prieto, and the communists had to comply, for the time being.

On 12 March Negrín went to Paris to meet French ministers, principally Blum, Daladier, Auriol and Cot. He was hoping to ask them to intervene in Spain with five divisions and 150 aircraft. The French military attaché in Spain, Colonel Morel, had already warned his government of the nationalists' overwhelming air superiority and the need to provide the republicans with at least 300 aircraft to restore the situation. But the French government was alarmed by the *Anschluss* between Nazi Germany and Austria, which Hitler carried out on the day Negrín reached Paris. They had no intention of intervening in Spain and risking a European conflagration. All that Negrín achieved was the agreement of the French government to open the border to allow through armament deliveries which had been held up.

On 16 March, on his return, Negrín called a cabinet meeting at the Pedralbes Palace in Barcelona. It happened to be the morning before the major Italian air raids. Just before the meeting, Negrín insisted that Prieto and Giral, who had also expressed his fears of inevitable defeat, should both support him. The next day, however, Azaña expressed his own concerns and asked Prieto to voice his views on the weakness of the People's Army, the critical situation in which the Republic found itself and the need to reach an agreement on ending the war. Prieto not only agreed, but painted a desolate and accurate picture of the opinions of the military commanders he had consulted. He went so far as to propose that the Republic should freeze its assets abroad to be ready for the needs of the future exiles. Negrín was completely undermined in his arguments with the president of the Republic, who considered him a '*visionario fantástico*' in his view that the Republic should fight on.

At this tense moment the council was informed that a huge demonstration had assembled outside the Pedralbes Palace. This had been prepared several days before at a meeting between communist leaders – Mije, La Pasionaria and Díaz – and representatives from the other working-class organizations, including the CNT and the FAI.[25] Negrín had been warned in advance of this demonstration to demand the resignation of 'defeatist' ministers. He left the room and went out to reassure the crowd that the struggle against the fascists would continue right up to the end. The demonstrators dispersed.

On 18 March, after the terrible bombing raids, representatives of the UGT and CNT signed an agreement submitting industrial planning to government control. It was probably the greatest concession the anarcho-syndicalists had made during the war. Promoted by Mariano Vázquez, it was the most explicit recognition of the state. On 29 March Prieto had a meeting with Negrín. He insisted that the war was lost and predicted the collapse of the Republic. Negrín was appalled. He said to a colleague, 'Now I don't know whether to tell my driver to take me home or to the frontier. That was how frightful Prieto's report was.'[26] According to Zugazagoitia, this report convinced Negrín that he had to ask Prieto to resign from the ministry of defence. He offered him a minor post in the government, but to the rejoicing of the communists, Prieto refused.[27] Prieto, the Cassandra of the Republic, was to be proved right within the year.

The departure of Prieto from government was strikingly reminiscent of that of his old rival, Largo Caballero. The anarchists also supported Prieto, despite their great ideological differences, out of a fear of the communists. The April government crisis created a bitter enmity between Prieto and Negrín, his former disciple, which was to continue on into exile.

When Negrín informed the president of the Republic of the crisis, Azaña called a meeting at the Pedralbes Palace, and in the course of a long speech, full of *sous-entendus*, he made clear that they would have to give up hope of prevailing through military strength.[28] He was already considering a government of capitulation headed by Prieto or Besteiro. Negrín confronted Azaña, insisting on his unshakeable determination to resist to the end. So did the communist leader, José Díaz, who blurted out with such vehemence that the president 'was on the point of abusing his constitutional powers' that Azaña was thoroughly disconcerted.

On 6 April 1938 Azaña asked Negrín once again to form a

government. It was supposed to be a 'government of unity', hoping to recreate the Popular Front, although it was described later as the 'war government'. Negrín took on the role of minister of defence as well as his presidency of the council of ministers.[29] The fact that only one communist remained in the cabinet had much to do with Stalin's reaction, alarmed by the Sino-Japanese war and Nazi expansionism. The hope of reaching an accommodation with Britain and France still remained the chief reason for keeping the communist profile as low as possible. (In France too, Maurice Thorez had been ordered by the Comintern not to be part of the Blum government.) Stalin, however, was persuaded to allow Uribe to stay in the cabinet.

Despite the government's outward impression of political unity, the real power was wielded by *negrínistas* and, above all, communists. Antonio Cordón was appointed under-secretary for war; Carlos Núñez under-secretary for air; Eleuterio Díaz Tendero the head of personnel in the ministry of defence; Manuel Estrada the head of information; Prados head of the naval staff; and Jesús Hernández commissar of the Army of the Centre. All were members of the Spanish Communist Party. But Negrín also appointed a couple of *prietistas*, such as Játiva, who became under-secretary of the navy, and Bruno Alonso, who was made commissar of the fleet.

The communists may not have controlled all the posts in the armed forces, but they certainly held the key administrative ones, to say nothing of the main field commands, with Juan Modesto, Enrique Líster, Valentín González, Etelvino Vega, Manuel Tagüeña, General Walter and so on. The air force and tank corps were also completely under Soviet control, so every military operation required communist approval. Palmiro Togliatti, in a report back to the Comintern, argued that the Spanish Communist Party should 'take over the whole apparatus of the ministry of defence and the whole of the army'. In the meantime the republican formations, which had been pushed back into Catalonia during the Aragón campaign, needed time to regroup and rearm, before they could hope to be effective in any way. The Aragón débâcle, following swiftly behind the enormous cost of Teruel, had virtually incapacitated the People's Army, as Prieto had warned. Little could be done to delay the advance of the Navarrese and Moroccan Corps across northern Aragón, and the loss of the hydroelectric plants in the Pyrenees to the west of the River Segre brought Catalonian industry to a standstill.

In the early part of 1938 the government of Neville Chamberlain (who had succeeded Baldwin in May 1937) took the policy of appeasement to such a point that Anthony Eden resigned as foreign minister on 20 February. This event confirmed the dictators in their belief that they had nothing to fear from Great Britain. Chamberlain's insistence on an Anglo-Italian treaty, in the hope of drawing her away from the influence of Germany, demonstrated convincingly that Axis intervention in Spain would not be challenged, whatever Negrín's government might propose at the League of Nations.

As soon as Lord Halifax succeeded Eden as foreign secretary the arrangements for the treaty went ahead, even though more British shipping had been sunk by Italian submarines at the beginning of the month. (Eden had ordered the anti-submarine patrols to be recommenced, noting that 'the Admiralty feared that this would impair the relations which they had established with General Franco's Admiral Moreno'.)[30] On 16 April Ciano recorded that 'at 6.30 p.m. the Pact with England was signed. Lord Perth was moved. He said to me: "You know how much I have wanted this moment to come." It is true – Perth has been a friend. Witness dozens of his reports which are in our hands.'[31] The date of the signing had been chosen to 'please Halifax as it is his birthday. All very romantic ...' the young fascist foreign minister added sarcastically.[32] The part of the treaty which affected Spain most directly was the provision that Italy should be allowed to keep its troops there until the end of the war. This agreement was not referred to the signatories of the non-intervention pact, although it was deemed to be still in force. It is not surprising that even Churchill, who had supported non-intervention strongly, later described it as 'an elaborate system of official humbug' which had 'been laboriously maintained'.

The Spanish republican government was horrified by the treaty. Two weeks after it was signed, Negrín launched a vain diplomatic offensive. He issued his 'Thirteen Points' plan for establishing what amounted to a caretaker government with free elections to follow.[33] It was intended as a formula for peace negotiations. According to Stepánov, they had been dictated to him by the central committee of the Spanish Communist Party. They consisted of the following:

1 Assure the absolute independence and integrity of Spain.
2 Liberation of Spanish territory from foreign forces.
3 The defence of the people's Republic and of a state based on democratic principles.
4 The calling of a plebiscite as soon as the war had ended.
5 Without undermining the unity of Spain, the protection and encouragement of the cultures of its various peoples.
6 Respect for citizens' rights: liberty of conscience and religious practice.
7 Respect for legal property and foreign capital.
8 A profound agrarian reform and democracy in the countryside.
9 Advanced social legislation to guarantee the rights of workers.
10 The improvement of the physical and moral culture of the nation.
11 An army independent of political parties and to be the instrument of the people.
12 The renunciation of war as an instrument of national policy.
13 A broad amnesty for all Spaniards.

Needless to say, there was not a single point which Franco would be prepared to consider. Time and again he had insisted that no peace deal was possible. Faupel had reported to Berlin in May 1937: 'Franco rejected any idea of a compromise as completely impossible, stating that the war would under all circumstances be fought to a final decision.'[34] Serrano Súñer said a few days later, 'Sooner or later there would have to be elections. Since red propaganda in Spain, however, is at present undoubtedly far more clever and effective than that of the whites and since, moreover, red propaganda would have the support of the Marxists, Jews and Freemasons of the entire world, these elections would necessarily lead to the formation of a government, the political composition of which would be decidedly leftist, openly anti-German, and anti-national socialist ... We cannot therefore have the slightest interest in a compromise solution in Spain.'[35] Once again Franco told Faupel that 'he and all Spanish nationalists would rather die than place the fate of Spain once again in the hands of a red or democratic government'.[36] Even the philo-communist Álvarez del Vayo told a French reporter that 'after so much blood had been shed he considered impossible any mediation between the two parties, as suggested by Mr Churchill'.[37]

So it is difficult to know what Negrín hoped to achieve in the way of a settlement. Was this just an appeal to the democracies to change their position, or a deliberate provocation of the nationalists, who were bound to reject every single one of his points? And yet Negrín, despite his overt rejection of the realism of Azaña and Prieto, was carrying out a number of secret overtures aimed at a peace settlement. It is impossible to tell, but one thing is certain. Negrín had great confidence in his diplomatic talents. He felt that all he needed was a single military victory to force the enemy to the negotiating table. This was to lead to the final, self-inflicted disaster of the Spanish Republic.

30
Arriba España!

Nothing deflected General Franco from his ultimate goal in the war: the total destruction of his enemies and the transformation of Spain. His collaborators in this grand project from the start had been his brother Nicolás, Generals Kindelán, Orgaz and Millán Astray, and then, from February 1937, his ambitious brother-in-law Ramón Serrano Súñer.

Faced with the simplicity of Franco's ideas, as well as those of the other generals, Serrano Súñer saw the possibilities for his own advancement in the hierarchy of the state. Their simple military government was effective enough to win the war (he called it the 'army camp state'), but it would hardly appear very convincing to the civilized world after the fighting was over.[1]

Once Franco had achieved absolute command of all the armed forces and had made himself the supreme leader of the National Movement, 'responsible only to God and to History', the time had come to replace the Junta Técnica of the early days with a formal government. On 30 January 1938, Franco constituted his first cabinet of ministers and established the Law for the Central Administration of the State. 'The presidency [of the council of ministers] remains tied to the chief of state. The ministers will constitute the government of the nation. The ministers will swear an oath of loyalty to the chief of state and to the nationalist regime.' And the chief of state assumed in addition 'the supreme power to dictate juridical norms of a general character'. This in effect meant that the nationalist head of state personally enjoyed total power, executive, legislative and judicial.

In the creation of the three key ministries, defence, public order and foreign affairs, all controlled by generals, the army camp was still clearly at work.[2] These senior officers and their departments were simply extensions of the Generalissimo's headquarters. The three ministries controlled by Falangists were linked to the ministry of the interior and the controlling influence of Serrano Súñer, who ran his domain with an iron hand. He achieved supremacy over the civil governors and moved two of his own supporters, José Antonio Giménez Arnau and Dionisio Ridruejo, to take over the direction of press and propaganda. Serrano Súñer even had a say in the appointment of his fellow ministers, suggesting most of the names himself. He somehow persuaded Franco to appoint Amado, a former colleague of Calvo Sotelo, as minister of finance, despite Franco's dislike of him for having been very critical of his brother Nicolás. He also managed to get the Caudillo to appoint the monarchist Sáinz Rodríguez, whom Franco suspected of being a Freemason.

The day after forming his new government in Burgos, Franco received members of the diplomatic corps, among whom was Robert Hodgson, then the British agent accredited to the nationalist government. Hodgson appears to have been charmed by the Caudillo.[3] On 12 February, in the Monastery de las Huelgas, the ministers swore their loyalty to Franco with the following declaration: 'I swear in the name of God and his holy evangelists to accomplish my duty as minister of Spain with the strictest loyalty to the head of state, the Generalissimo of our glorious forces, and to the constitutional principles of the national regime to serve the destiny of the Fatherland.' There was no mention either of a republic or of a monarchy, only of the Generalissimo himself, who would define the national regime as he saw fit.

During March, General Franco approved all the decrees which Serrano Súñer passed him to sign, including those abolishing the liberty of meeting or of association. The ministries of justice and education went to work reversing all republican legislation to do with the Church or teaching. Schools were handed over to the ecclesiastical authorities to control. Crucifixes would hang in every classroom. The most important decree was the Fuero del Trabajo, or Right of Work, which was a combination of the Church's social doctrine, as expressed in the encyclical *Rerum Novarum*, the 26 points of the Falange and some elements of the Italian fascist *Carta del Lavoro*. Above all, it decreed the disappearance of class struggle in Spain, which would be replaced by a vertical association of bosses and workers. It also emphasized the desire of the regime to exercise a completely dirigiste control of the economy.

Over the following months the legislative machinery did not halt.

Decrees were issued covering every aspect of life, from abolishing republican public holidays and choosing new ones to the design of the currency and postage stamps (usually the effigies of El Cid or the Catholic monarchs Ferdinand and Isabella, or the symbols of the new state). The Statute of Catalonia was abolished on 5 April and on 22 April the Law of the Press was introduced, placing all publications at the service of Franco. The purpose was to punish 'any piece of writing which, directly or indirectly, tended to diminish the prestige of the nation, or of the regime, undermine the work of government in the new state or sow pernicious ideas among those of feeble intellect'. The Law of the Press, although introduced as a wartime provision, according to Serrano Súñer, remained in force until 1966. On 21 May Castilian was pronounced the only official language. Basque or Catalan could no longer be spoken in public. On 7 July the sentence of death was rather belatedly made official again. Meanwhile, Pedro Sáinz Rodríguez began to overhaul primary education, with classes of religious and patriotic education. All foreign influences were rooted out, even in sport. Only recognizably Spanish sports, such as the game of *pelota*, were to be allowed.

In May the Portuguese government formally recognized Franco's government and the Vatican appointed Cardinal Cicognani as papal nuncio. Franco also annulled all republican decrees expelling the Jesuits. He returned their properties and privileges. The head of the order, Vladimir Ledochovsky, thanked the Caudillo, declaring that 'at the moment of his death, the 30,000 Jesuits in the world would give three masses for the soul of the Generalissimo',[4] an exchange very much to the advantage of the Company of Jesus. Franco, however, intended to make sure that the Church in Spain was no more than another lobby, along with the Carlists, the Falangists and his own generals.[5] He insisted that he should have the right to confirm or reject the appointment of bishops, the old prerogative of the monarchy.

Another question which preoccupied Franco during the spring of 1938 was the treatment of prisoners of war. Following the collapse of the republican northern front and the offensive in Aragón, there were another 72,000 of them, bringing the total captured to more than 160,000, according to the head of the Inspección de Campos de Concentración de Prisioneros, which came directly under Franco's headquarters.[6] By the end of the war the figure reached 367,000. Prisoners were held in ordinary jails, camps, castles, convents, monasteries, cinemas and prison ships. The problem was how to identify the '*irrecuperables*', who were usually executed, and those who had been led astray and could be re-educated back to the nationalist cause.

Since the *coup d'état* in 1936 had been successful in the main regions of agricultural production, nationalist Spain, unlike the republican zone, never suffered from food shortages, even in 1938 when the economy declined. Industrial production also increased and not just because of the conquest of the north.[7] This was because factory owners and managers had not fled. A similar process took place in the conquered territories. In addition, the nationalists carried out a very effective commercial and economic policy, such as Queipo de Llano's development of Andalucian trade. The nationalist authorities maintained an iron grip and centralized control over agricultural and industrial production, and of international trade. Monetary policy was also tightly controlled. By the end of the war, the nationalist peseta had lost only 27.7 per cent of its value.[8]

Food was not in short supply for those who could pay for it. In provincial cities of the nationalist zone such as Burgos, Pamplona, Corunna, Seville or Bilbao, well-dressed people strolled in the streets before taking an aperitif or having dinner. Bars and restaurants were as full as churches and bullrings.[9]

Franco's main suppliers (unlike those of the Republic) did not press the nationalists to pay in advance, nor did they overcharge. The nationalists did not have anything like enough in hard currency to pay, so Franco effectively mortgaged Spain's mineral wealth. His most voracious creditors, but also the purveyors of his most effective aid, were the Germans. Hermann Göring, the head of the Nazis' 'Four Year Plan' as well as the Luftwaffe, was the key figure. The origins of the German commercial organization, HISMA/ROWAK, have already been mentioned. It rapidly gained control of a virtual monopoly of Spanish nationalist imports and exports. Yet Göring, preoccupied by the scale of nationalist debt and determined to take control of Spanish mining output on a more permanent basis, created a special affiliate of HISMA, called the Montana Project. Montana would oversee the exploitation and export to Germany of iron, mercury, pyrites, tungsten and antimony from 73 Spanish mines.

On 10 January 1938 von Stohrer, the German ambassador in Salamanca, called a meeting to discuss HISMA/ROWAK's operations in 1937, which reached a total of 2,584,000 tons sent to Germany.[10] Fifteen days later Count Jordana, the foreign minister, told German representatives that the Montana project could not go ahead because existing (in fact, republican) legislation insisted on a study mine by mine first and could not be applied to 73 of them at once. Also, according to this same law, foreign capital invested in Spanish mines could not exceed 20 per cent. Jordana asked them to be patient until a new law could be passed. But the nationalists also came under heavy pressure from Great Britain which, as the largest importer of iron and pyrites from Spain, wanted to protect its own interests. Before July 1936 five British companies, including the Rio Tinto company, accounted for 65 per cent of British pyrite imports, which were essential for the armaments industry.

Franco's national pride reacted against the German demands and he asked for an increase in military aid, while playing for time. Eventually, the infuriated Germans threatened to cut off all aid and he had to sign the new mining law in July 1938. The Germans nevertheless immediately reinforced the Condor Legion, which happened to be just in time for the battle of the Ebro.

Franco had a much easier time with his Italian allies. Mussolini's megalomania led him into prodigal gestures of munificence, which reduced his minister of finance to despair. He never pressed the nationalists for payment or tried to exploit Spanish mineral wealth. Italian aid to nationalist Spain was disastrous to the economy. The cost of Mussolini's adventure in Spain rose to 8,500 million lire (the equivalent of three billion euros).

In 1938, as well as devoting his energies to rebuilding the political and economic structure of Spain, Franco had to concentrate on finishing the war. After the devastating advance of the nationalists across Aragón to the sea, his allies expected the fall of Barcelona to follow, yet Franco turned away from this prize. General Vigón and the other nationalist commanders could not understand why the Generalissimo should fail to seize the opportunity when his troops were almost at the gates of the Catalan capital. Nor could his republican opponents. General Rojo himself admitted that Barcelona could have been taken with 'less force and in less time' than when it finally took place in January 1939.[11]

The reason for Franco's timidity is indeed strange. Since the autumn of 1936 he had been convinced that the French were playing an ambitious game. He thought that French officers were serving secretly with the republican forces and that France planned to annex Catalonia. He had told a German representative in September 1936 that 'France was the actual ruler of Catalonia'.[12] He continued to believe, quite wrongly, that the French would annex Catalonia 'to prevent nationalist Spain from being too powerful', as he stated to Richthofen in November 1937.[13] It must be said that even the Germans were concerned for a short time in March 1938 that the French were moving troops to the south-west of the country and that the French Mediterranean squadron had 'received orders to be prepared for action'.[14] But Franco's fears persisted long after his allies had discounted the threat entirely. As late as 17 January 1939, with nationalist troops advancing on Barcelona, Richthofen again had to reassure Franco that the French would not intervene.[15] All this was despite the fact that Chamberlain had warned France clearly that if the Nazis reacted furiously to a French intervention in Catalonia, Great Britain would not come to her aid. In addition, Franco had heard that the French general staff was opposed to involvement in Spain, partly because few of its members sympathized with the Republic, and because they feared a conflict which could lead to war on two fronts.

Mussolini was fluctuating, once again, between enthusiasm and pessimism. He was becoming weary of the war in Spain. He had begun to set his sights on the coast of Albania across the Adriatic and was exasperated by Franco's lack of gratitude. In addition, Ciano had been deeply angered by the nationalist attitude. 'I talked to Nicolás Franco about our aid for 1938,' he recorded in his diary at the end of March. 'They want a billion lire worth of goods, payment to be mostly in kind and very problematical. We must keep our tempers. We are giving our blood for Spain – do they want more?'[16]

Relations between the national contingents were not helped by mistakes, however genuine: Italian bombers mistook targets and Condor Legion Messerschmitts attacked nationalist Fiats, which they had thought were Chatos. The Italian troops were becoming very unpopular in the rear. Even officers were frequently involved in brawls with Spaniards after mutual insults. Also an increasing number of Legionaries were deserting to the enemy and their commanders were making money on the black market. 'It seems from reports we have had', Ciano noted, 'that a bad impression is being created by the sight of Italian troops filling the cabarets and brothels in the rear areas, while the Spaniards are fighting a grim battle ... The soldiers of fascism must not, at any moment or for any reason, set an example of indifference to the struggle.'[17]

Meanwhile, the German minister of war gave instructions to General Volkmann to push Franco into carrying out the offensive towards Barcelona. But Franco obstinately refused to be shifted from his decision. Some suspect that he wanted a more drawn-out war so as to crush all opposition, bit by bit, in the conquered territories. According to Dionisio Ridruejo, a short war for him 'inevitably signified negotiations and concessions to finish it. A long war meant total victory. Franco chose the crueller option which, from his point of view, was also more effective.'[18]

Instead of deploying the Army of Manoeuvre in a swift offensive against the Catalan capital, Franco decided to widen the corridor to the sea and launch his troops south-westwards towards Valencia. This strategy lost all the momentum which they had achieved in the Aragón campaign and gave the defeated republican forces which had retreated into Catalonia the opportunity to reorganize and rearm with the supplies just delivered across the reopened French frontier. Also, the heavy rain in March and April greatly reduced the effectiveness of his air force. But most important of all, his troops were now sent against fresh republican formations in good defensive positions.

On 25 April, eight days after the Carlists reached the sea, the offensive towards Valencia began with Varela's Army Corps of Castile, Aranda's Galician Corps, and García Valiño's formation. They first occupied Aliaga to create a salient for an advance into the sierras of El Pobo and La Garrocha. This initial push took four days and then the bad weather forced them to suspend operations. On 4 May the offensive recommenced. The Corps of Castile attacked along two axes: from north to south towards Alcalá de la Selva and from Teruel towards Corbalán. Meanwhile, the Galician Corps advanced southwards down the coast road towards Benicassim and Castellón de la Plana. García Valiño's attacked from Morella towards Mosqueruela. The plan was to form a line from Teruel to Viver, Segorbe and Sagunto, but the nationalist advance was hard, because of the breadth of the front and because the republicans had established a strong line of defence – the XYZ Line – anchored on the left in the Sierra de Javalambre and which extended across the Sierra de Toro to the heights of Almenara, next to the coast. The nationalists launched attack after attack, but not even with 1,000 field guns and air attacks could they break the front. The well-prepared defence line gave the republican troops confidence in their flanks.

The painful experience of air and artillery bombardments had at last taught the republicans the necessity of solid trenches and bunkers. They had also learned to plan their fields of fire better to prevent infiltration of their positions via dead ground. Their artillery batteries prepared fire plans to bombard the most likely forming-up areas for enemy attacks. The nationalist advance prevailed slowly along the coast, taking Castellón on 13 June and Villarreal the next day. But the resistance of the republicans in the Sierra de Espadan prevented the nationalists from reaching their objective of the Segorbe–Sagunto line.

Nationalist commanders were deeply disconcerted by the strength of the resistance and their casualties, especially after such a crushing victory as the Aragón campaign.[19] Kindelán tried to persuade Franco of the difficulties of advancing further in the sector and begged him to abandon the operation in view of their heavy losses, but the Generalissimo ordered for the attacks to continue. The nationalists did not have any airfields within striking distance and the Condor Legion, withdrawn from the fighting until the mining law came into effect, played no part. Nevertheless, Franco had just received fresh support from Italy in the form of 6,000 more soldiers and new aircraft: 25 Savoia-Marchetti 81s, 12 Savoia-Marchetti 79s and 7 Br-20s.[20] At the beginning of July Franco ordered the front to be reinforced with the Italian CTV, led by General Berti, and formed the new Turia Corps of four divisions commanded by Solchaga. The Generalissimo ordered that Valencia was to be taken by 25 July, the feast of Saint James the Apostle, patron saint of Spain. Opposing the five nationalist army corps, which totalled fourteen divisions in all (some 125,000 men), the republicans had six corps,[21] but numbers were roughly equal on both sides, because the People's Army's formations were usually under strength.

On 13 July, the fourth and final phase of the battle began with an attack down the Teruel–Sagunto road, with the CTV and the

Army Corps of Turia and Castile. At the same time the Galician Corps and García Valiño's formation tried to advance down the coast. Such concentrations of forces hindered the nationalists in this 'absurd manoeuvre'.[22] For ten days the nationalists tried in vain to break the republican defences under the blazing sun of the Levante, with waves of infantry and intense bombing raids.

To their surprise, the nationalists found that these novice republican divisions were able to inflict severe damage on their attackers without the heavy losses which the troops of Modesto were accustomed to suffering. As a result, this purely defensive operation proved to be a far greater victory for the Republic than that of Guadalajara. With 20,000 nationalist casualties against only 5,000 republican, the slogan 'to resist is to win' finally achieved some sense. The tragic fact, however, was that even at this late stage of the war the republican leadership still failed to learn the lesson and continued to give priority to political and propaganda motives over those of military effectiveness. The battle of the Ebro, which was to begin soon afterwards, exceeded even that of Brunete in its disastrous attempts to create a spectacular success. It would lead directly to the final destruction of the republican army.

The fierce fighting north of Valencia had not been the only action of the early summer. After many months of inactivity, General Queipo de Llano put an end to the comparative calm in the west of Spain. On 20 July he launched an offensive from Madrigalejo to cut off the republican salient which pointed at the Portuguese frontier from either side of the River Guadiana. Queipo's five divisions and a cavalry brigade broke through the weakly held republican lines, manned by ill-armed and untrained troops. On 23 July the nationalists took Castuera, and Don Benito and Villanueva de la Serena on the next day. This cut off the republican salient in Estremadura. But Queipo de Llano's operation was brought to a halt on 25 July, because the republican army in Catalonia launched its great offensive on the Ebro. Franco's headquarters needed every battalion it could lay its hands on.

Just one week before, on 18 July, the second anniversary of the *coup d'état*, the government in Burgos decided to 'raise to the dignity of Captain-General of the Army and the Fleet, the Head of State and Generalissimo of the armed forces, and National Chief of the Falange Española Tradicionalista y de las JONS, the most Excellent Señor Don Francisco Franco Bahamonde'. In the military mind this appointment held great significance. Captain-general was the rank reserved for Spanish monarchs. Franco was on a path which would lead him not to the throne, but to the role of an all-powerful regent.

On that day of march-pasts through the streets of Burgos, hung with bunting and huge portraits of the Generalissimo, there was a 'mixture of fascist and medieval elements'.[23] In the ancient captain-generalcy of Burgos, the new captain-general made a speech, referring to the revolution of October 1934, paying homage to the 'absent one', José Antonio Primo de Rivera, denouncing the conspiracy of atheist Russia against Catholic Spain, recounting the crimes of the reds and announcing the final victory of his military crusade.[24] 'This imposes on every Spaniard the duty of cultivating remembrance. The harsh lesson must not be lost, and the benevolence of Christian generosity, which has no limits for those who have been led astray, and for the repentant who come in good faith to join us, must nevertheless be controlled by prudence to prevent infiltration by recalcitrant enemies of the Fatherland, whose health, like that of the body, needs to be quarantined from those coming from the camp of pestilence ... In their name [those of the nationalist dead] and that of sacred Spain, I sow today this seed in the deep furrow which our glorious army has ploughed. Spaniards all: *¡Arriba España! ¡Viva España!*'[25]

31
The Battle of the Ebro

After the collapse in Aragón during the spring, the republican government had set out to reconstitute an army from the formations pushed back into the isolated eastern zone. They had the River Segre to the west and the Ebro to the south as reasonable defence lines behind which they could reorganize. They also had the 18,000 tons of war matériel which came over the French frontier between March and mid June. And they had more time to reorganize than they could have reasonably expected, thanks to Franco's ill-judged offensive towards Valencia.

During the late spring and early summer the call-up was extended to the classes of 1925–9 and 1940–1. Twelve new divisions were formed. The conscripts ranged from sixteen-year-olds (which veterans called the *quinta del biberón*, the baby's bottle call-up) to middle-aged fathers. To these were added nationalist prisoners of war and many skilled technicians, who were now drafted because the loss of the hydroelectric plants in the Pyrenees had cut Catalonian production dramatically. Yet since there were insufficient rifles to go round, the government's militarization decrees seem to have had more to do with creating an impression of resolute resistance than with military requirements. The new war matériel was of most use to the air force, special arms and machine-gun companies. The small arms did no more than replace those lost by front-line divisions at Teruel or in Aragón.

After the failure of his peace overtures Negrín, supported by the communists, felt that international attention must be aroused by a great heroic action. If it were successful the Republic could negotiate from a position of greater strength. This reasoning, however, contained several basic flaws. European attention was much more preoccupied with events in the east, especially Hitler's designs on Czechoslovakia. There was no prospect of Franco changing his refusal to compromise,[1] nor of Chamberlain coming to the aid of the Republic.

The military justification for the project consisted of a vain plan to recapture the nationalists' corridor to the sea and link the two republican zones again. But this was wildly optimistic and demonstrated that the government and the communists still refused to learn from their own disastrous mistakes. The pattern was entirely predictable. Even if the republican attackers achieved surprise, the nationalist armies, with their American trucks, would redeploy rapidly to halt the offensive. And once again nationalist air and artillery superiority would crush them in the open. In addition, this attack across a major river, with all the problems of resupply that entailed, represented a far more dangerous risk than even the offensives of Brunete and Teruel. The loss of aircraft and equipment would also be far more catastrophic than before, since there was little chance of any further replacements arriving, now that the French border had closed again. Negrín also refused to see that another battle involving heavy casualties would damage republican morale irretrievably. Altogether it was a monumental gamble against very unfavourable odds and bizarrely incompatible with Negrín's hope that the Republic would still be resisting strongly when a European war broke out.

An Army of the Ebro was specially formed for this offensive. As at Brunete, it was communist dominated and received nearly all the armour, artillery and aircraft. Modesto was the army commander, with V Corps under Líster, and XV Corps under the 26-year-old communist physicist Manuel Tagüeña. His right flank was covered by XII Corps, which defended the bottom part of the River Segre from Lérida to where it joined the Ebro opposite Mequinenza.[2]

The curve of the Ebro between Fayón and Cherta was the sector chosen for the main assault, with XV Corps on the right and V Corps on the left. Two subsidiary actions were added – the 42nd Division crossing to the north, between Fayón and Mequinenza in order to impede a counter-attack from the right flank, and the French XIV International Brigade crossing downriver at Amposta. The total strength of the assault force was about 80,000 men.[3] The greatest weakness was in artillery as a result of losses in Aragón. The whole army had no more than 150 field guns, some of which dated from the last century. In addition, the 76mm anti-aircraft ammunition was known to be defective, although the soldiers were not informed 'for reasons of morale'.[4]

The nationalist troops facing them from the right bank of the Ebro consisted of the 50th Division commanded by Colonel Luis Campos Guereta, who had his headquarters in Gandesa, Barrón's 13th Division in reserve and the 105th Division, which covered the front from Cherta to the sea.[5] These divisions of Yagüe's Moroccan Corps consisted of about 40,000 men. Over the last few days before the republican attack, Colonel Campos passed back intelligence reports to Yagüe, warning that his men had observed troop movements and preparations on the opposite bank of the Ebro. These observations were confirmed by air reconnaissance, but the nationalist high command did not take the threat seriously. It seemed unthinkable to them that the republican army, which had been so severely mauled in Aragón, would be ready to undertake any sort of offensive, especially one across a broad river.

On 24 June Colonel Franco-Salgado, the Generalissimo's aide, had been informed that the republicans were preparing rafts to cross the river as well as pontoon bridges, and that the majority of the International Brigades were concentrated in Falset.[6] This intelligence was confirmed by the interrogation of deserters and prisoners, but Franco did no more than tell Yagüe to maintain a state of alert.[7]

The crossing of the Ebro was prepared in minute detail for a whole week, with the republican troops practising in ravines, rivers and on the coast. The engineer corps mocked up the crossing with bridges built in Barcelona or bought in France. Meanwhile, reconnaissance troops from the specialist XIV Corps of commandos slipped across the river at night. They made contact with peasants on the other side to obtain information on nationalist positions. The seventeen-year-old Rubén Ruiz, the son of La Pasionaria, was one of them. He was finally killed as a major in the Red Army in 1942 during the retreat into Stalingrad.

In the very early hours of 25 July commandos went across silently and knifed the sentries on the far bank. They also fastened lines for the assault boats to follow. Six republican divisions then began to cross the Ebro, with the point units in assault boats, guided by local peasants who knew the river. The bulk of the forces followed using twelve different pontoon bridges set up by the engineers. Above Fayón, the 226th Brigade from the 42nd

Division cut the road from Mequinenza, and the rest of XV Corps crossed the river at Ribarroja and Flix to establish a bridgehead along the line of Ascó–La Fatarella. At the same time V Corps crossed near Miravet to take Corbera d'Ebre on their line of advance to Gandesa, and also near Benissanet to attack Móra d'Ebre and link up with the flank units of XV Corps.

Much further downriver, almost on the sea, XIV International Brigade tried to cross the river, but only a small number reached the other shore alive. The Riffian Rifles of the 105th Division inflicted heavy casualties. XIV International Brigade lost 1,200 men in 24 hours, shot or drowned. Pierre Landrieu of the Henri Barbusse Battalion recorded that it was not possible to cross the river to help their comrades trapped on the far bank, who yelled for help in vain.[8]

In the centre the republican troops advanced rapidly and captured some 4,000 men from the 50th Division. On the following day they approached Villalba dels Arcs and Gandesa, after occupying Puig de L'Àliga, between the sierras of Pàndols and Cavalls, the key to the Terra Alta, as this dry mountainous region was called. It included the infamous Point 481, which became known as 'the heights of death', or the 'pimple', as the International Brigades called it.[9] In a little more than 24 hours, Modesto's troops had seized 800 square kilometres. But Yagüe, who had not forgotten Modesto's mistakes at Brunete and Belchite, ordered Barrón's 13th Division to move at greatest speed to the defence of Gandesa. The forced march of 50 kilometres under the July sun killed a number of men through heat exhaustion. The feet of many others were in a pitiful, bloody mess after this feat.[10] Nevertheless, by the early hours of 26 July, the 13th Division was deployed to defend the town. General Volkmann, the new commander of the Condor Legion, who visited Yagüe at his headquarters at this point, observed how calm he was. Yagüe was undoubtedly the nationalists' most capable field commander.

Franco had heard of the offensive within hours of it beginning on 25 July, the anniversary of the end of the battle of Brunete and the festival of Saint James: the day on which he had hoped to take Valencia. His reaction was typical. He rejected any idea of allowing the republicans to hold any territory, whatever the cost of winning it back. Operations on the Levante front were halted immediately and eight divisions were turned round to march against the republican bridgehead. The Condor Legion, the Italian Legionary Air Force and the Brigada Aérea Hispana were tasked immediately for operations on the Ebro front. By the early afternoon of the first day nationalist planes were over the Terra Alta and attacking the crossing points over the river. The pontoon bridges were given the highest priority. Altogether, 40 Savoia 79s, 20 Savoia 81s, 9 Breda 20s, 30 Heinkel 111s, 8 Dornier 20s, 30 Junker 52s and 6 Junker 87 Stukas, as well as 100 fighters, went into action. The republican air force was nowhere to be seen.[11]

Franco, having been assured by an engineer that no permanent damage would be done to industry in Barcelona,[12] ordered the dams at Tremp and Camasara up in the Pyrenees to be opened. The flood water which resulted raised the river by two metres and swept away the pontoon bridges on which Modesto's troops relied for supply and reinforcements. Republican engineers managed to repair them within two days, but the timing had been disastrous. Only a small number of tanks and guns had crossed the river. They were not enough to defeat Barrón's troops in Gandesa.

Throughout the battle the constant bombing of the bridges taxed the republican engineers to the limit. Each night they repaired the damage done during the day, a veritable task of Sisyphus. The most useful weapon which the nationalists had against the narrow bridges was the Stuka dive-bomber, but the Condor Legion never used more than two pairs at a time, and then with a strong fighter escort. The Luftwaffe was extremely concerned about losing one on enemy territory and the remains being sent to the Soviet Union. Even nationalist officers were not allowed to go near them. Stukas had been used for the first time during the Aragón offensive, but there had been little danger then, with the republicans retreating rapidly, because a downed aircraft could be recovered.

At dawn on 27 July republican aircraft had still not appeared, yet Modesto ordered his few T-26 tanks to attack Gandesa. General Rojo was appalled at the inexplicable absence of republican air cover. On 29 July he wrote to his friend Colonel Manuel Matallana with the Army of the Centre: 'The Ebro front is almost paralysed ... Once again we are facing the phenomenon in all our offensives of people seeming to be deflated.'[13] This was hardly surprising. The plan was deeply flawed from the start, and once the initial advantage of surprise had worn off, the communist field commanders had no idea how to handle the situation. They reverted to their usual practice of wasting lives for no purpose, because they could not admit that their operation had failed. In the first week alone their troops had suffered a huge number of casualties, decimated by bombing and strafing, but also by dysentery and typhus.[14] There was, too, a problem of physical and moral exhaustion, especially among the International Brigades. Dimitrov reported to Voroshilov and Stalin, 'The soldiers of the International Brigades are extremely exhausted by the continuous battles, their military efficiency has fallen off, and the Spanish divisions have significantly outstripped them in fighting value and discipline.'[15]

On 30 July Modesto reorganized the formations in the central sector and took personal command of operations. He concentrated the tanks and artillery which had managed to cross the Ebro around Gandesa. But the tanks presented an excellent target for the Condor Legion's 88mm anti-aircraft guns, which had been ordered to take them on whenever there were no aircraft around. Meanwhile its *Kampfgruppe* of Heinkel 111 bombers concentrated on the bridges, with over 40 sorties that day. They destroyed two bridges and one footbridge from a height of 4,000 metres. One of the bridges was repaired and again destroyed in a night bombing run. And the Stuka flight attacked the bridges at Asco and Vinebre, with eight of their 500kg bombs, achieving a direct hit on the latter.[16] But the Stukas had less luck next day when they attempted to smash the tunnel exit four kilometres east of Mora la Nueva.

Modesto ordered a relentless bombardment of Gandesa with his thirteen batteries and launched his infantry into the attack. They reached the cemetery and came close to the heavily defended building of the agriculture syndicate, but they could not get to grips with Barrón's men. Meanwhile the 3rd Division attacked Villalba dels Arcs. But all during daylight hours nationalist and allied aircraft continued to strike at troop concentrations and supply lines, still without opposition from the republican air force. Only on 31 July did republican planes appear in an attack on Gandesa.

The largest air battles of the whole war then took place over the Ebro front. On 31 July alone, no less than 300 missions were flown with fighter aircraft mixed in dogfights and attacking bombers to prevent them dropping their loads on comrades on the ground. 'The place stank because of the corpses,' wrote Edwin Rolfe, an American International Brigader. 'Enemy bombers returned to our position in the valley killing the wounded being evacuated and the stretcher-bearers, and attacking the wells ... The bullets whistled over our heads, red tracers which seemed to move slowly through the air ... It was the longest day of my life.'[17]

The experience was terrifying for those on the ground, but the last four weeks had also been disastrous for the Republic in the air, despite their absence from the Ebro front. The Condor Legion and the nationalists claimed for the month of July alone 76 republican aircraft destroyed and nine probables. But the battle of the Ebro provided an even better opportunity for the nationalists and their allies to destroy the republican air force once and for all.[18]

Rojo, Modesto and Tagüeña estimated that everything which had happened up to this point was a tactical victory. They had no doubt about the effect of the battle on an international audience as well as on the republican zone. But in fact the only thing they had achieved was to send their bull into the ring, with little chance of survival. Even if they had taken Gandesa, there would have been no further chance to advance because of the rapid concentration of nationalist troops against them. In this first week they had exhausted all their advantages, of surprise, speed and audacity.[19] Once again a great republican offensive collapsed without achieving its aims because of a lack of follow-through due to wasting time on crushing points of enemy resistance instead of pushing on towards the main objective. Yagüe's rapid reaction to the attack had given the nationalists enough time to bring up eight divisions of reinforcements. The situation of the republicans was even worse than that at Brunete. They had the river behind them and this created a far greater problem in bringing forward supplies and ammunition. There was also even less water for drinking.

On 1 August Modesto ordered the Army of the Ebro to go on to the defensive. They had lost 12,000 men to gain an area of desolate, scorched terrain of no strategic value. The heat increased. On 4 August the Condor Legion recorded temperatures of 37 degrees in the shade and 57 in the sun. Even the night brought little relief.[20] For the republicans, defence was hardly an easy option. It was impossible to dig trenches in the iron-hard earth and rocky landscape of the Terra Alta. They could protect themselves only with parapets and sangars made from stones, and they soon found that artillery shells were far more lethal in such surroundings than in open countryside for each explosion turned stones into shrapnel.

To continue the battle in such circumstances had no military justification at all, especially when the Republic was so vulnerable and there was no hope of achieving the original purpose of the offensive. But instead of withdrawing their best troops in good order to fight again, the republican command continued to send more men across the Ebro. And all this was because Negrín believed that the eyes of Europe were upon them and he could not acknowledge a defeat. Once again, political and propaganda considerations led to yet another self-inflicted disaster. The only consolation, perhaps, was that Franco was obsessed with destroying the force which had taken nationalist territory. The Army of the Ebro was thus saved the logical nationalist counter, an attack across the Segre in the rear of its right flank.[21]

Committed to a 'blind battle of sheep',[22] the nationalist forces were obliged to launch six counter-offensives against the republican positions. The first, which began on 6 August, was aimed against the bridgehead of Fayón defended by the 42nd Division. Over two days the Condor Legion flew 40 sorties against this target and dropped a total of 50 tons of bombs. 'The red losses are very high,' its war diary noted.[23] This onslaught lasted until 10 August, when the nationalists forced the republicans back across the river. The next attack, which began on 11 August, targeted the 11th Division in the Sierra de Pàndols. This was a bad decision, considering that the republicans occupied the high ground and could inflict heavy casualties on those climbing to the attack. For the next week the Condor Legion concentrated all its forces, including the Stukas, against bridges again to cut off supplies. Perhaps the nationalists counted on the fact that Líster's men were exhausted, dehydrated in the high temperatures and almost starving due to the interruption of their supplies. The shortage of water meant that they had to urinate into the water jackets round the barrels of their Maxim machine-guns.

During the day the bombs, shells and bullets never seemed to cease. The republicans had no choice but to wait for nightfall. Bodies could not be buried and there was no shade in that treeless waste.[24] The troops took it, the propaganda version goes, because they were disciplined anti-fascist fighters. The sceptic, on the other hand, might ponder the cold hysteria of commanders like Modesto and Líster, who were willing to shoot anyone 'who loses an inch of ground'. Their stubborn bravery, however, was more likely to have been an inarticulate expression of their hatred of the enemy.

On 13 August, during the nationalist assault on the Sierra de Pàndols, a deadly battle developed in the skies above the Terra Alta between the republican air force and nationalist fighters: three squadrons of Messerschmitts and a swarm of Fiats took on Chatos and Supermoscas, an up-gunned and up-engined version of the Soviet monoplane. Meanwhile the Heinkel 111s of the Condor Legion and the Junkers 52s of the Brigada Aérea Hispana continued to bomb the river crossings, when they were not acting as 'flying artillery' to hammer troop positions in the sierra.

The aerial battles were an unequal duel, with the republicans outnumbered by at least two to one. While the Moscas and Chatos in V formations fought with Fiats in the old-fashioned way, the Messerschmitt squadrons were trying out new tactics. They fought in pairs, a system later adopted by both sides during the battle of Britain. The great danger in such chaotic air battles was from collision or fire from friendly aircraft. The great nationalist air ace García Morato was shot down for the first time in the war by one of his own pilots.

On 18 August the nationalists again opened dams on the Segre. The wall of water, raising the level of the river by 3.5 metres, carried away the bridges at Flix, Móra d'Ebre and Ginestar. The next day 'the long-awaited' nationalist counter-attack began against the main Ebro bridgehead, with six divisions and a cavalry brigade. Condor Legion 88mm guns supported the ground troops, while the Stukas went for republican artillery batteries. The Heinkel 111 *Kampfgruppe* attacked the bridges again. The greatest success went to the Messerschmitt squadron, which shot down four Moscas (or Ratas as the nationalists called them) on that one day for no losses. One of the pilots was Oberleutnant Werner Mölders, later a great Luftwaffe ace of the Second World War. Having achieved fourteen kills in Spain, the highest score on the nationalist side, he became the first Luftwaffe fighter pilot to be credited with a hundred victories.[25]

Yagüe ordered his troops against the republican positions round Villalba dels Arcs and captured the heights of Gaeta. This time the nationalist planes dropped leaflets calling on the republicans to surrender, followed by heavy bombs. Over five days of fierce fighting Yagüe's divisions were hurled against well-defended positions manned by experienced troops who could deal with the waves of infantry. Nationalist tactics were often no better than those of the commanders on the republican side.

On 26 August Modesto was promoted to colonel, the first officer from the militia to achieve such rank. But the Army of the Ebro could do no more than hold on. Visits were paid by the friendly journalists of former battles: Hemingway, Matthews and Capa, but also Joseph North of the New York *Daily Worker*, Daniel Roosevelt of the *Brooklyn Daily Eagle*, Louis Fischer of *The Nation* and the German poet Ernst Toller.[26]

From the Coll del Moro, where Yagüe had his command post, General Franco studied the battlefield through his binoculars: on the right the Sierra de Pàndols; in the middle Gandesa and the sierras of Cavalls and Lavall de la Torre; Corbera on the left and beyond flowed the River Ebro on its last stretch to the sea. 'All within 35 kilometres', Franco said euphorically to his aide, Luis M. de Lojendio, 'I have the best of the red army trapped.'[27] But in Italy Mussolini did not see things in the same way. 'Today, 29 August,' he said to Ciano, 'I predict the defeat of Franco. That man either does not know how to make war or doesn't want to.'[28]

On 31 August the nationalists launched their third counter-offensive. It was aimed between Puig de l'Àliga and the road from Alcañiz to Tarragona. They wanted to take the Sierra de Cavalls at any cost and advance towards Corbera d'Ebre. Their frontline troops had now been reinforced with García Valiño's Maestrazgo Corps and stood at eight divisions, 300 guns, 500 aircraft and 100 tanks. Facing them were the 35th Division between Corbera and Gandesa, the 11th Division around Cavalls and the 43rd Division in Puig de l'Àliga. (According to Tagüeña, the telephone line from corps headquarters had to be repaired 83 times in a morning because of shell bursts.) Republican soldiers hung pieces of wood from their necks to bite on during the bombardments. Shell-shock and battle fatigue appear to have been far more prevalent on the republican than on the nationalist side, which was hardly surprising with the intensity of air bombardment.

On 3 September, exactly a year before the outbreak of the Second World War, the nationalists launched their fourth attack, this time against Líster's men in the sierra. After hammering the republican lines relentlessly with their artillery, the nationalists advanced from

Gandesa towards La Venta de Camposines and captured Corbera the following day. They had deployed 300 field guns on that sector as well as the German 88mm anti-aircraft guns firing directly at ground targets.[29]

During this attack Yagüe's forces managed to break the republican line on the boundary between the sectors of V Corps and XV Corps. Modesto had no choice but to throw in his only reserve, the 35th Division, to seal the breach. Modesto's orders at this time emphasize the madness of the republican decision to hold on. 'Not a single position must be lost. If the enemy takes one, there must be a rapid counter-attack and as much fighting as necessary, but always making sure that it remains in republican hands. Not a metre of ground to the enemy!'[30]

Two weeks later, between 19 and 26 September, the nationalists fought their way from rock to rock to take the heights of the Sierra de Cavalls, held by the exhausted soldiers of Modesto's army. Rojo was desperate because Menéndez, the commander of the Army of the Levante, and Miaja did nothing to launch an offensive on their side of the corridor to alleviate pressure on the Army of the Ebro. On 2 October, after capturing the heights of Lavall, the nationalists reached La Venta de Camposines. And a couple of weeks later they captured in a night attack Point 666, the key to the Sierra de Pàndols. They totally cleared the defensive position of Cavalls, leaving republican formations exposed, and carried out a pincer movement, with Yagüe attacking towards La Faterella and García Valiño in the direction of Ascó and Flix.

The republicans, after losing huge casualties, were left with only a small strip of territory on the right bank of the Ebro. At 4.30 in the morning of 16 November, taking advantage of a heavy river mist, the last men of the 35th Division recrossed the Ebro by the iron bridge at Flix. Fifteen minutes later Tagüeña gave the order to blow it up. 'A dry explosion, a flash, a thundering from fragments of iron falling into the water announced the end of the Battle of the Ebro, 113 days after its beginning.'[31] General Rojo supported Tagüeña's decision to withdraw. The mistake was not to have done it at least 100 days earlier. Modesto's Army of the Ebro had virtually ceased to exist. Its remnants returned to the same positions which they had occupied on 24 July.

The Terra Alta had been a harsh battlefield for a pitiless conflict – a summer counterpart to the winter horrors of Teruel.

The nationalists had sustained 60,000 casualties, the republicans 75,000, of whom 30,000 died, many of them unburied in the sierras which Modesto's army had been forced to abandon. Apart from the terrible loss of human life, almost all the weapons needed for the defence of Catalonia had been lost on this grotesque gamble.

Non-communist officers were the most vocal critics of the Ebro campaign and the way it had been handled. General Gámir Ulíbarri argued that the fall of Catalonia had taken place on the Ebro. Others, such as Colonel Perea, the commander of the Army of the East, who was furious with Rojo, had harsh words for the lack of military sense in the whole operation. The Comintern agents, on the other hand, tried to blame Rojo and the general staff. Togliatti informed Moscow that the Army of the Ebro had received no support from the central front because of 'sabotage and the malevolent action of General Miaja and the other commanders of the centre'.[32]

Following the distorting pattern of his usual Stalinist paranoia, Stepánov attacked the general staff and Rojo for having prolonged the operation, 'calculating that by exhausting the Army of the Ebro, they would debilitate and incapacitate it'.[33] The fact that the whole strategy had been agreed between Negrín and the communists, and the army had been commanded by a communist who refused to retreat, were of course ignored. So was the fact that the whole plan had been ill thought-out. To attack a sector so close to the bulk of the nationalist Army of Manoeuvre meant that the enemy could counter-attack rapidly; to choose to fight with a large river just behind your front line when the enemy had a crushing air superiority to smash your supply lines was idiotic; and to refuse to pull back after a week when it was clear that you had no chance of achieving your objective was bound to lead to the useless sacrifice of an army which could not be replaced. It was beyond military stupidity, it was the mad delusion of propaganda.

32

The Republic in the European Crisis

During the slaughter on the Ebro front, the vastly over-optimistic propaganda bulletins had raised exaggerated hopes in the rear areas. Even the normally pessimistic Azaña had been encouraged by the initial reports. But few people back in Barcelona realized that the offensive had in fact failed by 1 August.

Negrín, meanwhile, was attempting to impose an even more authoritarian stamp on his government. On 5 August he called a meeting of the council of ministers. He demanded their agreement to the confirmation of 58 death sentences; he presented a draft decree militarizing the war industries of Catalonia under the orders of the under-secretary of armaments; he set before them another decree planned to set up a special court to try those accused of smuggling and exporting capital; and he produced one more to militarize the emergency tribunals. But these measures provoked strong protests from five ministers, including Manuel de Irujo and Jaime Aiguader (the brother of the Artemi Aiguader involved in the events of May 1937). Irujo roundly attacked the activities of the SIM and the drift towards dictatorship, while Aiguader protested that Negrín's decree violated the Catalan statute of autonomy. Negrín, however, won the vote in the cabinet despite the protests. The censorship department tried to keep the affair quiet. Even Azaña was not informed of the confirmation of the death sentences. But when news of the clash leaked out, the communists hastened to attack the Basque Irujo and the Catalan Aiguader for being involved in 'a separatist plot'.

On 11 August Irujo and Aiguader resigned. The death sentences were carried out and two days later a shaken Azaña wrote in his diary, 'Tarradellas told me that yesterday they shot 58 people. Irujo sent me details. It's horrible. I feel indignation about the whole affair. Eight days after [I gave a speech] on pity and forgiveness, they kill 58. Without telling me anything nor seeking my opinion. I only found out from the press after the deed was done.'[1] Negrín, without turning a hair, left that night to visit the Ebro front.

Everyone began discussing the government crisis. *La Vanguardia* (perhaps at Negrín's own suggestion) published an article warning that a *coup d'état* might remove him and bring in a defeatist government to seek peace with the nationalists. Troops in communist formations were asked to send telegrams of support for the head of the government. On 16 August, in a meeting with Azaña which the president described as 'unforgettable', Negrín, in a scarcely veiled threat, brandished the claim that the leaders of the army were behind him. Certainly, the communists were. Two days before, *Frente Rojo* had proclaimed, 'Faced with all this manoeuvring, the workers, the soldiers, the whole people are firmly on the side of the government and its leader, Negrín.'

It can hardly have been a coincidence that on the day of Negrín's meeting with Azaña a military parade through the streets of Barcelona, with tanks and aircraft flying low overhead, was mounted by XVIII Army Corps, commanded by the communist José del Barrio. This blatant show of strength in the rear was especially provocative at a time when the republicans were fighting for their lives beyond the Ebro. Negrín's former liberal and social-democrat allies were outraged. Prieto condemned the prime minister for 'imposing his will over the composition of the government with a military show of strength through Barcelona streets'. Their protests were too late. In any case, Negrín's action was overshadowed by graver events. The appalling sacrifice on the Ebro was virtually ignored by Europe as it moved to the brink of war over Czechoslovakia in the late summer of 1938.

Negrín's next move represented a curious form of brinkmanship. He went to the residence of the president of Catalonia for a meeting. Apart from Companys, there were also present Tarradellas, Sbert, Bosch Gimpera and Pi y Súñer. Negrín announced that he was exhausted and intended to resign. He suggested that Companys should replace him. Negrín, a man of voracious appetites in women and food, apparently claimed to Companys (who related it to Azaña) that he was 'an animal and needed his hands free for his desires. Every ten days, a new woman.'[2]

Companys, although having fiercely attacked Negrín, said that he should continue to lead the government of the Republic, yet maintain a dialogue with the Generalitat to sort out their differences. In fact, there was no possible alternative to Negrín. His close alliance with the communists remained the only way to prevent the military machine, then involved in the most desperate battle of the whole war, from becoming totally paralysed. Yet there was little chance of agreement over Catalan autonomy. Negrín was almost as much of a centralist as Franco. 'I am not fighting Franco', he had said in July, 'so that a stupid and childish separatism resurfaces. I am fighting the war for Spain and on behalf of Spain ... There is only one nation: Spain!'[3]

Negrín decided to form a new government, but he restricted the changes in his cabinet to replacing Aiguader and Irujo with José Moix of the Catalan communist PSUC and Tomás Bilbao, of Acción Nacionalista Vasca. He then left for Zurich, officially to take part in an international medical conference, but also to have secret talks either with 'some pro-Franco Germans', according to Azaña,[4] or with the German ambassador to France, Count Welczek, according to Hugh Thomas,[5] or as has often been said with the Duke of Alba, to try to find a negotiated settlement of the war. Whichever the case, Negrín was attempting to find a way to finish the war while attacking his opponents as defeatists.

The Anglo-Italian treaty of April 1938, which signified the tacit acceptance of Italian intervention, had been a serious blow to the Republic's hopes of winning international support. The Munich agreement of September was far more serious. This climax of appeasement did not only signify that British policy towards Spain would not change, it also led to Stalin's decision that the Soviet Union's best interests lay in a *rapprochement* with Hitler. Soviet support for the Republic was starting to be an embarrassment.

The Munich agreement marked, too, the postponement of the European war on which Negrín was counting to force Great Britain and France to aid the Republic. In fact, it was rash of him to believe that even then their intervention would have been worth much. There would be little incentive for the British government to aid a severely weakened Republic at a time when all available armaments would be needed for its own forces. Moreover, active participation would have exposed Gibraltar to Franco's forces before a programme for improving the Rock's defences had started.

On the other hand the Republic's other potential ally, France, was starting to resent the British government's domination of its foreign policy. The French had been forced consistently from one compromise to another in what they had thought was the cause of democratic unity. Yet Chamberlain was in some ways closer to Franco, Mussolini and Hitler in his belief that France was politically and morally decadent. Fear of their traditional German enemy, combined with resentment against the anti-French attitude prevalent in the British government, had made even some conservative army officers feel they should intervene in Catalonia on the Republic's behalf. But the French general staff was firmly opposed to any move which might result in a war on two fronts. It was therefore greatly relieved, during the Czechoslovakian crisis, when Franco (on British advice) assured them of Spanish neutrality in the event of a European war, and also gave his guarantee that Axis troops would not approach the Pyrenean frontier. Ciano was sickened by this pandering to France, but the German and Italian regimes were at least reassured that France, as well as Great Britain, would do nothing to hinder their intervention in Spain. Yet Franco, as already mentioned, continued to fear it obsessively.

In fact, the proceedings of the Non-Intervention Committee had never given them cause for alarm. The sittings continued as before, despite the Anglo-Italian pact in April. 'The entire negotiation in the committee', the German representative reported, 'has something unreal about it since all participants see through the game of the other side ... The non-intervention policy is so unstable and is such an artificial creation that everyone fears to cause its collapse by a clear "no", and then have to bear the responsibility.'[6] The plan for the withdrawal of volunteers, which the British had originated as a formula to retard the granting of belligerent rights, had been undermined in the Anglo-Italian pact. Lord Halifax had deemed a partial withdrawal of troops sufficient to satisfy the spirit of the non-intervention agreement.

Franco had been unsure how to react to the revised British plan for the withdrawal of foreign forces from Spain, once it had been agreed by the committee in London on 5 July. He had asked his allies for advice, and they counselled him to accept in principle, but delay in practice. On 26 July Negrín's government accepted the withdrawal proposals, even though it was deeply disturbed at the prospect of the nationalists' being awarded belligerent rights. This meant that even ships flying the

British flag would become liable to search, thus allowing the blockade to become completely effective. Eventually, on 16 August, Franco made his reply to the British representative, Robert Hodgson. He demanded belligerent rights before the British minimum figure for withdrawal of 10,000 men on each side had been reached. His attitude was almost certainly encouraged by the fact that the British had pressured the French into closing the frontier to republican war matériel.

Against this background, Negrín made a speech to the League of Nations on 21 September to announce the unconditional withdrawal of the International Brigades. His surprise gesture had little of the dramatic effect upon which he had counted to focus sympathy for the Republic. Concern over the Czechoslovakian crisis, then reaching a climax, had turned Spain into a sideshow which diplomats in Geneva preferred to forget, since it was an embarrassing reminder of the worst aspects of international relations. Ciano was perplexed by Negrín's move. 'Why are they doing this?' he asked in his diary. 'Do they feel themselves so strong? Or is it merely a demonstration of a platonic nature? So far as we are concerned, I think this robs our partial evacuation of some of its flavour. But it has the advantage that the initiative is not made to appear ours – this would certainly have lent itself to disagreeable comments about Italian weariness, betrayal of Franco, etc.'[7]

Mussolini, on the other hand, although infuriated at times by Franco's 'serene optimism' and his 'flabby conduct of the war', offered fresh divisions. At that stage there were about 40,000 Italian troops in Spain. Eventually it was agreed that the best of them should stay and be concentrated in one over-strength division, while the remainder would be repatriated. In order to make up for this withdrawal, Mussolini promised additional aircraft and artillery, which were what Franco had really wanted in the first place. The Italian government was then able to point to its infantry withdrawals and insist on the implementation of the Anglo-Italian pact. Chamberlain asked for a brief delay, so that it would not look to the House of Commons, in Ciano's words, 'as if Mussolini has fixed the date'. This was necessary as Italian attacks on ships flying the British flag had continued sporadically. The first Italian troops disembarked in Naples to an orchestrated welcome on 20 October. Lord Perth asked permission for his military attaché to witness the event, which prompted Ciano to note, 'No objection in principle on our part – so long as the thing is useful to Chamberlain for the parliamentary debates.'[8]

Ciano had every reason to feel that he could afford to be patronizing in the wake of Munich. The prospect of a European war (which had frightened both Mussolini and Ciano, despite all their bombastic statements) had receded. Mussolini claimed that 'with the conquest of Prague, we had already practically captured Barcelona'. This remark underlines the way that Britain had sacrificed the Spanish Republic in its misguided desperation to avoid war, just as it went on to sacrifice the Czechs. Soviet policy towards the Republic changed from cautious support to active disengagement. The betrayal of Czechoslovakia finally convinced Stalin that he could not count on Great Britain and France as allies against Hitler and so must cover his vulnerability by an alliance with Germany. But it would be misleading to link the fate of the Republic entirely with that of Czechoslovakia. The final destruction of the Republic's hope of survival had begun with the fighting across the Ebro, at least a month before the Munich agreement.

Chamberlain, however, was convinced that the Munich agreement had been a diplomatic triumph. He was so pleased with his efforts that, just before Mussolini and Ciano left Munich, he suggested 'the possibility of a Conference of Four to solve the Spanish problem'.[9] Evidently he felt that the Spanish republicans could be made to see reason like the Czechs and be persuaded to sacrifice themselves in the cause of what he thought was European stability. The late 1930s were years in which statesmen were particularly tempted to cultivate inflated ideas of their diplomatic abilities. A diplomatic coup in times of tension offers the dazzling prospect of political stardom. As Anthony Eden commented about Chamberlain, 'This is a form of adulation to which Prime Ministers must expect to be subject: it is gratifying to indulge, and hard to resist.' This observation was also true of Negrín who, perhaps because of his undeniable talents in many fields, gravely overestimated what could be achieved by personal reputation and the power of persuasion. It is difficult otherwise to understand how he could have taken such an unjustified gamble as the Ebro offensive to serve as the backing for his diplomatic ventures.

In fact, Negrín's declaration on 21 September to the League of Nations did not represent a great sacrifice for the Republic because the number of foreigners serving in the ranks of the People's

Army had greatly reduced already. The 'International Military Commission to Observe the Withdrawal of non-Spanish combatants in Government Spain' observed, 'It may be said that the decision of the Negrín government to withdraw and send away the international volunteers and to let this happen under the supervision of the League of Nations was a way to make a virtue out of necessity.'[10] It was an astute propaganda move, because both the Republic and the nationalists had greatly exaggerated their role. In September 1938, only 7,102 foreigners were left in the International Brigades. The balance had been made up with Spaniards.

The stories of communist heresy hunting and the treatment of volunteers who wanted to leave, which had circulated in the second half of 1937, affected recruiting so seriously that the handfuls of new arrivals had done little to replace the losses suffered at Teruel and in Aragón. (The death rate among non-Spaniards in the International Brigades was just under 15 per cent up to the end of the Aragón campaign according to Soviet army statistics. A total casualty rate of 40 per cent is the figure most frequently cited.) The international military commission, which supervised their withdrawal, was later surprised to find how old many of the foreign volunteers were. The Swedish Colonel Ribbing paid particular attention to his own countrymen. 'As for the *Swedes*, whom I checked in Sant Quirze de Besuara, I noted: "Remarkably many in and around their forties."'[11]

On the Ebro front, Negrín's plan to withdraw foreigners was not communicated to the Americans, Canadians and British of XV International Brigade, because they were about to attack Point 401 on the following day and the news might affect their morale. During the last week of September, the survivors were brought back from the front to Barcelona for their official farewell, although more than half of them were given Spanish nationality and transferred to the People's Army. They usually consisted of those men for whom the secret police would be waiting in their home country: Germans, Italians, Hungarians and those from other dictatorships in Europe and Latin America.[12]

André Marty, however, rewrote the last editorial of the International Brigade newspaper, *Volunteer for Liberty*, telling the 'antifascist fighters' to return to their home countries to lead the struggle against fascism there. It was a way of saying that only selected senior cadres would be given refuge in the USSR. Marty was also terrified that proof of his summary executions might threaten him in the future, and headquarters personnel at Albacete only just escaped with their lives in his mania to suppress the truth.[13]

On 28 October, seven weeks after their withdrawal from the front, the International Brigades assembled for a dramatic farewell parade down the Diagonal in Barcelona past President Azaña, Negrín, Companys and General Rojo, along with many other republican leaders. There were 300,000 people lining the streets and aircraft flew overhead ready to defend them against a nationalist raid. La Pasionaria said in her speech, 'Comrades of the International Brigades! Political reasons, reasons of state, the welfare of that same cause for which you offered your blood with boundless generosity, are sending you back, some of you to your own countries and others to forced exile. You can go proudly. You are history. You are legend. You are the heroic example of democracy's solidarity and universality. We shall not forget you and, when the olive tree of peace puts forth its leaves again, mingled with the laurels of the Spanish Republic's victory – come back!'[14]

It was a moving occasion. Even the passionless expression on a huge portrait of the Soviet leader who was secretly considering an alliance with Hitler could not belittle the emotion of internationalism which made the tears of the Brigaders and the crowd flow. They were leaving behind 9,934 dead, 7,686 missing and had suffered 37,541 wounded.[15]

The international commission overseeing the withdrawal of foreign volunteers was clearly shocked later to find about 400 International Brigaders in prisons in and around Barcelona, including Montjuich and the 'Carlos Marx' prison. Colonel Ribbing, the Swedish member of the commission, reported, 'As regards the international volunteers, they had sometimes been convicted for pure trifles, sometimes for definite and seriously undisciplined behaviour. Many stated that they were accused of espionage or sabotage; most of them protested their complete innocence.' Even though the Negrín government had agreed to the repatriation of International Brigade prisoners as well, the commission found that there were still around 400 of them held in mid January 1939, just as the nationalists were advancing on Barcelona. This was more probably due to incompetence or bureaucratic inertia in a chaotic situation than to a deliberate attempt to leave them to the mercies of the enemy.[16]

The beginning of the departure of foreign communists in the second half of 1938 did not change Party policy outwardly. The Spanish communists may have been relieved that the exporters of the show-trial paranoia were returning home but this is uncertain. Spanish communist leaders later claimed that they had on several occasions argued against the orders of Moscow, not necessarily because they disliked Soviet methods, but because they considered them to be 'premature', as La Pasionaria put it. There is, however, little evidence of this claimed opposition in Russian files. More strikingly, there is nothing to show in the Comintern files that Dimitrov ever warned the Soviet advisers in Spain that their urge to take over the government completely was against Stalin's policy of reassuring the bourgeois democracies.

On his return from Zurich, Negrín summoned the Cortes to a meeting in the monastery of Sant Cugat del Vallès above Barcelona on 30 September and 1 October. The head of the government gave a speech in which he paid tribute to the soldiers who had died on the Ebro, without admitting, of course, that the plan had been disastrous. He then reviewed the governmental crisis, the relationship between the central government and the Generalitat, and re-emphasized the slogan 'to resist is to win'. He did not mention his own secret attempts to find a negotiated solution, but proclaimed his readiness to seek an agreement with the nationalists on the basis of his Thirteen Points, even though they were clearly unacceptable to Franco.

Many of the deputies did not hide their concerns at Negrín's designs. He had also made veiled references, which Prieto and Zugazagoitia interpreted as a threat to resign. After an adjournment in which Negrín assembled his ministers and spoke of a new governmental crisis which could be definitive, he recalled the Cortes and took up the debate again in violent terms. Faced with his hard position, opposition collapsed and the chamber gave him a vote of confidence, although this was, as Zugazagoitia later wrote, 'without enthusiasm and out of necessity. Negrín and the parliament recognized that they were enemies.'[17]

The trial of the POUM leaders[18] began on 11 October before the Tribunal of Espionage and High Treason, over fifteen months after the murder of Andreu Nin. Most Spanish communists realized that, although the process set in motion had to be followed through, it was unwise to be implacable. Even so, a remarkably unsubtle case was presented based on crudely forged documents linking the POUM to a nationalist spy organization in Perpignan. The communists also prepared a reserve line by adding the events of May 1937 to their charge of high treason. They claimed that the POUM had made a 'non-aggression pact with the enemy' so that their 29th Division could participate in the Barcelona fighting. The trials ended in something of a compromise verdict. The Republic's reputation could not be dragged through the mud at such a moment by a show trial, so the most outrageous charges were rejected; but the POUM's role in the events of Barcelona was used to justify imprisoning its leaders.

The onset of winter in republican Spain was bleak. Food supplies had diminished even further, and industrial production was down to about one-tenth of 1936 levels as a result of raw material shortages and the lack of electricity in Barcelona. There was little fuel for heating. Cigarettes and soap had been generally unobtainable for many months. Defeatism was rife and even those who had, in desperation, convinced themselves that the struggle would eventually end in victory could not now avoid the truth. They realized that the next battle would be the last and faced the prospect with bitter resignation.

In Barcelona the population was by now on the edge of starvation. The ration, if obtainable, was down to about 100 grams of lentils per day as winter approached. People collapsed from hunger in the bomb-scarred streets and diseases such as scurvy increased. The propaganda broadcasts sounded increasingly hollow to their ears. They kept going only because there seemed to be no alternative. Workers weak from lack of food carried on in factories with virtually no electricity or raw materials for the same reason that the army kept fighting: it was less painful than thinking about the consequences of stopping.

In late November and early December Negrín's government issued more mobilization decrees. They served little purpose because there were no spare weapons. Many of the new conscripts went home again, despite the shooting of deserters. Only a tiny proportion were caught because the administration was unable to cope with the new intake.

Even the army, where morale was usually higher than in the rearguard, looked beaten before the battle of Catalonia began,

December 1937.
The winter fighting
of Teruel.

An International Brigade
officer at Teruel.

Prieto (third from right) observes the fighting at Teruel.

The nationalists' devastating offensive in Aragón, 1938. Condor Legion Stukas with nationalist markings.

Panzer Mark Is advancing.

On 15 April 1938, the nationalists reach the sea at Vinaròs cutting the republican zone in two.

Summer 1938. Condor Legion 37mm anti-aircraft guns were also found to be effective against tanks and vehicles.

Republican soldiers under bombardment during the Battle of the Ebro.

A republican hospital train behind the Ebro front, summer 1938.

General Rojo (left) Juan Negrín (second left) and Líster (fourth left) at a farewell parade for the International Brigades, October 1938.

The anti-communist coup of March 1939, which ended the war. Colonel Casado (left) listens while Julián Besteiro broadcasts the manifesto of the National Council of Defence.

Republican refugees swarm across the French frontier in the Pyrenees, January 1939.

Republican prisoners in the French internment camp of Le Vernet.

19 May 1939. Condor Legion standard dipped in salute to Franco at the victory parade.

The indoctrination of republican orphans.

October 1940. Hitler and Franco meet at La Hendaye, a photo-montage after the event.

The Spanish Blue Division in Russia on the Leningrad front.

though this did not mean that they could not once again astonish the enemy with actions of brilliant and ferocious resistance. Apart from some 75,000 men dead or wounded on the Ebro, the republican forces in Catalonia had little equipment left. The Army of the Ebro and the Army of the East, with an estimated total strength of more than a quarter of a million men, were left with only 40 tanks, fewer than 100 field guns, 106 aircraft (of which only about a half were serviceable, due to a shortage of spare parts) and only 40,000 rifles to face the nationalist onslaught.

Soviet advisers, meanwhile, appear to have been taking things easily. Perhaps they thought that with the Republic's imminent defeat, they would not be in Spain for much longer and should therefore enjoy their 'holiday' while they could. 'Things are still the same with me,' an interpreter wrote home, 'that is, things are very good. I've turned into an inveterate gambler (dominoes), we play "goat" in the evenings. We listen to the gramophone ... My appetite clearly isn't normal (it is too great) ... One takes a nap after lunch, for an hour or two, that's why I've put on weight ... I am reading a lot here.'[19]

Negrín, however, was thinking about the future, but not discussing anything with his ministers. As Gerö pointed out to Dimitrov, 'the ministers complain that they cannot see Negrín and cannot resolve questions about their departments with him'.[20] In fact, Negrín appears to have been seeing only leading communists and Soviet officials. In an interview on 17 November with Marchenko, the Soviet chargé d'affaires, Negrín raised 'the question of our neighbouring workers in Spain', a euphemism for the NKVD. He said that 'a connection between Comrade Kotov and his workers with the Ministry of Internal Affairs and the SIM was inexpedient. He proposed that Comrade Kotov maintain an indirect connection with him, Negrín, because he is creating a special apparatus attached to him. The fact that Negrín, who is always extremely delicate with regard to our people, considered it necessary to make such a remark undoubtedly indicates the great pressure on him from the Socialist Party, the anarchists and especially the agents of the Second International concerning the "interference" of our people in police and counter-intelligence work.'[21]

At another meeting on 10 December, Negrín outlined his far from democratic vision, which was entirely in agreement with communist policy. He had discussed with Díaz and Uribe the idea of 'a united national front, which seemed to him to be a sort of distinctive new party. This idea came to him after he lost faith in the possibility of uniting the socialist and communist parties ... The most that might be expected is that the Socialist Party will be absorbed by the Communist Party at the end of the war.' Negrín realized that to 'depend on the Communist Party is unfavourable from the international standpoint. The existing republican parties have no future. The Popular Front does not have a common discipline and is torn apart by inter-party struggle. What is needed, therefore, is an organization that would unify all that is best in all of the parties and organizations and would represent a fundamental support of the government ... There is no returning to the old parliamentarism; it will be impossible to allow the "free play" of parties as it existed earlier, for in this case the right might once again force its way into power. This means that either a unified political organization or a military dictatorship is necessary. He does not see any other way.'[22] Negrín's plan for a 'National Front' party was more or less a left-wing counterpart to what Franco had achieved with his Movimiento Nacional.

33
The Fall of Catalonia

At the beginning of December, two weeks after the last republican units slipped back across the Ebro, the nationalist Army of Manoeuvre redeployed along the two river frontiers of the Republic's north-eastern zone. The republican general staff, foreseeing this development, prepared the defence of Catalonia and planned attacks in the west and south to divert the enemy's attention.[1]

Negrín also had to pay attention to feelings in the rearguard. Very few parties supported his policy of resistance to the very end. The republican alliance was split between his supporters, chiefly the communists,[2] and the other factions led by Prieto, Largo Caballero and Besteiro. Besteiro in particular disliked Negrín's position. On 16 November he had left Madrid for Barcelona to see the president of the Republic. He told Azaña of his conviction that Negrín was completely bound up with the communists. At the executive committee of the Socialist Party he had said to the head of government, 'I consider you to be an agent of the communists.'[3]

During a dinner with the new British representative, R. C. Shrine Stevenson, Negrín managed to convince him that his attitude to communism was purely a question of necessity. Stevenson reported to Lord Halifax afterwards how Negrín argued that communism was the wrong ideology for Spaniards. The republican government had only worked with the communists because they were the best organized force in the early days, and because the Soviet Union was the only country which had been able to provide solid support. The communists had been the most enthusiastic and energetic in their support of the government, and for that reason the government needed them, but if the Republic could obtain from France and Britain what it needed, then as soon as that happened, he could crush the Communist Party in a week.[4] But these sentiments which Negrín expressed are rather hard to reconcile with his own approach on 10 December to the communists about forming a United National Front to have done with party politics.

At the beginning of January Negrín tried again to persuade the French to help the Republic *in extremis*. On 7 January he travelled in secret to Paris where he met the British and the American ambassadors as well as seeing Georges Bonnet, the foreign minister. He told them that in order to resist, they needed 2,000 machine-guns and 100,000 rifles.[5] The French authorities not only failed to reply to this desperate and ingenuous request. Bonnet collaborated with Franco's representative in Paris, Quiñones de León, in partially blocking the last delivery of Soviet arms which reached Bordeaux on 15 January.[6]

Faced with the huge nationalist concentration of forces on the River Segre, the republican general staff put into effect its plan of diversionary attacks, agreed on 6 December. On 8 December republican forces advanced on the Córdoba-Peñarroya front towards Seville, while another effort was to be made on the north side of the Estremaduran front. An amphibious assault in reinforced brigade strength was also planned for the same day against the Andalucian coast near Motril, but it was called off just as the troops were ready to leave. The Estremaduran offensive did not begin for another four weeks, by which time the nationalist onslaught on Catalonia had commenced.

The nationalist offensive in the east was due to begin on 10 December, but torrential rain forced a postponement. Franco did not want to take any risk and insisted that flying conditions should be good enough for their 'flying artillery' to operate. The nationalists had deployed 340,000 men, around 300 tanks, more than 500 aircraft and 1,400 guns. Their only concern was the danger of a desperate resistance in Barcelona. The Italians were once again in two minds. 'Things seem to be going well and the campaign in Catalonia could have a decisive character,' wrote Ciano in his diary on 6 December. 'I am a little sceptical. This phrase has been used too many times to be believable.'[7]

Meanwhile, foreign statesmen like Roosevelt, who admitted that the arms embargo 'had been a grave mistake',[8] and Churchill and Eden, who had previously held aloof in disapproval of the Republic, now realized what its extinction signified. The few democracies left on the Continent included France, Switzerland, the Low

Countries and Scandinavia; even the pessimists did not imagine that most of these had only eighteen months left. Attempts to mediate in Spain were made by many foreign governments, but Franco rejected all approaches. The attitude of the British government left him feeling secure enough to continue to insist on belligerent rights before volunteers were withdrawn. Italian infantry he could do without, but the Condor Legion was his guarantee of victory.

The eventual outcome of the campaign was hardly in doubt, short of French intervention. Ciano warned London on 5 January (soon after the despatch of more Italian fighters and artillery) that 'if the French move, it will be the end of non-intervention. We will send regular divisions. That is to say, we will make war on France on Spanish soil.'[9] His posturing proved unnecessary, for Lord Halifax immediately told Paris once again that if the Axis powers were provoked over Spain, Great Britain would not help France. Franco's concern that Catalonia might declare itself independent and ask for French protection was also groundless. Negrín was almost as much of a centralist as he himself was. There was never a serious possibility of French troops being sent to intervene, despite the dramatic mutterings of those Frenchmen who felt humiliated by the betrayal of Czechoslovakia.

The nationalist air forces had benefited from having more than a month to reorganize for the Catalonian campaign. Nearly 400 new Spanish pilots, fresh from flying school, were posted to the Fiat squadrons. At the same time the Condor Legion began to hand over the Messerschmitt 109b fighters to the more experienced Spanish pilots, as their own squadrons were to be re-equipped with the 109e. Another Spanish squadron was equipped with the Heinkel 112, which had been beaten by the Messerschmitt in the Luftwaffe comparison trials. The Italians tried to rush in their latest fighter, the Fiat G.50 monoplane, to be battle-tested in the closing stages, but it never saw action.[10]

To face this force the seven republican fighter squadrons now had far fewer Moscas than Chatos. This was because the Moscas had to come from the Soviet Union. Only Chatos were manufactured at Sabadell. The 45 aircraft which they produced in the last three months of 1938 did little to make up their losses over the Ebro. Republican ground forces were suffering from an acute shortage of spare parts in almost every field, and machines, weapons and vehicles were being cannibalized ruthlessly so as to ensure a bare operational presence.

On the eve of the battle for Catalonia, the Republic's eastern army group mustered 220,000 men, of whom only 140,000 were in organized mixed brigades.[11] Many were without rifles. Of their 250 field guns, half were unserviceable and few of their 40 tanks were in battleworthy condition.

The nationalists deployed along the Segre the newly formed Army Corps of Urgel, commanded by Muñoz Grandes, the Army Corps of Maestrazgo, commanded by García Valiño, and the Army Corps of Aragón, commanded by Moscardó. Near the confluence of the Segre with the Ebro was the renamed Cuerpo Legionario Italiano, mustering 55,000 men under General Gambara, and Solchaga's Army Corps of Navarre, while Yagüe's Army Corps of Morocco was concentrated along the Ebro. The priority given to the Segre showed that the nationalist general staff had at last learned that that was their best start line. It is not hard to detect the hand of General Vigón in this improvement.

Despite the Vatican appeal for a Christmas truce, the nationalist offensive was launched on 23 December. It was a bright, cold day, with snow showers, a contrast to the rain and wind of the previous two weeks. The Navarre Corps and the Italians attacked from their bridgeheads towards Montblanc and Valls, supported by the Condor Legion. They were faced by the 56th Division of XII Corps. Although these *carabineros* were the best armed in the People's Army, they withdrew immediately. The breach in the line led to the collapse of that sector and allowed the *requetés* and Italians to penetrate sixteen kilometres towards Granadella in the rear of the Ebro front. The next day they entered Mayals, although on 25 December their advance was blocked by formations from V and XV Corps.

Also on the morning of 23 December the nationalists made another major attack on the left flank, south of Tremp, aiming for Artesa de Segre and Cervera. Then the Corps of Maestrazgo and that of Urgel, backed by a massive artillery bombardment, came up against the 26th Division, the former Durruti column, which maintained, according to Rojo, a 'magnificent resistance', and only conceded a little ground. A breakthrough on the western flank would have been catastrophic. After five days of heavy fighting, General Vigón felt obliged to change the main point of attack to the sector of Balaguer, some 30 kilometres downstream. He moved the Aragón Corps there and ordered the Maestrazgo to advance along the south bank of the bend in the Segre with maximum artillery support, all the available tanks and three anti-aircraft detachments of the Condor Legion.[12]

The real threat to Catalonia remained the thrust near the corner of the two fronts, where the Italians and the Carlists were fighting a reconstituted corps under Líster. This force, particularly the 11th Division, managed to slow the nationalists near Granadella on Christmas Day. Both they and the other formations defending the Ebro had been extremely fortunate that Yagüe's troops were held back by floodwater from the Pyrenees. But the war in the air had also been going badly for the Republic. Nearly a whole squadron of Natashas were wiped out in one battle on Christmas Eve, and about 40 fighters had been lost in the first ten days of the campaign. Only a handful of fragmented squadrons remained.

The crucial day was 3 January 1939. Solchaga's Carlists pushed forward to reach the Borjas Blancas–Montblanc road, some 50 kilometres behind the Ebro front. Also on that day the offensive from the Balaguer sector overran the key town of Artesa. Yagüe's troops finally crossed the Ebro and established a bridgehead opposite Asco in the centre of the bulge which had been occupied by the People's Army in the autumn.

Over the next few days the two Army Corps of Urgel and Maestrazgo widened their salient in the middle of the Segre front, while the Aragón Corps advanced from Lérida to protect the left flank of the Italians in their attack on Borges Blanques, which fell on 5 January. The Italians were fighting much better than on previous occasions. Richthofen, however, retained his rather jaundiced view. '5 January. Artesa taken,' he wrote in his diary. 'Hard resistance. Today the offensive in [the west] started. Hopefully, Franco will keep his nerve.'[13]

That morning, in Estremadura, the republicans' XXII Corps launched a surprise attack and broke the nationalist front line in the Hinojosa del Duque sector, opening a breach eight kilometres long. On the following day the republicans managed to break the second line and occupied Fuenteovejuna, but the bulk of the nationalist troops, some 80,000 men backed up by 100 guns, halted them at the Hill of the Saints, preventing them from reaching Peñarroya.

*

In Catalonia, General Solchaga's troops took Vinaixa on 6 January, but Richthofen was unimpressed. He sent an ultimatum to General Vigón. 'If tomorrow Agramunt is not attacked then the Condor Legion will not provide support any longer.'[14] The next day, he wrote, '7 January. Corps Valiño fails again. Three times the reds are thrown from their positions by [German] flak and air attack. Instead of the possible fifteen kilometres only two kilometres are taken. Of the whole Corps comprising 36 battalions, only two battalions attack.' Richthofen saw this as 'bad faith' and ceased operations, because he considered that the nationalists were letting the Condor Legion do all the work. The next day at a meeting he told Franco, Dávila and Vigón what he thought about the lack of Spanish leadership at Artesa. 'Good troops and miserable generals who are only battalion commanders, which is a natural consequence of the way things develop here. The Spaniards complain that they could relieve commanders but they do not have better ones.'

On 9 January the Aragón Corps and Gambara's Italians joined up at Mollerusa. The republican V and XV Corps were unable to block the Carlist *requetés* and the Italians. The northern part of the Ebro front collapsed in disorder with this threat to its rear. It was a bitter ending for those who had fought so hard for so little on the Ebro.

The day before, 8 January, the nationalists had begun the second phase of their offensive with the bombardment of Montsant. On 12 January they took Montblanc. On 13 January the republicans suffered another disaster. 'Our fighters destroy ten red fighters on the airfield at Vendrell,' Richthofen noted.[15] On 14 January the nationalists took Valls. Solchaga's Carlist troops turned south towards Tarragona, which was being battered by the Condor Legion. At dusk on 15 January the Navarre Corps joined up round Tarragona with the Moroccan Corps, which had just carried out another of its 50-kilometre forced marches, all the way from Tortosa in a single day. The Aragón and Maestrazgo Corps managed to take Cervera at the same time.

The nationalists had taken 23,000 prisoners and inflicted casualties of 5,000 dead and 40,000 wounded. The battle of Catalonia was already decided after a third of the territory was conquered, yet Franco did not want to repeat the mistake of the Aragón campaign: he intended never to allow the enemy a real chance to reorganize.

Meanwhile, in Estremadura the republican offensive had come to a halt in heavy rain after taking some 500 square kilometres. The attack never managed to gain momentum again, mainly because of enemy aircraft, but also because the tanks and guns were bogged down in the mud. The nationalists counter-attacked and seized back Peraleda del Saucejo on 22 January and three days later retook Fuenteovejuna.

In Catalonia the republican general staff had designated fall-back lines, but they were purely theoretical. 'Only when Tarragona fell', wrote Stepánov, 'did we realize that there was no Maginot Line round Barcelona, as some of our military leaders seemed to think. There was not even a kilometre of trenches.'[16]

The republican authorities had called up reserves on 9 January from the classes of 1922 and 1942, and a week later they ordered the general mobilization of all citizens of both sexes between 17 and 55 years old. All industry and transport was also militarized.[17] But these measures came far too late to have any effect. They were just gestures of defiance. The republican forces found themselves outnumbered six to one. Many were out of ammunition or without weapons. A defence of the city was also impossible because the morale and determination of 1936 had completely disappeared. Resistance might have taken place only if the city was surrounded, but an escape route to the French frontier remained open.

Since the fall of Tarragona the nationalist air forces never ceased bombing the city, yet Franco was still nervous about French intervention. On 17 January Richthofen had to reassure him again that it was simply too late for them to send in troops. The nationalists and their allies were now convinced that they could prosecute the campaign to the bitter end without the slightest worry of international reaction.

On the republican side, Negrín called an emergency meeting of the council of ministers on 18 January, to which Companys and Martínez Barrio were also invited. He proclaimed a state of war after two and a half years of fighting, a curiously empty gesture. For Federica Montseny, as for almost everyone else, the war was clearly lost. 'The Spanish people could do no more,' she wrote.

'Any solution aimed at saving lives ... seemed to us to be a collective salvation.'[18]

On the morning of 22 January General Rojo told Negrín that the front had ceased to exist.[19] The same day Negrín ordered all government departments to abandon Barcelona and make their way to Gerona and Figueras. The divisions of Solchaga and Yagüe were crossing the River Llobregat, the two corps of Muñoz Grandes and of García Valiño were attacking Sabadell and Tarrasa, while Gambara's Italians were advancing on Badalona. 'Barcelona, 48 hours before the entrance of the enemy,' wrote Rojo, 'was a dead city.'[20]

On the night of 25 January, Lluís Companys rang his friend Josep Andreu i Abelló, president of the Appeal Court of Catalonia, to invite him to dinner. Afterwards the two men drove to the centre of the old town through deserted streets. Leaflets appealing for resistance to the bitter end blew in the wind, along with identity cards that had been thrown away. 'It was a night which I will never forget,' recounted Abelló many years later. 'The silence was total, a terrible silence, of the sort which comes at the culminating point of a tragedy. We went to the Plaza de Sant Jaume and we made our farewell to the Generalitat and the city. It was two in the morning. The vanguard of the nationalist army was already in Tibidabo and close to Montjuich. We never believed that we would return.'[21]

Companys would return, but against his will, when the Gestapo found him in France in the autumn of the following year. He would be handed over to nationalist representatives and brought back over the border. The president of the Generalitat was to be declared guilty of 'military rebellion', sentenced to death and executed in the moat of Montjuich on 15 October 1940.

A large part of the population of Barcelona, seized by fear, abandoned the city. So many documents were being burned around the city that many minor fires broke out.[22] Shops were looted by people wanting food to take with them on the hard journey ahead. The coast road eastwards was jammed with buses, heavy lorries, vans, motor cars and horse-drawn carts piled with mattresses and domestic utensils, trunks and suitcases as well as exhausted women and children. Some men pushed their family belongings on hand-carts, but it was hard to see them having the strength to cross the Pyrenees.

The military convoys full of soldiers cast an even greater shadow over the sadness of departure. Teresa Pàmies, a young militant of the communist PSUC, described what she saw: 'Of the flight from Barcelona on 26 January, I will never be able to forget the wounded who crawled out of the Vallcarca hospital. Mutilated and covered in bandages, half-naked despite the cold, they pushed themselves towards the road, yelling pleas that they should not be left behind to fall into the hands of the victors ... Those who had lost their legs crawled along the ground, those who had lost an arm raised the other with a clenched fist, the youngest crying in fear, the older ones shouting in rage and cursing those of us who were fleeing and were abandoning them.'[23]

Also on 26 January the fifth column, right-wing men and women who had remained hidden for two and a half years, appeared in the streets to settle accounts. They mixed with the advance detachments of nationalist troops entering the city, particularly Yagüe's *regulares*, who were allowed several days of looting – their 'war tax' – in shops and apartment buildings, without worrying whether the owners were reds or whites. Although the republicans had released most of their prisoners before the downfall, the nationalists and their supporters killed some 10,000 people in the first five days of 'liberation'.[24] Italian officers were shaken by these massacres in cold blood, but obeyed the orders of Mussolini that any captured Italian who had fought in republican ranks should be executed immediately, 'because dead men tell not tales'.[25]

General Dávila, the commander-in-chief of the nationalist troops who had occupied Barcelona, published on that day an edict which 'reintegrated the city of Barcelona and other liberated territory of the Catalan provinces within the sovereignty of the Spanish state'. All appointments and decrees made since 18 July 1936 were annulled and gave 'the Catalan provinces the honour of being governed on an equal footing with their counterparts in the rest of Spain'.[26]

General Eliseo Álvarez Arenas, under-secretary of public order, and now chief of the occupation authority, published a decree which indicated that the nationalists saw themselves as an invading army in conquered territory. The Falangist Dionisio Ridruejo, who was in charge of propaganda, had prepared leaflets in Catalan. General Álvarez Arenas, on discovering this, gave orders that they should all be destroyed. The Catalan language was forbidden by law. 'It is a city which has sinned greatly,' he told Ridruejo, 'and now it must be cleansed. Altars should be erected in every street of the city and masses said continually.'[27] In less liturgical terms, Serrano Súñer told the special correspondent of the Nazi *Völkischer Beobachter*, 'The city is totally bolshevized. The decomposition is absolute. The population, whose deeds I myself have checked up on, is morally and politically sick. Barcelona and its citizens will be treated by us in the way one would attend to someone who is ill.'[28]

On the day of the fall of Barcelona no newspaper appeared in the city. All were requisitioned, passing under the control of the 'Press of the Movement'. On 27 January the first issue of *Hoja Oficial de Barcelona* came out, in which was written, 'Yesterday Barcelona was liberated! At two in the afternoon, without firing a shot, nationalist forces under the command of General Yagüe, entered Barcelona.' On the same day *La Vanguardia* and *El Correo Catalán* also reappeared. The former now called itself *La Vanguardia Española* and had changed its motto of 'Daily paper in the service of democracy' for 'Daily paper in the service of Spain and Generalissimo Franco'. Posters were displayed on walls proclaiming 'If you are Spanish, speak Spanish', and 'Speak the language of the empire!'. Books censored by the Church or the army were burned.

A few republican officers and officials had not fled to the frontier, but also stayed hidden waiting for the nationalist troops. They included Antonio Rodríguez Sastré, the chief of republican intelligence, who had been working for Franco and later became Juan March's lawyer. Others also remained either because they felt they had nothing to fear, or because of exhaustion and apathy. There was a numb relief that the fighting was at last over and they told themselves that nothing could be worse than recent months. For most, though, the atmosphere of downfall before the arrival of the enemy contributed greatly to their panic. Some nationalist prisoners, other than those left behind in Barcelona, had been herded ahead of the retreating forces. A number were shot by their guards, who either lost their heads or acted out of the bitterness of defeat. The victims included the Bishop of Teruel and Colonel Rey d'Harcourt, who had surrendered the town.

On 28 January, at eleven in the morning, nationalist troops paraded through Barcelona. Richthofen observed, no doubt with amusement, that the Italian commanders were furious that the nationalists were not allowing them to take part in the triumphal entry. A squadron of Condor Legion Messerschmitts flew overhead as an umbrella in case republican fighters tried to make a hit-and-run raid. The next day the Luftwaffe fighter pilots switched to making low-level attacks on railways and roads, which were packed with at least as many refugees as fleeing soldiers. 'The successes they had were excellent,' the Condor Legion reported, 'and the pilots are gradually getting a taste for it.'[29]

The few formations of the republican army which remained intact carried out desperate rearguard actions, such as the defence of Montsec, or fell back from one position to another, ambushing their pursuers. The Italians took five days to cover the 30 kilometres between Barcelona and Arenys de Mar. Meanwhile, in the castle of Figueras Negrín tried to manage the remains of the republican administration, split between different towns.

On 1 February the Cortes met in the stables of the castle of Figueras. Only 64 deputies out of the full 473 were present. In his speech, Negrín laid down three minimum conditions for peace negotiations: the independence of Spain from all foreign interference; the holding of a plebiscite so that the Spanish people could decide the form of government it wanted; and the renunciation of all reprisals and political repression after the end of the war. Negrín hoped that the democracies might support this, but Franco would never have accepted the last two.

On the following day the nationalists entered Gerona. Their progress had been held up by bridges blown up in the retreat or destroyed by their own bombers. The Condor Legion reported, 'The number of prisoners increases in an extraordinary way, just as the resistance in certain sectors.' Among the prisoners were two Sudeten Germans. If they were handed over to the nationalists, 'the best they could hope for was a bullet'. The Condor Legion's main task was to intercept any republican pilots trying to fly back to the central zone. In two days they destroyed another fifteen aircraft.[30]

During the battle for Catalonia International Brigaders waiting for repatriation had clamoured since early January to be allowed to rejoin the fighting. The republican authorities refused because this would break the agreement undertaken on the withdrawal of foreign volunteers. The volunteers, exasperated with their forced idleness, then appealed to the Spanish Communist Party. Only some 5,000 of them were fit to fight and they were finally given permission. One of them was a Latvian called Emil Shteingold and he recorded what happened: 'Soldiers and officers were distributed hastily in platoons, companies and battalions. We were put on trains in a great rush, and moved off towards Barcelona. It was cold on the train, as the wind pierced the carriages completely. Glass had long ago disappeared from the windows. Walls and partitions, too, were sometimes missing. Our carriage was moaning like a wounded beast when the train moved. We huddled against one another in an attempt to keep warm. At dawn we arrived at Granollers. As the train was not going any further, we started to disembark. Barcelona had fallen, and Italian motorized divisions were moving along all the roads heading north. Exhausted refugees with children and household belongings were trudging along the roads.'

A truck arrived with weapons and ammunition. These were distributed and the International Brigaders moved off as quickly as possible. They cleaned the grease from the rifles as they marched. After half an hour they took up positions either side of a small bridge to cut off the road. 'Some time later the enemy's reconnaissance appeared. There were two motorbikes, and after them an ambulance with officers. When we tried to capture them, the motorcyclists turned back and we killed them at the turn of the road. The ambulance also turned back, but was surrounded by our soldiers ... Officers surrendered and were taken to the headquarters of the brigade.' Then a short column of motorized infantry appeared. They halted them by knocking out the first and the last vehicles, and started firing with their rifles and machine-guns. The Italian troops panicked. 'Soldiers were pouring down from the truck like peas. Many fell and never got up again. Those who were still alive turned to flee, hiding behind vehicles which caught fire, and the ammunition and petrol on board began exploding. The corpses of these Italian fascists received a free cremation.'

But this was a short-lived success. They were soon attacked by fighters and then outflanked by stronger forces. They had to retreat over the hills by paths to find another ambush position. It was raining and they had received little food. 'Our boots were wet and torn by sharp gravel, they started to fall apart. After the sleepless nights, people were falling asleep while on the march. No one was allowed to sit down, as it would be impossible to get them up again.' This pattern of ambush and retreat repeated itself for at least a week, until the order finally came to withdraw over the French border.[31]

On 5 February Negrín, accompanied by President Azaña and his wife, crossed the frontier with Martínez Barrio, Giral, Companys and Aguirre. Azaña wanted to resign at that point, but he was persuaded to remain a little longer. He went to stay, supposedly incognito, in the Spanish embassy in Paris. Meanwhile, the endless caravan of refugees moved painfully towards the French frontier.

The nationalist rejoicing at having captured the second city of Spain slowed their advance and allowed the fugitives more time. The official cars of government functionaries tried to make a way through the crowds of refugees on foot. In the general atmosphere of *sauve qui peut*, some bureaucrats and politicians commandeered ambulances for themselves and their families, while the wounded had to make it on foot. 'A human mass,' wrote Julián Zugazagoitia, the socialist ex-minister who would also be handed back to Franco and shot, 'scattered across the countryside and slept on the hard winter ground, heating themselves with fires made from wood from the carts and branches. Some died of cold during the night. Mothers refused to let go of dead babies and women who had just given birth stood little chance.'[32]

The nationalist troops pursuing them were also tired from the long marches of the campaign, yet the main concern of the nationalist general staff focused on the remaining republican fighters. They did not want to allow them to rejoin squadrons in the central zone. All the nationalist and allied fighter and bomber groups were tasked to attack the last enemy airfields.

The French government faced a huge wave of refugees, without having done anything to prepare for the catastrophe, short of sending to the border gendarmes, *gardes mobiles* and Senegalese troops.[33] Its first decision was to close the frontier and refuse the republican government's request to allow through 150,000 old people, women and children. But the pressure of the multitude was so great that the French government was obliged to open the border on 28 January to civilians. Troops and men of military age were forbidden to cross. More than 200,000 people came through, as well as thousands of others who slipped across in the mountains, escaping the attention of the Senegalese battalions.

On 3 February nationalist units arrived within 50 kilometres of the frontier and it was evident that the republican rearguard could not hold them. The French government faced fierce opposition from the right-wing press and politicians. France was already sheltering many exiles, both from Spain and from the totalitarian states to the east and south. Since 1936, 344 million francs had been spent on supporting political refugees. But the government either had to let the republican troops through or attempt to keep the frontier closed with machine-guns against a well-armed force.

On 8 February General Rojo signed the order to republican troops to fall back on the frontier passes. The Condor Legion reported that white flags could be seen everywhere, yet that very morning French 105mm anti-aircraft batteries had fired warning shots at their aircraft flying close to the frontier.[34] 'German arms have also played a decisive role in this victory,' Colonel von Richthofen wrote in his war diary. The next day he added, 'We think of our brave comrades, who happily gave their lives for the destruction of the red world-pest and for the peace and honour of our Fatherland.'[35]

For the French government, which already had a bad conscience over the betrayal of Czechoslovakia, there was no choice. On 5 February it announced that the remains of the People's Army could cross into France. Altogether, from 28 January around half a million people crossed the border. Another 60,000 did not arrive in time and fell into nationalist hands. Negrín witnessed the entry into France of the first units of the People's Army. V and XV Corps crossed at Port-Bou; XVIII Corps at La Junquera; the 46th Division at Le Perthus; the 27th Division at La Vajol; and the 35th Division, which covered the withdrawal of the Army of the Ebro, and XI Corps finally crossed the frontier near Puigcerdá, on 13 February.

The sight of these gaunt, shivering masses was often tragic and pitiful. But many observers noted that their manner was of men and women who still refused to admit defeat. Some republican units marched across and piled arms on French soil under the directions of the gendarmes while the colonial troops from Senegal stood with rifles at the ready, not understanding the situation. A *garde mobile*, in a scene now famous, prised open the fist of a refugee to make him drop the handful of Spanish earth which he had carried into exile.[36] The republican diaspora had begun.

34

The Collapse of the Republic

On 9 February, just as the nationalists completed their occupation of Catalonia, the republican government, forced from Barcelona into France, met briefly in Toulouse to discuss the possibility of continued resistance. At the end of the meeting Negrín received a message from General Miaja, who a few days earlier had been promoted and made commander of all three services, requesting authorization to start negotiations with the enemy to end the war.[1] Negrín made no reply.

Accompanied by Álvarez del Vayo, he then managed to elude journalists before taking a chartered Air France plane to Alicante. On his arrival Negrín immediately had a meeting with Miaja, accompanied by Matallana who had taken over as commander of the armies in the remaining central and southern zone. Negrín wanted to know his reasons for starting negotiations. Only a few ministers, generals and senior officials returned to the remaining central-southern zone. Azaña was shortly to resign the presidency, when Great Britain and France recognized the Franquist regime, and his provisional successor, the leader of the Cortes, Martínez Barrio, refused to return to Spain.

Another meeting had taken place on 8 February in Paris. Mariano Vázquez, Juan García Oliver, Segundo Blanco, Eduardo Val and other CNT leaders had also come together to discuss the situation. For García Oliver, Negrín's policies had been a resounding failure and in his opinion there was no alternative but to seek peace with the nationalists, although not at any price. It had to be an 'honourable' agreement and needed a new government to negotiate it. Eduardo Val, secretary of the defence committee of the central region, supported this, saying that Negrín had been telegraphing in code to his closest colleagues warning them to evacuate the republican zone. From this it appeared that Negrín was playing a dirty game. They unanimously decided to push for the formation of a new government from which Negrín would be excluded. On returning to Madrid, Eduardo Val, who did not have complete confidence in the determination of his comrades, decided to act on his own account.[2]

During the first part of February the Comintern agent Stepánov tried to convince the cadres of the Spanish Communist Party in Madrid that the only course possible was a 'revolutionary democratic dictatorship'.[3] He proposed to replace the government with a 'special council of defence, work and security', made up of two ministers and two soldiers, 'reliable and energetic',[4] not to make peace, but to continue the war and win it. The Madrid communists accepted this at their conference, which took place from 9 to 11 February.

La Pasionaria also declared her determination to win the war and came up with another of her slogans: 'Spain will be the torch which will light the road of liberation for people subjugated by fascism.'[5] Palmiro Togliatti was dismayed. He tried to warn them of the divide between the leaders and the people, who were exhausted to the point of nausea by the war and only wanted to hear of peace.[6] Togliatti realized that the communists had lost support, largely because of the disastrous military strategy and because their methods had made them more enemies than friends. Officers, who had leaned towards the Party early in the war, now opposed them in secret. Many of them believed that the communists constituted the main barrier to peace. Above all, the commanders of the republican armies left in the centre had no illusions about their inability to resist any longer. The lack of armament was not as serious as in Catalonia, but they knew they had no chance against the crushing nationalist superiority in artillery, tanks and aircraft.

No assistance could be expected from the British. Chamberlain wanted the war to be finished as quickly as possible. On 7 February, with the collaboration of the nationalists, the British consul in Mallorca, Alan Hilgarth, arranged for the island's surrender on board HMS *Devonshire*. The British simply wanted to make sure that the Balearic Islands remained Spanish, with no Italian presence.[7]

On 12 February Negrín came to Madrid, where he summoned a council of ministers for the following day. During the session, Negrín called once again for the unity of the Popular Front and re-emphasized his decision to resist until the end: 'Either we all save ourselves, or we all sink in extermination and dishonour.'[8] On the same day General Franco published in Burgos his Law of Political Responsibilities. Its first article declared 'the political responsibility of those who from 1 October 1934 and before 18 July 1936 contributed to create or to aggravate the subversion of any sort which made Spain a victim, and all those who have opposed the nationalist movement with clear acts or grave passivity'. The law could thus apply to practically any republican, whether a combatant or not. The British consul in Burgos informed the Foreign Office that, in his opinion, the law gave not the slightest guarantee that those who had served in the republican army or been a member of a political party – which implied no criminal responsibility – would not be punished.[9]

Despite his calls for resistance, Negrín did not install his government in either Madrid or Valencia. He went to live in a villa near Elda, close to the port of Alicante, guarded by 300 communist commandos from XIV Corps. From there, by telephone and teleprinter, he sent a frenetic series of instructions, on one hand attempting to invigorate the defence of the republican zone, and on the other making preparations for evacuation and exile. This confused everyone, because he never gave his reasons, but Negrín was cut off from reality in his solitary world. He threatened to shoot anyone who disagreed with him and was attacked on all sides.[10]

It was hardly surprising that despite Franco's intransigent attitude, people believed that some sort of agreement must be possible. The International Military Commission had reported hearing frequent statements along two themes: 'If Spaniards alone were left here on both sides, we'd probably be able to reach agreement'; and 'We on this side are tired of revolutionary freedom, and the others of strict fascist order. It should not be hard to agree.'[11] In fact, the only argument on the republican side for continuing the war was that it was better to go down fighting than to face Franco's firing squads.

Negrín's supporters, especially the communists, tried to claim that if the Republic held out until the autumn, they would be saved by an Anglo-French intervention. But this did not take into account the obvious fact that with the destruction of the Republic's capacity to wage war after the battle of the Ebro there was no point in

Britain and France coming to its aid, even if they had wanted to. They simply could not spare the troops or weapons with the threat from Nazi Germany and the prospect of war looming in Europe. They were bound to prefer a neutral Spain under Franco to a debilitated and needy ally in the form of the Republic.

On 27 February the British and French governments formally recognized the nationalist government in Burgos. Marshal Philippe Pétain, who called Franco 'the cleanest sword in the Western world', was appointed the ambassador of France to Spain. In Paris, José Félix de Lequerica presented his letters of accreditation to President Lebrun. Daladier then handed over all the republican arms and matériel retained in France, as well as the republican gold deposits at Mont de Marsan.[12] He also guaranteed that his government would allow no activity against the nationalists from French soil. In London the Duke of Alba became the Spanish ambassador at the Court of St James. Chamberlain misled the House of Commons by saying that Franco had renounced all political reprisals, just two weeks after the Law of Political Responsibilities had been published. The United States government recalled its ambassador to the Republic, Claude Bowers, so that it could establish relations with Franco.[13]

On 26 February, a Sunday, Manuel Azaña left the Spanish embassy in Paris. He received a telegram from Negrín requesting him to return to Spain to continue in his duties. But Azaña decided to resign on 28 February after hearing of Britain's and France's recognition of the nationalist government. He informed Diego Martínez Barrio, who as leader of the Cortes was obliged to succeed him temporarily until he could convene the deputies to elect a successor. In his letter of resignation, Azaña made use of General Rojo's statement that the war was lost. He asked Negrín to arrange peace terms with General Franco and explained that he was resigning now that the Western democracies had recognized Franco and in any case the apparatus of the Republic, especially the Cortes, had ceased to function.[14] Negrín was left in a constitutional void.

Martínez Barrio met with sixteen deputies of the permanent commission of the Cortes at the Lapérouse restaurant on the Quai des Grands-Augustins. In this haunt of grand men of letters, the republican deputies discussed the rather academic question of presidential elections. There was not a single communist among them. They decided to send a telegram to Negrín, stating that

Martínez Barrio was prepared to come to the central zone to carry out the requirements of the constitution and organize the election of a new president of the Republic, but only to ensure the negotiation of a peace accord. Apparently the telegram received no response. Martínez Barrio and others, including General Rojo, then made their final decision not to return.

In the remaining republican zone of Spain, meanwhile, Negrín had summoned military leaders from all services to the aerodrome of Los Llanos outside Albacete. They included Miaja and Matallana, as well as General Menéndez of the Army of Levante, General Escobar of the Army of Estremadura, Colonel Casado and Admiral Buiza, the commander of the republican fleet.[15] Negrín urged them to fight on, assuring them that he was seeking peace. He also made the incredible claim that in a short time the arms blocked in France would arrive and war would break out in Europe. His generals were clearly unconvinced. Matallana warned that their troops were handicapped by the terrible lack of supplies and arms, and Buiza said that without an immediate solution, the fleet would have to abandon Spanish waters, which was what his officers and sailors wanted. Camacho, the air force commander, told him that they had no more than three fighter squadrons and five bomber squadrons in a serviceable state. Only Miaja, irritated that Negrín had not asked him to speak first, said to everyone's astonishment that he was ready to fight on. This sudden passion of his would not last long.

Over the last few months, Madrid had been increasingly cut off from the decision-making process of the Republic. The parties of the Popular Front had become more and more united in their dislike of Negrín and the communists, and began to seek an independent solution to put an end to the war. An alliance grew up between the socialist professor Julián Besteiro, professional officers, especially in the Army of the Centre, liberal republicans and the anarchists. There were many reasons for their anger. The communists' conduct of military affairs, however much they claimed to have had the interests of the war at heart, seemed to have had more to do with augmenting their own power. The arrogance of Soviet advisers, the 'Kléberist' arrogance of the International Brigades, the Stalinist persecutions through the NKVD and SIM, had all produced a strong reaction. It was also impossible to believe

Negrín's claim that the weapons waiting in France would soon be with them. Negrín must have known that the French government would never let them through, even if he did not yet know that they would be handed over to Franco the moment they recognized his government.

Perhaps one of the deepest suspicions, however, was that while Negrín called for resistance, they found it hard to imagine him and the communist leaders sharing the fate of their followers. Specifically, there were strong fears that the communists might use their military superiority and their control of republican shipping to ensure that their members got away, while those belonging to other parties and organizations would be left to face the nationalist revenge on their own.

The commander of the Army of the Centre, Colonel Segismundo Casado, a professional cavalry officer of peasant birth and austere tastes, had been one of the few career officers to have opposed the communists since the beginning of the war. He got on well with the anarchists and was particularly close to Cipriano Mera, with whom he had shared the tension before the battle of Brihuega.[16]

Mera still commanded IV Corps, which held the Guadalajara and Cuenca fronts. The other three corps in the Army of the Centre were all commanded by communists. The liaison committee of the libertarian movement had criticized Mera for adopting an independent political line and taking decisions on his own account. Mera defended himself throwing back at them the CNT's collaboration with Negrín, who had ignored the anarchists altogether. When Negrín visited the Guadalajara front at the end of February, Mera told him what he thought of a government which told its people to resist when they had no means of doing so, and of 'those who talk so much of resistance, while they collect valuables and goods to sell abroad and get their own families out of Spain'.[17]

Like other commanders and senior officers, Colonel Casado thought there might be a chance of professional army officers obtaining better terms for surrender than a regime controlled by Negrín and the communists. He was not one of those who hoped to save their lives, and perhaps also their professional careers, through a last-minute betrayal. But he was naive to believe that their military links and a record of anti-communism would sway Franco. The last thing that Franco wanted was for anyone else to be in a position of claiming that they had saved Spain from communism.

At the instigation of his brother César, a lieutenant-colonel of cavalry, Casado agreed to enter into contact with nationalist agents of the Servicio de Información y Policía Militar (SIPM). It is not known exactly when these first steps were made, but on 1 February Casado contacted Franco Ricardo Bertoloty and Diego Medina.[18] After telling them that it was necessary to fix the conditions for the surrender of the Army of the Centre, he sent a message to General Franco asking for assurance that the men with whom he was talking were authentic nationalist emissaries. He was prepared to accept as confirmation a letter from his contemporary at military college, General Barrón.

The same day Casado met Generals Miaja, Menéndez and Matallana in Valencia. They agreed with his plans. On the following day, back in Madrid, he went to see Besteiro at his home and they agreed to set up an alternative junta to the government. A few days later Eduardo Val offered the support of the anarchists in Madrid in accordance with what had been agreed at the meeting in Paris.[19] Casado also stayed in touch with the various British agents, such as Denis Cowan, the representative of Sir Philip Chetwode, president of the international commission who supervised the exchange of prisoners. Cowan met Besteiro on 16 February and Casado four days later. Casado also met Stevenson, the British chargé d'affaires, who offered British mediation to prevent reprisals if Casado surrendered the central zone or help in evacuating republicans, if it came to that.

On 5 February Casado was approached by Lieutenant-Colonel José Centaño, who informed him that he had been the head of 'Green Star', a secret nationalist organization in Madrid, since the beginning of 1938. Casado asked him to obtain from Burgos Franco's conditions for surrender and the letter which he had requested from Barrón. Franco himself dictated to Barrón the terms and these were sent to Casado in Madrid on 15 February via agents of the SIPM.

Franco's conditions were those of a conqueror. The republicans had lost the war and all resistance was criminal. Nationalist Spain demanded unconditional surrender, offering a pardon for those who had been 'tricked into fighting'. Those who laid down their arms would be spared and judged according to the support they might give in the future to the 'cause of nationalist Spain'. Safe conducts would be given to leave Spanish territory. After vague promises of humanitarian treatment, the letter finished with a clear threat: 'Delay in surrender and a criminal and futile resistance to our advance will carry a grave responsibility, which we will exact on the grounds of the blood spilled uselessly.'[20]

Negrín, of course, was extremely suspicious, but he did nothing to forestall the coup, probably because he was exhausted and it would clear him of responsibility for the final collapse.[21] Whatever the case, on 2 March Negrín ordered Casado and Matallana to come to see him at Elda. There he told them that he was preparing to reorganize army commands. Both Casado and Matallana outlined their objections and left. They went straight to Valencia to warn Menéndez and planned to bring forward their coup.

The next day, 3 March, Negrín published in the *Diario Oficial* a list of promotions and new appointments of communist officers: Francisco Galán was made commander of the naval base at Cartagena; Etelvino Vega governor of Alicante; Leocadio Mendiola military commandant of Murcia; and Inocencio Curto military commandant of Albacete. He promoted Modesto and Cordón to the rank of general, and Cordón was made secretary-general of the ministry of defence. At the same time Miaja was moved to the symbolic position of inspector-general, Matallana made chief of the general staff and Casado was also promoted to general. The conspirators were not taken in by the sops offered to them. In their eyes it was no coincidence that the communists were being given the active commands and control of the Mediterranean coast from where any evacuation would take place. Their worst fears that the communists would ensure their own escape and prevent that of their opponents seemed to be confirmed. The announcement of 3 March alarmed Franco as much as the conspirators, although for slightly different reasons. Communist command of the People's Army implied a vicious struggle to the end.

When Francisco Galán arrived in Cartagena on the night of 4 March to take over his command, a revolt broke out in various military units and in the fleet. Galán was arrested during dinner with his predecessor, General Bernal, who had received him with an air of normality. The fifth column took advantage of the situation and made an alliance with officers who wanted to save themselves as the war ended. Falangists and marines seized the coastal batteries of Los Dolores and the radio station, from where they broadcast appeals for help from the nationalists.

The situation was very confused, with two rebellions mixed up – one of republicans who wanted peace and the other of secret nationalist sympathizers. In the middle of the revolt, on 5 March at eleven in the morning, five Savoia bombers flew in from the sea and began to bomb the naval base and harbour where ships of the republican fleet lay at anchor. Admiral Buiza, who was observing the rebellion in the streets of Cartagena, threatened that his ships would shell the port installations if Galán and other prisoners were not released. But before the nationalist air attack, guns of the coastal batteries had been seized by rebels. That event, and the danger that nationalist warships would arrive to assist the uprising, made the admiral decide to order the fleet to head for the open sea. Galán, released in the confusion, just managed to get aboard one of the ships at the last moment.

The Condor Legion, informed of events, flew reconnaissance flights with Dorniers throughout 6 March to track the republican fleet. Relays of bombers also attacked shipping in the harbour of Valencia. They did not bomb Cartagena itself, however, in the belief that nationalist troops had already been landed by sea, when in fact they were still on their way.[22]

At dawn on 7 March, troops loyal to Negrín and the communists in the form of the 206th Brigade arrived on the orders of Hernández. They seized back the radio station, crushed the rebellion in the city and were just in time to turn the coastal batteries on two nationalist ships loaded with troops, who were arriving to support the rebellion. The crew of the first of them, the *Castillo de Olite*, did not spot anything amiss and the shore batteries, firing at close range, sank her in a matter of minutes. Altogether, 1,223 soldiers died and another 700 were taken prisoner.[23] But even though the rising was crushed, the republican fleet did not return to port. Franco sent an urgent message to Count Ciano, requesting that the Italian fleet and air force prevent the ships from heading to Odessa, but that was not Buiza's destination. He was steaming for Bizerta, where the crews were interned by the French authorities. It was a futile escape. The warships were later handed over to the nationalists.

Meanwhile, at dusk on 5 March Colonel Casado, after rejecting the renewed appeals of Negrín, set up a National Council of

Defence in the cellars of the ministry of finance. He appointed himself provisional president of the council and councillor for defence; Julián Besteiro took over as councillor of state; and Wenceslao Carrillo, the socialist father of Santiago Carrillo, as councillor of the interior. The other proto-ministers were left republicans, moderate socialists and anarchists.[24] Another present at the act of inauguration was Cipriano Mera. He had brought one of his formations to Madrid, the 70th Division, whose men were already guarding the ministry, the military governor, General Martínez Cabrera, and the head of the SIM in Madrid, who had joined the plotters.

At midnight the members of the council broadcast to the country via Radio España and Unión Radio de Madrid. Negrín, who was still having dinner at Elda with other members of the government, broke off his meal on hearing the tremulous voice of Julián Besteiro addressing his 'Spanish fellow citizens'. Besteiro announced that the moment of truth had arrived. The Negrín government had neither legal nor moral authority, and the only legitimate power for the moment would be military power. After Besteiro had spoken, the manifesto of the council was read out, accusing Negrín and his associates of calling on the people to resist while they prepared 'a comfortable and lucrative flight'. Later Mera and Casado spoke in a similar vein.[25] There was, as Azaña observed, a strong element of parody in the fact that the justification for their rebellion was to forestall a communist coup.[26] And there is no doubt that Casado was naive to think that Franco might be persuaded to come to an agreement, but Negrín's plan to fight on when it was utterly hopeless would have led to even more useless bloodshed.

As soon as the speeches finished, all those at the dinner table in Elda rushed to telephones to call Madrid. Towards one in the morning Negrín spoke to Casado, who confirmed that he had indeed risen in revolt against him. Negrín, fulminating uselessly down the telephone, stripped him of any position. Giner de los Ríos then called Besteiro, and Paulino Gómez and Segundo Blanco also spoke to Casado, but all these calls were nothing more than a dialogue of the deaf. By telephone and teleprinter, ministers tried to get in touch with other military commanders to evaluate the situation, but the replies were not encouraging. General Menéndez even warned that if General Matallana was not allowed to leave

Elda he would send troops from Valencia to free him. Matallana left shortly afterwards.

Around four in the morning on 6 March Negrín, who had just been informed of the departure of the fleet from Cartagena, asked Colonel Camacho to send transport aircraft from Los Llanos. He then dictated a teleprinter message to the council in Madrid in which he deplored their action, describing it as 'impatient'. This implied that he was already considering, or had actually entered into contact with the nationalists. He then asked that 'any eventual transfer of powers be carried out in a normal and constitutional manner'.[27]

Meanwhile, the recently appointed military governor of Alicante, the communist Etelvino Vega, had been arrested in the city by Casado's followers. News of this was brought to Elda by Tagüeña. On hearing what had happened Negrín, who after the departure of the fleet from Cartagena had planned on Alicante as the last redoubt for evacuation, murmured to Álvarez del Vayo in German so that the others would not understand: '*Ich, auf alle Fälle, werde gehen* [I, in any case, am off].'[28]

Negrín waited until two in the afternoon in case Casado replied to his signal, then gave instructions to his entourage to go to the airfield to await the aircraft from Los Llanos. From there Negrín, Álvarez del Vayo, Giner de los Ríos, Blanco, Paulino Gómez, González Peña, Cordón, Dolores Ibárruri, Rafael Alberti and María Teresa León left Spain on board three Douglas aircraft. During the flight to Toulouse, Negrín decided on a meeting of ministers in Paris for 15 March. It would be the day when the Condor Legion was able to write in its war diary: '08.00 First news from home: German troops march into Czechoslovakia.'[29]

In a hangar at the same airfield the executive committee of the Spanish Communist Party met under the chairmanship of Pedro Checa. Those present included Uribe, Claudín, Líster, Modesto, Tagüeña and Togliatti. Líster and Modesto, when asked about the possibilities of overthrowing Besteiro's and Casado's council by force, replied that this was out of the question. They then decided that Checa, Claudín and Togliatti would remain in Spain to direct the remains of the Party and prepare for an underground existence in the future.[30] The others boarded the last aeroplanes just before troops loyal to Casado occupied Elda and the airfield. The three communist leaders assigned to stay in Spain were arrested, but later in Alicante they were freed and eventually they too escaped from Spain by air.[31]

The National Council of Defence made a series of approaches to arrange peace, or at least to buy time so that republican forces could retreat towards the Mediterranean ports not yet taken by the nationalists. Negrín's decrees of 3 March were annulled as well as the call-up of the classes of 1915 and 1916. All the promotions were also declared null and void, including that of Casado, with the idea of telling the nationalists that Negrín's decisions were regarded as illegal.

Colonel Prada was appointed commander of the Army of the Centre and communists, including commanders of its I, II and III Corps, were relieved. Communists were purged from other posts, the Party newspaper, *Mundo Obrero*, was closed and red stars were removed from uniforms. Communist power in republican Spain was at an end.

The council, now headed by General Miaja, who had reached Madrid on 6 March, proceeded to order the arrests of communist commissars and militants wherever they were found. Mera's troops carried out the order and went straight to the main communist centres. One commissar, Domingo Girón, managed to escape arrest at the headquarters of the Army of the Centre and warned Colonel Bueno, the commander of II Corps, of what was happening. Bueno it seems was ill, but his chief of staff, Major Guillermo Ascanio, marched on Madrid at the head of a column of troops. Daniel Ortega, another communist commissar, who had escaped the round-up by jumping out of a window, warned Tagüeña, who left Madrid.[32]

Luis Barceló, the communist commander of I Corps, appointed himself commander of the Army of the Centre and the leader of forces opposing the Council. After setting up his command post in the Pardo Palace, he sent his men to Casado's headquarters near the airfield of Barajas, where they arrested members of his staff, brought them back to El Pardo and executed them on Barceló's orders. Meanwhile, the troops led by Ascanio reached the heart of Madrid, where they came up against the anarchists of the 70th Division and *carabineros* guarding the buildings occupied by the Council. Soon afterwards the bulk of Mera's IV Corps arrived to support the defenders, and furious fighting began in the centre of

Madrid between *casadistas* and communists. Julián Marías, working for Besteiro, described a mother sitting on a bench under the trees on the Castellana as her children played nearby and communist tanks advanced against one of the positions held by troops loyal to the Junta. 'I did not know which was more admirable,' he wrote, 'the heroism or the insouciance of the Madrileños.'[33] This struggle lasted until Sunday, 12 March, when Mera's forces crushed the communist troops, who agreed to a ceasefire. Apart from the overwhelming superiority of the anarchists, Barceló had not been able to communicate with Togliatti or Checa to obtain instructions, because Casado's supporters controlled the telephone network. In any case, the main outcome of the struggle, in which 2,000 had been killed, was a military tribunal that sentenced Barceló and his commissar to death.

Once peace was restored to the streets of Madrid on 12 March, the National Council of Defence met to prepare peace negotiations and organize the evacuation of the republican army. In the note sent to Franco, they explained that they had not been able to get in touch while crushing the revolt and restoring order. They wished to establish conditions for laying down arms and ending the war. But once again the insistence on national independence and the idea that Casado might have saved the country from communism was bound to irritate Franco deeply. They asked for no reprisals of any form against civilians or soldiers and a period of 25 days to allow anyone who wanted to leave Spain to do so. Casado and Matallana were appointed negotiators.

On the next day, 13 March, Casado summoned Lieutenant-Colonel Centaño and entrusted him with the conditions to be passed to Franco. Six days later Franco replied in cutting and glacial terms: 'Unconditional surrender incompatible with negotiations and presence in nationalist zone of senior enemy commanders.'[34] Centaño advised Casado to appoint two other officers, and the Council decided to send to Burgos Lieutenant-Colonel Antonio Garijo and Major Leopoldo Ortega. Despite the cold reception of his earlier message, Casado drew up another document addressed to the nationalists in which he emphasized the dangers they had run in taking on the communists and the risks they faced if they confounded the hopes which 'everyone has placed in this Council'.

On 21 March, agents of the SIPM informed Casado that the nationalist supreme command had agreed to the visit of Garijo and

Ortega to Burgos two days later. The two officers went and were told that on 25 March the whole of the republican air force must be surrendered, and two days later the republican army must raise the white flag in unconditional surrender. When this was known, some republican commanders, feeling angered and humiliated, considered fighting on, but it was too late to reverse the emotional process of surrender. Casado, meanwhile, sent another letter to Franco, but it too was doomed to failure.

When 25 March arrived, bad weather and the problem of unserviceable aircraft made it impossible to hand over the air force. The two republican emissaries went back to explain the situation, but their nationalist intermediaries were ordered by Franco's headquarters to send them away. Instructions for the final offensive were issued to nationalist commanders immediately.

The next day, nationalist formations began to advance on all fronts. They encountered no resistance. The Army of the South signalled at 2 p.m.: 'Many prisoners, including Russians.'[35] '27 March 1939,' wrote Richthofen in his personal war diary the next day. 'Artillery begins at 05.50. No movement in the red lines. Our first bombing attack at seven o'clock very good. At the same time reconnaissance flights over red positions which had been bombed. Artillery gets going as never before in Spain. 06.00 Infantry moves ahead with tanks after Condor Legion has made bombing attacks in front of their positions. The reds have evacuated. Only a few people left in the front lines. But they all run away. Our fire magic has really worked. After a 24-kilometre advance the infantry runs out of breath. News that there are white flags and units are surrendering everywhere round Madrid. THE WAR IS OVER!!! End for the Condor Legion.'[36] This declaration, not surprisingly with the impatient Richthofen, was a little premature. But by the next morning the republican fronts had suffered a spontaneous collapse. Soldiers embraced each other. Surrounded republican troops were ordered to pile arms, before they were marched off to bullrings or open-air camps. Others who were not captured at this time threw away their weapons and set off for home on foot.

The Condor Legion wasted no time in sending 'propaganda flights' over Madrid during the morning. At four in the afternoon the last entry was made in the official Condor Legion war diary: 'In the course of the day radio stations and transmitters in all provincial towns offer their submission and express their devotion to nationalist Spain and its Caudillo. The war can be said to be at an end.'[37]

With its attempts at negotiation completely thwarted, the National Council of Defence collapsed. Julián Besteiro decided to remain in Madrid awaiting his fate (which would be death in prison a year later). Miaja fled to Orán in his aeroplane on 28 March. Casado went to Valencia, having given orders that formal surrender would take place at 11 a.m. on 29 March.[38]

Nationalist formations continued their advance to the main ports, where thousands and thousands of people were jammed trying desperately to board one of the few boats. The pleas for help which Casado had sent to the British and French governments had received no reply, and in any case there had been too little time to organize such an evacuation. There was also still the danger of Italian submarines torpedoing any ships in the area. When Casado reached Valencia he encountered total chaos. Only one ship, the *Lézardrieux*, managed to get away loaded with refugees. In the port of Alicante the *Maritime* and the *African Trade* sailed without taking on passengers, unlike the *Stanbrook*, which left on 28 March loaded with 3,500 refugees. From Cartagena only the *Campilo* managed to sail. Casado carried on to Gandía where the next day he was allowed to board the British cruiser HMS *Galatea*, which was there to evacuate Italian prisoners as part of an exchange arrangement.

Meanwhile, thousands of soldiers, union members and politicians still tried to get to Alicante, despite the blocked traffic of coaches, trucks and vehicles of all sorts. More than 15,000 were rounded up by Gambara's Italian troops on 30 March. Many committed suicide, but the vast majority were marched off by nationalist troops to prisons, bullrings and camps.

The first nationalist troops to enter Madrid were those on the Casa de Campo front on the morning of 28 March. Later, at midday, a column led by General Espinosa de los Monteros arrived, followed by trucks with food and 200 justice officials and military police who, assisted by the Falange, began to take part in the repression of the defeated. On balconies the flag of 'Old Spain' appeared, while fifth columnists rushed out into the streets, shouting nationalist slogans with their right arm raised in the Falangist salute. 'They smashed portraits [of republican leaders] and tore down posters, they pulled down street signs and those on buildings, and they dismantled barricades. Yet apparently on that first night Falangists patrolled the streets to prevent revenge killings. Priests and monks appeared blessing everyone, also civil guards who had hidden away their old uniforms.'[39] The Spanish capital was transformed even more dramatically than on 19 July 1936. Julián Marías, who had assisted Besteiro in the Junta, felt bemused. The slogans of the Popular Front were replaced by their nationalist counterparts. Language itself changed. People went back to saying 'my wife' instead of the left-wing '*mi compañera*', and '*Buenos días*' instead of '*¡Salud!*'.[40]

On 31 March Franco's armies reached their ultimate objectives. 'Lifting our hearts to God,' ran Pope Pius XII's message of congratulation to Franco, 'we give sincere thanks with your Excellency for the victory of Catholic Spain.'[41] Ciano wrote in his diary that 'Madrid has fallen and with the capital all the other cities of red Spain. It is a new formidable victory for fascism, perhaps the greatest one so far.'[42] In London on 20 April, exactly three weeks after Franco's conquest, the Non-Intervention Committee dissolved itself at its thirtieth plenary session.

PART SEVEN

Vae Victis!

35
The New Spain and the Franquist Gulag

On 19 May 1939 the grand victory parade of nationalist Spain took place in Madrid along the Castellana, now renamed the Avenida del Generalissimo. A huge construction of wood and cardboard had been erected to form a triumphal arch on which the word 'Victory' was displayed. On each side the name 'FRANCO' was repeated three times, and linked with the heraldic arms of the Catholic monarchs.

Franco took the salute at this march-past from a large tribune. He wore the uniform of captain-general, but the dark blue collar of a Falangist shirt could be seen underneath and on his head the red beret of the Carlists. Below him in front of the stand his personal bodyguard of Moroccan cavalry was drawn up.

Altogether 120,000 soldiers – including legionnaires, *regulares*, Falangists and *requetés* – took part in the parade, with artillery and tanks. The rear was brought up by Portuguese *viriatos* and the Condor Legion. The German contingent was led by Colonel von Richthofen. 'I am driving at the front,' he wrote in his diary. 'The spectators go wild. "*¡Viva Alemania!*"'[1] In the sky above, aircraft formed the initials of '*Viva Franco*'.

The next day Cardinal Gomá, primate of Spain, gave Franco the wooden cross to kiss at the door of the church of Santa Bárbara, where the Caudillo entered under a canopy, as the kings of Spain used to do. In the middle of a solemn ceremony, imbued with heavy medieval imagery, Franco laid his victorious sword in front of the miraculous Christ of Lepanto, brought especially from Barcelona for the occasion. All the trappings and incantations represented the sentiments and self-image of the crusading conqueror. In his struggle to defeat the Marxist hydra Franco had been fighting against the past as well as the present: against the nineteenth century poisoned by liberalism; against the eighteenth century which had produced the Enlightenment and Freemasonry; and against the defeats of the seventeenth century. Only in an earlier period could the Caudillo find the roots of a great and united Spain, the Spain of Ferdinand and Isabella.

Franco was now master in his own country, but he could not ignore the debts to barons and clans who had helped him achieve the victory. In feudal style, he knew that he could maintain the loyalty of his generals by making them ministers, under-secretaries and military governors. But there were a few – Kindelán, Varela, Aranda – who only accepted his power as a form of regency until the Alphonsine line was restored. Others, such as Queipo de Llano or Yagüe, had their own plans.

Franco heard from Beigbeder that Queipo was openly conspiring to install a military junta. With the garrulous viceroy of Andalucia, he did not have to wait long for Queipo to make a mistake. On 17 July, at the celebrations of the third anniversary of the rising, he presented the cross of San Fernando to the city of Valladolid. This irritated Queipo, since he considered that Seville (personified by himself) had played a far more important role in the rising. Queipo could not desist from making the most disobliging remarks in all directions about 'Paca, the fat-arsed'. Franco summoned him to Burgos for consultations and at the same time sent General Saliquet to Seville to take command there as soon as Queipo arrived to see his Caudillo. Queipo was promptly sent off on a military mission to Rome. He had lost his power base.[2]

On 8 August, in a move to consolidate his political position, Franco issued the law of the head of state, which gave him the right to sanction laws or decrees in cases of emergency, without deliberation by the council of ministers. Two days later Franco approved the formation of his second government with another master stroke. He made Colonel Juan Beigbeder minister of foreign affairs; Ramón Serrano Súñer minister of the interior; General Varela minister of the army; but then, to everyone's stupefaction, he made General Yagüe minister of air. This dismayed both Yagüe and especially Kindelán, who had commanded the air force throughout the war. Kindelán was sent to the Balearic Isles as military governor, where he would find it difficult to conspire with other monarchists. And Yagüe, given a task which he was unlikely to perform well, would find it difficult to be a credible standard-bearer for the Falangists.[3] No doubt Serrano Súñer played a part, for he was still advising his brother-in-law on most appointments and would continue to play the most influential role until 1942.

The generals, after almost three exhausting years under arms and in the field, were now content with a more sedentary role in the political barracks of Franquist Spain. The country, however, was in a terrible state. Its economy was in ruins, with both agrarian and industrial production below the already low levels of 1935. This did not take into account the massive destruction of the country's infrastructure – railways, roads, bridges, ports, power lines and telephone systems. Some 60 per cent of rolling stock had been lost and 40 per cent of the merchant fleet. A quarter of a million buildings had been destroyed and a similar number severely damaged.[4] The new state had almost no foreign exchange and had lost all its gold reserves, so the monetary system was in chaos. There were also the war debts to the nationalists' allies to be paid off. And the loss of manpower, some 3.5 per cent of the working population, did not take into account the prisoners and the exiles.

One of the regime's first priorities was to return land to its former owners, not just the farms taken over during the revolution of 1936, but also those affected by the agrarian reforms under the Republic.[5] Wages were fixed and in the countryside were reduced to half of what they had been under the Republic. They would not again reach the level of 1931 until 1956. The sale of agricultural production was controlled by the state, which fixed prices. This, of course, encouraged the black market to flourish, whatever the punishments threatened under military tribunals. In Madrid, a kilo of flour was selling at 12 pesetas as opposed to the official price of 1.25. Beans, meat, olive oil, all were selling at prices up to more than three times the official level.[6] The opportunities for corruption escalated rapidly in such conditions. Meanwhile, the lack of tools and the failure to invest in farm machinery meant that agricultural production fell over a number of years, with disastrous results in 1941 and 1945, when many areas were close to famine.

State control of industry was designed to create a form of autarchy, in which priority was given to military needs in case Spain found itself involved in a European war. Owners and managers returned to find themselves in a form of barracks dirigisme. They could control their workforces, since strikes were outlawed, militants purged and working hours extended at fixed salaries; but the factory owners had little say in obtaining raw materials or the sale of their finished product.[7]

On 25 September 1941 the decree of the Instituto Nacional de Industria (INI), the main mechanism for economic control and autarchy, was established.[8] It covered almost everything: war production, mineral prospection, coal, iron and steel, copper and non-ferrous metals, chemicals, explosives, rubber etc. The INI intervened in aircraft production and later in all types of vehicles, as well as synthetic oil production, a concept which greatly appealed to Franco, who saw autarchy as a particularly Spanish virtue as well as a necessity. The fact that it was far from cost-efficient does not appear to have dawned on him or his ministers until 1950. He proclaimed that 'Spain is a privileged country which can survive on its own. We have everything we need to live and our production is sufficiently abundant to assure our survival. We do not need to import anything.'[9] Autarchy would only diminish after the bulk of the nationalist debts to Germany and Italy had been settled. To pay its debts to Germany required, between 1939 and 1943, the equivalent of 12 per cent of the value of all its imports and 3 per cent in the case of Italy.[10]

Franco also liked the idea of cheap energy and agricultural irrigation from hydroelectric dams, the great projects which had appealed to Calvo Sotelo during Primo de Rivera's dictatorship and nearly bankrupted Spain. On 7 October 1939 he launched a plan for their construction and republican prisoners of war were put to work.[11] The financing of such projects as well as much of the nationalist economy had created a very close relationship between the regime and the five major Spanish banks. In return for their co-operation they were protected from competition – no new banks were set up in Spain until 1962 – and given great power in the economy, allowing them to amass huge profits and create veritable commercial empires.[12] As one historian wrote, 'The architectural symbol of the new Spain was not the church, as Carlists wanted before the war, but the bank.'[13]

This anti-communist state also proceeded to nationalize the railway network, paying its owners in shares which were worth nothing.[14] At a time when the shortage of petrol and its high cost appeared to favour railways, the RENFE managed to achieve pitiful results due to appalling management. Some commentators have observed that the effects of Franco's nationalization programme were very similar to those of Soviet satellite states after 1945.[15]

*

Another paradoxical parallel between Franquism and Stalinist Russia was the obsessive fear of foreign ideological contagion. While most of the senior Soviet advisers from Spain were being forced to confess by the NKVD to treasonous contacts abroad and then shot, in nationalist Spain the rhetoric called for drastic surgery to save the body politic. The Bishop of Vic called for 'a scalpel to drain the pus from Spain's entrails'.[16] Franco's press attaché, the Count de Alba y Yeltes, said during the war to one Englishman that they had to rid Spain of the virus of bolshevism, if necessary by eliminating a third of the male population of Spain.[17] Now that the nationalists had almost all the republican prisoners in their power, they could embark on their thorough cleansing.

Prison camps were set up all over the country. Including temporary and transit camps, there were 190 of them, holding between 367,000 and half a million inmates.[18] During the final offensive 45,000 had been taken in the central zone, 60,000 in the south and 35,000 in Levante.[19] When the summer of 1939 arrived, numbers had to be reduced, especially in the temporary camps. Some prisoners were given provisional liberty, 90,000 were sent off to 121 labour battalions, and 8,000 put to work in military workshops. Executions, suicides and escapes also reduced the total. Certain 'special' camps were maintained, such as those at Miranda de Ebro and San Pedro de Cardeña, for foreign combatants in the International Brigades. Some of those prisoners were sent off to rebuild Belchite – 'You destroyed Belchite and you will rebuild it,' they were told.

In January 1940 the supervision of prison camps came under General Camilo Alonso Vega, the director-general of services in the ministry of the army. Alonso Vega, who had been head of the Civil Guard, later became minister of the interior. Those condemned by military tribunals were sent to military penal colonies for reconstruction work, or to mine coal in Asturias, León and the Basque country; some had to extract mercury, and many thousands were sent to dig canals and work on other projects close to Franco's heart. Much of this forced labour proved far from cost-effective, as was the case in Beria's Gulag,[20] but later the work was subcontracted to various companies who made better use of the unpaid labour than the military authorities. Prisoners were also hired out to landowners who were able to improve their properties with irrigation and other schemes impossible before. The rest who remained in prison, 270,719 of them according to ministry of justice figures, were spread around jails with a capacity for only 20,000.

The 150,000 republicans who returned across the French frontier to nationalist Spain found a society still in a state of war, even though the trenches had been abandoned. Repressive laws, such as that of 26 April 1940, insisted on exacting revenge for everything that had happened 'in the red zone since 18 July 1936, until the liberation'. Investigations were aimed not just at crimes against the person, but also those of a 'moral' nature committed 'against religion, culture, art and the national patrimony'.[21]

The 'attribution of responsibilities' was aimed at 'the physical destruction of the cadres of the parties of the Popular Front, of the workers' unions and the Masonic organizations' and the 'extirpation of the political forces which had sponsored and sustained the Republic'.[22] We do not have a final figure for the Franquist terror, but recent researches in more than half the provinces of Spain indicate a minimum there of 35,000 official executions.[23] This suggests that the generally accepted figure of 50,000 after the war may be low. If one adds on the unofficial and random killings, and those who died during the war from execution, suicide, hunger and sickness in prison,[24] the total figure probably approaches 200,000.

Once again, another unanswerable question needs to be asked. If the Republic had won, how many would have been executed and might have died in their camps? As several historians have pointed out, the winner of a civil war always kills more than the losers. Everything would have depended on the republican regime which would have emerged. If it had been a communist regime, then to judge by other communist dictatorships, it would have been very high because of the paranoid nature of the system. But in Spain, much would also have depended on whether it was a Stalinist version, or whether a more Spanish variety would have evolved, as Negrín seemed to think.

The Caudillo used to read through the sentences of death when taking his coffee after a meal, often in the presence of his personal priest, José María Bulart. He would write an 'E' against those he decided should be executed, and a 'C' when commuting the sentence. For those who he considered needed to be made a conspicuous example, he wrote '*garrote y prensa*' (garrotting and press coverage). After coffee, his aide would send off the sentences to be passed to the military governor of each region of each province, who would communicate them by telegram to the head of the prison. The sentences would then be read out in the central gallery of the prison. Some officials enjoyed reading out the first name, then pausing if it was a common one, such as José or Juan, to strike fear into all those who bore it, before adding the family name. In the woman's prison of Amorebieta one of the nuns who acted as warders would perform this duty.[25]

Those who escaped a death sentence faced many years of terrible conditions in one of the 500 penitentiaries. The director of the Model Prison of Barcelona, Isidro Castrillón López, said to his charges, 'You should know that a prisoner is a ten millionth part of shit.'[26] Prisoners were made to suffer from thirst as well as hunger. Sometimes they received no more than the equivalent of a small can of water in three days. There were epidemics of typhus and dysentery even in prisons holding mothers and small children where washing facilities hardly existed and the smell was overpowering.[27] The poet Miguel Hernández suffered from pneumonia in the prison of Palencia, bronchitis in the prison of Ocaña, and typhus and tuberculosis, of which he died, in Alicante prison.

Even by the standards of many prison systems, the corruption among warders and indeed senior officials was striking. In the penal colony of San Simón in Pontevedra provisional liberty was sold and, most appalling of all, a death sentence could be given to somebody else if a very large sum was paid. The family of a doctor from Vigo struggled desperately to raise the 400,000 pesetas which a senior official had demanded for this service.[28] Those captured after 1 April 1939 were known as the '*posteriores*'. They were often political militants or members of the guerrilla resistance to the regime. Many of them were subjected to terrible tortures, near-drowning in '*la bañera*' or electric shocks, to force them to give the names of others in their organization. Both *posteriores* and *anteriores* were sometimes lined up on identity parades for widows of nationalist victims, accompanied by Falangists. Any suspected of having been involved in the death of a husband were simply 'disappeared'.

The notion of a bolshevik infection, as an explanation of left-wing views, was given a spurious scientific basis. Major Antonio

Vallejo Nágera, a professor of psychiatry at Madrid University, had founded in the summer of 1938 a centre of psychological investigation with fourteen clinics in the nationalist zone to study the '*psiquismo del fanatismo marxista*'. His conclusions were that the only way to prevent the racial dissolution of Spanishness was the removal of children from suspect parents to be schooled in nationalist values. In 1943 there were 12,043 children taken from their mothers and handed over to the Falangist Auxilio Social, to orphanages and to religious organizations. Some of these children were passed on for adoption to selected families, a pattern followed 30 years later in Argentina under the military dictatorship there.[29]

Nationalist Spain was little more than an open prison for all those who did not sympathize with the regime. Various departments of secret police were set up. Franco's obsession with Freemasonry even led to the creation of the Servicio de Información Especial Antimasónico in March 1940. Freemasons, in his view, were responsible for the loss of the Spanish empire, the fall of the monarchy and numerous 'state crimes' during the period of the Republic. On 29 March 1941 a law for the 'Security of the State' was introduced, which targeted illegal propaganda, criminal association including strikes and the spreading of rumours unfavourable to the regime, all of which were regarded as tantamount to 'military rebellion'. Later, in April 1947, the law for the Repression of Banditry and Terrorism, aimed at the guerrilla resistance, represented a further turn of the screw on individual liberties.

The mania for total mastery of everything extended even to the nationalist movement itself. The state political movement combining the Falange and Carlists, the FET y de las Jons, was given a crucial role in the network of repression and social control. Serrano Súñer made sure that the 'old shirts', with their anti-capitalist rhetoric, should not offend the military and the rich. Franco was given total authority – 'before God and History' – to direct its ideology. Prominent Falangist 'old shirts' were sent abroad as ambassadors or given out-of-the-way posts in Spain. Candidates for membership of the national council of the movement were carefully chosen for their blind obedience to the Caudillo. At the end of the civil war in 1939, the party had 650,000 members. By

1945 this figure had almost doubled. As in Germany and the Soviet Union, it was essential to become a member if you wanted promotion within the bureaucracy which directed every aspect of national life.

In September 1939 the Spanish University Union was founded, to which every student in higher education had to belong. The universities themselves were turned into an extension of the state bureaucracy. Youth and even employers' organizations were treated in a similar fashion. The Falangist trade union, the Organización Sindical, which wielded immense power, had little interest in the rights of workers. Its task was to ensure that the labour force ran on almost military lines in the service of the state. Women, meanwhile, were expected to stay at home, unless they were involved in the Feminine Section, an evolution of the Falangist charity Winter Help, copied from the Nazi *Winterhilfe*. The primary role of such an organization was to train women in their household tasks and obedience to their husbands. In a counterpart to national service in the armed forces, young women had to work for Auxilio Social for six months, either looking after the children in its institutions or serving in the equivalent of soup kitchens.[30]

The defeat of the republicans also obliged them to submit themselves to the authority of the Church as well as to their temporal masters. Franco had been extremely generous in restoring all the Church's privileges and wealth, as well as its power in education, but in return he expected the priesthood to act virtually as another arm of the state. With Church control over primary schools re-established, Franco's minister for education purged thousands of teachers and hundreds of university lecturers and professors who were thought to have fallen under Masonic, Jewish or Marxist influences. Universities were controlled by the Falange, but with strong guidance from ecclesiastical authorities. The precepts of the nationalist movement were imposed on all subjects from history to architecture. Censorship of cultural life in all its forms was also rigorously exercised. This had started with the Law of the Press in 1938. Military and ecclesiastical censors went through libraries, destroying forbidden works.

Those republicans who had not been arrested and those freed from prison discovered that their life was still severely restricted. Many found it impossible to take up their previous employment. Priority was always given to former members of the nationalist armies. And there was also the risk of being denounced to the authorities by a jealous neighbour or a rival. The population was encouraged to accuse people as part of its patriotic duty. Concierges and caretakers became police spies, as in every dictatorship, and priests noted those who did not turn up to mass. They were regarded as part of what was called 'the sixth column', traitors to the cause by thought rather than by identifiable deed.

All this made the struggle for survival even harder. For example, those regarded as politically unreliable were not allowed to open a shop. Unable to scrape a living in their home town, many emigrated to the larger cities where they were unknown. The post-civil war years formed a period of great suffering and little hope of change. Franco's regime appeared impregnable.

36

The Exiles and the Second World War

The 450,000 republicans who crossed the French frontier in February 1939 as Catalonia fell were not the first refugees from the civil war.[1] Nor were they the last. Another 15,000, who managed to escape from Mediterranean ports in March during the final collapse of the Republic, reached the French colony of Tunisia, where they were interned in the camps of Getta and Gafsa near Tunis, and in others near Bizerta and Argelia. The conditions were described as sub-human. The French colonial authorities did not welcome this influx of 'reds'. One of the many prisoners there was Cipriano Mera, the former bricklayer who had become commander of IV Corps and Casado's military companion in the coup. Like many other republicans, Mera was handed over to nationalist Spain after the fall of France in 1940, but his sentence of death was commuted.[2]

Those refugees who had crossed the frontier in February and March 1939 were divided between the women, children, the old and the sick on one hand, and soldiers and men of military age on the other. The former, some 170,000, went to camps at Prats de Molló, La Tour-de-Carol, Le Boulu, Bourg-Madame and Arles-sur-Tech, and later were spread over 70 French *départements*. The latter were interned in improvised camps mostly on the beaches of south-west France.

The places to which the defeated republicans were sent consisted of stretches of coast, wet, salty and without any protection from the wind. The first camp to open, in the middle of February, was at Argelès-sur-Mer. It was little more than a marshland divided into rectangles of a hectare apiece and surrounded by a perimeter of barbed wire guarded by Senegalese troops. There was a shortage of drinking water, many resorted to drinking sea water, and nothing was done to provide washing facilities or latrines. The food they received was scarce and of bad quality. The men suffered from scabies and lice. The 77,000 refugees, many without proper clothing, belongings, money or food, had to build huts for the sick and wounded. The rest dug into the sand to shelter from the wind. Only after the first few weeks were they given drinking water in cans and wood to make latrines next to the sea.

Emil Shteingold, the Latvian International Brigader, described the largest, Saint-Cyprien, where up to 90,000 men were herded. 'Imagine a gloomy sandy spit of land with no vegetation, which was about two kilometres long, and about 400–500 metres wide. It was washed by the Mediterranean Sea on one side and ended up in a swamp on the other. This area was fenced by barbed wire and divided into square corrals. Machine-guns were placed along the perimeter of the camp. A latrine was erected on the beach, which consisted of a long log fixed on piles, under which the tide flowed back and forth. This was how we were welcomed by republican France with its socialist government. As a sign of gratitude for this warm welcome, we decided to call the latrine area "The Daladier Boulevard" ... The sand looked dry, but it was only dry on the surface. We had to sleep out on it in groups of five to ten men. Some of the greatcoats and blankets we put underneath, and with other coats and blankets we covered ourselves. It was not a good idea to turn from one side to another, as the wet side would freeze in the cold wind, and this could lead to pneumonia ... Wounded and sick men were brought here, too. The mortality was very high, it reached 100 people every day.'[3]

The other camps in the south were fairly similar and new ones opened up. In April, Basques, aviators and International Brigaders were transferred to Gurs. Barcarès was slightly better, because the people sent there had indicated their willingness to be repatriated to Spain. The much smaller Bram, near Carcassonne, was one of the very few good ones. It even had a sanatorium of 80 beds. In an attempt to improve the wretched conditions in the large camps, the French authorities tried to move some of their inmates to the initial sorting camps of Arles and Prats de Molló in the mountains, but they had to stop the practice because too many died literally of cold.[4]

The camp of Vernet-les-Bains, situated between Saverdun and Foix, was a punishment camp from the First World War cut off from the outside world. About 50 hectares in area, and divided into three sections all surrounded by barbed-wire fences, it held those republicans the French authorities considered 'a danger to public safety', among them the survivors of the 26th Division, the old Durruti column and 150 International Brigaders segregated in a sector known as the 'leper colony'. Under the Vichy government the camp passed to the Germans, who rebuilt it according to their own concentration camp guidelines. Yet Arthur Koestler wrote that 'from a point of view of food, installations and hygiene, Vernet was worse than a Nazi concentration camp'.[5] In such conditions it was predictable that many thousands of refugees should have died. Suspected male political activists in other camps were transferred to the Templar castle of Collioure and women militants to the camp of Rieucros.

The French authorities had never prepared for such an influx, but even when the scale of the human disaster was apparent, they were very slow and reluctant to move. This was not entirely surprising since the cost of looking after so many refugees rose to seven million francs a day. The right-wing press constantly attacked Daladier's government for having allowed in so many left-wingers and *Candide* complained about feeding them.[6] The French authorities encouraged refugees to return to Spain and surrender themselves to the nationalists. Only those with relations in France and who were prepared to sign a form that they would never ask for state aid were allowed out of the camps. The alternatives, apart from returning to Spain, were re-emigration to the New World or any other country that would accept them; or to 'volunteer' for the French Foreign Legion or the labour battalions, which were being used on improving fortifications and other projects as the threat of war increased.[7]

By the end of 1939 between 140,000 and 180,000 had decided to go back to Spain and take their chances.[8] Some 300,000 chose exile in France, in other European countries or in Latin America. The Mexican government of President Lázaro Cárdenas had already welcomed children evacuated from the republican zone. Thousands more of all ages were to follow in different waves, including José Giral and General Miaja. Some went to Chile, then under a popular front government, others to Dominica and then on to Venezuela and Cuba. Argentina allowed in only 2,500, giving priority to Basques. In Europe Belgium took 5,000, but Britain restricted immigration to only a few hundred. The Soviet Union took no more than 3,000 and most of those were senior members of the Spanish Communist Party. Of the 50,000 to 60,000 who stayed in France, most were enrolled in Companies of Foreign Workers, a semi-militarized organization, which put them to work in the mines, war industry or in agriculture.[9]

Republican leaders seldom suffered the same rigours and frustrations of the ordinary exiles. Azaña, badly stricken with heart disease, died at Montauban on 4 November 1940. Juan Negrín and Indalecio Prieto, the former friends who had become bitter enemies, continued their struggle in France. Although Negrín had summoned a meeting of the permanent delegation of the Cortes in Paris on 31 March 1939, Prieto organized another on 27 July to dissolve formally the government of the Republic, but Negrín refused to accept the vote.

The confrontation became increasingly bitter when Prieto and the permanent delegation set up the JARE, the Council for Aid to Spanish Republicans.[10] Prieto demanded that Negrín hand over control of the valuables and currency which the republican government held in Europe and North America, among them the famous 'treasure' of the yacht *Vita*. Negrín had allocated this to his own organization, the SERE, the Service of Evacuation for Spanish Republicans. The treasure – jewels, bonds and other valuables worth some $300 million – came from the confiscations ordered against nationalist supporters by the People's Tribunal of Civil Responsibilities. It was stored on the *Vita*, which had been Alfonso XIII's private yacht and was guarded by a detachment of Negrín's *carabineros*.

The *Vita* sailed from Le Havre for Mexico and reached Veracruz a few days earlier than expected. As a result, Dr José Puche, a confidant of Negrín's, was not at the dockside to take charge of the contents. Enrique Puente, the commander of the *carabineros*, telephoned Prieto to ask him what he should do and Prieto seized the whole consignment with the approval of President Cárdenas. The treasure was taken to Mexico City under the control of the JARE, and thus Prieto made off with it from under the noses of Negrín and the communists.

Yet even after this blow, Negrín and his associates never exactly found themselves in a state of poverty. He personally controlled a trust made up of funds confiscated under his government and was able to buy a large country house near London where he lived until 1945, providing lodgings there for up to a dozen republican politicians. Other leaders were not nearly so fortunate. Once France was occupied by German troops in the summer of 1940, General Franco asked Marshal Pétain to extradite 3,617 republican leaders. The Vichy regime agreed to very few, but it did hand over to the Gestapo seven leaders, including the president of the Generalitat, Lluís Companys; Joan Peiró, the former anarchist minister; Francisco Cruz Salido and Julián Zugazagoitia. These four were executed, the other three sentenced to life imprisonment. Largo Caballero was captured by the Gestapo and, after being interrogated in Berlin, was sent to the concentration camp of Sachsenhausen. He was barely alive at the liberation in 1945 and died soon afterwards.

Foreign communists in France followed Comintern orders and were obliged to remain silent when the Nazi–Soviet pact was signed in August. Those left in Spain tried to set up underground organizations, but the Franquist secret police managed to smash one network after another, usually as the result of extracting names under torture.

The Second World War was to put Franco's statecraft to its greatest challenge. When Germany invaded Poland on 1 September 1939, Franco issued a decree imposing 'the strictest neutrality on Spanish subjects'. Yet two months later, on 31 October, he summoned the Junta de Defensa Nacional to announce that he had decided on an ambitious plan to rearm the forces and increase the army to 150 divisions through conscription. This would mean a target of two million men under arms. He ordered the general staff to prepare to close the Straits of Gibraltar by concentrating artillery on the coast there. He also wanted them to reinforce the army in Morocco in readiness to invade the much larger French zone. The navy was to prepare a blockade of French maritime traffic in the Mediterranean, including their North African ports, and to interrupt British shipping, if necessary by blockading the Portuguese coast as well.[11]

Spanish coasts and territorial waters were put at the disposal of the German Kriegsmarine, which apart from its base in Cádiz, was to resupply 21 submarines from Vigo. Tankers and supply ships would come and go replenishing the U-boats. Italian ships and submarines, watching the Straits of Gibraltar, routinely used Spanish territorial waters, both on the Mediterranean and Atlantic sides.[12]

In April 1940 Mussolini decided to enter the war on the German side. On 12 June, during the Fall of France, Franco changed from neutrality to a state of 'non-belligerency'. Forty-eight hours later he ordered the occupation of Tangier. That same day, in a meeting with the German ambassador von Stohrer, he passed a message to Hitler expressing his desire to enter the war if the Führer had need of him. In mid July he sent General Vigón to see Hitler and Ribbentrop, then at the Château de Acoz in Belgium, to communicate his desire to enter the war on the side of the Axis. He wanted to negotiate the conditions. As well as arms, fuel, ammunition and food, he wanted in compensation 'Morocco, Oran, the Sahara as far as the twentieth parallel, and the coastal zone of Guinea as far as the Niger delta'.[13]

The Nazis, stupefied at the price Franco put on entering the war, showed little enthusiasm, but a few days later Hitler sent a message via Richthofen that he should prepare to collaborate in an imminent operation against Gibraltar, which would coincide with Operation Sealion, the invasion of Britain. Richthofen and Vigón met to coordinate plans of attack, but on 31 July Sealion was suspended because Admiral Raeder warned the Führer that the Kriegsmarine could not guarantee success.

Hitler's attention soon started to turn towards his ultimate ambition, the invasion of the Soviet Union. Offering Spain as a bastion for the Axis in the Atlantic, Franco wrote to Mussolini on 15 August, asking him to intercede with Hitler to persuade him to agree to his conditions so that Spain could enter the war 'at the favourable moment'. But Hitler did not want to give Franco power over the western Mediterranean, since the sea was to be maintained as the preserve of Italy.[14]

Hitler decided to have a private meeting with Franco on 23 October at Hendaye on the French frontier. Unfortunately, Franco was travelling by the Spanish railway system and arrived late, which deeply irritated the Nazi leader. Hitler again refused to give in to Franco's claims over the French empire in North Africa. He was due to see Marshal Pétain the following day and wanted to consolidate the Vichy regime's collaboration. In the end a protocol was drawn up stating that Franco would enter the war when requested, that Gibraltar would be given to Spain and vague affirmations were made about compensating him with some undefined African territories at a later date.

In December Hitler sent Canaris to see Franco to tell him that the Wehrmacht was preparing a force of fifteen divisions to seize Gibraltar in Operation Felix. Franco expressed his concern that the British would reply by attacking the Canary Islands and demanded guarantees. Hitler was furious when he heard of Franco's 'treason' to the agreement made in Hendaye. On 6 February 1941 Hitler sent Franco another letter, polite but imperative. This crossed with a memorandum from Franco asking for so much artillery, spare parts, signals equipment, trucks, locomotives and wagons, that German civil servants considered the list beyond the capacity of Germany.[15] Hitler then wrote to Mussolini asking him to arrange things with Franco, thinking that the 'Latin charlatans' would understand each other.

Mussolini had a meeting with Franco on 12 February in the Villa Margherita at Bordighera. Serrano Súñer, now minister for foreign affairs, was also present. Franco said that he was afraid of entering the war too late and complained that the Germans were so slow giving him the weapons that he needed. Mussolini told Hitler of the results of the meeting and recommended that Franco should not be pushed any further. It is certainly possible that Mussolini did not want Franco as a rival in the Mediterranean.[16]

On their return to Madrid Serrano Súñer, who had recently met Hitler and had held five meetings with Ribbentrop, felt himself to be the man of the moment. But he failed to realize how much he was hated by the Spanish generals and by the 'old shirts' of the Falange. In recent months the British secret service had been paying large bribes to the more monarchist and religious generals to encourage them to oppose Franco and his brother-in-law. From the middle of 1940 to the end of 1941 some 30 generals between them had received $13 million and continued to be given more. Aranda alone was given $2 million in 1942. The financial arrangements were made by the great smuggler Juan March, who had now allied himself with the British.[17] General Vigón had a private interview with the Caudillo in which he warned him of the deep resentment of generals at the enormous power which Serrano Súñer had accumulated, and added that rumours were running around Spain saying that it was his brother-in-law who controlled everything.

Even some Falangists began to turn against Serrano Súñer, but others were determined to increase their power. The situation was becoming dangerous, because German agents were encouraging them. Serrano Súñer felt that his best way to advance was to put increased pressure on Franco to enter the war as soon as possible. The Germans in that spring of 1941 had just conquered Yugoslavia and Greece, and captured Crete.

Franco moved in stages with a series of changes at the top level. Serrano Súñer found that not only had he lost the ministry of the interior and control of the Movement, but his conduct of foreign affairs was being questioned in government circles. Then, on 22 June, the Wehrmacht invaded the Soviet Union. Two days later Falangists launched themselves on to the streets in a great demonstration shouting slogans against 'atheist communism'. Serrano Súñer thought that this was his chance. In uniform, he made a speech from the balcony of the General Secretariat of the Movement which overlooked the Calle de Alcalá: 'Russia is guilty! Guilty of our civil war! ... The extermination of Russia is demanded by history and by the future of Europe!' The Falangist demonstrators, in a bellicose frenzy, went on to yell at the British embassy, 'Gibraltar is Spanish!'

Serrano Súñer thought that he could recover all his power if he managed to channel the onrush of Falangist energy. A move then occurred to him, which seemed to offer a resounding triumph in the eyes of Spaniards and Germans alike. He went to see Franco and spoke to him of the need to form a division of volunteer Falangists to go to Russia alongside the Wehrmacht to fight the 'apocalyptic beast'. But the senior generals, using Varela as their spokesman, made it clear that they opposed Serrano's attempt to meddle in military affairs, especially since this also involved the Falange. Franco once again adopted a double-edged solution. He would agree to a Falangist volunteer division, but it should be commanded by one of his generals.

On 13 July the 'División Española de Voluntarios', usually known as the 'División Azul', or Blue Division, began to leave for the training camp of Grafenwöhr in Germany. Commanded by General Agustín Muñoz Grandes, it became the 250th Infantry Division in the German army and was sent to the Volkhov front near Lake Ilmen, east of Leningrad.[18] A few days after their departure Franco made a speech on the anniversary of the rising in which he linked Spain's destiny to Nazi victory and said that the Allies had lost. This speech, combined with the despatch of the Blue Division, alarmed the British and they began to prepare Operation Pilgrim, the invasion of the Canary Islands. In the end,

Churchill cancelled it, but increased the pressure on Franco's regime by reducing oil and wheat deliveries, and demanding that exports of wolfram to Germany should cease.

Even after Hitler's check before Moscow in December 1941, and the entry of the United States into the war, Serrano Súñer became increasingly confident. But on 16 August 1942, just as Hitler's armies began to advance on Stalingrad and strike into the Caucasus, a curious incident happened in Bilbao. During a religious festival at the shrine of the Virgin of Begoña, a confrontation took place between Carlist traditionalists and Falangists. The clash developed from insults and shoving into something more deadly. A Falangist, Juan Domíngo, threw a hand grenade, which wounded 30 people. General Varela, a traditionalist, took the disturbance as an assassination attempt against himself, and announced that it constituted 'an attack against the whole army' and sent telegrams to all the captaincy-generals. Domíngo was accused of being an agent provocateur in the service of the British and was executed. For Franco, this presented the perfect occasion for his policy of divide and rule. On 3 September he accepted Varela's resignation in protest at the 'Falangization' of the regime, but to balance the account he also dismissed Serrano Súñer. He replaced him as foreign minister with General Gómez-Jordana, an anglophile. His brother-in-law's political career was at an end.

When the Allies launched Operation Torch, their landings in North Africa, in November 1942, Gibraltar was used as their main base. Roosevelt sent Franco a letter to reassure him about Allied intentions towards Spain and its possessions in Morocco. Meanwhile the British encouraged Kindelán to put pressure on Franco to restore the monarchy, but without success. Franco, under pressure abroad and at home, could only contemplate the collapse of his imperial dreams and of the hopes of the Axis. After the Allied success in North Africa, which completely changed the balance of power in the western Mediterranean, Field Marshal Paulus capitulated at Stalingrad at the end of January 1943. Then, in July, the Red Army during the battle of Kursk smashed the Wehrmacht's armoured strength and the Allies landed in Sicily, which soon led to the fall of Mussolini. The following summer saw the Allied invasion of Normandy and the destruction of the Wehrmacht's Army Group Centre in Belorussia. France was liberated by the end of August, and at the end of the year the last major German offensive was crushed in the Ardennes. In May 1945, the Third Reich finally collapsed.

Franco had adapted to these dramatic geopolitical changes by modifying his policy towards the Allies, using Gómez-Jordana. On 16 March 1943 he had opened the Franquist version of the Cortes with a speech calling for an agreement with the Allies to defend 'Western civilization' from the Soviets and in November his withdrawal of the Blue Division was accompanied by a return to neutrality from his position of 'non-belligerency'. In May 1944 he closed the German consulate in Tangier and halted exports of wolfram to Germany. In August, following the death of Jordana, he appointed José Felix de Lequerica as foreign minister, who showed the same obsequious approach to the Allies that Serrano Súñer had adopted towards the Axis.

At home, he adopted a tougher policy. Following the pressure to restore the monarchy in June 1943, he declared to his senior generals that this was a Masonic conspiracy designed to subvert the regime of 18 July 1936. And in September of that year he dismissed a group of monarchist generals, afraid that he might face the same downfall as Mussolini at the hands of the Fascist Grand Council. On 4 November 1944 he gave an interview to United Press in which he declared that nationalist Spain had never been fascist or national socialist and had never been allied to the Axis powers. When Hitler heard of this he said that 'the nerve of señor Franco' had no limits.[19]

Once the Second World War was over, Franco on 17 July 1945 issued a decree on the Rights of Spaniards, which conceded a general pardon for political prisoners from the civil war. He calmed the large landowners and senior generals alike, and turned once more to the Church. On 18 July 1945 he formed a new government, giving key posts to Catholic politicians, thus achieving a transition to national Catholicism which sidelined the Movement. On 13 December 1946, the United Nations Organization recommended the withdrawal of ambassadors from Spain, yet the start of the Cold War, which was to last over 40 years, would prove the salvation of his regime. On 17 April 1948 General Franco ended the state of war in Spain. It was nearly twelve years after the beginning of the civil war.

37
The Unfinished War

For many Spanish republicans, especially those in France, the Second World War had been an equally tough continuation of the civil war. Once the war began, many republican refugees enlisted to fight against the common enemy. One of the formations which contained the highest proportion of Spanish republicans (1,000 out of 2,500) was the 13th Half-Brigade of the French Foreign Legion. Many other units, French and British, had Spaniards fighting in their ranks, in North Africa and elsewhere. A company of Spanish republicans fought with Colonel Robert Laycock's commandos in the final phase of the battle of Crete.

Perhaps the best-known contingent formed part of the 3rd March Battalion of Chad, fought in General Leclerc's 2nd Armoured Division all the way to Paris. The 9th Company – known as 'La Nueve', even by the French – under the command of Captain Raymond Dronne, was the first to enter the French capital to the sound of pealing bells on the night of 23 August 1944. Their tanks bore such names as *Madrid*, *Teruel*, *Ebro*, *Guernica* and *Don Quixote*.[1]

Their less fortunate companions in France were either sent to camps in Germany or used as forced labour by the Organisation Todt. In Mauthausen the 7,200 Spaniards were made to wear a triangle of Falangist blue on their striped uniforms, even though they were 'reds'. Some 5,000 of them died there. Dachau, Buchenwald, Bergen-Belsen, Sachsenhausen-Oranienburg and Auschwitz also held many Spanish republican prisoners.[2]

In the Soviet Union some 700 Spanish republicans served in the Red Army and an equal number as partisans. Many others attempted to enlist but were told that they had fought in their own war and would serve the Soviet Union better by working in factories.[3] Altogether 46 pilots, most of whom had been training in the Soviet Union at the end of the civil war, were sent to aviation regiments after appealing to La Pasionaria and other communist leaders of 'the Moscow emigration' to intercede on their behalf.[4] More surprisingly, considering the Stalinist suspicion of foreign communists, 119 Spanish men and six women served in the OMSBON (the Separate Motorized Infantry Brigade of Special Designation of the NKVD of the USSR), which was the key praetorian unit in Moscow to defend the Kremlin. Six of them were officers and one became a company commander.[5]

Others served in the 1st Special Air Brigade of NKVD Frontier Guards, stationed at Bykovo twenty kilometres south of Moscow, ready to defend the Soviet capital. Another 700 joined partisan units in the German rear, many of them parachuted in. They included a group of Catalans led by José Fusimaña, while another detachment of eighteen fought with Medvedev, one of the most renowned of all the Soviet partisan leaders.[6] A number of republican soldiers who spoke good Russian served in the front-line Red Army as if they were Soviet citizens. La Pasionaria's son, Rubén Ruiz Ibárruri, was made a Hero of the Soviet Union and died in the fighting before Stalingrad, while two others were awarded the Order of Lenin. It is also said that 150 Spanish orphans took part in the defence of Leningrad.[7]

Many other republican refugees fought in the French resistance and the Forces Françaises de l'Intérieur (FFI). During the first phase, until November 1942, their networks co-operated with Allied intelligence and helped with the escape routes for shot-down aircrews. Libertarians and poumistas were also active, such as Francisco Ponzán ('François Vidal'), a former anarchist member of the Council of Aragón, who took part in the Pat O'Leary group. Captured by the Germans in August 1944, he was shot and his body was burned in a wood. Josep Rovira of the POUM managed to escape.

During 1943 and the first half of 1944 there was a certain unification of Spanish resistance groups under Spanish communist direction in the south-west of France. In the last phase of the resistance in France, republican groups formed an important element during what became a virtual civil war against the Vichy Milice. As soon as the fighting in France was over they began looking at the Spanish frontier, expecting the imminent collapse of the Franquist regime.

After the German invasion of the Soviet Union in June 1941,

and following Comintern orders, the Spanish Communist Party had made urgent calls from Independent Spanish Radio and from Radio Toulouse to establish an anti-fascist front of all Spanish republican forces, including the CNT. The communists called this the Unión Nacional Española and it became the political arm of XIV Guerrilla Corps. From the start of 1944, XIV Corps controlled almost all Spanish units in 31 *départements* in the southern half of France. In May 1944 its name was changed to the Group of Spanish Guerrillas, and over the following months it took over all Spanish state property, consuls and trade councils in the region, hoisting the republican flag. The UNE called for a general mobilization on both sides of the border ready to 'reorganize our patriotic army for the reconquest of Spain'.[8] But Franco's Spain would never be overthrown.

Those who had taken to the hills, '*los hombres de la sierra*', having escaped from prison or labour battalions, formed small, scattered groups which could not communicate effectively. Yet the first examples of armed resistance to nationalist conquest had started from the very beginning of the civil war. In Galicia, where so many had escaped the brutal Falangist repression, groups had formed in the hills, especially the Sierra do Eixe. In 1937 there were some 3,000 fugitives around Vigo and Tuy. There were other bands in León, Asturias, Santander, Cáceres, Badajoz, Granada, Ronda and Huelva, but they too were improvised and acted more for reasons of survival than as a co-ordinated resistance force. Most of those in the south were annihilated in 1937, but in the north the struggle continued until the end of the war and beyond. When the Asturias front had collapsed in 1937, over 2,000 soldiers fled to the mountains and the nationalists needed to deploy fifteen *tabors* of *regulares* and eight battalions of infantry for many months hunting them down.

In the central zone during the war the fugitives grouped themselves in the mountains of Toledo under a former socialist mayor, Jesús Gómez Recio, and the communist José Manzanero, who had also escaped from prison, in his case on the day he was due to be executed after terrible tortures. From 1941, after many of the groups had been broken, the Civil Guard became the principal force engaged in anti-guerrilla operations. The guerrillas, having to survive by stealing food, often alienated the local population and helped the Franquist regime in its attempts to brand them as common brigands. The police also sent agents, pretending to have escaped from prison, to infiltrate their groups.

After the liberation of France in 1944 the Spanish Communist Party prepared a double plan for its 'reconquest' of Spain – one was to invade across the Pyrenees, the other was to send small detachments of guerrillas into Spain to link up with other groups and organize a more co-ordinated resistance. The vain hope was that this would encourage the victorious Allies to take a more robust line against Franco's regime. In September 1944 the communist leader Jesús Monzón gave the order to attack from the Valle de Arán, and from there advance on Lérida, with the idea of establishing a bridgehead in which a 'government of national union' could be set up to lead a mass rising across Spain. The operation was entrusted to the so-called 204th Division, which consisted of less than 4,000 men, under the command of Colonel Vicente López Tovar.

On 19 October, at six in the morning, they crossed the frontier while other diversionary attacks were carried out at different points along the Pyrenees. In this first stage the invading force managed to penetrate several dozen kilometres into Spain, occupying small villages, capturing a few Civil Guard posts and taking 300 prisoners. But following the usual republican mistake, they spent time laying siege to Viella, the main town of the Valle de Arán. Once again the nationalists reacted rapidly, sending in 40,000 Moroccan troops under Generals Yagüe, Garcia Valiño, Monasterio and Moscardó. López Tovar gave the order to withdraw back across the frontier on 28 October. The operation ended in a resounding defeat, with the loss of 200 killed and 800 taken prisoner. Another 200 managed to slip away into the interior of Spain.[9] Similarly, the attempt to produce a rising, with so-called 'corps' and 'guerrilla armies', inside Spain failed dismally. But guerrilla activity still carried on. In Galicia it continued until 1950. In Asturias the movement was split by disagreements between socialists and communists. In Levante and upper Aragón the guerrilla groups were kept going by more small detachments crossing the French border to join them.

An attempt was made by Jesús Monzón in Madrid to set up a guerrilla army of the centre and operations started in urban areas, such as an attack on the Falangist headquarters in Cuatro Caminos.

But the pitiless methods of the Civil Guard and the secret police took a heavy toll. In Catalonia the communist PSUC set up another 'guerrilla army', but this too was broken up in 1947, with 78 members tried before the largest court martial ever assembled in Spain. The most famous guerrillas in Catalonia, however, were anarchists such as Francisco Sabaté Llopart ('El Quico'), Ramon Vila Capdevila ('Caraquemada'), Luis Facerías and Marcelino Massana. Massana managed to flee to France in 1950. Facerías took refuge in Italy in 1952, but returned to Barcelona where he was killed by the police in August 1957.

'Quico' started his guerrilla activity in 1945, when on 20 October he managed to free three anarchist prisoners escorted by police. He spent periods in Spain, then rested in France before crossing the border again. In March 1949 he organized an attempted assassination of the brutal police commissioner Eduardo Quintela, but he attacked the wrong car and killed its occupants. On his return to France he was arrested by gendarmes and imprisoned until 1955. Later, towards the end of 1959, he returned to Spain, but in January 1960 the Civil Guard surrounded him and some companions in a farmhouse in the province of Gerona. The exchange of fire left a number wounded, including 'Quico' himself, yet he managed to break through the encirclement. He hijacked a train a few days later and escaped again, but his wound had become gangrenous. He sought medical help, but was recognized and was killed on 5 January. 'Caraquemada', his comrade, was surrounded on 6 August 1963 and shot by civil guards.[10]

The repression of the guerrillas between 1947 and 1949 was relentless. Altogether some 60,000 people were arrested during the decade following the civil war, yet in fact the guerrilla resistance involved only a tiny minority of the population, probably fewer than 8,000 within the whole of Spain. Among the very last survivors were Francisco Blancas, who led a group between Ciudad Real and Cáceres until 1955, when he fled to France; Patricio Serra in Badajoz who lasted until April 1954; and in the first and last stronghold of Galicia, Benigno Andradé, who was executed in July 1952, José Castro Veiga, shot down by the Civil Guard in March 1965, and Mario Rodríguez Losada, who finally escaped to France in August 1968. By then, foreign tourists packed the beaches of the southern coast and Franco's Spain found itself being subverted more by new values from without than by the old ideologies within.

*

While the struggle continued in Spain, the republican leaders in exile had pursued their vicious and self-destructive rivalries abroad. In November 1943 Indalecio Prieto had set up a political coalition in Mexico which brought together the PSOE, Unión Republicana and the Catalan parties under the leadership of Martínez Barrio.[11] The anarchists and communists were excluded.

In August 1945, Negrín moved from London to Mexico to take part in the session of the Cortes in exile, called by Martínez Barrio at Prieto's instigation. Negrín formally announced his resignation as president of the council of ministers, six years after the fact, and Martínez Barrio was elected president of a republic which had ceased to exist. Negrín put himself forward as the new head of government, but Prieto vetoed this and José Giral stepped forward to take on the task. In his phantom administration there were again no communists and no anarchists. Even with a Labour government in power in London, there was still no hope of achieving recognition by either Britain or France. Ernest Bevin, the foreign secretary, nevertheless arranged a meeting in October 1947 between Prieto and Gil Robles, the former leader of the CEDA, his enemy at the time of the rising of October 1934. After tense and difficult discussions, a pact was signed in Saint Jean de Luz near the Basque border. This demanded among other things an amnesty in Spain, the end of reprisals and the right of Spaniards to choose their own government. It was almost ten years since the same three points had been made at Figueras.

The pact was to have little effect. Five days after it was signed the son of Alfonso XIII, Don Juan, the Count of Barcelona, met Franco aboard the yacht *Azor* off San Sebastián. He agreed that his son, Prince Juan Carlos, would follow his studies in Spain under Franco's tutelage. This boy, then less than ten years old, would become the Caudillo's heir. But after Franco's death in 1975 he would preside over Spain's successful return to democracy and freedom.

38
Lost Causes

In June 1937, Cardinal Gomá had described the Spanish Civil War as 'an armed plebiscite'. It was indeed an extension of politics by military means. Yet the violence of the conflict created a great impression abroad. Stereotypical assumptions about Hispanic passions were sometimes strengthened by the male Spaniard's own image of himself. 'I am not pretending', El Campesino wrote later, 'that I was not guilty of ugly things myself, or that I never caused needless sacrifice of human lives. I am a Spaniard. We look upon life as tragic. We despise death.'[1] But such statements are not merely a grotesque self-indulgence, they are profoundly misleading. Violence is often the product of a distorted expression of fear. And the more that fear is suppressed out of a need to show bravery, the more explosive the result.

The cults of virility and death went hand in hand as the imagery of Queipo de Llano, the Falange and the Foreign Legion demonstrated. Nationalist leaders also revelled in the language of the stern patriarchal surgeon, whose diagnosis and proposed treatment for the country could not be questioned because the patient did not know what was best for him. Foreign contagions and cancers had to be cut out. National regeneration could only come through pain, in the medieval manner of trial by ordeal.

Ideological and religious invocations deliberately tried to make the violence abstract. There was said to have been a sweet-natured youth among Moscardó's defenders at Toledo, who was called the Angel of the Alcázar because before firing his rifle he used to cry, 'Kill without hate!' This depersonalization existed on the republican side as well. David Antona, a CNT leader, said that 'the bullets which ended the lives of the officers at the Montana barracks did not kill men, they killed a whole social system'. People were encouraged to submerge their identity and individual responsibility into causes with either mystical or superhuman auras. Carlist *requetés* were told that they would have a year less in purgatory for every red they killed, as if Christendom were still fighting the Moors. It was this dehumanization of the enemy which made the war so terrible, along, of course, with modern weapons and the tactics of terror aimed against civilian populations.

The destruction of Guernica became the internationally recognized symbol of the new horror, yet even more chilling were the motives behind the Nazi campaign in Spain. There has been a great debate over the comparative weight and timing of foreign intervention on either side during the war. But arguing over the exact numbers of aircraft, tanks and military advisers misses the point. So much depended on the standard of training and the quality of the equipment. There can be no doubt, for example, that German pilots and aeroplanes were considerably superior to their Soviet adversaries, a fact re-emphasized with terrifying effect in June 1941 when the Luftwaffe destroyed over 2,000 Soviet aircraft, most of them on the ground, in less than 48 hours. The Italian contribution to Franco's victory was indeed large, but the haphazard nature of its bombing and its general unreliability rather diminished its military potential.

The Spanish Civil War, as the Nazi government recognized right from the start, offered the perfect testing ground for weaponry and tactics. The Red Army also saw the opportunities, but because of Stalinist military orthodoxy following Marshal Tukhachevsky's execution, it was unable to take much advantage. The Luftwaffe's Condor Legion, on the other hand, was meticulous in its reports on the effects of new weapons systems. For example, their squadrons discovered that during an offensive it was very effective to strafe enemy trenches as soon as the artillery bombardment ceased to keep the republicans' heads down while the nationalist infantry charged the last few hundred metres. Enemy artillery positions were also attacked to prevent counter-battery fire, and bomber squadrons were directed against forming-up areas and rear communications to prevent reinforcements from being brought forward.

When it came to fighter tactics the Luftwaffe Messerschmitt squadrons abandoned the traditional V formation during the air battles over the Ebro. Their aircraft began to fight in double pairs instead, a tactic which RAF Fighter Command was forced to imitate two years later during the battle of Britain. But perhaps the most important psychological weapon which the Condor Legion tested in Spain was the Junkers 87, or Stuka. During the advance across Aragón in the spring of 1938 the Condor Legion bombed towns and villages – including Albocacer, Ares del Maestre, Benasal and Villar de Canes – then photographed them carefully afterwards, from the air and on the ground, to measure bomb patterns and destruction caused. They were above all interested in assessing the accuracy of Stuka bombing with 500kg bombs. In Benasal, which they hit with nine 500kg bombs, they took many photographs of the large church there, which they had completely gutted. Much of this investigative work was carried out by Major Count Fugger, from an ancient family of Augsburg bankers.[2]

On the ground the Germans learned important lessons which aided them greatly over the next few years. Their tanks needed to be more heavily armed and concentrated in armoured divisions for '*Schwerpunkt*' breakthroughs. They also discovered in Spain the accuracy and power of their 88mm anti-aircraft gun when used against tank targets. It was later installed in the much feared Tiger tank. In fact, it was as a result of the war in Spain that the German army saw the need to increase the size and power of its tank force. In Spain, the Soviet tanks deployed there – the T26 and the BT-5 – proved more effective than the German Panzer Mark I, while the Italian Fiat-Ansaldo miniature tank looked and performed more like a clockwork toy. Yet the Soviet advisers could not advocate modern armoured tactics after the show trial of Marshal Tukhachevsky, so their tank brigade was often misused, if not squandered.

The need for much closer liaison between advancing ground troops and their air support had also become obvious to both sides by the time of the battle of Jarama, yet the Red Army refused to install radios in non-command tanks throughout the Second World War and for most of the Cold War. The only real lesson that Soviet advisers learned was on the advantage of concentrating centrally controlled, long-range artillery, a tactic which finally had a chance to pay off during the battle of Stalingrad.[3]

One of the most debated questions is whether foreign intervention was decisive or not. Hitler's decision to send Junkers 52 transports to help Franco carry the first detachments of *regulares* and Foreign Legion across the Straits of Gibraltar was certainly important, but it is hard to say that it was decisive. The republican navy's incompetence and lack of initiative during the revolutionary chaos of the early weeks meant that the Army of Africa would have got across eventually. And since the republican forces were incapable of launching an offensive, time was not as crucial as it would otherwise have been. The argument that the rebellion of the generals would have collapsed in the summer of 1936 is unconvincing, unless one brings in that other form of intervention, the supply of ammunition from Portugal. Franco and his fellow rebel generals had gone too far to pull back, and so long as they had enough ammunition the battle would have continued until a critical mass of *africanistas* had reached the mainland.

Soviet intervention may well have helped save Madrid for the Republic in November 1936, as Franquist historians claim, but overall, there can be no doubt that German and Italian forces greatly shortened the war in the nationalists' favour. To say that they won the war for Franco entirely would be going too far. The Condor Legion above all accelerated the conquest of the north, a development which enabled the nationalists to concentrate their forces in the centre of Spain. But the truly devastating effectiveness of the Condor Legion came in countering the major republican offensives of 1937 and 1938, battles which were to break the back of the republican armed forces. These perfect opportunities for the deployment of air power to maximum effect were, however, provided by the disastrous leadership of the communist commanders and their Soviet advisers.

The organization and objectives which the People's Army assumed in the winter of 1936 were moulded more by internal and external political pressures than by military considerations. The communists' demands for a unified command and discipline were entirely logical from a military point of view (while, of course, presenting them with the best way to seize the levers of power). But the idea that the only possible strategy consisted of set-piece offensives, straight out of French training manuals from the First World War, proved to be almost as grave a liability as the militias' belief in the triumph of revolutionary morale. Even worse, the decisions to take the offensive were not guided by coherent thinking. In almost all cases these attacks were vain attempts to take the pressure off other threatened sectors and were launched for propaganda considerations. Once the attack had achieved surprise, the People's Army commanders then allowed the momentum of the offensive to be lost by besieging villages and small towns. In a matter of a few days the nationalists managed to redeploy their troops and the Condor Legion.

The Condor Legion, as its war diaries confirm, found that Soviet pilots and the republican air force lacked confidence in combat and proved more of a nuisance than a danger. So its squadrons were able to bomb and strafe the People's Army's elite formations at will, since they were usually trapped in a small area on a completely exposed terrain. Yet the republican leadership, even though all surprise and momentum had been lost, could not withdraw its precious troops and tanks, because of the grossly exaggerated propaganda claims that had been made when announcing the offensive. Thus the battles of Brunete, Belchite, Teruel and the Ebro were all disastrous repetitions. To make matters far worse, the Stalinist paranoia of the Soviet advisers and Spanish communist leaders attributed all reverses to Trotskyite treason and 'fifth columnists'. Preposterous theories were concocted, innocent officers and soldiers arrested and shot, and reports were sent back to Moscow which revealed delusions that went well over the edge of sanity. It is hardly surprising that republican morale suffered so desperately.

The only two successes the Republic enjoyed were Guadalajara, a victory which resulted basically from a collapse in Italian morale, and the defence of the XYZ line in the summer of 1938. The latter proved to be the most cost-effective battle of the whole war for the republicans, inflicting four times as many casualties as they received. It has presumably received so little attention because none of the star communist formations was involved and little propaganda effort was attached to a battle that did not conform to 'the active war policy of the Negrín government'.

All this suggests that a far more effective conduct of the war would have been to combine a strong defensive strategy with short, sharp probing attacks at different points to confuse the nationalists. The People's Army's tank forces should have been held back in an armoured reserve ready to counter-attack any nationalist break-through. The Republic could not simply have abandoned orthodox warfare for unorthodox, as some militia idealists dreamed. The conditions for a universal guerrilla war simply did not exist. The best-suited regions, with the right terrain, were insufficient to have stretched nationalist forces beyond capacity. But on thinly held fronts, many more nationalist troops could have been held down by commando actions. This would have hampered General Franco's brutally unsubtle strategy far more effectively. Franco did not so much win the war: the republican commanders, with the odds already stacked heavily against them, squandered the courage and sacrifice of their troops and lost it.

The British-inspired policy of non-intervention has, not surprisingly, generated a great deal of passion and moral outrage. For republicans, it seemed unthinkable that the legitimately elected government of a country should not be allowed to buy arms to defend itself. There can also be little doubt about the hypocrisy of maintaining a policy which was manifestly failing to work, while the committee in London, including the three main interventionist powers, Germany, Italy and the Soviet Union, pretended otherwise. The main anger is understandably reserved for the British government which, even if it did not officially propose the non-intervention plan, was certainly the main force behind it. The motives of the two prime ministers, Baldwin and Chamberlain, and the two foreign secretaries, Eden and Halifax, are frequently ascribed to a conservative plot to support Franco. Although extremely plausible, considering their personal friendships and tastes, this is probably a distortion of the truth.

None of them had any sympathy for the left-wing, if not revolutionary, nature of republican Spain, and certainly in the early days, they would have preferred a rapid nationalist success rather than what they saw as a slide towards the horrors of bolshevism. But their principal concerns lay elsewhere. They no more wanted Spain to be controlled by Nazi Germany or fascist Italy, Britain's chief rival in the Mediterranean, than for the country to fall under Soviet influence. Above all, they were deeply concerned that the Spanish conflagration would prove to be another Sarajevo, creating a widening ripple of involvement which would turn into the next European war. The British Foreign Office was nevertheless totally wrong to assume the lofty role of international policeman when it was secretly prepared to sacrifice the Spanish people, just as it sacrificed the Czechs in 1938.

One must also look at the effective results of the non-intervention policy, which prevented the Republic from purchasing arms openly. The republicans' greatest needs were for aircraft, tanks and automatic weapons. French equipment was generally of poor quality and the British aircraft available at that date were obsolete. Probably the only country capable of satisfying their needs, apart from the Soviet Union, was the United States. Roosevelt and Cordell Hull may have been influenced by the non-intervention agreement, but it was the Catholic lobby that led Congress to block arms supplies to the Republic. Thus, apart from a few aircraft purchases, Mexican rifles and ammunition, and Czechoslovakian machine-guns bought privately, it might appear that, even without the Non-Intervention Committee, the Republic had no alternative to the Soviet monopoly of arms supplies. Nevertheless, the decision to send Stalin the Republic's gold reserves was one of the most critical of the war.

The Archbishop of Burgos, who justified the cruelty of the war as being ultimately less cruel because it meant a shorter conflict, was clearly wrong, both morally and logically. Neither side could be terrified into submission. The polarization of political beliefs meant that both parties felt that everything in which they believed, as well as their very existence, was at stake. This transmuted fear into desperate bravery. The war was only likely to end when a decisive lack of troops, armaments and munitions demonstrated that defeat was inescapable. This came about for the Republic after its catastrophic defeat on the Ebro.

The only possible reason for continuing the struggle would have been to achieve better surrender terms from Franco, but this was a vain hope. Negrín failed utterly with his thirteen points and there were no grounds to expect that Franco was likely to shift his position; in fact, he was bound to become even more inflexible the closer he came to victory. Any decision to fight on could lead only to a useless loss of life. An International Brigader wrote later, 'It was all very fine for the left in Europe and America to beat their breasts and demand that the common people of Spain should fight to the last man, but once it had become apparent that the war could not be won it should have been terminated.'[4] Whether or not an earlier surrender might have mitigated the vicious revenge of the victors is impossible to say, but it is doubtful. All one can be sure of is that it would have saved many of the tens of thousands of lives lost in the hopeless battle for Catalonia.

Little more need be said about the Franquist vengeance, a process which was frequently justified on the basis of sentences for 'military rebellion', a reversal of judicial logic that speaks for itself. Facts gathered so painstakingly by Spanish historians over recent years leave little further doubt about its scale or its cruelty. The only question left to answer covers the thought processes of those who perpetrated such a regime. But to speculate about the mental state of such oppressors, whether Nazi, Soviet or nationalist, is to risk assuming the dubious mantle of a long-distance psychiatrist.

The repression extended throughout the population as a whole, creating a terrible claustrophobia, exceeded only by the harshness of living conditions imposed by the regime. One of the great debates of recent years has been the degree to which Franco's policy of autarchy and centralized financial direction laid the ground for Spain's subsequent economic transformation. The argument for the economic policy established under Franco is very hard to fathom since it created a deadening form of state control which some commentators have compared to the Soviet satellite states of the Cold War years. In the case of Franco's Spain, however, the degree of corruption and waste was perhaps equalled only by Ceauşescu's Romania. The partial economic liberalization which came about in the 1960s was in many ways more a case of accident due to foreign influences than of design.

The pertinent question, however, is what would a republican victory have produced? If the People's Army had achieved victory in, say, 1937 or 1938, what form of government would have ensued – the left-liberal administration of early 1936 or a hard-line communist regime? The accelerated collapse of the republican government in the spring and summer of 1936 and the onset of civil war, which triggered the revolutionary upheaval, followed a different path from the chaos that ensued from the First World War. Yet there was one similarity to the Russian revolution: this was the communist determination to eliminate their left-wing allies once the war had been won against the right. In September 1936, soon after his arrival, General Vladimir Gorev reported to Moscow: 'A struggle against the anarchists is absolutely inevitable after victory over the whites. This struggle will be very severe.'[5] André Marty, the Comintern representative, stated on 10 October, 'After victory we will get even with them [the anarchists], all the more so since at that point we will have a strong army.'[6] And *Pravda* declared on 10 December that the 'cleaning up of Trotskyist and anarcho-syndicalist elements will be carried out with the same energy as in the USSR'. As numerous reports back to Moscow made clear, the Popular Front strategy was merely a strategy 'for the moment'. The Comintern representatives in Spain were clearly seeking communist hegemony in Spain and, even though this was not in line with Stalin's general strategy, it is significant that no reproof or warning about this from Dimitrov appears in the communications between Moscow and Spain.

Stalinists, by the very nature of their own ideology, were not prepared to share power with anybody else in the longer term. Only one factor was likely to mitigate this in Spain, and that was the question of the Soviet Union's interests elsewhere on the international stage. Stalin had already demonstrated his readiness to sacrifice a foreign communist party if it happened to be in the interests of the 'Socialist Motherland'. In the case of Spain, it was mainly events in central Europe which determined Soviet policy. The British appeasement of Hitler in 1938 over his demands on Czechoslovakia prompted Stalin to prepare a new course, even if that eventually meant an alliance with Hitler himself. The post-war years would have been desperate, whatever government was in power. But everything afterwards would have depended on the form of regime which emerged. A fully democratic government would presumably have received Marshall Plan aid from the United States in 1948. Then, with a reasonably unfettered economy, recovery would almost certainly have begun by 1950, like elsewhere in Western Europe. But with an authoritarian leftist, perhaps overtly communist, government, Spain would probably have been left in a similar state to those Central European or Balkan people's republics until after 1989.

The Spanish Civil War is, however, best remembered in entirely human terms: the clash of beliefs, the ferocity, the generosity and selfishness, the hypocrisy of diplomats and ministers, the betrayal of ideals and political manoeuvres and, above all, the bravery and self-sacrifice of those who fought on both sides. But history, which is never tidy, must always end with questions. Conclusions are much too convenient.

BIBLIOGRAPHY

Abad de Santillán, Diego, *Porqué perdimos la guerra*, Buenos Aires, 1940
——, *Memorias, 1897–1936*, Barcelona, 1977
Abella, Rafael, *La Vida Cotidiana durante la Guerra Civil*, 2 vols, Barcelona, 1978
Abellán, José Luis (ed.), *El exilio español de 1939*, 6 vols, Madrid, 1976–8
——, *Historia crítica del pensamiento español*, 2 vols, Madrid, 1988
Acosta, Gonzalo, et al., *El canal de los presos. Trabajos forzados: de la represión política a la explotación económica*, Barcelona, 2004
Aguilar Fernández, Paloma, *Memoria y olvido de la guerra civil*, Madrid, 1996
Akin, Mohammed Ibn A., *La actitud de los moros ante el Alzamiento*, Málaga, 1997
Alba, Victor, *Histoire du POUM. Le marxisme en Espagne (1919–1939)*, Paris, 1975
Alcalá Zamora, Niceto, *Memorias*, Barcelona, 1977
Alexander, Bill, *British Volunteers for Liberty. Spain 1936–1939*, London, 1982
'Alfredo', see Togliatti, Palmiro
Alpert, Michael, *El ejército republicano en la guerra civil*, Paris, 1977
——, *La reforma militar de Azaña: 1931–1933*, Madrid, 1982
——, *La guerra civil española en el March*, Madrid, 1987
Alted, Alicia, 'Los niños de la guerra civil' in *Anales de Historia Contemporánea*, 2003
Álvarez, Santiago, *Negrín, personalidad histórica*, Madrid, 1994
Álvarez del Vayo, Julio, *Freedom's Battle*, London, 1940; *En la lucha*, Mèxico, 1974
Álvarez Rodriguez and López Ortega, R. (eds), *Poesía anglo-norteamericana de la guerra civil española*, Salamanca, 1986
Araquistáin, Luis, *El comunismo y la guerra de España*, Carmaux, 1939
Arasa, Daniel, *La invasión de los maquis*, Barcelona, 2004
Aróstegui, Julio (ed.), *Historia y memoria de la Guerra Civil. Encuentro de Castilla y León*, 3 vols, Valladolid, 1988
——, 'Violencia y politica en España' in *Ayer*, 13, Madrid, 1994
Aróstegui, Julio and Martínez, J. A., *La Junta de Defensa de Madrid*, Madrid, 1984
Asociación de Historia Contemporánea, 'La Guerra Civil', *Ayer*, 50, Madrid, 2003
Atholl, Katherine Duchess of, *Searchlight on Spain*, Harmondsworth, 1938
Atkin, Nicholas and Tallett, F., *Priests, Prelates and People*, London, 2003

Azaña, Manuel, *Causas de la guerra de España*, Barcelona, 1986
——, *Diarios completos. Monarquía, República, Guerra Civil*, Barcelona, 2000
——, *Discursos políticos*, Barcelona, 2003
Azcárate, Pablo de, *Mi embajada en Londres durante la guerra civil española*, Barcelona, 1976
Aznar, Manuel, *Historia militar de la guerra civil de España*, Madrid, 1940
——, *Pensamiento literario y compromiso antifascista de la inteligencia española republicana*, Barcelona, 1978

Bachoud, André, *Los españoles ante las campañas de Marruecos*, Madrid, 1988
——, *Franco*, Barcelona, 2000
Bahamonde, Angel and Cervera, J., *Así terminó la guerra de España*, Madrid, 1999
Bahamonde, Antonio, *Un año con Queipo. Memorias de un nacionalista*, Barcelona, 1938
Balfour, S. and Preston, Paul, *España y las grandes potencias en el siglo XX*, Barcelona, 2002
Banc, Ivo (ed.), *The Diary of Georgi Dimitrov, 1933–1949*, New Haven, 2003
Barciela, Carlos (ed.), *Autarquía y mercado negro*, Barcelona, 2003
Barea, Arturo, *La forja de un rebelde*, Madrid, 2000
Ben-Ami, Shlomo, *Los orígenes de la Segunda República*, Madrid, 1990
Benet, Josep, *Catalunya sota el règim franquista*, Paris, 1973
Bennassar, Bartolomé, *La guerre d'Espagne et ses lendemains*, Paris, 2004
Benson, F. R., *Writers in Arms*, London, 1968
Berdah, Jean-François, *La democracia asesinada: España 1931–1939. La República española y las grandes potencias*, Barcelona, 2002
Bernal, Antonio Miguel, *Economía e historia de los latifundios*, Madrid, 1988
Bernanos, Georges, *Les grandes cimetières sous la Lune*, Paris, 1938
Bernecker, Walter L., *Colectividades y revolución social. El anarquismo en la guerra civil española, 1936–1939*, Barcelona, 1983
Bessie, Alvah, *Men in Battle: A History of Americans in Spain*, New York, 1939
Blanco Escolá, Carlos, *La incompetencia militar de Franco*, Madrid, 2000
——, *Vicente Rojo, el general que humilló a Franco*, Barcelona, 2003
——, *Falacias de la guerra civil. Un homenaje a la causa republicana*, Barcelona, 2005
Blaye, Eduardo de, *Franco ou la Monarchie sans Roi*, Paris, 1974
Blinkhorn, Martín, *Aragón en la revolución española*, Barcelona, 1983
Bolín, Luis, *Spain: The Vital Years*, London, 1967; *Los años vitales*, Madrid, 1967
Bolloten, Burnett, *The Spanish Revolution: The Left and the Struggle for Power*, London, 1979 and Barcelona, 1980
Bonamusa, Francesc, 'L'administració de Justicia a Catalunya de setembre a desembre de 1936' in *Recerques*, 4, Barcelona, 1974
——, *Andreu Nin y el movimiento comunista en España, 1930–1937*, Barcelona, 1977

——, *Política i finances republicanes, 1931–1939*, Tarragona, 1997
Borkenau, Franz, *The Spanish Cockpit*, London, 1937; Ann Arbor, 1963
Bosch, Aurora, *Ugetistas y libertarios. Guerra civil y revolución en el país Valenciano*, Valencia, 1983
Bosch Gimpera, Pere, *Memòries*, Barcelona, 1980
Bowers, Claude, *My Mission to Spain*, New York, 1954; *Misión en España*, Barcelona, 1977
Boyarsky, V. I., *Partizansvo vchera, segodnya, zavtra*, Moscow, 2003
Bozal, Valeriano, *Pintura y escultura española del siglo XX*, 2 vols, Madrid, 1991
Brademas, John, *Anarcosindicalismo y revolución en España*, Barcelona, 1974
Brenan, Gerald, *The Spanish Labyrinth*, Cambridge, 1969; *El laberinto español*, Paris, 1962
Bricall, Josep María, *La política económica de la Generalitat (1936–1939)* 2 vols, Barcelona, 1979
Broué, Pierre and Témime, E., *La Révolution et la guerre d'Espagne*, Paris, 1961
Brown, C. G., *El siglo XX. Del 98 a la guerra civil*, Barcelona, 1993
Brusco, Ramón, *Les milícies antifeixistes i l'Exèrcit popular a Catalunya (1936–1937)*, Lérida, 2003
Buckley, Henry, *Vida y muerte de la República española*, Madrid, 2004
Bullejos, José, *La Comintern en España. Recuerdos de mi vida*, México, 1972
Bullón de Mendoza and Álvaro de Diego, *Historias orales de la guerra civil*, Barcelona, 2000
Busquets, Julio, *El Militar de Carrera en España*, Barcelona, 1971
Busquets, Julio and Losada J. C., *Ruido de sables. Las conspiraciones militares en la España del siglo XX*, Barcelona, 2003

Cabanellas, Guillermo, *La guerra de los mil días*, Barcelona, 1973
Cabrera, Mercedes, *La patronal ante la II República Organizaciónes y estrategia, 1931–1936*, Madrid, 1983
——, *Con luz y taquígrafos*, Madrid, 1999
Cabrera, Mercedes and Del Rey, F., *El poder de los empresarios. Política e intereses Económicos en la España contemporánea, 1875–2000*, Madrid, 2002
Cabrera Castillo, F., *Del Ebro a Gandesa. La batalla del Ebro*, Madrid, 2002
Callahan, William J., *La Iglesia católica en España, 1875–2002*, Barcelona, 2002
Cambó, Francesc, *Memorias (1876–1936)*, Madrid, 1987
Caminal, Miguel, *Joan Comorera. Catalanisme i socialisme, 1913–1936*, Barcelona, 1984
——, *Joan Comorera: Guerra i revolució, 1936–1939*, Barcelona, 1985
Campbell, Roy, *Light on a Dark Horse*, London, 1951
Canales, Antonio F., *La llarga posguerra*, Barcelona, 1997
Capponi, N., *I legionari rossi. Le Brigate Internazionali nella Guerra civile spagnola (1936–1939)*, Rome, 2000

Carbajosa, Mónica y Pablo, *La corte literaria de José Antonio*, Barcelona, 2003
Cárcel Orti, Vicente, *La gran persecución. España 1936–1939*, Barcelona, 2001
——, *Breve historia de la Iglesia en España*, Barcelona, 2003
Cardona, Gabriel, *El poder militar y la España contemporánea hasta la guerra civil*, Madrid, 1983
——, *El gigante descalzo: El ejército de Franco*, Madrid, 2003
Cardona, Gabriel and Losada, J. C., *Aunque me tires el Puente*, Madrid, 2004
Carnero, Teresa (ed.), *El reinado de Alfonso XIII*, Madrid, 1997
Carr, Raymond, *Spain 1808–1939*, Oxford, 1968
——, *Estudios sobre la República y la guerra civil española*, Barcelona, 1973
——, *España 1808–1975*, Barcelona, 1984
Carreras, Albert and Tafunell, X., *Historia económica de la España contemporánea*, Barcelona, 2004
Carrion, Pascual, *La reforma agraria de la Segunda República y la situación actual de la agricultura español*, Barcelona, 1973
Carroll, Peter N., *The Odyssey of the Abraham Lincoln Brigade: Americans in the Spanish Civil War*, Stanford, 1998
Carulla, Jordi and Carulla, A., *La guerra civil en 2000 carteles*, Barcelona, 1997
Casado, Segismundo, *The Last Days of Madrid*, London, 1939; *Así cayó Madrid*, Madrid, 1968
Casanova, Julián, *Anarquismo y revolución social en la sociedad rural aragonesa (1936–1938)*, Madrid, 1985
——, *De la calle al frente. El anarcosindicalismo en España (1931–1939)*, Barcelona, 1997
Casanova, Julián, et al., *Morir, matar, sobrevivir. La violencia en la dictadura de Franco*, Barcelona, 2002
Casares, Maria, *Residente Privilégiée*, Paris, 1980
Castells, Andreu, *Las Brigadas Internacionales en la Guerra de España*, Barcelona 1974
Castro, Luis, *Burgos durante la guerra civil* (in preparation)
Castro Delgado, Enrique, *Hombres made in Moscú*, Barcelona, 1965
Cattell, David T., *Communism and the Spanish Civil War*, New York, 1965
Cenarro, Ángela, *La sonrisa de Falange*, Barcelona, 2005
Cervera, Javier, *Madrid en Guerra. La ciudad clandestina 1936–1939*, Madrid, 1998
Chalmers-Mitchell, Peter, *My House in Malaga*, London, 1938
Chapaprieta, Joaquín, *La paz fue possible*, Barcelona, 1971
Chaves, Julián, *La guerra civil en Extremadura*, Badajoz, 1997
Chomsky, Noam, *American Power and the New Mandarins*, New York, 1969
Churchill, Winston, *Step by Step, 1936–1939*, London, 1939
Ciano, Galeazzo, *Diarios, 1937–1943*, Barcelona, 2004
Cierva, R. de la, *Historia actualizada de la Segunda república y la guerra civil, 1931–1939*, Madrid, 2003
Ciutat, Francisco, *Relatos y reflexiones de la guerra de España, 1936–1939*, Madrid, 1978

Cobb, Christopher, *La cultura y el pueblo: España 1930–1939*, Barcelona, 1981

Colodny, Robert, *El Asedio de Madrid*, Paris, 1970

Comín, Francisco, Hernández, M. and Llopis, E. (eds), *Historia económica de España*, Barcelona, 1997

Congreso Internacional de Escritores para la Defensa de la Cultura, *Literatura española y antifascismo (1927–1939)*, Valencia, 1987

Connelly Ullman, Joan, *La Semana Trágica*, Barcelona, 1972

Connolly, Cyril, *The Golden Horizon*, London, 1953

Commissariat XV Brigade, *Book of XV International Brigade*, Madrid, 1938 and Graham, Frank (ed.); Newcastle, 1975

Cordón, Antonio, *Trayectoria. Memorias de un militar republicano*, Barcelona, 1977

Corral, Pedro, *Si me quires escribir. Gloria y castigo de la 84a Brigada Mixta del Ejército Popular*, Barcelona, 2004

Coverdale, John R, *La intervención italiana en la guerra civil española*, Madrid, 1979

Cowles, Virginia, *Looking for Trouble*, London, 1941

Cox, Geoffrey, *The Defence of Madrid*, London, 1937

Crespo, Jesús, *Purga de maestros en la guerra civil*, Valladolid, 1987

Cruells, Manuel, *Els fets de maig. Barcelona, 1937*, Barcelona, 1970

——, *El sis d'Octubre a Catalunya*, Barcelona, 1976

Cruz, Rafael, *El Partido Comunista de España en la Segunda República*, Madrid, 1987

——, *Pasionaria. Dolores Ibárruri historia y símbolo*, Madrid, 1999

Cubero, José, *Les Républicains espagnols*, Pau, 2003

Cuevas, Tomasa, *Mujeres en las cárceles franquistas*, Madrid, 1979

——, *Cárcel de mujeres*, Barcelona, 1985

Cunard, Nancy (ed.), 'Authors Take Sides' in *Left Review*, London, 1937

Cunningham, Valentine, *Spanish Civil War Verse*, Harmondsworth, 1980

——, *Spanish Front – Writers on the Spanish Civil War*, Oxford, 1986

De Felice, Renzo, *Mussolini il duce*, 2 vols, Turin, 1974–81

De la Granja, J. L. and Garitaonaindía, C. (eds), *Gernika: 50 años después (1937–1987)*, Lejona, 1987

De la Mora, Constancia, *Doble esplendor*, Barcelona, 1977

De Luis, Francisco, *La FETE en la guerra civil española (1936–1939)*, Barcelona, 2002

De Pablo, S., 'La guerra civil en el País Vasco' in *Ayer*, Madrid, 2003

De Pablo, S., Mees, L. and Rodríguez, J. A., *El péndulo patriótico. Historia del Partido Nacionalista Vasco*, 2 vols, Barcelona, 1999 and 2001

Delpierre de Bayac, Jacques, *Les Brigades Internationales*, Paris, 1968

Díaz, José, *Tres años de lucha*, Paris, 1970

Díaz, Lorenzo, *La radio en España 1923–1997*, Madrid, 1997

Díaz del Moral, Juan, *Historia de los agitaciones campesinos andaluzas*, Madrid, 1973

Doña, Juana, *Desde la noche y la niebla: mujeres en las cárceles franguistas*, Madrid, 1978

Dos Passos, John, *Journeys Between Wars*, New York, 1938

Dreyfus-Armand, Geneviève, *El exilio de los republicanos españoles en Francia*, Barcelona, 2000

Eden, Anthony (Earl of Avon), *The Eden Memoirs*, vol. i, *Facing the Dictators*, London, 1962

Ellwood, Sheelagh, *Prietas las filas. Historia de la Falange Española, 1933–1983*, Barcelona, 2001

Elorza, Antonio and Bizcarrondo, M., *Queridos camaradas. La Internacional Comunista y España*, Barcelona, 1999

Elpatievsky, A. V., *Ispanskaya emigratsiya v SSSR*, Moscow, 2002

Enzensberger, Hans Magnus, *El corto verano de la anarquía. Vida y muerte de Buenaventura Durruti*, Barcelona, 1977

Esch, P. van der, *Prelude to War: The International Repercussions of the Spanish Civil War*, The Hague, 1951

Escolar, Hipólito, *La cultura durante la guerra civil*, Madrid, 1987

Espinosa, Francisco, *La guerra civil en Huelva*, Huelva, 1996

——, *La columna de la muerte. El avance del ejército franquista de Sevilla a Badajoz*, Barcelona, 2003

——, *La justicia de Queipo*, Barcelona, 2005

Esteban Infantes, Emilio, *General Sanjurjo*, Barcelona, 1957

Estruch, Joan, *Historia oculta del PCE*, Madrid, 2000

Fernández, Alberto, *Emigración republicana española (1939–1945)*, Algorta, 1972

Fernández, Carlos, *El general Franco. Un dictador en un tiempo de infamia*, Barcelona, 2005

Ferrerons, R. and Gascón, A., *Huesca: La bolsa de Bielsa*, Huesca, 1991

Figueres, J. M. (ed.), *Madrid en guerra. Crónica de la batalla de Madrid, 1936–1939*, Barcelona, 2004

Foltz, Charles, *Masquerade in Spain*, Boston, 1948

Fonseca, Carlos, *Trece rosas rojas*, Madrid, 2004

Fontana, Josep and Nadal, Jorgi, 'España 1914–1970' in C. M. Cipolla (ed.), *Historia económica de Europa*, vol. vi, Barcelona, 1980

Fontana, Josep (ed.), *Visions de guerra i reraguarda*, Barcelona, 1977

——, *España bajo el franquismo*, Barcelona, 1986

Franco Bahamonde, Francisco, *Palabras de Franco. I año triunfal*, Bilbao, 1937

——, *Palabras del Caudillo. 19 de abril 1937–7 de diciembre 1942*, Madrid, 1943

——, *Apuntes personales sobre la República y la guerra civil*, Madrid, 1987

Franco Salgado-Araujo, Francisco, *Mis conversaciónes privadas con Franco*, Barcelona, 1976

Fraser, Ronald, *The Blood of Spain*, London, 1979; *Recuérdalo tú y recuérdalo a otros. Historia oral de la guerra civil española*, Barcelona, 1979

——, *In Hiding. The life of Manuel Cortés*, London, 1972; *Escondido: el calvario de Manuel Cortés*, Valencia, 1986

Fusi, Juan Pablo, *Franco: autoritarismo y poder personal*, Madrid, 1985

——, *El País Vasco, 1931–1937*, Madrid, 2002

Fusi, Juan Pablo and Palafox, J., *España, 1808–1996, El desafio de la modernidad*, Madrid, 1997

Galland, Adolf, *Die Ersten und die Letzten. Jagdflieger im Zweiten Weltkrieg*, Darmstadt, 1953

Gárate Córdoba, José M., *Alféreces provisionales*, Madrid, 1976

García Delgado, José Luis, 'Modernización económica y democracia en España. Una recapitulación' in *Anales de la Real Academia de Ciencias Morales y Politicas*, n. 81, vol. i, Madrid, 2004

García Delgado, José Luis (ed.), *La II República española. El premier bienio*, Madrid, 1987

——, *La II República española. Bienio rectificador y Frente Popular, 1934–1936*, Madrid, 1988

García Delgado, José Luis; Fusi, J. P.; Juliá, Santos; Malefakis, E.; Payne, Stanley G., *Franquismo. El juicio de la historia*, Madrid, 2000

García Oliver, Juan, *De julio a Julio: Un año de lucha*, Barcelona, 1937

——, *El eco de los pasos*, Paris, 1978

García Pradas, José, *La traición de Stalin: como terminó la guerra de España*, New York, 1939

García Valiño, Rafael, *Guerra de liberación española (1938–1939). Campañas de Aragón y Maestrazgo. Batalla de Teruel. Batalla del Ebro*, Madrid, 1949

Garitaonaindía, C., *José Antonio Aguirre, primer lehendakari*, Bilbao, 1990

Garosci, Aldo, *Los intelectuales y la Guerra de España*, Madrid, 1981

Garriga, Ramón, *El General Yagüe*, Barcelona, 1985

Germán, L.; Lopis, E.; Maluquer de Motes, J., and Zapata, S., *Historia económica regional de España siglos XIX y XX*, Barcelona, 2001

Gibson, Ian, *Granada en 1936 y el asesinato de Federico García Lorca*, Barcelona, 1979

——, *En busca de José Antonio*, Barcelona, 1980

——, *La noche en que mataron a Calvo Sotelo*, Barcelona, 1982

——, *Paracuellos: cómo fue*, Barcelona, 1983

——, *Queipo de Llano. Sevilla, verano de 1936*, Barcelona, 1986

——, *Federico García Lorca*, 2 vols, Barcelona, 1998

Gil Andrés, Carlos, *Lejos del frente. Guerra civil y violencia política en La Rioja, 1933–1945* (in preparation)

Gil Pecharromán, Julio, *Historia de la Segunda República Española (1931–1936)*, Madrid, 2002

——, *José Antonio Primo de Rivera. Retrato de un visionario*, Madrid, 1996

Gil Robles, José Maria, *No fue posible la paz*, Barcelona, 1968

Gillain, Nick, *El mercenario. Diario de un combatiente rojo*, Tangier, 1939

Godicheau, François, 'La légende noire du Service d'Information Militaire de la République dans la guerre civile espagnole, et l'idée de contrôle politique'

in *Le Mouvement Social*, Paris, 2002
——, 'Los hechos de mayo de 1937 y los presos antifascistas: identificación de un fenómeno represivo' in *Historia Social*, Barcelona, 2002
——, *La guerre d'Espagne. République et Révolution en Catalogne (1936–1939)*, Paris, 2004
Goloviznin, Mark, 'Dnevnik sovetskogo generalnogo konsula v Barselone' in *Tetradi rabochego dvizheniya, Daidzhest*, Vypusk 1, Moscow, 1991
Gómez Aparicio, P., *Historia del periodismo español*, Madrid, 1981
Gómez Navarro, José Luis, *El régimen de Primo de Rivera*, Madrid, 1991
González, Miguel, 'La conjura del 36 contada por Franco', *El País*, Madrid, 2001
González, Valentin ('El Campesino'), *Listen Comrades*, London 1952
——, *Mis memorias de la Guerra*, Madrid, 1968
González Calvet, María Teresa, *La dictadura de Primo de Rivera. El directorio militar*, Madrid, 1987
González Cuevas, P. C., *Acción Española. Teología política nacionalismo autoritario en España, 1931–1936*, Madrid, 1998
Gorkín, Julián, *Caníbales políticos: Hitler y Stalin en España*, México, 1941
Graham, Frank, *The Battle of Jarama, 1937*, Newcastle, 1987
Graham, Helen, *Socialism and War. The Spanish Socialist Party in Power and Crisis (1936–1939)*, Cambridge, 1991
——, 'Against the State: the genealogy of the Barcelona May Days (1937)', in *European History Quarterly*, vol. 29, 4, 1999
——, *The Spanish Republic at War (1936–1939)*, Cambridge, 2002
Graham, Helen and Labanyi, J. (eds), *Spanish Cultural Studies. An Introduction. The Struggle for Modernity*, Oxford, 1995
Grimau, Carmen, *El cartel republicano en la guerra civil*, Madrid, 1979
Gubern, Román et al., *Historia del cine español*, Madrid, 1995
Guerin, Daniel, *L'Anarchisme*, Paris, 1965
Gurney, Jason, *Crusade in Spain*, London, 1974
Guzmán, Eduardo de, *Madrid rojo y Negro*, Barcelona, 1938

Hanrez, Marc, *Les écrivains et la guerre d'Espagne*, Madrid, 2004
Hedilla, Manuel, *Testimonio de Manuel Hedilla*, Barcelona, 1972
Heiber, Helmut (ed.), *Hitler y sus generales*, Barcelona, 2004
Heiberg, Morten, *Emperadores del Mediterráneo. Franco, Mussolini y la guerra civil española*, Barcelona, 2003
Heiberg, Morten and Pelt, Mogens, *Los negocios de la guerra. Armas nazis para la República española*, Barcelona, 2005
Heine, Harmutt, *La guerrilla antifranquista en Galicia*, Vigo, 1980
——, *La oposición política al franquismo*, Barcelona, 1983
Helsey, G., *Anarcosindicalismo y estado en Aragón, 1930–1938*, Madrid, 1994
Hemingway, Ernest, *The Spanish War*, London, 1938
Henríquez Caubín, Julián, *La batalla del Ebro*, Mexico, 1966
Hernández, Jesús, *La Grande Trahison*, Paris, 1953; *Yo fuí ministro de Stalin*, Mexico, 1953

Herreros, Isabelo, *El Alcázar de Toledo. Mitología de la cruzada de Franco*, Madrid, 1995

Hidalgo de Cisneros, Ignacio, *Cambio de rumbo (Memorias)*, 2 vols, Bucharest, 1964

Higuera, A. G. de la and Molina, L., *Historia de la revolución española*, Cádiz, 1940

Hoare, Samuel, see Templewood, Viscount

Holguín, Sandie, *República de ciudadanos. Cultura e identidad nacional en la España republicana*, Barcelona, 2003

Hormiga, *La Historia del Sindicalismo Español*, Paris, 1975

Howson, Gerald, *Arms for Spain*, London, 2000; *Armas para España*, Barcelona, 2000

Hubbard, J. R., 'How Franco financed his War' in *Journal of Modern History*, Chicago, 1953

Ibárruri, Dolores (ed.), *Guerra y revolución en España*, 3 vols, Moscow, 1971

Internatsionalnaya brigada, Moscow, 1937

Iribarren, J. M., *El general Mola*, Madrid, 1963

Jackson, Gabriel, *La República española y la guerra civil*, Barcelona, 1976

——, *Entre la reforma y la revolución. La República y la guerra civil 1931–1939*, Barcelona, 1980

——, *Juan Negrín*, Barcelona, 2004

Jackson, Gabriel et al., *Octubre 1934, Cincuenta años para la reflexión*, Madrid, 1985

Jackson, Gabriel and Alba, V., *Juan Negrín*, Barcelona, 2004

Jensen, Geoffrey, *Irrational Triumph. Cultural Despair, Military Nationalism and the Ideological Origins of Franco's Spain*, Reno, 2002

Jiménez de Aberasturi, Luis M., *Crónica de la guerra en el Norte (1936–1937)*, San Sebastián, 2003

Jones, Thomas, *A Diary with Letters (1931–1950)*, Oxford, 1954

Jover, José M.; Gómez-Ferrer, G.; and Fusi, J. P., *España. Sociedad, política y civilización, (siglos XIX–XX)*, Madrid 2000

Juliá, Santos, *La izquierda del PSOE (1935–1936)*, Madrid, 1977

——, *Orígenes del Frente Popular en España (1934–1936)*, Madrid, 1979

——, 'El fracaso de la Segunda República' in *Revista de Occidente*, 7–8, Madrid, 1981

——, *Madrid 1931–1934. De la fiesta popular a la lucha de clases*, Madrid, 1984

——, *Historia del socialismo español (1931–1939)*, Barcelona, 1989

——, *Manuel Azaña: una biografía política: del Ateneo al Palacio Nacional*, Madrid, 1990

——, 'Política en la Segunda República' in *Ayer*, 20, Madrid, 1995

——, *Historias de las dos Españas*, Madrid, 2004

Juliá, Santos (ed.), 'Fracaso de una insurreción y derrota de una huelga: los hechos de Octubre en Madrid' in *Estudios de Historia Social*, Madrid, 1984

——, *Escritos de la República: notas históricas de la guerra en España (1917–1940)*, Madrid, 1985

——, *Victimas de la guerra civil*, Barcelona, 1999

Juliá, Santos; García Delgado, J. L.; Jiménez, J. C.; Fusi, J. P.; *La España del siglo XX*, Madrid, 2003

Junod, Marcel, *Warrior without Weapons*, New York, 1951

Kaminski, H., *Ceux de Barcelone*, Paris, 1937; *Los de Barcelona*, Barcelona, 2002

Kemp, Peter, *Mine Were of Trouble*, London, 1957

Kindelán, General Alfredo, *Mis cuadernos de guerra*, Madrid, 1945; Barcelona, 1982

Koestler, Arthur, *Spanish Testament*, London, 1937

Koltsov, M, *Ispansky dnevnik*, Moscow, 1957. *Diario de la guerra de España*, Paris, 1963

Kowalsky, Daniel, *La Unión Soviética y la guerra civil española*, Barcelona, 2004

Krivosheev, G. F. (ed.), *Rossiya i SSSR v voihakh 20 veka. Poteri vooruzhennykh sil*, Moscow, 2001

Kuznetsov, Nikolai G., *Bajo la bandera de la España republicana*, Moscow, 1967

La guerra civil a Catalunya (1936–1939), 4 vols., Barcelona, 2005

Lacomba, Juan Antonio, *La crisis española de 1917*, Madrid, 1970

Lafuente, Isaías, *Tiempos de hambre. Viaje a la España de posguerra*, Madrid, 1999

——, *Esclavos por la patria*, Madrid, 2001

Langdon-Davies, John, *Behind Spanish Barricades*, London, 1936; *Detrás de las barricadas españolas*, Santiago de Chile, 1937

——, *La Semana Tràgica de 1937: Els fets de maig*, Barcelona, 1987

Largo Caballero, Francisco, *Mis Recuerdos*, México, 1956

Lefebvre, Michel and Skoutelsky, R., *Las Brigadas Internacionales. Imágenes recuperadas*, Barcelona, 2003

Leval, Gaston, *Collectives in the Spanish Revolution*, London, 1975

Líster, Enrique, *Nuestra Guerra*, Paris, 1966

——, *Memorias de un luchador*, Madrid, 1977

Little, Douglas, *Malevolent Neutrality, the United States, Great Britain and the origins of the Spanish Civil War*, Ithaca, 1985

Lojendio, Luis María de, *Operaciónes militares de la guerra de España*, Barcelona, 1940

Lorenzo, César M., *Les anarchistes espagnols et le pouvoir (1868–1969)* Paris, 1969

Luca de Tena, Catalina (ed.), *El periódico del siglo Cien firmas – cien años*, Madrid, 2002

MacDougall, Ian (ed.), *Voices from the Spanish Civil War*, Edinburgh, 1986

Madariaga, María Rosa de, *Los moros que trajo Franco*, Madrid, 2002
Madariaga, Salvador de, *Spain*, London, 1946
Maiz, Félix, *Mola, aquel hombre*, Barcelona, 1976
Maldonado, José María, *Alcañiz, 1938. El bombardeo olvidado*, Saragossa, 2003
Malefakis, Edward E., *Agrarian Reform and Peasant Revolution in Spain*, Yale, 1970; *Reforma agraria y revolución campesina en la España del siglo XX*, Barcelona, 1971
Malerbe, Pierre; Tuñón de Lara, M.; García Nieto, M. C.; and Mainer Baqué, J-C., *La crisis del Estado: Dictadura, Républica y guerra (1923–1939)*, vol. ix of *Historia de España*, Manuel Tuñón de Lara (ed.), Barcelona, 1981
Mallett, Robert, *Mussolini and the origins of the Second World War, 1933–1940*, London, 2003
Malraux, André, *L'Espoir*, Paris, 1939; *La esperanza*, Barcelona, 1978
Manzanara, Elías, *Documento histórico. La columna de hierro*, Barcelona, 1981
Marías, Julián, *Una vida presente Memorías (1914–1951)*, Madrid, 1989
Mariñas, Francisco Javier, *General Varela*, Barcelona, 1956
Martín Aceña, Pablo, *El oro de Moscú y el oro de Berlin*, Madrid, 2001
Martín Blázquez, J., *I Helped to Build an Army*, London, 1939
Martín Jiménez, Ignacio, *La guerra civil en Valladolid (1936–1939)*, Valladolid, 2000
Martín Ramos, Josep Lluís, *Els orígens del Partit Socialista Unificat de Catalunya (1930–1936)*, Barcelona, 1977
Martínez Bande, J. M., *Los cien ultimos días de la Républica*, Barcelona, 1973
——, *La ofensiva sobre Segovia y la batalla de Brunete*, Madrid, 1972
Martínez Barrio, Diego, *Páginas para la historia del Frente Popular*, Madrid, 1937
——, *Memorias*, Barcelona, 1983
Martínez Cuadrado, Miguel, *Elecciónes y partidos políticos en España, 1808–1931*, Madrid, 1969
Martínez Reverte, Jorge, *La Batalla del Ebro*, Barcelona, 2003
——, *La Batalla de Madrid*, Barcelona, 2004
Matesanz, José A., *Las raíces del exilio, México ante la guerra civil española, 1936–1939*, México, 1999
Matthews, Herbert, *The Education of a Correspondent*, New York, 1946
Maura, Miguel, *Así cayó Alfonso XIII*, Barcelona, 1966
Maurice, Jacques, *El anarquismo andaluz. Campesinos y sindicalistas, 1868–1936*, Barcelona, 1990
McDermott, Kevin and Agnew, J., *The Comintern*, New York, 1997
Meaker, Gerald H., *The Revolutionary Left in Spain 1914–1923*, Stanford, 1974
Mera, Cipriano, *Guerra, exilio y carcel de un anarcosindicalista*, Paris, 1976
Merino, Ignacio, *Serrano Súñer. Conciencia y poder*, Madrid, 2004
Mezquida i Gene, Lluís M., *La batalla del Ebro*, Tarragona, 2001
Millán Astray, José, *Franco, el Caudillo*, Salamanca, 1939

Mínev, Stoyán ('Stepánov'), *Las causas de la derrota de la República española*, Madrid, 2003
Mintz, Frank, *L'Autogestion dans l'Espagne Révolutionnaire*, Paris, 1976
Mintz, Jerome R., *Los anarquistas de Casas Viejas*, Cádiz, 1994
Mir, Conxita, *Vivir es sobrevivir. Justicia, orden y marginación en la Cataluña rural de posguerra*, Lérida, 2000
Miralles, Ricardo, *Juan Negrín. La República en guerra*, Madrid, 2003
Modesto, J., *Soy del Quinto Regimiento*, Paris, 1969
Mola, Emilio, *Obras completas*, Valladolid, 1940
Molinero, Carme and Ysàs, P., *'Patria, justicia, y pan'. Nivell de vida i condicións de treball a Catalunya 1939–1951*, Barcelona, 1985
Molinero, C.; Sala, M.; and Sobrequés, J. (eds), *Una inmensa prisión. Los campos de concentración y las prisiones durante la guerra civil y el franquismo*, Barcelona, 2003
Monjo, Anna and Vega, Carmen, *Els treballadors i la guerra civil. Història d'una indústria catalana collectivitzada*, Barcelona, 1986
Montagut, Lluís, *Yo fuí soldado de la República 1936–1945*, Barcelona, 2003
Montero, Antonio, *Historia de la persecución religiosa de España 1750–2000*, Barcelona, 2003
Montero, José R., *La CEDA. El catolicismo social y politico en la Segunda República*, 2 vols, Madrid, 1977
Moradiellos, Enrique, *Neutralidad benévola el gobierno británico y la insurreción militar española de 1936*, Oviedo, 1990
——, *La perfidia de Albíon. El gobierno británico y la guerra civil española*, Barcelona, 1996
——, *El reñidero de Europa. Las dimensiones internacionales de la guerra civil española*, Barcelona, 2001
——, *1936. Los mitos de la guerra civil*, Barcelona, 2004
Morán, Gregorio, *Miseria y grandeza del Partido Comunista de España, 1939–1985*, Barcelona, 1986
Moreno, Gómez, Francisco, *La resistencia armada contra Franco. Tragedia del maquis y la guerrilla*, Barcelona, 2001
Moreno, Xavier, *La División Azul. Sangre española en Rusia 1941–1945*, Barcelona, 2004
Morente, Francisco, *La escuela y el Estado Nuevo. La depuración del magisterio nacional, 1936–1943*, Valladolid, 1997
Morodo, Raúl, *Origenes ideológicos del franquismo: Acción Española*, Madrid, 1985

Nadal, Jordi, Carreras, A. and Sudrià, C., *La economía española en el siglo XX. Una perspectiva histórica*, Barcelona, 1987
Nadal Sánchez, A., *Guerra civil en Málaga*, Málaga, 1984
Nash, Mary, *Mujeres Libres: España 1936–1939*, Barcelona, 1975
——, *Rojas. Las mujeres republicanas en la Guerra Civil*, Madrid, 1999
Nerín, Gustau, *La guerra que vino de África*, Barcelona, 2005
Neves, Mário, *A chacina de Badajoz*, Lisbon, 1985

Nicolson, Harold, *Diaries and Letters, 1930–1939*, 3 vols, London, 1966–8

Nin, Andreu, *Los Problemas de la revolución española*, Paris, 1971

Nora, Eugenio G. de, *La novela española contemporánea (1898–1962)*, 3 vols, Madrid, 1958–71

Nothomb, Paul, *Malraux en España*, Barcelona, 2001

Ojeda Revah, Mario, *México y la guerra civil española*, Madrid, 2005

Olmos, Victor, *Historia del ABC*, Barcelona, 2002

Orlov, Aleksandr, *Tainaya istoriya stalinskikh prestupleny*, Saint Petersburg, 1981

Orwell, George, *Homage to Catalonia*, London, 1938; *Homenaje a Cataluña*, Barcelona, 1970

——, Collected Essays, *Journalism and Letters*, London, 1968

Ossorio, Ángel, *Vida y sacrificio de Companys*, Buenos Aires, 1943

Pages, Pelai, *El movimiento trotskista en España 1930–1935*, Barcelona, 1977

Palafox, Jordi, *Altraso económico y democracia. La Segunda República, 1931–1936*, Barcelona, 1995

Palomares, Jesús M., *La guerra civil en Palencia. La eliminación de los contraries*, Palencia, 2002

Pàmies, Teresa, *Quan érem capitans. Memòries d'aquella guerra*, Barcelona, 1974

Paniagua, Xavier, *La sociedad libertaria. Agrarismo e industrialización en el anarquismo español, 1930–1939*, Barcelona, 1982

Payne, Stanley G., *Falange. Historia del fascismo español*, Paris, 1965

——, *The Spanish Revolution*, London, 1970; *La revolución española*, Barcelona, 1971

——, *La primera democracia española. La Segunda República, 1931–1936*, Barcelona, 1995

——, *Unión Soviética, comunismo y revolución en España (1931–1939)*, Barcelona, 2003; *The Spanish Civil War, the Soviet Union and Communism*, London, 2004

——, *El colapso de la República*, Madrid, 2005

Paz, Abel, *Durruti en la revolución española*, Madrid, 1996

Peirats, José, *La CNT en la revolución española*, 3 vols, Paris, 1971

Peiró, Joan, *Perill a la reraguardia*, Barcelona, 1936

Pérez, Joseph, *Historia de España*, Barcelona, 1999

Pérez Baró, Albert, *Trenta mesos de collectivisme a Catalunya*, Barcelona, 1970

——, *Història de les cooperatives a Catalunya*, Barcelona, 1989

Pérez Galán, Mariano, *La enseñanza en la Segunda República española*, Madrid, 1975

Pérez Lopez, E. A., *Guerrilla Diary of the Spanish Civil War*, London, 1972

Petit Pastor, D., *La cinquena columna a Catalunya (1936–1939)*, Barcelona, 1974

——, *Los dossiers secretos de la Guardia Civil*, Barcelona, 1978

Pettifer, James (ed.), *Cockburn in Spain – Despatches from the Spanish Civil War*, London, 1986
Pi y Suñer, Carlos, *La República y la Guerra. Memorias de un político catalán*, México, 1975
Pike, D. W., *Vae Victis! Los republicanos españoles refugiados en Francia*, Paris, 1969
——, *Les français et la guerre d'Espagne*, Paris, 1975
Pla Brugat, Dolores, 'El exilio republicano español' in *Aula. Historia social*, 2004
Plenn, Abel, *Wind in the Olive Trees*, New York, 1946
Poblet, J. M., *Vida i mort de Lluís Companys*, Barcelona, 1976
Pons Prades, E., *Guerrillas españolas 1939–1960*, Barcelona, 1977
——, *Los niños republicanos en la guerra de España*, Madrid, 2004
Prados de la Escosura, Leandro, *El progreso económico de España (1850–2000)*, Madrid, 2003
Preston, Paul, *The Coming of the Spanish Civil War*, London, 1978
——, *La destrucción de la democracia en España. Reforma reacción y revolución en la Segunda República*, Madrid, 1978
——, *Las derechas españolas en el siglo XX: Autoritarismo, fascismo y golpismo*, Madrid, 1986
——, *Franco, caudillo de España*, Barcelona, 1994
——, *Las tres Españas del 36*, Barcelona, 1998
——, *La República asediada. Hostilidad internacional y conflitos internos durante la guerra civil*, Barcelona, 1999
——, *La guerra civil española*, Barcelona, 2000
——, *Palomas de guerra*, Barcelona, 2001
Prieto, Indalecio, *Convulciones de España*, 3 vols, México, 1967–9
——, *Discursos fundamentales*, Madrid, 1976
——, *Cómo y porqué salí del Ministerio del Defensa Nacional*, Barcelona, 1989
Primo de Rivera, José Antonio, *Obras completas*, Madrid, 1976

Quevedo, A., *Queipo de Llano. Gloria e infortunio de un general*, Barcelona, 2001
Quintanilla, Luis, *Los rehenes del Alcázar de Toledo*, Paris, 1967

Radosh, Ronald; Habeck, M. R.; and Sevostianov, G., *España traicionada. Stalin y la guerra civil*, Barcelona, 2002; *Spain Betrayed – The Soviet Union in the Spanish Civil War*, New Haven, 2001
Raguer, Hilari, *La espada y la cruz: La iglesia 1936–1939*, Barcelona, 1977
——, *El general Batet*, Barcelona, 1996
——, *La pólvora y el incienso*, Barcelona, 2001
Ramos Oliveira, Antonio, *Historia de España*, 3 vols, Mexico, 1943
Ranzato, Gabriele, *L'eclissi della democrazia. La guerra civile spagnola e le sue origine, 1931–1939*, Turin, 2004
Razvedka i kontrrazvedka v litsakh, Moscow, 2002

Read, Herbert, *Collected Poems*, London, 1943
Reig Tapia, Alberto, *Ideología e historia: sobre la represión franquista y la guerra civil*, Madrid, 1986
——, *Memoria de la guerra civil. Los mitos de la tribu*, Madrid, 1999
Regler, Gustav, *The Great Crusade*, New York, 1940
——, *The Owl of Minerva*, London, 1959
Requena Gallego, M., *Los sucesos de Yeste*, Albacete, 1983
Requena, Manuel and Sepúlveda, R. M., *Las brigadas internacionales. El contexto internacional, los medios de propaganda, literatura y memorias*, Cuenca, 2003
Richards, Michael, *Un tiempo de silencio. La guerra civil y la cultura de la represión en la España de Franco*, Barcelona, 1999
Ridruejo, Dionisio, *Escrito en España*, Buenos Aires, 1964
——, *Casi unas memorias*, Barcelona, 1976
Rivas, F., *El Frente Popular*, Madrid, 1976
Rivas Cherif, Cipriano, *Retrato de un desconocido. Vida de Manuel Azaña*, Barcelona, 1980
Rodimtsev, Aleksandr Ilyich, *Dobrovoltsy – internatsionalisty*, Sverdlovsk, 1976
Rodrigo, Javier, *Cautivos. Campos de concentración en España franquista*, Barcelona, 2005
'Rogeby', Sixten (Olsson, Sixten), *Spanska frontminnen*, Arbetarkultur, Stockholm, 1938
Rojo, Vicente, *Alerta los pueblos!*, Barcelona, 1974
——, *España Heroica*, Barcelona, 1975
——, *Así fue la defensa de Madrid*, Madrid, 1987
——, *Elementos del arte de guerra*, Madrid, 1988
Rolfe, Edwin, *The Lincoln Battalion: The Story of the Americans who fought in the International Brigades*, New York, 1939
Romero, Luis, *Tres días de Julio*, Barcelona, 1967
——, *Desastre en Cartagena*, Barcelona, 1971
——, *El final de la guerra*, Barcelona, 1976
Romilly, Esmond, *Boadilla*, London, 1971
Rosado, Antonio, *Tierra y libertad. Memorias de un campesino anarcosindicalista andaluz*, Barcelona, 1979
Rosal, Amaro del, *El oro del Banco de España y la historia del Vita*, Mexico, 1976
Rosas, Fernando (ed.), *Portugal e a guerra civil de Espanha*, Lisbon, 1996
Rosenthal, Marilyn, *Poetry of the Spanish Civil War*, New York, 1975
Rovighi, A. and Stefani, F., *La partizipazione italiana alla guerra civil spagnola*, Rome, 1993
Rubio, Javier, *La emigración de la guerra civil de 1936–1939*, 3 vols, Madrid, 1977
Ruíz Ramón, F., *Historia del teatro español: siglo XX, Madrid, 1975*
Russell, Bertrand, *Roads to Freedom*, New York, 1948

Saborit, Andrés, *Julián Besteiro*, Buenos Aires, 1967
Sáinz Rodríguez, Pedro, *Testimonio y recuerdos*, Barcelona, 1978
Sala Noguer, Ramón, *El cine en la España republicana durante la guerra civil*, Bilbao, 1993
Salas Larrazábal, Jésus, *La guerra de España desde el aire. Dos ejércitos y sus cazas frente a frente*, Barcelona, 1970
Salas Larrazábal, Ramón, *Pérdidas de la guerra*, Barcelona, 1972
——, *Historia del Ejército Popular de la República*, 4 vols, Madrid 1973
——, *Los datos exactos de la guerra civil*, Madrid, 1980
——, *Historia general de la guerra de España*, Madrid, 1986
Salcedo, Emilio, *Vida de Don Miguel*, Salamanca, 1964
Sallés, Anna (ed.), *Documents 1931–1939*, 2 vols, Barcelona, 1976
Saña, Heleno, *El franquismo sin mitos. Conversaciónes con Serrano Súñer*, Barcelona, 1981
Sanabre, José M., *Martirologio de la Iglesia en la diócesis de Barcelona durante la persecución religiosa*, Barcelona, 1943
Sánchez Asiaín, José Ángel, *La Banca española en la guerra civil (1936–1939)*, Madrid, 1992
——, *Economía y finanzas en la guerra civil española, 1936–1939*, Madrid, 1999
Sánchez Recio, Glicerio, *Guerra civil y franguismo en Alicante*, Alicante, 1990
——, *Justicia y guerra en España: los tribunales populares (1936–1939)*, Alicante, 1991
Sartorius, Nicolás and Alfaya, Javier, *La memoria insumisa. Sobre la dictadura de Franco*, Barcelona, 2002
Saz, Ismael, *Mussolini contra la Segunda República*, Valencia, 1986
Schwartz, Fernando, *La internacionalización de la guerra civil española*, Barcelona, 1972
Schwarzstein, Dora, *Entre Franco y Perón. Memoria e identidad del exilio republicano español en Argentina*, Barcelona, 2001
Seco, Carlos, *Alfonso XIII y la crisis de la Restauración*, Barcelona, 1969
Segala, Renzo, *Trincee di Spagna*, Milan, 1938
Seidman, Michael, *A ras de suelo Historia social de la República durante la guerra civil*, Madrid, 2003
Serge, Victor, *Memoirs of a Revolutionary*, Oxford, 1967
Serrano, Secundino, *Maquis. Historia de la guerrilla antifranquista*, Madrid, 2001
Serrano Súñer, Ramón, *Entre Hendaya y Gibraltar*, Barcelona, 1973
——, *Entre el silencio y la propaganda. La historia como fue*, Barcelona, 1977
——, *Memorias*, Barcelona, 1977
Servicio Histórico Militar, *La marcha sobre Madrid*, Madrid, 1968
——, *La lucha en torno a Madrid*, Madrid, 1968
——, *La guerra en el norte*, Madrid, 1969
——, *La batalla del Ebro*, Madrid, 1978
Silva, Emilio and Macías, S., *Las fosas de Franco*, Madrid, 2003

Skoutelsky, Rémi, *L'espoir guidait leurs pas. Les volontaires français dans les Brigades Internationales, 1936–1939*, Paris, 1988

Solano, Fernando, *La tragedia del Norte*, Barcelona, 1938

Solé i Barju, Queralt, *A los presos de Franco*, Barcelona, 2004

Solé i Sabaté, Josep María, *La repressió franquista a Catalunya (1938–1953)*, Barcelona, 1985

Solé i Sabaté, J. M. and Joan Villarroya, *España en llamas. La guerra civil desde el aire*, Madrid, 2003

Sommerfield, John, *Volunteer in Spain*, London, 1937

Sopeña, Andrés, *El florido pensil. Memoria de la escuela nacionalcatólica*, Barcelona, 1994

Soria, George, *Trotskyism in the Service of Franco: Facts and documents on the Activities of the POUM*, London, 1939

Soriano, Antonio, *Éxodus. Historia oral del exilio republicano en Francia, 1939–1945*, Barcelona, 1989

Souchy, Augustin, *Die Soziale Revolution in Spanien*, Berlin, 1974

——, *With the Peasants of Aragon*, Minneapolis, 1982

Southworth, H., *Mythe de la Croisade de Franco*, Paris, 1964; *El mito de la cruzada de Franco*, Barcelona, 1986

——, *La destrucción de Guernica. Periodismo, diplomacia, propaganda e historia*, Paris, 1977

——, *El lavado de cerebro de Francisco Franco*, Barcelona, 2000

Stafford, David, *Churchill and Secret Service*, London, 1997

Steer, G. L., *The Tree of Gernika*, London, 1938

'Stepánov', see Mínev, Stoyán

Suárez, Luis, *Franco: la historia y sus documentos*, 20 vols, Madrid, 1986

——, *Franco*, Barcelona, 2005

Suárez, Manuel (ed.), *La restauración, entre el liberalismo y la democracia*, Madrid, 1997

Subirats, Josep, *Pilatos 1939–1941. Prisiones de Tarragona*, Madrid, 1993

Sueiro, Daniel, *El Valle de los Caídos. Los secretos de la cripta franquista*, Barcelona, 1983

Suero, Luciana, *Memorias de un campesino andaluz en la revolución española*, Madrid, 1982

Tagüeña, Manuel, *Testimonio de dos guerras*, Mexico, 1973

Talón, Vicente, *Memoria de la guerra de Euzkadi de 1936*, Barcelona, 1988

Tarancón, Vicent Enrique, *Recuerdos de juventud*, Barcelona, 1984

Tavera, Susanna, 'La historia del anarquismo español: una encrucijada interpretativa' in *Ayer*, 45, Madrid, 2002

——, *Federica Montseny. La indomable (1905–1994)*, Madrid, 2005

Templewood, Viscount (Samuel Hoare), *Ambassador on Special Mission*, London, 1946

Thomas, Gordon and Witts, Max Morgan, *The Day Guernica Died*, London, 1975

Thomas, Hugh, *La guerra civil española*, 2 vols, Barcelona, 1976; *The Spanish Civil War*, London, 2003
Thomàs, J. M., *Lo que la Falange*, Barcelona, 1999
Togliatti, Palmiro, *Escritos sobre la guerra de España*, Barcelona, 1980
Torres, Estanislau, *La batalla de l'Ebre i la caiguda de Barcelona*, Lérida, 1999
Townson, Nigel, *The Crisis of Democracy in Spain*, Brighton, 2000
Townson, Nigel (ed.), *El republicanismo en España (1830–1977)*, Madrid, 1994
Trapiello, Andrés, *Las armas y las letras. Literatura y guerra civil (1936–1939)*, Barcelona, 1994
Trevor-Roper, H. (ed.), *Las conversaciónes privadas de Hitler*, Barcelona; *Hitler's Table Talk*, London, 2003
Tuñón de Lara, Manuel, *La España del siglo XX*, Paris, 1966
——, *La II República*, 2 vol, Madrid, 1976
——, *La guerra civil 50 años después*, Barcelona, 1985
Tuñón de Lara, Manuel (ed.), *Historia de España*, 10 vols, Barcelona, 1981–3
Tusell, Javier, *La Segunda República en Madrid: Elecciónes y partidos políticos*, Madrid, 1970
——, *Las elecciónes del Frente Popular en España*, 2 vols, Madrid, 1971
——, *Historia de la democracia cristiana en España*, 2 vols, Madrid, 1974
——, *Los católicos en la España de Franco*, Madrid, 1990
——, *Franco en la guerra civil. Un biografia politica*, Barcelona, 1992
——, *Franco, España y la II Guerra Mundial – Entre el Eje y la neutralidad*, Madrid, 1995
——, *Historia de España en el siglo XX*, Madrid, 1999
——, *Vivir en guerra*, Barcelona, 1986
——, *Dictadura franquista y democracia, 1939–2004*, vol. xiv of *Historia de España*, John Lynch (ed.), Barcelona, 2005
Tusell, Javier and Queipo de Llano, G., *Los intelectuales y la República*, Madrid, 1990

United States Senate, *Report on Scope of Soviet Activity*, Washington DC, 1954
Urquijo, José Ramón, *Gobiernos y ministros españoles (1808–2000)*, Madrid, 2001

Valdesoto, Fernando de, *Francisco Franco*, Madrid, 1943
Vázquez Montalbán, Manuel, *Pasionaria y los siete enanitos*, Barcelona, 1995
Vega, Eulàlia, *Entre revolució i reforma: la CNT a Catalunya (1930–1936)*, Lérida, 2004
Vega Sonbría, Santiago, *De la esperanza a la persecución. La repressión franquista en la provincia de Segovia, 1936–1939*, Barcelona, 2005
Vetrov, A., *Volontyory svobody*, Moscow, 1972
Vidarte, Juan-Simeón, *Las Cortes constituyentes de 1931 a 1933*, Barcelona, 1976

——, *No queríamos al rey. Testimonio de un socialista español*, Barcelona, 1977

——, *Todos fuimos culpables. Testimonio de un socialista español*, Barcelona, 1978

Vigón, Jorge, *General Mola*, Barcelona, 1957

Vilar, Pierre, *Historia de España*, Barcelona, 1978

Villares, Romón, *Historia de Galicia*, Vigo, 2004

Villarroya i Font, Joan, *Els bombardeigs de Barcelona, durant la guerra civil (1936–1939)*, Barcelona, 1981

Viñas, Ángel, *Guerra, dinero, dictadura. Ayuda fascista y autarquía en la España de Franco*, Barcelona, 1974

——, *La Alemania nazi y el 18 de Julio*, Madrid, 1977

——, *El oro de Moscú*, Barcelona, 1979

——, *Franco, Hitler y el estallido de la guerra civil*, Madrid, 2001

Viñas, Ángel and Collado Seidel, C., 'Franco's request to the Third Reich for Military Assistance' in *Contemporary European History*, Cambridge, 2002

Viñas, Ángel; Viñuela, J.; Eguidazu, F.; Pulgar, C. F.; and Florensa, S., *Política commercial exterior en España (1931–1975)*, 2 vols, Madrid, 1979

Vinyes, Ricard, *Irredentas. Las presas politicas y sus hijos en las cárceles de Franco*, Madrid, 2002

Watson, Peter, *Historia intelectual del siglo* XX, Barcelona, 2002

Whitaker, John, *We Cannot Escape History*, New York, 1943

Wintringham, Tom, *English Captain*, London, 1939

Woolsey, G., *Málaga en llamas*, Madrid, 1998

Wulff, Fernando, *Antigüedad y franquismo (1936–1975)*, Málaga, 2003

Zugazagoitia, Julián, *Guerra y vicisitudes de los españoles*, Barcelona, 1977

SOURCES

APRF	Arkhiv Prezidiuma Rossiyskoy Federatsii (Archive of the Presidium of the Russian Federation), Moscow
BA-MA	Bundesarchiv-Militärarchiv, Freiburg-im-Breisgau
DGFP	*Documents on German Foreign Policy*, Series D, vol. iii, *Germany and the Spanish Civil War 1936–1939*, HMSO, London, 1951, otherwise *Akten zur Deutschen Auswärtigen Politik 1918–1945*, Serie D, Band III, Baden-Baden, 1951
GARF	Gosudarstvenny Arkhiv Rossiiskoy Federatsii (State Archive of the Russian Federation), Moscow
KA	Krigsarkivet, Stockholm
RGAE	Rossiisky Gosudarstvennyi Arkhiv Ekonomiki (Russian State Economic Archive)
RGASPI	Rossiisky Gosudarstvenny Arkhiv Sotsialno-Politeskoi Istorii (Russian State Archive for Social-Political History), Moscow (formerly RTsKhIDNI)
RGVA	Rossiisky Gosudarstvenny Voenny Arkhiv (Russian State Military Archive), Moscow
RTsKhIDNI	see RGASPI
TNA	The National Archives (formerly the Public Record Office), Kew, England
TsAMO	Tsentralny Arkhiv Ministerstva Oborony (Central Archive of the Ministry of Defence) Podolsk, Moscow

NOTES

INTRODUCTION

1 'Estamos perdidos. Cuando Marx puede más que las hormonas, no hay nada que hacer.' (Julián Marías, *Una vida presente Memorias I*, p. 188.) I am most grateful to Javier Marías for sending me his father's memoirs.

CHAPTER 1: Their Most Catholic Majesties

1 For this development in the Spanish army, see Julio Busquets, *El Militar de Carrera en España*, Barcelona, 1971, pp. 56–61.

2 78.7 per cent of all properties in Galicia were less than ten hectares. At the other end of the scale, the large landholdings of Andalucia (more than 100 hectares) occupied 52.4 per cent of the land. See Edward Malefakis, *Reforma agraria y revolución campesina en la España del siglo XX*, Barcelona, 1971.

3 These statistics are taken from Albert Carreras y Xavier Tafunell, *Historia económica de la España contemporánea*, Barcelona, 2004; Manuel Tuñón de Lara (ed.), *Historia de España*, vol. viii., *Revolución burguesa oligarquía y constitucionalismo (1843–1923)*, Barcelona, 1983; Jordi Palafox, *Atraso económico y democracia. La Segunda República y la economía española, 1892–1936*, Barcelona, 1991; and Mercè Vilanova and Xavier Moreno, *Atlas de la evolución del analfabetismo en España de 1887 a 1981*, Ministerio de Educación y Ciencia, Madrid, 1992.

4 See Carreras and Tafunell, *Historia económica de la España contemporánea*, pp. 201–4. Banks took such an active role in the financing of industrial companies that in 1921, the seven largest banks in Spain controlled half the capital of all Spanish limited companies.

5 Company profits reached four billion pesetas. A large part of this, converted into gold, sat in the reserves of the Banco de España. See Francisco Comín, *Historia de la hacienda pública, II (España 1808–1995)*, Barcelona, 1996, pp. 81 and 133.

CHAPTER 2: Royal Exit

1 Following an armed clash, the conservative government of Antonio Maura decided to send reservists to Morocco. In Barcelona, this produced spontaneous protests and a general strike lasted from 26 July to 1 August 1909, during which barricades were erected and 42 convents and churches

were damaged or destroyed. See Joan Connelly Ullman, *La Semana Trágica*, Barcelona, 1972.

2 José Luis García Delgado and Santos Juliá (eds), *La España del siglo XX*, Madrid, 2003, pp. 309–11.

3 Javier Tusell (ed), *Historia de España. 2. La Edad Contemporánea*, Madrid, 1998, pp. 252–3.

4 Figure for 1915, Julio Busquets, *El militar de carrera en España*, Barcelona, 1967, p. 37.

5 Santos Julíá (ed.), *La España del siglo XX*, Madrid, 2003, p. 18.

6 This company which supplied electricity to Barcelona and the trams was in fact called the Barcelona Traction Light & Power company, but was known by its original name of La Canadiense.

7 Between 1921 and 1923 some 152 people were killed in Barcelona. In 1923 the labour lawyer Francesc Layret and the anarcho-syndicalist Salvador Seguí were assassinated, and also the Archbishop of Saragossa, Cardinal Soldevilla.

8 Juan Díaz del Moral, *Historia de las agitaciones campesinas andaluzas*, Madrid, 1973, pp. 265 ff.

9 Between 1917 and 1923 there were 23 major government crises and 30 lesser interruptions.

10 Using the Patronato del Circuito Nacional de Firmes Especiales, the dictatorship improved 2,500 kilometres of highway. For the hydroelectric projects, it set up the Confederaciónes Sindicales Hidrográficas del Ebro, Duero, Segura, Guadalquivir and Eastern Pyrenees, although only that of the Ebro went ahead under the supervision of the engineer Manuel Lorenzo Pardo, and the direction of the minister concerned, the Count de Guadalhorce. See José Luis García Delgado and Santos Juliá (eds), *La España del siglo XX*, pp. 319ff.

11 The exact results are not certain. See M. Martínez Cuadrado in *Eleccíónes y partidos politicos en España, 1808–1931*, Madrid, 1969, vol. 2, pp. 1,000–1. In Madrid the republicans received three times more votes than the monarchists and four times more in Barcelona.

12 'Una fiesta popular que tomó el aire de una revolución', Santos Juliá (ed.), *La España del siglo XX*, Madrid, 2003, p. 15.

13 'Mucho, antes de su caída, la Monarquía se había evaporado en la conciencia de los españoles', Miguel Maura, *Así cayó Alfonso XIII*, Barcelona, 1966, p. 329.

CHAPTER 3: The Second Republic

1 The provisional government consisted of: Niceto Alcalá Zamora (DLR), president; Miguel Maura (DLR), minister of the interior; Alejandro Lerroux (PRR), minister of state; Diego Martínez Barrio (PRR), minister of communications; Manuel Azaña (AR), minister of war; Santiago Casares Quiroga (FRG), minister of marine; Lluís Nicolau d'Olwer (PCR), minister for economic affairs; Álvaro de Albornoz (PRRS), minister of development;

Marcelino Domingo (PRRS), minister of education; Fernando de los Ríos (PSOE), minister of justice; Indalecio Prieto (PSOE), minister of finance; Francisco Largo Caballero (PSOE), minister of labour and social security.

2 Exports fell by nearly half between 1930 and 1933, and industrial production declined by 17 per cent (Carreras and Tafunell, *Historia económica de la España contemporánea*, pp. 251–2).

3 For example in Italy, Portugal, Austria, Hungary, Yugoslavia and soon in Germany.

4 Between 1 April and 30 June 1931, 13 per cent of the total deposits in banks were transferred. The peseta fell 20 per cent in value.

5 Prieto introduced a tax on share dealings, investigated the flight of capital and arranged the import of cheaper oil from the Soviet Union instead of from US oil companies (Gabriel Jackson, *La República española y la guerra civil*, Barcelona, 1976, p. 54).

6 Those who took advantage of the 'Azaña law' included 84 generals and 8,738 officers. The plan was for the new army to consist of 7,600 officers and 105,000 men in the Peninsula and 1,700 officers and 42,000 men in North Africa (Michael Alpert, *La reforma militar de Azaña, 1931–1933*, Madrid, 1982).

7 The men of this 30,000-strong force, commanded by army officers, were never posted to their home province. Forbidden to mix with the local population, they were regarded as an occupying force of outsiders, which protected only the interests of the landowners and the clergy.

8 The Church had declared property to the value of 244 million pesetas, but its real wealth was in fact much greater. It possessed a well-organized structure of cultural institutions, media outlets, charities, societies and educational centres. It controlled primary education, part of secondary education and higher education through technical schools and universities. Between 1909 and 1931 under the monarchy, the Church had built 11,128 primary schools. The Republic in its first year built 9,600 (Jackson, *La República española* . . ., p. 74).

9 See Miguel Maura, *Así cayó Alfonso XIII*, pp. 293ff.

10 The Socialists obtained 117 seats; the Radicals, 94; the Radical-Socialists, 58; Esquerra Republicana de Catalunya, 26; ORGA, 21. In all, the left and centre-left occupied 400 of the 470 seats in the Cortes (Nigel Townson, *The Crisis of Democracy in Spain*, Brighton, 2000, p. 57).

11 The Company of Jesus in Spain was finally dissolved on 24 January 1932. It had some 2,500 members in the country and considerable wealth in property and shares. Only its lawyers, of whom the Catholic politician Gil Robles was one, knew the exact size of its portfolio (Jackson, *La República española* . . ., pp. 71–2).

12 On 3 June 1931, Pope Pius XI published his encyclical *Dilectissima nobis*, which compared the situation in Spain with the persecution the Church had suffered in Mexico and the Soviet Union (Callahan, *La Iglesia católica en España*, p. 239).

13 See Pascual Carrión, *La reforma agraria de la Segunda República y la situación actual de la agricultura española*, Barcelona, 1973.

14 Manuel Azaña (AR), prime minister (president of the council of ministers) and minister of war; José Giral (AR), minister of marine; Luis Zulueta (indep.), minister of state; Jaume Carner (AC), minister of finance; Santiago Casares Quiroga (ORGA), minister of interior; Álvaro de Albornoz (PRRS), minister of justice; Marcelino Domingo (PRRS), agriculture, industry and commerce; Fernando de los Ríos (PSOE), education; Indalecio Prieto (PSOE), public works; and Francisco Largo Caballero (PSOE), minister of labour.

15 In October 1931, the Alfonsine monarchists, headed by Antonio Goicoechea, set up Acción Nacional (which later became Acción Popular). Carlist monarchists, who supported their own pretender, Alfonso Carlos, belonged to their own organization, the Traditionalist Communión. Goicoechea later set up Renovación Española with other monarchists, such as Ramiro de Maeztu, Pedro Sáinz Rodríguez and José María Pemán. Gil Robles, who later split from Acción Nacional in March 1933, formed the major parliamentary Catholic coalition of the right, known as the CEDA, Confederación Española de Derechas Autónomas.

16 The first manifestations of fascism in Spain existed in two reviews: *La Gaceta literaria*, edited by Ernesto Giménez Caballero, and *La conquista del Estado*, directed by Ramiro Ledesma Ramos, and published by a group which joined itself with the very Catholic and conservative Juntas Castellanas de Acción Hispánica, founded by Onésimo Redondo. This union made up Las Juntas de Ofensiva Nacional Sindicalista (JONS). There was also a strange fascist party, although Catholic and monarchist, the Partido Nacionalista Español, founded by Dr José María Albiñana, which almost immediately merged with the Bloque Nacional of Calvo Sotelo. José Antonio Primo de Rivera, Rafael Sánchez Mazas and Julio Ruiz de Alda started the Movimiento Español Sindicalista which in October 1933 would be refounded with the name Falange Española.

17 Azaña appointed General Miguel Cabanellas as head of the Civil Guard in Sanjurjo's place.

18 Emilio Esteban Infantes, *General Sanjurjo*, Barcelona, 1957, p. 235.

19 The law of agrarian reform applied only to Salamanca, Estremadura, La Mancha and Andalucia, where estates of more than 250 hectares accounted for more than half of all land. The slow process, opposed at every turn by landowners, exasperated the landless peasants. By the end of 1934 no more than 117,000 hectares had been expropriated and only 12,000 families out of the 200,000 planned for in the programme had been resettled (Carrión, *La reforma agraria* ... p. 129).

20 Manuel Azaña, *Discursos políticos*, Barcelona, 2004, pp. 179–219.

21 Jerome R. Mintz, *Los anarquistas de Casas Viejas*, Diputación Provincial, Cádiz, 1994.

22 The CEDA obtained 24.4 per cent of the votes and the Partido Republicano Radical 22 per cent. In total, the right won 204 seats and the centre 170.

The left won only 93, largely because of the weighting given in the electoral law to favour coalitions (Julio Gil Pecharromán, *Historia de la Segunda República Española (1931–1936)*, Madrid, 2002, p. 179).

23 *El Socialista*, 3 January 1934, quoted in Payne, *The Spanish Civil War, the Soviet Union and Communism*, London, 2004, p. 46.

24 Payne, ibid.

25 In 1933, both Salazar in Portugal and Dollfuss in Austria had introduced corporatist regimes, strongly influenced by Catholicism, and had suppressed socialist organizations. It was not surprising, therefore, that the PSOE should suspect Gil Robles, who had assumed some of the fascist imagery then fashionable, of similar intentions. But Largo Caballero completely rejected the warnings of moderates within his own party. Gil Robles, although initially impressed by Hitler and National Socialism in Germany, rapidly turned against it.

26 A. Saborit, *Julián Besteiro*, Buenos Aires 1967, pp. 238–40.

27 Azaña, *Obras completas*, vol. iv, Mexico, 1967, p. 652.

28 Marías, *Una vida presente*, p. 175.

29 'La aparación del juvenilismo, y por tanto de la violencia, en la política española.' ibid. p. 148.

30 La Federación Nacional de Trabajadores de la Tierra (FNTT).

31 Hugh Thomas, *The Spanish Civil War*, London, 1977, p. 133.

32 Santos Juliá, 'Fracaso de una insurrección y derrota de una huelga: los hechos de octubre en Madrid' in *Estudios de historia social*, 1984, p. 40.

33 Franco wrote in 1956: 'La revolución de Asturias fue el primer paso para la implantación del comunismo en nuestra nación ... La revolución había sido concienzudamente preparada por los agentes de Moscú' (Jesús Palacios, *La España totalitaria*, Barcelona, 1999, p. 29).

34 Jackson, *La República española y la guerra civil*, Barcelona, 1976, p. 141.

35 The Spanish Foreign Legion (Tercio de Estranjeros) contained fewer foreigners than its French counterpart. Its basic unit was the *bandera* of several hundred men with their own light artillery. Its counterpart for Moroccan colonial troops serving as *regulares* was the *tabor*, which had only 250 men.

36 Quoted Bartolomé Bennassar, *La guerre d'Espagne et ses lendemains*, p. 51.

37 General Goded was made head of the air force and General Mola was given command of the army in Morocco.

38 Two Dutch businessmen, Strauss and Perl (whose two names created the new word 'estra-perlo'), patented a game of roulette which they wanted to introduce to Spain. Since games of chance had been prohibited since the dictatorship of Primo Rivera, they tried to obtain authorization through bribery. The affair involved corrupt members of the Radical Party such as Sigfrido Blasco Ibáñez (son of the writer) and also Lerroux's adopted son Aurelio.

39 This scandal involved payments by the entrepreneur Antonio Tayá who obtained a government contract which was not respected.

CHAPTER 4: The Popular Front

1 Quoted in Bennassar, p. 51.

2 José María Gil Robles, *No fue posible la paz*, Barcelona, 1968, p. 404. In Catalonia the alliance was represented by the Front Català d'Ordre which included the Lliga, Acció Popular de Catalunya, Renovación Española, Carlists, and Radicals.

3 'Armamento de la canalla, incendio de bancos y casas particulares, reparto de bienes y tierras, saqueos en forma, reparto de vuestras mujeres' (Paul Preston, *La destrucción de la democracia en España*, Madrid, 1978, p. 279).

4 William J. Callahan, *La Iglesia católica en España (1875–2002)*, Barcelona, 2002, pp. 262ff.

5 Ibid., pp. 263–4.

6 The Frente Popular included Izquierda Republicana, Unión Republicana, Partido Socialista Obrero Español, Juventudes Socialistas, Partido Comunista de España, Partido Obrero de Unificación Marxista, the Partido Sindicalista and the Unión General de Trabajadores. In Catalonia, the Esquerra Republicana, Acció Catalana Republicana, Partit Nacionalista Republicà Català, Unió Socialista de Catalunya, Unió de Rabassaires and the small communist groups made up the Front d'Esquerres. The PNV also applied, despite pressure from the Vatican to join the Bloque Nacional. In Galicia the Partido Galeguista joined the Popular Front without suffering a split with its right wing.

7 The figures vary bewilderingly. The left in Spain has always convinced itself that there were 30,000, but Stanley Payne has calculated that it was closer to 15,000. See *La primera democracia española*, p. 305, n. 21.

8 Diego Martínez Barrio, *Páginas para la historia del Frente Popular*, Madrid, 1937, p. 12.

9 See Payne, *The Spanish Civil War, the Soviet Union and Communism*, New Haven, 2004, pp. 67–8.

10 Ibid., p. 81.

11 Kevin McDermott and Jeremy Agnew, *The Comintern*, New York, 1997, p. 132.

12 'Decisión sobre la cuestión española', RTsKhIDNI 495/18, quoted in Daniel Kowalsky, *La Unión Soviética y la guerra civil española*, Barcelona, 2004, p. 23.

13 Secretariat of the Executive Committee of the Communist International, 23 July 1936, RGASPI 495/18/1101, pp. 21–2.

14 Quoted Radosh and Habeck, *España traicionada*, p. 8.

15 14 October 1936, RGASPI 495/74/199, p. 63.

16 Estimates of union membership figures vary considerably. Some historians put the UGT at 1.5 million and the CNT at 1.8 million, but others attribute much lower numbers to CNT and much higher to the UGT, for example Ramón Tamames, *La República, La era de Franco*, Historia de España, vol. vii, Madrid, 1973, p. 29.

17 The results were as follows based on a total number of voters of 9,864,783,

which represented 72 per cent of the electoral register:

Popular Front: 4,654,116
Nacionalistas vascos: 125,714
Centre: 400,901
Right: 4,503,524

Of the more important parties, the PSOE won 99 seats; Izquierda Republicana (an amalgam of Acción Republicana, Partido Republicano Galeguista and the radical-socialists of Marcelino Domingo), 87 seats; Unión Republicana of Martínez Barrio (an offshoot from Lerroux's Radical Party), 38; the Spanish Communist Party, 17; and Esquerra Republicana of Catalonia, 21. On the right, the CEDA kept 88 seats, the monarchists of the Bloque Nacional won 12; the Carlist Traditionalists, 10; the Catalan Lliga, 12; and the Radical Party, 5. In the middle, the Centrist Party of Portela Valladares won 16 seats and the Basque Nationalist Party, 10 (Javier Tusell, *Las elecciónes del Frente Popular*, Madrid, 1972, ii, pp. 190 and 243).

18 Miguel González, 'La conjura del '36 contada por Franco', *El País*, Madrid, 9 September 2001.
19 Manuel Azaña, *Diarios completos*, Barcelona, 2000, p. 933.
20 Teodoro Rodríguez, quoted in Callahan, op. cit., p. 259.
21 *Ahora*, Madrid, 21 February 1936.
22 Pedro C. González Cuevas, *Acción española. Teología política y nacionalismo autoritario en España*, 1913–1936, Madrid, 1998, pp. 172–4.
23 Ismael Saz, *Mussolini contra la Sunda República*, pp. 139ff.
24 Sheelagh Ellwood, *Historia de Falange Española*, Barcelona, 2001, pp. 65ff.
25 Martin Blinkhorn, *Carlismo y contrarrevolución en España, 1931–1939*, Barcelona, 1979, p. 288.
26 Ibid.

CHAPTER 5: The Fatal Paradox

1 Francisco Comín, Mauro Hernández and Enrique Llopis, op. cit., p. 285.
2 See M. Requena Gallego, *Los sucesos de Yeste*, Albacete, 1983.
3 Edward Malefakis, *Reforma agraria y revolución campesina en la España del siglo XX*, Barcelona, 1971, p. 434.
4 Unemployment in Spain at this time was around 17 per cent, but it was closer to 30 per cent in Andalucia. In the summer of 1936 out of a total population of 24 million, 796,341 were unemployed and of those 522,079 (65 per cent) were agricultural workers (ibid., p. 331).
5 'Cuando querrá el Dios del cielo que la justicia se vuelva / y los pobres coman pan y los ricos coman mierda'.
6 '¿No habéis oído gritar las muchachas españolas estos días "¡Hijos, sí; maridos, no!"?' José Antonio Primo de Rivera, 'Carta a los militares de España' in *Obras completas*, pp. 669–74.
7 Indalecio Prieto, *Discursos fundamentales*, Madrid, 1976, pp. 272–3.

8 There was an unusually high turnout of 70 per cent, with nearly a million votes in favour and little more than 6,000 against.

9 Pedro Gómez Aparicio, *Historia del periodismo español*, Madrid, 1981, vol. iv, p. 467. Gabriel Jackson argues that the figure given for burned churches, considering that they were buildings made of stone, is highly improbable. In some cases people had merely lit a pile of newspapers on the steps as a gesture (Gabriel Jackson, *La República española y la guerra civil*, Barcelona, 1976, pp. 202–3).

10 José Antonio Primo de Rivera, *Obras completas*, pp. 645–53. These parallels seem bizarre, since if followed through, they suggest that General Franco would have fared little better than General Kornilov, whose failed *coup d'état* helped trigger the bolshevik revolution.

11 Gabriel Cardona, 'Las operaciónes militares' in M. Tuñón (ed.), *La guerra civil española 50 años después*, Barcelona, 1985, p. 205.

12 The majority of the plots were being organized by members of the Unión Militar Española (UME), founded in 1933 by Captain Barba Hernández (the one who had accused Azaña over the Casas Viejas affair) and by a Falangist, Lieutenant-Colonel Rodríguez Tarduchy. The UME consisted of serving and retired officers. They did not represent more than 10 per cent of the officer corps, but maintained excellent relations with the Carlists, with Renovación Española, with the Juventudes de Acción Popular, with the Falange and with plotting generals. The UME held aloof from the ridiculous plot which Colonel Varela had planned for 19 April. Varela ended up in prison in Cádiz and General Orgaz who supported him was confined in Las Palmas (Carlos Blanco Escolá, *Falacias de la guerra civil. Un homenaje a la causa republicana*, Barcelona, 2005, p. 72).

13 Sanjurjo was to be known as the chief – 'el Jefe' – and Valentín Galarza as the 'Técnico'.

14 'Instrucciónes y directivas para el arranque de la conspiración, primero, y de un posible alzamiento, después', Felix Maiz, *Mola, aquel hombre*, Barcelona, 1976, pp. 62–4.

15 For details on Franco's military career, see Paul Preston's *Franco, caudillo de España*, Barcelona, 1994, and the highly critical Carlos Blanco Escolá, *La incompetencia militar de Franco*, Madrid, 2000, p. 21.

16 See also Juan Pablo Fusi, *Franco*, Madrid, 1985, p. 26, and Herbert R. Southworth, *El lavado de cerebro de Francisco Franco*, Barcelona, 2000, pp. 187ff.

17 The organization was created at the end of 1935 and its leading spirit was Captain Díaz Tendero, who was to die later in the concentration camp of Mauthausen.

18 Julio Busquets and Juan Carlos Losada, op. cit., pp. 63ff.

CHAPTER 6: The Rising of the Generals

1 Juan Campos, quoted by Ronald Fraser, *Recuérdalo tú y recuérdalo a otros*, p. 49.

2 Gustau Nerín, *La guerra que vino de África*, Barcelona, 2005, p. 178.
3 Hugh Thomas, *La guerra civil española*, Barcelona, 1976, i, p. 239.
4 General Romerales would be sentenced to death by a court martial on 26 August, accused of 'sedition' and 'treason' (J. Casanova et al., *Morir, matar, sobrevivir*, Barcelona, 2002, p. 62).
5 Luis Romero, *Tres días de Julio*, Barcelona, 1967, p. 12.
6 José Millán Astray, *Franco el Caudillo*, Salamanca, 1939, pp. 22–6.
7 J. Casanova et al., op. cit., p. 62.
8 Quoted in Manuel Tuñón de Lara, *La España del siglo xx*, Paris, 1966, p. 429.
9 Julián Zugazagoitia, *Guerra y vicisitudes de los españoles*, Barcelona, 1977, p. 58.
10 See Francisco Espinosa, *La columna de la muerte. El avance del ejército franquista de Sevilla a Badajoz*, Barcelona, 2003, p. 4.
11 *ABC* de Sevilla, special supplement of 22 July 1936.
12 Quoted by Fraser, *Recuérdalo tú* ..., pp. 205–6.
13 Quoted in Burnett Bolloten, *La Revolución española*, Barcelona, 1979, pp. 205–6.
14 Eduardo de Guzmán, *Madrid rojo y negro*, Barcelona, 1938, p. 37.
15 *Hoy*, México, D.F., 27 April 1940.
16 Marías, *Una vida presente*, pp. 190–1.
17 José Peirats, *La CNT en la Revolución española*, Paris, 1973, vol. i, p. 182.
18 On the subject of the time Franco took to reach Morocco out of prudence, see Carlos Blanco Escolá, *La incompetencia militar de Franco*, pp. 216–18, and also Paul Preston, *Franco*, pp. 187–90.
19 Carlos Blanco Escolá, *Falacias de la guerra civil*, p. 120.
20 DGFP, Wegener to Foreign Ministry, pp. 3–4.
21 Manuel Tuñon de Lara, *Historia de España*, vol. xii, pp. 456–9.
22 'Dame la boina / dame el fusil / que voy a matar más rojos / que flores tienen / mayo y abril'.
23 Gabriel Jackson, *La República española* ..., p. 215.
24 Marcel Junod, *Warrior without Weapons*, New York, 1951, p. 98.
25 Ignacio Martín Jiménez, *La guerra civil en Valladolid, 1936–1939*, Valladolid, 2000, pp. 47ff.
26 There cannot have been very many. According to Josep Fontana no more than 346 civilians in Barcelona took up arms against the Republic (*Visions de guerra de reraguardia*, Barcelona, 1977, prologue).
27 'Soy el general Goded. Declaro ante el pueblo español que la suerte me ha sido adversa. En adelante, aquellos que quieran continuar la lucha no deben ya contar conmigo', quoted in Tuñon, *La España del siglo XX*, p. 432.

CHAPTER 7: The Struggle for Control

1 Ian Gibson, *Queipo de Llano*, Barcelona, 1986, p. 76.
2 Luis Romero, *Tres días de Julio*, p. 50.

3 In 1919, when the French sent a squadron to the Black Sea during the Russian civil war to support the White Army, sailors of the battleships *France* and *Jean Bart* mutinied in support of the bolsheviks. André Marty, the French Comintern representative in Spain, had made an almost mythical reputation there when he played a leading part.
4 Voelckels to Foreign Ministry, Alicante, 16 October 1936, DGFP, p. 112.
5 Small bodies of troops had been flown before, including British soldiers sent from Cyprus to Iraq in 1932, but the transport of Franco's troops across the Straits of Gibraltar is generally regarded as the first major air bridge.
6 H. R. Trevor-Roper (ed.), *Las conversaciónes privadas de Hitler*, Barcelona, 2004.
7 Santos Juliá (ed.), *Victimas de la guerra civil*, Madrid. 1999, pp. 87–8.
8 Zugazagoitia, *Guerra y vicisitudes*, p. 70; Fraser, *Recuérdalo tú y recuérdalo a otros*, pp. 80, 86–7.
9 Jack Lindsay, 'On guard for Spain!', Junta de Castilla y León, Salamanca, 1986, p. 132.
10 Luis Romero, op. cit., p. 555.
11 Ian Gibson, *Granada en 1936 y el asesinato de García Lorca*, Barcelona, 1979, p. 75.
12 Antonio Bahamonde, *Un año con Queipo*, or *Memoirs of a Spanish Nationalist*, London, 1939.
13 Ronald Fraser, op. cit., p. 152.
14 The rebels controlled approximately 235,000 square kilometres of the peninsular territory with eleven million people, and the Republic 270,000 with fourteen million.
15 The Army of Africa included 15,000 *regulares* and 4,000 legionnaires, as well as 12,000 members of the Sultan's forces and 1,500 Ifni riflemen. See Gustau Nerín, *La guerra que vino de África*, Barcelona, 2005, p. 170.
16 See Pierre Vilar, *La guerra civil española*, Barcelona, 1986, p. 66; Enrique Moradiellos, *1936. Los mitos de la guerra civil*, Barcelona, 2004, p. 83; and Ramón Salas Larrazábal, *Los datos exactos de la guerra civil*, Madrid, 1980, pp. 62–3.

CHAPTER 8: The Red Terror

1 Callahan, *La Iglesia católica en España*, p. 282.
2 Schwendemann, Salamanca, 27 December 1936 to Foreign Ministry, DGFP, p. 189.
3 The Rev. Dr Gerhard Ohlemüller, Secretary-General of the Protestant World Council, protested to the Wilhelmstrasse on 28 November 1936, but the nationalist government refused to answer a German Foreign Ministry request to investigate (DGFP, pp. 144–5).
4 See José M. Sanabre Sanromá, *Martirologio de la Iglesia en la diócesis de Barcelona durante la persecución religiosa*, Barcelona, 1943; Hilari Raguer,

La espada y la cruz: La Iglesia, 1936–1939, Barcelona, 1977; *La pólvora y el incienso*, Barcelona, 2001; Julián Casanova, *La iglesia de Franco*, Madrid, 2001.

5 '*Checa*' was the acronym for Chrezvichainaia Komissia, the 'Extraordinary Commission' to fight counter-revolutionary activities and sabotage. It was led by Feliks Dzherzhinsky, and became the forerunner of the OGPU, the NKVD and the KGB.

6 The official Francoist account, *Causa general*, states that there were more than 200 *checas* in Madrid alone. See Santos Juliá (ed.), *Víctimas de la guerra civil.*

7 Maria Casares, *Residente privilégiée*, Paris, 1980.

8 Santos Juliá, *Víctimas* ..., p. 131.

9 Among the dead were the Falangists Julio Ruiz de Alda and Fernando Primo de Rivera; José María Albiñana, founder of the Nationalist Party, and the former ministers, Ramón Alvarez Valdés, Manuel Rico Avellot and José Martínez de Velasco and the old Melquíades Alvarez (Juliá, *Victimas* ..., p. 73).

10 Manuel Azaña, 'Cuaderno de la Pobleta' in *Diarios completos*, pp. 943ff.

11 José Peirats, *La CNT en la Revolución española*, Toulouse, 1953, vol. i, p. 182.

12 *La guerra civil a Catalunya (1936–1939)*, vol. i, p. 152.

13 For the repression by the left in Catalonia see J. M. Solé i Sabaté and J. Villarroya, *La repressió a la reraguarda de Catalunya (1936–1939)*, Barcelona, 1989, two volumes.

14 In Huelva the civil governor, Diego Jiménez Castellano, did all that he could to protect the right-wingers put behind bars. On 12 August, in La Nava de Santiago (Badajoz), the municipal council stopped a crowd from setting fire to the church with 63 right-wing prisoners inside (Francisco Espinosa, *La columna de la muerte*, pp. 165–6). In Zafra the mayor, González Barrero, saved the prisoners just before Major Castejón's troops arrived (Espinosa, *La columna de la muerte*, p. 30). In Pozoblanco the head teacher, Antonio Baena, prevented an attack on the town jail (Juliá, *Víctimas* ..., p. 165).

15 Ibid., p. 412; see also G. Sánchez Recio, *Justicia y guerra en España. Los tribunales populares*, Alicante, 1991. Enrique Moradiellos raises the figure to 60,000 victims (*1936. Los mitos de la guerra civil*, p. 129).

CHAPTER 9: The White Terror

1 Mohammad Ibn Azzuz Akin, *La actitud de los moros ante el Alzamiento*, Algazara, 1997, p. 102.

2 Dionisio Ridruejo, *Escrito en España*, Buenos Aires, 1964, p. 94.

3 Casanova, *Morir, matar* ..., p. 11.

4 Santos Juliá, *Victimas* ..., p. 92.

5 This profession was one of the most heavily punished in the nationalist repression. Several hundred teachers were murdered in the first few weeks;

20 in Huelva, 21 in Burgos, 33 in Saragossa, 50 in León, etc. See Jesús Crespo, *Purga de maestros en la guerra civil*, Valladolid, 1987; F. Morente 'La represió sobre el magisteri' in *Actes del IV Seminari sobre la República i la guerra civil*, pp. 80ff.

6 Santos Juliá, *Victimas* ..., p. 94.

7 Julián Casanova, *Morir, matar, sobrevivir*, p. 106.

8 Ibid., p. 107.

9 Manuel Tuñón de Lara, *La España del siglo XX*, p. 451.

10 Jackson, *La República española y la guerra civil*, p. 271.

11 The same happened in Palencia, where the rising was immediately successful. In 1936 the freelance executions resulted in the death of 103 people, to which should be added the 169 sentences of death by military tribunals. In Soria 281 were killed and in Segovia, where little had happened before the war to justify the repression, 358 were executed and another 2,282 imprisoned. See Jesús M. Palomares, *La guerra civil en Palencia*, Palencia, 2002, pp. 121–44; Santiago Vega Sombría, *De la esperanza a la persecución. La repressión franquista en la provincia de Segovia*, Barcelona, 2005, p. 279.

12 Juliá, op. cit., p. 101.

13 Emilio Silva and Santiago Macías, *Las fosas de Franco*, Madrid, 2003, pp. 317ff.

14 Ibid., pp. 151ff.

15 Fraser, *Recuérdalo tú*, p. 369.

16 Ibid., p. 211.

17 Ibid., p. 213.

18 When, in September 1936, a Falangist column reached Andavalo, where many of the miners for Rio Tinto worked, they killed 315 of the inhabitants. See Luciano Suero Sánchez, *Memorias de un campesino andaluz en la revolución española*, Madrid, 1982, p. 84.

19 Espinosa, *La columna de la muerte*, p. 30.

20 For the events at Badajoz see Espinosa, *La columna de la muerte*; Mário Neves, *A chacina de Badajoz, Lisbon*, 1985; Julián Chaves, *La guerra civil en Extremadura*, Editora Regional de Extremadura, 1997; Alberto Reig Tapia, *Memoria de la guerra civil*, Madrid, 1999; and Justo Vila, *Extremadura: La guerra civil*, Badajoz, 1983. The journalists who gave the news to the world soon afterwards included: Mario Neves, Marcel Dany of Havas, Jacques Berthet of *Temps*, Jean d'Esme of *l'Intransigéant*, René Brut, a cameraman with Pathé Newsreels, Jay Allen of the *Chicago Tribune* and John T. Whitaker of the *New York Herald Tribune*.

21 The figure of 6,610 was compiled by Francisco Espinosa, but he added that the figure might well prove to be twice as high (*La columna de la morte*, p. 321).

22 John Whitaker, *We Cannot Escape History*, New York, 1943, quoted by Reig Tapia, *Memoria de la guerra civil*, pp. 140–1.

23 Lorca was killed on 18 August along with the teacher Dióscoro Galindo González and the anarchist banderilleros Joaquín Arcollas and Francisco

Galadí, in Fuente Grande, next to the gully of Víznar, where the bodies of hundreds of victims lay (Ian Gibson, *Federico García Lorca*, vol. i, Barcelona, 1998, p. 485). Before ordering the killing of the poet, the new governor, Colonel José Valdés Guzmán, head of the Falangist squads, telephoned Queipo de Llano to consult him. He apparently replied, 'Give him coffee, a lot of coffee.' Café, it must be remembered, was formed by the initials of 'Camaradas: Arriba Falange Española'. The death certificate stated: 'died in the month of August 1936 as a result of war wounds'. See Ian Gibson, *Granada en 1936 y el asesinato de Federico García Lorca*, Barcelona, 1979.

24 TNA, FO 371/39742, 9903.

25 Juliá, *Victimas* . . ., p. 201.

26 A. Nadal Sànchez, *Guerra civil en Málaga*, Málaga, 1984.

27 See Ignacio Martín Jiménez, *La guerra civil en Valladolid, 1936–1939*, Valladolid, 2000.

28 Fraser, *Recuérdalo tú* . . ., p. 219.

29 Ibid., p. 217.

30 Juliá, *Victimas* . . ., pp. 411–12.

31 Article of 25 July 1936, quoted by Ian Gibson, *Queipo de Llano*, p. 83.

CHAPTER 10: The Nationalist Zone

1 The junta assumed 'all the powers of the state and legitimately represented the country to foreign powers' (*Boletin Oficial del Estado* of 25 July 1936).

2 Constancia de la Mora, *Doble esplendor*, Barcelona, 1977, p. 247.

3 Manuel Tuñón de Lara, *La España del siglo xx*, p. 479.

4 The full text of the pastoral letter is in Antonio Montero, *Historia de la persecución religiosa en España, 1936–1939*, Madrid, 1961.

5 Bahamonde, p. 34.

6 *La Unión*, Seville, 15 August 1936.

7 In October the Falange had 35,000 members, which represented 54 per cent of the nationalist militias and 19 per cent of the total nationalist forces, many more than the Carlist *requetés*.

8 Messerschmitt of the Export Cartel for War Matériel, 8 September 1936, DGFP, p. 88.

9 G. Sánchez Recio et al., *Guerra civil y franquismo en Alicante*, Alicante, 1990, p. 27; Gil Pecharromán, *José Antonio Primo de Rivera*, p. 455.

10 Voelckers to Foreign Ministry, 17 October 1936, DGFP, pp. 114–15.

11 Ellwood, *Prietas las filas*, pp. 90–1.

12 For Queipo's direction of the Andalucian economy see Banco Exterior de España, *Política commercial exterior en España (1931–1975)*, Madrid, 1979, pp. 144ff.

13 For a study of Millán Astray see Geoffrey Jensen, *Irrational Triumph. Cultural Despair, Military Nationalism and the Ideological Origins of Franco's Spain*, Reno, 2002, pp. 140ff.

14 Cervantes's satire on chivalry in *Don Quixote* was said to have been

partially inspired from his wounds received at Lepanto in 1571.

15 No exact record of Unamuno's speech was published. The Salamanca papers next day reported every other speech, but not his. This version was written down soon afterwards. See Emilio Salcedo, *Vida de don Miguel*, Salamanca, 1964; and Luis Portillo, 'Unamuno's Last Lecture' in Cyril Connolly, *The Golden Horizon*, London, 1953.

CHAPTER 11: The Republican Zone

1 Pierre Vilar, *La guerra civil española*, Barcelona, 1986, p. 104.

2 The Spanish Communist Party in a report to the Comintern on 15 February 1937 claimed 250,000 members, 'of whom 135,000 are at the front' (RGASPI 495/120/259, p. 3).

3 Manuel Azaña, 'La revolución abortada' in *Obras completas*, México, 1967, vol. iii, p. 499.

4 Fernando Solano, *La tragedia del Norte*, Barcelona, 1938, p. 73.

5 The Basque government consisted of four PNV councillors, three from the PSOE, one for the ANV, one from Izquierda Republicana, one from Unión Republicana and one member of the PCE.

6 See Santiago de Pablo, Ludger Mees and José A. Rodríguez Ranz, *El péndulo patriótico. Historia del Partido Nacionalista Vasco, II 1936–1979*, Barcelona, 2001.

7 John Langdon-Davies, *Behind Spanish Barricades*, London, 1937. p. 63.

8 For example, Josep Tarradellas, quoted in Walther L. Bernecker, *Colectividades y revolución social*, Barcelona, 1983, p. 386n.

9 *Solidaridad Obrera*, 18 July 1937.

10 Diego Abad de Santillán, *Por qué perdimos la guerra*, Buenos Aires, 1940, p. 169.

11 Bernecker, *Colectividades y revolución social*, pp. 437–48.

12 The committee went under its Catalan name of the Comitè Central de Milícies Antifeixistes. Of their five posts, the libertarians allocated three to representatives of the CNT (Durruti, García Oliver and Asens) and two to the FAI (Abad de Santillán and Aurelio Fernández). Durruti and other libertarian leaders left for the front on 23 July, thus further reducing their influence (John Brademas, *Anarcosindicalismo y revolución en España, 1930–1937*, Barcelona, 1974, p. 175.)

13 Ossorio, *Vida y Sacrificio de Companys*, p. 172.

14 For the relationship between the Generalitat and the anarchists in the field of finance and industry, see Francesc Bonamusa in *La guerra civil a Catalunya*, vol. ii, pp. 54ff.

15 Fraser, *Recuérdalo tú ...*, p. 393.

16 See Mary Nash, *Mujeres libres: España, 1936–1939*, Barcelona, 1975.

17 Sandie Holguín, *República de ciudadanos*, Barcelona, 2003, pp. 209ff.

18 RGASPI 495/120/259.

19 The UGT or UGT-CNT organized about 15 per cent of the collectives in New Castile and La Mancha, the majority in Estremadura, very few in

Andalucia, about 20 per cent in Aragón and about 12 per cent in Catalonia.

20 The loss of markets and shortage of raw materials led to a 40 per cent decline in textile output, but engineering production increased by 60 per cent over the next nine months.

21 Josep Maria Bricall, 'Les collectivitzacions' in Anna Salles (ed.) *Documents 1931–1939*.

22 Franz Borkenau, *The Spanish Cockpit*, Michigan, 1963, p. 90.

23 Ibid., p. 103.

24 Brademas, *Anarcosindicalismo*, pp. 204–9.

25 José Borrás, *Aragón en la revolución española*, Viguera, Barcelona, 1983, pp. 174ff.

26 The areas expropriated for collectives included 65 per cent of the agricultural land in the province of Jaén, 56.9 per cent in Ciudad Real, 33 per cent in Albacete and only 13.18 per cent in the whole of the province of Valencia. See Aurora Bosch, *Ugetistas libertarios. Guerra Civil y revolución en el País Valenciano*, Valencia, 1983.

27 Borkenau, pp. 155–6.

28 G. Helsey, *Anarcosindicalismo y estado en Aragón, 1930–1938*, Madrid, 1994.

CHAPTER 12: The Army of Africa and the People's Militias

1 Tuñón, *La España del siglo xx*, p. 438.

2 Jackson, *La República* ..., p. 248.

3 Fraser, *Recuérdalo tú* ..., p. 252.

4 Tuñón, *La España del siglo xx*, p. 474.

5 Kuznetsov, *Bajo la bandera de la España republicana*, p. 160.

6 Zugazagoitia, *Guerra y vicisitudes* ..., p. 135.

7 Borkenau, *The Spanish Cockpit*, p. 159.

8 Marty report to Comintern, 10 October 1936, RGVA 33987/3/832, pp. 70–107.

9 Espinosa, *La columna* ..., p. 52.

10 Ibid. p. 77.

11 Nationalist historians claim that Yagüe fell ill on 20 September.

12 Reig Tapia, *Memoria de la guerra civil*, pp. 149–87.

13 Robert Mallett, *Mussolini and the Origins of the Second World War, 1933–1940*, London 2003, p. 101.

14 See H. R. Southworth, *El mito de la cruzada de Franco*, Barcelona, 1986, pp. 93–116; and Reig Tapia, pp. 149–87.

15 According to Luis Quintanilla (*Los rehenes del Alcázar de Toledo*, Paris, 1967), they were shot and their bodies used to block shell holes in the wall, but this too may have been a myth.

16 John Whitaker, *We Cannot Escape History*, pp. 113–114.

17 Isabelo Herreros, *El Alcázar de Toledo. Mitología de la cruzada de Franco*, Madrid, 1995, p. 75.

18 Preston, *Franco*, p. 235.

19 RGVA 33987/3/845, pp. 14, 17–18.
20 According to Hugh Thomas, Cortés's men lived from robbing the local area (*La guerra civil española*, p. 334).
21 See Seidmann, *A ras del suelo*, pp. 59–61.
22 Abad de Santillán, *Por qué perdimos la guerra*, Madrid, 1975, p. 85.
23 Ramón Brusco, *Les milícies antifeixistes i l'Exèrcit popular a Catalunya, 1936–1937*, Lérida, 2003, pp. 81–98.
24 Bolloten, *La revolución española*, p. 368.
25 Bill Alexander, *British Volunteers for Liberty*, London, 1982, pp. 73–4.
26 Salas, *Historia del ejército popular de la República*, vol. i, pp. 1147–8.

CHAPTER 13: Arms and the Diplomats

1 Bennassar, *La guerre d'Espagne et ses lendemains*, Paris, 2005, p. 133.
2 Bachoud, *Franco*, Barcelona, 2000, p. 150.
3 D. W. Pike, *Les français et la guerre d'Espagne*, Paris, 1975, p. 81.
4 Welczeck to Foreign Ministry, DGFP, p. 4.
5 Wegener to Foreign Ministry, 25 July 1936, DGFP, p. 9.
6 Howson, *Armas para España*, pp. 45–6.
7 On 7 and 8 August, thirteen fighters and six bombers were sent to Spain, but they were stripped of weapons and equipment. The French Potez bombers were in any case completely obsolete. Nationalist claims of large numbers of aircraft being sent earlier are without foundation.
8 Eden, *Facing the Dictators*, London, 1962, p. 402.
9 Balfour and Preston (eds), *España y las grandes potencias*, p. 81.
10 Director of Legal Department, Foreign Ministry, to the German Legation in Lisbon, 7 September 1936 (DGFP, p. 78).
11 Faupel to Wilhelmstrasse, 5 May 1937, DGFP, pp. 282–3.
12 J. M. Keynes, *The Economic Consequences of the Peace*, London, 1920.
13 Kirkpatrick, Ivone, *The Inner Circle*, London, 1958.
14 Eden, *Facing the Dictators*, p. 433.
15 Bolín, *Spain: The Vital Years*, London, 1967.
16 Heiberg, *Emperadores del Mediterráneo*, pp. 57–60.
17 Renzo de Felice, *Mussolini il duce*, vol. ii, *Lo stato totalitario*, p. 366.
18 Coverdale, *La intervención italiana en la guerra civil española*, Madrid, 1979.
19 Johannes Bernhardt and Adolf Langenheim, both members of the Nazi Party and based in Morocco, were accompanied by one of General Kindelán's officers, Captain Francisco Arranz Monasterio. For the seizure of the Lufthansa aircraft in Las Palmas to take General Orgaz to Tetuán, and then the arms delegation on to Berlin, see DGFP, pp. 7–8.
20 See Memorandum of the Director of the Political Department, Dr Hans Heinrich Dieckhoff, arguing that 'it is absolutely necessary that at this stage German governmental and Party authorities continue to refrain from any contact with the two officers. Arms deliveries to the rebels would become known very soon' (Dieckhoff, 25 July 1936, DGFP, p. 11).

21 Angel Viñas and Carlos Collado Seidel, 'Franco's Request to the Third Reich for Military Assistance' in *Contemporary European History*, II, 2 (2002), Cambridge University Press.
22 Howson, *Armas para España*, p. 35.
23 Balfour and Preston (eds), *España y las grandes potencias*, p. 100.
24 Viñas, *Guerra, dinero, dictadura*, p. 170.
25 Spanish industry had been dominated by foreign capital since its retarded start in the mid nineteenth century. The railways and basic services such as electricity, engineering and mining all depended on heavy foreign investment. American ITT owned the Spanish telephone system and Ford and General Motors had little competition in the motor industry. British companies owned the greatest share of Spanish business with nearly 20 per cent of all foreign capital investment. The United Kingdom was also the largest importer of Spanish goods, including over half of her iron ore (Comin, Hernández and Llopis (eds), *Historia económica de España*, p. 221).
26 J. R. Hubbard, 'How Franco financed his war' in *Journal of Modern History*, Chicago, 1953, p. 404.
27 In conversation with Charles Foltz, correspondent of Associated Press: *The Masquerade in Spain*, Boston, 1948, pp. 46–8.
28 AP RF 3/74/26, p. 51.
29 Radosh, Habeck and Sevostianov (eds), *España traicionada*, p. 56.
30 Blanco Escolá, *Falacias de la guerra civil*, p. 167.
31 RGVA 35082/1/185, p. 148.

CHAPTER 14: Sovereign States

1 Other influential officers present included Generals Orgaz, Kindelán, Dávila, Saliquet and Gil Yuste, as well as Colonels Muntaner and Moreno Calderón.
2 Iribarren, *Mola*, p. 232.
3 Gil Robles, *No fue posible la paz*, p. 776, n. 25.
4 *Boletín Official del Estado* of 30 September 1936. Paul Preston does not believe that Nicolás Franco actually deleted the words '*del gobierno*' from the document drawn up by the lawyer, José Yanguas Messía, but thinks that the words were not read out. The qualification 'for the duration of the war' does appear to have been deleted by Franco himself. The important point is that the newspapers faithfully published a verbatim version of the speech, not the text. The best account is in Preston, *Franco*, pp. 221–53.
5 'Caudillo' was Franco's new title, a Spanish term for leader roughly approximate to Führer or Duce.
6 The various departments of the Junta Técnica were divided between Burgos, Valladolid and Salamanca, where Franco set up his headquarters with the Secretariat-General and departments for foreign affairs, as well as press and propaganda directed by Millán Astray with the help of Ernesto Giménez Caballero. The poet and president of Acción Española, José

María Pemán, took over the Commission of Culture and Education. There, with the assistance of Enrique Súñer, he began a systematic purge of university professors and lecturers.

7 Zugazagoitia, *Guerra y vicisitudes*, p. 153.
8 Koltsov, *Ispanskii Dnevnik*, quoted by Bolloten, *La revolución española*, p. 189.
9 RGVA 33987/3/852, p. 46.
10 Marty's report to the Executive Committee of the Comintern, 10 October 1936, RGVA 33987/3/832, pp. 70–107; Radosh and Habeck, pp. 40–55.
11 The cabinet consisted of president of the council of ministers and minister of war, Francisco Largo Caballero; foreign affairs, Julio Álvarez del Vayo; minister of the interior, Angel Galarza; finance, Juan Negrín; navy and air, Indalecio Prieto; industry and commerce, Anastasio de Gracia (all PSOE); justice, Mariano Ruiz Funes (Izquierda Republicana); agriculture, Vicente Uribe (communist); education, Jesús Hernández (communist); work and health, Josep Tomàs i Piera (Esquerra Republicana); communications and mercantile marine, Bernardo Giner de los Ríos (Unión Republicana); minister without portfolio, José Giral (Izquierda Republicana). A few days later Julio Just (Izquierda Republicana) became minister of works. Prieto wanted to bring the conservative Basque PNV into the central government and to strengthen Madrid's influence in the north, but Aguirre, the Basque president, refused. The Basques wanted the statute of autonomy, frozen since 1934, passed as soon as possible. Manuel de Irujo joined the government as a minister without portfolio on 17 September, after the Basques had set up their own government (Santiago del Pablo (ed.), *El péndulo patriótico*, ii, pp. 15–18).
12 RGVA 33987/3/832 pp. 70–107.
13 Brusco, *Les milícies antifeixistes i l'Exèrcit popular*, pp. 101–103.
14 Vilar, *La guerra civil española*, p. 103
15 RGVA 33987/3/832 p. 70
16 Pablo de Azcárate, *Mi embajada en Londres*, p. 141.
17 Eden, *Facing the Dictators*, pp. 415 and 408.
18 Bowers, *Mission in Spain.*

CHAPTER 15: The Soviet Union and the Spanish Republic

1 The PSUC in Catalonia increased during this period of a year from 5,000 members to 45,000 and the Communist Party of Euzkadi from 3,000 to 22,000, which made an approximate total of 300,000, more than the PSOE and all the republican parties together. According to José Díaz, the breakdown was as follows:

industrial workers (including engineers and technicians): 87,660
agricultural workers: 62,250
landowning peasants: 76,700

middle class: 15,485
intellectuals: 7,045
women: 19,300
Total: 268,440

It is significant that the communists attracted more landowning peasants than agricultural workers (Joan Estruch, *Historia oculta del PCE*, Madrid, 2000, pp. 132–5).

2 Antonio Elorza and Marta Bizcarrondo, *Queridos camaradas. La Internacional Comunista y España, 1919–1939*, Barcelona, 1999, p. 305.

3 Ivo Banac (ed.), *The Diary of Georgi Dimitrov, 1933–1949*, Yale University Press, New Haven, 2003, pp. 28 and 32.

4 The main works on the subject, making use of the former Soviet archives since 1992, include: R. Radosh, M. R. Habeck and G. Sevostianov (eds), *Spain Betrayed, The Soviet Union in the Spanish Civil War*, Yale, 2001; Yury Rybalkin, *Operatsiya 'X': Sovetskaya voennaya pomoshch respublikanskoi ispanii (1936–1939)*, Moscow, 2000; Daniel Kowalsky, *La Unión Soviética y la guerra civil española. Una revisión crítica*, Barcelona, 2003; Gerald Howson, *Armas para España. La historia no contada de la guerra civil española*, Barcelona, 2000; Michael Seidman, *A ras de suelo. Historia social de la República durante la guerra civil*, Madrid, 2003; A. Elorza and M. Bizcarrondo, *Queridos camaradas. La Internacional Comunista y España, 1919–1939*, Barcelona, 1999; and of course the archives themselves have shed further light: principally, the RGVA, RGASPI and GARF.

5 Kowalsky, pp. 73–4.

6 Orlov was a *nom de guerre*. His NKVD name was Lev Lazarovich Nikolsky, but his real name was Felbin, Leiba Lazarovich. Most Jews who joined the NKVD were ordered to take less recognizably Jewish names (GARF R-9401/12/55, pp. 211–12).

7 From the papers of S. P. Litvinov, the radio operator for the Intelligence Department of the Red Army and then the chief of radio communications at the Republican Tank Brigade under the command of D. G. Pavlov (Yury Rybalkin, *Operatsiya 'X'*, p. 39).

8 See Kowalsky, pp. 42ff.

9 There has been much debate over figures of Soviet armament supplied during the war, but Gerald Howson, to whom I am most grateful, has established that in almost all essential respects the Soviet figures match the receipts of the Spanish Republican government. They amount to 623 combat aircraft, including 92 SB Katiuska bombers; 131 I-15 Chato fighters (of which 15 were delivered to Vizcaya); 276 I-16 Mosca fighters; 31 R-5SSS Rasante light bombers; 93 RZ Natacha light bombers. Another 30 I-152 Super Chato fighters which arrived too late to be used are excluded from the total. Altogether 331 tanks, 60 armoured cars and between 737 and 755 peices of artillery of various sorts were supplied during the course of the war.

10 Howson, p. 181.

11 RGVA 35082/1/185, p. 352.

12 See Ángel Viñas, *El oro de Moscú*, Barcelona, 1979 and *Guerra, dinero, dictadura*, Barcelona, 1984; and also Pablo Martín Aceña, *El oro de Moscú y el oro de Berlin*, Madrid, 2001.
13 Gabriel Jackson, however, argues that the idea of sending the gold to Moscow took the Soviet authorities by surprise and that Négrin had to explain the idea in detail to Rosenberg, the Soviet ambassador (*Juan Negrín*, p. 75).
14 Its value was 598 million gold pesetas, the equivalent of $195 million (Viñas, *Guerra, dinero, dictadura*, p. 170).
15 GARF 7733/36/27, pp. 25–6.
16 Viñas, *El oro de Moscú*, pp. 289–92. These figures do not, however, take into account the numismatic value of many of the coins, which was considerable in the case of old Spanish and Portuguese pieces.
17 During the course of 1937 another $256 million were transferred to the account of Eurobank in Paris. Another $131,500,000 served to pay the Soviet Union for the matériel which it had supplied. The balance of the gold from the Banco de España ran out early in 1938, according to the Soviet version, and in March of that year the Republic had to request from the USSR a credit of $70 million and in December another $85 million (Kowalsky, pp. 232–3).
18 Seidman, *A ras de suelo*, p. 112; Comín et al., *Historia económica de España*, p. 335.
19 RGASPI 17/120/263, pp. 2–3.
20 Ibid., pp. 16–1.
21 Antonov-Ovseyenko's diary, RGASPI 17/120/84, pp. 58–79.
22 Antonov-Ovseyenko's confession was published in *Izvestia*, 24 August 1936.
23 RGASPI 17/120/259, pp. 73–4.
24 RGASPI 17/120/84, pp. 75–6.
25 RGASPI 17/120/263, pp. 32.
26 Ibid., pp. 16–17.

CHAPTER 16: The International Brigades and the Soviet Advisers

1 Claims arising from French Communist Party sources that Maurice Thorez, their secretary-general, had somehow put forward the idea at a Comintern meeting of 26 July appear to have been completely discredited. See Rémi Skoutelsky, *L'Espoir guidait leurs pas. Les voluntaires françaises dans les Brigades Internationales, 1936–1939*, Paris, 1998, pp. 50–1.
2 Quoted in Elorza and Bizcarrondo, p. 303.
3 Andreu Castells, *Las Brigadas Internacionales*, Barcelona, 1974, p. 449.
4 The most accurate figures by country, but still uncertain, are as follows:

France: 8,962
Poland: 3,113

Italy: 3,002
United States: 2,341
Germany: 2,217
Balkan countries: 2,095
Great Britain: 1,843
Belgium: 1,722
Czechoslovakia: 1,066
Baltic states: 892
Austria: 872
Scandinavian countries: 799
Netherlands: 628
Hungary: 528
Canada: 512
Switzerland: 408
Portugal: 134
Others: 1,122

Michel Lefebvre and Rémi Skoutelsky, *Las Brigadas Internacionales*, Barcelona, 2003, p. 16.

5 Kowalsky, p. 267.
6 Esmond Romilly, *Boadilla*, London, 1971.
7 Castells, *Las Brigadas Internacionales*, p. 80.
8 Jason Gurney, *Crusade in Spain*, London, 1974.
9 George Orwell, *Collected Essays, Journalism and Letters*, London, 1968.
10 Abad de Santillán, *Por qué perdimos la guerra*, p. 175.
11 Bennassar believes that Marty was responsible for the death of the French commander Gaston Delassale and a dozen International Brigaders, 'but not, however, of systematic executions' (*La guerre d'Espagne et les lendemains*, p. 146). Soviet documents, on the other hand, indicate that Marty's obsession with 'fifth column' infiltration and the executions of deserters and 'cowards' may well have contributed to the very high rate of executions.
12 Castells, p. 73n.
13 Commissariat XV International Brigade, *Book of XV International Brigade*, Madrid, 1938.
14 TsAMO 132/2642/77, p. 47.
15 RGASPI 545/3/309, p. 2.
16 RGVA 33987/3/870, p. 346.
17 The figures in Soviet files do not entirely agree, mainly because of differences in category definition. One of the clearest breakdowns states that in addition to the Red Army advisers attached to various headquarters, a total of 772 Soviet pilots, 351 tankists, 100 artillerists, 77 sailors, 166 signals experts, 141 military engineers and technicians, and 204 interpreters served in Spain (RGVA 33987/3/1143, p. 127). There were about 150 advisers in 1937 and about 250 in 1938. In January 1939 their number was reduced to 84 (RGVA 35082/1/15, pp. 47–9). For casualty figures,

see G. F. Krivosheev (ed.), *Rossiya i SSSR v voihakh 20 veka. Poteri vooruzhennykh sil* (Russia and the USSR in the wars of the twentieth century. Losses of the armed forces), Moscow, 2001.

18 TsAMO 132/2642/192, p. 1.

19 Rybalkin, p. 56.

20 TsAMO 132/2642/192, p. 15.

21 Ibid., p. 32.

22 RGVA 35082/1/40, p. 78.

23 RGVA 9/29/315, p. 70; 33987/3/1149, p. 172.

24 RGVA 33987/3/960, pp. 180–9, quoted in Radosh and Habeck, p. 127.

25 RGVA 35082/1/185, pp. 356 and 408.

26 See Rybalkin, pp. 38–42 and RGVA 33987/3/870, pp. 341–2; RGVA 33987/3/961 p. 166; RGVA 35082/1/18, pp. 49, 64–6; RGVA 33987/3/961, pp. 155–6; TsAMO 16/3148/5, pp. 23–5. According to Rybalkin, p. 42, the experience gained in this operation was later used in the Soviet planning and organization of transport during the Second World War and then later in 1962 when Soviet weapons and troops were transported to Cuba as part of Operation Anadyr, an enterprise directed by the then minister of defence, Marshal Rodion Malinovsky, who had himself served in Spain.

27 RGASPI 545/3/302, p. 118.

CHAPTER 17: The Battle for Madrid

1 The first line, some 30 kilometres out from Madrid, linked Navalcarnero with Valdemoro passing by Batres, Griñón and Torrejón de Velasco; the second, about twenty kilometres out, consisted of Brunete, Villaviciosa, Móstoles, Fuenlabrada and Pinto; the third, at about ten kilometres out, went from Villaviciosa de Odón to Cerro de los Ángeles; and the fourth, at the gates of the capital, consisted of fortifying Pozuelo, la Casa de Campo, Campamento, Carabanchel, Villaverde and Vallecas (José Manuel Martínez Bande, *La guerra en el norte*, Madrid, 1969, p. 130).

2 Preston, *Franco, caudillo de España*, p. 255.

3 These first mixed brigades came under the División Orgánica de Albacete, commanded by Colonel Segismundo Casado. The first was led by Major of Militia Enrique Líster; the second by Major Jesús Martínez de Aragón; the third, composed of *carabineros*, by José María Galán; the fourth, commanded by an infantry captain, Eutiquiano Arellano, was made up of conscript soldiers; the fifth, also *carabineros*, was led by Fernando Sabio; and the sixth, of reserve soldiers based in Murcia, was commanded by Miguel Gallo Martínez.

4 Rodimtsev, Aleksandr Ilyich, *Dobrovoltsy–internatsionalisty*, Sverdlovsk, 1976, p. 31.

5 Louis Aragon, the French poet and communist, and his partner, Elsa Triolet, a writer, were regarded as 'the royal couple' of the French Communist Party. Koltsov, *Ispansky dnevnik*, Moscow, 1957, p. 199.

Many people suspected Triolet of being an NKVD agent, but no documentary proof has emerged.

6 Francisco Largo Caballero, *Arenga a las fuerzas armadas*, 28 October 1936, reported in the daily press.

7 The republican tank force was formed on the basis of a brigade which arrived from the Belorussian military district; 60 per cent of the unit were Soviet 'volunteer' tankists. RGVA 31811/4/28, pp. 104–10. The brigade was commanded by Colonel D. G. Pavlov, who was executed in 1941 as a scapegoat when the Wehrmacht smashed the Red Army in its invasion. Arman was not the son of Lenin's close friend Inessa Armand, as some people think.

8 *Ispansky dnevnik*, Moscow, 1957, p. 231.

9 Letter from Federica Montseny to Bolloten: *La revolución española*, p. 288.

10 *Ispansky dnevnik*, p. 235.

11 Azaña, *Diarios completos*, p. 956.

12 For this massacre and those from other prisons, such as Antón, Porlier and Ventas, see Gibson, *Paracuellos cómo fue*, pp. 185ff., which gives a total figure of 2,400 murders between 7 November and 4 December 1936. Javier Cervera (*Madrid en guerra. La ciudad clandestin*, Madrid, pp. 84–103) states that there were more than 2,000 killed at Paracuellos and Torrejón.

13 See Martínez Reverte, *La batalla de Madrid*, Barcelona, 2004, pp. 226–7, 240. The document is reproduced on pp. 577–81.

14 RGVA 35082/1/185, p. 365.

15 R. Salas Larrazábal, *Historia del Ejército Popular*, p. 574 and General Alonso Baquer, *El Ebro. La batalla decisiva de los cien días*, La Esfera, Madrid, 2003, p. 33.

16 'French direction had been unmistakably evident on the side of the reds in their whole tactical procedure' (DGFP, p. 259).

17 Paul Schmidt, *Hitler's Interpreter, The Secret History of German Diplomacy, 1939–1945*, London, 1951.

18 J. Delperrie, *Las brigadas internacionales*, Madrid, 1978, p. 94.

19 *Hoy*, Las Palmas, 24 July 1936.

20 Blanco Escolá, *El general Rojo*, p. 173.

21 Karl Anger, alias Dobrovolsky, RGVA 35082/1/189, p. 83.

22 RGVA 35082/1/95, pp. 33–58.

23 Rodimtsev, *Dobrovoltsy–internatsionalisty*, p. 46,

24 Koltsov, *Ispansky dnevnik*, Moscow, 1957, p. 279.

25 RGVA 35082/1/189, p. 103.

26 A biographer of Durruti suggests that the doctors did not dare intervene surgically when they might have saved him. He died of an internal haemorrhage (Abel Paz, *Durruti en la revolución española*, Madrid, 2004, p. 678).

27 J. Salas Larrazábal, *La guerra de España desde el aire*, p. 140.

28 See Solé Sabaté, pp. 48–9.

29 BA-MA RL 35/38.

30 *Venid a ver la sangre por las calles,*
venid a ver
la sangre por las calles,
venid a ver la sangre
por las calles!

'Explico algunas cosas' in *Poesía política*, Santiago de Chile, 1953, I, p. 60.

31 RGASPI 495/120/261, p. 14.

32 Cowles, *Looking for Trouble*, p. 18.

33 Dobrovolsky (Karl Anger), RGVA 35082/1/189, p. 126.

34 Richthofen, BA-MA RL 35/38. The request, supported by General Faupel, was rejected in Berlin on both political and technical grounds, principally the problem of shipping such a large body of men past Britain without being seen. See Dieckhoff's memorandum of December 1936, DGFP, pp. 155–6, 162, 165 and 168.

CHAPTER 18: The Metamorphosis of the War

1 Chargé d'affaires in Madrid, v. Tippelskirch, to Foreign Ministry, 23 September 1936, DGFP, p. 94.

2 Faupel to Foreign Ministry, 10 December 1936, DGFP, p. 159.

3 Richthofen personal war diary, BA-MA RL 35/38.

4 Karl Anger (Dobrovolsky), RGVA 35082/1/189.

5 Koltsov, *Ispansky dnevnik*, p. 309.

6 RGVA 35082/1/185, pp. 400, 407.

7 Ibid., pp. 680–95.

8 Castells, *Las Brigadas Internacionales*, pp. 130–1.

9 *The Owl of Minerva*, London, 1959.

10 Gillain, *La Marseillaise*, p. 16.

11 Preston, *La guerra civil española*, Barcelona, 1999, p. 125.

12 See Gabriele Ranzato, *L'eclissi della democrazia. La guerra civile spagnola e le sue origine*, Turín, 2004, pp. 372–3.

13 *Diarios 1937–1943*, Barcelona, 2004, p. 15.

14 When Villalba returned to nationalist Spain after the war, his claims of '*negligencia deliberada*' were fully accepted and he was restored to the rank of full colonel, with pension. See 'Rectificaciones' in vol. iv of *Crónica de la guerra española*, Buenos Aires, 1966, p. 491.

15 Richthofen personal war diary, BA-MA RL 35/38.

16 Borkenau, *The Spanish Cockpit*, p. 227.

17 23 March 1937, RGVA 33987/3/991, pp. 81–96, quoted in Radosh and Habeck, p. 162.

18 RGVA 33987/3/960, pp. 180–9, quoted in Radosh and Habeck, p. 127.

19 RGVA/33987/3/1010, p. 300.

20 Marchenko to Litvinov, 22 February 1937, RGVA 33987/3/960, pp. 303–15.

21 Brusco, p. 114.
22 *El péndulo patriótico*, vol. ii, p. 22.
23 'Adelante!', *Internatsionalnaya brigada*, Moscow, 1937, pp. 106–18.
24 *Krasnaya Zvezda*, 15 September 1993.
25 Alpert, *El Ejército de la República*, p. 65.
26 *Guerra, exilio y cárcel*, Paris, 1976.
27 J. Martínez Reverte, *La batalla de Madrid*.

CHAPTER 19: The Battles of the Jarama and Guadalajara

1 Richthofen war diary, BA-MA RL 35/38.
2 Regler, *The Great Crusade*, pp. 243–63.
3 Castells, *Las Brigadas Internacionales*, p. 166.
4 Wintringham, *English Captain*, London, 1939.
5 Alexander, *British Volunteers*, p. 95.
6 Richthofen war diary, BA-MA RL 35/38.
7 Kemp, *Mine Were of Trouble*, London, 1957.
8 RGVA 33987/3/912, pp. 127–8.
9 RGVA 35082/1/185, p. 379.
10 Sixten Rogeby, *Spanska frontminnen*, Arbetarkultur, Stockholm, 1938.
11 RGVA 35082/1/185, p. 361.
12 According to Salas, *La guerra de España desde el aire*, p. 164, eight Chatos were downed.
13 Marty to Dimitrov, 28 March 1937, RGVA 33987/3/991, pp. 150–88.
14 Blanco, *La incompetencia militar de Franco*, p. 344.
15 Segala, *Trincee di Spagna*, p. 116.
16 Renzo de Felice, *Mussolini il duce*, vol. ii., *Lo stato totalitario*, p. 404.
17 Rodimtsev, *Dobrovoltsy*, p. 57.
18 Castells, *Las Brigadas Internacionales*, p. 187.
19 Rodimtsev, op. cit., pp. 73–4.
20 RGASPI 533/6/102, p. 110.
21 Karl Anger (Dobrovolsky), RGVA 35082/1/189, p. 188.
22 Koltsov, *Ispansky dnevnik*, p. 450.
23 *Mi embajada en Londres*, pp. 321–3.
24 Rodimtsev, pp. 94–6.
25 Mera, *Guerra, exilio y cárcel*, Paris, 1976.
26 Karl Anger (Dobrovolsky), RGVA 35082/1/189, p. 190.
27 Rodimtsev, p. 102.
28 RGVA 33987/3/1082, p. 206.
29 RGVA 33987/3/961, p. 123.
30 *Two Wars and More to Come*, p. 264.
31 Renzo de Felice, *Lo stato totalitario*, p. 392.
32 Mussolini, probably echoing Franco's own conviction that French regular officers were directing operations, told the German ambassador in Italy on 25 March that 'French direction has been unmistakably evident on the side of the reds in their whole tactical procedure' (DGFP, p. 259).

33 DGFP, p. 265.

CHAPTER 20: The War in the North

1 The government consisted of Aguirre, Jesús María Leizaola, Heliodoro de la Torre and Telesforo Monzón (all PNV); three socialists (Santiago Aznar, Juan Gracía and Juan de los Toyos); a member of ANV (Gonzalo Nárdiz), one from the Izquierda Republicana (Ramón Maria Aldasoro), another from Unión Republicana (Alfredo Espinosa) and Juan Astigarrabía, a communist.
2 S. de Pablo et al., *El péndulo patrótico*, vol. ii, p. 19.
3 Luis María Jiménez de Aberasturi, *La guerra en el Norte*, p. 118.
4 RGVA 35082/1/189, pp. 8–9.
5 Aberasturi, op. cit., p. 163.
6 BA-MA RL 35/3.
7 Richthofen war diary, BA-MA RL 35/38.
8 Ibid.
9 According to the republican chaplain José María Basabilotra, people tried to seek refuge in the cemetery. Fraser, *Recuérdalo tú* ..., pp. 549–50.
10 Vicente Talón, *Memoria de la guerra de Euskadi*, p. 398.
11 Richthofen war diary, BA-MA RL 35/38.
12 Ibid.
13 Ibid.
14 Ibid.
15 Luis Michelena, quoted in Fraser, *Recuérdalo tú* ..., p. 552.
16 Richthofen war diary, BA-MA RL 35/38.
17 Sole Sabaté and Villarroya state that three Savoia S-79s had already dropped 36 bombs of 50 kilograms each (*España en llamas*, pp. 84–5).
18 Between 200 and 300 according to V. Talón, *Memoria* ..., pp. 34–5, and around 200 according to S. De Pablo, 'La guerra civil en el País Vasco'.
19 See Southworth, *Guernica*, pp. 22–4, and Steer, *The Tree of Gernika*.
20 Ángel Viñas, *Guerra, dinero, dictadura*, p. 122.
21 *ABC*, 29 April 1937.
22 Ibid. A slightly different version was reported by Faupel, the German ambassador, on 5 May 1937. It included the sentence: 'Aguirre planned the destruction of Guernica with the devilish intention of laying the blame before the enemy's door and producing a storm of indignation among the already conquered and demoralized Basques' (DGFP, p. 281).
23 A. Rovighi and F. Stefani, *La participazione italiana alla guerra civile spagnola*, Estado Mayor del Ejército, Roma, 1993, quoted by Ranzato, *Leclissi della democrazia*, p. 492.
24 Virginia Cowles, *Looking for Trouble*, p. 75.
25 Richthofen war diary, BA-MA RL 35/38.
26 For the destruction of Guernica see Gordon Thomas and Max Morgan Witts, *The Day Guernica Died*, London, 1975; H. R. Southworth, *Guernica*

el mito; A. Viñas, *Guerra, dinero, dictadura*; and J. L. de la Granja and C. Garitaonandía (ed.), *Gernika: 50 años después*.

27 *Diarios completos*, p. 974.

28 Richthofen war diary, BA-MA RL 35/38.

29 Aberasturi, *La guerra en el norte*, pp. 234–5.

30 The German ambassador in Rome, Ulrich von Hassell, reported as early as 13 January 1937 that 'through the mediation of the Vatican negotiations are being carried on in the north with the Basque separatists at Bilbao' (DGFP, p. 221).

31 Franco's headquarters, however, announced: 'Vizcaya front. This afternoon at 3.10 p.m. troops entered the capital of Vizcaya. Bilbao is once again part of Spain.'

32 For the 'Pact of Santoña', the relations between the Basque government and Valencia and the diplomatic discussion, see S. De Pablo, *El péndulo patriótico*, pp. 29–41.

33 Ciano, *Diarios 1937–1943*, p. 15.

CHAPTER 21: The Propaganda War and the Intellectuals

1 H. R. Southworth, *El lavado de cerebro de Francisco Franco*, pp. 21–186.

2 Blanco Escolá, *Falacios de la guerra civil*, p. 105.

3 The Catholic Church declared that the murdered priests were martyrs. This position continued right up to John Paul II's visit to Spain in May 2003, when he maintained that the killing of priests was a 'bloody and planned religious persecution'. In Madrid, he beatified the teacher Pedro Poveda, killed there on 27 July 1936. He still made no mention of the Basque priests killed by the nationalists (*El País*, 5 May 2003).

4 'Carta colectiva del Episcopado español a los obispos del mundo entero', 1 July 1937, quoted in Antonio Montero, *Historia de la persecución religiosa en España, 1936–1939*, Madrid, 1961.

5 Southworth, *El mito*, p. 169.

6 Luis Bolín, *Spain: The Vital Years*, London, 1967

7 Peter Kemp, *Mine Were of Trouble*, pp. 49–50.

8 Virginia Cowles, pp. 77–80.

9 Peter Kemp, *Mine Were of Trouble*.

10 Arthur Koestler, *Spanish Testament*, London, 1937.

11 Southworth, *El mito*, p. 238.

12 Bennassar argues that 'the two camps behaved like agencies of disinformation and rumour factories' (*La guerre d'Espagne et ses lendemains*, p. 323).

13 Quoted in Noam Chomsky, *American Power and the New Mandarins*, p. 115.

14 For the part played by intellectuals in the Spanish Civil War, see among others: Southworth, *El mito de la cruzada de Franco*; R. Álvarez and R. López (eds), *Poesia anglo-norteamericana de la guerra civil española*, Salamanca, 1986; Robert Payne, *The Civil War in Spain, 1936–1939*,

London, 1962; and Francisco Rico (ed.), *Historia y crítica de la literatura española*, vol. 7, Barcelona, 1984.

15 'Writers Take Sides', in *New Left Review*.

16 Bertrand Russell, *Roads to Freedom*, London, 1948.

17 Supporters included Claudio Sánchez Albornoz, Américo Castro, Pau Casals, Rodolfo Halffter, Blas Cabrera, Alberto Jiménez Fraud, Josep Ferrater Mora, Alfonso Rodríguez Castelao, Pere Bosch Gimpera, Luís Buñuel, Pablo Picasso and Joan Miró. Writers and others who took an active role, either in the trenches or behind the lines, included Antonio Machado, Juan Ramón Jiménez, Jorge Guillén, Pedro Salinas, Vicente Aleixandre, Rafael Alberti, Luis Cernuda, José Bergamín, León Felipe, Max Aub, José Moreno Villa, Ramón J. Sender, Miguel Hernández, Salvador Espriu, Juan Marichal, Francisco Ayala, Antonio Buero Vallejo, María Zambrano, Rafael Dieste, Juan Gil-Albert, Ramón Gaya, Teresa León, José Herrera Petere, Antonio Sanchez Barbudo, Manuel Altolaguirre, Emilio Prados, Pedro Garfias, Rosa Chacel, Antonio Agraz, Félix Paredes, Leopoldo Urrutia, Lorenzo Varela, José María Morón, Benigno Bejarano, Eduardo Zamacois, Rafel Vidiella, Julio Sesto, A. Martínez de Luzenay, Silvia Mistral, Clemente Cimorra, Roger de Flor, Gabriel Baldrich, Manuel Cabanillas, Juan Usón ('Juaninus').

On the nationalist side supporters included Eugenio d'Ors, Manuel Machado, José María Pemán, Francisco Cossío, Concha Espina, José Muñoz San Román, Rafael García Serrano, Ricardo León, Wenceslao Fernández Flórez, Cecilio Benítez de Castro, Francisco Camba, Evaristo Casariego, Tomás Borrás, Josep Pla, Eduardo Marquina, Federico de Urrutia, José Camón Aznar, José María Castroviejo, Ignacio Agustí, Alvaro Cunqueiro, Pedro Laín Entralgo, José L. López Aranguren, Antonio Tovar, Luis Díez del Corral, Antonio Maravall, Gerardo Diego, Leopoldo Panero, Luis Rosales, Luis Felipe Vivanco, Gonzalo Torrente Ballester, Félix Ros, Pedro Muñoz Seca and of course the literary court of José Antonio Primo de Rivera: Rafael Sánchez Mazas, Ernesto Giménez Caballero, Eugenio Montes, Agustín de Foxá, Jacinto Miquelarena, Pedro Mourlane Michelena, José María Alfaro, Luys Santa Marina, Samuel Ros and Dionisio Ridruejo.

18 Agustín Sánchez Vidal in F. Rico, *Historia y crítica de la literatura española*, vol. vii, p. 759.

19 On the intellectuals and the 'cause of the people' see Santos Juliá, *Historias de las dos Españas*, Madrid, 2004.

20 The Mangada column had *Avance*, the communists on the Somosierra front; *¡No pasarán!* and *El miliciano rojo* on the Aragón front; *Octubre* for the battalion of that name; *Komsomol* for the Communist Youth of La Mancha; socialists, anarchists and republicans all had their own. The International Brigades had a dozen of their own: *Le Volontaire de la Liberté, Our Fight, Il Garibaldino* and *Freiheit Kämpfer*. Even the Scandinavian company with the Thaelmann Battalion produced its own paper, edited by a journalist called Lise, who had accompanied them to Spain

(Conny Andersson in Sixten Rogeby, *Spanska frontminnen*, Arbetarkultur, 1938).

The nationalists, meanwhile, had *ABC* in Seville; *El Heraldo de Aragón* in Saragossa; *El Norte de Castilla* in Valladolid; *Ideal* in Granada; the *Gaceta regional* in Salamanca; *El Faro* in Vigo; *La Voz de Asturias* in Oviedo; *El Pensamiento Navarro* in Pamplona and the *Diario de Burgos*. In the early part of the war the besieged nationalist garrison in Toledo had produced the roneoed *El Alcázar*. The main Falangist publication was *¡Arriba España!*, but also *Jerarquía*; *Fotos*, which was close to Manuel Hedilla; *Vértice*, published by the Delegación de Prensa y Propaganda; *Fe* in Seville; *Patria* in Granada; *Odiel* in Huelva; *Sur* in Malaga; *Destino*, the publication of the Catalans in Burgos; and the satirical review *Ametralladora*. In November 1938 the nationalist administration created an official news service, EFE, financed by Juan March and other bankers. For the press on both sides see Rafael Abella, *La vida cotidiana durante la guerra civil*, Planeta, Barcelona, 1975.

21 Phrase used in *El Socialista*, October 1936.

22 Josep Renau, Carles Fontseré, Lorenzo Gomis, Ramón Gaya, José Bardasano, Josep Obiols, Lola Anglada, Martí Bas, José Luis Rey Vila ('Sim'), Antoni Clavé, Emeterio Melendreras, Helios Gómez and Luis Quintanilla. On the nationalist side the best-known designers were Carlos Sáenz de Tejada, a great draughtsman, and Teodoro Delgado. See Jordi and Arnau Carulla, *La guerra civil en 2000 carteles*, 2 vol, Barcelona, 1997; Carmen Grimau, *El cartel republicano en la guerra civil*, Madrid, 1979.

23 The republicans had Unión Radio, Radio España and the many transmitters belonging to political parties and trade unions. La Voz de España was the station for propaganda aimed abroad. The nationalists used Radio Tetuán, Radio Ceuta and Radio Sevilla (known as Queipo de Llano's 'plaything'), as well as the foreign broadcasts of their allies in Rome, Berlin and Lisbon. The radio station attached to the Generalissimo's headquarters soon became the most important in nationalist Spain. When the nationalists conquered a sector of republican territory, they immediately put the radio station there to work for their own side. See C. Garitaonandía, 'La radio republicana durante la guerra civil' in *Historia y memoria de la guerra civil*, vol. i, pp. 391–400.

24 Most were by Ramon Biadiu: *Delta de l'Ebre; Els tapers de la Costa; Transformació de la indústria al servei de la guerra* and *Vail d'Aran* (Santos Zunzunegui and Eduardo González Calleja, *Comunicación cultura y política durante la Il República y la guerra civil*, vol. ii, Bilbao, 1990, pp. 475–493); see also Daniel Kowalsky, *La Unión Soviética y la guerra civil española*.

25 For the exhibition, see Manuel Aznar, *Pensamiento literario y compromiso antifascista de la inteligencia española republicana*, Barcelona, 1978.

26 André Malraux, Julián Benda, Tristan Tzara, André Chamson, Anna Seghers, Ilya Ehrenburg, Alexis Tolstoy, Stephen Spender, Malcolm Cowley, Jef Last, Ernest Hemingway, Frank Pitcairn, Eric Weinert, Pablo

Neruda, Nicolás Guillén, Octavio Paz, César Vallejo, Vicente Huidobro, Juan Marinello, Raúl González Tuñón, José Mancisidor, Enrique Díez Canedo, Antonio Machado, Rafael Alberti, Corpus Barga, Eugenio Imaz, Wenceslao Roces, Manuel Altolaguirre, Emilio Prados, José Bergamín, Juan Chabás, Juan Gil Albert and Miguel Hernández (International Anti-Fascist Congress of Writers in Spain, GARF 1117/04/37).

27 Victor Serge, *Memoirs of a Revolutionary*, Oxford, 1968.

28 Churchill, *Step by Step*, p. 304.

CHAPTER 22: The Struggle for Power

1 Faupel to Wilhelmstrasse, 14 April 1937, DGFP, p. 269.

2 Cowles, p. 80.

3 In his last despatch of 9 April 1937 the Italian ambassador to Franco, Roberto Cantalupo, described with great clarity the Generalissimo's plans to amalgamate the political parties and establish 'his own position as future head of state, head of government and head of all the political and union organizations in the future totalitarian Spain'. Quoted by Ranzato, *L'eclissi della democrazia*, p. 527.

4 Decreto no. 255, published in the *Boletín Oficial* of 20 April 1937. The text was drafted by Serrano Súñer and Ernesto Jiménez Caballero who, needless to say, did not consult either Hedilla or Rodezno.

5 Ellwood, *Prietas las filas*, p. 111. The Carlists were in charge of only nine provincial organizations, while the Falangists took over 22. See J. Tusell, *Franco en la guerra civil*, Tusquets, Barcelona, 1992.

6 Heleno Saña, *El franquismo sin mitos. Conversaciones con Serrano Súñer*, Barcelona, 1982, p. 69. Leonardo Painador, the prosecutor of the popular tribunal which condemned to death the two brothers of Serrano Súñer, was shot early in 1940 (Bullón and De Diego, *Historias orales de la guerra civil*, p. 191).

7 Manuel Hedilla, *Testimonio*, pp. 529–33.

8 TsAMO 132/2642/77, pp. 45–6.

9 Elorza and Bizcarrondo, *Queridos camaradas*, p. 341 and Dimitrov, *Diarios*, 20 March 1937, p. 58.

10 RGVA 33987/3/960, pp. 14–15.

11 RGVA 33987/3/961, pp. 34–56, quoted in Radosh and Habeck, pp. 403–4.

12 TsAMO 132/2642/192, p. 42, quoted in Rybalkin, p. 48.

13 Bolloten, *La Revolución española*, p. 322.

14 *Frente Rojo*, 17 April 1937, quoted in Bolloten, p. 337.

15 Petrov, battalion commander, 17 May 1937, RGVA 35082/1/185, p. 374.

16 A project of close collaboration between the PSOE and the Spanish Communist Party was first put forward by Ramón Lamoneda on 26 December 1936. This proposal consisted of creating a joint supervisory committee. See Graham, *Socialism and War*, p. 75.

17 *Treball*, 22 December 1936. For the food supply situation in Barcelona, see E. Ucelay da Cal, *La Catalunya populista. Imatge, cultura i politica en l'etapa republicana 1931–1939*, Barcelona, 1982.
18 *Treball*, 8 April 1937.
19 *Solidaridad Obrera*, 8 April 1937.
20 *La Batalla*, 11 April 1937.
21 See L. Trotsky, *La revolución española 1930–1940*, Barcelona, 1977, vol. i, p. 333.
22 Elorza and Bizcarrondo, *Queridos camaradas*, p. 364.

CHAPTER 23: The Civil War within the Civil War

1 See J. Pous and J. M. Solé, *Anarquia i república a la Cerdanya (1936–1939)*, Barcelona, 1988.
2 Many suspected that the killing was a communist provocation, arguing that Roldán Cortada objected to the PSUC attacks against the CNT and the POUM. See Thomas, *The Spanish Civil War*, 2003, p. 635; José Peirats, *Los anarquistas en la crisis política española*, Buenos Aires, 1964, pp. 241–3; and Felix Morrow, p. 87.
3 Bolloten, p. 557.
4 'Kein Wagen, der nicht zur CNT gehörte dürfte passieren und mehr als 200 Polizisten and Sturmgardisten wurden entwaffnet' (12 May 1937, RGASPI 495/120/259, p. 4).
5 Orwell, *Homage to Catalonia*.
6 García Oliver's address was astonishingly emotional and sentimental. He spoke twice of bending over the dead 'to kiss them'. The libertarian rank and file referred scornfully to his speech as 'the legend of the kiss'.
7 Gabriele Ranzato says that Berneri and Barbieri were killed probably by communists, but that one cannot rule out the theory of García Oliver that they might have been killed by agents of Mussolini's secret police, the OVRA (*L'eclessi della democrazia*, p. 453). The simultaneous killing of prominent Catalan anarchists would, however, suggest that these crimes were more likely to have been the work of communists.
8 In an interview with John Brademas, *Anarcosindicalismo y revolución ...*, p. 246.
9 Casanova, *De la calle al frente*, p. 222.
10 Personal account of Hidalgo de Cisneros in Bolloten, p. 570.
11 RGASPI 495/74/204, p. 129.
12 RGASPI 495/120/259, p. 117.
13 Ibid., p. 118.
14 RGASPI 495/120/261, p. 4.
15 Ibid., p. 6.
16 Faupel to Wilhelmstrasse, 11 May 1937, DGFP, p. 286.
17 For the establishment of republican justice in the face of revolutionary disorder see François Godicheau, *La guerre d'Espagne. République et Révolution en Catalogne (1936–1939)*, Paris, 2004. Of the 3,700 'anti-

fascist prisoners' still in jail in January 1939, 90 per cent were from the CNT-FAI.

18 The Pueblo Español (Montjuich), Vandellós, L'Hospitalet de l'Infant, Omelles de na Gaia, Concabella, Anglesrola and Falset. François Godicheau, 'Los hechos de mayo de 1937 y los "presos antifascistas": identificación de un fenómeno represivo' in *Historia social*, n. 44, 2002, pp. 39 and 55, and *La guerra civil a Catalunya (1936–1939)* vol. ii, pp. 212ff.

19 José Díaz, *Tres años de lucha*, p. 433.

20 Helen Graham argues convincingly that the Spanish Communist Party and the republicans had worked closely together, with the joint aim of opposing Largo Caballero (*Socialism and War*, p. 91).

21 Ibid., pp. 100–2.

22 RGASPI 17/120/263, p. 32.

23 The other main portfolios were José Giral, minister of state; Bernardo Giner de los Ríos, public works; and Jaime Aiguader, minister of work and public assistance.

24 *Diarios completos*, pp. 959–60.

25 For the POUM and the Nin affair see Francesc Bonamusa, *Andreu Nin y el movimiento comunista en España (1930–1937)*, Barcelona, 1977, and Elorza and Bizcarrondo, *Queridos camaradas*.

26 *Diarios completos*, p. 1054.

27 Diego Abad de Santillán, *Por qué perdimos la guerra*, Buenos Aires, 1940. See J. Pous and J. M. Solé, *Anarquia i república a la Cerdanya (1936–1939)*, Barcelona, 1988.

CHAPTER 24: The Battle of Brunete

1 RGVA 33987/3/969, p. 266.

2 R. Salas Larrazábal, 'Génesis y actuación del Ejército Popular de la República' in Carr (ed.), *Estudios sobre la República y la guerra civil española*, p. 222.

3 'Mein Bruder ist ein Flieger / Unserm Volke fehlt's an Raum / Und Grund und Boden zu kriegen, ist / Bei uns ein alter Traum. / Der Raum, den mein Bruder eroberte / Liegt in Guadarramamassiv. / Er ist lang einen Meter achtzig / Und einen Meter fünfzig tief (Bertolt Brecht, 'Mein Bruder war ein Flieger' in *Gedichte 1931–1941*, Frankfurt, 1961 p. 31).

4 Castells, *Las Brigadas Internacionales*, p. 214.

5 RGVA 35082/1/95, pp. 33–58, quoted in Radosh and Habeck, p. 436.

6 J. Salas Larrazábal, *La guerra de España desde el aire*, p. 222.

7 J. Salas, p. 223.

8 Nick Gillain, *Le mercenaire*, p. 59.

9 Castells, p. 217.

10 García Morato, who had fired his machine-guns at another black car, believed that he had killed Lukács, when in fact he had killed Doctor Heilbrun, the head of medical services.

11 RGVA 35082/1/95, pp. 35–58, quoted in Radosh and Habeck, p. 436.

12 Castells, p. 225.
13 D. Kowalski, *La Unión Soviética y la guerra civil española*, p. 340.
14 Azaña, p. 1003.
15 Ibid., p. 1073.
16 Colonel Rudolf Xylander, September 1937, RGASPI 545/2/185, p. 9.
17 Ibid.
18 Ibid.
19 Ibid.
20 F. Ciutat, *Relatos y reflexiones de la guerra de España 1936–1939*, Madrid, 1978, p. 71.
21 J. Salas, p. 241.
22 Colonel Rudolf Xylander, September 1937, RGASPI 545/2/185, p. 9.
23 Castells, p. 241.
24 Richthofen war diary, BA-MA RL 35/38.
25 BA-MA RL 35/42.
26 Richthofen war diary, BA-MA RL 35/38.
27 Report G. Stern, 8 October 1937, RGVA 35082/1/21, p. 12.
28 RGVA 35082/1/95, pp. 33–58, quoted in Radosh and Habeck, p. 437.
29 Richthofen war diary, BA-MA RL 35/38.
30 V. Rojo, *España heroica*, p. 87.
31 Alexander, p. 118.
32 RGVA 35082/1/95, pp. 33–58, quoted in Radosh and Habeck, p. 440.
33 Rodimtsev, *Dobrovoltsy*.
34 Azaña, p. 1054.
35 Radosh and Habeck, p. 267.
36 Preston, *Franco*, pp. 355–6.
37 Castells, pp. 246–9.
38 RGVA 35082/1/42, pp. 249–55.
39 RGVA 33987/3/1149, p. 262.
40 Ibid., pp. 221–6, quoted in Radosh and Habeck, p. 481.
41 23 June 1937, RGVA 33987/3/1056, pp. 27–8.
42 RGVA 35082/1/90, p. 533.
43 Meretskov and Simonov to Voroshilov, 21 August 1937, RGVA 33987/3/1033.
44 RGVA 33987/3/1149, p. 261.

CHAPTER 25: The Beleaguered Republic

1 P. Azcárate, *Mi embajada en Londres*, pp. 145–9.
2 Ibid., p. 155.
3 Cowles, p. 80.
4 Chargé d'affaires in US to Wilhelmstrasse, DGFP, pp. 208–9.
5 J-F Berdah, *La democracia asesinada*, pp. 292–8.
6 Ciano, *Diarios*, p. 13.
7 Ibid., p. 19.
8 H. Nicolson, *Diaries and Letters 1930–1939*, London, 1966.

9 Ribbentrop to Wilhelmstrasse, 22 June 1937, DGFP, pp. 364–5 and 366–7.
10 Azcárate, p. 192.
11 Eden, *Facing the Dictators*, p. 412.
12 RGVA 33987/3/1015, pp. 92–113, quoted in Radosh and Habeck, pp. 219–33.

CHAPTER 26: The War in Aragón

1 Bolloten, *La Revolución española*, pp. 337–9.
2 Casanova, *De la calle al frente*, p. 233.
3 Fraser, *Recuérdalo tú . . .*, p. 481.
4 F. Mintz, *L'autogestion dans l'Espagne révolutionnaire*, Paris 1970; Bernecker, op. cit.; Casanova, op. cit.
5 *La revolución popular en el campo*, p. 17, quoted in Bolloten, *La Revolución española*, pp. 339–40,
6 Líster, *Nuestra guerra*, pp. 151–5.
7 Antonio Cordón, *Trayectoria*, pp. 301–2.
8 TsAMO 132/2542/192, p. 61.
9 Blanco Escolá, *Falacias de la guerra civil*, p. 238.
10 Cordón, op. cit.
11 Castells, *Las Brigadas Internacionales . . .*, p. 272.
12 TsAMO 132/2542/192, p. 61.
13 RGVA 33987/3/1149, pp. 211–26, quoted in Radosh and Habeck, p. 484; and RGVA 33987/3/1149, p. 229.
14 M. Dunbar, *The Book of the XV Brigade*, p. 266. For the course of the battle see Cordón, pp. 302–14; Rojo, *España heroica*, pp. 115–27; and Martínez Bande, *La gran ofensiva*, pp. 77ff.
15 Castells, *Las Brigadas Internacionales*, p. 283.
16 RGVA 33987/3/1149, pp. 211–26, quoted in Radosh and Habeck, p. 483.
17 *Mundo Obrero*, 4 September 1937.

CHAPTER 27: The Destruction of the Northern Front and of Republican Idealism

1 Salas, *La guerra de España desde el aire*, p. 270.
2 It was at this point that the Council of Asturias ordered the evacuation of 1,200 children to the French port of Saint-Nazaire, from where they were taken to Leningrad. Already 14,000 children had been evacuated from the Basque country, most of them going to Britain, France, Belgium and the Soviet Union. In all, the republican government arranged the evacuation abroad of 33,000 children. See Alicia Altea, 'Los niños de la guerra civil' in *Anales de Historia Contemporánea*, 19, 2003, pp. 43ff.
3 Viñas, *Guerra, dinero, dictadura*, pp. 141–52.
4 Tuñón, *Historia de España*, vol. x, pp. 401–4.

5 *El Socialista*, 30 October 1937.
6 Salas, *La guerra de España desde el aire*, p. 272.
7 Thomas, *La guerra civil española*, p. 846.
8 Zugazagoitia, *Guerra y vicisitudes de los españoles*, p. 343.
9 Cordón, *Trayectoria*, p. 340.
10 Tuñón, *Historia de España*, vol. x, p. 400.
11 Graham, *Socialism and War*, pp. 130–1.
12 The SIM incorporated the intelligence and counter-intelligence services, especially the DEDIDE (Departamento Especial de Información del Estado) and the SIEP (Servicio de Información Especial Periférico). For the creation, organigram and evolution of the SIM see François Godicheau, 'La légende noire du Service d'Information Militaire de la République dans la guerre civil espagnole, et l'idée de contrôle politique' in *Le Mouvement Social*, No. 201, October–December 2002. Also D. Pastor Petit, *La cinquena columna a Catalunya (1936–1939)*, Barcelona, 1978 and *Los dossiers secretos de la guerra civil*, Barcelona, 1978.
13 Skoutelsky, *Les Brigades Internationales*, p. 254.
14 Azaña, *Diarios completos*, p. 1232.
15 Peirats, *La CNT en la Revolución española*, III, p. 278.
16 François Godicheau, 'La légende noire du SIM . . .', pp. 38–9.
17 Ibid.
18 Ibid., p. 46.
19 IKKI report, RGASPI, 495/120/261, p. 7.
20 Thomas, *La guerra civil española*, p. 722n.
21 RGVA 33987/3/1149, pp. 211–26.
22 Castells, *Las Brigadas Internacionales*, pp. 258–9.
23 Ibid., p. 262.
24 Ibid., p. 265.
25 From the speech by the secretary of the Madrid branch of the Spanish Communist Party at the Plenum of Central Committee, December 1937, RGASPI 495/120/259, p. 112.

CHAPTER 28: The Battle of Teruel and Franco's 'Victorious Sword'

1 Among the 'garrison' or front-holding formations were V Army Corps in Aragón commanded by Moscardó; the Army of the South under Queipo de Llano, which included II and III Army Corps; the Army of the Centre, led by Saliquet, which consisted of I Corps on the Madrid Front and VII Corps along the Guadarrama. In the Army of Manoeuvre there were: the Moroccan Army Corps under Yagüe, with the major part of the Foreign Legion and the *regulares* in Barrón's 13th Division and Sáenz de Buruaga's 150th Division; Solchaga's Army Corps of Navarre with the Carlist *requetés*; Varela's Army Corps of Castile and Aranda's Army Corps of Galicia. After the fall of the Asturias the Italian CTV, now commanded

by General Berti, was sent to Aragón as reserve force. These corps were massively strong, and on the republican side only V Corps and XVIII Corps were in any way comparable.

2 The nationalist squadrons were reorganized into 1st Hispanic Air Brigade under the command of Colonel Sáenz de Buruaga, with the fighter ace García Morato as chief of operations. The fighter squadrons had nine aircraft each and the bomber squadrons twelve (Sabaté y Villarroya, *España en llamas*, p. 17).

3 GARF 4459/12/4, p. 268.

4 Salas, *La guerra* . . ., pp. 282–3.

5 Ibid., p. 280.

6 Richthofen war diary, BA-MA RL 35/38; see also Ranzato, *L'eclissi della democrazia*, p. 553, for details of the row. The Italians suspected that Franco was hoping for an internal collapse of the Republic and was avoiding a military victory.

7 Vicente Rojo, *Elementos del arte de la guerra*, p. 433.

8 The main formations were the 11th Division (Líster), 25th (García Vivancos), 34th (Etelvino Vega), 39th (Alba), 40th (Andrés Nieto), 41st (Menéndez), 42nd (Naira), 64th (Martínez Cartón), 68th (Triguero) and 70th (Hilamón Toral). In reserve were the 35th Division (Walter) and the 47th Division (Durán).

9 RGVA 35082/1/95, pp. 33–58, quoted in Radosh and Habeck, pp. 444, 459 and 448.

10 Ciutat, pp. 113–14.

11 A. Vetrov, *Volontyory svobody*, Moscow, 1972, p. 178.

12 RGVA 33987/3/912, p. 126.

13 Castells, *Las Brigadas Internacionales*, p. 298.

14 Richthofen war diary, 15 December, BA-MA RL 35/38.

15 BA-MA RL 35/39.

16 BA-MA RL 35/38.

17 Herbert Matthews, *The Education of a Correspondent*, New York, 1946.

18 Bernardo Aguilar, quoted by Pedro Corral, *Si me quieres escribir*, Barcelona, 2004.

19 Zugazagoitia, *Guerra y vicisitudes* . . ., p. 358.

20 Corral, *Si me quieres escribir*, p. 160.

21 Zugazagoitia, *Guerra y vicisitudes* . . ., p. 354.

22 Castells, *Las Brigadas Internacionales* . . ., pp. 298–9.

23 Salas, *La guerra* . . ., p. 292.

24 BA-MA RL 35/39.

25 Ibid.

26 Salas, *La guerra* . . ., p. 294.

27 Zugazagoitia, *Guerra y vicisitudes* . . ., p. 354.

28 RGVA 33987/3/1149, pp. 211–26, quoted in Radosh and Habeck, p. 484.

29 BA-MA RL 35/39.

30 *Crónica de la guerra de España*, vol. iv, p. 442.

31 R. de la Cierva, *Francisco Franco, un siglo de España*, p. 56. Rey d'Harcourt was treated very badly by Franco. The republican government gave orders that the colonel should be taken to the rear with the local bishop, Anselmo Polanco, and his chaplain, Felipe Ripoll. The three men were executed on 7 February 1939 by republicans during the final collapse of Catalonia.
32 RGVA 35082/1/95, pp. 33–58, quoted in Radosh and Habeck, p. 447.
33 Corral, *Si me quieres escribir*, p. 213.
34 BA-MA RL 35/39.
35 Seidman, *A ras de suelo*, p. 243.
36 BA-MA RL 35/39.
37 Zugazagoitia, *Guerra y vicisitudes . . .*, p. 354.
38 Palmiro Togliatti, *Escritos sobre la guerra de España*, Barcelona, 1980, p. 189.
39 Stepánov, *Las causas de la derrota*, p. 108.
40 'Count Rossi' was a fascist whose real name was Aldobrando Bonaccorsi. Ciano put him in charge of the Balearic Islands, especially Mallorca. His crimes and reign of terror became infamous. Mussolini and Ciano wanted him to bring the local Falange under Italian fascist influence. See Ranzato, *L'eclissi della democrazia*, pp. 554ff.
41 Delperrié du Bayac, *Les Brigades Internationales*, Paris, 1985, p. 331. Von Thoma had four tank battalions, each of three companies with fourteen tanks. See Blanco Escolá, *Falacias de la guerra civil*, p. 241.
42 RGVA 33987/3/1149, pp. 211–226, quoted in Radosh and Habeck, p. 485.
43 RGVA 33987/3/1149, p. 230.
44 BA-MA RL 35/40.
45 Stepánov, p. 109.
46 Skoutelsky, *Les Brigades Internationales*, p. 99.
47 José M. Maldonado, *Alcañiz 1938. El bombardeo olvidado*, Saragossa, 2003.
48 Tagüeña, *Testimonio de dos guerras*, p. 107.
49 *ABC* of Seville, 16 April 1938.

CHAPTER 29: Hopes of Peace Destroyed

1 On 30 June 1936, Spanish banknotes in circulation amounted to 5,399 million pesetas. In April 1938 they reached 9,212 million in just the republican zone (Joan Sardà, *Banco de España*, p. 432). Exacerbated by military disasters and the export of the gold reserves, the republican peseta had fallen catastrophically. At the end of 1936 it had depreciated by 19.3 per cent of its value and one year later by 75 per cent. By the end of 1938 it had lost 97.6 per cent of its original value. In December 1936 the exchange rate was 42 pesetas to the pound sterling. A year later, just before the battle of Teruel, the exchange rate was 226 to the pound sterling, but after the nationalist campaign in Aragón it fell to between 530 and 650 to the pound. See also, A. Carreras and X. Tafunell, *Historia*

económica de la España contemporánea, Crítica, Barcelona, 2004, pp. 270–1; Ángel Viñas et al., *Política comercial exterior en España (1931–1975)*, Banco Exterior de España, Madrid, 1979.

2 The main arms-buying teams were headed by Dr Alejandro Otero Fernández (replaced later by Antonio Lara), José Calviño Ozores and Martí Esteve in Paris; Antonio Bolaños, Daniel Ovalle and Francisco Martínez Dorrién in Belgium; Carlos Pastor Krauel in Britain; Ángel Pastor Velasco in Czechoslovakia; Félix Gordón Ordás, with Fernando de los Ríos, in Mexico and the US. They had to do business with traffickers such as Josef Veltjens, Prodromos Bodosakis-Athanasiades, John Ball, Jack A. Billmeir, Stefan Czarnecki, Kazimierz Ziembinski, Stefan Katelbach and others of their type. See Howson, *Armas para España*.

3 The work by Professors Morten Heiberg and Mogens Pelt for their book, *Los negocios de la guerra*, has finally confirmed the details of an outrageous paradox which had previously just been suspected.

4 The Nationalists estimated that Göring received the equivalent of one pound sterling for each rifle supplied. Morton Heiberg and Mogens Pelt in *Los negocios de la guerra*, pp.190–3, quote the letter of 10 August 1938 from the Marquis de Magaz, the Nationalist ambassador in Berlin, to Count Jordana, Franco's foreign minister. Magaz gleaned this figure from 'confidential sources' in Paris.

5 Colonel Ribbing's report from Spain, General Staff, Former Secret Archive, Foreign Department, KA E III 26, vol., p. 20.

6 The nationalist debt to Nazi Germany rose to RM 372 million, but it was paid off over a long period and mainly in kind, through raw materials from mining and other produce.

7 Heiberg and Pelt, *Los negocios de la guerra*.

8 Howson, *Armas para España*.

9 See Chapter 19.

10 In five shipments, $15 million worth of silver was sold. Another $5 million was disposed of in other ways.

11 Viñas, *Guerra, dinero, dictadura*, p. 174.

12 For the whole episode see Villas, *El oro de Moscú*; Viñas, *Guerra, dinero, dictadura*; Howson, *Armas para España*; and Kowalsky, *La Unión Soviética y la guerra civil española*. The Republic paid for: 31 Katiuska bombers; 26 Tupolev bombers; 121 I-16 (Moscas); 25 T-26 tanks; 149 75mm field guns; 32 anti-aircraft guns; 254 anti-tank guns; 4,158 machine-guns; 125,050 rifles; 237,349 shells; 132,559,672 rounds of ammunition. All the arms and ammunition which left the Soviet Union after August 1938 never reached the Republic. Most of it was handed over to Franco at the end of the war by the French government. See Chapter 35 below.

13 AVP RF 18/84/144, p. 5.

14 Ibid., pp. 14–15.

15 Jackson, *La República española ...*, p. 387.

16 Ibid., p. 388.

17 Rafael Abella, *La vida cotidiana durante la guerra civil. La España republicana*, Barcelona, 2004, p. 359.

18 Ciano, *Diarios*, p. 87.
19 Jackson, *La República española ...*, p. 387.
20 Sole Sabaté and Villarroya, *España en llamas*, p. 170.
21 Ciano, *Diarios*, p. 109.
22 During the course of the war, Barcelona was bombed 113 times by the Aviazione Legionaria, 80 by the Condor Legion. (40 times between 21 and 25 January 1939) and once by the Brigada Aérea Hispana. Altogether, these bombing attacks caused 2,500 deaths, 1,200 of them between March and December 1938 (Joan Villarroya, *Els bombardeigs de Barcelona durant la guerra civil*, Barcelona, 1981).
23 Ibid.
24 He did the same thing in *La Vanguardia* under the pseudonym Juan Ventura, describing Prieto as an 'impenitent pessimist'.
25 Mije, La Pasionaria and Díaz for the Spanish Communist Party; Mariano Vázquez and García Oliver for the CNT; Herrera and Escorza for the FAI; Vidarte and Pretel for the UGT; Serra Pàmies for the PSUC; and Santiago Carrillo for the JSU.
26 To José Prat, under-secretary of the cabinet. Quoted by Miralles, *Juan Negrín*, p. 198.
27 Prieto always maintained (*Cómo y por qué salí del Ministeri de Defensa Nacional*, and in his bitter correspondence with Negrín collected in *Epistolario Prieto–Negrín*) that Negrín forced him out of the ministry of defence at the insistence of the communists.
28 Those present included Negrín, Martínez Barrio as president of the Cortes, Lluís Companys as president of the Generalitat, Quemades of the Izquierda Republicana, González Peña of the PSOE, José Díaz of the PCE, Monzón of the PNV and Mariano Vázquez of the CNT.
29 Negrín appointed Méndez Aspe (Izquierda Republicana) as minister of finance; González Peña (PSOE) as minister of justice; Paulino Gómez Sáez (PSOE), minister of the interior; Álvarez del Vayo (PSOE, but pro-communist) as minister of state; Giral (Izquierda Republicana) and Irujo (PNV) as ministers without portfolio; Giner de los Ríos (Unión Republicana) as minister of communications and transport; Velao (Izquierda Republicana) as minister of public works; Blanco (CNT) as minister of education (in the place of Jesús Hernández, PCE); and kept Ayguadé (ERC) as minister of work and Uribe (PCE) as minister of agriculture.
30 Eden, *Facing the Dictators*, p. 571.
31 Ciano, *Diarios*, p. 221.
32 Ibid., p. 117.
33 These were presented to the council of ministers on 30 April 1938. He described them as part of his new programme 'for the knowledge of his compatriots and as an announcement to the world', to emphasize the national character of his political programme and as the basis of a future compromise between all Spaniards.
34 Faupel to Wilhelmstrasse, 5 May 1937, DGF, p. 282.

35 Faupel to Wilhelmstrasse, 11 May 1937, DGF, pp. 284–5.
36 Faupel to Wilhelmstrasse, 23 May 1937, DGF, p. 294.
37 Faupel to Wilhelmstrasse, 11 May 1937, DGF, p. 284.

CHAPTER 30: Arriba España!

1 Luis Suárez, *Franco: la historia y sus documentos*, p. 94.
2 This first government was made up as follows: vice-president and minister for foreign affairs, General Gómez Jordana; minister of the interior and secretary-general of the council, Ramón Serrano Súñer; minister of justice, Tomás Domínguez; minister without portfolio, Count de Rodezno; minister of national defence, General Fidel Dávila; minister of public order, General Martínez Anido; minister of finance, Andrés Amado; minister of public works, Alfonso Peña Boeuf; minister of national education, Pedro Sáinz Rodríguez; minister of agriculture, Raimundo Fernández Cuesta; minister of organization and unions, Pedro González Bueno; minister of industry and commerce, Juan Antonio Suanzes.
3 Preston, *Franco, caudillo de España*, p. 371.
4 Carlos Fernández, *El General Franco*, p. 109.
5 Callahan, *La Iglesia católica en España*, p. 302.
6 Colonel Martín Pinillos, see Javier Rodrigo, *Prisioneros de Franco*.
7 Coal and steel production underwent a 'rapid recovery and by 1938 volume output surpassed those of 1935'. See J. M. Bricall, 'La economia española, 1936–1939' in Tuñón de Lara, *La guerra civil española 50 años después*, p. 377.
8 Carreras and Tafunell, *Historia económica de la España contemporánea*, p. 267.
9 Abella, *La vida cotidiana* . . ., p. 241.
10 Luis Suárez, *Franco: la historia y sus documentos*, vol. iii, p. 67.
11 Rojo, *Alerta los pueblos*, p. 40.
12 8 September 1936, DGFP, p. 87.
13 Richthofen war diary, 21 November 1937, BA-MA RL 35/38.
14 German ambassador in France to Wilhelmstrasse, 17 March 1938, DGFP, p. 621.
15 Richthofen war diary, 17 January 1939, BA-MA RL 35/38.
16 Ciano, *Diarios*, p. 166.
17 Ibid., p. 167.
18 Fraser, *Recuérdalo tú* . . ., p. 659.
19 Jesús Salas, *La guerra de España desde el aire*, p. 332.
20 Coverdale, *La intervencíon italiana* . . ., p. 317.
21 XVI Corps under Palacios, García Vallejo's XVII, Vidal's XIX, Durán's XX, and Ibarrola's XXII, as well as Group 'A' under Güemes and Group 'B' under Romero, together made up the Army of Levante under Colonel Leopoldo Menéndez.
22 Ciutat, *Relatos y reflexiones*, p. 199.
23 Preston, *Franco, caudillo de España*, p. 387.

24 Francisco Franco, *Palabras del Caudillo*, Vicesecretaría de Educación Popular, Madrid, 1943.
25 'Spain arise! Long live Spain!'

CHAPTER 31: The Battle of the Ebro

1 Franco cracked down on anybody who favoured negotiation with the enemy. He saw it as treason to the nationalist cause. See Saña, *Serrano Súñer*, p. 91.
2 V Corps consisted of the 11th, 45th and 46th Divisions; XV Corps of the 3rd, 35th and 42nd Divisions; and XII Corps (commanded by Etelvino Vega) of the 16th and 44th Divisions.
3 Each division in theory had 10,000 men with 5,000 rifles, 255 machine-guns, 30 mortars, four anti-tank guns, three artillery groups of nine field guns, and a battalion of engineers to organize the crossing.
4 For the progress of the battle, see Francisco Cabrera Castillo, *Del Ebro a Gandesa. La batalla del Ebro, Julio–noviembre 1938*, Madrid, 2002; Julián Henríquez Caubín, *La batalla del Ebro*, México, 1966; J. M. Martínez Bande, *La batalla del Ebro*, Madrid, 1988; Lluís M. Mezquida i Gené, *La batalla del Ebro*, Tarragona, 2001; Estanislau Torres, *La batalla de l'Ebre i la caiguda de Barcelona*, Lérida, 1999; Gabriel Cardona and Juan Carlos Losada, *Aunque me tires el Puente*, Madrid, 2004; and above all, Jorge M. Reverte, *La batalla del Ebro*, Barcelona, 2003.
5 The 50th Division was commanded by Colonel Luís Campos Guereta and the 105th Division by Colonel Natalio López Bravo.
6 Francisco Franco-Salgado, *Mis conversaciónes privadas con Franco*, pp. 262-3.
7 Blanco, *La incompetencia militar …*, p. 476.
8 Skoutelsky, *L'espoir guidait leurs pas*, p. 104.
9 Castells, *Las Brigadas Internacionales*, pp. 355ff.
10 Fraser, *Recuérdalo tú …*, p. 661.
11 Jesús Salas, *La guerra desde el aire*, pp. 356ff.
12 Miguel Mateu, personal testimony.
13 Quoted by Reverte, *La batalla del Ebro*, p. 112.
14 Castells, *Las Brigadas …*, p. 358.
15 RGVA 33987/3/1149, p. 284.
16 Legion Condor *Lageberichte* BA-MA RL 35/5 H 7202.
17 Rolfe, *The Lincoln Battalion*, p. 131.
18 Legion Condor *Lageberichte* BA-MA RL 35/5 H 7162.
19 Reverte, *La batalla del Ebro*, p. 141.
20 BA-MA RL 35/5 H7197.
21 See Tagüeña, *Testimonio de dos guerras*, p. 230,
22 Ramón Salas, *El Ejército Popular de la República*, p. 1974.
23 Legion Condor *Lageberichte* BA-MA RL 35/5 H7175.
24 Reverte, *La batalla del Ebro*, p. 219.
25 Legion Condor *Lageberichte* BA-MA RL 35/5 H7122.

26 Castells, *Las Brigadas*, p. 359.
27 Luís María de Lojendio, *Operaciones militares de la guerra de España*, Madrid, 1940.
28 Ciano, *Diarios*, p. 168.
29 *Crónica*, vol. v, p. 111.
30 Boletín del V Cuerpo del Ejército del Ebro.
31 Reverte, *La batalla del Ebro*, p. 564.
32 Togliatti, *Escritos sobre la guerra de España*, p. 253.
33 Stepánov, *Las causas de la derrota ...*, p. 142.

CHAPTER 32: The Republic in the European Crisis

1 Azaña, *Diarios completos*, p. 1238.
2 Ibid., p. 1240.
3 Negrín to Rafael Méndez (Rafael Méndez in *Indice*, November–December 1971).
4 Azaña, *Diarios completos*, p. 1240.
5 Thomas, *La guerra civil española*, p. 911.
6 DGFP, p. 629.
7 Ciano, *Diarios*, p. 180.
8 Ibid., p. 183.
9 Azcárate, *Mi embajada ...*, p. 240.
10 Colonel Ribbing's report from Spain, General Staff, Former Secret Archive, Foreign Department, KA E III 26, vol. 1, p. 22.
11 Ibid.
12 Also in the United States, the FBI investigated US nationals who had served in the International Brigades, and later, during Senator McCarthy's 'witch-hunts', Milton Woff, Alvah Bessie, Edwin Rolfe, John Gates, Robert Thompson, Irving Margollies and other members of the Lincoln Brigade were persecuted, with some imprisoned, while others found it very hard to obtain employment.
13 Finally in 1952, André Marty was expelled from the French Communist Party.
14 Ibárruri. Pamphlet published in Barcelona in 1938, quoted by Thomas, *La guerra civil española*, p. 916.
15 Castells, *Las Brigadas ...*, pp. 383–4. Many of those communists who fought in Spain played important roles in their home countries during and after the war: Pietro Nenni, who became minister of foreign affairs in Italy; Luigi Longo, vice-president of the Italian Communist Party; Charles Tillon, minister for air in France between 1945 and 1948; Rol-Tanguy, the communist leader of the Paris uprising just before its liberation in August 1944; Enver Hodja, the dictator of Albania; Walter Ulbricht, the leader of East Germany; Josip Broz 'Tito', the leader of Yugoslavia; Erno Gerö, 'Pedro', minister of communications in Hungary; Ladislas Rajk, minister of the interior in Hungary and a number of others. Many would be purged. In Stalin's eyes, service in Spain signified foreign contagion.

16 Colonel Ribbing's report from Spain, General Staff, Former Secret Archive, Foreign Department, KA E III 26, vol. 1, p. 14.
17 Zugazagoitia, *Guerra y vicisitudes*, p. 487.
18 Gorkín, Arquer, Andrade, Escuder, Rebull, Adroher and Bonet.
19 15 December 1938, RGVA 35082/1/221, p. 2.
20 25 November 1938, RGVA 33987/3/1081, pp. 30–44, quoted in Radosh and Habeck, p. 506.
21 RGVA 33987/3/1081, p. 16.
22 Ibid., p. 80, quoted in Radosh and Habeck, pp. 498–9.

CHAPTER 33: The Fall of Catalonia

1 The Army of the Centre had around 100,000 men, while the Estremadura front had 50,000 and Andalucia 20,000. The Army of Levante had 21 under-strength divisions and four and a half in reserve. At the beginning of December 1938 the People's Army possessed no more than 225,000 rifles, 4,000 light machine-guns and 3,000 machine-guns (Ramón Salas, *Historia del Ejército Popular*).
2 Negrín could also count on the support of a small group within the CNT around Mariano Vázquez, a larger group within the UGT and a fraction of the PSOE, led by its general secretary, Ramón Lamoneda.
3 Saborit, *Julián Besteiro*, Buenos Aires, 1967, p. 421.
4 Stevenson to Lord Halifax, 31 October 1938 in *BDFA*, vol. 27, Spain, July 1936–January 1940, p. 222.
5 Miralles, *Juan Negrín*, p. 302.
6 Ibid., p. 303. Negrín had asked for this arms shipment on 11 November in a letter delivered personally to Stalin by Hidalgo de Cisneros. Five annexes to the letter listed their needs, including 2,150 field guns, 120 anti-aircraft guns, 400,000 rifles, 10,000 machine-guns, 260 fighters, 150 bombers, 300,000 shells and so on. The shipment left Murmansk and reached Bordeaux on 15 January, by which time Tarragona had already fallen. Only a small part crossed the frontier and the republicans did not even have time to open the crates.
7 Ciano, *Diarios*, p. 223.
8 Thomas, *La guerra civil española*, p. 940.
9 Ciano, *Diarios*, p. 235.
10 At the end of 1938 the nationalists and their allies mustered fourteen squadrons of Fiat CR 32 fighters and three squadrons of Messerschmitts with twelve aircraft each. Added to the Fiat force based in the Balearics, this gave them over 200 fighters (a total roughly equal to their combined bomber forces of Junkers 52s, Heinkel IIIs and Savoia-Marchettis).
11 Salas, *La guerra de España*, pp. 445–6.
12 Ibid., p. 404.
13 Richthofen war diary, BA-MA RL 35/38.
14 Ibid.
15 Ibid.

16 Stepánov, *Las causas de la derrota*, p. 150.
17 Cordón, *Trayectoria*, p. 375.
18 Bolloten, *La Revolución española*, p. 932.
19 Rojo, *¡Alerta los pueblos!*, p. 121.
20 Ibid., p. 125.
21 Quoted in *Recuérdalo tú* . . ., p. 674.
22 Abella, *La vida cotidiana . . . La España republicana*, p. 415.
23 *Quan érem capitans*, Barcelona, 1974, p. 149.
24 Guillermo Cabanellas, *La guerra de los mil días*, Barcelona, 1973, vol. ii, p. 1047.
25 Ciano, *Diarios*, p. 258.
26 Benet, *Catalunya sota el règim franquista*, Paris, 1973, vol. i, p. 222.
27 Fraser, *Recuérdalo tú* . . ., p. 674.
28 Benet, *Catalunya sota el règim franquista*, p. 229.
29 BA-MA RL 35/7.
30 Ibid.
31 Emil Voldemarovich Shteingold, 'My Last 10 Days in Spain', RGVA 35082/3/32, pp. 1–5.
32 Zugazagoitia, *Guerra y vicisitudes* . . ., p. 523.
33 Daladier had proposed that a free zone was established on Spanish soil in which to intern refugees, but this was rejected by Negrín as well as by Franco.
34 BA-MA RL 35/8.
35 BA-MA RL 35/7.
36 Regler, *Owl of Minerva*, p. 321.

CHAPTER 34: The Collapse of the Republic

1 Luis Romero, *El final de la guerra*, Barcelona, 1976, p. 134.
2 Ibid., pp. 124–5.
3 Elorza and Bizcarrondo, *Queridos camaradas*, p. 430.
4 Stepánov, *Las causas de la derrota* . . ., pp. 168–9.
5 *Mundo Obrero*, 12 February 1939.
6 Togliatti, *Escritos sobre la guerra de España*, p. 275.
7 Tuñón, *Historia de España*, vol. ix, p. 506.
8 *ABC*, Madrid, 14 February 1939.
9 Alpert, *El ejército republicano*, p. 313.
10 See Miralles, *Juan Negrín*, p. 311; Togliatti, *Escritos* . . ., p. 279; Elorza and Bizcarrondo, *Queridos camaradas*, p. 431.
11 Colonel Ribbing's report from Spain, General Staff, Former Secret Archive, Foreign Department, KA E III 26, vol. 1, p. 22.
12 The gold handed over was worth almost $27 million. See Joan Sardà, *El Banco de España*, p. 452.
13 *Memoirs*, New York, 1948.
14 Azaña, *Obras Completa*, vol. iii, p. 567.
15 Also Colonel Moriones, of the Army of the Centre, Colonel Camacho,

head of the air force in the zone, and General Bernal, commander of the naval base of Cartagena.

16 Casado's first acquaintance with anarchists had come during the dictatorship of Primo de Rivera, when Casado was imprisoned and became friends with libertarians in jail. See Alpert, *El ejército republicano*, pp. 301ff.

17 Romero, *El final de la guerra*, p. 138.

18 See Luis Suárez, *Francisco Franco*, in preparation, and Martínez Bande, *Los cien últimos días de la República*.

19 Romero, *El final de la guerra*, p. 123.

20 Ibid., p. 138.

21 See Martínez Bande, *Los cien últimos días de la República*.

22 BA-MA RL 35/8.

23 For the most thorough account of the uprising, see Luis Romero, *Desastre en Cartagena*, Barcelona, 1971.

24 Other appointments included González Marín, CNT, finance; Miguel San Andrés, Izquierda Republicana, justice and propaganda; Eduardo Val, CNT, communications and public works; José del Río, of Unión Republicana, education and health; and Antonio Pérez, of the UGT, labour. Melchor Rodríguez, of the CNT, became the new mayor of Madrid.

25 All the speeches are printed in full in Romero, *El final de la guerra*, pp. 261–8.

26 Cipriano Rivas Cherif, *Retrato de un desconocido*, p. 437.

27 Luis Romero, *El final de la guerra*, pp. 274–5.

28 Miralles, *Juan Negrín*, p. 324.

29 BA-MA RL 35/8.

30 Elorza and Bizcarrondo, *Queridos camaradas*, p. 434.

31 Togliatti, *Escritos sobre la guerra de España*, p. 297.

32 Tagüeña, *Entre dos guerras*, p. 310.

33 Marías, p. 248.

34 Tuñón, *Historia de España*, ix, p. 526.

35 BA-MA RL 35/7.

36 Richthofen war diary, BA-MA RL 35/38.

37 BA-MA RL 35/37.

38 Casado, *The Last Days of Madrid*, p. 259.

39 Marías, p. 255.

40 Marías, p. 261.

41 *ABC*, 2 April 1939, Romero, *El final de la guerra*, p. 421.

42 Ciano, *Diarios*, p. 276.

CHAPTER 35: The New Spain and the Franquist Gulag

1 Richthofen war diary, BA-MA RL 35/38. The Condor Legion reached Hamburg by ship on 31 May and on 6 June it paraded through Berlin.

2 Luis Suárez, *Franco: la historia y sus documentos*, iv, p. 33.

3 Among the other appointments were Esteban Bilbao, minister of justice;

José Larraz, minister of finance; Vice-Admiral Moreno, minister of marine; Luis Alarcón de la Lastra, minister for industry and commerce; Joaquín Benjumea, minister of agriculture and labour; Juan Ibáñez Martín, minister of national education; Alfonso Peña Boeuf, minister of public works.

4 Javier Tusell, *Dictadura franquista y democracia*, p. 45.

5 This was overseen by the Servicio Nacional de Reforma Económica y Social de la Tierra, set up by the nationalists in 1938.

6 See Carlos Barciela (ed.), *Autarquía y mercado negro*, Barcelona 2003, pp. 55ff.

7 Glicerio Sánchez and Julio Tascón (eds), *Los empresarios de Franco*, Barcelona, 2003, pp. 237ff.

8 See Elena San Román, *Ejército e industria: el nacimiento del INI*, Barcelona, 1999.

9 Franco statement to Henri Massis, published in *Candide*, 18 August 1938.

10 Suárez, *Franco*, pp. 119ff.

11 Joan Clavera (ed.), *Capitalismo español: De la autarquía a la estabilización, 1939–1959*, Madrid, 1978, pp. 179ff.

12 Tusell, *Dictadura franquista y democracia*, p. 98.

13 Blinkhorn, *Carlismo y contrarrevolución*, p. 411.

14 Carreras and Tafunell, *Historia económica de la España contemporánea*, p. 277.

15 See for example, Robert Graham, *A Nation Comes of Age*, London, 1984.

16 Antonio F. Canales, *La llarga postguerra*, Barcelona, 1997, p. 178.

17 Kemp, *Mine Were of Trouble*, pp. 49–50.

18 Rodrigo, *Cautivos*, p. 209.

19 Ibid.

20 See Anne Applebaum, *Gulag*, London, 2003.

21 Casanova (ed.), *Morir, matar, sobrevivir*, p. 31.

22 Michael Richards, *Un tiempo de silencio*, p. 30; and Dionisio Ridruejo, *Escrito en España*, p. 93.

23 For example, around 5,000 were killed in the province of Valencia; 4,000 in Catalonia; in Madrid's East Cemetery 2,663 executions were registered up to 1945; in Jaén, 1,280 up to 1950; in Albacete 1,026 between 1939 and 1953; and so on. Casanova, *Morir, matar, sobrevivir*, pp. 19ff; Santiago Vega Sombría, *De la esperanza a la persecución*, p. 279. Paul Preston has pointed out that 92,462 individually named victims have been identified in just 36 of Spain's 50 provinces.

24 For example, in the notorious San Marcos prison in León, more than 800 died of hunger and cold.

25 Vinyes, *Irredentas*, p. 114.

26 Francisco Moreno, *Víctimas de la guerra civil*, p. 278.

27 Juana Doña, *Desde la noche y la niebla*.

28 Francisco Moreno, *Víctimas de la guerra civil*, p. 278.

29 Richards, *Un tiempo de silencio*; and Vinyes, *Irredentas*.

30 Ángela Cenarro, *La sonrisa de Falange*, in preparation.

CHAPTER 36: The Exiles and the Second World War

1 Between 1936 and 1938, there had been three waves of different sizes: the first in the summer of 1936; the second following the fall of Santander and the Asturias in June 1937; and the third as a result of the Aragón campaign in the spring of 1938. The first wave of 15,000 refugees came mainly from the Basque country when the nationalists attacked Irún and San Sebastían. The second amounted to 160,000, and the third of 14,000, including 7,000 men of the 42nd Division cut off in the Bielsa pocket in the Pyrenees. Of these three waves, most returned to republican territory, leaving just 40,000 in France at the end of 1938 (Dolores Pla Brugat, 'El exilio republicano español' in *AULA Historia social*, no. 13, Valencia, Spring, 2004; Bartolomé Bennassar, *La guerre d'Espagne et ses lendemains*, Paris, 2004, p. 363).

2 Mera was released from prison in 1946. He made contact with old friends from the CNT and then had to flee to France again, where he died in 1975.

3 Emil Voldemarovich Shteingold, 'My Last 10 Days in Spain', RGVA 35082/3/32, p. 1.

4 Antonio Soriano, *Éxodos, Historia oral del exilio republicano en Francia 1939–1945*, Barcelona, 1989, p. 23.

5 Arthur Koestler, *La lie de la terre*, Paris, 1946, p. 148.

6 *Candide*, 8 February 1939.

7 See Geneviève Dreyfus-Armand, *El exilio de los republicanos españoles en Francia*; Bennassar, *La guerre d'Espagne et ses lendemains*; Tusell, *Dictadura franquista y democracia*, p. 36.

8 Dreyfus-Armand, p. 79; Tusell, *Dictadura franquista y democracia*, p. 36.

9 See Bennassar and Dreyfus-Armand, who do not agree over figures.

10 Junta de Auxilio a los Republicanos Españoles.

11 Manuel Ros, *La guerra secreta de Franco*, Barcelona, 2002, p. xxiv.

12 Suárez, *Franco: la historia y sus documentos*, vol. v, p. 87.

13 Ibid., pp. 153–4.

14 Heiberg, *Emperadores del Mediterráneo*; and Preston, *Franco*.

15 Preston, *Franco*, pp. 524–5.

16 Heiberg, *Emperadores del Mediterráneo*.

17 Ros, *La guerra secreta de Franco*, pp. 146–52; for the role of Captain Alan Hillgarth RN, see David Stafford, *Churchill and Secret Service*, pp. 237–8.

18 The Blue Division was withdrawn by an ever-cautious Franco in 1943, when the war was clearly going against the Axis. But 2,200 men stayed behind in the Legión Azul, which in turn would be dissolved in January 1944. Its survivors became the Legion Española de Voluntarios, although most were attached to SS units until the end of the war. Total Spanish losses in the Soviet Union out of 45,500 participants were approximately 5,000 dead, 8,700 wounded, 2,137 maimed, 1,600 cases of severe frostbite, 7,800 sick and 372 prisoners, who did not return to Spain until April

1954 aboard the *Semiramis*. The total cost of 613,500,000 pesetas was offset against the Spanish debt for the Condor Legion. See Xavier Moreno Juliá, *La División Azul. Sangre española en Rusia, 1941–1945*, Barcelona, 2005.

19 Helmut Heiber (ed.), *Hitler y sus generales*, Barcelona, 2005, p. 398.

CHAPTER 37: The Unfinished War

1 Pierre Vilar, *La guerra civil española*, p. 176.

2 They included Jorge Semprún, a member of the resistance who would later become minister of culture in the new democratic Spain after Franco's death in 1975.

3 RGASPI 495/120/236, p. 57.

4 A. V. Elpatievsky, *Ispanskaya emigratsiya v SSSR*, Moscow, 2002.

5 Order of People's Commissar for Internal Affairs, 1942, No. 3498, 16 November 1942, Moscow, GARF P-9401/9/896.

6 GARF 2306/1/5991, p. 7.

7 GARF 307/1/272, p. 27.

8 *Reconquista de España*, supplement, 18 July 1944.

9 Daniel Arasa, *La invasión de los maquis*, Barcelona, 2004; Richards, *Un tiempo de silencio*; Serrano, *Maquis*; Francisco Moreno, *La resistencia armada*.

10 Casanova, *Morir, matar, sobrevivir*, p. 227; Antonio Telez, *Sabaté*, London, 1974, pp. 171–8.

11 The JEL, Junta Española de Liberación.

CHAPTER 38: Lost Causes

1 Valentín González (El Campesino), *Listen Comrades*, London, 1952.

2 BA-MA RL 35/34.

3 RGVA 33987/3/991, p. 68.

4 Gurney, p. 175.

5 Goriev to Moscow, 25 September 1936, quoted in Radosh and Habeck (eds), *Spain Betrayed*, London 2002, p. 60.

6 RGVA 33987/3/832, p. 107.

INDEX